A Faithful Guide to Philosophy

'Peter Williams has provided an invaluable text for Christians who wish to engage with philosophy. This isn't the usual abstract overview, but rather provides the reader with a human experience where their commitment to Christ is nurtured and their needs as a learner are embraced whilst also achieving academic rigour. Every Christian student of philosophy ought to have this book both on their desk and at their bedside.'
Dr Trevor Cooling, Professor of Christian Education at Canterbury Christ Church University and co-editor of the *Journal of Education and Christian Belief*

'*A Faithful Guide to Philosophy* is faithful, not only in the sense of being reliable, but also in the sense of being infused with a Christian world and life view. It is encouraging to see that this text is centered in natural theology and the philosophy of mind, for these are two areas of vital importance to the Christian faith, for which we must contend vigorously in our increasingly secular society. Williams' focus is well chosen and his arguments interesting and persuasive.'
Dr William Lane Craig, Research Professor of Philosophy at the Talbot School of Theology

'Peter S. Williams is a sure-footed guide to philosophy in general, and philosophy of religion in particular. He picks his way through knotty arguments with exemplary clarity lightened by a dry sense of humour. Although he is open about his own Christian commitment, he is equally rigorous in his assessment of arguments for theism as he is with arguments against. The addition of detailed bibliographies including YouTube videos and Web resources make this book a sure-fire winner for students and for Christian ministers and laypeople alike.'
Dr Daniel J. Hill, Lecturer, Department of Philosophy, Liverpool University

'This is an excellent book for introduction to the study of philosophy from the perspective of the Christian faith . . . The writer models the "love of wisdom" he recommends by his open, engaging and balanced approach, and shows abilities as both a thinker and communicator. His discussion with the New Atheists throughout the book makes it engaging and up to date. Both teachers and students will also appreciate the resource list after each chapter, pointing to a lot of high quality video, audio and written material . . . The book clearly shows the importance of philosophy for Christians, and the relevance of the Christian faith to philosophy.'
Bjørn Hinderaker, Assistant Professor at Gimlekollen School of Journalism and Communication in Norway

'This book is a highly accessible, stimulating introduction to logic, the nature of argument and philosophy written from a Christian perspective by an author who understands his subject and knows how to communicate it at the right level. This book, which is a delight to read and is full of useful references to books, articles, websites and other media, has the potential to de-mystify philosophy for a generation of young people and provide an excellent resource to enable them to articulate their faith in God with renewed confidence in a way that demonstrates its reasonableness against all New Atheist claims to the contrary.'
Professor John C. Lennox, Fellow in Mathematics and Philosophy of Science at Green Templeton College, Oxford

'*A Faithful Guide to Philosophy* is an extremely well-researched book that is tightly argued, excellent in topic selection, deep in coverage yet readable in style. Williams had done a masterful job of producing a book that is now a must read for Christians who want to explore the intellectual underpinnings of their faith. I highly recommend this delightful volume.'
Dr J.P. Moreland, Distinguished Professor of Philosophy at Biola University in La Mirada, California and author of *Love Your God With All Your Mind*

'Peter S. Williams has a real gift of clarity and communication. He makes the complex accessible and interesting, without distorting the issues.'
Stefan Gustavsson, Director of Credo Academy, Stockholm

A Faithful Guide to Philosophy

A Christian Introduction to the Love of Wisdom

Peter S. Williams

Paternoster:
thinking faith

26 25 24 23 22 19 18 17 16 15 14 13   12 11 10 9 8 7 6 5 4 3 2 1

First published 2013 by Paternoster
Paternoster is an imprint of Authentic Media Limited
52 Presley Way, Crownhill, Milton Keynes, MK8 0ES.
www.authenticmedia.co.uk

British Library Cataloguing in Publication Data

A catalogue record for this book is available from the British Library

ISBN 978-1-84227-811-6
978-1-78078-310-9 (e-book)

Cover Design by David McNeill (www.revocreative.co.uk)
Printed and bound by CPI Group (UK) Ltd., Croydon, CR0 4YY

This book is dedicated to the Christian scholars who first illuminated the path of philosophy for me (especially William Lane Craig, Michael Durrant, Norman L. Geisler, C.S. Lewis, J.P. Moreland, H.P. Owen, Richard Swinburne and Keith Ward) and to my goddaughter, Abigail Rebecca Price (b. 2011), in the hope that some day she'll be blessed to explore a little of the same path:

Open your ears, and hear the words of wise people,
and set your mind on the knowledge I give you.
It is pleasant if you keep them in mind
so that they will be on the tip of your tongue,
so that your trust may be in the LORD.
Today I have made them known to you, especially to you
(Proverbs 22:17–19 GW).

Contents

Introduction

A Faithful Guide to Philosophy

The pursuit of wisdom especially joins man to God in friendship.
Thomas Aquinas[1]

This book offers 'a faithful guide to philosophy' both in the sense that I seek to represent my subject accurately[2] and that I write as a philosopher who follows Jesus of Nazareth. I don't offer a historical overview of philosophy[3] or a supposedly neutral review of other philosophers' ideas. Rather, I offer attentive readers a good grounding in philosophical method and a range of philosophical topics of particular relevance to the Christian worldview. Above all, I hope readers will fall in love with philosophy and more in love with the Divine Subject who is the Ultimate Object of the quest upon which we are about to embark.

I invite an inquisitorial attitude from readers:

Questioning means that your mind is hungry. If your body isn't hungry, you won't eat, and if you don't eat, you won't grow. If your mind is not hungry – if you don't have wonder and the desire to know – then you won't ask questions, and if you don't ask questions, you won't find truth – and that means that your mind and soul and spirit won't grow. Truth is your mind's food.[4]

If you disagree with a conclusion, you must think my argument for it commits a logical fallacy and/or that it rests upon at least one false truth-claim. Those are the rules to which every disagreement should pay respect. As the apostle Paul says: 'Test everything. Hold on to the good' (1 Thessalonians 5:21).

Part I (The Love of Wisdom) covers the nature and basic tools of philosophy. Chapter 1 introduces philosophy as the love of wisdom. It also looks at truth, knowledge and the relationship between faith and reason. Chapter 2 looks at how philosophical arguments are supposed to work. By illustrating a clutch of fallacies with quotes from prominent atheists, chapter 3 will show that certain so-called 'sceptics' could stand a few lessons in logic.

Part II (Some Arguments for God) introduces five types of theistic argument: cosmological, teleological, moral, ontological and experiential (don't worry if you find some of these terms off-putting. Every subject has specialist language, and philosophy is no exception. I'll explain as we go along). We'll meet several other arguments for God in the context of topics introduced by parts III and IV. As Peter Kreeft observes:

> The question of God . . . is not a scientific question . . . though some scientific evidence is relevant to it . . . It is not a historical question . . . though some historical evidence is relevant to it . . . It is a philosophical question, a question about wisdom. Is it wise or unwise to believe we have an invisible Creator and Lord?[5]

I think it's wise to believe in God. Indeed, as a Christian I don't just believe in 'an invisible Creator', but in a God who personally invites us to engage in an eternal relationship with him in and through Jesus Christ (see my book *Understanding Jesus: Five Ways to Spiritual Enlightenment*, Paternoster, 2011). History brings relevant data to the table here, but *what we make of historical data depends upon our philosophy*.

Part III (The Philosophy of Mind) is about the finite minds of embodied persons. We'll look at the relationship between mind and body, see how mind points to God and investigate free will.

Part IV (Broadening Our Horizons) begins with the nature of beauty and some arguments for God from beauty, before addressing key objections to theism having to do with the relationship between science and theology and with the existence of evil.

These chapters are laced with questions designed to cement and deepen your understanding, as well as summary points and recommended resources to watch, listen to and/or read. Each chapter ends with some recommended resources (if you don't know where to begin, follow the * symbol). Many of these resources are online, and while the URLs were correct at the time of writing I can't guarantee their longevity. It may be simpler to enter the author and title into your favourite 'search engine'. I don't agree with everything I recommend, but at the very least I think it has stimulating content. As these resources indicate, there's more to be said both for and against the thesis advanced herein than can be covered in the space available.

This book is based, with permission, upon material written between 2008 and 2011 for the Good Book College's short course modules on 'Philosophy and Christian Belief' (cf. www.thegoodbookcollege.co.uk/).

Introduction

I'd like to thank everyone who provided me with support and feedback during the long writing and rewriting process, especially: Helen Thorne (for editing much of the original material), commissioning editor Dr Mike Parsons (for championing this project at Paternoster), copy- editor Mollie Barker, production manager Peter Little, Chris Knight, Phil Lenton, Sophie Lister, Luke Pollard, Lizzie Pollard and my parents.

Peter S. Williams
Southampton
March 2013

Part I

The Love of Wisdom

Good philosophy must exist, if for no other reason,
because bad philosophy needs to be answered.
C.S. Lewis, 'The Weight of Glory'

Philosophy, remarks Alvin Plantinga with dry wit, is 'just thinking hard about something.'[1] So 'doing good philosophy will be a matter of learning to think well.'[2] Logic helps us think well, and 'while many modern anti-theists argue for the irrationality of religion, Jesus is an exemplar of reason, rationality and logic.'[3] Christians should emulate Jesus' *rationality* as well as his *morality* – indeed these qualities are interlinked (cf. Romans 12:1–2; 15:14; Philippians 1:9; 2 Peter 1:3–8).

Philosopher David A. Horner holds up a book first published in 1724 and entitled *Logic: Or the Right Use of Reason in the Inquiry after Truth with a Variety of Rules to Guard against Error in the Affairs of Religion and Human Life, as Well as in the Sciences*.[4] This book 'was the most influential logic text of its time, the standard one used at Oxford, Cambridge, Harvard and Yale universities. And its influence continued for many decades, printed in some twenty editions.'[5] Horner invites his audience to describe the book's author:

> Typical answers include: he was very smart; he was analytical; he was boring . . . a philosopher, a logician. No one has suggested that the author was likely a pastor, a theologian or a devotional writer. Or a writer of hymns. Yet the author of *Logic* was all of those. His name is Isaac Watts . . . composer of such beloved works as 'Joy to the World,' 'When I Survey the Wondrous Cross' and seven hundred more. He was also a pastor in active ministry and a significant theological and devotional writer. And the most influential logician of his time.[6]

Horner comments: 'Those were days when Christians did not simply assume that one must choose between a sharp mind and a passionate heart.'[7] Indeed, a passionate heart should be partially devoted to a sharp mind, for as Proverbs observes: 'Desire without knowledge is not good – how much more will hasty feet miss the way!' (19:2 NIV) and 'The heart of the discerning acquires knowledge, for the ears of the wise seek it out' (18:15 NIV). We should pray with the psalmist for God to teach us 'knowledge and good judgment' (Psalm 119:66 NIV). Amen.

1. Philosophy and Faith

The fear [i.e. awe] of the LORD is the beginning of knowledge, but fools despise wisdom and discipline (Proverbs 1:7).

Introduction: Searching Questions

Let's begin with some searching questions:

- Why should you believe in God when the world's so full of pain?
- Do you need to believe in God in order to be a good person?
- How can you believe in God when there isn't any evidence?
- Does having faith in God mean ignoring reason?

These are the typical sorts of questions people ask about theism (belief in God), and honest questions demand honest answers. Talking of honesty, don't *Christians* ask questions like these that deserve honest answers? People in the Bible were always asking God questions (e.g. Exodus 6:30; Judges 6:13; Psalm 10:1). Why would contemporary believers be any different? I wrestled with some doubts of my own while writing this book. As Timothy Keller writes:

> A faith without some doubts is like a human body without any antibodies in it. People who blithely go through life too busy or indifferent to ask hard questions about why they believe as they do will find themselves defenseless against either the experience of tragedy or the probing questions of a smart skeptic. A person's faith can collapse overnight if she has failed over the years

to listen patiently to her own doubts, which should only be discarded after long reflection.[1]

How can we square belief in God with the reality of suffering? What *does* God have to do with morality? *Are* there good arguments for the existence of God? What *is* the relationship between 'faith' and 'reason'? If we want to give honest, satisfying answers to such questions, we need to ask and answer them *for ourselves*. And to seek true answers to significant questions like these – whether as a believer or a non-believer – means not merely 'doing philosophy', but *being* a *philosopher*!

Watch:
Lee Strobel, 'Faith Involves Doubt' www.leestrobel.com/videoserver/video.php?-clip=CCNT1687.
Greg Koukl, 'Can a Christian Have Doubts?'
http://youtu.beljvwoQZADOYE.

Question:
American Sociologist Brad Wright interviewed fifty people who had recently left the church: 'One of his most surprising findings is that . . . 42 out of 50 people who left the church did so because their doubts were not handled well!'[2] In a survey of over 14,000 people, c. 73% referenced a lack of answers to questions as part of the reason for their diminishing church attendance: 'People want churches to emphasise the many reasons why believing in God and Christianity makes sense and to challenge a doubting society' www.churchsurvey.co.uk Why do churches often fail to meet the needs of people with questions?

1.1 What Is a Philosopher?

'Philosophy' has usually meant the love of wisdom and the desire to find truth and understanding in fundamental matters of inquiry.
Chad Meister[3]

A philosopher is *someone dedicated to the wise pursuit and dissemination of true answers to significant questions through the practice of good intellectual habits.* The word 'philosophy' comes from two ancient Greek words: *philo* means 'brotherly love'; *sophia* means 'wisdom'. Philosophy is literally *philo-sophia*, the brotherly love of wisdom. Hence Thomas V. Morris defines philosophy as 'the love of wisdom, along with an unending desire to find it, understand it, put it into action and pass it on to others.'[4]

There are many references to wisdom in the Bible:

> the Bible contains a whole genre of books called 'wisdom literature,' about how to live a rational, intelligent life. It reflects an approach to reason that is embraced by a growing number of contemporary philosophers. On a wisdom model . . . being rational is more than just looking for good reasons for holding the beliefs you do, although that's part of it. Being rational – being wise – includes the whole package of one's moral and intellectual habits and patterns of thinking and acting.[5]

Scripture teaches that Jesus is the Christian's brother (cf. Hebrews 2:11–12) 'in whom are hidden all the treasures of wisdom and knowledge' (Colossians 2:3). Hence Paul K. Moser argues that 'if it is the job of philosophy to understand, explore, and expand upon knowledge in the realm of ultimate truth . . . and if God is the locus of such truth, then philosophers (knowingly or not) pursue divine truth.'[6] With J.P. More-land:

> I repeatedly return to the conviction that Jesus of Nazareth is simply peer-less. He is the wisest, most virtuous, most influential person in history. I can't even imagine what the last two thousand years would have been like without his influence. There is no one remotely like him. The power of his ideas, the quality of his character, the beauty of his personality, the uniqueness of his life, miracles, crucifixion, and resurrection are so far removed from any other person or ideology that, in my view, it is the greatest honor ever bestowed on me to be counted among his followers.[7]

Douglas Groothuis points out that, among other things, Jesus was a philosopher.[8] David A. Horner comments that although 'Jesus was not a scholar in the modern, professional sense of the term . . . he was a learned rabbi and teacher. His arguments were logically sound, he winsomely out-thought those who opposed him, and he graciously led his followers into penetrating truth about all of life.'[9] Dallas Willard expresses his judgement that 'the life and words that Jesus brought into the world came in the form of information and reality. He and his early associates overwhelmed the ancient world because they brought into it a stream of life at its deepest, along with the best information possible on the most important matters.'[10]

Philosophers seek to know and defend truth by thinking carefully and arguing well. As medieval philosopher and theologian Thomas Aquinas wrote: 'the twofold office of the wise man [is] to mediate and speak forth . . . truth . . . and to refute the opposing error.'[11] According to the Bible, people are created in the 'image' of God (Genesis 1:26) and so are all deserving of respect. But the 'golden rule' (Leviticus 19:18; Mark 12:31) applies only to people; *it doesn't apply to ideas.* Some ideas are better than others, and should be treated as such. Applying the golden rule to *ideas* is the central mistake of postmodernism.[12] For instance, the idea that all ideas are equal is much worse than the idea that all ideas are not equal. Hence philosophy is 'the critical examination of the basis for fundamental beliefs as to what is true, and the analysis of the concepts we use in expressing such beliefs.'[13]

Of course, people disagree about which fundamental beliefs are true and how best to articulate them. Christians must remember that they should be 'speaking the truth in love' (Ephesians 4:15). Because we should love our neighbour as ourselves, we should tolerate our neighbour's right to believe and argue for things with which we disagree. But toleration doesn't mean celebration. Indeed, one can only tolerate that with which one disagrees: 'Tolerance of the views of others [means] that even though we might think those views wrong and will argue against them, we will defend the rights of others to argue their cases.'[14] Proverbs 27:17 says:

> As iron sharpens iron,
> so one man sharpens another.

There's a sense in which the philosopher welcomes disagreement, but only *as a means to the end of discovering truth.* The wise make their pursuit of truth a communal activity: 'philosophy is best done among groups where there is an authentic spirit of friendship or camaraderie.'[15]

Philosophy is an art developed through practice. Philosophy isn't so much about learning a body of knowledge as it is about *learning good intellectual habits* (of course, philosophers trust that good intellectual habits increase our long-term chances of learning and defending a body of philosophical knowledge). These good intellectual habits are studied by *rhetoric,* the art of good argumentation defined by Aristotle as 'the *detection of the persuasive aspects of each matter.*'[16] Rhetoric also encompasses the principles of how best to communicate these objective observations. Hence, as Stratford Caldecott comments: 'Rhetoric . . . is not a set of techniques to impress (oratory, eloquence), nor a means of manipulating the will and emotions of others (sophistry, advertising), but rather a way of liberating the freedom of others by showing them the truth in a form they can understand.'[17]

Aristotle held that rhetoric encompasses three interrelated aspects of communication: 'Of those proofs that are furnished through the speech there are three kinds. Some reside in the *character* of the speaker, some in a certain *disposition* of the audience and some in the *speech* itself, through its demonstrating or seeming to demonstrate.'[18] These three aspects of rhetoric are known by the Greek terms *ethos*, *pathos* and *logos* (from which we get our word 'logic').

According to the Roman orator Cicero, the ideal speaker 'is he who . . . will speak in such a way as to achieve proof, delight and influence.'[19] These outcomes not only relate to the rhetorical elements of *logos* ('proof'), *pathos* ('delight') and *ethos* ('influence'), but to the corresponding transcendental (overarching) values of truth ('proof'), beauty ('delight') and goodness ('influence').

Watch:
Conor Neill, 'The Three Pillars of Persuasion' http://youtu.be/aEZWKkv48MY.

Good rhetoric (i.e. rhetoric dedicated to seeing and communicating the objectively persuasive aspects of each matter as judged by the transcendental values) is crucial for persuasive evangelism (i.e. apologetics) as well as for philosophy, as the apostle Paul makes clear: 'Please pray that I will make the message as clear as possible. When you are with unbelievers, always make good use of the time. Be pleasant and hold their interest when you speak the message [i.e. *use good ethos and pathos*]. Choose your words carefully and be ready to give answers to anyone who asks questions [i.e. *to communicate good logos*]' (Colossians 4:4–6 CEV).

While the rhetorical habits of thinking carefully and arguing well are transferable skills, philosophers are interested in applying these skills in the quest to truthfully answer the most important questions about reality. These are questions that can't be answered by science. Science is great, but it can't explain why something rather than nothing exists to be studied by science. Science can't say why scientific study is a good thing, or how scientific study is to be defined, or how it should be related to theology, etc. All *these* questions are philosophical: 'Science can be classified as a "first-order" activity, concerned with discovering the truth about the physical world . . . Philosophy, in contrast, is a "second-order" activity, one that examines the assumptions lying behind first-order activities.'[20]

Once you've learned the rules of logic (cf. chapters 2 and 3), philosophy is simply a matter of applying them over and over again to different subjects; which is a bit like saying that once you've learned musical notation and the fingering of an instrument, being a musician is just a matter of applying that knowledge to one piece of music after another! Philosophy is an artistic discipline, and for the Christian it should be *a spiritual discipline*. After all, Jesus endorsed the idea that true spirituality requires one to 'love the Lord your God with all your heart and . . . *with all your mind* and with all your strength' and to 'love your neighbour as yourself' (Mark 12:30,31, my italics; cf. Matthew 22:37,39; Luke 10:27; Deuteronomy 6:5). Horner comments: 'We use our minds for distinguishing between truth and falsity, learning, evaluating, memorizing, communicating, planning, inventing and deciding. In fact, we use our minds in doing everything else that we do. Loving God with our mind, then, is doing *all* of those things – the best we can, for the glory of God, as an expression of gratitude, love and worship of Him.'[21]

Christians can and should philosophize with the 'mind of Christ':

> To have 'the mind of Christ' . . . is to embrace and inhabit a way of life, within a set of divine and human relationships characterized by faith, hope, and love. To do philosophy with Christ's mind is, minimally, to have Christ-like attitudes, but it is also to work out the meaning of faithful, hopeful, and loving relationships in one's present circumstances . . . This involves philosophical activities that not only articulate and defend beliefs . . . but also offer to Christian communities the clarification, interpretation and critical appraisal of their beliefs.[22]

Our 'mind' or 'understanding' is an essential element of our spirituality, for as Glen Schultz explains: 'At the foundation of a person's life, we find his beliefs. These beliefs shape his values, and his values drive his actions.'[23] Thus Paul urges: 'Do not conform . . . to the pattern of this world, but be transformed *by the renewing of your mind*. Then you will be able to test and approve what God's will is – his good, pleasing and perfect will' (Romans 12:2, my italics). However, we can't engage our minds without thereby engaging our whole selves. As Paul Copan observes: 'the quest for wisdom isn't merely intellectual fact-gathering; it's also a *virtuous* and *spiritual* endeavor, requiring certain attitudes and character qualities.'[24] What Bill Smith says of Christian spirituality actually goes for *all* spiritualities: 'spirituality is holistic in the truest sense. It encompasses reason and feeling . . . we need to proclaim and live a [spirituality] that integrates the mind (orthodoxy), the heart (orthopathy) and the hands (orthopraxy).'[25] All spiritualities (including atheistic spiritualities)[26] can be analyzed in terms of this three-part structure.

Fig. 1.

Spirituality =

Practices (Orthopraxy: Actions – 'strength')
⇧
Attitudes (Orthopathy: Attitudes – 'heart')
⇧
Worldview (Orthodoxy: Beliefs – 'mind')

Fig. 2. The relationships between spirituality, the transcendental values and rhetoric

Spirituality	*Judged by*	Transendental Values	*Communicated by*	Classical Rhetoric
Actions	Judged by	Goodness	Communicated by	*Ethos*
Attitudes	Judged by	Beauty	Communicated by	*Pathos*
Beliefs	Judged by	Truth	Communicated by	*Logos*

As theologian Alister McGrath comments:

> We cannot allow Christ to reign in our hearts if he does not also guide our thinking. The discipleship of the mind is just as important as any other part of the process by which we grow in our faith and commitment. The defense of the intellectual credibility of Christianity has become increasingly important in recent years, not least on account of the rise of the new atheism. We must see ourselves as standard-bearers for the spiritual, ethical, imaginative and intellectual vitality of the Christian faith, working out why we believe that certain things are true and what difference they make to the way we live our lives and engage with the world around us.[27]

1.2 What Is Truth?

We will examine the nature of goodness and beauty in later chapters, but as Pontius Pilate asked Jesus: 'What is truth?' (John 18:38). The word 'truth' actually has two meanings. One refers to the accurate saying of things about reality. The other refers to the reality about which things are said. That is, we must distinguish a) true beliefs *about reality* from b) the truth *of reality* that true beliefs accurately represent.

✔ True statements correspond to the facts; they tell it like it is

For example, if the cat is on the mat then this is a truth of reality. That's one sense of the 'truth': *what reality is*. If the cat is on the mat and I *believe* that the cat is on the mat, then *the truth of my belief* is another sense of the term 'truth'. My belief is *true to* the *truth of* reality (because it accurately represents the way things are). As C.S. Lewis wrote: 'Reality is that *about which* truth is.'[28] Likewise, Aquinas observed: 'it is from the fact that a thing is or is not, that our thought or word is true or false, as [Aristotle] teaches.'[29]

Fig. 3.[30]

In 3.1 the statement 'The cat is on the mat' is true because the cat is on the mat.

In 3.2 the statement 'The cat is on the mat' is false, because it isn't.

3.1 'The cat is on the mat'   3.2 'The cat is on the mat'

Aristotle's definition of the primary meaning of truth can be given in words of one syllable: 'If one says of what is that it is, or of what is not that it is not, he speaks the truth; but if one says of what is that it is not, or of what is not that it is, he does not speak the truth.'[31] All theories of truth presuppose this commonsense notion of truth (called the correspondence theory of truth) because any theory of truth must claim that it is really true, i.e. that it corresponds to the actual nature of truth.

This 'correspondence' meaning of truth refers to a quality of beliefs. It's not a quality of *all* beliefs, but only of those that *correspond to the truth of reality*: 'truth in the mind . . . isn't determined by how the mind sees things but by how things are: for *statements* – and the understanding they embody – *are called true or false inasmuch as things are or are not so.*'[32] As Aristotle wrote: 'it is by the facts of the case, by their being or not being so, that a statement is called true or false.'[33] The facts of the case (like the cat being or not being on the mat) are *the truth of reality*, and it is the truth of reality that determines whether or not our *beliefs about reality* are *true to reality*. Reality calls the shots: 'We may be entitled to our own opinions, but we are not entitled to our own facts. Believing a statement is one thing; that statement being true is another.'[34]

Watch:
Norman L. Geisler, 'Truth and Relativism'
http://youtu.be/KSLrK6cWcMM.

Turning from the meaning of 'truth' to the philosopher's *attitude* towards truth, recall that philosophy means the 'brotherly love of wisdom.' According to Jacques Maritain, 'it was Pythagoras who first invented the term *philosophy* . . . observing that wisdom belongs in the strict sense to God alone, and for that reason not wishing to be called a wise man, but simply a friend or lover of wisdom. His modesty was itself a mark of great wisdom.'[35] Wisdom is more about *our attitude towards truth* than about *how much we know*. A philosopher's main motive in seeking truth is not to make reality conform to how they think it should be. Rather, it's to conform their belief to how reality is. A philosopher doesn't merely seek *knowledge*, but *understanding*. To have understanding means 'standing under' the authority of the truth to dictate what we believe. Hence: 'the consideration of the wise man aims principally at truth.'[36]

11

> **Question:**
> Jesus said, 'I am the way and *the truth* and the life' (John 14:6, my italics). How does this claim relate to the two senses of 'truth' distinguished by Aquinas?

1.3 What Is Knowledge?

At bottom, knowing and loving significantly overlap each other.[37]

God warns, 'my people are destroyed from lack of knowledge' (Hosea 4:6), but what is knowledge? Many textbooks will tell you that knowledge is 'justified (or warranted) true belief.' That's not 'justified' in the theological sense, but in the sense of being *backed up* by reason or evidence, or by some rationally appropriate (or at least not inappropriate) method of belief-formation. Hence Douglas Groothuis defines knowledge as 'a warranted awareness of reality as it is.'[38] However, while philosophers agree about the 'true belief' bit (you can't know something you don't believe, and you can't know what isn't so), they disagree about the 'justified/warranted' bit. Some think that to know something *just is* to have a true belief.[39] On this 'minimalist' account of knowledge, justification/warrant remains *desirable*, but it isn't something *required* for knowledge.

✔ Philosophers disagree about whether having a true belief is a sufficient or merely necessary condition of knowledge

Quite apart from debating the minimalist account of knowledge, philosophers debate what it *means* for a belief to be 'justified' or 'warranted.'[40]

Philosophers disagree about what knowledge is. But they know they disagree! This fact reveals that we can know things *even if we don't know how we know them*. To think otherwise would be to commit what J.P. Moreland dubs the 'the centipede fallacy':

> The centipede knows very well that he can walk, even though he can't give you all the details about how he does so. Most people know well what 'God' means, and they use it to refer, even if they cannot give you a complete theory of reference and meaning to explain this . . . I'm not sure I could define to everyone's satisfaction what a number is. And I couldn't define to everyone's satisfaction what God is nor how I refer to any of these entities. Nonetheless, it does seem reasonable that I could know something about these things, whether or not I could give an exhaustive treatment of how those terms get meaning. We can know them truly without knowing them exhaustively.[41]

The fact is that there are things that we know, and we know it: 'We know that we all possess knowledge' (1 Corinthians 8:1). How could anyone claim to *know* 'that we cannot know anything' with a straight face? Our ability to know is a 'properly basic' belief that we must acknowledge at the foundation of philosophical inquiry:

> I can know some things directly and simply without having to have criteria for how I know them and without having to know how or even that I know them. We know many things without being able to prove that we do or without fully understanding the things we know. We simply identify clear instances of knowledge without having to possess or apply any criteria for knowledge. We may reflect on these instances and go on to develop criteria for knowledge consistent with them and use these criteria to make judgements in borderline cases of knowledge, but the criteria are justified by their congruence with specific instances of knowledge, not the other way around.[42]

So, while the precise nature of knowledge is itself one of those significant things about which philosophers want to know the truth, this isn't a barrier to the process of philosophy. The glass of human understanding isn't full, but nor is it empty. We can *understand* even though we cannot *comprehend*. In theological terms, while we are created in the 'image' of an omniscient God (Genesis 1:26) only 'a little lower than the angels' (Hebrews 2:7), we should nevertheless think of ourselves 'with sober judgment' (Romans 12:3) because 'now we see through a glass, darkly' (1 Corinthians 13:12 AV).

Philosophers agree that in order to have knowledge you must have a belief that's true. They disagree about whether or not you need something in addition to a true belief in order to know something. Most do think that justification/warrant is required, but there's disagreement about what this means. Many would say that knowledge is a true belief that's been *arrived at in a rationally appropriate or reliable manner:* 'We have knowledge of something when we are representing it (thinking about it, speaking of it, treating it) as it actually is, on an appropriate basis of thought and experience. Knowledge involves truth or accuracy of representation, but it must also be truth based upon adequate evidence or insight. The evidence or insight comes in various ways, depending on the nature of the subject matter.'[43]

Question: People can become discouraged when they discover philosophers spend much of their time disagreeing with each other. List as many reasons as you can as to why people might be discouraged by this disagreement. Are there good counter-arguments to each point on your list? For example, does disagreement about the truth necessarily mean that there isn't any truth worth disagreeing about?

1.4 What Is the Relationship between Christian Faith and Philosophy?

Truly loving God with your mind means being intentional about your intellectual life, learning to think well.
David A. Horner[44]

Atheist Richard Dawkins defines religious faith as 'blind trust, in the absence of evidence, even in the teeth of evidence.'[45] Dawkins is right to object to holding beliefs 'in the teeth of evidence' (assuming that the counter-evidence is strong enough). However, he is wrong to think that 'faith' *means* belief in the face of overwhelming counter-evidence. McGrath comments that Dawkins':

> idiosyncratic definition simply does not stand up to serious investigation. In fact, it is itself an excellent example of a belief tenaciously held and defended 'in the absence of evidence, even in the teeth of evidence' . . . the classic Christian tradition has always valued rationality, and does not hold that faith involves the complete abandonment of reason or believing in the teeth of evidence. Indeed, the Christian tradition is so consistent on this matter that it is difficult to understand where Dawkins has got the idea of faith as 'blind trust' from.[46]

Nevertheless, Julian Baggini defines faith as 'belief in what there is a lack of strong evidence to believe in. Indeed, sometimes it is belief in something that is contrary to the available evidence.'[47] Likewise, according to A.C. Grayling, 'faith is a commitment to belief contrary to evidence and reason.'[48] Both atheists misrepresent the story of doubting Thomas (John 20:24–31) as endorsing 'the principle that it is good to believe what you have no evidence to believe.'[49] However, Jesus commends people who believe *without having to see for themselves.* He doesn't commend those who believe *without evidence.* Indeed, earlier in John's gospel Jesus challenged people to '*believe on the evidence* of the miracles' (John 14:11, my italics; cf. John 11:42).

Thomas wasn't asked to believe *without evidence.* He was asked to believe on the basis of the other disciples' testimony. Thomas initially lacked *the first-hand experience of the evidence that had convinced them*; but that's the position of most people throughout history! Moreover, the reason John gives for recounting these events is that what he saw is *evidence* for the truth of the gospel: 'Jesus did many other miraculous signs in the presence of his disciples, which are not recorded in this book. But these are written that you may believe that Jesus is the Christ, the Son of God, and that by believing you may have life in his name' (John 20:30–31).

Watch:
Francis A. Schaeffer, 'Faith, Seeing and Believing' http://youtu.be/1eKdw32_wJE.

J.P. Moreland writes:

> The essence of faith – biblical or otherwise – is confidence or trust, and one can have faith in a thing (such as a chair) or a person (such as a parent, the president, or God), and one can have faith in the truth of a proposition . . . When trust is directed toward a person/thing, it is called 'faith in'; when it is directed toward the truth of a proposition, it is called 'faith that.' . . . It is a great misunderstanding of faith to oppose it to reason or knowledge. Nothing could be further from the truth. In actual fact, faith – confidence, trust – is rooted in knowledge.[50]

Moreland defines faith as 'a trust in and commitment to what we have reason to believe is true.'[51] This is perfectly compatible with the observation that 'faith is being sure of what we hope for and certain of what we do not see' (Hebrews 11:1). There's nothing here about faith meaning to be sure of what we believe *despite evidence to the contrary*. There's nothing here about faith meaning to be certain of something that we *have no reason to think is true*. Read in context, the writer of Hebrews exhorts Christians to cling to their warranted trust in Jesus despite the temptation to abandon *what they know to be true* under the pressure of persecution.

Watch:
Gregory Koukl, 'What Is Faith?' www.youtube.com/watch?v=bRuxYaiTg4g&feature=related.

Listen:
Peter S. Williams, 'Blind Faith in Blind Faith' www.damaris.org/cm/podcasts/618.

C.S. Lewis defined faith as 'the art of holding onto things your reason has once accepted, in spite of your changing moods.'[52] For moods change whatever view your reason takes:

> Now that I am a Christian I do have moods in which the whole thing looks very improbable: but when I was an atheist I had moods in which Christianity looked terribly probable . . . unless you teach your moods 'where to get off,'

you can never be a sound Christian or even a sound atheist, but just a creature dithering to and fro, with its beliefs really dependent on the weather and the state of its digestion . . .[53]

Moreover:

When we exhort people to Faith as a virtue, to the settled intention of continuing to believe certain things, we are not exhorting them to fight against reason . . . If we wish to be rational, not now and then, but constantly, we must pray for the gift of Faith, for the power to go on believing not in the teeth of reason but in the teeth of lust and terror and jealousy and boredom and indifference that which reason, authority, or experience, or all three, have once delivered to us for truth.[54]

When the New Testament talks positively about faith, 'it *only* uses words derived from the Greek root [*pistis*] which means "to be persuaded."'[55] Faith and reason are *not* competitors. As Michael J. Wilkins and J.P. Moreland affirm: 'the modern view of faith as something unrelated or even hostile to reason is a departure from traditional Christianity and not a genuine expression of it.'[56]

> **Question:**
> What does the Bible say about the meaning of 'faith' and the roles of reason, wisdom, knowledge and evidence in discipleship? (You may find www.biblegateway.com a useful resource.)

Consider a sampling of what the Bible says about evidence and reason (all italics mine):

* The cosmos is created by a rational God who made humans in his own 'image' (Genesis 1:27; John 1:1)
* God says to humans: 'let us *reason* together' (Isaiah 1:18)
* Samuel stood before Israel and said: 'I am going to *confront you with evidence* before the LORD' (1 Samuel 12:7)
* Jesus said: *'believe on the evidence* of the miracles' (John 14:11)
* When John the Baptist questioned if Jesus was the Messiah, Jesus likewise *appealed to the evidence of his works* (cf. Matthew 11:4–6)
* Paul wrote of '*defending* and *confirming* the gospel' (Philippians 1:7)
* Paul '*reasoned . . . explaining* and *proving*' (Acts 17:2–3)
* 'Every Sabbath [Paul] *reasoned* in the synagogue, trying to *persuade* Jews and Greeks . . . Paul entered the synagogue and spoke boldly there for three months, *arguing persuasively* about the kingdom of God. But

some of them became obstinate; they refused to believe and publicly maligned the Way. So Paul left them. He took the disciples with him and had *discussions* daily in the lecture hall of Tyrannus' (Acts 18:4; 19:8–9)

- Paul urges Christians to '*stop thinking like children*. In regard to evil be infants, but *in your thinking be adults*' (1 Corinthians 14:20)
- Paul advises Christians: 'Choose your words carefully and be ready to *give answers* to anyone who asks questions' (Colossians 4:6 CEV)
- Peter commands Christians to 'always be prepared to *give an answer* to everyone who asks you to give the *reason* for the hope that you have . . . with gentleness and respect' (1 Peter 3:15)

The Greek translated as 'give an answer' in 1 Peter 3:15 is *apologia* – from which we get the word 'apologetics.' Apologetics isn't apologizing in the sense of saying sorry! An *apologia* is literally 'a word back', but the term means a 'defence' or 'vindication.' Apologetics can be defined as 'the art of persuasively advocating Christian spirituality across spiritualities, as objectively true, good and beautiful, through the responsible use of classical rhetoric.'[57] Apologetics is part of 'spiritual warfare' wherein we '*demolish arguments* and every pretension that sets itself up against the *knowledge* of God' (2 Corinthians 10:5). Spiritual warfare 'is against unbelief, not unbelievers . . . [Its goal] is not victory but truth. Both sides win.'[58] The Bible is clearly against belief contrary to evidence and reason. For example, Paul says: 'Test everything. Hold on to the good' (1 Thessalonians 5:21).

Norman L. Geisler and Paul D. Feinberg note that some Christians are suspicious of philosophy and advise others to stay away from the subject. However, this isn't wise advice: 'Christianity *can* stand up to the intellectual challenge mounted against it. The result of such a challenge should not be the loss of faith, but the priceless possession of a well-reasoned and mature faith.'[59] Failure to be aware of contemporary thought patterns can have serious consequences for the Christian who avoids philosophy, for 'the Christian most likely to fall prey to false philosophy is the ignorant Christian.'[60] Indeed, in today's message-saturated world everyone would benefit from some philosophical savvy.

Colossians 2:8 (ESV) warns against being taken 'captive by philosophy and empty deceit according to human tradition . . . and not according to Christ,' but this 'is not a prohibition against philosophy as such, but against . . . a specific false philosophy, a kind of incipient Gnosticism . . . the definite article "this" in [the] Greek indicates a particular philosophy.'[61] Apostles such as John and Paul clearly engage in philosophical activities (cf. John 1; Acts 17), as does Jesus himself. Groothuis argues that Jesus' own use of reason 'brings into serious question the indictment that Jesus praised uncritical faith over reasoning.'[62] With Mark Mittelberg:

I would urge my fellow believers to not let go of one of the most important things God has given us: logic, evidence, old-fashioned apologetics, which Jesus often appealed to when he was questioned. He would say, 'Don't just listen to my words, but look at my works, look at my miracles, look at the fact that I am fulfilling the roles of the Messiah in the prophecies. Look to the fact that I will rise from the dead.' And then to Thomas the doubter, he said, 'Look at the holes in my hands and in my side. Look at me; it's Jesus.' Over and over he pointed to the facts, the evidence, as did the apostles and other writers of Scripture.[63]

1.5 Philosophy, Natural Theology and Beyond

Mortimer J. Adler observes that 'more consequences for thought and action follow from the affirmation or denial of God than from answering any other basic question.'[64] Hence, after introducing the ground rules of logic in the next two chapters, much of this book is dedicated to examining various arguments for (and against) belief in God. For as John Wesley[65] said in his 'Address to the Clergy':

> Some knowledge of the sciences also, is, to say the least . . . expedient. Nay, may we not say, that the knowledge of one . . . is even necessary next, and in order to, the knowledge of the Scripture itself? I mean logic. For what is this, if rightly understood, but the art of good sense, of apprehending things clearly, judging truly, and reasoning conclusively? What is it, viewed in another light, but the art of learning and teaching; whether by convincing or persuading? What is there, then, in the whole compass of science, to be desired in comparison of it? . . . Should not a Minister be acquainted too with at least the general grounds of natural philosophy? Is not this a great help to the accurate understanding of several passages of Scripture? Assisted by this, he may himself comprehend, and on proper occasions explain to others, how the invisible things of God are seen from the creation of the world; how 'the heavens declare the glory of God, and the firmament showeth his handiwork;' till they cry out, 'O Lord, how manifold are thy works! In wisdom hast thou made them all.'[66]

The Catholic Church holds that 'God . . . can, by the natural light of human reason, be known with certainty from the works of creation.'[67] This statement has generally been understood as giving the thumbs-up to 'natural theology', which John Polkinghorne defines as 'the attempt to learn something of God from the exercise of reason and the inspection of the world – in other words, from reflection on general experience.'[68] Like Psalm 19 and Romans 1:18–20 this claim could be read as affirming that God can be *perceived* through contemplating creation, rather than *proved*. Nevertheless, such scriptural and theological assertions lay a foundation upon which natural theology may build, for as Geisler writes: 'It should not seem strange to those who believe in God's manifestation in His creation (Rom. 1:19–29; Ps. 19:1) that it is possible to arrive at knowledge of God by inference from these manifestations.'[69] The question of God's existence offers an interesting introduction to the art of philosophy and quickly introduces a wide range of interrelated philosophical topics.

Question:
Heeding the call for the discipleship of the mind can mean swimming against the stream, not only of 'the world' but also of 'the church', for 'the present age has been described as the most anti-intellectual period in all church history. Pietism and fideism are rampant in the evangelical world.'[70] With this in mind, imagine a Christian expresses a heartfelt concern that they would put their faith at risk by studying philosophy. They worry about being taken captive by vain human tradition rather than by Christ (Colossians 2:8), about being tempted to lean on their own understanding rather than upon God (Proverbs 3:5), and that philosophy will cause them to abandon the childlike faith necessary for salvation (Mark 10:15). How might you graciously respond to these concerns using the resources of the Christian tradition itself?

Conclusion

As C.S. Lewis wrote: 'Good philosophy must exist, if for no other reason, because bad philosophy needs to be answered.'[71] Correctly understood and conducted, philosophy is a spiritual discipline (and one with deep scriptural roots). Philosophy is an intrinsically valuable art underpinned by transferable rhetorical skills (skills of use to all those who strive to worship God with their minds and to serve him in the persuasive communication of the gospel). Our next two chapters will focus upon the foundational *logos* element of good rhetoric, which is the subject of the philosophical discipline of logic.

Film to watch and discuss:
Serenity, directed by Joss Whedon (Universal Pictures, 2005) (PG-13) – What does this film (a stand-alone conclusion to the TV series *Firefly*) have to say about the power and importance of truth? cf. Emily Russell, 'Serenity: Discussion Guide' www.damaris.org/content/content.php?type=1&id=314.

Recommended Resources

Video

Fr. Barron. 'Evangelizing Through Beauty' http://youtu.be/bBMOwZFpZX0.
Geisler, Norman L. 'Truth and Relativism' http://youtu.be/kSLrK6cWcMM.
Groothuis, Douglas. 'A Biblical View of Truth' http://saddleback.com/mc/m/97a67/.
Lennox, John. 'The Christian Use of the Mind' http://johnlennox.org/index.php/en/resource/the_christian_use_of_the_mind/.
*Moreland, J.P. 'Faith and Reason' www.veritas.org/Talks.aspx#!/v/250.
— 'What Is Truth?' www.youtube.com/watch?v=kOJ9GDpQBUI&feature=related.
Neill, Conor. 'The Three Pillars of Persuasion' http://youtu.be/aEZWKkv48MY.
*Reynolds, John Mark. 'Finding Christ in Culture' http://vimeo.com/30333189.
— 'The War of Worldviews' http://youtu.be/6F5DE11X8yY.
Plantinga, Alvin. 'Truth and Worldviews' http://youtu.be/oz7zDliggYQ.
Strobel, Lee. 'Faith Involves Doubt' www.leestrobel.com/videoserver/video.php?-clip=CCNT1687.
Willard, Dallas. 'What Is Truth?' www.youtube.com/watch?v=I7Mq6KNw9OQ&feature=relmfu.
*Williams, Peter S. 'Apologetics in 3D' http://vimeo.com/33805834.
*— 'A Pre-Modern Perspective on Postmodernism: A Tale of Three Mirrors' (Eastern European Bible College)' http://youtu.be/Mhf6-H6l2K4.
*— 'Faith and Reason' YouTube Playlist
www.youtube.com/playlist?list=PLQhh3qcwVEWgaO33qUCPRYWqkDn2nomC5.

Audio

Geisler, Norman L. 'Christians and Philosophy' http://youthofcbc.com/podcast_item/21/27/Geisler+16+-+Christians+and+Philosophy.mp3.
Groothuis, Douglas. 'Truth Decay' www.thethingsthatmattermost.org/gallery06042006.htm.
Horner, David A. 'Apologetics 315 Interview' http://j.mp/Apologetics315-InterviewDavidHorner.
Iona. 'Wisdom', from *Journey into the Morn* (Forefront, 1996) http://youtu.be/TOXQFb-HXYtM.
Moreland, J.P. 'The Importance of the Christian Mind' www.veritas.org/Media.aspx#/v/62.
Ortberg, John. 'Faith and Doubt' www.thethingsthatmattermost.com/Sound/11-16-08.mp3.
Willard, Dallas. 'Why We Can Trust Spiritual Knowledge' www.thethingsthatmattermost.com/Sound/05-31-09.mp3.
*Williams, Peter S. 'Understanding Spirituality: The Jesus Way' (1st Delivery) www.damaris.org/cm/podcasts/770 (2nd Delivery) www.damaris.org/cm/podcasts/771.

*— 'Apologetics and Flourishing' www.damaris.org/cm/podcasts/702.
— 'Apologetics in 3D' www.damaris.org/cm/podcasts/554.
*— 'Blind Faith in Blind Faith' www.damaris.org/cm/podcasts/618.
— 'Interview on Apologetics in 3D' www.damaris.org/cm/podcasts/556.
— 'Introduction to Philosophy' www.damaris.org/cm/podcasts/527.
— 'A Pre-Modern Perspective on Postmodernism: A Tale of Three Mirrors' (Eastern European Bible College) www.damaris.org/cm/podcasts/707.
— 'The Values of Our Answers' www.damaris.org/cm/podcasts/748.

Online papers

Copan, Paul. 'True for You, but Not for Me' www.bethinking.org/truth-tolerance/introductory/thats-true-for-you-but-not-for-me-relativism.htm.
Craig, William Lane. 'In Intellectual Neutral' www.reasonablefaith.org/site/News2?page=NewsArticle&id=6597.
— 'The Revolution in Anglo-American Philosophy' www.reasonablefaith.org/site/News2?page=NewsArticle&id=5352.
*DeWeese, Garry and Joseph E. Gorra. 'Doing Philosophy as a Christian' www.epsociety.org/userfiles/DeWeese_Doing_Philosophy_Interview.pdf.
Fellows, Andrew. 'Recovering Goodness, Beauty and Truth' www.labri.org/england/resources/05052008/AF02_Goodness_Beauty_3E64FE.pdf.
Geisler, Norman L. 'The Nature of Truth: Part One' www.ankerberg.com/Articles/_PDFArchives/theological-dictionary/TD1W1099.pdf.
— 'The Nature of Truth: Part Two' www.ankerberg.com/Articles/_PDFArchives/theological-dictionary/TD2W1099.pdf.
Marian, David. 'The Correspondence Theory of Truth' http://plato.stanford.edu/entries/truth-correspondence/.
*Moreland, J.P. 'Academic Integration and the Christian Scholar' http://ai.clm.org/articles/moreland_integration.html.
— 'Christianity and Non-Empirical Knowledge' www.jpmoreland.com/articles/christianity-and-non-empirical-knowledge/.
— 'How Evangelicals Became Over-Committed to the Bible and What Can Be Done about It' www.kingdomtriangle.com/discussion/moreland_EvangOverCommBible.pdf.
— 'Philosophical Apologetics, the Church, and Contemporary Culture' www.afterall.net/index.php/papers/23.
— 'What Is Knowledge?' www.jpmoreland.com/articles/what-is-knowledge/.
Moser, Paul. 'Christ-Shaped Philosophy: Wisdom and Spirit United' www.epsociety.org/userfiles/art-Moser%20%28Christ-Shaped%20Philosophy%29.pdf.
Plantinga, Alvin. 'Advice to Christian Philosophers' http://ai.clm.org/articles/plantinga_advice.html.
— 'Christian Philosophy at the End of the 20th Century' www.calvin.edu/academic/philosophy/virtual_library/articles/plantinga_alvin/christian_philosophy_at_the_end_of_the_20th_century.pdf.
— 'Spiritual Autobiography' www.calvin.edu/125th/wolterst/p_bio.pdf.
Weitnauer, Carson. 'How Churches Can Respond to Doubt' www.apologetics315.com/2012/08/how-to-get-apologetics-in-your-church-2_30.html#more.
Wesley, John. 'An Address to the Clergy' http://wesley.nnu.edu/john_wesley/10clergy.htm.
Williams, Peter S. 'A Sceptical Tea Party' http://philosophynow.org/issues/24/A_Sceptical_Tea_Party.

*— 'Apologetics in 3D: Persuading across Spiritualities with the Apostle Paul', *Theofilos* (2012:1) pp. 3-24, www.bethinking.org/what-is-apologetics/advanced/apologetics-in-3d.htm.

Books

Beckwith, Francis J., William Lane Craig and J.P. Moreland, eds. *To Everyone an Answer: A Case for the Christian Worldview* (Downers Grove, IL: IVP, 2004), 'Part 1: Faith, Reason and the Necessity of Apologetics'.

Beilby, James and David K. Clark. *Why Bother with Truth? Arriving at Knowledge in a Skeptical Society* (Norcross, GA: RZIM, 2000).

Boa, Kenneth and Robert Bowman Jr. *Faith Has Its Reasons: Integrative Approaches to Defending the Christian Faith* (Milton Keynes: Paternoster Press, 2006) www.apologetics315.com/2009/03/faith-has-its-reasons-by-ken-boa-rob.html.

Clark, Kelly James, ed. *Philosophers Who Believe: The Spiritual Journeys of 11 Leading Thinkers* (Downers Grove, IL: IVP, 1993).

DeWeese, Garrett J. *Doing Philosophy as a Christian* (Downers Grove, IL; IVP Academic, 2011).

Evans, C. Stephen. *Pocket Dictionary of Apologetics and Philosophy of Religion* (Downers Grove, IL: IVP, 2002).

Groothuis, Douglas. *On Jesus* (London: Thomson/Wadsworth, 2003).

— *Truth Decay: Defending Christianity against the Challenges of Postmodernism* (Leicester: IVP, 2000).

Horner, David A. *Mind Your Faith: A Student's Guide to Thinking and Living Well* (Downers Grove, IL: IVP Academic, 2011).

Kostenberger, Andreas, ed. *Whatever Happened to Truth?* (Wheaton, IL: Crossway, 2005).

Koukl, Gregory. *Tactics: A Game Plan for Discussing Your Christian Convictions* (Grand Rapids, MI: Zondervan, 2009).

Levin, Margarita Rosa. 'A Defence of Objectivity.' Pages 549-559 in *Classics of Philosophy: Volume III – The Twentieth Century* (ed. Louis P. Pojman; Oxford University Press, 2001).

McGrath, Alister. *The Passionate Intellect: Christian Faith and the Discipleship of the Mind* (Downers Grove, IL: IVP, 2010).

Moreland, J.P. *The Kingdom Triangle* (Grand Rapids, MI: Zondervan, 2007) cf. www.kingdomtriangle.com/book/kingdom-triangle-sample.pdf.

— *Love Your God with All Your Mind: The Role of Reason in the Life of the Soul* (Colorado Springs, CO: NavPress, 2nd edn, 2012); for 1st edn cf. www.navpress.com/images/pdfs/9781576830161.pdf.

*— and Mark Matlock. *Smart Faith: Loving Your God with All Your Mind* (Colorado Springs, CO: Think, 2005).

Morris, Thomas V., ed. *God and the Philosophers: The Reconciliation of Faith and Reason* (Oxford University Press, 1994).

Muehlhoff, Tim and Todd V. Lewis. *Authentic Communication: Christian Speech Engaging Culture* (Downers Grove, IL: IVP Academic, 2010).

Pearcey, Nancy. *Saving Leonardo: A Call to Resist the Secular Assault on Mind, Morals and Meaning* (Nashville, TN: B&H, 2010).

Reynolds, John Mark. *When Athens Met Jerusalem: An Introduction to Classical and Christian Thought* (Downers Grove, IL: IVP Academic, 2009).

Willard, Dallas. *Knowing Christ Today: Why We Can Trust Spiritual Knowledge* (New York: HarperOne, 2009).

Williams, Peter S. *Understanding Jesus: Five Ways to Spiritual Enlightenment* (Milton Keynes: Paternoster Press, 2011).

Wood, W. Jay. *Epistemology: Becoming Intellectually Virtuous* (Leicester: Apollos, 1998).

2. Making a Good Argument

Another part of my trade, too, made me sure that you weren't a priest . . . You
attacked reason . . . It's bad theology.
Father Brown[1]

Introduction: Common Ground

When Paul wanted to talk about Jesus with fellow Jews, he began where
they were: on the common ground of the Hebrew Scriptures. When he
wanted to introduce Jesus to Greeks in Athens, the Hebrew Scripture
was no longer common ground. Paul still began where his audience was,
but he quoted from Greek philosophers and poets (cf. Acts 17).[2] Paul's
method – starting where his audience was, before trying to move them to
where he was – highlights the importance of common ground for rational
discussion.

✔ Look for common ground when arguing

Some common ground takes the form of language, or culture (like the
poets Paul quoted, or the latest film everyone's talking about). Some
common ground runs deeper than that: 'philosophy, whatever else it
may be, is the investigation of significant truth claims through rational
analysis. In that light, the necessary and sufficient conditions for being
a philosopher . . . are a strong and lived-out inclination to pursue truth

about philosophical matters through the rigorous use of human reasoning and to do so with some intellectual facility.'[3]

The inherent structure of logic, which determines whether our pursuit of truth is rigorous, is an essential part of the common ground required by any human interaction.

When someone asks a question, they *necessarily* make assumptions. For example, they assume that truth is obtainable and that paying attention to rational argumentation is a good way to seek it. These unavoidable rational assumptions are *common ground* on the basis of which debate takes place. As Aquinas observed: 'against the Jews we are able to argue by means of the Old Testament, while against heretics we are able to argue by means of the New Testament. But the Mohammedans and the pagans accept neither the one nor the other. We must, therefore, have recourse to the natural reason, to which all men are forced to give their assent.'[4]

Sometimes a person may need to explicitly recognize their previously implicit trust in the principles of logic before fruitful debate can take place. Nevertheless, whether this common ground needs to be dusted off a little, or lies waiting in eager anticipation of the next 'game' of reason, common ground exists. As Thomas Nagel explains: 'Certain forms of thought can't be intelligibly doubted because they force themselves into every attempt to think about anything . . . There just isn't room for scepticism about basic logic, because there is no place to stand where we can formulate or think it without immediately contradicting ourselves by relying on it.'[5]

Question:
Someone asks you a question. List as many 'common ground' assumptions you share with them as you can think of.

The analogy of philosophy as a 'game' taking place on the common ground of rationality isn't meant to imply that arguments have winners and losers. If both sides have a greater commitment to *the* truth than to *their* truth, then both sides emerge as winners. One side will be pleased to have been freed from ignorance and delusion, and the other will be glad they could help (and will respect the 'loser' for having the courage to admit they were wrong).

✔ A philosopher should value truth more than being right

Arguments attack assertions, not people. Rational debate is one 'game' where everyone can be a winner, if they stick to the rules:

The idea of good defeats – those in which you learn, or give, or allow the better to flourish – is an important one. Spinoza wrote that weapons never conquer minds, only magnanimity and love; to be conquered by these things is a great victory in itself, because it is a response to what is best. To recognize an argument as sound, and to defer to it, or to grasp the justice of another's cause and to make way for it, are likewise victorious defeats.[6]

2.1 The Laws of Reason

Philosophers often disagree concerning what the truth about reality is, but this disagreement presupposes that there *is* such a thing as 'truth,' that humans *can* know truth (even if we don't know *how* we know), that beliefs that contradict the truth are false and that self-contradictory beliefs (e.g. 'I know it is true that knowledge is impossible') *cannot* be true! Hence, while the pursuit of truth results in disagreement, it presupposes a fundamental agreement about truth, knowledge and the rules by which they can and should be pursued.

Aquinas pointed out that from the mere acceptance that *there is a fact* followed the truths of logical thought. He observed that a 'something' is a something *rather than a nothing*. He therefore insisted that along with the possibility of affirmation (i.e. 'X is') there instantly and necessarily enters the possibility of contradiction (i.e. 'No, it isn't'). That is, the reality of *being* entails the nature of *truth* (correspondence with being) and *falsehood* (contradiction of being). As G.K. Chesterton explains, the instant we admit that 'there *is* an Is':

> there has already entered *something* beyond even the first fact of being; there follows it like its shadow the first fundamental creed or commandment; that a thing cannot be and not be. Henceforth, in common or popular language, there is a false and true. I say in popular language, because Aquinas is nowhere more subtle than in pointing out that being is not strictly the same as truth; seeing truth must mean the appreciation of being by some mind capable of appreciating it . . . two agencies are at work; reality and the recognition of reality . . .[7]

The basic laws of reason, revealed by the recognition that 'there *is* an Is', include:

* The Law of [Non-]Contradiction – 'Nothing can both be and not be'
* The Law of Excluded Middle – 'Everything must either be or not be'[8]
* The Law of Identity – 'A thing is identical to itself'

As Bertrand Russell noted: 'what is important is not the fact that we think in accordance with these laws, but the fact that things behave in accordance with them', so that when we think in accordance with them[9] 'we think truly'.[10] The most basic of these laws is the law of non-contradiction, because the most basic distinction is between something *rather than* nothing existing. Indeed, as Gregory E. Ganssle writes: 'the laws of logic are expressions of who God is and how he thinks. To say that the law of non-contradiction is most basic is another way of stating the simple fact that God is exactly who he is and he is not otherwise.'[11]

Watch:
Frank Turek, 'The Law of Non-Contradiction'
www.youtube.com/watch?v=B8CLXh9G-1c.
Ravi Zacharias, 'Law of Non-Contradiction'
www.youtube.com/watch?v=JWVzHOhGSC0&feature=related.

2.2 The Noetic Structure of Basic and Non-Basic Beliefs

A person's beliefs form what philosophers call a 'noetic structure' (from the Greek word for 'mental' – *nous*). A house has a structure. The roof depends upon the top floor, the top floor depends upon the ground floor and the ground floor depends upon the foundations. Likewise, beliefs have a structure. Some beliefs depend upon other beliefs, while others do not. For example, the belief that 'umbrellas are useful' depends upon beliefs about the existence of rain, the preferability of being dry rather than wet, and so on. In the absence of these other beliefs, you wouldn't believe that umbrellas are useful.

Fig. 1.

'Umbrellas are useful'

'There is such a thing as rain' + 'Being rained on makes you wet' + 'I don't like being wet'

Your belief that umbrellas are useful is less *fundamental* or *basic* in your noetic structure than beliefs like 'There is such a thing as rain' and 'Being rained on makes you wet.'

27

How fundamental a belief is in one's noetic structure depends upon how many other beliefs are based upon it. The more your noetic structure would change if you gave up a belief, the more fundamental that belief is for you. A belief in the usefulness of the umbrella isn't particularly fundamental in anyone's noetic structure.

Some beliefs in one's noetic structure are unsupported by *any* other beliefs. These are 'basic beliefs.' A basic belief is a belief 'that one holds but not on the basis of other beliefs that one holds.'[12] Basic beliefs form the *foundation* of one's noetic structure. For example, your belief that 'being rained on makes you wet' probably isn't something you believe on the basis of other, more foundational beliefs. Rather, it's something you believe simply because you remember getting wet in the rain. Indeed, memories and perceptual beliefs are both prime examples of basic belief. Perceptual beliefs are acquired immediately, without being based upon other beliefs: 'one simply *finds oneself believing* the sky is blue when one is in the *appropriate circumstances*: one is outside, one looks at the sky, and the sky is blue.'[13] Likewise, I don't *argue* my way to the conclusion that I had coffee with friends yesterday. I simply *remember* drinking coffee with friends yesterday.

Notice that while I *could* argue that I had coffee with friends yesterday (e.g. by doing some forensic science), I don't *need* an argument in order to make my memory-based belief that I did (or your belief that I did, based on my testimony) a rational belief. Some basic beliefs simply *are not* held on the basis of other beliefs, *even though they could be*. Other basic beliefs (e.g. belief in the laws of reason) *cannot* be held on the basis of other beliefs. Either way, basic beliefs provide a basis for holding other, 'non-basic' beliefs. Such 'non-basic' beliefs are, of course, always held on the basis of other beliefs (and however long or short, the chain of beliefs always track back to basic beliefs). Hence: 'Some of our beliefs are basic, beliefs not believed on the basis of other beliefs we hold, and some beliefs are non-basic, beliefs that are acquired and maintained by the evidential support of other beliefs.'[14] In the case of basic beliefs, 'one simply finds oneself believing them in certain circumstances.'[15] By contrast, one always comes to hold non-basic beliefs on the basis of considering the relationship between other beliefs one has; that is, *by considering arguments*.

✔ Non-basic beliefs depend upon other beliefs, but basic beliefs don't

2.3 Properly Basic Beliefs

As a matter of fact, a basic belief isn't held on the basis of other beliefs (even if it could be held on the basis of other beliefs). However, the mere fact of being held basically doesn't necessarily make a belief rational or 'warranted' (let alone true). We might say that although a given basic belief *isn't* supported by other beliefs, it *should* be, in the sense that it is irrational in the absence of such non-basic support. For example, someone might have a basic belief that a certain set of numbers will come up trumps in next week's lottery. The mere fact that this belief is basic (i.e. isn't supported by any other beliefs they hold) doesn't mean that it's a rational belief! Philosophers therefore distinguish between basic beliefs that are and are not *properly* basic, where being 'properly basic' means being 'a belief that it is rational to hold basically' (i.e. without supporting beliefs).

I don't have to have independent evidence that I drank coffee with friends yesterday for my memory-based belief that I did to be reasonable. Hence, unlike a basic belief that a certain set of numbers will win next week's lottery, my memory of having coffee with friends yesterday is a 'properly basic belief', a basic belief that's *prima facie* (i.e. 'on the face of things') rational for me to hold in a basic manner. I don't flout any rational obligations when I believe that I had coffee with friends yesterday simply because I remember doing so.

✔ A 'properly basic belief' is any belief that's rational to hold without its being based on any other beliefs

Like memory-beliefs, fundamental moral beliefs are 'properly basic': 'Somewhere in one's moral reasoning one reaches a set of beliefs that are bearers of intrinsic value; they are not valued as a means to some other end or for some extrinsic reason. At this level one reaches one's basic moral beliefs.'[16] Many other kinds of beliefs are properly basic: 'There are, for example, elementary *truths of logic* . . . There are certain *mathematical beliefs*. And there are certain framework or fundamental beliefs such as *belief in an external world, belief in the self*, etc. These are foundational beliefs that we typically reason from and not to.'[17]

In short, many beliefs appear to be rational *without their being based on other beliefs* (even if some of them *can* be based on other beliefs). Such beliefs are 'properly basic' or 'warranted' beliefs.

The existence of *some* properly basic beliefs in our noetic structure is a necessity. As Roy Clouser argues:

it is *impossible* that the only beliefs we have the right to be certain about are the ones that we have proven . . . First, if everything needed to be proven, then the premises of every proof would also need to be proven. But . . . it makes no sense to demand that everything be proven because an infinite regress of proofs is impossible. So when the premises of an argument are themselves in need of proof, the series of arguments needed to prove its premises must eventually end with an argument whose premises are all 'basic', that is, not in need of proof . . . not all beliefs need proof, and proving anything depends on having beliefs that don't need it . . . A second reason why not every belief needs proof is that the rules for drawing inferences correctly . . . cannot them-selves have proofs because they are the very rules we must use in order to prove anything. If we were to use them to construct proofs of themselves, the proofs would already be assuming the truth of the very rules we were trying to prove! So proofs need belief in unproven *rules* as well as *premises* that we can know without proof . . .[18]

Clouser uses the term 'intuition' to describe 'our [fallible] capacity to recognize a state of affairs as in fact the case and to form the belief that it is so without any mediating process of reasoning.'[19]

A properly non-basic belief is a belief it is within one's epistemic rights ('epistemic' comes from the same root as 'epistemology', meaning 'theory of knowledge') to hold *on the basis of the relationship between other beliefs that one has an epistemic right to hold*. For example, because I believe that Socrates is a man and that all men are mortal, I am within my epistemic rights to hold the non-basic belief that Socrates is mortal. A properly basic belief is a basic belief that one is within one's epistemic rights to hold in a basic manner (e.g. *without its being held in a properly non-basic manner*). For example, because I remember that rain is wet, I am within my epistemic rights in believing that rain is wet.

While it would obviously be irrational to pick basic beliefs at random (since we know this is an unreliable method of belief formation), the class of properly basic beliefs is nevertheless larger than the basic laws of logic beloved of the 'rationalist' or the basic data of sense impressions beloved of the 'empiricist.' Beliefs that appear to be properly basic should be accepted as such *until and unless there is sufficient reason to doubt them*. Many properly basic beliefs are open to defeat by stronger evidence, *but the burden of proof is always on the sceptic rather than the believer*.

Properly basic beliefs that aren't open to defeat by stronger evidence because they cannot be doubted (e.g. because they are self-contradictory to doubt) might be called 'inescapably properly basic' beliefs. Not all properly basic beliefs are inescapable (perhaps you could prove I was hypnotized into having a false memory of drinking coffee with friends yesterday). However, noting the existence of some inescapable properly basic beliefs, Aquinas argued that Christians must see faith and reason as two sides of the same coin:

> For that with which the human reason is naturally endowed [i.e. inescapably properly basic beliefs] is clearly most true; so much so, that it is impossible for us to think of such truths as false . . . Since, therefore, only the false is opposed to the true, as is clearly evident from an examination of their definitions, it is impossible that the truth of faith should be opposed to those principles that the human reason knows naturally. Furthermore, that which is introduced into the soul of the student by the teacher is contained in the knowledge of the teacher – unless his teaching is fictitious, which it is improper to say of God. Now, the knowledge of the principles that are known to us naturally has been implanted in us by God; for God is the Author of our nature. These principles, therefore, are also contained by the divine Wisdom. Hence, whatever is opposed to them is opposed to the divine Wisdom, and, therefore, cannot come from God . . . From this we evidently gather the following conclusion: whatever arguments are brought against the doctrines of faith are conclusions incorrectly derived from the first and self-evident principles imbedded in nature . . . And so, there exists the possibility to answer them.[20]

Question:
Can belief in God be properly basic? If belief in God is properly basic, is it in principle open to defeat by stronger evidence, or is it an 'inescapably properly basic' belief?

2.4 Faith in Reason

All argument rests upon a properly basic trust in certain inescapable principles of logic. These principles can't be doubted without thereby being affirmed. However, neither can they be proved in a way that doesn't rely upon their truth (and so the attempt to prove these basic principles is 'question begging'). As Roy Abraham Varghese explains:

> it is a fact of universal and immediate experience that human beings are . . . endowed with a knowledge-base encompassing essential and ultimate principles of reality. It is this knowledge-base that underlies all thought and rationality and every exercise of the human mind . . . How do we know that these affirmations are true and how can we demonstrate their truth? Well, we know them to be true because that is what our minds tell us – instinctively, immediately – but we cannot demonstrate them to be true because all demonstrations would presuppose their truth . . . Nevertheless, we know that these affirmations

are true affirmations and if any interlocutor wishes to deny them the burden of proof lies with the interlocutor . . .[21]

Many of our beliefs appear to be properly basic and require no argument, even if they *can* be argued for. Some of our properly basic beliefs (e.g. in the laws of logic) cannot be rationally doubted (and hence cannot be argued for) – they are 'inescapably properly basic.'

✔ An 'inescapably properly basic' belief is a properly basic belief that's self-contradictory to doubt

Other properly basic beliefs can be doubted, but the burden of proof always rests with the doubter.

✔ The burden of proof is always on the person who doubts a properly basic belief

Whether one is debating the merits of a basic belief, or thinking about non-basic beliefs, the ability to argue well according to the laws of reason is key for the practice of philosophy.

2.5 How Arguments Work

Humans communicate many things in many ways (e.g. with spoken and written words, pictures, sign language, body language, and even with music). Sometimes we communicate 'propositions.' A proposition is *a proposal about how things are*. In other words, a proposition is the claim that a particular understanding of reality is true. For a particular understanding of reality to be true is for it to correspond to the facts. For example, asked if I am happy, I may claim that I am. I may claim this by nodding and smiling, by saying or writing 'I'm happy' in various languages, etc. However I make this claim, my claim has the same 'propositional content' (that I am happy). If I claim to be happy when I am happy, my claim is true. If I claim to be happy when I am not, my claim is false.

Philosophers pay particular attention to our use of *language* to discover and express truth. Because language can communicate more than 'body language' it can also miscommunicate more. You probably wouldn't mistake my smile for my name. But if I *say* 'I'm happy', you *might* think 'Happy' is my name rather than my frame of mind (perhaps I know a girl called Snow White)! Nevertheless, if we take good care of language (by avoiding misunderstandings), language takes good care of us, because it enables us to communicate very complex and specific truth claims.

We can use language to combine words into grammatical sentences that communicate propositions. These propositions have meanings that are either clear (intelligible and unambiguous) or unclear (unintelligible and/or ambiguous). A proposition that's clear enough to make a truth claim is either true or false. For example, the sentence 'This is a spludge' contains an unclear term: 'spludge.' This might be nonsense. If I stipulate that 'spludge' means 'sentence', then we have a clear proposition ('This is a sentence') – in this case one that's true.

Combining several propositions (which, under the circumstances, are called 'premises') with the aim of supporting yet another proposition (a proposition that, under the circumstances, is called a *conclusion*) produces an *argument*. As William Lane Craig writes: 'An argument is a set of statements which serve as premises leading to a conclusion.'[22]

Fig. 3.

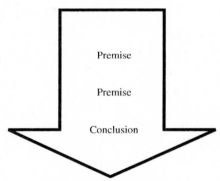

Premise

Premise

Conclusion

The simplest form of argument uses two propositions (premises) tied together with logic to support belief in a third proposition (the conclusion). A proposition on its own is just an assertion. An assertion may be true or false, but it isn't an argument.

✔ The smallest unit of argument, consisting of two premises and a conclusion, is called a syllogism

Of course, while a good argument has at least two premises and a conclusion, having two premises and a conclusion isn't enough to guarantee that you have a good argument. For example:

Premise 1) Footballs are round
Premise 2) Onions are round
Conclusion) Therefore, footballs are onions

Clearly, having two premises and a conclusion is necessary for a good argument, but not sufficient. Only if both premises are clear, *and* true, *and* the conclusion really follows from the premises, is an argument a good one.

A good argument (one that gives some support to its conclusion) is called a 'sound' argument. Bad arguments are called 'unsound'. Think of the way in which a wooden boat might be said to be 'soundly built' if it is capable of taking you from shore to shore, and 'unsound' if it will not. A sound argument is a logically valid argument (one where the conclusion really does follow from the premises), with premises all of which are not only clear, but also true. Such an argument takes you safely from the familiar shore of its premises to the previously undiscovered country of its conclusion. Here's a famous example of a sound syllogism often attributed to Aristotle:

Premise 1) Socrates is a mortal
Premise 2) All mortals die
Conclusion) Therefore, Socrates will die

Of course, people don't always present their arguments as syllogisms. They might say, 'Socrates will eventually "pop his clogs". After all, he's only mortal, and no one lives for ever.' So it's a good idea to develop the skill of rearranging arguments in ordinary prose into syllogistic form. This often means recognizing and separating out a string of syllogisms the feed into one another, the conclusion of one syllogism becoming in turn a premise in the next:

Fig. 3.

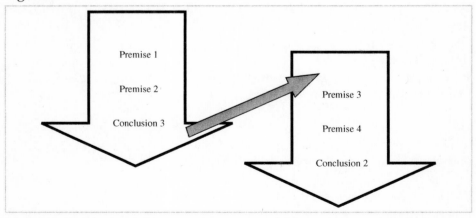

This diagram might represent the following two-syllogism argument:

1) Fred is a human
2) Eventually, all humans die
3) Therefore, eventually, Fred will die
4) Fred will die eventually (the conclusion of the previous syllogism)
5) Dead men don't talk
6) Therefore, eventually, Fred won't talk

It would be more usual to condense such an argument like this:

1) Fred is a human
2) Eventually, all humans die
3) Eventually, Fred will die
4) Dead men don't talk
5) Therefore, eventually, Fred won't talk

Here step 3 in the argument ('Eventually, Fred will die') is both the conclusion to one syllogism and the first premise in a second syllogism.

2.6 Three Tests for a Good Argument

A philosopher considering an argument will ask whether it passes three tests:

- Are all the premises clear (intelligible and unambiguous)?
- Does the conclusion really follow (with logical validity) from the premises?
- Are all the premises true?

If the premises are unclear, then either no argument has been given (because it's unintelligible) or the argument is in danger of being invalid due to an ambiguity in its terms (in which case one would want to see how the argument fares when this ambiguity is ironed out).

If the premises are clear but the conclusion doesn't follow from them, then the argument is unsound due to logical invalidity. Committing a logical 'fallacy' like this makes the argument 'fallacious.'

If the premises are clear and the conclusion would be true if the premises were true (the argument is logically valid), *but one or more of the premises are not true*, then the argument is still unsound.

For an argument to work, *everything* in it has to work; if just one thing goes wrong, then the argument fails. Think of the three tests above as three legs on a stool: you'd only feel confident about sitting on a stool if all three legs are in place!

When assessing an argument, the philosopher will test it using these three criteria. Any argument that passes all three criteria is a sound argument that supports its conclusion to some degree. Any argument that fails one or more of these criteria is unsound:

Fig. 4.

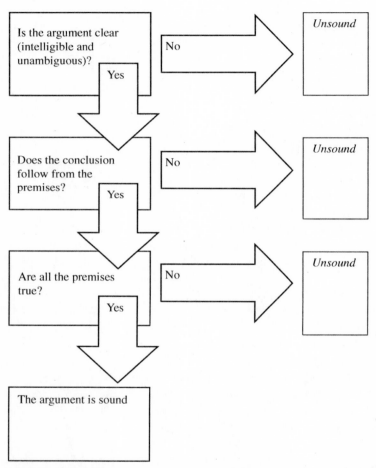

✔ A sound argument has a conclusion that really follows from premises that are both clear and true

2.7 How Strong Is Your Argument?

The strength of support given by an argument to its conclusion depends upon how sure we are about the answers we give to the above string of questions. If we're sure that the answer is 'yes' in every case, then we should be sure that the conclusion is true. But suppose we are only *pretty* sure that Fred is a man (rather than an alien). In that case, we could only be *pretty* sure about our conclusion *on the basis of this argument* (we might nevertheless be sure about the truth of the conclusion on other grounds). For an argument to be a good argument:

> it isn't required that we have 100% certainty of the truth of the premises. Some of the premises in a good argument may strike you as only slightly more plausible than their denials . . . But so long as a statement is more plausible than its negation, then you should believe it rather than its negation, and so it may serve as a premise in a good argument . . . The question is not whether the denial of a particular premise in the argument is possible (or even plausible); the question is whether the denial is as plausible or more plausible than the premise. If it isn't, then we should believe the premise.[23]

We might think that Fred is probably a man because he looks like a man, and things that look like men usually are. But suppose someone presented us with an argument strong enough to convince us that that premise 1 ('Fred is a man') is probably false (they might show us a video of an alien putting on its realistic-looking 'Fred' disguise). Nevertheless, we might argue:

Premise 1) 'Fred' is biologically alive
Premise 2) Everything biologically alive dies
Conclusion) Therefore, 'Fred' will die

Whether or not Fred is an alien, we can be more certain of Fred's eventual death on the basis of our second argument than on the basis of our first argument, because it's harder to doubt that Fred is biologically alive than it is to doubt that he is a man (Fred's being biologically alive is a more fundamental belief within our noetic structure than is his being a man).

An argument asks one to choose between:

a) accepting the conclusion
b) rejecting the clarity of at least one premise
c) rejecting the logical validity of the argument
d) rejecting the truth of at least one premise

You could think of an argument as a set of weighing scales with a conclusion in one balance pan connected via the logical mechanism of the scales to two or more propositions in the remaining balance pan. A good argument links premises together that raise the plausibility of, or weigh in favour of, its conclusion being true.

Arguments ideally use the most fundamental relevant beliefs possible to affect someone's noetic structure. As Aquinas pointed out, arguments convince by following 'a development from the more manifest to the less manifest.'[24] For example, the *kalam* cosmological argument (cf. chapter 5) tries to establish a connection between the universe having a finite past and the existence of God. *If* one acknowledges that the *kalam* argument is both clear and logically valid, and *if* one thinks that the proposed link between the universe having a finite past and the existence of God is true, but one nevertheless wants to deny the conclusion (because atheism is deeply embedded in your noetic structure), *then* one can and must deny that the universe has a finite past: 'in this way you can reduce someone from knowledge to ignorance by giving him an argument he sees to be valid from premises he knows to be true.'[25]

Reversing an argument for God into an argument against one of its premises is a logically valid manoeuvre; but it's a manoeuvre that should only be attempted by someone willing to pay the philosophical 'price tag' involved: 'The arguments [for theism] can be rejected, but the person who rejects them pays a price. For to deny a proposition is logically equivalent to asserting another proposition [and] the assertions required to reject theistic arguments may be troublesome ones.'[26] Rejecting the conclusion of an argument always carries an intellectual 'price tag' – the higher the 'price tag', the stronger the argument.

Question:
Pick an advert (you may find it helpful to record an ad-break on TV or buy a newspaper or magazine) and *syllogize the argument/s it presents*, whether explicitly or (more likely) implicitly: How does the advert's argument fare when assessed by the criteria for a good argument?

For example, you may find that an advert for a car implicitly argues as follows:

1. If you own this car, good-looking members of the opposite sex will be attracted to you
2. You want good-looking members of the opposite sex to be attracted to you
3. Therefore, you want to buy this car

You might point out that the conclusion doesn't follow from the premises (since you don't have to buy this car in order to own a car that's equally adept at attracting members of the opposite sex) and that you are sceptical about the truth of both premises (is there really a cause-and-effect link between owning this car and being found attractive by good-looking members of the opposite sex? Mightn't I be more concerned to attract a spiritually compatible mate than a 'good-looking' one? Or mightn't I prefer to spend my money on more important things than being attractive?).

Conclusion

Peter Kreeft and Ronald Tacelli summarize how arguments work:

> The inherent structure of human reason manifests itself in three acts of the mind: 1) understanding, 2) judging and 3) reasoning. These three acts of the mind are expressed in 1) terms, 2) propositions and 3) arguments. Terms are either clear or unclear. Propositions are either true or untrue. Arguments are either logically valid or invalid. A term is clear if it is intelligible and unambiguous. A proposition is true if it corresponds to reality . . . An argument is valid if the conclusion follows necessarily from the premise.[27]

They observe: 'To disagree with the conclusion of any argument, it must be shown that either an ambiguous term or false premise or logical fallacy exists in the argument.'[28] Of course, the fact that an argument is unsound doesn't necessarily mean that its conclusion is false, only that the conclusion is unsupported by this particular argument.

* * *

Recommended Resources

Video

Craig, William Lane. 'What Is a Properly Basic Belief?' http://youtu.be/4b7pQ3v4T2A.
Plantinga, Alvin. 'Sure Faith without Proof or Argument' http://youtu.be/oygakf85XUE.
— 'What Is a Properly Basic Belief?' http://youtu.be/f7377jU2a8Y.
*Williams, Peter S. 'Critical Thinking'
    www.youtube.com/playlist?list=PLQ3qcwVEWjunXMo96VWNyJgx-XAn8fp.

Audio

Nash, Ronald. 'The Law of Non-Contradiction' www.biblicaltraining.org/law-non-contradiction/christian-apologetics.
*Williams, Peter S. 'A Good Argument' www.damaris.org/cm/podcasts/731.
— 'That's a Good Argument' www.damaris.org/cm/podcasts/596.

Online papers

Auten, Brian. 'A Basic Logic Primer' www.apologetics315.com/2009/05/basic-logic-primer.html.
Clark, James Kelly. 'Religious Epistemology' www.iep.utm.edu/relig-ep/.

*— 'Without Evidence or Argument' www.calvin.edu/academic/philosophy/virtual_library/articles/clark_kelly_j/without_evidence_or_argument.pdf.

*Chesterton, G.K. 'Philosophy for the Schoolroom' www.chesterton.org/discover-chesterton/selected-works/the-philosopher/philosophy-for-the-schoolroom/.

Moreland, J.P. 'How Did Jesus Argue? Jesus and Logic' www.scriptoriumdaily.com/2007/08/06/how-did-jesus-argue-jesus-logic/.

Plantinga, Alvin. 'Intellectual Sophistication and Basic Belief in God' www.leaderu.com/truth/3truth03.html.

— 'Reason and Belief in God' http://philosophy.nd.edu/people/all/profiles/plantinga-alvin/documents/ReasonandBelief.pdf.

Willard, Dallas. 'Jesus the Logician' www.dwillard.org/articles/artview.asp?artID=39.

Books

Adler, Mortimer J. *How to Speak/How to Listen* (New York: Macmillan, 1983).

— and Charles Van Doren. *How to Read a Book: The Classic Guide to Intelligent Reading* (New York: Touchstone, rev. edn, 1972).

*Carter, Joe and John Coleman. *How to Argue Like Jesus: Learning Persuasion from History's Greatest Communicator* (Wheaton, IL: Crossway, 2009).

DeWeese, Garrett J. and J.P. Moreland. *Philosophy Made Slightly Less Difficult* (Downers Grove, IL: IVP, 2005).

Geisler, Norman L. and Ronald Brooks. *Come Let Us Reason: An Introduction to Logical Thinking* (Grand Rapids, MI: Baker, 1990).

Geisler, Norman L. and Paul D. *Feinberg. Introduction to Philosophy: A Christian Perspective* (Grand Rapids, MI: Baker, 1997).

Moreland, J.P. and William Lane Craig. *Philosophical Foundations for a Christian Worldview* (Downers Grove, IL: IVP, 2003).

Shand, John. *Arguing Well* (London: Routledge, 2000).

Stokes, Mitch. *A Shot of Faith to the Head: Be a Confident Believer in an Age of Cranky Atheists* (Nashville, TN: Thomas Nelson, 2012).

3. Making a Bad Argument

The study of logic increases one's ability to understand,
analyse, evaluate, and construct arguments.
C. Stephen Layman[1]

Introduction

Suppose you responded to a request to provide some reason for belief in the existence of God by stating, 'The Cosmological Argument . . . is a philosophical argument for the existence of God which explains that everything has a cause, that there must have been a first cause, and that this first cause was itself uncaused.'[2]

Unfortunately, this way of putting the argument is *fallacious*. That is, it fails to support its conclusion because it commits a logical fallacy. The problem in this instance is that if 'everything has a cause' then any purported 'first cause' *must itself have a cause* – but then, of course, it can't possibly be a 'first' cause! In other words, this particular summary of the cosmological argument *contradicts itself*.

This chapter will provide you with a working knowledge of some common ways in which arguments can go wrong. Let's start with the most important way in which an argument or assertion can go wrong (the fallacy committed by the cosmological argument examined above): self-contradiction.

3.1 Self-Contradiction

If a statement applies to itself and fails to meet its own conditions for truth or rationality, then it's 'self-contradictory' and *it cannot be true*. For example, the claim 'There is no truth' is self-contradictory, for it is a truth-claim (a claim that reality is a certain way) which claims that it is true that no truth-claims can be true!

According to physicists Stephen Hawking and Leonard Mlodinow, 'philosophy is dead. Philosophy has not kept up with modern developments in science, particularly physics. Scientists have become the bearers of the torch of discovery in our quest for knowledge.'[3] But as John C. Lennox points out: 'Hawking's statement about philosophy is itself a philosophical statement. It is manifestly not a statement of science: it is a metaphysical statement about science. Therefore, his statement that philosophy is dead contradicts itself.'[4]

The claim 'You should never believe anything without evidence' is self-contradictory. If we ask *why* we should believe it, no evidence can be given. (Try it! Of any evidence or argument you provide, we could ask, 'And why should we believe *that*?') The assertion that we should 'never believe anything without evidence' generates an infinitely recurring series of demands for evidence that can never be met. This means that the claim 'You should never believe anything without evidence' fails to meet its own standard of rational acceptability. In other words, this claim is self-contradictory and must be rejected (i.e. one must believe *something* without evidence – something 'properly basic' – in order to believe *anything* on account of evidence).

Scottish philosopher David Hume wrote:

When we run over libraries, persuaded of these principles, what havoc must we make? If we take in hand any volume; of divinity or school metaphysics, for instance; let us ask, Does it contain any abstract reasoning concerning quantity or number? No. Does it contain any experimental reasoning concerning matters of fact or existence? No. Commit it to the flames: For it can contain nothing but sophistry and illusion.[5]

This principle (known as 'Hume's fork') is self-contradictory. Does Hume's fork contain any abstract reasoning concerning number? No. Does it contain any experimental reasoning concerning existence? No. In which case, Hume would have to commit his own truth-claim 'to the flames' as containing 'nothing but sophistry and illusion'! As Norman L. Geisler observes: 'Hume's contention that all meaningful statements are either a relation of ideas or else about matters of fact is itself neither of these. Hence, on its own grounds it would be meaningless.'[6] Therefore, it must be possible to make a meaningful statement that is neither a relation of ideas nor a matter of experimental reasoning. For example, despite the fact that they contain no abstract reasoning concerning numbers nor any experimental reasoning about existence, the statements 'Rainbows are beautiful', 'Murder is wrong' and 'Hume's fork is self-contradictory' are all meaningful statements.[7]

> **Watch:**
> Frank Turek, 'The Road-Runner Tactic' http://youtu.be/VaGNRP6Q-6Q.

3.2 Formal Fallacies

Sound arguments need true premises and a logically valid form. For an argument to have a logically valid form means for it to be laid out according to a logical structure whereby the conclusion of the argument really follows from the premises. An argument can be unsound by having formally invalid logic (a concept into which we will incorporate arguments that are unsound because of an ambiguity of terms) or by having premises that are not true. Arguments can of course suffer from both problems:

> it is possible to have a valid argument where both the premises and the conclusion are false [e.g. All humans are goldfish, all goldfish can ride a bike, therefore all humans can ride a bike]. It is also possible to have a valid argument with a true conclusion and false premises [e.g. Some humans are goldfish, all goldfish can ride a bike, therefore some humans can ride a bike]. It is impossible, however, to have a valid argument with true premises and a false conclusion.[8]

But what about *invalid* arguments? Let us first of all consider three *valid* forms of syllogism and the formal logical fallacies that might be made when using them:

3.2.1 Modus ponens – *MP ('the mood of affirming')*

In *modus ponens* one *affirms* that the truth of an antecedent (i.e. prior) truth-claim (P) ought to lead one to *affirm* the truth of a consequent truth-claim (Q), and one *affirms* the truth of the antecedent truth-claim (P) in order to thereby *affirm* the truth of the consequential truth-claim (Q). The antecedent truth-claim (P) is, as it were, the ancestor of (that which leads to the affirmation of) the consequent truth-claim (Q). In syllogistic form:

1. If P then Q (→Q)
2. P
3. Therefore, Q

For example:

1. If it is raining (P) then it is wet (Q)
2. It is raining (P)
3. Therefore, it is wet (Q)

Or:

1. If you have faith in Jesus Christ (P) then you are saved (Q)
2. You have faith in Jesus Christ (P)
3. Therefore, you are saved (Q)

Jesus implicitly used this *modus ponens* form of argument when responding to John the Baptist's question: 'Are you the one who was to come, or should we expect someone else?' (Matthew 11:3). Jesus sends John a message: 'Go back and report to John what you hear and see: the blind receive sight, the lame walk, those who have leprosy are cured, the deaf hear, the dead are raised, and the good news is preached to the poor. Blessed is the man who does not fall away on account of me' (Matthew 11:4–6, cf. Luke 7:22–23). In other words, Jesus appeals to his works of healing and teaching as evidence for his being the Messiah, because they fulfil the Messianic predictions of the Scriptures (cf. Isaiah 26:19; 35:5–6; 61:1).[9] In syllogistic form, Jesus argues:

Making a Bad Argument

1. If someone does P, then they are the Messiah (Q)
2. I am doing P
3. Therefore, I am the Messiah (Q)

In these arguments P is the 'antecedent' and Q the 'consequent' (i.e. if P is true, then Q is true as a consequence).

Watch:
Lee Strobel, 'Did Jesus Fit the Old Testament Description of the Messiah?' http://youtu.be/suMMz4E5tas.
— 'Did Jesus Really Fulfil Prophecy?' http://youtu.be/ZKUurWrlZcM.

In an argument with the MP logical form it is a fallacy to affirm the consequent instead of the antecedent:

1. If P then Q
2. Q
3. Therefore, P

Arguments that follow this invalid form can have true premises but a false conclusion. For example:

1. If it is raining (P), then it is wet (Q)
2. It is wet (Q)
3. Therefore, it is raining (P)

Although it can't rain without being wet, it might be wet for reasons besides rain (perhaps a water main has burst)! Rain is a *sufficient* condition of it being wet (it's enough to make it wet), but not a *necessary* condition (it's not the only possible cause).

3.2.2 Modus tollens – MT ('the mood of denying')

In *modus tollens* one affirms that the truth of an antecedent (i.e. prior) truth-claim (P) ought to lead one to affirm the truth of a consequent truth-claim (Q), but one *denies* that this consequent truth-claim is the case (~Q), in order to thereby *deny* the antecedent (~P):

1. If P then Q (P→Q)
2. Not Q (~Q)
3. Therefore, not P (~P)

For example:

1. If it is raining, then it is wet
2. But it isn't wet
3. Therefore, it isn't raining

Or:

1. If Jesus' claim to divinity was insincere (P), then he was a bad man (Q)
2. But Jesus was not a bad man (~Q)
3. Therefore, Jesus' claim to divinity was not insincere (~P)

Which is to say that Jesus' claim to divinity was sincere.
The formal fallacy associated with MT is called *denying the antecedent*:

1. If P, then Q
2. Not P
3. Therefore, not Q

For example:

1. If it is raining, then it is wet
2. It isn't raining
3. Therefore, it isn't wet

But of course, it might be wet without rain (perhaps a water main has burst).

3.2.3 Disjunctive syllogism – DS

In a disjunctive syllogism one claims concerning some particular question that there are a finite number of competing possible answers, and then one claims that all of the alternative answers *except one* are false, in order to justify the conclusion that the only remaining answer must be true. This is an indirect way of arguing for something by a process of elimination. The simplest form of this type of argument is when there are only two competing truth-claims, and so the elimination of one necessarily concedes victory to the other, like so:

1. Either P or Q (PvQ)
2. Not P (~P)
3. Therefore, Q

For example:

1. Jesus' claim to divinity was either insincere or sincere (PvQ)
2. Jesus' claim to divinity wasn't insincere (~P)
3. Therefore, Jesus' claim to divinity was sincere (Q)

But of course, there may be many alternative options that need to be taken into account, like so:

1. Either P or Q or R or S or T
2. Not P or R or S or T
3. Therefore, Q

The formal logical mistake to watch out for with a DS is a contradiction between the conclusion and the second premise. For example:

1. Either P or Q
2. Not P
3. Therefore, P

Premise 2 and the conclusion can't both be true since the claim that they are is self-contradictory!

Fig 1: Formally valid and associated formally invalid argument forms

	Modus Ponents	*Modus Tollens*	Disjunctive Syllogism
Formally Valid	If P, then Q P Therefore, Q	Of P, then Q Not Q Therefore, not P	Either P or Q Not P Therefore, Q
Formally Invalid	Of P, then Q Q Therefore p	If P, then Q Not P Therefore, not Q	Either P or Q Not P Therefore, P

3.3 Combining Forms

The more likely mistake with a DS syllogism is reliance upon a *false dilemma* (wherein P and Q are not the only alternatives and so eliminating P doesn't justify the conclusion Q). For example, the critic might suggest that Jesus' presumed claim to divinity could be legendary (i.e. unhistorical) rather than a matter of historical fact. One could back up the first DS syllogism about Jesus with an MP syllogism:

1. If there's sufficient evidence to support the premise that 'Jesus laid claim to divinity', then we should accept that premise (If P, then Q)
2. There is sufficient evidence to support the premise that Jesus laid claim to divinity (P)
3. Therefore, we should accept the premise that Jesus laid claim to divinity (Q)

Watch:
William Lane Craig, 'Did Jesus Claim to Be God in His Teachings?' www.leestrobel.com/videoserver/video.php?clip=strobelT1214.
Craig A. Evans, 'Did Jesus Claim to Be Deity?' http://youtu.be/4yURUoBvPJw.
Gary R. Habermas, 'Did Jesus Ever Consider Himself to Be God?' http://youtu.be/TvNVisB79U0.
Lee Strobel, 'Did Jesus Claim to Be God?' http://youtu.be/1Flt1i7Rp98.

Having rebutted the critic's attack on the DS syllogism about Jesus, one could then cap things off with a MT syllogism:

1. If a sincere claim to divinity is wrong, then the person issuing the claim is mad (P→Q)
2. Jesus was not mad (~Q)
3. Therefore, Jesus' sincere claim to divinity was not wrong (~P)

And of course, if Jesus' sincere historical claim to divinity wasn't wrong, then it was right. This is a version of the *aut deus aut homo malus* – 'Either God or a bad man' – argument for the deity of Jesus.

Listen:
Peter S. Williams, 'Who Did Jesus Think He Was?' www.damaris.org/cm/podcasts/63.

Read:
Peter Kreeft, 'The Divinity of Christ' www.peterkreeft.com/topics/christ-divinity.htm.

We can construct a logically valid argument interweaving all three (MP, DS *and* MT) syllogistic forms:

1. If there's sufficient evidence to support the premise that 'Jesus laid claim to divinity', then we should accept that premise
2. There is sufficient evidence to support the premise that Jesus laid claim to divinity
3. Therefore, we should accept the premise that Jesus laid claim to divinity

4. If Jesus laid claim to divinity, then his claim was either sincere or insincere
5. Therefore, Jesus' claim to divinity was either sincere or insincere
6. Jesus' claim to divinity was not insincere
   i) If Jesus' claim to divinity was insincere, then he was a bad man (a liar and blasphemer)
   ii) But Jesus wasn't a bad man
   iii) Therefore, Jesus' claim to divinity was not insincere
7. Therefore, Jesus' claim to divinity was sincere
8. If Jesus' claim to divinity was sincere but wrong, then Jesus was mad
9. Jesus wasn't mad
10. Therefore, if Jesus' claim to divinity was sincere, it wasn't wrong
11. Therefore (via premise 7), Jesus' claim to divinity wasn't wrong (i.e. it was right)

Like all long arguments this can be broken down into a series of over-lapping syllogisms: 1–3 is *modus ponens*; 3–5 is a *modus ponens* syllogism, the conclusion of which is a disjunction of possibilities; 5–7 is a disjunctive syllogism; 6i–6iii is a subsidiary *modus tollens* syllogism in support of premise 6; 8–10 is a *modus tollens* syllogism; and premise 10 draws upon premise 7 to form a *modus ponens* syllogism that completes our argument with the conclusion stated in 11. This argument uses formally valid syllogistic logic (by abstracting the logical form of each syllogism from the content, you can check the formal validity of the argument for yourself). Hence the crucial question becomes the truth of those premises (i.e. 1, 2, 4, 6, 8 and 9) that aren't conclusions. If all of these premises are true, then the conclusion of this argument is true.

> **Question:**
> According to Scottish preacher John Duncan (1796–1870), 'Christ either deceived mankind by conscious fraud, or He was Himself deluded and self-deceived, or He was Divine. There is no getting out of this trilemma. It is inexorable.'[10] How would you turn Duncan's claim into a single disjunctive syllogism? How many objections to this argument can you express using syllogistic logic? Can you rebut the objections?

3.4 A Dozen Informally Bad Ways to Argue

A formal fallacy is exhibited by any argument with a faulty logical structure that means that the conclusion doesn't follow from the premises. An informal fallacy is any bad way of trying to win an argument that isn't a formal logical fallacy. You can think of an informal fallacy as a logical problem stemming from the content of the premises of an argument rather than from its logical form or structure: 'Formal fallacies are types of deductive argument that instantiate an invalid inference pattern [see above]. Informal fallacies [see below] are types of . . . argument the premises of which fail to establish the conclusion because of their content.'[11]

3.4.1 False dilemma

A false dilemma occurs 'when someone sets up a dichotomy [a choice] in such a way that it appears there are only two possible conclusions when in fact there are further alternatives not mentioned.'[12] For example, atheist Roy Hattersley argues as follows:

> God is in this room because God is everywhere. 'Well, if God's in this room, what does he sound like?' Well, you can't hear him. 'If God's in this room, what does he look like?' Well, you can't see him. 'If God's in this room, what would he feel like if you touched him?' Well, you can't touch him. And then the ultimate question, 'How does God being in this room differ from God not being in this room?' And there's no answer to the question. And that's good enough, for me, to convince me that he isn't in this room, or anywhere else.[13]

Hattersley's argument uses a disjunctive syllogism:

1. *Either* God can be detected directly by our physical senses, *or* he doesn't exist
2. God can't be detected directly by our physical senses
3. Therefore, God doesn't exist

This argument is formally valid (there's no contradiction between the conclusion and the second premise), and premise 2 is true by definition. However, premise 1 is a false dilemma. Premise 1 should read:

1. a) *Either* God can be detected directly by our physical senses, or he doesn't exist, or God exists without being directly detectable by our physical senses

But with 1a as the first premise, the conclusion that follows from the addition of the fact that:

2. God can't be detected directly by our physical senses

is:

3. a) Therefore, *either* God doesn't exist, *or* God exists without being directly detectable by our physical senses

Hardly the result Hattersley was aiming for!

God's being in (i.e. present to) the room differs from his not being in the room by the meaningful proposition 'God is in this room' being true in the one instance and false in the other. Moreover, if the proposition 'God is in this room' is true, it would follow that various other propositions are also true that would not otherwise follow (e.g. 'God *could* work a miracle in this room'). Hattersley seems to think that a proposition is false unless its truth would make *an empirically detectable difference to* reality – but this assumption is self-contradictory (the truth of this assumption wouldn't make an empirically detectable difference to reality).

Richard Dawkins tries to dispense with the argument for Jesus' deity examined in section 3.3 by suggesting that it rests upon a false dilemma, because Jesus could simply have been 'honestly mistaken'. In other words, Dawkins claims that premise 8 is false. But as Mike King responds: 'anyone "honestly mistaken" in such a way would inevitably be considered insane. But why should Dawkins *et al* not be content to simply dismiss Jesus as mad or bad? Quite clearly, it is because even a rudimentary flick through Jesus' life demonstrates both of these possibilities to be untenable.'[14]

> **Watch:**
> Example of a false dilemma http://youtu.be/Dln3DJEcghY.

3.4.2 *The genetic fallacy*

The genetic fallacy is committed 'whenever an idea is evaluated based upon irrelevant history.'[15] Noting that a witness has a history of lying is relevant to assessing the worth of their testimony. Noting that a truth-claim is old (e.g. 'That idea is medieval') is irrelevant to its truth-value. That medieval people thought that love was a good thing doesn't undermine the claim that love is a good thing! C.S. Lewis dubbed this particular type of genetic fallacy 'chronological snobbery.' Noting that someone only believes in God because that's what their parents taught them doesn't do anything to show that God doesn't exist.

> **Watch:**
> William Lane Craig, 'The Genetic Fallacy'
> www.reasonablefaith.org/site/News2?page=NewsArticle&id=9172.

3.4.3 Ad hominem

Ad hominem is 'a Latin phrase meaning "to the person" . . . [The fallacy involves] shifting attention from the point in question to some non-relevant aspect of the person making it.'[16] Arthur Schopenhauer warned against becoming 'personal, insulting, rude . . . passing from the subject of dispute . . . to the disputant himself, and in some way attacking his person.'[17] Mortimer J. Adler advises:

> Never make irrelevant references to the other person's grandmother, his nationality, his business or political associates, his occupation, or his personal habits. All such tactics are instances of the fallacious ad hominem argument. The most exasperating form of this fallacy is the bedfellow argument. You say to someone, 'So you agree with Hitler,' as if this suffices to discredit the point he is trying to make. Hitler may be in ill repute with everyone present, but that does not mean he is necessarily wrong about everything.[18]

Like the genetic fallacy, the *ad hominem* argument is a 'fallacy of relevance', since it asks us to evaluate an idea based upon irrelevant data concerning the person proposing it.

> **Watch:**
> William Lane Craig, 'Argument Ad Hominem' www.reasonablefaith.org/site/News2?page=NewsArticle&id=9177.
> 'Poisoning the Well' http://youtu.be/djDh_M-03Zs.

Antony Flew, 'an icon and champion for unbelievers for decades,'[19] and a scholar dubbed 'the world's most influential philosophical atheist,'[20] announced in January 2004 that he had come to believe in God because 'the case for an Aristotelian God who has the characteristics of power and also intelligence, is now much stronger than it ever was before.'[21] Unfortunately, prominent atheists (including Dawkins and Hattersley) responded to Flew's change of mind with *ad hominem* attacks about his losing his marbles in his dotage,[22] or about his hedging his bets with respect to the afterlife (although Flew didn't believe in an afterlife!). Commenting on the latter accusation, Flew wrote:

> When reports of my change of mind were spread by the media . . . some commentators were quick to claim that my advanced age had something to do with my 'conversion.' It has been said that fear concentrates the mind powerfully, and these critics had concluded that expectations of an impending entrance into the afterlife had triggered a deathbed conversion. Clearly these

people were familiar with neither my writings on the non-existence of an afterlife nor with my current views on the topic . . . I do not think of myself 'surviving' death.[23]

Even if Flew *were* 'losing his marbles', or 'hedging his bets', such facts *about Flew* are not facts *about Flew's arguments* for belief in God that show they were unsound. To dismiss Flew's beliefs by attacking Flew rather than his arguments is fallacious.

Watch:
'Flew's Conversion to Theism' http://youtu.be/f_nzleTFqGQ.

Read:
Gary R. Habermas, 'My Pilgrimage from Atheism to Theism: An Exclusive Interview with Former British Atheist Professor Antony Flew' http://epsociety.org/library/articles.asp?pid=33&mode=detail.

The *ad hominem* arguments suffered by Flew are a verbal form of the *ad baculums* fallacy (literally 'appeals to the stick'), which encompasses any attempt 'to establish a conclusion by threat or intimidation.'[24] If you argue for something unpopular or politically incorrect, some people will attack you personally and drag your name through the mud (cf. Matthew 5:11), for as Tertullian lamented: 'Truth and hatred of truth come into our world together. As soon as truth appears, it is regarded as an enemy. It has as many foes as are strangers to it.'[25] Christians hold some views that are frowned upon in the wider culture. At the very least this means swimming against the tide of that most informal *ad hominem* argument: *peer pressure*.

3.4.4 The abuse of authority

Mortimer J. Adler observes: 'What great or wise men have said deserves our consideration. But great and wise men have sometimes made mistakes, just like the rest of us.'[26] While arguments from authority aren't infallible, they aren't necessarily fallacious: 'appeals to authority are fallacious if they demand uncritical acceptance of the authority's statements without evidence of the authority's reliability.'[27] Hence 'an appeal to authority is relevant (and hence reasonable) in proportion to the reliability of the authority in the corresponding field.'[28]

Quoting a scientist speaking within their field of expertise would be an appropriate use of the argument from authority. Quoting the same scientist on something outside their field of expertise (for example, on philosophical issues like the existence of God) would be an abuse of the argument from authority. Thus physicist Stephen Hawking is an appropriate authority to quote on cosmology, but not on the question of God's existence.[29] Likewise, celebrity endorsements in adverts are often an abuse of the argument from authority, because being a celebrity doesn't necessarily make one an authority on whatever is being sold.

Question:
Is the quotation from Adler at the start of 3.4.4 an appropriate appeal to authority?

3.4.5 Rash generalization

Generalization is an inductive form of argument, that is, an argument that goes from an accumulation of particulars (e.g. observations) to a general conclusion. For example, in an inductive argument, I might reason like this: 'Every time I tasted chocolate in the past I liked it; therefore, there being no reason to treat the present differently from the past with respect to my food preferences, if I taste chocolate now I will probably like it.'

A *rash generalization* is 'a general statement based on insufficient evidence.'[30] It would be rash to generalize as follows: 'Since humans can run a mile in four minutes, they can run eight miles in thirty-two minutes.' Or as follows: 'Since natural selection can explain why the proportion of large to small beaks in finches changes over generations, it can explain the origin of birds.' As Sean B. Carroll observes: 'A long-standing issue in evolutionary biology is whether the processes observable in extant populations and species (microevolution) are sufficient to account for the larger-scale changes evident over longer periods of life's history (macroevolution).'[31]

Watch:
William Lane Craig, 'The Sheer Lack of Evidence for Darwinism' http://youtu.be/9iOgHK70kSI.

3.4.6 Begging the question

This fallacy (also known as 'arguing in a circle') occurs 'when a disputant uses his conclusion as one of the premises employed to establish that conclusion.'[32] For example, if someone said, 'I know the Bible is the word of God because the Bible says it is the word of God, and that must be true because, as the word of God, everything the Bible says is true' they'd be guilty of begging the question. If the Bible is 'the word of

God' (as this phrase is understood by some Christians),[33] then it follows that everything it claims must be true; but one can't prove that the Bible is 'the word of God' simply by quoting the Bible without arguing in a circle.

Even young-earth creationists accept the microevolutionary observation that biological systems can change somewhat over time through the accumulation of beneficial mutations via natural selection. Richard Dawkins explains that 'the larger the leap through genetic space, the lower the probability that the resulting change will be viable, let alone an improvement. [Hence] evolution must in general be a crawl through genetic space, not a series of leaps.'[34] He likens this gradual approach to attaining biological complexity to 'climbing Mount Improbable.'[35] Mount Improbable has a sheer cliff on one side that could never be conquered in one go, but the back of Mount Improbable is a gradual series of attainable steps leading to the summit. Dawkins argues that evolution by natural selection must have climbed a gradual series of steps from biological simplicity to complex biological diversity *because this is the only hypothesis able to fill the explanatory gap left by the philosophical exclusion of design*. Dawkins asserts that although we've no idea what gradual 'path' organisms took up Mount Improbable, *they must have done so*: 'however daunting the sheer cliffs that the adaptive mountain first presents, graded ramps can be found the other side and the peak eventually scaled.'[36] But how does Dawkins know that these 'graded ramps can be found' *without having found them*? 'Without stirring from our chair, we can see that it must be so,'[37] he explains, 'because nothing except gradual accumulation could, in principle, do the job.'[38] That is, the job of explaining life *without design*. Hence Dawkins argues for macroevolution by *begging the question against design*, rather than by providing evidence that evolution can do the job assigned to it. Dawkins' argument for macroevolution is question begging, as he implicitly admitted in a 2005 interview:

> There cannot have been intermediate stages that were not beneficial . . . There's got to be a series of advantages all the way . . . If you can't think of one, then that's your problem, not natural selection's problem. Natural selection – well, *I suppose that is a sort of matter of faith on my part* since the theory is so coherent and so powerful.[39]

Watch:
'Darwin and Dawkins Dilemma: Climbing Mt Improbable' http://youtu.be/h38Xi-Jz9yk.

Astonishingly, Dawkins proceeds to *beg the question against theism* by proclaiming that there's no reason to believe in God because evolution can explain away the apparent design of nature (a conclusion that also represents a 'false dilemma')!

3.4.7 Double standard

This is 'a fallacy in which a person applies standards, principles, rules, etc. to others while taking herself (or those she has a special interest in) to be exempt, without providing adequate justification for the exemption.'[40] Jesus objected to double standards:

> Why do you look at the speck of sawdust in your brother's eye and pay no attention to the plank in your own eye? How can you say to your brother, 'Let me take the speck out of your eye,' when all the time there is a plank in your own eye? You hypocrite, first take the plank out of your own eye, and then you will see clearly to remove the speck from your brother's eye (Matthew 7:3–5; cf. Luke 6:41–42).

Dawkins thinks that 'God' is a redundant explanation: 'To explain the origin of the DNA / protein machine by invoking a supernatural designer is to explain precisely nothing, for it leaves unexplained the origin of the designer.'[41] However, *this objection counts against all scientific explanations!* As atheist Daniel Came points out: 'One might as well say that evolution by natural selection explains nothing because it does nothing to explain why there were living organisms on earth in the first place; or that the big bang fails to explain the cosmic background radiation because the big bang is itself inexplicable.'[42] Dawkins just wants to exclude design, but that involves him in a double standard.

I've lost count of the number of students who have told me that they are atheists because 'there's no scientific evidence' for God. Setting aside the questionable assumptions that a) belief in God requires scientific evidence and that b) such evidence is lacking, Steven Lovell points out that this 'Insufficient Evidence' argument often involves a double standard: 'if we reject belief in God due to (alleged) insufficient evidence, then we would be irrational to accept atheism, if the evidence for God's non-existence were similarly insufficient. It would be a radical [double standard]. If theistic belief requires evidence, so must atheistic belief.'[43]

3.4.8 Shifting the burden of proof

Issues to do with the burden of proof can be just as important to philosophers as they are to lawyers. According to Robert A. Harris, 'a common sense look at the world, with all its beauty, apparent design, meaning, and vibrancy, would seem to predispose a neutral observer to presume that God exists unless good evidence for his non-existence could be brought to bear.'[44] On grounds such as these, one might say that theism is a properly basic belief and that the burden of proof is therefore on the non-theist.

On the other hand, atheist Richard Norman asserts that 'the onus is on those who believe in a god to provide reasons for that belief. If they cannot come up with good reasons, then we should reject the belief.'[45] Flew likewise urged that the 'onus of proof must lie upon the theist,'[46] and that in the absence of reasons for God's existence there should be a 'presumption of atheism'. However, by 'atheism' Flew only meant 'non-theism', which includes agnosticism. The presumption of atheism is therefore not very interesting unless (as with Norman) it really is the presumption of *atheism*. However, such a presumption appears to involve a double standard: 'Clearly, if we reject belief in God due to (alleged) insufficient evidence, then we would be irrational to accept atheism, if the evidence for God's non-existence were similarly insufficient . . . If we have no evidence either way, then the logical conclusion would be agnosticism.'[47]

Read:
Paul Copan, 'The Presumptuousness of Atheism' www.equip.org/articles/the-presumptuousness-of-atheism/.

3.4.9 Equivocation

An equivocation (ambiguity) is where a term that gets repeated in an argument needs to mean the same thing each time it appears for the argument to work, but it actually means different things. An equivocation is like a bad logical pun. Consider comedian Groucho Marx's quip: 'One morning I shot an elephant in my pyjamas. How he got in my pyjamas I don't know!'[48] Equivocation makes for good humour and bad logic.

Watch:
Groucho Marx, 'Groucho's Elephant'
http://youtu.be/2mTqopwPTvU.
'The Fallacy of Equivocation'
http://youtu.be/MmhhYcJirl8.

Richard Dawkins distinguishes between objects that are clearly designed and objects that are not designed but look a bit like they are designed, which he calls '*designoid*'[49] and illustrates with a craggy hillside that suggests the profile of the late President Kennedy: 'Once you have been told, you can just see a slight resemblance to either John or Robert Kennedy. But some don't see it and it is certainly easy to believe that the resemblance is accidental.'[50] Dawkins contrasts this Kennedy-esque hillside with the presidents' heads carved into Mt Rushmore, which 'are obviously not accidental: they have design written all over them.'[51] Dawkins asserts that biological organisms are (at most) designoid: 'Designoid objects look designed, so much so that some people – probably, alas, most people – think that they *are* designed. These people are wrong . . . the true explanation – Darwinian natural selection – is very different.'[52]

The meaning of Dawkins' crucial term shifts in the course of his argument. Dawkins' original definition of a 'designoid' was of something with the *superficial* appearance of design. Later, Dawkins wants to convince us that, although some biological objects give such a strong appearance of design that 'most people'[53] intuitively think that they are designed, they are actually designoid. Dawkins thus *equivocates* between 'things that look a bit like they might be designed, but on closer inspection obviously are not' and 'things that give every appearance of being designed, but are not.'

3.4.10 Misusing Occam's razor

William of Occam (sometimes spelt 'Ockham') introduced a principle of reason stating that *we should always accept the simplest adequate explanation* of the available evidence. Following the razor doesn't guarantee the truth of our beliefs, but it prevents us from adopting complicated non-basic beliefs without a reason.

If some money is missing from a safe covered by unknown fingerprints and led up to by muddy footprints, the simplest adequate explanation would seem to be that a thief with muddy feet and no gloves opened the safe and stole the money. The truth might be that two thieves, one who had muddy feet but wore gloves and one who did not have muddy feet but did not wear gloves, stole the money. But it would be unreasonable to *believe* in two thieves if all the available evidence is adequately explained by the 'one thief' theory. If there were *two* different sets of prints on the safe, then the more complex theory would be *more adequate* than the simpler theory (while being simpler than a 'three thieves' theory).

Occam's razor is *misused* when people suggest we should believe the *simplest* available theory rather than the simplest *adequate* theory available. Ironically, this is an oversimplification of Occam's razor, which lays out two criteria: adequacy of explanation on the one hand and simplicity of explanation on the other – of which adequacy is the more important. Should we accept atheism simply because it is *simpler* than theism? No, because while atheism is simpler than theism, it must be shown rather than assumed that atheism is the more *adequate* theory.

Read:
Paul Copan, 'Is Naturalism a Simpler Explanation than Theism?'
http://enrichmentjournal.ag.org/201201/201201_108_Naturalism.cfm.

3.4.11 Argument from ignorance

An argument from ignorance confuses a lack of evidence against a belief with the existence of positive evidence for that belief. Atheist Nigel Warburton explains: 'Although no one has provided conclusive evidence that there is no life after death it would be extremely rash to treat this as a conclusive proof that there is.'[54] Warburton observes:

> in some courts of law a defendant is presumed innocent until proven guilty. In other words, lack of evidence against someone is taken as proof, for the purposes of the court, that they did not commit the crime. However, as many cases of guilty people being freed because of lack of evidence show, this isn't really a proof of innocence, but merely a practical, if imprecise, way of protecting innocent people from wrongful conviction.[55]

For example, just because doctors can't explain why someone has recovered from an illness doesn't mean that their recovery was a miracle.

3.4.11.1 Gaps, ignorance and God

It might be useful to say something about the 'God-of-the-gaps' accusation sometimes levelled at arguments for God (especially design arguments). A genuine God-of-the-gaps argument proposes God as an explanation for gaps in a scientific account of nature *simply on the grounds that no non-divine explanation is currently available*. As such, a genuine God-of-the-gaps argument is simply an argument from ignorance. (Of course, to propose that nature can bridge a gap in our scientific account, simply because there's no evidence that it can't, would likewise be to make an argument from ignorance.)

The 'God-of-the-gaps' phrase is often used as a caution against the fragility of belief in God based merely on the provision of explanations for natural phenomena. If science later provides a non-divine explanation for the phenomena in question, this God-of-the-gaps is apt to appear an unnecessary hypothesis. (Such a change in explanation does not of course *contradict* belief in God.) This is taken to imply that God is thereby rendered an unnecessary hypothesis to be dispensed with by Occam's razor. However, this doesn't follow, except in the case of theism lacking any warrant for belief in God besides the 'gap' argument in question. Any warranted theistic believer will interpret the collapse of a 'gap' argument as simply providing a more accurate picture of the nature of God's relationship with the aspect of reality in question, not as disproving the hypothesis that God has *some sort of relationship* with the aspect of reality in question.

Moreover, to assume that all empirical data must be best explained without teleology turns science into an exercise in applied materialism rather than a search for truth. In short, a God-of-the-gaps explanation, *when it isn't an argument from ignorance*, isn't necessarily unsound.[56] The 'gap' in question might be a genuine gap in the self-explanatory abilities of the natural world, a gap that can never be 'filled in' with a naturalistic explanation.[57] No one thinks we commit a 'designer of the gaps' fallacy when we reckon that an engineer explains the existence of an aircraft, because there's an obvious gap between the creative capacities of nature as understood by contemporary science and the aircraft as understood by contemporary science. The design inference in this instance (as in any other) isn't a deductive proof, but a falsifiable inference to the best explanation. Hence 'gaps' are legitimate data for both 'intelligent design theory' and 'natural theology' *if and when* they have at least a *prima facie* claim, *based on what we know*, to being gaps in nature. As J.P. Moreland argues:

> if one discovered [that] living systems bear certain features that usually result from personal agency (e.g., information in DNA, different kinds of design such as beauty, order, etc.), and if one has grounds for thinking that it is improbable that a naturalist mechanism will be found to account for this, then one could legitimately see the origin of life as a gap in the history of the universe due to a primary causal act of God.[58]

Those 'grounds for thinking that it is improbable that a naturalist mechanism will be found' to account for the 'gap' in question may be falsifiable, but they are nevertheless *grounds*, rather than the *lack of grounds* that feature in an argument from ignorance. As Phil Dowe argues:

We must draw conclusions based on the evidence we have. All scientific reasoning works like that – it is by nature defeasible [open to revision]. That it is defeasible is no reason to ignore the conclusions as we now see them. The same may sometimes be true of reasons for God. If the reason is removed at a later time, then unless that was our only evidence for God, that is no reason to think God does not exist, and should, logically, be no reason to doubt.[59]

The lack of a naturalistic explanation can represent a defeasible failure to rebut a properly basic belief, an argument by analogy, an argument from the principle of credulity,[60] or an inference to the best explanation. Hence philosopher of science Robert Larmer concludes: 'there is nothing wrong with the reasoning typically involved in [so-called] "God of the gaps" arguments.'[61]

> **Watch:**
> William Lane Craig, 'Is Intelligent Design a "God-of-the-Gaps"?' http://youtu.be/d6c78a_REpA.

3.4.12 *Straw man*

This fallacy is committed 'when an arguer distorts an opponent's position for the purpose of making it [easier] to destroy, refutes the distorted position, and concludes that his opponent's actual view is thereby demolished.'[62]

The straw man may be committed *intentionally* or *unintentionally*: 'Sometimes [a straw man] is a deliberate ploy; in which case it is a disreputable form of rhetoric. More often it involves a degree of wishful thinking stemming from widespread reluctance to attribute great intelligence or subtlety to someone with whom you strongly disagree.'[63] As seen in chapter 1, many atheists attack a straw-man definition of Christian 'faith' by defining it non-biblically as belief without evidence.

> **Watch:**
> The Straw Man Fallacy' http://youtu.be/v5vzCmURh7o.
> 'How the New Atheists Misrepresent Faith' http://youtu.be/54Y1zt3-iRA.

✔ Arguments with a valid syllogistic structure must still avoid fallacies in their premises if they are to be considered logically valid arguments

> **Question:**
> How many informal logical fallacies can you spot in Bertrand Russell's 1927 paper 'Why I Am Not A Christian' (in Bertrand Russell, *Why I Am Not a Christian* [London: Routledge, 2nd edn, 2004]; cf. www.positiveatheism.org/hist/russell0.htm)?

Conclusion

As Peter Kreeft warns: 'There are honest ways to persuade people (by appealing to objective evidence and logic) and also dishonest ways (by appealing to anything other than truth and goodness, for example, fear, force, prejudice, lust, greed, pride, and so on).'[64] Rhetoric is a powerful tool, and like any tool it can be misused:

> Sophistry is always a misuse of the skills of rhetoric, always an unscrupulous effort to succeed in persuading by any means, fair or fowl. The line Plato drew to distinguish the sophist from the philosopher, both equally skilled in argument, put the philosopher on the side of those who, devoted to truth, would not misuse logic or rhetoric to win an argument by means of deception, misrepresentation, or other trickery.[65]

*   *   *

Recommended Resources

Video

'Flew's Conversion to Theism' http://youtu.be/f_nzleTFqGQ

Craig, William Lane. 'Did Jesus Claim to Be God in His Teachings?' www.leestrobel.com/videoserver/video.php?clip=strobelT1214.

— 'Is Intelligent Design a "God-of-the-Gaps"?' http://youtu.be/d6c78a_RepA.

— 'The Sheer Lack of Evidence for Darwinism' http://youtu.be/9iOgHK70kSI.

Discovery Institute. 'Darwin and Dawkins Dilemma: Climbing Mt Improbable' http://youtu.be/h38Xi-Jz9yk.

Evans, Craig A. 'Did Jesus Claim to Be Deity?' http://youtu.be/4yURUoBvPJw.

Habermas, Gary R. 'Did Jesus Ever Consider Himself to Be God?' http://youtu.be/TvNVisB79U0.

'How the New Atheists Misrepresent Faith' http://youtu.be/54Y1zt3-iRA.

Koukl, Gregory. 'Bad Arguments against Christianity' http://youtu.be/PEdq-01Yt3c.

— 'Common New Atheist Fallacies – Part 1' http://youtu.be/ICSjHdFYVss; 'Part 2' http://youtu.be/Lenm0eVHx40; 'Part 3' http://youtu.be/kPT-TzIBT2c; 'Part 4' http://youtu.be/4Qkc1cr7hB0.

Licona, Michael. 'Who Was Jesus? (Part 2)' http://youtu.be/CBDzzuTGdT4.

Marx, Groucho. 'Groucho's Elephant' http://youtu.be/2mTqopwPTvU.

Strobel, Lee. 'Antony Flew - The Honest Ex-Atheist' http://youtu.be/fbyTwmaJArU.

— 'Did Jesus Claim to Be God?' http://youtu.be/1Flt1i7Rp98.

— 'Did Jesus Fit the Old Testament Description of the Messiah?' http://youtu.be/suMMz4E5tas.

— 'Did Jesus Really Fulfil Prophecy?' http://youtu.be/ZKUurWrlZcM.

*Williams, Peter S. 'Critical Thinking' YouTube Playlist www.youtube.com/playlist?list=PLQhh3qcwVEWjunXMo96VWNyJgx-XAn8fp.

Audio

Auten, Brian. 'Logical Fallacies' http://itunes.apple.com/podcast/logical-fallacies/id317371051?mt=2.
— 'Logical Fallacies 2' http://itunes.apple.com/us/podcast/logical-fallacies-2/id322147415?mt=2.
Flannagan, Matthew. 'Fallacy Friday' http://itunes.apple.com/us/podcast/fallacy-friday/id422160633?mt=2.
Ramsden, Michael. 'Logic and Fallacies: Thinking Clearly' www.bethinking.org/resource.php?ID=445.
Strobel, Lee. '*The Case for the Real Jesus*: Challenge 1' http://youtu.be/0QfKVMNp08M.
*Williams, Peter S. 'Who Did Jesus Think He Was?' www.damaris.org/cm/podcasts/63.

Online papers

Afterall. 'The Illogic Primer' http://afterall.net/illogic.
Bohlin, Raymond G. 'Limits to Evolvability' www.4truth.net/fourtruthpbscience.aspx?pageid=8589952921.
Collins, Jack. 'Miracles, Intelligent Design, and God-of-the-Gaps'. *Perspectives on Science and Christian Faith* 55:1 (March 2003) www.asa3.org/ASA/PSCF/2003/PSCF3-03Collins.pdf.
Copan, Paul. 'Is Naturalism a Simpler Explanation Than Theism?' http://enrichmentjournal.ag.org/201201/201201_108_Naturalism.cfm.
— 'The Presumptuousness of Atheism' www.equip.org/articles/the-presumptuousness-of-atheism/.
Habermas, Gary R. 'My Pilgrimage from Atheism to Theism: An Exclusive Interview with Former British Atheist Professor Antony Flew' http://epsociety.org/library/articles.asp?pid=33&mode=detail.
*Kreeft, Peter. 'The Divinity of Christ' www.peterkreeft.com/topics/christ-divinity.htm.
Larmer, Robert. 'Is There Anything Wrong with "God of the Gaps" Reasoning?' www.newdualism.org/papers/R.Larmer/Gaps.htm.
Moreland, J.P. 'Complementarity, Agency Theory, and the God-of-the-Gaps' http://afterall.net/papers/490579.
O'Leary-Hawthorne, John. 'Arguments for Atheism' www.colorado.edu/philosophy/heathwood/pdf/hawthorn.pdf.
Shalkowski, Scott A. 'Atheological Apologetics' http://commonsenseatheism.com/wp-content/uploads/2010/02/Shalkowski-Atheological-Apologetics.pdf.
Snoke, David. 'In Favour of God-of-the-Gaps Reasoning' www.cityreformed.org/snoke/gaps.pdf.
*Williams, Peter S. 'Darwin's Rottweiler and the Public Understanding of Scientism' www.bethinking.org/science-christianity/intermediate/darwins-rottweiler-and-the-public-understanding.htm.
— 'Reviewing the Reviewers: Pigliucci et al. on "Darwin's Rottweiler and the Public Understanding of Science"' www.arn.org/docs/williams/pw_pigliucci_reviewingreviewers.htm.

Books

*DeWeese, Garrett J. and J.P. Moreland. *Philosophy Made Slightly Less Difficult* (Downers Grove, IL: IVP, 2005).

Horner, David A. 'Aut Deus Aut Malus Homo: A Defense of C.S. Lewis' "Shocking Alternative".' Pages 68–84 in *C.S. Lewis as Philosopher: Truth, Goodness and Beauty* (ed. David Baggett, Gary R. Habermas and Jerry L. Walls; Downers Grove, IL: IVP Academic, 2008).

Howard-Snyder, Francis, Daniel Howard-Snyder and Ryan Wasserman. *The Power of Logic* (New York: McGraw-Hill, 4th edn, 2008).

Kreeft, Peter. *Beyond Heaven and Hell* (Downers Grove, IL: IVP, 2nd edn, 2008).

Overman, Dean L. *A Case for the Divinity of Jesus: Examining the Earliest Evidence* (New York: Rowman & Littlefield, 2009).

Pirie, Madsen. *How to Win Every Argument: The Use and Abuse of Logic* (New York: Continuum, 2006).

Schopenhauer, Arthur. *The Art of Always Being Right* (London: Gibson Square, 2005).

Warburton, Nigel. *Thinking from A to Z* (London: Routledge, 3rd edn, 2007).

*Williams, Peter S. *C.S. Lewis vs the New Atheists* (Paternoster, 2013).

*— *Understanding Jesus: Five Ways to Spiritual Enlightenment* (Milton Keynes: Paternoster Press, 2011).

Many of the arguments critiqued in this chapter come from antitheistic 'new atheists'. Here are some key responses to the new atheism:

Watch:
Peter S. Williams, 'Concerning the "New Atheism"' YouTube Playlist, www.youtube.com/playlist?list=PLQhh3qcwVEWifP3P_gIS8MMsRXLOGDiG_.

Listen:
William Lane Craig, Daniel Dennett and Alister McGrath, 'Evidence for God's Existence' http://youtu.be/_Wzol00G2MM.

John Lennox, 'God, the Universe and Stephen Hawking' www.brianauten.com/Apologetics/john-lennox-god-universe-stephen-hawking.mp3.

Alvin Plantinga vs Daniel Dennett, 'Science and Religion: Are They Compatible?' http://youtu.be/fLb7UQp_gn4.

Peter S. Williams, 'A Sceptic's Guide to the New Atheists' www.damaris.org/cm/podcasts/694.

— 'C.S. Lewis vs the New Atheists (ELF 2012)' www.damaris.org/cm/podcasts/716.

— 'C.S. Lewis vs the New Atheists (Oxford C.S. Lewis Society, 2013)' www.damaris.org/cm/podcasts/794.

Read:
William Lane Craig and Chad Meister, eds, *God Is Great, God Is Good: Why Believing in God Is Reasonable and Responsible* (Downers Grove, IL: IVP, 2009).

Gregory E. Ganssle, *A Reasonable God: Engaging the New Face of Atheism* (Waco, TX: Baylor, 2009).

David Glass, *Atheism's New Clothes: Exploring and Exposing the Claims of the New Atheists* (Downers Grove, IL: IVP, 2012).

David Bentley Hart, *Atheist Delusions: The Christian Revolution and Its Fashionable Enemies* (Yale University Press, 2010).

Alvin Plantinga, 'The Dawkins Confusion' www.christianitytoday.com/bc/2007/002/1.21.html.

Mark D. Roberts, 'God Is Not Great by Christopher Hitchens: A Response' www.patheos.com/blogs/markdroberts/series/god-is-not-great-by-christopher-hitchens-a-response/.

Keith Ward, *Why There Almost Certainly Is a God: Doubting Dawkins* (Oxford: Lion, 2008).

Peter S. Williams, *C.S. Lewis vs the New Atheists* (Milton Keynes: Paternoster Press, 2013).

— 'A Christian Response to Against All Gods' www.arn.org/docs/williams/pw_contragrayling.htm.

— *A Sceptic's Guide to Atheism* (Carlisle: Paternoster Press, 2009).

— 'A Universe from Someone: Against Lawrence Krauss' A Universe from Nothing' www.bethinking.org/science-christianity/advanced/a-universe-from-someone-against-lawrence-krauss.htm.

— 'Who's Afraid of the Big Bad Wolf? Richard Dawkins' Failed Rebuttal of Natural Theology' www.arn.org/docs/williams/pw_goddelusionreview2.htm.

Part II

Some Arguments for God

The evidence for theism has never been so clear and so strong as it is now.
Robert C. Koons[1]

To most people, the existence of God is simply obvious. The Bible observes that the heavens declare the glory of God (Psalm 19:1) and that God's power is perceived through the things he has created (Romans 1:20). Moreover, 'numerous thinkers have proposed theistic arguments not only for the purpose of (a) persuading atheists [and agnostics] to become theists, but also . . . for the purpose of (b) vindicating the rationality of human beings' spontaneous belief in a higher power.'[2] This is the project of *natural theology*: 'the attempt to provide rational justification for theism using only those sources of information accessible to all inquirers, namely, the data of empirical experience and the dictates of human reason.'[3]

Natural theology underwent a renaissance in the late twentieth century, such that 'all of the traditional arguments for God's existence, as well as creative new arguments, find prominent, intelligent proponents among contemporary philosophers.'[4] Agnostic David Berlinski acknowledges that there's been a 'revival of natural theology,'[5] and highlights the importance of 'the consolidation of theoretical cosmology,'[6] including the discoveries that the universe had a temporal beginning and that its physical laws and initial conditions are 'fine tuned' for life.

Antony Flew (1923–2010), 'a legendary British philosopher and atheist [who was] an icon and champion for unbelievers for decades,'[7] renounced atheism in 2004 after concluding that 'the case for an Aristotelian God who has the characteristics of power and also intelligence, is now much stronger than it ever was before.'[8] Of course, as William C. Davis observes: 'a determined skeptic will always be able to find a reason – even if somewhat implausible – for persisting in unbelief,'[9] but there exist 'good arguments . . . that firmly connect the belief that God exists with other beliefs that are something like obviously true.'[10]

4. Cosmological Arguments I: Explaining a Dependent Cosmos

A family of arguments for the existence of God that postulate God's existence
as the ultimate cause or ground or explanation of the cosmos.
C. Stephen Evans[1]

Introduction

Christians believe that *God is in some sense the Creator of everything except himself*. The 'except himself' part is important because Christians believe that God himself is an uncreated being. The 'in some sense' part is important because different meanings can be given to the term 'create'. For example, there's a world of difference between:

1. Creating a new form of reality using pre-existing 'stuff' (e.g. God creating humanity 'from the dust of the ground' [Genesis 2:7])

which is a matter of rearranging existing things into new relationships, and:

2. Creating a new form of reality, like a universe, *without using pre-existing 'stuff'* (e.g. Genesis 1:1)

The first type of creation isn't the subject of cosmological arguments (but of 'design' arguments). Cosmological arguments are concerned exclusively with the second kind of creation. They focus upon the mere *existence* of things, leaving discussion of their *structure* to design arguments.

✔ Cosmological arguments concern the existence, not the structure, of the universe

Philosophers call the second type of creation *creatio ex nihilo*, which is Latin for 'creation not out of anything'. *Creatio ex nihilo* does *not* mean 'creation out of nothing', as if 'nothing' were a something used to create the cosmos! To create *ex nihilo* is not a matter of rearranging things, but of *arranging for there to be things* of some sort or other (beside God) *in the first place.*

Theists believe God is an uncreated being who created the universe *ex nihilo*. They believe the universe is the sort of thing that needs to be created if it is to exist, while God is the sort of thing that doesn't need to be created (note that any existing thing either does or does not need creating – i.e. causing) in order to exist. To believe in a Creator God is thus to say something both about the nature of the deity in which one believes and about the nature of the cosmos.

Atheists disagree with theists about the nature of the cosmos, believing that it is *not* the sort of thing that needs to be caused, and/or that causes can be multiplied indefinitely without the need to bring God into the picture as a 'First Cause'. The argument in favour of the theistic side of this debate is the 'First Cause' or *cosmological* argument.

The term 'cosmological' comes from two Greek words: *cosmos* and *logos*. *Cosmos* means 'ordered beauty' (think cosmetics); *logos* means 'reason' (hence 'logic'). 'Cosmological' literally means 'reasoning about ordered beauty'. Design arguments are *literally* 'cosmological', but design arguments have their own Greek term ('teleological') and are concerned with the *structure* rather than the mere *existence* of reality. 'Cosmological' has come to mean 'a family of arguments for the existence of God that postulate God's existence as the ultimate cause or ground or explanation of the cosmos.'[3] As C. Stephen Evans and R. Zachary Manis comment: 'there is no such thing as *the* cosmological argument or *the* teleological argument . . . many different versions of each of these arguments have been proposed, and some differ radically from others in the same category. For this reason alone one should be wary of claims to have been given a final refutation of one of these types of arguments.'[4]

4.1 Three Types of Cosmological Argument

Philosophers distinguish three subclasses of cosmological argument, two of which are often named after philosophers who gave particularly famous versions of that type of argument (i.e. Thomas Aquinas and Gottfried Leibniz). The third type of argument is named after an ancient tradition of Islamic philosophical discourse. This chapter will examine Thomistic and Leibnizian-type cosmological arguments. Chapter 5 will examine the third, *'kalam'* type of cosmological argument. These three types of argument aren't in competition with one another. They are three independent and complementary causal arguments for the existence of God.

✔ The different types of cosmological arguments are complementary

4.2 The General Form of Cosmological Arguments

Cosmological arguments, of whatever subcategory, take a general form that we can examine by substituting the placeholders X and Y for the specific causal terms that would appear in a specific argument. The meaning of our placeholders is provided in italics in the first premise, after which their use saves a lot of repetition:

1. At least one thing exists, and it is either *the sort of thing the existence of which requires the existence of something outside of itself* (an X), or it isn't (and *to be an existing thing but not an X is by definition to be a Y*).
2. It's implausible to think that any thing of type X can be accounted for only in terms of things of type X.
3. Therefore, whether or not one or more things of type X exist, it's plausible to think that there exists something of type Y.

Let's review this generalized cosmological argument one step at a time:

1. At least one thing exists, and it is either *the sort of thing the existence of which requires the existence of something outside of itself* (an X), or it isn't (and *to be an existing thing but not an X is by definition to be a Y*).

It's impossible to claim coherently that nothing exists. To claim that nothing exists is self-contradictory. It's hard (but perhaps not impossible) to claim that nothing of type X exists. X and Y might be more specifically defined in terms of:

- Being (X) 'an effect' or (Y) 'a cause'; being (X) 'contingent' or (Y) 'necessary'; being (X) 'dependent' or (Y) 'independent' (the Thomistic argument)
- (X) 'failing to contain the sufficient reason for one's existence', or (Y) 'containing the sufficient reason for one's existence' (the Leibnizian argument)
- Being (X) a thing 'that has a beginning', or 'that comes into being', or that 'has a finite past'; versus being (Y) a thing that doesn't have a beginning, which doesn't come into being and/or which exists atemporally (the *kalam* argument)

On the one hand, if nothing of type X (on any definition) exists, but something does exist (and it's self-contradictory to claim that nothing exists), then it must be something of type Y (under some definition thereof). On the other hand:

2. It's implausible to think that any thing of type X can be accounted for *only* in terms of the existence of things of type X

Another way to put this premise would be to claim that it's *implausible* to think that 'the existence of an X does not imply the existence of a Y.' It might be said that since Xs always demand further explanation, one can never *completely* explain an X simply by mentioning more Xs (that just makes the problem worse). In fact, trying to take this route entails the existence of an infinite regress of Xs, and it might be argued that this regress is factually false (e.g. the universe did have a beginning), or even that it is impossible (e.g. that there can't be an infinite regress of causes). But if the number of Xs in one's explanation of things is (or must) be finite, then it's implausible to deny that, since Xs don't account for themselves, the existence of an X implies the existence of a Y:

3. Therefore, whether or not one or more things of type X exists, it's plausible to think that there exists something of type Y.

Since, however, X and Y are defined in the different types of cosmological argument, and being Y is by definition more Godlike than being X, any argument supporting the existence of something that is Y is thereby an argument that supports the theistic worldview. Moreover, one can provide further arguments that tease out further Godlike properties of being a Y rather than an X.

> **Question:**
> From the fact that something exists displaying the properties of some 'Y' given above,
> what else can be plausibly concluded about the nature of 'Y'?

4.3 Who Made God?

Faced with any cosmological argument, a particularly popular objection is to raise the question 'Who made God?' or 'What caused God?' J.P. Moreland counters:

> we can consistently hold that all events need causes and that God does not need a cause because God is not an event. Furthermore, the question 'What or who made God?' is a pointless category fallacy, like the question 'What colour is the note C?' The question 'What made X?' can only be asked of Xs that are by definition makeable. But God, if he exists at all, is a necessary being, the uncreated Creator of all else. This definition is what theists mean by 'God,' even if it turns out that no God exists. Now, if that is what 'God' means, then the question 'What made God?' turns out to be 'What made an entity, God, who is by definition un-makeable?'[5]

It's useful to understand that the 'Who made God?' question arises from an all-too-common misrepresentation of the cosmological argument. Many atheists attack a 'straw man' (cf. chapter 3, 3.4.12) of the cosmological argument that goes something like this:

1. Everything has a cause
2. The universe (the sum total of material reality) is a thing
3. Therefore, the universe has a cause (God)

For example, Nigel Warburton asserts: 'The First Cause Argument states that absolutely everything has been caused by something else prior to it . . . If we follow this series back we will find an original cause . . . This first cause, so the First Cause Argument tells us, is God.'[6] Warburton objects that if every thing has a cause, 'God' must have a cause. But then how can he be God? If we deny that God is caused, we contradict the premise that 'every thing has a cause.' However, without this premise, the argument falls apart:

> The First Cause Argument begins with the assumption that every single thing was caused by something else, but it then proceeds to contradict this by saying that God was the very first cause . . . It invites the question 'And what

caused God?' . . . If the series of effects and causes is going to stop somewhere, why must it stop at God? Why couldn't it stop earlier in the regression, with the appearance of the universe itself?[7]

However, 'the cosmological argument does *not* say: "everything must have a cause, therefore the Universe has a cause"; but "for contingent (dependent) things to exist, 'necessary' (self-existent) being must exist, but contingent being (the Universe) *does* exist, *therefore* necessary being (God) exists."'[8] Warburton's discussion includes the premise that 'absolutely everything has been caused by something else', but genuine cosmological arguments rely on *precisely the opposite premise*!

Sam Harris writes:

> The argument runs more or less like this: everything that exists has a cause; space and time exist; space and time must, therefore, have been caused by something that stands outside of space and time; and the only thing that transcends space and time, and yet retains the power to create, is God . . . As many critics of religion have pointed out, the notion of a creator poses an immediate problem of an infinite regress. If God created the universe, what created God? To say that God, by definition, is uncreated simply begs the question.[9]

The cosmological argument does *not* beg the question against the universe being uncreated. The cosmological argument *argues* for the conclusion that there must exist an uncaused cause of the universe precisely by pointing out the 'problem of an infinite regress' that arises if one denies this conclusion! Harris fails to distinguish between the straw-man premise that 'everything that exists has a cause' and the premise that 'space-time is the sort of thing that has a cause.'

Daniel Dennett critiques:

> The Cosmological Argument, which in its simplest form states that since everything must have a cause the universe must have a cause – namely, God . . . Some deny the premise [that everything must have a cause] . . . Others prefer to accept the premise and then ask: What caused God? The reply that God is self-caused (somehow) then raises the rebuttal: If something can be self-caused, why can't the universe as a whole be the thing that is self-caused?[10]

Indeed, *theists* deny both the premise that everything must have a cause *and* the incoherent suggestion that anything, including God, can be 'self-caused'![11] As Edward Feser complains: 'that is *not* what the Cosmological Argument for the existence of God says. In fact, *not one* of the best-known defenders of the Cosmological Argument in the history of philosophy ever gave this stupid "everything has a cause" argument.'[12] The cosmological argument proper doesn't contain the stipulation that 'everything must have a cause.' Rather, it contains the stipulation that all caused things (all effects) must (by definition) have a cause. The conclusion of the argument is not that there exists a 'self-caused' cause (nothing can cause itself), but that there exists an *uncaused* cause. In summary, according to many atheists, the cosmological argument says:

1. Everything has a cause
2. The universe is a thing
3. Therefore, the universe has a cause ('God')

This straw man naturally invites the 'Who caused God?' objection. But we can easily avoid this problem. For example:

1. At least one caused reality exists
2. It's impossible for *everything* to be caused (there can't be an infinite regress of causes)
3. Therefore, there must exist an uncaused cause ('God')

The first premise of this logically valid argument seems to be beyond dispute (e.g. you exist and you are caused). The question is whether or not it is possible for everything that exists to be caused. As soon as one asks, 'Caused by what?' one can see the problem with saying that everything is caused. Outside of *everything* is nothing, and 'from nothing, nothing comes'. The important point to note is that the cosmological argument actually depends upon the *denial* of the very premise – namely 'everything has a cause' – falsely attributed to it by many atheists!

✔ Watch out for atheists attacking straw-man cosmological arguments that lead to the question 'Who made God?'

Watch:
'Atheists with Attention Deficit Disorder' http://youtu.be/DQ5XsgJp9g4.
John Lennox, 'Who Created the Creator?' http://youtu.be/1W18m966MX8.

4.4 Dawkins' Doubts

Faced with a cosmological argument that relies upon the premise that an infinite regress is impossible, Richard Dawkins complains that it makes 'the entirely unwarranted assumption that God himself is immune to the regress.'[13] In other words, Dawkins asks, 'Who made God?' Dawkins fails to recognize that the cosmological argument is *an argument for* the existence of a being that's 'immune to the regress' of cause and effect! The only alternative to acknowledging the existence of something 'immune to the regress' is not simply to stop 'with the appearance of the universe itself' (as Warburton suggests). Rather, it is to accept the reality of an infinite regress of causes. This is highly implausible.

But why identify this 'something that's immune to the regress of causality' with God? Dawkins complains that, even if the cosmological argument were sound, 'there is absolutely no reason to endow that terminator [of the causal regress] with any of the properties normally ascribed to God.'[14] Again, this is incorrect. One of the properties normally ascribed to God is being the uncreated Creator of the universe, and the cosmological argument (assuming it is sound) shows that there is a being with precisely this divine property! Moreover, in conjunction with other sound examples of natural theology, Occam's razor (cf. chapter 3, 3.4.10) guides us into building up a composite picture of this uncreated Creator. Dawkins' 'divide and conquer' approach to natural theology is unreasonable. Several arguments that individually fail to warrant belief in God may do exactly that when taken together, just as several clues that are individually insufficient to warrant conviction in a court of law may be jointly sufficient to that end. As atheist J.L. Mackie advised: 'It will not be sufficient to criticize each argument on its own by saying that it does not prove the intended conclusion . . . For a set of arguments of each of which, on its own, this adverse comment is true may together make the conclusion *more* likely than not.'[15]

✔ Cosmological arguments can tell us something about God without telling us everything!

It's time we turned our attention away from straw men set up by atheists intent upon blowing away easy targets. Instead we will take a look at two genuine articles (our third genuine article, the *kalam* cosmological argument, will occupy our attention in chapter 5).

4.5 Cosmological Arguments from Dependency

We should dispose of unsound cosmological arguments based upon the false premise that 'every thing needs a cause'; but we can easily formulate cosmological arguments that avoid the 'Who made God?' objection. For example:

1. By definition, every dependent thing needs something to depend upon
2. The universe (i.e. the sum total of dependent things) is a dependent thing
3. Therefore, the universe needs something to depend upon (i.e. God)

This type of cosmological argument – similar to arguments made by Thomas Aquinas in his *Summa Theologica* – avoids the 'Who made God?' problem by replacing 'Every thing needs a cause' with 'Every *dependent* thing needs something to depend upon.' We can then answer the 'Who made God?' question by noting that *'God' is not a dependent thing*. In other words, a good answer to the 'Who made God?' question is: 'If God exists, then he isn't the sort of being that could be made; but let's talk about the universe, because it sure seems like the sort of thing that would need to be made . . .'

✔ If God exists, then he can't have been created – but the same thing can't plausibly be said of the universe . . .

The existence of a necessary and/or independent unmade Maker (God) is the theist's answer to the question 'Why does the universe exist?' Some atheists ask why we need to take this question seriously, suggesting that the regress of causes stops 'with the appearance of the universe itself.' In other words, why not say that the universe is a necessary and/or independent, uncaused thing? Both theists and atheists can be committed to the existence of an independent thing. The point at issue is whether that independent thing is the universe, or something the universe depends upon. However, to rationally stop 'with the appearance of the universe itself', atheists must show that denying the premise 'The universe is a dependent thing' is at least as reasonable as affirming it. However, this denial looks *less plausible* than its affirmation.

It seems just as reasonable to argue that 'if every dependent thing needs something to depend upon, then the sum total of dependent things (the universe) needs something to depend upon' as it does to argue that 'if a wall is built using only red bricks, then the whole wall will be red.'

As Richard Taylor argues: 'it would certainly be odd to maintain that everything in the world owes its existence to something . . . and then to deny this of the world itself . . . we find nothing whatever about the world, any more than in its parts, to suggest that it exists by its own nature.'[16]

Peter Kreeft and Ronald K. Tacelli frame the dependency argument as a *reductio ad absurdum* ('reduction to absurdity'):[17]

> Are all things caused to exist by other things right now? Suppose they are. That is, suppose there is no Uncaused Being . . . Then nothing could exist right now. For remember, on the [no Uncaused Being] hypothesis, all things need a present cause outside of themselves in order to exist. So right now, all things, including all those things which are causing other things to be, need a cause. They can give being only so long as they are given being. Everything that exists, therefore, on this hypothesis, stands in need of being caused to exist. But caused by what? Beyond everything that is, there can only be nothing. But that is absurd: all of reality dependent – but dependent on nothing! The hypothesis that all being is caused, that there is no Uncaused Being, is absurd. So there must be something uncaused, something on which all things that need an efficient cause of being are dependent.[18]

'The point here,' notes W. David Beck, 'is that everyone can see that certain things owe their existence to other things.'[19] The idea that some things owe their existence to other things is surely more plausible than its denial. However, nothing can owe its existence to itself, for then its existence would have to precede its existence, which is contradictory. The causal relation of 'transitivity' exists when A is caused by (owes its existence to) B, but only because B is caused in turn by C: 'Every physical object we know of possesses this sort of contingency: it exists and functions only as it is caused by other objects in the chain.'[20] Can this chain be infinite?

Consider a train carriage. Why is it moving? It is pulled by the carriage in front. And why is *that* carriage moving? It is tempting to settle the question of causal explanation by noting that each carriage is being pulled by the one in front:

> It may well be true that [carriage] A is pulled by [carriage] B. But B can pull A only because B is, in turn, pulled by C . . . and so on . . . But now something important becomes obvious. An infinity of [carriages] will still leave unsolved the problem of explaining why the first [carriage] is moving and hence why any are. The problem is not with the arrangement of [carriages], nor is it a matter of the number of [carriages]. The problem is that no [carriage] in the

chain has the capacity to generate or initiate its own motion. It can pass on the pulling, but it does not initiate it.[21]

As with carriages moving, so with dependent things existing. Dependent things can be *given* existence, and they can *pass on* existence once they've been given it, but they can't pass on what they don't have. Hence the existence of dependent things ultimately requires the existence of something that is *independent*.

4.6 Leibnizian Cosmological Arguments

If anything exists, then it does so either necessarily or contingently. Something is necessary if its non-existence is impossible. Something is contingent if its existence is not necessary (i.e. its non-existence is possible). The existence of something contingent that does not *have* to exist (e.g. a chicken) raises the question of *why* it exists. The existence of the universe raises the same question. As David S. Oderberg points out: 'if *anything* cries out for an explanation, contingent existents do. The universe is contingent. So it too requires an explanation, moreover one that does not appeal to itself or any of its parts on pain of circularity.'[22]

The question of 'contingent existents' seems to assume the truth of some sort of 'principle of sufficient reason' (PSR). For a reason to be 'sufficient' means that it is enough of a reason to account for whatever it is meant to explain. Suppose you know I want a chicken, and that the only available chicken costs £10. Your observation of a chicken in my garden wouldn't sit comfortably with my explaining that I'd given the chicken's previous owner £5. This isn't a *sufficient* explanation of my chicken-owning status. On the other hand, the explanation that I had paid £10 for the chicken (or stolen it!) would be a sufficient explanation. In short, given a state of affairs requiring explanation, the explanation must be a *sufficient explanation*, i.e. *one that's actually up to the job of explaining what needs to be explained*.

✔ A sufficient explanation is one that's 'big enough' to explain what needs to be explained

Let's examine two cosmological arguments that depend upon two different formulations of the principle of sufficient reason.

4.6.1 William Lane Craig's Leibnizian cosmological argument

Watch:
William Lane Craig, 'Leibniz's Argument for the Existence of God?' http://youtu.
be/sdSVypgj88M.

William Lane Craig defends a Leibnizian-type cosmological argument
that can be put as follows:

1. Everything that exists has an explanation of its existence, either in the
   necessity of its own nature or in an external cause
2. The universe exists
3. Therefore, the universe has an explanation of its existence
4. If the universe has an explanation of its existence, that explanation is
   God
5. Therefore, the explanation of the universe's existence is God

This argument depends upon three crucial premises. The first is a form of
the principle of sufficient reason:

1. Everything that exists has an explanation of its existence (either in the
   necessity of its own nature or in an external cause).

The other two crucial premises are:

2. The universe exists

and:

4. If the universe has an explanation of its existence, that explanation is God.

From premises 1 and 2 it follows logically that

3. Therefore, the universe has an explanation of its existence.

And from 3 and 4 the conclusion follows:

5. Therefore, the explanation of the universe's existence is God.

Anyone who wants to remain an atheist must hold that one of the crucial
three premises is false: 'Premise [2] is undeniable for any sincere seeker

after truth. So the atheist is going to have to deny either 1 or [4] if he wants to remain an atheist and be rational.'[23]

Question:
What would you say to someone who questioned the existence of the universe?

Craig argues that premise 1 is self-evident:

> Imagine that you're hiking through the woods one day and you come across a translucent ball lying on the forest floor. You would naturally wonder how it came to be there. If one of your hiking partners said to you, 'It just exists inexplicably. Don't worry about it!', you'd either think that he was crazy or figure that he just wanted you to keep moving. No one would take seriously the suggestion that the ball existed there with literally no explanation. Now suppose you increase the size of the ball in this story so that it's the size of a car. That wouldn't do anything to satisfy or remove the demand for an explanation . . . Suppose it were the size of the entire universe. Same problem. Merely increasing the size of the ball does nothing to affect the need of an explanation.[24]

Some atheists respond that while premise 1 is true of everything *in* the universe it isn't true *of* the universe as a whole. Craig replies: 'It would be arbitrary for the atheist to claim that the universe is the exception to the rule. The illustration of the ball in the woods showed that merely increasing the size of the object to be explained, even until it becomes the universe itself, does nothing to remove the need for some explanation of its existence.'[25]

Then again:

> Some atheists have tried to justify making the universe an exception to premise 1 by saying that it's *impossible* for the universe to have an explanation of its existence. For the explanation of the universe would have to be some prior state of affairs in which the universe did not yet exist. But that would be nothingness, and nothingness cannot be the explanation of anything . . . This line of reasoning . . . assumes that the universe is all there is, so that if there were no universe there would be nothing . . . the objection assumes that atheism is true! The atheist is thus begging the question . . .[26]

Hence Craig concludes that 'premise 1 is more plausibly true than false, which is all we need for a good argument.'[27]

What about premise 4? This is synonymous with the standard atheistic claim that if God doesn't exist, then the universe has no explanation of its existence. If the physical universe has a cause, that cause can't be something physical and so it must be something non-physical. There are only two possible types of non-physical thing: so-called 'abstract' objects (some philosophers think that numbers are abstract objects) and un-embodied mind. But abstract objects can't cause anything: 'The number 7, for example, can't cause any effects. So the cause of the existence of the universe must be a transcendent Mind, which is what believers understand God to be.'[28]

✔ The only type of non-physical thing that can cause effects is a mind

The atheist seems to have only one alternative at this point: he or she can admit the universe *does* have an explanation of its existence, but then claim that this explanation is that the universe exists *by a necessity of its own nature*. However, according to Craig: 'this would be a very radical step for the atheist to take, and I can't think of any contemporary atheist who has in fact adopted this line.'[29] Craig reckons: 'The reason atheists are not eager to embrace this alternative is clear. As we look about the universe, none of the things that make it up . . . seems to exist necessarily. They could all fail to exist.'[30] He notes that:

> matter itself is composed of tiny particles called 'quarks' . . . couldn't a different collection of quarks have existed instead of this one? Does each and every one of these quarks exist necessarily? Notice what the atheist cannot say at this point. He cannot say that the quarks are just configurations of matter which could have been different, even though the matter of which the quarks are composed exists necessarily . . . quarks . . . just *are* the basic units of matter . . . Now it seems obvious that a different collection of quarks could have existed instead of the collection that does exist. But if that were the case, then a different universe would have existed . . . made up of different quarks, even if identically arranged as in this universe . . . It follows, then, that the universe does not exist by a necessity of its own nature.[31]

Suppose I ask you to loan me a certain book, but you say, 'I don't have a copy right now, but I'll ask my friend to lend me his copy and then I'll lend it to you.' Suppose your friend says the same thing to you, and so on. Two things are clear. First, if the process of asking to borrow the book goes on *ad infinitum*, I'll never get the book. Second, if I get the book, the process that led to me getting it can't have gone on *ad infinitum*. Somewhere down the line of requests to borrow the book, someone *had* the book *without having to borrow it*. Likewise, argues Richard Purtill, consider any contingent reality: 'the same two principles apply. If the process of everything getting its existence from something else went on to infinity, then the thing in question would never [have] existence. And if the thing has . . . existence then the process hasn't gone on to infinity. There was something that had existence without having to receive it from something else.'[32]

Hence, 'given the truth of the three premises the conclusion is logically inescapable: *God is the explanation of the existence of the universe.*'[33]

Does God's existence have an explanation? Yes: in the necessity of his own nature.

Watch:
'The Intellectual Laziness of Lawrence Krauss (as Well as Others)' http://youtu.be/JNcr63dlelc.

4.6.2 Alexander R. Pruss's Leibnizian cosmological argument

Alexander R. Pruss adds an interesting addendum to the cosmological argument that accommodates rejection of the principle of sufficient reason: 1) The principle of sufficient reason is either true or not. 2) If it is true, God exists by the cosmological argument. 3) If it is not true, then it is a puzzling fact that all observed things have causes, a puzzling fact best explained in terms of God. 4) So, at least probably, God exists.[34]

Consider the 'restricted principle of sufficient reason' (RPSR) proposed by Pruss:

If p is a true proposition and possibly p has an explanation, then p actually has an explanation'[35]

(The weaker principle that 'if p is a true proposition and possibly p has an explanation, then p *probably* has an explanation' would serve almost as well.) RPSR entails that *if* the proposition 'Chickens exist' is true (it is), and *if* it is possible that the existence of chickens has an explanation (and surely this is possible), *then* there must be an explanation for the existence of chickens (which seems right). This RPSR has intuitive force (while it makes no sense to ask for an explanation for the existence of a necessary being, it does seem to make sense to ask for an explanation of a contingent being like a chicken). This principle (like Craig's) also allows for popular counter-examples to Leibniz's original 'non-restricted' PSR (which stated that '*every* contingent true proposition necessarily has an explanation', and which some people argue is contradicted by the existence of free will).

✔ The principle of sufficient reason can be defined so that it is compatible with the existence of freely willed choices

If one accepts that 'There is a contingent being' is a true proposition that possibly has an explanation, then, according to RPSR, it must have an explanation; but 'since the agency of a contingent being cannot, without vicious circularity, explain why there exists at least one contingent, it follows that the explanation of *p* invokes the agency of a necessary being which is a first cause.'[36] In syllogistic form:

1. (RPSR) If *p* is a true proposition and possibly *p* has an explanation, then *p* actually [or probably] has an explanation
2. 'There is a universe' is a true proposition *p* that possibly has an explanation
3. Therefore, 'There is a universe' is a true proposition *p* that actually [or probably] has an explanation
4. If there is an explanation for the universe, the most plausible explanation is its creation *ex nihilo* by the agency of a necessary being which is a first cause (i.e. God)
5. Therefore the hypothesis that the universe was created *ex nihilo* by God is more plausible than its denial

The controversial premises in this argument are likely to be premise 2 (note that this premise doesn't claim that the universe has an explanation, only that it *could* have one) and premise 4.

> **Question:**
> What could one say in defence of premises 2 and 4 of the above argument?

Conclusion

It's easy to construct logically valid cosmological arguments that don't invite the question 'Who made God?' Indeed, there seem to be several logically valid cosmological arguments with premises that are all more plausible than their denials. No cosmological argument proves everything the theist believes about God, but each proves something that chimes with the theistic belief in *creatio ex nihilo*.

> **Question:**
> Taking any of the cosmological arguments in this chapter, what proposition/s would an atheist need to accept in order to avoid the conclusion? In other words, what philosophical price tag is attached to denying the conclusion of the argument?

* * *

Recommended Resources

Video

Williams, Peter S. and William Lane Craig vs Andrew Copson and Arif Ahmed. 'Cambridge Union: This House Believes God Is Not a Delusion' www.bethinking.org/who-are-you-god/advanced/cambridge-union-society-debate-an-analysis.htm.

*Williams, Peter S. 'Cosmological Arguments for God' YouTube Playlist www.youtube.com/playlist?list=PLQhh3qcwVEWjEXjiEjnCCbr_Qnu-1UbAa.

Audio

Beck, W. David. 'Cosmological Argument' www.4truth.net/fourtruthpbgod.aspx-?pageid=8589952708.

Craig, William Lane. 'The Argument from Contingency' www.rfmedia.org/RF_audio_video/Defender_podcast/20040425ArgumentfromContingency.mp3.

— 'Creation out of Nothing' www.reasonablefaith.org/creation-out-of-nothing.

— 'Lawrence Krauss on Creation out of Nothing' www.reasonablefaith.org/lawrence-krauss-on-creation-out-of-nothing.

— Defenders Podcast, series 2, parts 1–5 www.reasonablefaith.org/defenders-2-podcast/s4.

Groothuis, Douglas. 'Cosmological Arguments' www.relyonchrist.com/Lecture/Audio/12.mp3, www.relyonchrist.com/Lecture/Audio/13.mp3 and www.relyon-christ.com/Lecture/Audio/14.mp3.

Williams, Peter S. 'Hawking and the Grand Designer (Exeter School)' www.damaris.org/cm/podcasts/566.

— 'Stephen Hawking and the Grand Designer (Bryanston School)' www.damaris.org/cm/podcasts/663.

— 'Stephen Hawking and the Grand Designer (Winchester)' www.damaris.org/cm/podcasts/682.

Online papers

*Albert, David. 'On the Origin of Everything' www.nytimes.com/2012/03/25/books/review/a-universe-from-nothing-by-lawrence-m-krauss.html.

*Aquinas, Thomas. 'Does God Exist?' from *Summa Theologica* http://newadvent.org/summa/100203.htm.

Beck, W. David. 'The Cosmological Argument' www.4truth.net/fourtruthpbgod.aspx-?pageid=8589952710.

Copleston, F.C. vs Bertrand Russell. 'A Debate on the Argument from Contingency' www.ditext.com/russell/debate.html and www.bringyou.to/apologetics/p20.htm (includes full debate transcript and audio of discussion on contingency).

Craig, William Lane. 'Argument from Contingency' www.reasonablefaith.org/site/News2?page=NewsArticle&id=5847.

Fesser, Edward. 'Not Understanding Nothing: A Review of *A Universe from Nothing*' www.firstthings.com/article/2012/05/not-understanding-nothing.

Koons, Robert C. Lectures on cosmological arguments at www.leaderu.com/offices/koons/menus/lecture.html.

Pruss, Alexander R. 'A Restricted Principle of Sufficient Reason and the Cosmological Argument' www.georgetown.edu/faculty/ap85/papers/RPSR.html and www.last-seminary.com/cosmological-argument/A%20Restricted%20Principle%20of%20Sufficient%20Reason%20and%20the%20Cosmological%20Argument.pdf.

Sadowsky, James A. 'Can There Be an Endless Regress of Causes?' www.anthonyflood.com/sadowskyendlessregress.htm.

*Taylor, Richard. 'The Cosmological Argument: A Defence' http://mind.ucsd.edu/syllabi/02-03/01w/readings/taylor.pdf.

*Williams, Peter S. 'A Universe from Someone: Against Lawrence Krauss' *A Universe from Nothing: Why There Is Something Rather Than Nothing*' www.bethinking.org/science-christianity/advanced/a-universe-from-someone-against-lawrence-krauss.htm.

— 'Who Made God?' www.bethinking.org/who-are-you-god/introductory/who-made-god.htm.

Books

*Beck, W. David. 'A Thomistic Cosmological Argument.' Pages 95–107 in *To Everyone an Answer* (ed. Francis J. Beckwith, William Lane Craig and J.P. Moreland; Downers Grove, IL: IVP, 2004).

Clarke, Samuel L. *A Demonstration of the Being and Attributes of God* (CUP, 1998) www.ccel.org/ccel/clarke_s/being.html.

*Craig, William Lane. *On Guard: Defending Your Faith with Reason and Precision* (Colorado Springs, CO: David C. Cook, 2010).

— *Reasonable Faith: Christian Truth and Apologetics* (Wheaton, IL: Crossway, 3rd edn, 2008).

—, ed. *Philosophy of Religion: A Reader and Guide* (Edinburgh University Press, 2002).

Craig, William Lane and J.P. Moreland, eds. *The Blackwell Companion to Natural Theology* (Oxford: Wiley-Blackwell, 2009).

Copan, Paul and Paul K. Moser, eds. *The Rationality of Theism* (London: Routledge, 2003).

Geivett, R. Douglas. 'Two Versions of the Cosmological Argument.' Pages 52–68 in *Passionate Conviction: Contemporary Discourses on Christian Apologetics* (ed. Paul Copan and William Lane Craig; Nashville, TN: B&H Academic, 2007).

Miethe, Terry L. and Antony Flew. *Does God Exist? A Believer and an Atheist Debate* (HarperSanFrancisco, 1991).

Nagasawa, Yujin. *The Existence of God: A Philosophical Introduction* (Oxford: Routledge, 2011).

Oderberg, David S. 'The Cosmological Argument.' Pages 342–50 in *The Routledge Companion to Philosophy of Religion* (ed. Chad Meister and Paul Copan; London: Routledge, 2010).

Reichenbach, Bruce R. *The Cosmological Argument: A Reassessment* (Springfield, IL: Charles C. Thomas, 1972).

Smart, J.J.C. and John Haldane. *Atheism and Theism* (Oxford: Blackwell, 2nd edn, 2002).
Swinburne, Richard. *The Existence of God* (Oxford: Clarendon Press, 2nd edn, 2004).

5. Cosmological Arguments II: The *Kalam* Cosmological Argument

[The world] has come-to-be. For it is visible, tangible, and possessed of body; all such things . . . have been shown to be things that come-to-be and have been brought-into-being.

Plato, *Timaeus*[1]

Introduction

Introduction

In chapter 4 we examined two different types of cosmological arguments, but we didn't examine the *kalam* cosmological argument. *Kalam* means 'speech' in Arabic, and cosmological arguments in this tradition claim both that the cosmos began to exist and that it's having a beginning entails that it was created *ex nihilo* (not out of anything) by God: 'This . . . argument originated in the attempts of early Christian philosophers . . . to rebut the Aristotelian doctrine of the eternity of the universe and was developed by medieval Islamic and Jewish theologians who bequeathed it to the Christian West.'[2]

William Lane Craig revived the *kalam* argument in the late twentieth century, discussing it in the light of modern scientific cosmology. Other scholars, notably J.P. Moreland, followed his lead.[3] Craig summarizes the argument: 'both philosophical and scientific evidence show that the universe began to exist. Anything that begins to exist must have a cause that brings it into being. So the universe must have a cause. Philosophical analysis reveals that such a cause must have several of the principal theistic attributes.'[4]

This chapter will say relatively little about the second step mentioned by Craig, that of drawing out the implications of the universe having a transcendent cause (cf. section 5.4.2). Our focus will be upon the primary step of establishing that the universe has a transcendent cause. That is:

1. Whatever begins to exist has a cause
2. The universe began to exist
3. Therefore, the universe has a cause

> **Watch:**
> William Lane Craig, 'What Is the Kalam Cosmological Argument?' http://youtu.be/Z5XvT0awYHk.
> Doug Powell, 'The Kalam Cosmological Argument' http://youtu.be/8V1hM-FaH3gM.

Let's examine both premises in order:

5.1 Does Whatever Begins to Exist Have a Cause?

To affirm . . . that the world or cosmos had an absolute beginning . . . would be tantamount to affirming the existence of God.
Mortimer J. Adler[5]

According to Moreland and Craig, premise 1 is, at the very least, more plausible than its denial: 'It is rooted in the metaphysical intuition that something cannot come into being from nothing. Moreover, this premise is constantly confirmed in our experience.'[6] Even the sceptical Scottish philosopher David Hume remarked that he 'never asserted so absurd a proposition as that something could arise without a cause.'[7]

Watch:
William Lane Craig, 'The Absurdity of Denying the First Premise of the Kalam Cosmological Argument' http://youtu.be/ssnEzF596IY.

We will return to premise 1 later.

5.2 Did the Universe Begin to Exist?

To claim that the universe 'began to exist' amounts to claiming that the universe has a past that's finite *rather than actually infinite*. There's an important distinction between the concepts of an *actual infinite* and of a *potential infinite*. An 'actual infinite' is any collection of things which at any given time has a number of members greater than any natural number {0, 1, 2, 3, etc.}. This notion contrasts with that of a 'potential infinite', which is any collection of things which at any given time has a number of members equal to some natural number or other, but members of which can increase in number endlessly over time. In other words: *a potential infinite* means something that's always finite and which can always get bigger, whereas an *actual infinite* means something that's never finite and which, therefore, can't get any bigger (infinity plus one equals infinity).

Support for the premise that the universe began to exist comes from both philosophy and science.

5.2.1 Two philosophical arguments for the premise that the universe had a beginning

Defenders of the *kalam* argument give two philosophical arguments for the premise that the universe had a beginning, that is, that it has a finite past. The first argument rests upon the claims that 1) actual infinities cannot have an objective existence in the real world, and that 2) a universe with no beginning would be a universe where an actual infinity existed in the real world. From these premises it follows that the universe has a beginning. The second argument rests upon the claims that 1) the past is a series of events formed by successive addition, and that 2) no series formed by successive addition can ever be actually infinite. From these premises it also follows that the universe has a beginning.

Before examining these arguments against the past being actually infinite, it's worth noting with Craig that 'when we speak of the infinity of God, we are not using the word in a mathematical sense to refer to an aggregate of an infinite number of parts. God's infinity is, if you will, qualitative, not quantitative. It means that God is metaphysically necessary, morally perfect, omnipotent, omniscient, eternal, etc.'[8]

5.2.1.1 *The impossibility of actual infinities*

The first philosophical argument for the finitude of the past runs as follows:

1. An actual infinite cannot exist
2. An infinite temporal regress of events is an actual infinite
3. Therefore, an infinite temporal regress of events cannot exist

It would seem to be true by definition that if the series of past events is infinite rather than finite, then 'the past' constitutes an actual infinity. But why believe that an actual infinity cannot exist in the concrete (i.e. *real*, not 'made of concrete'!) world?

First, we need to clarify the distinction between talking about an actual infinity as *an abstract idea* that mathematicians use in their thinking, and as *a concrete reality* in the world outside of minds. As Norman L. Geisler and Frank Turek explain: 'there's a difference between an abstract infinite series and a concrete one. The one is purely theoretical, the other is actual ... You can conceive of an infinite number of mathematical points between two bookends on a shelf, but you could not fit an infinite number of books between them. That's the difference between an abstract and a concrete.'[9]

The term 'actual' in the phrase 'actual infinite' does *not* mean 'having a concrete existence'! According to Craig: 'although infinite set theory and transfinite arithmetic each constitutes a logically consistent universe of discourse, given their axioms and conventions, the existence of an actual infinite in the real world leads to intolerable absurdities'[10] that should not be accepted. In other words, although mathematicians can think about the idea of an actual infinite in their 'ivory towers' all they like, architects had better not try to design any actual infinities into the building plans of any towers they actually want to build!

Consider a thought experiment about a day in the working life of 'Hilbert's Hotel', named after mathematician David Hilbert and built by an architect who spurns this advice about avoiding actual infinities in their building plans. That is, suppose that there existed (as a concrete reality you could visit) a hotel with an *actually infinite* number of rooms and an actually infinite number of guests. Every room in Hilbert's Hotel is booked out to a guest. The sign in the entrance lobby reads: 'No Vacancies.' It also says: 'Guests Welcome'! When a new guest arrives, the manager asks the person in room #1 to move into room #2, and so on, in order to free up room #1 for the new arrival. Before this new guest checked into the hotel there were no vacancies, because an actually infinite number of guests had booked out each and every one of the hotel's actually infinite number of rooms. After the new guest has been *added* to the guest list, that guest list is *no longer* than before! The hotel contains the same indefinite number of guests before and after the new guest checks in, namely, 'an actual infinity'! This story about Hilbert's Hotel is consistent with the theoretical definition of an *actual infinity*. However, is it plausible to believe that Hilbert's Hotel could actually exist in the real world? If I claimed to have visited such a hotel, would you believe me? David Hilbert wouldn't, and stated that 'the infinite is nowhere to be found in reality . . . The role that remains for the infinite to play is solely that of an idea.'[11] As Moreland and Craig conclude:

> Hilbert's Hotel certainly seems absurd. Since nothing hangs on the illustration's involving a hotel, the argument, if successful, would show in general that it is impossible for an actually infinite number of things to exist in spatiotemporal reality . . . if an actual infinite cannot exist in the real, spatiotemporal world and an infinite temporal regress of events is such an actual infinite, we can conclude that an infinite temporal regress of events cannot exist, that is to say, the temporal series of past physical events had a beginning.[12]

The concept of an actual infinite is by definition the concept of something *indefinite*; whereas one might argue that for anything to exist in concrete reality is necessarily for it to be *a definite something or other*. For example, one might argue that for a brick wall to exist it must be made of *a definite number of bricks*. It must be theoretically possible to give the question 'How many bricks are there in that wall?' a definite answer. However, this is just what we cannot do when talking about a wall of actually infinite length or dimensions. An actually infinite wall might be precisely ten bricks high (rather than nine or eleven bricks high), but it isn't *any* definite number of bricks long (or vice versa). The question 'How many bricks are there in that wall?' has no *definite* answer here. We can progressively knock off however many bricks we like from a wall that's of actually infinite length (e.g. 1, 10, 100 bricks, etc.) while continuously giving the identical *indefinite* answer concerning the precise composition of the wall, i.e. 'It is composed of *infinitely* many bricks'! Likewise, one would think that an actual wall must be composed of either an even number of bricks or an odd number of bricks; but no actually infinite wall can be composed of any particular even number of bricks *or* any particular odd number of bricks! Thus we can argue:

1. To be an actually infinite anything is by definition to be an at least partially *indefinite* something, whereas to exist in concrete reality is by definition to be a wholly *definite* something or other
2. Nothing can be both wholly definite and not wholly definite in the same sense and at the same time
3. Therefore, nothing actually infinite can exist in concrete reality

✔ 'Although one may conceive of an actual infinite, any attempted actual instantiation appears to be absurd'[13]

5.2.1.2 *The impossibility of forming an actual infinity*

The second philosophical argument for the finitude of the past runs as follows:

1. The temporal series of events is a collection formed by successive addition
2. A collection formed by successive addition cannot be an actual infinite
3. Therefore, the temporal series of events cannot be an actual infinite

Moreland and Craig explain:

> Even if an actual infinite can exist, it is argued that the temporal series of events cannot be such, since an actual infinite cannot be formed by successive addition, as the temporal series of events is . . . To say that the infinite past could have been formed by successive addition is like saying that someone has just succeeded in writing down all the negative numbers, ending with -1.[14]

Consider an infinitely deep well containing a ladder with an *actually infinite* number of rungs. If you started at the top of the ladder and climbed down some finite number of rungs or other, you could climb out again one rung at a time. However, suppose your task was to climb out of the well one rung at a time, but that there was no particular finite number of rungs that you had to climb past in order to get to the top. Could you climb out? Don't imagine that as there's *no* particular finite number of rungs that you must climb in order to exit the well this somehow means that you are already at the top and therefore have no climbing to do! You *are* in the well, and you *do* have climbing to do. It's simply that there's no *finite* number of rungs between your present position and the top of the well. In this analogy, the well stands for the past, the rungs on the ladder stand for each and every past event, and the top of the well stands for the present time. If climbing out of an actually infinite well one rung at a time is impossible, then so too is arriving at the present time if the past is actually infinite. And yet we *have* arrived at the present time one event at a time. In which case, it is plausible to conclude that the past is not actually infinite. David S. Oderberg delves behind this analogy:

> Wittgenstein thought it ridiculous that one might come across a person saying, '-5, -4, -3, -2, -1, 0!' and who, when asked what he was doing, claimed that he had just finished reciting the series of negative numbers backwards from infinity . . . this sort of scenario would violate the Principle of Sufficient Reason: if the reciter claimed to have finished his job on April 9, 2006, surely we would be entitled to ask why he had finished *then* rather than, say . . . November 30, 1363 or January 12, 5041. The very date of completion requires an explanation, yet if the scenario were real, an explanation would be in principle impossible.[15]

> **Question:**
> Do you find either of the philosophical arguments against actual infinites more convincing than the other? Why?

5.2.2 Two scientific arguments for the premise that the universe has a finite past

There are at least two scientific arguments for the premise that the universe has a finite past.

5.2.2.1 The second law of thermodynamics

Thermodynamics (the science of heat and work) underlies our understanding of the fact that if you leave your coffee too long before drinking, it gets cold. If you walk into a room and find a warm mug of coffee there, then you know that coffee wasn't made very long ago. It certainly hasn't been sitting there for an actually infinite number of days, because if it had, it would have gone cold by now! Something analogous can be argued of the universe.

In point of fact, as coffee gets cooler the world around it consequently gets warmer *until the temperatures inside and outside the coffee balance out*, reaching a state of equilibrium: 'According to the second law of thermodynamics, processes taking place in a closed system always tend toward a state of equilibrium. In other words, unless energy is constantly being fed into a system, the processes in the system will tend to run down and quit.'[16]

Thermodynamics is a well-established scientific theory, as cosmologist Arthur Eddington explained:

> The law that entropy increases – the Second Law of Thermodynamics – holds, I think, the supreme position among the laws of Nature. If someone points out to you that your pet theory of the universe is in disagreement with Maxwell's equations – then so much for Maxwell's equations. If it is found to be contradicted by observation – well, experimenters do bungle things sometimes. But *if your theory is found to be against the Second Law of Thermodynamics I can give you no hope; there is nothing for it but to collapse in deepest humiliation.*[17]

The theory that the universe has an *actually infinite* past appears to have 'no hope' in the face of the second law of thermodynamics. A naturalistic universe would, considered as a whole, be a closed system to which the second law must apply: 'The universe is, on the atheistic view, a gigantic closed system, since it is everything there is and there is nothing outside it. What this seems to imply then is that, given enough time, the universe and all its processes will run down, and the entire universe will come to equilibrium.'[18] Yet here we are in a universe that clearly *hasn't* reached equilibrium! Thus Norman L. Geisler and Frank Turek argue: 'the universe would be out of energy by now if it had been running down from all eternity. But here we are – the lights are still on, so the universe must have begun sometime in the finite past. That is, the universe is not eternal – it had a beginning.'[19]

> **Watch:**
> Muse, *The 2nd Law* (2012), 'Unsustainable' http://youtu.be/EF_xdvn52As.

5.2.2.2 The 'Big Bang' theory

The second scientific theory for the premise that the universe has a finite past is the 'Big Bang' theory. Geisler and Turek explain:

> It's important to understand that the universe is not expanding into empty space, but space itself is expanding – there was no space before the Big Bang. It's also important to understand that . . . there was no matter before the Big Bang. In fact, chronologically, there was no 'before' the Big Bang because there are no 'befores' without time . . . Time, space, and matter [started] at the Big Bang.[20]

The Big Bang model is considered by the majority of cosmologists to be the best explanation of a wide range of data (including the red shift of light from stars and the cosmic microwave background radiation). Philosopher of science John Lennox reports: 'There is . . . a remarkable consensus of opinion nowadays, that the universe had a beginning.'[21] Atheist physicist Victor J. Stenger confirms: 'every year that goes by, and more astronomical data comes in, it's more and more consistent with at least the general Big Bang picture.'[22] At the 2012 State of the Universe conference honouring Stephen Hawking's seventieth birthday,[23] atheist cosmologist Alexander Vilenkin argued that 'all the evidence we have says that the universe had a beginning.'[24] A *New Scientist* editorial on the conference commented:

> The big bang is now part of the furniture of modern cosmology . . . Many physicists have been fighting a rearguard action against it for decades, largely because of its theological overtones. If you have an instant of creation, don't you need a creator? Cosmologists . . . have tried on several different models of the universe that dodge the need for a beginning while still requiring a big bang. But recent research has shot them full of holes. It now seems certain that the universe did have a beginning. Without an escape clause, physicists and philosophers must finally answer a problem that has been nagging at them for the best part of 50 years: how do you get a universe, complete with the laws of physics, out of nothing.[25]

As Vilenkin states elsewhere: 'It is said that an argument is what convinces reasonable men and a proof is what it takes to convince even an unreasonable man. With the proof now in place, cosmologists can no longer hide behind the possibility of a past-eternal universe. There is no escape, they have to face the problem of a cosmic beginning.'[26]

Question:
Which argument for the universe having a finite past do you find the most convincing? Why?

Agnostic philosopher Anthony Kenny observes that 'according to the Big Bang theory, the whole matter of the universe began to exist at a particular time in the remote past. A proponent of such a theory, at least if he is an atheist, must believe that the matter of the universe came from nothing and by nothing.'[27]

Atheist Peter Atkins admits:

> If at any stage an agent must be invoked to account for what there is, then science will have to concede the existence of what we have agreed to call a

God . . . The task before science in this connection will be to show how some-thing can come from nothing without intervention . . . The unfolding of abso-lutely nothing . . . into something is a problem of the profoundest difficulty.[28]

Indeed, the difficulties involved in not invoking an agent to 'account for what there is' ultimately drive Atkins to the self-contradictory claim that *there is literally nothing in existence* to explain in the first place!

Watch:

'Atkins' Atheism: The Argument from Nothing' www.youtube.com/watch?v=Li4G-bixCf4A&feature=related.

'Do Atheists Believe We're Nothing?' www.youtube.com/watch?v=HXke0dURBZQ.

In *A Universe from Nothing: Why There Is Something Rather Than Nothing* (Free Press, 2012), atheist Lawrence M. Krauss redefines 'nothing' in terms of increasingly incorporeal somethings (from 'empty space' to reified 'laws of physics') as if this undermined the metaphysical principle that 'out of nothing nothing comes' (a claim that goes back to Parmenides of Elea in the fifth century BC). That's like arguing that since it's possible to live on less and less food each day it must be possible to live on no food! As Sam Harris commented during an interview with Krauss:

You have described three gradations of nothing – empty space, the absence of space, and the absence of physical laws. It seems to me that this last condition – the absence of any laws that might have caused or constrained the emer-gence of matter and space-time – really is a case of 'nothing' in the strictest sense. It strikes me as genuinely incomprehensible that anything – laws, energy, etc. – could spring out of it.[29]

Krauss resorts to rejecting metaphysics in the name of science: 'The meta-physical "rule," which is held as an ironclad conviction by those with whom I have debated the issue of creation, namely that *"out of nothing nothing comes,"* has no foundation in science.'[30] This scientistic objection is self-contradictory. Krauss relies upon the metaphysical rule that 'meta-physical rules with no foundation in science aren't true', but this rule *has no foundation in science.*

Listen:

William Lane Craig, 'Lawrence Krauss: A Universe from Nothing' (parts 1–3) www.reasonablefaith.org/a-universe-from-nothing.

5.3 Ironing out a Possible Ambiguity

Craig says that his *kalam* argument 'is valid and very simple . . . the question is, are there good reasons to believe that each of the steps is true?'[31] However, the logical validity of this argument is not *quite* as obvious as Craig suggests, for there is a possible ambiguity (or equivocation) in its use of the term 'began.'

Craig appears to shift in his writings between describing the universe as something that 'began to exist' a) in the sense that the universe *has a finite past* and b) in the sense that it *came into being* a finite time ago. On the one hand, to say that E 'has a finite past' is to say that we could go back in time to the first second that E had existence. On the other hand, to say that E 'came into being' is to describe a situation where there was already a *pre-existing* set of existing things *into which* E was *added* at some time; and this 'adding of E' *to the already existing set of existing things* is the 'coming *into being*' of E.

The 'coming into being of E' is *not* the situation described by modern science, or supported by philosophical arguments for the finitude of the past. The arguments offered in support of the second premise of the *kalam* argument all support the premise that the universe *has a finite past*. They do *not* support the premise that the universe *came into existence*.[32]

To avoid ambiguity, both premises of the *kalam* argument must talk about things that 'begin' to exist requiring causes, and about the universe 'beginning' to exist, *in the same sense of 'begin/beginning'* (whether sense 'a' or sense 'b').

This is where, as promised, we return to considering the first premise of the *kalam* argument. Together with the premise 'The universe is not eternal in the past', the premise that 'Whatever is not eternal in the past has a cause of its existence' entails the conclusion that 'The universe has a cause of its existence' (or at least that the universe *had* a cause of its existence, which may then be argued to exist atemporally, or to continue to exist eternally).[33] But although the arguments offered by Craig for his first premise do a good job of supporting the claim that 'Whatever beings to exist *in the sense of coming into existence* has a cause of its existence', do they support the distinct claim that 'Whatever begins to exist *in the sense that it is not eternal in the past* has a cause of its existence'? It is this latter claim that Craig really needs to defend if his argument is to be logically valid, because all the arguments for the second premise support the claim that the universe *has a finite past*, not that the universe *came into existence.*

Consider the following arguments:

1. Whatever begins to exist *in the sense of coming into existence* has a cause of its existence
2. The universe began to exist *in the sense that it came into existence*
3. Therefore, the universe has a cause of its existence

And:

4. Whatever begins to exist *in the sense that it is not eternal in the past* has a cause of its existence
5. The universe began to exist *in the sense that it is not eternal in the past*
6. Therefore, the universe has a cause of its existence

Ironing out the equivocation between our two different senses of 'beginning' (i.e. 'coming into being' and 'having a finite past'), senses that are used interchangeably by Craig, *both of these arguments are logically valid.* We can therefore move on to the question of whether these arguments have true premises.

On the one hand, while argument 1–3 has a well-supported first premise, it has a second premise that isn't supported by any of the arguments Craig offers. On the other hand, while argument 4–6 has a second premise (5) that is supported by the arguments Craig gives for his second premise, it has a first premise (4) that isn't obviously supported by Craig's arguments for his first premise.

Our experience relates to things that have a finite past *and* which come into existence. Hence we cannot *empirically* settle the question of whether things have causes *because they come into existence*, or *because they have finite pasts*, or indeed *because they exhibit both properties*. But of course, empirically based reasoning isn't the only way to support a truth-claim. Craig has addressed the concern that his *kalam* argument is invalid due to the equivocation between 'comes into being' and 'has a finite past.' He basically argues that premise 4 is *intuitively* more plausible than its denial, and so argument 4–6 is sound. 4–6 thus represents the way Craig thinks his original *kalam* argument syllogism should be consistently interpreted.[34]

> **Question:**
> What could you say to try to convince someone with doubts that whatever has
> existed for a finite amount of time must have a cause of its existence? If you find it
> hard to think of anything to say, does this show that this premise is less plausible than
> its denial? Or does it show that this premise is so intuitively plausible that it counts
> as a basic belief?

Despite the possible ambiguity in Craig's original formulation of the
kalam argument, then, there is a logically valid version of his argument
that should convince anyone who thinks that both of its premises are
more plausible than their denials.

In 2011 William Lane Craig introduced a reworded causal premise in
formulating the *kalam* argument:

1. The universe began to exist
2. If the universe began to exist, then the universe has a transcendent
    cause
3. Therefore, the universe has a transcendent cause[35]

While one can interpret this argument in line with 4–6 above, one might
give reasons for premise 2 in addition to Craig's claim that anything with
a finite past must have a cause of its existence . . .

5.4 Another *Kalam* Argument

> We can attribute no *physical* cause to the big bang.
> Paul Davies[36]

Richard Swinburne points out that 'in showing that the universe had a
beginning in time, we would have shown that its first stage S_f had no
scientific explanation in terms of a cause which was a prior state of the
universe. There are then two alternatives – either S_f just happened (it had
no cause) or S_f had a personal explanation.'[37]

Moreland likewise focuses upon the fact that the temporal finitude
of the universe entails the existence of *a first physical event*: 'events have
a definite beginning and end, and do not happen without something
causing them . . . The first event, then, needs a cause.'[38] Moreland doesn't
argue that the universe must have a cause *because it came into existence*, or
because it has a finite past, but rather because its having a finite past means
there was a first physical event, and all physical events have causes: 'There is no

reason to deny what we experience as true every day. Events have causes. So did the first one.'[39] That is:

1. Since the universe has a finite past, there was a first physical event
2. All physical events have at least one cause outside and independent of themselves
3. Therefore, the first physical event (and thus the universe) had at least one cause outside and independent of itself

Dallas Willard frames a similar version of the *kalam* argument as a disjunctive syllogism: 'there was a beginning of the physical universe . . . If this is so, we are faced with a stark alternative. *Either* the physical universe was not produced by anything *or* it was produced by something that is not physical – something spiritual in that minimal sense. The former cannot be, so the latter is the case.'[40] Against the former 'no cause' option Willard observes:

> every constituent of the physical world about us comes into existence in a *context* of other physical things, not in the context of nothing. Is the physical world as a whole an exception to this general rule? . . . there is at the very least no reason to think that this requirement of a prior causal condition or 'source' does not apply to it as well. And there is good reason to think it does apply, for it too is a *physical* reality.[41]

After all, 'if you allow that the entire physical universe originated "from nothing," then there is no reason why physical things and events would not continue to arise "from nothing." If the entire universe could originate from nothing, then surely a cup of tea could originate from nothing.'[42]

Hence, as Moreland writes: 'it seems reasonable to hold to the well-established law of cause and effect. Surely the burden of proof is on those who deny that law.'[43] Indeed, a physical event is surely a contingent event, and a *contingent* event is by definition contingent *upon something beyond itself*. Thus Willard argues that 'the dependent character of all physical states, together with the completeness of the series of dependencies underlying the existence of any given physical state, logically implies at least one self-existent, and therefore nonphysical, state of being.'[44]

5.4.1 A quantum rebuttal?

Quantum fluctuations are supposed to involve particles emerging from a pre-existing space-time structure, not a genuine vacuum.
David S. Oderberg[45]

It might be suggested that quantum mechanics poses a counter-example to the premise that all physical events have at least one cause outside and independent of themselves. According to this objection there's an ultimate 'indeterminacy' within subatomic nature that would apply to the Big Bang (because when the universe began it was of subatomic size). Moreland observes:

> not all philosophers and physicists are agreed as to how to interpret quantum mechanics. A number of thinkers . . . argue that the laws and theoretical entities of quantum mechanics should be treated in non-realist terms. This involves taking the statements of quantum mechanics as statements about our knowledge (or language) of reality, and not about mind-independent reality itself [i.e. in the subatomic realm we can know conditioning but not necessitating causes]. Thus, nature is not really indeterminate; we just do not know – perhaps cannot know – the underlying [necessitating] causes of quantum phenomena . . . in the absence of a clear consensus on quantum interpretation, it seems reasonable to hold to the well-established law of cause and effect. Surely the burden of proof is on those who deny that law, and if quantum mechanics can be understood in a way which preserves the law of cause and effect, then that interpretation of quantum theory is preferable for that reason.[46]

Moreover, as R. Douglas Geivett points out, even granting for the sake of argument that quantum events are indeterminate:

> the typical example of a quantum event is said to be indeterminate relative to a set of possible events, given certain specifiable conditions . . . such an event is not indeterminate with respect to the disjunction of all the members of the set of events made possible by conditions C. Consider a simple case where there is exactly one alternative to a particular quantum event, E1, that actually occurs under conditions C. The rule would seem to be roughly as follows: if conditions C is obtained, then either event E1 or event E2 will occur. That one or the other quantum event will occur is determined by conditions C, even if conditions C don't determine which event will occur.[47]

Our scientific experience of quantum events is set against a background of physical conditions that causally condition, even if they don't causally necessitate, the events in question. However, *the obtaining of condition/s C – relative to which a quantum event might be considered causally conditioned but not causally necessitated – would itself count as a physical event.*[48] Craig observes:

While the mathematical core of quantum theory has been confirmed to a fantastic degree of precision, there are at least ten different physical interpretations of the mathematics, and no one knows which of these, if any, is correct, since they are all empirically equivalent. Only some of these, principally the so-called Copenhagen Interpretation, are causally indeterministic. Others are fully deterministic . . . Moreover, even in the Copenhagen Interpretation things don't come into being without a cause. It's true that in this interpretation so-called virtual particles can arise spontaneously out of the quantum vacuum. But . . . the quantum vacuum is not nothing; rather it's a sea of fluctuating energy that serves as the indeterministic cause of such virtual particles . . . Thus, even in the disputed Copenhagen Interpretation, the quantum vacuum is a physical cause of the entities it is alleged to spawn.[49]

Atheist Quentin Smith admits that quantum considerations 'at most tend to show that acausal laws govern the *change of condition* of particles . . . They state nothing about the causality or acausality of absolute beginnings, of beginnings of the existence of particles.'[50] Hence we may conclude that 'we are far from having any empirical basis for believing that events occur in a totally conditionless void.'[51]

✔ 'Quantum fluctuations need a context of space and time'[52]

Indeed, on the atheistic theory that the first physical event was something that occurred *without any causal context or precondition whatsoever*, there's literally no reason why the universe exists *rather than just a tea set*!

> **Listen:**
> William Lane Craig, 'Do Virtual Particles Prove Something Can Come from Nothing?' www.youtube.com/watch?v=7oQVAj8HxP0.
> — 'Doesn't Quantum Physics Prove Something Came from Nothing?' http://youtu.be/g6kMWSo-Jz0.

5.4.2 Events and causes

The failure of the quantum rebuttal leaves our *kalam* argument unscathed. This argument claims that any physical reality with a finite temporal duration (a 'physical event') has at least one cause independent and outside of itself. But if there was a first physical event, this means that there must be at least one cause outside and independent of the first physical event, a cause that must therefore lie outside the physical world. As physicist Paul Davies muses:

103

What caused the big bang? . . . One might consider some supernatural force, some agency beyond space and time as being responsible for the big bang, or one might prefer to regard the big bang as an event without a cause. It seems to me that we don't have too much choice. Either . . . something outside of the physical world [or] an event without a cause.[53]

One cannot posit a *physical* cause for the *first* physical event. In order to deny that the first physical event had a non-physical cause one must either reject the premise 'All physical events have at least one cause', or else claim that all physical events must be the effect of nothing but *physical* causation. The latter claim leads to an infinite regress of physical causes (thereby amounting to a rejection of the first premise of our argument). It also amounts to begging the question in favour of naturalism. However, to make an exception to the proposition that all physical events have at least one cause only when it comes to the *first* physical event is obviously *ad hoc* (that is, a move expressly designed to avoid the conclusion of an argument and which has nothing else going for it). Therefore, we should recognize the existence of a first physical event that should be explained *in terms of a non-physical cause:*

1. There was a first physical event
2. All physical events have at least one cause outside and independent of themselves
3. Therefore, the first physical event had at least one cause outside and independent of itself
4. The cause of the first physical event cannot have been a physical cause
5. Therefore, since causes can only be either physical or non-physical, the first physical event had a non-physical cause outside and independent of itself

Moreover, as Moreland and Craig argue: 'there are two types of causal explanation . . . explanations in terms of laws and initial conditions and personal explanations in terms of agents and their volitions. A first state of the universe *cannot* have [an explanation in terms of laws and initial conditions] since there is nothing before it, and therefore it can be accounted for only in terms of personal explanation.'[54]

Hence our final formulation of the *kalam* argument:

1. There was a first physical event
2. All physical events have at least one cause outside and independent of themselves
3. Therefore, the first physical event had at least one cause outside and independent of itself

4. The cause of the first physical event cannot have been a physical cause
5. Therefore (since causes can only be either physical or non-physical), the first physical event had a non-physical cause outside and independent of itself
6. The non-physical cause of the first physical event must be a personal cause
7. Therefore the first physical event must have had a non-physical, personal cause outside and independent of itself (and this, of course, is a part of what theists mean by 'God')

Conclusion

We've examined two logically valid versions of the *kalam* cosmological argument from the finitude of the past, arguments that should convince anyone who thinks that all of their premises are more plausible than their denials. The *kalam* cosmological argument is a particularly popular subject in contemporary philosophy of religion and apologetics. Both versions of the argument examined above can be formulated as simple syllogisms (although these need to be extended to unpack the nature of the cosmic cause deduced), and both receive scientific support (e.g. from the well-known 'Big Bang' theory), which allows the argument to be presented without reference to abstract philosophical arguments about actual infinites.

* * *

Recommended Resources

Video

Craig, William Lane. 'Did God Create from Nothing? Part 1' www.closertotruth.com/video-profile/Did-God-Create-From-Nothing-Part-1-of-3-William-Lane-Craig-/994.
— 'Did God Create from Nothing? Part 2' www.closertotruth.com/video-profile/Did-God-Create-From-Nothing-Part-2-of-3-William-Lane-Craig-/993.
— 'Did God Create from Nothing? Part 3' www.closertotruth.com/video-profile/Did-God-Create-From-Nothing-Part-3-of-3-William-Lane-Craig-/992.
— 'How Did the Universe Begin?' www.rfmedia.org/RF_audio_video/Other_clips/Saddleback-How-Did-Universe-Begin/index.php.
— vs Peter Atkins. 'Does God Exist?' http://idpluspeterswilliams.blogspot.co.uk/2012/04/craig-v-atkins-does-god-exist.html.
— vs Lawrence M. Krauss. 'Is There Evidence for God?' www.reasonablefaith.org/media/craig-vs-krauss-north-carolina-state-university.

God: New Evidence. www.youtube.com/user/godnewevidence.

*Pollard, Luke, William Lane Craig and Peter S. Williams. 'The Cosmological Argument' www.damaris.org/schools/alevelrs.

Spitzer, Robert J. 'God and Modern Physics' www.magisreasonfaith.org/library/videos/.

Strobel, Lee, William Lane Craig and Jay Richards. 'How Did the Universe Begin?' www.leestrobel.com/videoserver/video.php?clip=strobelT2041.

*Williams, Peter S. 'Cosmological Arguments for God' YouTube Playlist www.youtube.com/playlist?list=PLQhh3qcwVEWjEXjiEjnCCbr_Qnu-1UbAa.

Audio

Brierley, Justin. '*Unbelievable*: A Universe from Nothing? Lawrence Krauss vs Rodney Holder' www.premierradio.org.uk/listen/ondemand.aspx?mediaid=%7B02949395-E52F-4784-BF29-3A3138738B0B%7D.

Craig, William Lane. 'Creation out of Nothing' www.rfmedia.org/RF_audio_video/RF_podcast/Creation-Out-of-Nothing.mp3.

— Defenders Podcast, series 2, parts 6–13 www.reasonablefaith.org/defenders-2-podcast/s4.

— 'Do Virtual Particles Prove Something Can Come from Nothing?' www.youtube.com/watch?v=7oQVAj8HxP0.

— 'Doesn't Quantum Physics Prove Something Came from Nothing?' http://youtu.be/g6kMWSo-Jz0.

— 'Has Hawking Eliminated God?' www.reasonablefaith.org/has-hawking-eliminated-god.

*— 'Lawrence Krauss: A Universe from Nothing', parts 1–3 www.reasonablefaith.org/a-universe-from-nothing.

Groothuis, Douglas. 'Douglas Groothuis Lectures on the Kalam Cosmological Argument' http://winteryknight.wordpress.com/2012/07/17/douglas-groothuis-lectures-on-the-kalam-cosmological-argument/.

Williams, Peter S. 'Hawking and the Grand Designer (Exeter School)' www.damaris.org/cm/podcasts/566.

— 'Stephen Hawking and the Grand Designer (Bryanston School)' www.damaris.org/cm/podcasts/663.

*— 'Stephen Hawking and the Grand Designer (Winchester)' www.damaris.org/cm/podcasts/682.

Online papers

Alberts, David. 'On the Origin of Everything: *A Universe from Nothing*, by Lawrence M. Krauss' www.nytimes.com/2012/03/25/books/review/a-universe-from-nothing-by-lawrence-m-krauss.html.

Borde, Arvind, Alan H. Guth and Alexander Vilenkin. 'Inflationary Spacetimes Are Not Past-Complete' http://arxiv.org/PS_cache/gr-qc/pdf/0110/0110012v2.pdf.

Craig, William Lane. Papers on the *kalam* cosmological argument www.reasonablefaith.org/site/PageServer?pagename=scholarly_articles_existence_of_God.

*Dembski, William A. and Stephen C. Meyer. 'Fruitful Interchange or Polite Chitchat? The Dialogue between Science and Theology' www.arn.org/docs/dembski/wd_fruitfulinterchange.htm.

Guthrie, Shandon L. 'Theism and Contemporary Cosmology' http://sguthrie.net/theism_and_contemporary_cosmology_2.pdf.

Koons, Robert C. 'Theism and Big Bang Cosmology' www.leaderu.com/offices/koons/docs/lec5.html.

Williams, Peter S. 'A Universe from Someone: Against Lawrence Krauss' *A Universe from Nothing: Why There Is Something Rather Than Nothing*' www.bethinking.org/science-christianity/advanced/a-universe-from-someone-against-lawrence-krauss.htm.

Books

Craig, William Lane. 'The Cosmological Argument.' Pages 112–31 in *The Rationality of Theism* (ed. Paul Copan and Paul K. Moser; London: Routledge, 2003).

*— *On Guard: Defending Your Faith with Reason and Precision* (Colorado Springs, CO: David C. Cook, 2010).

— *Reasonable Faith: Christian Truth and Apologetics* (Wheaton, IL: Crossway, 3rd edn, 2008).

— and J.P. Moreland, eds. *The Blackwell Companion to Natural Theology* (Oxford: Wiley-Blackwell, 2009).

Geisler, Norman L. and Frank Turek. *I Don't Have Enough Faith to Be an Atheist* (Wheaton, IL: Crossway, 2004).

Geivett, R. Douglas. 'The Kalam Cosmological Argument.' Pages 61–76 in *To Everyone an Answer* (ed. Francis J. Beckwith, William Lane Craig and J.P. Moreland; Downers Grove, IL: IVP, 2004).

*Moreland, J.P. *Love Your God With All Your Mind* (Colorado Springs, CO: NavPress, 2012).

— *Scaling the Secular City* (Grand Rapids, MI: Baker, 1987).

Oderberg, David S. 'The Cosmological Argument.' Pages 342–50 in *The Routledge Companion to Philosophy of Religion* (ed. Chad Meister and Paul Copan; London: Routledge, 2010).

*Willard, Dallas. *Knowing Christ Today: Why We Can Trust Spiritual Knowledge* (New York: HarperOne, 2009).

— 'The Three-Stage Argument for the Existence of God.' Pages 212–24 in *Contemporary Perspectives on Religious Epistemology* (ed. Douglas Geivett and Brendan Sweetman; Oxford University Press, 1992).

6. Teleological Arguments I: Paley, Hume and Design

Every thing is adjusted to every thing. One design prevails throughout the whole. And this uniformity leads the mind to acknowledge one author.
David Hume[1]

Introduction
6.1 Paley's Design Detection Criteria
      6.1.1 Irreducible complexity
      6.1.2 Added beauty
6.2 Paley's Limited Conclusion
6.3 Hume's Critique
6.4 Rebuttal of Eight Objections
      6.4.1 Rebuttal 1: The ignorance objection
      6.4.2 Rebuttal 2: The 'what sort of designer?' objection
      6.4.3 Rebuttal 3: The imperfection objection
      6.4.4 Rebuttal 4: The useless parts objection
      6.4.5 Rebuttal 5: The 'complicated things happen all the time' objection
      6.4.6 Rebuttal 6: The 'principle of order' objection
      6.4.7 Rebuttal 7: The subjectivity objection
      6.4.8 Rebuttal 8: The 'God-of-the-gaps' objection
6.5 Assessing Paley's Contribution
Conclusion

Introduction

For the last two chapters we've been looking at the cosmological argument for the existence of an uncreated being with the power to create the cosmos *ex nihilo*. We will now turn our attention to arguments for the existence of an intelligent designer of the cosmos. Cosmological and design arguments point to different aspects of the Creator's nature. The cosmological argument points primarily to the Creator's universe-causing power and uncreated existence, whereas the design argument points to the Creator's intelligence, purposiveness, and even (as we will see) his artistic awareness.

The design argument is the oldest and most popular of theistic evidences. Plato argued that all things are 'under the dominion of the mind which ordered the universe.'[2] It's an argument reflected in several biblical passages (e.g. Psalm 19; Romans 1:20; Hebrews 3:4). A recent study revealed that while only 6% of those polled thought that theists believe in God because of a perception of design in the universe, such a perception of design is in fact the most common reason given by theists for their belief (28.6%).[3] The design argument is important because it gives a rationally persuasive framework to something that is already intuitively persuasive to many people. As Henry Melvill Gwatkin observes: 'The appearance of design in the world is undisputed . . . the *prima facie* inference is from the appearance of design to its reality.'[4]

Perhaps because it's the most empirical theistic argument, the design argument receives respectful notice from non-theists with an otherwise dismissive attitude to natural theology. For example, Bertrand Russell wrote: 'This argument has no formal logical defect; its premises are empirical, and its conclusion professes to be reached in accordance with the usual canons of empirical inference. The question whether it is to be accepted or not turns, therefore, not on general metaphysical questions, but on comparatively detailed considerations.'[5]

The Greek word for the 'end' a designer has in mind when they create something for a purpose is *telos*. Hence design arguments are technically called *teleological* arguments. By inferring the existence of an intelligence behind nature *from* nature, the teleological argument also infers the existence of an objective purpose *for* nature. As Kant wrote:

> This proof always deserves to be mentioned with respect. It is the oldest, the clearest and the most accordant with the common reason of mankind. It enlivens the study of nature, just as it itself derives its existence and gains every new vigour from that source. It suggests ends and purposes . . . and extends our knowledge of nature by means of the guiding concept of a special unity, the principle of which is outside nature. This knowledge . . . so strengthens the belief in a supreme author of nature that the belief acquires the force of an irresistible conviction.[6]

In recent decades the teleological argument has gained new vigour from our increased scientific knowledge of nature.[7]

Although we'll keep one eye on relevant aspects of contemporary 'Intelligent Design Theory' (which will be the focus of chapter 7), this chapter is mainly a commentary upon the first chapter of William Paley's classic book *Natural Theology* (1802). Our focus will be on the *philosophical* aspects of Paley's argument rather than any purported *examples* of design from the natural world (possible examples abound).

> **Watch:**
> 'Cell Animation' http://youtu.be/ZDH8sWiUsAM.
> 'The Inner Life of the Cell' http://youtu.be/zrXykvorybo.

6.1 Paley's Design Detection Criteria

Paley begins with an illustration: 'In crossing a heath, suppose I pitched my foot against a *stone*, and were asked how the stone came to be there, I might possibly answer, that, for any thing I knew to the contrary, it had lain there for ever: nor would it perhaps be very easy to [demonstrate] the absurdity of this answer.'[8] To demonstrate the absurdity of this answer (once made by Bertrand Russell about the universe as a whole) one must provide a *kalam cosmological* argument. Paley continues: 'But suppose I had found a *watch* upon the ground, and it should be enquired how the watch happened to be in that place, I should hardly think of the answer I had before given . . . Yet why should not this answer serve for the watch, as well as for the stone?'[9]

The answer, of course, is that unlike the stone *the watch is obviously the product of intelligent design*. Distinguishing between rock and watch in this way is a matter of common sense. Beliefs about objects being designed are typically 'properly basic', rather than the product of rational argument. You see a watch and naturally form the belief that it is the product of design. You don't have to argue your way to this conclusion (although you can) to rationally believe that a watch is designed. Properly basic beliefs should be accepted until we are given sufficient reason for doubt. Hence any lack of plausibility in natural explanations for apparently designed facets of nature is simply a failure to rebut a properly basic belief in design grounded in observation. As a properly basic intuition, belief in design is innocent until proven guilty (hence the design argument is *not* an 'argument from ignorance').

✔ The belief that nature is the product of design carries the presumption of truth

Let's look at two design detection criteria used by Paley – that is, tests we can apply to check if it is reasonable to conclude that an object or event is the product of design.

110

6.1.1 Irreducible complexity

Although it is rational to believe in design on the basis of intuition, Paley offers two design detection criteria that allow us to move beyond the *prima facie* ('on-the-face-of-it') case for design. Having such criteria is clearly very useful for engaging in rational argumentation about design. Talking about the watch, Paley observes:

> if the several parts had been differently shaped from what they are, or of different size from what they are, or placed after any other manner, or in any other order, than that in which they are placed, either no motion at all would have been carried on in the machine, or none which would have answered the use, that is now served by it.[10]

With the benefit of hindsight, this first criterion given by Paley is very close to the contemporary concept of 'irreducible complexity'. Biologist Michael J. Behe defines an 'irreducibly complex' system as 'a single system composed of several well-matched, interacting parts that contribute to the basic function, wherein the removal of any one of the parts causes the system to effectively cease functioning.'[11] The interesting thing about any 'irreducibly complex' (IC) system is that it *cannot* evolve *directly* by natural selection (because its function isn't obtained unless all its parts are present and correct); and the more parts such a system has, the less likely it is to evolve *indirectly* (by shifting its function as it evolves).

✔ Anything 'irreducibly complex' *can't evolve directly*, and is *unlikely to evolve indirectly*

The best explanation for the existence of anything irreducibly complex is design. Paley's first criterion of design detection thus sets the ground for a rebuttal to the suggestion that evolution by natural selection can adequately explain, and thereby explain away, the appearance of design in at least some natural things.[12]

Watch:
'Dawkins on Irreducible Complexity' http://youtu.be/WG0RCVB629Y.
'The Evidence of Biological Machines' http://youtu.be/_u_LYJGDopA.

6.1.2 *Added beauty*

'the widespread presence of gratuitous beauty – beauty that seems to serve no
additional function besides just being beautiful – is powerful evidence for a
Grand Artist.'
J.P. Moreland[13]

Paley notes that a watch may exhibit what Dr Stuart Burgess[14] (professor of design and nature, and head of the Department of Mechanical Engineering at the University of Bristol) calls 'added beauty': 'the wheels are made of brass, in order to keep them from rust; the springs of steel, no other metal being so elastic; over the face of the watch there is placed a glass.'[15] The watch exhibits a pattern that more than 'scrapes by', which exceeds the evolutionary requirement of 'doing the job just well enough to be an advantage', and which includes beautiful but mechanically superfluous aspects that have no practical necessity to them (removing these aspects of the watch doesn't affect its proper functioning). This means that the watch consists of an 'irreducibly complex' *core* together with 'added beauty', and that there are thus two independent arguments to design from the watch. Burgess explains:

> Inherent beauty is a beauty that exists as a by-product of mechanical design. In contrast, added beauty is a type of beauty which has the sole purpose of providing a beautiful display. The two types of beauty can be seen in man-made products like buildings and bridges . . . A suspension bridge has a curved cable structure because this is an efficient way of supporting a roadway. However, the end result can be a very elegant and beautiful design. An example of added beauty can be seen in the decoration of a classical column . . . There is no mechanical reason for a classical column to be any more than a plain cylinder . . . yet the designers embellish the column with elaborate patterns just for the sake of adding beauty . . . added beauty . . . represents very strong evidence for design because there is no mechanical reason for the beautiful appearance.[16]

Finding 'added beauty' in nature would likewise be evidence of (aesthetically aware) design. Burgess argues that nature contains 'added beauty' and that this is evidence for design.[17]

✔ 'Added beauty' is difficult to explain with reference to survival value

> **Question:**
> Arguments by analogy reason that analogous (similar) effects have analogous causes.
> The teleological argument can be constructed as an argument by analogy, where the
> strength of the argument depends largely upon the strength of the analogy it draws
> upon. Paley's design argument is often presented as an argument by analogy (e.g. 'A
> watch is designed; things in nature are analogous to a watch, and therefore probably
> have an analogous cause'). Is this an accurate representation of Paley's argument?
> If it is inaccurate, is his actual argument stronger or weaker than an argument by
> analogy?

6.2 Paley's Limited Conclusion

Paley argues that by reasoning from observation of a watch's 'irreducible complexity' and 'added beauty' we can show that 'there must have
existed, at some time and at some place or other, an artificer or artificers
who formed it for the purpose which we find it actually to answer, who
comprehended its construction, and designed its use.'[18] Paley goes on
to argue (later in his book) that 'every manifestation of design, which
existed in the watch, exists in the works of nature; with this difference,
on the side of nature, of being greater and more.'[19] The conclusion drawn
by Paley is that nature is (at least in some of its aspects) the product of
intelligent design. In other words, Paley's argument might be framed as
a logically valid MP syllogism, as follows:

1.   If something exhibits 'irreducible complexity' and/or 'added beauty',
     then it is probably the product of design
2.   Various aspects of nature exhibit 'irreducible complexity' and/or
     'added beauty'
3.   Therefore, various aspects of nature are probably the product of
     design

Note that this conclusion does *not* justify the conclusion that other aspects
of nature are *not* the product of design.

6.3 Hume's Critique

David Hume (1711–76) is Scotland's most famous philosopher. Hume
remains an influential philosophical voice today, primarily because
many contemporary atheists embrace his scepticism and empiricism.[20]
However, as Nicholas Capaldi states: 'In none of his writings does
Hume say or imply that he does not accept the existence of God.[21] On

the contrary, Hume says in several places that he accepts the existence of God.'[21] What Hume did reject was *arguments* for God. This is unsurprising given his general scepticism about metaphysics.[22]

Hume's objections to the design argument are a mixed bag,[23] but his good points are 'slimming' rather than 'starving' (that is, they render the conclusions of the arguments in question more limited in scope without rendering the arguments defunct). For example, Hume objected that '[if] a great number of men join in building a house or a ship, in rearing a city, in framing a commonwealth, why may not several deities combine in framing a world?'[24] Belief in design is indeed compatible with belief in several designers (divine or otherwise). However, as Stephen T. Davis argues, one designer is a simpler adequate explanation: 'If there is more than one designer, exactly how many are there? And why do they cooperate? Those questions do not need to be asked if there is but one designer.'[25] Richard Swinburne comments: 'If there were more than one deity responsible for the order of the universe, we should expect to see characteristic marks of the handiwork of different deities in different parts of the universe, just as we see different workmanship in the different houses of a city.'[26] Hence it's more plausible to think that the source of design inherent within the cosmos is the God of biblical monotheism than it is to think that it is the work of a bunch of gods. As Hume himself admitted: 'All things of the universe are evidently of a piece. Every thing is adjusted to every thing. One design prevails throughout the whole. And this uniformity leads the mind to acknowledge one author.'[27]

✔ The best explanation of design within nature is a single designer

We should distinguish between 'the design inference' (for the conclusion of intelligent design) and 'the design argument' (for the conclusion of theism); that is, between:

a) Inferences from evidence to intelligent design

and:

b) Inferences from intelligent design to a transcendent, supernatural designer (e.g. theism)

While the design argument depends upon the design inference, the design inference stands independently of the design argument. As Hume (like Aquinas before him) pointed out, there's a gap between the proposition that something in nature is designed and the conclusion that the designer is divine. After all, one can make a design inference from the portraits of American presidents carved into Mount Rushmore in America, but one certainly need not conclude that the designer in this instance was God! One has to *argue* that the most plausible source of design in any given case is God. But as Hume warned: 'When we infer any particular cause for an effect we must proportion the one to the other, and can never be allowed to ascribe to any cause any qualities, but what are exactly sufficient to produce the effect.'[28] Hence, filling in the gap between 'designed by some designer or other' and 'designed *by God*' takes us beyond the 'design inference' and into the 'design argument'.

✔ The *design argument* extends the *design inference* into an argument for God

John Earman concludes that 'Hume was a theist, albeit of a vague and weak-kneed sort. He seems to have been convinced by the argument from design of the proposition "That the cause or causes of order in the universe probably bear some remote analogy to human intelligence." But he was also convinced that the argument does not permit this undefined intelligence to be given further shape or specificity.'[29] Nevertheless, a 'weak-kneed' theism is strong enough to exclude atheism.

> **Question:**
> How much can the design argument tell us about the designer? How close to the biblical concept of 'God' can the argument bring us?

6.4 Rebuttal of Eight Objections

Paley rebuts eight objections to his design inference:

6.4.1 Rebuttal 1: The ignorance objection

> Nor would it . . . weaken the conclusion, that we had never seen a watch made; that we had never known an artist capable of making one; that we were altogether incapable of executing such a piece of workmanship ourselves, or of understanding in what manner it was performed: all this being no more than what is true of some exquisite remains of ancient art, of some lost arts, and, to the generality of mankind, of the more curious productions of modern manufacture.[30]

The design inference from applying detection criteria (such as irreducible complexity) to some object or event (e.g. a watch) wouldn't be weakened if we'd never seen a watch made, didn't know how the design was implemented, and/or couldn't duplicate the design ourselves. Despite our ignorance on the points, the hallmarks of design would still justify a design inference. Likewise, a design inference from something in nature isn't weakened if we can't reproduce the design, if we don't know how it was implemented, have never seen such designs before, or never seen them implemented before. Given reliable design detection criteria, and given something that passes the criteria, one has a sound argument for design:

1. Anything passing criterion X is probably the product of intelligent design
2. Y passes criterion X
3. Therefore, Y is probably the product of intelligent design

6.4.2 Rebuttal 2: The 'what sort of designer?' objection

> Nor can I perceive that it varies at all the inference, whether the question arise concerning a human agent, or concerning an agent of a different species, or an agent possessing, in some respects, a different nature.[31]

Design can be detected independently of knowledge about the nature of the designer (besides the obvious fact that the designer must have been capable of causing the observed marks of design). Beyond this point, the design inference cannot take us, and other discussion is strictly beside the point as far as the design inference is concerned. Intelligence is intelligence, and is capable of producing the hallmarks of intelligence – be that 'irreducible complexity', 'added beauty', etc. – whatever other characteristics it may have (including whether or not the designer is embodied like ourselves).

One cannot argue that, since 'God' is so different from human (or alien) designers we can't detect design caused by God. The matter must be approached in what physicist-theologian John Polkinghorne calls a 'bottom up' manner. First we detect design by making a design inference. Then we ask who the best designer candidate is in this particular case. Whatever the answer (and we might remain agnostic about *this*), it doesn't affect the fact that we have evidence for design by *something capable of producing the design in hand.*

Some people think 'crop circles' are made by aliens. Some think that humans make them. Both groups agree crop circles are designed; and it would be silly to argue: 'Since aliens don't exist crop circles must, despite appearances, be the product of unintelligent causes'! Likewise, it would be silly to argue: 'Since God doesn't exist everything in nature must, despite appearances, be the product of unintelligent causes.' And once design in nature is acknowledged, God is a good candidate for the best explanation of this design.

6.4.3 Rebuttal 3: The imperfection objection

> Neither . . . would it invalidate our conclusion, that the watch sometimes went wrong, or that it seldom went exactly right . . . It is not necessary that the machine be perfect, in order to shew with what design it was made.[32]

The objection here is that some features of purportedly designed things don't fit our expectations about what a perfectly good and wise designer would design, and that therefore no perfectly good and wise designer exists, and that therefore there is no designer (or design). This objection (a variation of the 'problem of evil', and susceptible to the same rebuttals) is fallacious.

The objection moves from asserting that X is imperfect to saying that no designer of X can be perfect, to saying that *therefore there is no design*. But since both imperfect designs and imperfect designers can and do exist, this argument is unsound. After all, cars rust (an 'imperfection'), but they are obviously designed.

More importantly (for any theistic design argument), this objection depends upon a risky extrapolation from 'I can't think of a good reason why a designer would make X that way' to the conclusion 'There is no good reason why a designer would make X that way.'

Design involves seeking the best trade-off among competing goals. The more battery life my laptop has, the heavier it is. Who would want a laptop with a year's battery life if they couldn't lift it? It would be silly to argue that, since a laptop didn't have the maximum possible battery life, it couldn't have been designed (or designed by a good and wise designer)!

Even granting that certain (supposedly indefensibly imperfect) things aren't designed (they are perhaps the by-product of design), this is compatible with the proposition that other things *are* designed. The argument that 'Natural object X isn't designed, therefore *nothing* natural is designed' is a *non sequitur* (an argument with a conclusion that doesn't follow from its premises) based on the false dilemma that either everything is designed or else nothing is.

6.4.4 Rebuttal 4: The useless parts objection

Nor . . . would it bring any uncertainty into the argument, if there were a few parts of the watch, concerning which we could not discover, or had not yet discovered, in what manner they conducted to the general effect; or even some parts concerning which we could not ascertain, whether they conducted to that effect in any manner whatsoever.[33]

Even if organisms *did* contain 'junk DNA'[34] (stretches of DNA that don't have a function) and/or 'vestigial organs'[35] (organs that lack a current function), this wouldn't 'bring any uncertainty into the argument' from structures which *do* serve functional requirements.

Paley observes: 'if, by the loss, or disorder, or decay of the parts in question, the movement of the watch were found in fact to be stopped, or disturbed, or retarded, no doubt would remain in our minds as to the utility or intention of these parts.'[36] Using gene knock-out experiments it is possible to determine which protein parts of a biomolecular machine are parts of its irreducibly complex (IC) core, being essential to its functioning. The existence of parts outside the IC core does not, Paley observes, furnish grounds to doubt the design inference from such a core. Indeed, superfluous parts may be candidates for design detection via 'added beauty': '[suppose] that there were parts, which might be spared without prejudice to the movement of the watch, and that we had proved this by experiment, – these superfluous parts, even if we were completely assured that they were such, would not vacate the reasoning which we had instituted concerning other parts.'[37]

Paley thus prefigured a) the modern concept of 'irreducible complexity', b) the idea of a system having an irreducible 'core', and c) the idea that this distinction could be made experimentally.

6.4.5 Rebuttal 5: The 'complicated things happen all the time' objection

> Nor . . . would any man in his senses think the existence of the watch . . . accounted for, by being told that it was one out of possible combinations of material forms; that whatever had been found in the place where he found the watch, must have contained some internal configuration or other; and that this configuration might be the structure now exhibited, viz. of the works of a watch, as well as a different structure.[38]

This objection ignores part of Paley's design detection criteria, which isn't focused upon mere *complexity* (low probability), but which requires that the relevant complexity be *irreducible*.

Irreducible complexity is one form of *specified complexity* (i.e. complexity that exhibits an independently given pattern). Suppose you see a poem written using scrabble tiles and infer design. Someone objects, saying that any sequence of tiles (of the same length) is equally complex or improbable (1 out of *n* possible sequences of tiles), and that since the tiles had to have some sequence or other, it might as well be a poem as one of the many non-poem sequences! But of course, it's far more likely that a non- designed sequence of titles would form gibberish (unspecified complexity) rather than a poem (specified complexity). Our objector missed the fact that your design inference wasn't based upon the mere *complexity* of the sequence of tiles, but upon the fact that it was both complex *and* specified. In other words, we can argue that 'specified complexity' is a reliable marker of design, and that it's no good to observe that a scrap heap is as *complex* as a watch when the watch, but not the scrapheap, is *specified* in its complexity (*watches tell the time and scrap heaps don't*).

In our experience, unintelligent forces often produce complex (i.e. unlikely) results – just tip a bag of scrabble letters out onto a table to see this. But it is our uniform experience that whenever something complex exhibits an independently given pattern (a 'specification') and we know how it came about, then it came about by design. Poems have poets, music has composers, buildings have architects, codes have code makers, watches have watchmakers, etc.

6.4.6 Rebuttal 6: The 'principle of order' objection

> Nor . . . would it yield his enquiry more satisfaction to be answered, that there existed in things a principle of order, which had disposed the parts of the watch into their present form and situation. He never knew a watch made by the principle of order; nor can he even form to himself an idea of what is meant by a principle of order, distinct from the intelligence of the watch-maker.[39]

The suggestion that some unknown law of nature is responsible for the specified, irreducible complexity of a watch is not a better explanation than design, because it is an *ad hoc* 'non-intelligent designer' of the gaps! Such a hypothesis is contradicted by our experience of the cause-and-effect structure of the world. Nature produces specified but un-complex things (you might draw 'C A T' out of a scrabble bag sight unseen), and complex unspecified things (just tip the bag out onto the table); but we never experience nature producing specified complexity. In our experience, whenever we know where something that exhibits specified complexity came from, it always came from intelligent design.

Moreover, an 'unknown law' hypothesis could be constructed against *every* design inference, including those accepted within uncontroversial scientific fields such as archaeology, cryptography, psychology and forensic science! Science must proceed on the basis of what we know, not on the basis of speculations that undermine proven methods of explanation.

6.4.7 Rebuttal 7: The subjectivity objection

> he would be surprised to be informed, that the mechanism of the watch was no proof of contrivance, only a motive to induce the mind to think so.[40]

The appearance of design in a watch isn't subjective – the watch is not (to use Richard Dawkins' term) 'designoid' (i.e. something giving the superficial and easily undermined appearance of design but which is not designed). The watch gives *every indication* of being designed – because of the type of complexity and beauty it exhibits – and if the watch is 'designoid', then material things cannot be configured in such a way as to provide objective evidence of design! But clearly, we *can* have objective evidence for design from at least some material arrangements – the watch is just such a case. Therefore, *if* we find something that exhibits the same (or greater) evidence for design as is exhibited by the watch, the inference to design would be likewise justified in such cases.

6.4.8 Rebuttal 8: The 'God-of-the-gaps' objection

> Neither . . . would our observer [of the watch] be driven out of his conclu-
> sion, or from his confidence in its truth, by being told that he knew nothing
> at all about the matter. He knows enough for his argument. He knows the
> utility of the end: he knows the subserviency and adaptation of the means
> to the end. These points being known, his ignorance of other points, his
> doubts concerning other points, affects not the certainty of his reasoning. The
> consciousness of knowing little, need not beget a distrust of that which he
> does know.[41]

This is Paley's response to the 'God-of-the-gaps' objection, the accusation that the design argument is merely an argument from ignorance that
leaps from 'We don't know how X came about' to 'God did it' (cf. chapter
3). Paley points out that this accusation wouldn't serve in the instance
of inferring design from the watch. If such an objection was as strong
as its proponents think, no inference to design on the basis of empirical evidence would ever be sound! But some such inferences are sound.
Therefore the 'God-of-the-gaps' objection can't be a strong objection to
the design inference.

There's a strong inference to design from observing that the watch
fits certain design detection criteria. Things exhibiting specified and/
or irreducible complexity are, in our experience, the product of intelligence whenever their causes are known. Here is something (a watch) that
exhibits such complexity. Therefore, the best explanation of the watch is
design. The design inference *per se* is a sound argument. Therefore no
argument can stand against it unless it is a sound argument of greater
strength. Since it clearly doesn't carry the day in every instance (e.g. the
instance of the watch-to-designer argument), the 'gaps' objection can't
be a sound deductive argument. And it is questionable whether it is an
inductive argument, let alone a sound one, let alone a stronger one. If
the watch grounds a good inductive design inference, and something
in nature grounds just as strong an inference, there is every reason to
accept the latter argument. Since the former inference wasn't beaten by
the 'gaps' objection, why think that the latter argument would be beaten
by the same objection?

All scientific arguments are conducted on the basis of the presently
available evidence; which is why such arguments are in theory falsifiable. Nevertheless, the 'principle of credulity'[42] means that the burden
of proof is clearly with the person who says, 'Of course the watch *looks*
designed, but actually it is not the product of design but of the operation of unintelligent but presently unknown natural forces (which may

themselves be designed).' Likewise in the case of inferring design from a radio signal from space listing prime numbers, or an autopsy of a man with a dagger through the heart, or an archaeological find of pottery, *or from nature.*

Watch:
William Lane Craig, 'Is Intelligent Design a "God-of-the-Gaps"?' http://youtu.be/dbc78q_REpA.

6.5 Assessing Paley's Contribution

William Lane Craig observes: 'Although most philosophers – who have undoubtedly never read Paley – believe that his sort of argument was dealt a crushing blow by David Hume's critique of the teleological argument, Paley's argument, which was written nearly thirty years after the publication of Hume's critique, is in fact not vulnerable to most of Hume's objections.'[43] Paley wrote *after* David Hume's critique of the design argument, and he was aware of evolutionary thinking. However, he wrote *before* Charles Darwin's particular theory of evolution by natural selection. The main drawback of this historical placing is that, having developed both:

a)   sophisticated design detection criteria

and:

b)   responses to objections to making design inferences using these criteria

Paley isn't as careful as he should have been to:

c)   distinguish between natural things to which these criteria do and do not apply

or to:

d)   adequately attend to how the design inference can be extended in support of the design argument for God.

Paley drifts from the careful design detection criteria given in his first chapter into thinking that anything complex must result from design. In this, he was caught in the same false dilemma that troubled Darwin: the idea that either *everything* is the direct result of design, or *nothing* is. This is a false dilemma. Whether or not some things in nature are the product of direct design, other things may be the product of a *designed* evolutionary process (a process that cannot have evolved itself).

✔ The prerequisites of evolution cannot themselves be the product of evolution

Contemporary Intelligent Design Theory (ID) is a much misunderstood and misrepresented scientific theory[44] which 'holds that there are tell-tale features of living systems and the universe that are best explained by an intelligent cause.'[45] ID has learned lessons from Hume's critique of the design argument as well as from Paley's contribution. ID theorists continue to develop sophisticated design detection criteria, and to respond to objections to making 'design inferences' using them. However, they carefully attend to the distinction between natural things to which these criteria do and do not apply. Moreover, they agree with Hume about the limited nature of the 'design inference', separating debate about 'the design inference' from debate about 'the design argument'. Still, as we have seen, the design inference is an indispensible element in the design argument.

> **Question:**
> Does Darwin's theory of evolution undermine Paley's design argument?

Conclusion

The impression of Paley's argument one gleans from many introductory philosophy books is that it is a weak argument by analogy that was dented by Hume's critique and then sunk by Darwin's theory of evolution by natural selection. It's actually a sophisticated, multifaceted and robust (if limited) teleological argument.

Recommended Resources

Video

The Case for a Creator. 'Dawkins on Irreducible Complexity' http://youtu.be/ WG0RCVB629Y.

Craig, William Lane. 'Nature's "Design Flaws" and "Cruelties"' http://youtu.be/ytyd-aXzl4zc.

— 'Philosophical and Theological Objections to Intelligent Design' http://youtu.be/ r5NVbyCAZB8.

'The Evidence of Biological Machines' http://youtu.be/_u_LYJGDopA.

Expelled. 'Cell Animation' http://youtu.be/ZDH8sWiUsAM.

'The Inner Life of the Cell' http://youtu.be/zrXykvorybo.

Minnich, Scott. 'Bacterial Flagella: A Paradigm for Design' http://youtu.be/0NXEln-MuTPI.

*Niles, Randall. 'Watch Design' www.randallniles.com/watch-design.htm.

TrueU. *Does God Exist? Building the Scientific Case* (Focus on the Family/Tyndale, 2012).

Woodward, Tom and James P. Gills. 'The Mysterious Epigenome' http://youtu.be/ RpXs8uShFMo.

Audio

*Richards, Jay. 'Paley, Hume, Argument by Analogy and Intelligent Design' http://intelligentdesign.podomatic.com/enclosure/2007-08-10T14_59_47-07_00.mp3.

Online papers

Burgess, Stuart. 'The Beauty of the Peacock Tail and the Problems with the Theory of Sexual Selection' www.creationontheweb.com/content/view/1832.

Deem, Rich. 'Did David Hume Really Defeat William Paley's Watchmaker Argument?' www.godandscience.org/evolution/hume_vs_paley_watchmaker.php.

*Dembski, William A. 'Irreducible Complexity Revisited' www.designinference.com/ documents/2004.01.Irred_Compl_Revisited.pdf.

'Do Biological Clocks Revive William Paley's Design Argument?' www.evolutionnews. org/2012/06/do_biological_c060411.html.

Luskin, Casey. 'Isn't Intelligent Design Just a Rehash of William Paley's 19th Century Design Arguments, Refuted by Hume and Darwin?' www.ideacenter.org/contentmgr/ showdetails.php/id/1166.

*Nelson, Paul. 'Jettison the Arguments, or the Rule? The Place of Darwinian Theological Themata in Evolutionary Reasoning' www.arn.org/docs/nelson/pn_jettison.htm.

'Sexual Selection Falsified in the Case of Peacock Feathers' www.arn.org/blogs/index. php/literature/2008/04/01/sexual_selection_falsified_in_the_case_o.

*Williams, Peter S. 'Atheists against Darwinism: Johnson's "Wedge" Breaks Through' http://epsociety.org/library/articles.asp?pid=66.

— 'Design and the Humean Touchstone' www.arn.org/docs/williams/pw_humean-touchstone.htm.

*— 'The Design Inference from Specified Complexity Defended by Scholars Outside the Intelligent Design Movement – A Critical Review'. *Philosophia Christi* 9:2 (2007): pp. 407–28. http://epsociety.org/library/articles.asp?pid=54; www.discovery.org/a/4499 and www.bethinking.org/science-christianity/advanced/the-design-inference---a-critical-review.htm.

— 'Intelligent Design, Aesthetics and the Design Argument' www.arn.org/docs/williams/pw_idaestheticsanddesignarguments.htm.

Witt, Jonathan. 'Panning God: Darwinism's Defective Argument against Bad Design' www.4truth.net/fourtruthpbscience.aspx?pageid=8589952945.

Books

*Behe, Michael J. *Darwin's Black Box* (New York: Free Press, 2nd edn, 2006).

Collins, Robin. 'The Teleological Argument.' Pages 352–61 in *The Routledge Companion to Philosophy of Religion* (ed. Chad Meister and Paul Copan; London: Routledge, 2010).

Davis, Stephen T. *God, Reason and Theistic Proofs* (Edinburgh University Press, 1997).

Hume, David. *Dialogues Concerning Natural Religion* (Mineola, NY: Dover, 2006).

*Paley, William. *Natural Theology* (Kila, MT: R.A. Kessinger Publishing Co., 2003) www.hti.umich.edu/cgi/p/pd-modeng/pd-modeng-idx?type=HTML&rgn=DIV1&byte=53054870.

Plantinga, Alvin. *Where the Conflict Really Lies: Science, Religion, and Naturalism* (Oxford University Press, 2011).

Swinburne, Richard. 'The Argument from Design.' Pages 201–11 in *Contemporary Perspectives on Religious Epistemology* (ed. R. Douglas Geivett and Brendan Sweetman; Oxford University Press, 1992).

7. Teleological Arguments II: Intelligent Design Theory

> I think there is some evidence for an intelligent designer, and in fact, I think
> that there is some evidence that the intelligent designer is God.
> Bradley Monton[1]

Introduction

Chapter 6 reviewed William Paley's classic formulation of the design argument with half an eye on recent developments in the debate about teleology; and we distinguished between the design inference *to some designer or other* and the design argument for a designing *deity*. The design argument is always an extension of the design inference, and recent decades have seen the emergence of a theory within the historical sciences dedicated to making design inferences. This theory of design detection is called 'Intelligent Design' (or 'ID' for short). According to the growing number of scientists and other academics (called 'design theorists') who constitute the ID movement:

a) Empirical evidence within nature justifies a design inference on the basis of reliable design detection criteria, and
b) Making this inference can be legitimately described as a *scientific* activity.

As J.P. Moreland and William Lane Craig note: 'The central aspect of ID theory is the idea that the designedness of some things that are designed can be identified as such in scientifically acceptable ways.'[2] In this broad sense: 'Intelligent Design is simply the science of design detection.'[3] Hence we should distinguish between ID as a general approach to design detection on the one hand and intelligent design *theory* as the specific application of ID to the question of *origins* on the other hand. As leading design theorist William A. Dembski explains:

> Many special sciences already fall under intelligent design, including archae- ology, cryptography, forensics, and SETI (the Search for Extraterrestrial Intelli- gence). Intelligent design is thus already part of science. Moreover, it employs well-defined methods for detecting intelligence. These methods together with their application constitute the theory of intelligent design [ID in the broad sense]. The question, therefore, is not whether intelligent design constitutes a genuine scientific theory but whether, as a scientific theory, it properly applies to [nature].[4]

Setting aside for the moment the issue of whether or not ID is science, ID can be advanced as a logically valid syllogism:

ID Claim 1) There exist one or more reliable tests for detecting intelligent design
ID Claim 2) Nature exhibits empirical data that pass one or more tests for reliably detecting intelligent design
ID Core Conclusion) Therefore, at least one aspect of nature reliably signals intelligent design

Neither an exercise in 'creation science',[5] nor natural theology,[6] ID theory states that 'intelligent agency, as an aspect of scientific theory making, has more explanatory power in accounting for the specified, and some- times irreducible complexity of some physical systems, including biolog- ical entities, and/or the existence of the universe as a whole, than the blind forces of . . . matter.'[7]

Watch:
William A. Dembski, 'Is Intelligent Design Scientifically Legitimate?' http://youtu. be/ZxYBYW6WzmI.

ID is compatible with any worldview that allows for the empirical detec- tion of genuine design within nature. Michael J. Behe explains that 'if one

127

wishes to be academically rigorous, one can't leap directly from design to a transcendent God. To reach a transcendent God, other, nonscientific arguments have to be made.'[8] That said, the design inferences made by intelligent design theory are obviously open to theistic interpretation, as William Lane Craig observes:

> The teleological argument for God's existence has come roaring back into prominence in recent years. The explanatory adequacy of the neo-Darwinian mechanisms of random mutation and natural selection with respect to the observed biological complexity has been sharply challenged, as advances in microbiology have served to disclose the breathtaking complexity of the micro-machinery of a single cell, not to speak of higher-level organisms. The field of origin of life studies is in turmoil, as all the old scenarios of the chemical origin of life in the primordial soup have collapsed, and no new, better theory is on the horizon. And the scientific community has been stunned by its discovery of how complex and sensitive a nexus of initial conditions must be given in order for the universe even to permit the origin and evolution of intelligent life.[9]

Let's review ID theory by examining its three core claims in turn.

7.1 ID Core Claim 1 – Reliable Design Detection Criteria

Design theorists defend several design detection criteria, including 'specified complexity',[10] 'irreducible complexity'[11] and Bayesian probability approaches.[12] We will attend to the concepts of 'specified complexity' and 'irreducible complexity' already mentioned in chapter 6.

7.1.1 Specified complexity

> Given words, they must come in some order or other;
> but if that order makes sense we infer design.
> Henry Melvill Gwatkin[13]

According to William A. Dembski: 'given an event, object, or structure, to convince ourselves that it is designed we need to show that it is improbably (i.e. complex) and suitably patterned (i.e. specified).'[14] Dembski has defended 'specified complexity' – or 'complex specified information' (CSI) – as a reliable design detection criterion in numerous writings,[15] including his peer-reviewed monograph *The Design Inference* (Cambridge University Press, 1998).

Watch:
William A. Dembski, 'How Do We Detect Design in Nature?' http://youtu.be/0T-FsnQo5LE4.

Imagine drawing scrabble tiles out of a scrabble bag. A long string of random letters – like bdvfajkdoeytwefasqeo – is *complex* (i.e. statistically unlikely) but it is not *specified* (it does not conform to any independent pattern that we haven't simply read off the object or event in question). A short string of letters could be specified – like 'this' or 'that' – but wouldn't be sufficiently complex to outstrip the ability of chance to explain this match (letters drawn at random from a scrabble bag will occasionally form a short word by chance). So, neither complexity without specificity, nor specificity without complexity compels us to infer design. However, if you saw a sonnet written out on a table in scrabble tiles, you would certainly infer that this was the product of design. A scrabble-tile sonnet is both specified (conforming to the functional requirements of grammatical English) *and* sufficiently complex (doing so at a level of complexity that makes it unreasonable to attribute this match to luck) to trigger a design inference on the grounds that 'in all cases where we know the causal origin of . . . specified complexity, experience has shown that intelligent design played a causal role.'[16]

Watch:
William Lane Craig, 'Specified Complexity' http://youtu.be/RiUJLHDYOBs.

Atheist Richard Dawkins admits that basing a design inference on *specified* complexity, rather than upon *mere* complexity, takes care of the objection that *any* arrangements of parts is going to be improbable: 'A pile of detached watch parts tossed in a box is . . . as improbable as a fully functioning, genuinely complicated watch. What is specified about a watch is that it is improbable in the specific direction of telling the time.'[17] Although any given arrangement of watch parts is equally improbable (i.e. one possible arrangement out of a huge number of possible arrangements), it is nevertheless highly improbable that the parts should happen to be arranged 'in the specific direction of telling the time' in the absence of design! Dawkins argues: 'Of all the unique and, with hindsight equally improbable, positions of the combination lock [that's *complexity*], only one opens the lock [that's *specification*] . . . The uniqueness of the [complex] arrangement . . . that opens the safe . . . is *specified*.'[18] The *best explanation* of an open safe is not that someone 'got lucky', but that someone knew the *specific* and *complex* combination required to open it *by intelligent design.*

> **Question:**
> Consider the events described in the following passages of Scripture – Genesis 44:33; Judges 6:36–40; Psalm 22; Matthew 17:27 and Acts 1:23–25 – and explain a) if/how specified complexity features in or can be applied to these episodes and b) what can be inferred from this fact?

7.1.2 Only positive evidence

Suppose an artist carefully weathered a hillside, cleverly mimicking natural processes, to produce a profile *vaguely* like that of a person. The 'specified complexity' criterion wouldn't detect the activity of intelligence in that hillside. As far as the 'specified complexity' test goes, the hillside *might* be the product of design, it might *superficially* look like objects that the test would attribute to design, but the test would give us no reason to think that it *must* be the product of design. On the other hand, if the hillside in question were carved into a detailed picture of four American presidents (like Mount Rushmore), then the test *would* detect design, because such a pattern (unlike the former example) is both complex and specified.

✔ The 'specified complexity' test *can't rule design out*, but *it can rule it in.*

7.1.3 Irreducible complexity

Michael J. Behe's most notable presentation of 'irreducible complexity' (IC) is *Darwin's Black Box: The Biochemical Challenge to Evolution* (Free Press, 1996/2006), where he defined his terms as follows:

> By *irreducibly complex* I mean a single system composed of several well-matched, interacting parts that contribute to basic function, wherein the removal of any one of the parts causes the system to effectively cease functioning. An irreducibly complex system cannot be produced directly . . . by slight, successive modifications of a precursor system, because any precursor to an irreducibly complex system that is missing a part is by definition non-functional.[19]

An 'irreducibly complex' system is a specific example of 'specified complexity.' The systems Behe considers require numerous components working together to achieve a given function. Hence they are complex. Moreover, these systems exhibit patterns – given by their function – that are independent of the actual living systems. Hence these systems are also specified.

Charles Darwin acknowledged: 'If it could be demonstrated that any complex organ existed which could not possibly have been formed by numerous, successive modifications, my theory would absolutely break down.'[20] Darwin made the universal negative bet that no such system would be discovered. Richard Dawkins agrees: 'Maybe there is something out there in nature that really does preclude, by its genuinely irreducible complexity, the smooth gradient of Mount Improbable . . . if genuinely irreducible complexity could be properly demonstrated, it would wreck Darwin's theory.'[21]

Any system that is IC cannot have evolved *directly* (retaining the same function) by a series of slight evolutionary improvements. Ruling out direct, incremental evolution doesn't exclude what Darwin called 'a sudden leap', but as Dawkins notes: 'The larger the leap through genetic space, the lower the probability that the resulting change will be viable, let alone an improvement.'[22]

Behe observes: 'Even if a system is irreducibly complex (and thus cannot have been produced directly) . . . one cannot definitely rule out the possibility of an indirect, circuitous route. As the complexity of an interacting system increases, though, the likelihood of such an indirect route drops precipitously.'[23]

Behe argues that at the biomolecular level of life there are many IC systems that are unlikely to have been formed by numerous, successive, unguided, indirect evolutionary modifications. For example, some bacteria swim using an outboard motor, spinning their 'flagella' at up to 100,000 rpm like a screw propeller: 'The rotary motor, with a diameter of only 30 to 40 [nanometres], drives the rotation of the flagellum at around 300 Hz, at a power level of 10^{-16} W with energy conversion efficiency close to 100%.'[24] As a rotary motor, the flagellum is obviously IC. A rotary motor without a propeller, or a drive shaft, or a motor, just won't work! Experiments show that a flagellum motor requires about fifty proteins, and 'the absence of any one of these proteins results in the complete loss of motor function.'[25]

Watch:
'Self Assembling Nano-Machine' http://youtu.be/uw0-MHI_248.

Given that IC systems resist evolutionary explanation, and given our everyday experience of intelligent agents easily producing IC systems,

Behe argues that the best explanation of such molecular machines is design: 'For discrete physical systems – if there is not a [plausible] gradual route to their production – design is evident when a number of separate, interacting components are ordered in such a way as to accomplish a function beyond the individual components.'[26]

Behe combines his argument with a positive design-detection criterion; hence, as atheist Bradley Monton recognizes: 'Behe's irreducible complexity argument is not a God-of-the-gaps argument at all.'[27]

✔ The design inference is *not* an argument from ignorance

Behe argues the burden of proof is on those who doubt that IC systems are designed:

> a person who conjectured that the statues on Easter Island . . . were actually the result of unintelligent forces would bear the substantial burden of proof the claim demanded. In those examples, the positive evidence for design would be there for all to see in the purposeful arrangements of parts to produce the images. Any putative evidence for the claim that the images were actually the result of unintelligent processes (perhaps erosion by some vague, hypothesized chaotic forces) would have to clearly show that the postulated unintelligent process could indeed do the job. In the absence of such a clear demonstration, any person would be rationally justified to prefer the design explanation.[28]

In other words, if it 'looks like a duck, walks like a duck, swims like a duck and sounds like a duck', then it should be assumed to *be* a duck, in the absence of sufficient evidence to the contrary.

✔ The burden of proof is on those who doubt design

But as biologist Franklin Harold admits: 'there are presently no detailed Darwinian accounts of the evolution of any biochemical or cellular system, only a variety of wishful speculations.'[29]

Design looks like the best explanation for IC systems, and Darwinists appear to be betting in the face of long odds. If they can meet the proper burden of proof by discovering indirect Darwinian pathways of sufficiently high probability that account for the emergence of systems like the flagellum, 'then more power to them',[30] says Dembski (the assertion that a given system is IC is a falsifiable claim): 'But until that happens . . . biologists who claim that natural selection accounts for the emergence of the bacterial flagellum are worthy of no more credence than compulsive gamblers who are forever promising to settle their accounts.'[31]

7.2 ID Core Claim 2 – Empirical Data Triggering Reliable Design Detection Criteria

The molecular machinery of the cell isn't the only evidence adduced by design theorists, who have proposed that design can be inferred from several facets of nature, including the specified complexity exhibited by:

- Cosmic fine-tuning
- The fine-tuning of our local cosmic habitat for life and scientific discovery
- The origin of life (including the information within DNA, RNA and epigenetics)
- The 'Cambrian explosion'
- Macroevolution
- The phenomenon of metamorphosis
- Irreducibly complex biomolecular systems

Watch:
The Case for a Creator, 'The Evidence of Biological Information' http://youtu.be/CamNoA6Cfjc.
— 'The Evidence of Biological Machines' http://youtu.be/_u_LYJGDopA.
— 'The Evidence of Physics' http://youtu.be/x3dOzC3G368.
— 'Planet Earth' http://youtu.be/0MVDiNl7bBM.
'The Mysterious Epigenome: What Lies beyond DNA' http://youtu.be/RpXs8u-ShFMo.
William Lane Craig, 'The Limits of Darwinism' http://youtu.be/QYSY3dUqC2c.
Illustra Media, 'Metamorphosis' http://youtu.be/9_FdB7pRbUU.
— 'The Mystery of the Cambrian Fossil Record' http://youtu.be/h38Xi-Jz9yk.

It's worth noting that while the final four items on this list (the Cambrian explosion, macroevolution, metamorphosis and irreducible complexity) call into question the explanatory sufficiency of evolution by natural selection, the first three items (cosmic fine-tuning, local fine-tuning and the origin of life including the information within DNA, RNA and the epigenome) concern preconditions for evolution. Let's briefly review the first of these preconditions: cosmic fine-tuning.

7.2.1 Cosmic fine-tuning

Physicists Stephen Hawking and Leonard Mlodinow acknowledge: 'the initial state of the universe had to be set up in a very special *and* highly improbable way . . . if the universe were only slightly different, beings like us could not exist. What are we to make of this fine-tuning? Is it

133

evidence that the universe, after all, was designed?'[32] The combination
of a 'highly improbable' event with a 'very special' pattern, as seen in
cosmic fine-tuning, is an example of 'specified complexity' best explained
by intelligent design. That is:

1. The fine-tuning of the universe exhibits specified complexity
2. If something exhibits specified complexity then it's probably the
   product of design
3. Therefore, the fine-tuning of the universe is probably the product of
   design

Watch:
Peter S. Williams, 'Can I Hack Your Bank Account?' www.youtube.com/watch?v=QK-grezenX4A.
— 'A Machine for Making Universes' www.youtube.com/watch?v=D8FKF_2PjG4.
— 'Our Existence Isn't Enough to Explain Fine-Tuning' www.youtube.com/watch?v=OS-0RQYIZmRU.

The most popular objection to this argument seeks to deny the complexity
of cosmic fine-tuning by invoking multiple universes with different
constants and initial conditions. However, this objection commits the
'inflationary fallacy' of multiplying probabilistic resources without independent evidence. It's like explaining a text by invoking enough monkeys
randomly typing away for long enough: in the absence of independent
evidence for the existence of enough time, typewriters and monkeys, the
'one author' explanation is clearly preferable. Likewise, even granting
that *if* there were 'multiple universes' *then* one could obtain the fine-
tuning of our universe by chance, in the absence of independent evidence
for the existence of 'multiple universes' the design explanation is clearly
rationally preferable.

Watch:
Peter S. Williams, 'No Evidence for Many Universes' www.youtube.com/watch?v=-JOfLLHIDwrc.

William Lane Craig argues that the 'many worlds' hypothesis is actually
disconfirmed by observation:

> If our world is just a random member of a world ensemble, then it's vastly
> more probable that we should be observing a much smaller region of order
> . . . the odds of our universe's initial low-entropy condition's existing by
> chance alone are one chance out of $10^{10^{(123)}}$. By contrast the odds of our

solar system's suddenly forming by the random collision of particles is one chance out of $10^{10 (60)}$ ... What that means is that it is *far* more likely that we should be observing an orderly universe no larger than our solar system, since a world of that size is unfathomably more probable than a fine-tuned universe like ours.[33]

Moreover, philosopher Robin Collins observes that 'if [a physically plausible] many-universe generator exists, it along with the back-ground laws and principles could be said to be an *irreducibly complex* system . . . with just the right combination of laws and fields for the production of life-permitting universes . . . the existence of such a system suggests design.'[34]

7.3 ID Core Claim 3 – ID as Science

It is worse than random guesswork to lay down the law, that life 'must' have
come from matter, not on evidence, but simply to round off a theory.
Henry Melvill Gwatkin[35]

As well as claiming that the 'core claim' of ID theory is sound, ID theorists additionally claim that:

ID Claim 3) Inferring intelligent design from empirical evidence using reliable tests is a *scientific* enterprise

Watch:
Stephen C. Meyer, 'Is Intelligent Design Science?' www.youtube.com/user/DiscoveryInstitute#p/u/32/hy0_Mn1s1xo.

Read:
Bruce L. Gordon, 'The Scientific Status of Design Inferences' www.4truth.net/fourthpbscience.aspx?pageid=8589952949.

The philosophical question of whether or not ID is science is not the same question as whether or not the 'core claim' of ID theory is true. Arguments may be sound without being scientific, and vice versa.

Question:
Which logical fallacy is committed by the claim 'Because Intelligent Design Theory isn't a scientific theory it can't be true'?

Whether or not ID should be called 'science' is an important question. Nevertheless, it's not a crucial question. The crucial question is whether both premises of the logically valid core argument of ID are true. As Stephen C. Meyer writes, what really matters 'is not whether a theory is scientific but whether a theory is true or false, well confirmed or not, worthy of our belief or not.'[36]

Philosopher of science Del Ratzsch observes:

> The scientific attitude has usually been characterised as a commitment to following the evidence wherever it leads. That does not look like promising ammunition for someone pushing an official policy of refusing to allow science to follow evidence to design no matter what the evidence turns out to be . . . it commits science to either having to deliberately ignore major (possibly even *observable*) features of the material realm or having to refrain from even considering the obvious and only workable explanation, should it turn out that those features clearly resulted from [intelligent] activity . . . any imposed policy of naturalism in science has the potential not only of eroding any self-correcting capability of science but of preventing science from reaching certain truths. Any imposed policy of methodological naturalism will have precisely the same potential consequences.[37]

Naturalism is the belief that nothing supernatural exists. 'Methodological naturalism' is not the belief that naturalism is true, but rather the belief that science should be done *as if* naturalism were true. Atheist philosopher of science Bradley Monton observes that 'if science really is permanently committed to methodological naturalism, it follows that the aim of science is not generating true theories. Instead, the aim of science would be something like: generating the best theories that can be formulated subject to the restriction that the theories are naturalistic . . . science is better off without being shackled by methodological naturalism.'[38]

However, we can distinguish between hard-line methodological naturalism (HMN) and soft methodological naturalism (SMN):[39]

- HMN holds that science must not appeal to personal agency *of any sort* in its explanations.
- SMN holds that while science can appeal to personal agency in its explanations, it cannot appeal to *supernatural* personal agency.

ID theory is incompatible with HMN; but then so are many subjects whose scientific status is uncontroversial (e.g. archaeology, cryptography, forensic science, parapsychology, psychology, SETI). ID (like forensic science etc.) is compatible with SMN: 'intelligent design does not investigate whether the designing intelligent agent was natural or supernatural because it assumes that things designed by an intelligence may possess certain perceptible properties regardless of whether that intelligent agent is a natural entity, or in some way supernatural.'[40]

Hence 'intelligent design, properly conceived, does not need to violate methodological naturalism.'[41] As Moreland argues: 'some branches of science, including SETI, archaeology, forensic science, psychology and sociology, use personal agency and various internal states of agents . . . as explanations for certain phenomena . . . Thus there is nothing non-scientific about appealing to personal agency and the like in a scientific explanation.'[42]

One needn't concede that even SMN draws a line between 'science' and 'pseudoscience.' Philosopher of science Larry Laudan notes: 'There is no demarcation line between science and non-science, or between science and pseudoscience, which would win assent from a majority of philosophers.'[43] Michael Ruse admits: 'It would indeed be very odd were I and others to simply characterize "science" as something which, by definition, is based on (methodological) naturalistic philosophy and hence excludes God.'[44] Richard Dawkins *affirms* the scientific status of ID: 'The presence or absence of a creative super-intelligence is unequivocally a scientific question, even if it is not in practice – or not yet – a decided one . . . The methods we should use to settle the matter . . . would be purely and entirely scientific methods.'[45] Atheist Victor J. Stenger likewise concedes: 'I agree with [Bradley] Monton (an avowed atheist, incidentally) that intelligent design is science.'[46]

Besides, *if* the core ID syllogism is sound, *then* advocates of the 'it's not science' critique of ID must either eat their proverbial hats, or else endorse transferring assets from university science departments to philosophy departments in the interests of furthering our understanding of nature! In other words, if ID is true, it's impractical not to call it 'science.'

7.4 From Design to God

I think a particular god like Zeus or Jehovah is as unlikely as the tooth fairy, but the idea of some kind of creative intelligence is not quite so ridiculous.
Richard Dawkins[47]

There's a logical gap between the *scientific* conclusion of intelligent design (which is compatible with SMN) and the *metaphysical* conclusion that the designer is God. As atheist Sam Harris says: 'Even if we accepted that our universe simply had to be designed by a designer, this would not suggest that this designer is the biblical God, or that He approves of

Christianity.'[48] This gap can be illustrated by thinking about crop circles. Crop circles are obviously the product of design (they exhibit specified complexity). Some people suggest that the source of crop circle design is extraterrestrial. No matter how sceptical we are about extraterrestrials, it would be irrational to argue that 'because extraterrestrials don't exist, crop circles are not the product of design'! Likewise, however sceptical someone is about the existence of God, it would be irrational to argue that 'since God doesn't exist, nothing in nature is the product of design'! The inference to design, whether from crop circles or nature, is prior to the inference to any particular designer, and stands or falls on its own merits. Behe explains:

> my argument is limited to design itself; I strongly emphasize that it is not an argument for the existence of a benevolent God . . . I recognize that philosophy and theology may be able to extend the argument. But a scientific argument for design in biology does not reach that far. Thus while I argue for design, the question of the identity of the designer is left open . . .[49]

Working with the distinctions between *intelligent, supernatural* and *divine* design is *not* a rhetorical move on the part of ID theorists. As Behe observes, 'diligence in making proper distinctions should not be impugned as craftiness.'[50]

It's a mistake to confuse the perceived metaphysical implications of a scientific theory with the theory itself. For example, the 'Big Bang' theory supports one premise of the *kalam* cosmological argument (cf. chapter 5). Together with a second (philosophical) premise, one might well think that the Big Bang theory supported the metaphysical conclusion that God exists. Nevertheless, this would surely not mean that the Big Bang theory *per se* posited the existence of God! The same holds for ID.

ID argues that there are natural entities that are very unlikely to occur by chance and/or physical necessity, and infers, *on the basis of experience*, that the best explanation of these features of reality is design (ID is not an 'argument from ignorance'). But whether or not the designer is supernatural, let alone divine, is a further question. After all, one could acknowledge intelligent design while remaining agnostic as to the nature of the source of design; or one could attribute design to the activity of Plato's Demiurge, to the finite gods of Egyptian, Greek or Norse polytheism, to angels, demons, aliens (whether from this or a parallel universe), or to time-travelling human scientists, rather than to God.

Design inferences, then, needn't be viewed as design arguments for God – at least, not without considerations from outside ID as a scientific theory being brought to bear: 'intelligent design theory by itself makes no claims about the nature of the designer, and scientists currently working within an intelligent design framework include Protestants, Catholics, Jews, agnostics, and others.'[51] Dembski comments: 'I've seen intelligent design embraced by Jews, Muslims, Hindus, Buddhists, agnostics and even atheists.'[52]

However, a valid design argument based upon the design inference can be constructed *by adding an additional premise to the core argument for ID*:

1. There exist one or more reliable tests for detecting intelligent design
2. Nature exhibits empirical data that passes one or more tests for reliably detecting intelligent design
3. Therefore, at least one aspect of nature reliably signals intelligent design
4. The best explanation for intelligent design within nature is theistic
5. Therefore, theism is probably true

The necessity for premise 4 gives the lie to the claim that ID is an inherently theistic or supernatural hypothesis. However, those who think that premise 4 is more plausible than its denial will view ID as a hypothesis capable of lending support to such a conclusion.

Why might one think that premise 4 is more plausible than its denial? Given the assumption that intelligence can be explained naturalistically (an assumption I don't accept), naturalism can be made *logically compatible* with inferring design from nature. *Perhaps*, as the naturalistic Raelian UFO cult believes,[53] aliens are responsible for life on earth. *Perhaps* the Big Bang was fine-tuned to produce a life-sustaining universe by aliens in a parallel universe! However, just as human agency is a better explanation for the specified complexity of crop circles than aliens (or supernatural agency), so supernatural agency is a better explanation of design in the texture of nature than aliens (or humans). Attributing specified complexity in nature to aliens:

*   Looks *ad hoc*[54]
*   Lacks independent confirmation (whereas theism is supported by numerous converging lines of evidence)
*   Is disconfirmed by empirical evidence (about the lack of suitable cosmic life-supporting bodies besides earth, and about the practical difficulties of long-distance space travel)
*   Implies an infinite regress of explanation not faced by theism with its uncaused First Cause

Since the universe exhibits signs of design that would otherwise imply an infinite regress of designers, it's reasonable to infer the existence of a designer who doesn't exhibit any signs of design (i.e. who contains no specified complexity), and so doesn't trigger a design inference. Therefore (in conjunction with Occam's razor), the best explanation of design in nature is the existence of a single, transcendent, uncaused, highly intelligent, knowledgeable and powerful agent whose existence (unlike any naturalistically acceptable designer) does *not* depend upon or contain specified complexity – which is as much as to say that this undesigned designer must be *immaterial* or *supernatural*.

Watch:
William Lane Craig, 'Who Designed the Designer?' http://youtu.be/jnhMmJPnnDo.

Conclusion

Many atheists (e.g. Richard Dawkins, Bradley Monton, Thomas Nagel, Victor J. Stenger) accept that ID is a scientific theory. However, debates about whether or not ID is *science* aren't as important as debates about whether it is *true*. ID theory advances a simple, logically valid syllogism. Even many people who disagree with ID (e.g. Richard Dawkins) accept the first premise, that there are reliable tests for design. After all, scientists search for signs of design every day in fields such as archaeology, cryptography, forensic science and the search for extraterrestrial intelligence. The crucial question is whether anything that is *an intrinsic part of nature* passes a reliable test for design (i.e. is the second core ID premise true?).

As Hume argued, to infer design isn't necessarily to infer God. Nevertheless, if Intelligent Design Theory is true, it provides the starting point for a philosophical argument with much to contribute to the case for theism and to debates between theists about how to understand the details of God's creative activity. Writing about ID, atheist Bradley Monton even admits: 'the arguments do have *some* force – they make me less certain of my atheism than I would be had I not heard the arguments.'[55]

Films to watch and discuss:
Prometheus, directed by Ridley Scott (Twentieth Century Fox, 2012) (15)

* **(Audio)** David Boze, 'Intelligent Design in *Prometheus*' http://intelligentdesign.podomatic.com/entry/2012-06-25T14_32_37-07_00.

Contact, directed by Robert Zemeckis (Warner Bros, 1997) (PG)

* * *

Recommended Resources

Video

Dembski, William A. 'The Challenge of Intelligent Design to Unintelligent Evolution' http://video.google.com/videoplay?docid=-6646238627774515357&hl=en.
God: New Evidence www.youtube.com/user/godnewevidence.
'A Rotary Nano-Engine' www.nanonet.go.jp/english/mailmag/2004/files/011a.wmv.
*TrueU. *Does God Exist? Building the Scientific Case* (Focus on the Family/Tyndale, 2012).
*Williams, Peter S. 'Intelligent Design' YouTube Playlist www.youtube.com/playlist?list=PLQhh3qcwVEWjckJboK1rfuBKPcHiMFTSO.

Audio

Behe, Michael. 'The Edge of Evolution' http://hw.libsyn.com/p/b/9/9/b99d841f6c507fb9/POI_2007_11_07_Michael_Behe.mp3?sid=677cb6068eaaf2dad-84fafd56cc82a0c&l_sid=18988&l_eid=&l_mid=1770278.
Boze, David. 'Intelligent Design in *Prometheus*' http://intelligentdesign.podomatic.com/entry/2012-06-25T14_32_37-07_00.
Collins, Robin. 'Apologetics 315 Interview on Fine-Tuning' http://apologetics315.s3.amazonaws.com/interview/interview-robin-collins.mp3.
Craig, William Lane. Defenders Podcast, series 2, parts 14–18 www.reasonablefaith.org/defenders-2-podcast/s4.
Holder, Rodney. 'Stephen Hawking and the Multiverse' www.cis.org.uk/upload/southampton/Rodney%20Holder%20-%20Multiverse%20talk.
*Luskin, Casey. 'Atheists Who Defend Intelligent Design: Interview with Bradley Monton' http://youtu.be/Et2VTJ1UBC4.
*Monton, Bradley. 'Think Lecture: Intelligent Design' http://web.mac.com/cookj3/ID_Podcast/ID_Podcast/Entries/2008/10/29_Sounds_at_the_beach.html.
— 'Think Lecture Q&A Time' http://web.mac.com/cookj3/ID_Podcast/ID_Podcast/Entries/2008/10/29_Dr._Brad_Monton%2C_Q_%26_A_after_lecture.html.
Unbelievable? 'Mike Behe and Michael Reiss Debate ID' www.premierradio.org.uk/listen/ondemand.aspx?mediaid={42F345D1-A875-41AD-8591-71515CB69803.
*Unbelievable? 'Signature in the Cell: Stephen C. Meyer vs Keith Fox' www.premierradio.org.uk/listen/ondemand.aspx?mediaid={D5D3E5D1-697C-4348-87E6-7B6EED18E0AC}.
*Williams, Peter S. 'Introduction to Intelligent Design Theory' www.damaris.org/cm/podcasts/434.
— 'Stephen Hawking and the Grand Designer (Bryanston School)' www.damaris.org/cm/podcasts/663.
— 'Stephen Hawking and the Grand Designer (Winchester)' www.damaris.org/cm/podcasts/682.

Websites

Access Research Network www.arn.org.
Centre for Intelligent Design www.c4id.org.uk/.
Designinference.com: Writings of William A. Dembski: http://designinference.com/dembski-on-intelligent-design/dembski-writings/.
Discovery Institute Centre for Science and Culture www.discovery.org/csc/.
Evolutionary Informatics www.evoinfo.org/.
ID Quest www.youtube.com/user/idquest?feature=results_main.
Illustra Media Website www.youtube.com/user/IllustraMedia.
Stephen C. Meyer www.stephencmeyer.org/.

The Bethinking debate on Intelligent Design Theory and theistic evolution

1) Alexander, Denis. 'Creation and Evolution? Section II – Hot Issues for the Twenty-First Century' www.bethinking.org/resource.php?ID=193.
2) Williams, Peter S. 'Theistic Evolution and Intelligent Design in Dialogue' www.bethinking.org/resource.php?ID=216.
3) Alexander, Denis. 'Designs on Science' www.bethinking.org/science-christianity/designs-on-science.htm.
4) Williams, Peter S. 'Intelligent Designs on Science: A Surreply to Denis Alexander's Critique of Intelligent Design Theory', part 1 www.bethinking.org/science-christianity/part-1-intelligent-designs-on-science-a.htm and part 2 www.bethinking.org/resource.php?ID=530&CategoryID=8 (cf. www.iscid.org/papers/Williams_IntelligentDesigns_073106.pdf).

Online papers

Barns, Luke A. 'The Fine-Tuning of the Universe for Intelligent Life' http://arxiv.org/PS_cache/arxiv/pdf/1112/1112.4647v1.pdf.
Bradley, Walter L. 'The Origin of Life' www.4truth.net/fourtruthpbscience.aspx?pageid=8589952963.
Collins, Robin. 'God, Design and Fine Tuning' http://home.messiah.edu/%7Ercollins/Fine-tuning/Revised%20Version%20of%20Fine-tuning%20for%20anthology.doc.
— 'Modern Cosmology and Anthropic Fine Tuning: Three Approaches' http://home.messiah.edu/~rcollins/Fine-tuning/Modern%20Cosmology%20in%20Philosophical%20and%20Theological%20Perspective.pdf.
— 'Stenger's Fallacies' http://home.messiah.edu/%7Ercollins/Fine-tuning/Stenger-fallacy.pdf.
— 'The Teleological Argument: An Exploration of the Fine Tuning of the Cosmos' http://home.messiah.edu/%7Ercollins/Fine-tuning/Abridged%20Version%20of%20Fine-tuning%20book.doc.
Craig, William Lane. 'Scepticism about the Neo-Darwinian Paradigm' www.reasonable-faith.org/site/News2?page=NewsArticle&id=6711.
— 'Scepticism about the Neo-Darwinian Paradigm – Re-Visited' www.reasonablefaith.org/site/News2?page=NewsArticle&id=6741.
*Dembski, William A. 'Intelligent Design: A Brief Introduction' www.4truth.net/fourtruthpbscience.aspx?pageid=8589952955.

— 'In Defence of Intelligent Design' www.designinference.com/documents/2005.06. Defense_of_ID.pdf.

— 'The Logical Underpinnings of Intelligent Design' http://designinference.com/documents/2002.10.logicalunderpinningsofID.pdf.

Fuller, Steve. 'Against the Faith' http://newhumanist.org.uk/1880.

Fodor, Jerry. 'Why Pigs Don't Have Wings' www.lrb.co.uk/v29/n20/fodo01_.html.

Gonzalez, Guillermo and Jay Richards. 'Designed for Discovery' www.4truth.net/fourtruthpbscience.aspx?pageid=8589952941.

Gordon, Bruce L. 'The Scientific Status of Design Inferences' www.4truth.net/fourtruthpbscience.aspx?pageid=8589952949.

Marks II, Robert J. 'Evolutionary Computation: A Perpetual Motion Machine for Design Information?' www.4truth.net/fourtruthpbscience.aspx?pageid=8589952931.

Menuge, Angus. 'The Role of Agency in Science' www.4truth.net/site/apps/nl/content3.asp?c=hiKXLbPNLrF&b=1171681&ct=1579247.

*Meyer, Stephen C. 'A Scientific History and Philosophical Defence of the Theory of Intelligent Design' www.discovery.org/a/7471.

— 'DNA and the Origin of Life' www.discovery.org/a/2184.

— 'The Origin of Biological Information and the Higher Taxonomic Categories' www.discovery.org/scripts/viewDB/index.php?command=view&id=2177&program=CSC%20-%20Scientific%20Research%20and%20Scholarship%20-%20Science.

— 'The Scientific Status of Intelligent Design' www.discovery.org/scripts/viewDB/index.php?command=view&id=2834&program=CSC%20-%20Scientific%20Research%20and%20Scholarship%20-%20History%20and%20Philosophy%20of%20Science.

Monton, Bradley. 'Is Intelligent Design Science? Dissecting the Dover Decision' http://philsci-archive.pitt.edu/archive/00002583/01/Methodological_Naturalism_2.pdf.

Nagel, Thomas. 'Public Education and Intelligent Design' http://as.nyu.edu/docs/IO/1172/papa_132.pdf.

Nelson, Paul. 'Intelligent Design' www.cmf.org.uk/printable/?context=article&id=1303.

Peer-Reviewed Support for Intelligent Design www.discovery.org/a/2640.

Plantinga, Alvin. 'Methodological Naturalism?' http://id-www.ucsb.edu/fscf/library/plantinga/mn/home.html.

*— 'Why Darwinist Materialism Is Wrong'. *The New Republic*, 16 November 2012 www.tnr.com/print/article/books-and-arts/magazine/110189/why-darwinist-materialism-wrong.

Ruse, Michael. 'Nonliteralist Antievolution'. AAAS Symposium: 'The New Antievolutionism', Boston, MA (1993) www.leaderu.com/orgs/arn/orpages/or151/mr93tran.htm.

*Williams, Peter S. 'Atheists against Darwinism: Johnson's "Wedge" Breaks Through' http://epsociety.org/library/articles.asp?pid=66.

*— 'The Design Inference from Specified Complexity Defended by Scholars

outside the Intelligent Design Movement – A Critical Review'. *Philosophia Christi* 9:2 (2007): pp. 407–28 http://epsociety.org/library/articles.asp?pid=54; www.discovery.org/a/4499 and www.bethinking.org/science-christianity/advanced/the-design-inference---a-critical-review.htm.

Books

Behe, Michael J. *Darwin's Black Box: The Biochemical Challenge to Evolution* (New York: Free Press, 2nd edn, 2006).

— *The Edge of Evolution: The Search for the Limits of Darwinism* (New York: Free Press, 2007).

Campbell, John Angus and Stephen C. Meyer, eds. *Darwinism, Design, and Public Education* (Michigan State University Press, 2003).

Dembski, William A. 'An Information Theoretic Design Argument.' Pages 77–94 in *To Everyone an Answer: A Case for the Christian Worldview* (ed. Francis J. Beckwith, William Lane Craig and J.P. Moreland; Downers Grove, IL: IVP, 2004).

— *The Design Revolution: Answering the Toughest Questions about Intelligent Design* (Downers Grove, IL: IVP, 2004).

*— and Sean McDowell. *Understanding Intelligent Design: Everything You Need to Know in Plain Language* (Eugene, OR: Harvest House, 2008).

— and Jonathan Wells. *The Design of Life: Discovering Signs of Intelligence in Biological Systems* (Dallas, TX: Foundation for Thought and Ethics, 2008).

Fuller, Steve. *Dissent over Descent: Intelligent Design's Challenge to Darwinism* (Cambridge: Icon, 2008).

Gonzalez, Guillermo and Jay Richards. *The Privileged Planet: How Our Place in the Cosmos Is Designed for Discovery* (Washington, DC: Regnery Publishing, 2005).

Gordon, Bruce L. 'Inflationary Cosmology and the String Multiverse.' Pages 75–102 in Robert J. Spitzer, *New Proofs for the Existence of God: Contributions of Contemporary Physics and Philosophy* (Cambridge: Eerdmans, 2010).

Johnson, Phillip E. *Darwin on Trial* (Downers Grove, IL: IVP, 20th anniv. edn, 2010) http://talebooks.com/images/bs/291.pdf.

Lennox, John C. *God and Stephen Hawking: Whose Design Is It Anyway?* (Oxford: Lion, 2010).

— *God's Undertaker: Has Science Buried God?* (Oxford: Lion, 2nd edn, 2009).

Meyer, Stephen C. *Signature in the Cell: DNA and the Evidence for Intelligent Design* (New York: HarperOne, 2009).

— *Darwin's Doubt: The Explosive Origin of Animal Life And The Case For Intelligent Design* (New York: HarperOne, 2013).

*Monton, Bradley. *Seeking God in Science: An Atheist Defends Intelligent Design* (Peterborough, ON: Broadview Press, 2009).

Moreland, J.P. *Love Your God with All Your Mind* (Colorado, CO: NavPress, 2012).

Moreland, J.P. and William Lane Craig. *Philosophical Foundations for a Christian Worldview* (Downers Grove, IL: IVP, 2003).

Nagel, Thomas. *Mind and Cosmos: Why the Materialist Neo-Darwinian Conception of Nature Is Almost Certainly False* (Oxford University Press, 2012).

— *Secular Philosophy and the Religious Temperament* (Oxford University Press, 2010).

Plantinga, Alvin. *Where the Conflict Really Lies: Science, Religion, and Naturalism* (Oxford University Press, 2011).

Ratzsch, Del. *Science and Its Limits: The Natural Sciences in Christian Perspective* (Downers Grove, IL: IVP, 2000).

Williams, Peter S. *I Wish I Could Believe in Meaning: A Response to Nihilism* (Southampton: Damaris, 2004).

Woodward, Tom and James P. Gills. *The Mysterious Epigenome: What Lies beyond DNA* (Grand Rapids, MI: Kregel, 2012).

8. The Moral Argument

Without God, there would be no good, no right and wrong.
The two are inseparably linked.
Luke Pollard[1]

Introduction

The main argument against theism, the 'problem of evil' (cf. chapter 17), can't be advanced without simultaneously raising one of the main arguments *for* theism, namely 'the moral argument.' *If* objective values stand or fall with the reality of a wholly good personal deity, as the moral argument claims, *then* the existence of objective evil actually proves the truth of theism! The moral argument can take either objective goodness or evil as its starting point, because it is based upon the general premise that *objective moral value is a reality*. This is one reason why the moral argument is important, because it is a natural dialogue partner of the problem of evil. Another reason is that it speaks to the wholly good moral character of God, and so lays a natural platform upon which to discuss issues of sin and salvation.

One version of the moral argument claims that morality is objective, that objective moral value requires the existence of a god, and that a god must therefore exist. This argument can be expressed in one logically valid (MP) syllogism:

1. If objective moral duties exist, then a god exists
2. Objective moral duties exist
3. Therefore, a god exists

This argument doesn't conclude with the full-blown God of classical theism, but it can establish some of his characteristics (e.g. that this 'god' is the necessarily existent and good source of objective moral duties, is unchanging in this respect, is personal, and has a relationship with us through moral requirements).

To defend the moral argument we first of all need to understand the distinction between moral objectivism and moral subjectivism. We will then counter two common arguments for moral subjectivism before considering several arguments for moral objectivism. Having defended the premise that objective moral values exist, we will then consider arguments for the premise that the existence of objective moral values entails the existence of a god. We will consider what can be known about this deity on this basis, before finally reviewing three common objections to the moral argument.

8.1 Objective Moral Values Exist

Moral values are either *objective* (independent of the subject) or *subjective* (not independent of, and therefore relative to, the subject – hence this view is also called 'moral relativism'). Moral objectivism claims that there are moral truths that don't depend upon our belief in them. For instance, one culture may believe that cannibalism is right, and another may think cannibalism is wrong. In order to argue that at least one of these cultures is *wrong*, one must be a moral objectivist (the objectivist needn't claim to know *which* culture is wrong to coherently claim that *one of them is wrong*).

Suppose one group of people thinks the sun goes around the earth, and another thinks the opposite. Scientists wouldn't say, 'These are equally true claims', but rather, 'At least one of these contradictory claims is wrong.' In this case, we know the earth goes around the sun; those who think otherwise, *however sincerely*, are simply mistaken. Moreover, our coming to know that the earth goes around the sun was a matter of *discovering* the truth, not *inventing* it. Likewise, moral objectivists see ethics as a matter of discovering objective moral facts about right and wrong, facts that hold even if we sincerely disagree with them. Hence, according to the objectivist, if there's a moral disagreement, the fact that some people think one way and others think another way simply means that some people's beliefs are mistaken.

William Lane Craig defines moral objectivism as the view that:

> moral values . . . are valid and binding whether anybody believes in them or not. Thus, to say, for example, that the Holocaust was objectively wrong is to say that it was wrong even though the Nazis who carried it out thought that it was right and that it would still have been wrong even if the Nazis had won World War II and succeeded in exterminating or brain-washing everyone who disagreed with them.[2]

As Thomas L. Carson and Paul K. Moser explain, *meta-ethical relativism* or *subjectivism* 'states that moral judgements are not objectively true or false and thus that different individuals or societies can hold conflicting moral judgements without any of them being mistaken.'[3] According to subjectivism, the belief that slavery is okay and the belief that it is not are *equally valid*, there being *no objective fact of the matter*. This contradicts the first premise of the moral argument, by claiming not merely that we cannot *know* what is objectively right in ethics (moral scepticism), but that *there is nothing that is objective in ethics to be known* (moral relativism or subjectivism).

Question:
Richard Dawkins says that there is a distinction 'between ideas that are false or true about the real world (factual matters, in the broad sense) and ideas about what we ought to do . . . for which the words "true" and "false" have no meaning' ('After-word', in *What Is Your Dangerous Idea?* [ed. John Brockman; Pocket Books, 2006], p. 307). Dawkins also asserts that religious faith is 'a major force for evil in the world' ('Imagine No Religion', http://old.richarddawkins.net/articles/1-imagine-no-religion). Which logical fallacy results from putting these two claims together?

✔ According to moral objectivism, moral truths exist independently of the knowing subject and are discovered rather than invented. Moral subjectivism denies this.

Let's examine two common arguments for subjectivism:

8.1.1 Outlook difference argument

One of the main arguments for subjectivism is the 'outlook difference argument',[4] an example of which is provided by Jordan, Lockyer and Tate in their textbook *Philosophy of Religion for A Level*: 'The fact that no one can establish the exact rules of this law [objective morality] calls its objectivity into question, thus supporting a human as opposed to divine origin.'[5]

Suppose one culture believes killing cows is wrong, and another culture believes it is acceptable. There's certainly a difference in moral opinion here; there is no *agreement* on what is right and wrong. It is sometimes argued that the mere fact of moral disagreement is evidence for moral subjectivism. However, to make the outlook difference argument valid, we'd have to supply the missing second premise. The most plausible candidate is: 'If a claim is subject to unresolved dispute among thoughtful people, then it isn't objectively true.' That is:

1. Claims about ethics are subject to unresolved dispute among thoughtful people
2. If a claim is subject to unresolved dispute among thoughtful people, then it isn't objectively true
3. Therefore, claims about ethics are not objectively true (i.e. subjectivism is correct)

However, the required additional second premise is false. As atheist Russ Shafer-Landau points out: 'we aren't entitled to conclude, from the fact that even brilliant physicists disagree amongst themselves, that there are no objective truths within fundamental physics . . . If scientific disagreements don't undermine the objective status of science, then moral disagreements shouldn't undermine the objective status of morality.'[6]

Moreover, advancing the outlook difference argument puts the subjectivist in a self-contradictory position. Since 1) moral subjectivism is itself the subject of unresolved dispute among thoughtful people, granting the principle that 2) 'if a claim is the subject of unresolved dispute among thoughtful people, then it isn't objectively true' leads to the conclusion that 3) moral subjectivism is not objectively true (i.e. it is false)! This conclusion is entailed by our two premises, and the first premise is clearly true, so moral subjectivists must reject the second premise. But once they do that, the outlook difference argument collapses.

There's no necessary link between what people *believe* to be the case and what is the case (as is proven by the fact that people can have false beliefs). Some people *believe* the Easter Bunny is real. This doesn't stop it being *objectively true* that the Easter Bunny isn't real!

✔ Just because people disagree about something doesn't mean that there's no fact of the matter

8.1.2 Objectivism is dangerous and intolerant

Another common argument for moral subjectivism is that moral objectivism is dangerous because it causes us to condemn other moral outlooks, whereas subjectivism is accepting of other viewpoints. Subjectivism avoids, so it is claimed, the persecutions and horrific acts that have so often been justified by an appeal to moral objectivism.

Objectivists point out that subjectivism avoids such outcomes at the expense of accepting all moral viewpoints, including viewpoints that endorse the horrific acts sometimes committed in the name of objectivism, acts to which only objectivists can coherently object. Moreover, subjectivism is *not* accepting of all viewpoints, for it refuses to accept the viewpoint of the objectivist.

The 'objectivism is dangerous' argument was well by put by Rebecca Massey-Chase: 'with relativism there is the danger of people not being able to enforce their views on others. But is this dangerous? The danger of religious fundamentalism seems to me a far greater one, if it means putting social laws in place to ensure no divergence without punishment from what is accepted by the religious majority as best for society.'[7]

There are several problems with this objection. First, it confuses *objectivism* with *absolutism*. Objectivism, which the moral argument depends upon, says that there are objective moral values. Absolutism, which the moral argument does not depend upon, is the claim to *know absolutely* what is right and wrong, and is sometimes accompanied by the idea that those who disagree should be forced to toe the line. Absolutism may be dangerous, but the supporter of the moral argument needn't be an absolutist.

Second, although a belief's being dangerous doesn't entail that it is false, it may be argued that it is in fact subjectivism rather than objectivism that's dangerous, because subjectivism eliminates moral debate between people or cultures. A subjectivist viewing the atrocities of Nazi Germany could not say that it was any worse than a liberal society, and therefore could not object to or interfere with that regime *on moral grounds*. They could only object and interfere on non-moral grounds (e.g. 'We don't like that and we're stronger than you'). Divorcing the decision to use force to interfere in situations we dislike from any consideration of moral grounds is surely a dangerous move.

Anyone condemning intolerance is either appealing to an objective moral value (that we objectively *ought* to be tolerant), or not. If they are appealing to an objective value, they cannot criticize moral objectivism without contradicting themselves. If they reject the *objective* value of tolerance, then they have to admit that *intolerance is not objectively wrong*. By definition, the subjectivist's condemnation of intolerance is a subjective condemnation *of equal status with the intolerance it condemns*. It would seem, therefore, that those who really value tolerance should embrace moral objectivism. Paul Copan explains:

> Although many accuse [objectivists] of intolerance, these accusers most likely have an unclear and distorted notion of what tolerance really is. They often are unaware that the concept of tolerance implies a close relationship to truth. Contrary to popular definitions, true tolerance means 'putting up with error' – not 'being accepting of all views.' We don't tolerate what we enjoy or approve of . . . By definition, what we tolerate is what we disapprove of or what we believe to be false and erroneous.[8]

Indeed, the traditional meaning of 'tolerance' *requires* moral objectivity: 'For we tolerate only real evils, in order to prevent worse evils. We do not tolerate good; we promote it.'[9]

✔ Only moral objectivists can coherently believe that they objectively should be appropriately humble, gentle and tolerant concerning matters of moral disagreement

Let us now examine a number of arguments for moral objectivism.

8.1.3 Subjectivism makes it impossible to criticize others

If one accepts subjectivism, and follows it through consistently, then one would have to acknowledge that all ethical standpoints are equally valid. In which case, one would have to regard the Nazi opinion that 'Jews are the plague of the earth and should be exterminated' as being just as valid as the opinion that 'Jews are human beings and should be treated as such'. This is surely a significant problem with subjectivism, for the simple reason that it conflicts with the moral intuitions that a) some moral claims are true and others are false (e.g. Jews deserve respect and should not be exterminated), and that b) false moral beliefs should be opposed. As Francis J. Beckwith and Gregory Koukl explain: 'When right or wrong are a matter of personal choice, we surrender the privilege of making moral judgements on others' actions. But if our moral intuition rebels against these consequences of relativism – if we're sure that some things must be wrong and that some judgements against another's conduct are justified – then relativism is false.'[10] If our moral intuition tells us that something like the Holocaust is objectively *wrong*, then we must reject subjectivism, because it directly contradicts this intuition (without adequate supporting reasons). However, if our intuitions don't tell us this, or if we're willing to forgo our moral intuitions, we can accept subjectivism with integrity. But in that case we cannot claim that any act, however atrocious, is objectively *wrong*. As atheist Stephen Law argues:

> The relativist who points a finger at the Westerner who judges female circumcision to be wrong and says 'It's wrong of you to judge!' ends up condemning themselves. For of course *they* are doing exactly what they are saying you shouldn't be doing . . . notice that it's only if we reject moral relativism that we are free to promote tolerance and open-mindedness as universal virtues . . . Relativists can't consistently condemn the intolerance of others. It's only those who *reject* relativism that are free to do that.[11]

8.1.4 Moral progress

It seems obvious that great moral reforms have come about when one person, or a group of people, has stood out against the ethical assumptions of their generation and by so doing have not merely changed things, but changed them *for the better*. The abolition of the slave trade was brought about because William Wilberforce and his friends believed that it was objectively wrong, and worked to convince other people of this fact.

But if subjectivism is accepted, then the change from a society that traded people to one that didn't was not *progress*, because for the subjectivist *there can be no moral progress, only change*. On the subjectivist's theory there is no objective value added between slave-trading Britain and non-slave-trading Britain, because there is no objective value to add. This is where the acceptance of subjectivism leads us. Here's the same ethical dilemma put in general terms:

- Does one maintain that subjectivism is true, and therefore accept that one cannot progress morally, or does one reject subjectivism in favour of objectivism and so comply with the intuition that a state without the slave trade is better than one with the slave trade?

One can't have it both ways. Either subjectivism or our intuition that some things are objectively wrong must go out the window. Which horn of the dilemma is most plausible? According to the objectivist, the proposition that some things are wrong (e.g. slavery, torturing babies for fun) is more plausible (one can simply take these as properly basic intuitions) than the claim that subjectivism is true. Indeed, because there seem to be no credible arguments *for* subjectivism, even a weak reason to accept objectivism would settle the dispute between the two views. But the intuition that it is objectively wrong to torture a baby for fun is surely quite a strong reason to think that objectivism is true! In other words, the burden of proof should be shouldered by the subjectivist, and that burden has not been met. As atheist Kai Nielsen argues: 'moral truisms . . . are as available to me or to any atheist as they are to the believer [in God]. You can be . . . confident of the correctness or, if you will, the [objective] truth of these moral utterances . . . They are more justified than any sceptical philosophical theory that would lead you to question them.'[12]

✔ Subjectivism shoulders a heavy burden of proof that it fails to meet

Remember, according to the moral argument, while non-theists can *recognize* and even *defend* the objectivity of morality without reference to God, they cannot coherently account for the *existence* of objective moral values.

8.1.5 Intuitions and objectivism

In working out which possibility is the case – objectivism or subjectivism – the only data we have to hand is our moral intuitions, which can be divided into several 'particular' moral intuitions and one 'general' moral intuition. The former are intuitions about *particular things* being objectively right or wrong (e.g. kindness or murder). The latter intuition is about *whether anything at all is objectively right or wrong.*

For example, I find myself with the properly basic intuition that torturing a baby for fun is wrong. Such torture isn't *merely* something that stops the baby functioning as it otherwise would (an empirical observation), or something I feel bad about because of my species' evolutionary history, or something my society has decided not to endorse. Torturing a baby for fun is *something that is objectively wrong. So at least one thing is objectively wrong.* Therefore, *subjectivism is false.*

I have a number of such properly basic moral intuitions (e.g. the slave trade was wrong, the Holocaust was wrong). I needn't take an *absolutist* attitude towards these truth-claims. I allow that I *could* be mistaken about these intuitions (although I don't think I am). However, even *this* admission of moral fallibility contains, and endorses, the *general* intuition that 'particular moral claims are either objectively true or objectively false.' If subjectivism were true, then none of my moral intuitions could be false! The intuition that it is possible to have mistaken moral opinions entails that subjectivism is false. Indeed, if people don't in fact share this intuition of objectivity, why do they worry so much about making *the right* ethical decision?

✔ If it's possible to have mistaken moral intuitions, then moral objectivism must be true

8.1.6 Arguments for moral subjectivism are not obligatory

If someone argues for subjectivism, they seem to rely upon assumptions they deny; for if there are no objective moral values then it can't be objectively true that I *ought* to consider the relativist's arguments, or that I *ought* to consider them fairly, or that I *ought* to value truth over falsehood in such a way that I *should* accept the relativist's conclusion if I find their arguments persuasive. The relativist might say that arguments can have the effect of persuading people even if no argument *ought* to persuade anyone (e.g. people may simply be in the habit of allowing arguments to change their minds), but this response drives a wedge between the acknowledgement that a proposition is true and the acknowledgement that one ought to believe it that's highly counterintuitive.

Indeed, since the subjectivist cannot say that we objectively *ought* to reject beliefs we have sufficient reason to doubt, why shouldn't I believe that objectivism is true *even if I were given sufficient reason to doubt it*? For the subjectivist there can be no *objective* moral 'shouldn't' about it! Knowing this, how could I view any argument against objectivism as requiring my attention, let alone my assent? To consider any such argument as objectively persuasive would be to embrace the self-contradictory position that: a) there are no objective moral values, and b) one objectively *ought* to accept subjectivism.

> **Listen:**
> Peter Kreeft, 'A Refutation of Moral Relativism' www.peterkreeft.com/audio/05_ relativism.htm.

8.2 If Objective Moral Values Exist, a God Exists

The moral argument claims that there's a link between moral objectivism on the one hand and the existence of a 'god' on the other. For morality to be objective, it cannot be rooted in finite persons, but must transcend individual and corporate humanity. As C.S. Lewis writes: 'The Law of . . . Right and Wrong, must be something above and beyond the actual facts of human behaviour. In this case, besides the actual facts, you have something else – a real law which we did not invent and which we know we ought to obey.'[13] However, because objective morality *prescribes* and *obligates* our behaviour, it must be rooted in *something personal*, since only persons can prescribe and obligate behaviour. Therefore, there must be a personal moral-law prescriber and obligator beyond individual and collective humanity.

In any true apprehension of the moral law we experience ourselves as the subject of a transcendent *intentionality* that is *about* what we should or should not do; and we recognize that this transcendent intentionality not only demands, but is worthy of our obedience. The reality of such a transcendent intentionality is incompatible with a naturalistic world-view. Hence atheist Michael Ruse states: 'if you stay with naturalism, then there is no foundation, and in this sense substantive ethics is an illusion.'[14] As Beckwith and Koukl note: 'A command only makes sense when there are two minds involved, one giving the command and one receiving it.'[15] If an objective moral duty is a command that humans receive and are obligated to obey, there must be an objective and personal moral commander. As H.P. Owen argues:

> On the one hand [objective moral] claims transcend every human person . . . On the other hand . . . it is contradictory to assert that impersonal claims are entitled to the allegiance of our wills. The only solution to this paradox is to suppose that the order of [objective moral] claims . . . is in fact rooted in the personality of God.[16]

Since it would be incoherent to ground objective moral duties in an *evil* personality, they must be grounded in a *good* personality. Indeed, as the ground of a moral law that requires and deserves our absolute adherence, the divine personality must be *wholly good*, such that 'the Good is determined paradigmatically by God's own character.'[17]

Watch:
J.P. Moreland, 'Arguing God from Moral Law' www.closertotruth.com/video-pro-file/Arguing-God-from-Moral-Law-J-P-Moreland-/222.

8.3 What Sort of 'God'?

What else can be concluded concerning the being who grounds moral values? For one thing, since the objective moral laws are necessary and eternal truths (e.g. the fact that it's wrong to torture babies is like the fact that 2 + 2 = 4) the transcendent personal being in which the moral law is rooted must likewise be necessary and eternal. For another, we *know about* this objective moral law (however imperfectly) through our moral intuitions, which enable us to grasp that 'I *ought* to do this' or 'I *ought not* to do that.' Our ability to intuit right and wrong is best explained by positing our creation as moral agents by the moral lawgiver. Our creator *relates* to us through our moral intuitions, since any 'ought' implies not merely an impersonal 'fact' but a duty-owing relationship to someone (e.g. 'I ought to keep my promise to help Fred study philosophy'). That is, in addition to having a duty to Fred, we have a duty to the personal objective lawgiver behind the objective rightness of keeping a promise to Fred.

Thus we have established the existence of an objective, transcendent, intentional, necessary and eternal, wholly good personal being who is the source of objective moral obligation, and who created humans as moral agents able to relate to their creator through their perception of the moral law.

8.4 Three Objections to the Moral Argument

There are a number of common objections to the moral argument besides the attempt to deny moral objectivism:

8.4.1 Falling short of God

Jordan, Lockyer and Tate observe that 'if we accept that morality points us to belief in a law-giver and belief in a source for our conscience, all we have established is that there is a law-giver of some description. It does not establish the existence of the omnipotent, omnibenevolent God of Classical Theism.'[18] If one expects the moral argument to take you to the God of classical theism, one has misunderstood it. No argument can take you further than the premises allow, and the premises of the moral argument only allow us to reach a personal, eternal source of objective morality who has a relationship with us through our moral intuitions. Hence the argument both disproves naturalism and supports a minimal form of theism; which is quite good going.

✔ The moral argument doesn't prove that the Christian God exists, but it does prove that theism is true whereas atheism is false!

8.4.2 Atheists can be good

Richard Dawkins responds to the moral argument by observing that belief in God isn't necessary for *knowing* about morality, or for *being* moral. Indeed; the apostle Paul wrote that 'when Gentiles, who do not have the law, do by nature things required by the law, they are a law for themselves, even though they do not have the law, since they show that *the requirements of the law are written on their hearts, their consciences also bearing witness,* and their thoughts now accusing, now *even defending them'* (Romans 2:14–15, my italics).

Dawkins' observations are beside the point. The moral argument doesn't claim that atheists can't *distinguish* between good and evil, or that they cannot be good without *belief* in God. Rather, the moral argument claims that there could not be such a thing as objective good (or evil) if a 'god' did not exist. As Paul Copan writes, the moral argument urges that although '*belief* in God isn't a requirement for being moral . . . the *existence* of a personal God is crucial for a coherent understanding of objective morality.'[19]

✔ Atheists can be good, but only because God exists!

Dawkins accepts the premise that if a god doesn't exist, then objective moral values don't exist: 'The universe that we observe has precisely the properties we should expect if there is, at bottom, no design, no purpose [that is, no god], *no evil, no good,* nothing but pitiless indifference.'[20] Again, Dawkins concedes that 'it is pretty hard to defend absolutist [i.e. objective] morals on grounds other than religious ones.'[21] Dawkins therefore evades the moral argument at the terribly high price of denying moral objectivism. This denial renders his moral critique of religion either self-contradictory (if it assumes objective moral values) or toothless (if it assumes subjectivism).

The denial of objective moral value also removes any basis for Dawkins' evident expectation that we *should* attend carefully to his arguments and that we *ought* to change our views if we find them convincing! How can anyone be convinced to adopt a worldview which denies that anyone *should* ever be convinced of anything? As Stephen Unwin comments: 'As for Dawkins' assertion that moral behaviour for believers is simply "sucking up to God", or that morality doesn't need faith . . . such observations miss the more fundamental question of why we have moral or aesthetic values at all – such as the ones by which Dawkins, myself and others venerate rational analysis.'[22]

8.4.3 Euthyphro's dilemma

In Plato's *Euthyphro* dialogue, Socrates asks: 'Is what is holy holy because the gods approve it, or do they approve it because it is holy?'[23] This question poses a dilemma: are God's commands arbitrary, or is there some standard of goodness independent of God's commands to which his commands must conform in order to be good? We either ground morality in God's commands or not. If we ground them in God's commands, morality becomes arbitrary (things are 'good' only because God commands it – and he could have commanded the opposite). If we don't ground morality in God's commands, morality must be independent of God's commands – in which case why bring God into our explanation of morality?

✔ The Euthyphro dilemma is a false dilemma: God's commandments flow from his wholly good moral character

Euthyphro's dilemma is a 'false dilemma.' There's a third option: that objective morality is part of God's unchanging character. Hence there *is* something above God's *commands*, but that something is God's *character*. God's commands must be 'in character', and his character paradigmatically defines 'the good.' The moral argument concludes with a being whose 'good' essence is necessary and eternal (thus objective) and from whom we inherit non-arbitrary moral duties. This avoids the Euthyphro 'dilemma':

> Plato himself saw the solution to this objection: you split the horns of the dilemma by formulating a third alternative, namely, God is the Good. The Good is the moral nature of God himself . . . God *is* necessarily holy, loving, kind, just, and so on, and these attributes of God comprise the Good. God's moral character expresses itself towards us in the form of certain commandments, which become for us our moral duties. Hence God's commandments are not arbitrary, but necessarily flow from his own nature. They are necessary expressions of the way God is.[24]

Watch:
William Lane Craig, 'What Is the Euthyphro Dilemma?' www.youtube.com/watch?v=IgGB4Oxs5VU.

Conclusion

The moral argument does *not* claim that humans can't *know about right and wrong* unless they know about God, or read the Bible. The moral argument does *not* claim that humans can't *make the right moral choices* unless they believe in God. The moral argument claims that there cannot *be such a thing as an objective right and wrong,* unless a transcendent, morally perfect and personal 'god' *exists* to 'ground' it. Only a person can prescribe and/ or obligate *moral* behaviour; but only a transcendent person can ground an *objective* moral prescription and/or obligation. Given that anything is objectively right or wrong (a claim it is self-contradictory to deny), it follows that such an all-good personal deity exists.

Watch:
Doug Powell, 'The Moral Argument' http://youtu.be/i2h7PFg5Dwk.

Films to watch and discuss:
Rope, directed by Alfred Hitchcock (Universal, 1948) (PG)
Amazing Grace, directed by Michael Apted (20th Century Fox, 2006) (PG) – Did Wilberforce and his friends simply *change* Britain, or did they change it *for the better*?

* * *

Recommended Resources

Video

CNN. 'Prominent Atheist Blogger Leah Libresco Converts to Catholicism' http://youtu.be/L5DOeokjHlU.
*Craig, William Lane. 'Can We Be Good without God?' http://winteryknight.wordpress.com/2012/06/21/william-lane-craig-lectures-on-the-moral-argument-at-georgia-tech/.
— vs Louise Antony. 'Is God Necessary for Morality? Part 1' www.rfmedia.org/av/video/is-god-necessary-for-morality-craig-vs-antony-1/ and 'Part 2' www.rfmedia.org/av/video/is-god-necessary-for-morality-craig-vs-antony-2/.
Greg Koukl vs John Baker. 'Do Moral Truths Exist?' http://youtu.be/yIgktzBG9Hk.
Turek, Frank vs Christopher Hitchens. 'Does God Exist?' www.youtube.com/watch?v=M-R2wtrD8HnM.
Williams, Peter S. and William Lane Craig vs Andrew Copson and Arif Ahmed. 'Cambridge Union: This House Believes God Is Not a Delusion' www.bethinking.org/who-are-you-god/advanced/cambridge-union-society-debate-an-analysis.htm.
*Williams, Peter S. 'The Moral Argument for God' YouTube Playlist www.youtube.com/playlist?list=PLQhh3qcwVEWhOfs_uQrFceuBRfMF1asf4.

Audio

Craig, William Lane. Defenders Podcast, series 2, parts 19–22 www.reasonablefaith.org/defenders-2-podcast/s4.
Koukl, Gregory. 'Relativism' www.apologetics315.com/2008/12/relativism-by-greg-koukl-mp3-audio.html.

— vs John Baker. 'Do Moral Truths Exist?' http://j.mp/Apologetics315-DebateKoukl-Baker.

*Kreeft, Peter. 'A Refutation of Moral Relativism' www.peterkreeft.com/audio/05_relativism.htm.

McDowell, Sean vs James Corbett. 'Is God the Best Explanation of Moral Values?' www.brianauten.com/Apologetics/mcdowell-corbett-debate.mp3.

Williams, Peter S. 'An Introduction to Ethics' www.damaris.org/cm/podcasts/646.

*— 'Meta-Ethics and God' www.damaris.org/cm/podcasts/528.

— 'The Problem of Goodness' www.damaris.org/cm/podcasts/588.

— and Christopher Norris. 'The Cardiff God Debate' www.damaris.org/cm/podcasts/786.

Online papers

Beckwith, Francis J. 'Why I Am Not a Moral Relativist' www.lastseminary.com/moral-argument/Why%20I%20am%20Not%20a%20Moral%20Relativist.pdf.

Copan, Paul. 'Can Michael Martin Be a Moral Realist?' www.paulcopan.com/articles/pdf/Michael-Martin-a-moral-realist.pdf.

— 'God, Naturalism and the Foundations of Morality' www.paulcopan.com/articles/pdf/God-naturalism-morality.pdf.

— 'The Moral Argument for God's Existence' www.4truth.net/fourtruthpbgod.aspx?pageid=8589952712.

— 'Morality and Meaning without God: Another Failed Attempt' www.paulcopan.com/articles/pdf/morality-meaning.pdf.

*Craig, William Lane. 'The Indispensability of Theological Meta-Ethical Foundations for Morality' www.reasonablefaith.org/site/News2?page=NewsArticle&id=5175.

Geisler, Norman L. 'Any Absolutes? Absolutely' www.equip.org/articles/any-absolutes-absolutely/.

Koukl, Gregory. 'Seven Things You Can't Do as a Moral Relativist' www.salvomag.com/new/articles/salvo1/koukl.php.

— and Francis Beckwith. 'What Is Moral Relativism?' www.bethinking.org/resource.php?ID=229&TopicID=10&CategoryID=9.

Kreeft, Peter. 'The Argument from Conscience' www.peterkreeft.com/topics/conscience.htm.

Lovell, Steven. 'God as the Grounding of Moral Objectivity: Defending against Euthyphro' http://myweb.tiscali.co.uk/annotations/euthyphro.html.

Moreland, J.P. 'The Ethical Inadequacy of Naturalism' www.lastseminary.com/moral-argument/The%20Ethical%20Inadequacy%20of%20Naturalism.pdf.

Williams, Peter S. 'Amazing Grace' www.bethinking.org/right-wrong/introductory/amazing-grace.htm.

*— 'Can Moral Objectivism Do without God?' www.bethinking.org/right-wrong/advanced/can-moral-objectivism-do-without-god.htm.

Books

Baggett, David and Jerry L. Walls. *Good God: The Theistic Foundations of Morality* (Oxford University Press, 2011).

*Beckwith, Francis J. and Gregory Koukl. *Relativism: Feet Firmly Planted in Mid-Air* (Grand Rapids, MI: Baker, 1998).

Copan, Paul. *Is God a Moral Monster? Making Sense of the Old Testament God* (Grand Rapids, MI: Baker, 2011).
— 'A Moral Argument.' Pages 108–23 in *To Everyone an Answer: A Case for the Christian Worldview* (ed. Francis J. Beckwith, William Lane Craig and J.P. Moreland; Downers Grove, IL: IVP, 2004).
— 'The Moral Argument.' Pages 362–72 in *The Routledge Companion to Philosophy of Religion* (ed. Chad Meister and Paul Copan; London: Routledge, 2010).
— and Mark D. Linville. *The Moral Argument* (New York: Continuum, 2013).
Craig, William Lane. *On Guard: Defending Your Faith with Reason and Precision* (Colorado Springs, CO: David C. Cook, 2010).
— and J.P. Moreland, eds. *The Blackwell Companion to Natural Theology* (Oxford: Wiley-Blackwell, 2009).
Garcia, Robert K. and Nathan L. King, eds., *Is Goodness without God Good Enough? A Debate on Faith, Secularism, and Ethics* (Lanham, MD: AltaMira Press, 2009).
Lewis, C.S. *The Abolition of Man* www.columbia.edu/cu/augustine/arch/lewis/abolition1.htm#1.
Owen, H.P. 'Why Morality Implies the Existence of God' from *The Moral Argument for Christian Theism* (London: George Allen & Unwin, 1965) in *Philosophy of Religion: A Guide and Anthology* (ed. Brian Davies; Oxford University Press, 2000).
Ritchie, Angus. *From Morality to Metaphysics: The Theistic Implications of our Ethical Commitments* (Oxford University Press, 2012).
Sorley, W.R. *Moral Values and the Idea of God* (Cambridge University Press, 2nd edn, 1921).
Williams, Peter S. *C.S. Lewis vs the New Atheists* (Milton Keynes: Paternoster Press, 2013).
— *The Case for God* (Crowborough: Monarch, 1999).
Wood, W. Jay. *God* (Durham: Acumen, 2011).

9. The Ontological Argument

If God is possible then God exists.
Stephen T. Davis[1]

Introduction

The Greek word *ontos* means 'being,' and the ontological argument for God (OA for short) begins with thinking about what sort of being God is supposed to be, particularly what manner of being or existence he's supposed to have if he exists.

Atheist Colin McGinn recalls being 'impressed with the argument'[2] when he first studied it, reporting: 'it left me with a disturbed feeling. A lot of philosophy is like that: gripping, momentous, but also worrying, naggingly so.'[3] He reveals that although the ontological argument doesn't convince him to believe in God, he doesn't 'think there is anything *obviously* wrong with it.'[4] McGinn admits to finding the OA 'as tantalizing as ever' and asks: 'Is this why philosophers sometimes feel as if they are being haunted? Or do I mean persecuted?'[5] Former atheist Trent

Dougherty explains that Alvin Plantinga's so-called 'modal' version of the ontological argument forced him to 'conclude, somewhat reluctantly, that God exists.' He goes on: 'I might add that I am a convert on this argument. I argued for years that the ontological argument was flawed until someone showed me the modal version. I have always followed Reason wherever it [led] and, as usual, it [led] to God.'[6]

The ontological argument was first given in 1078 by a Benedictine monk named Anselm. Philosophers have critiqued and defended many versions of the OA, but Anselm's central insight was that 'God' can be defined as 'a being than which nothing greater can be conceived.' If one could think of a being greater than 'God,' then that greater being, rather than the lesser being, would deserve the title 'God'. Hence *if* God exists, *then* he is *by definition* 'the greatest possible being' or 'the maximally great being' (these superlative phrases mean the same thing).

✔ To say 'God' exists is to say that 'the greatest possible being' exists

A 'great-making property' *is any objective property which* a) *is intrinsically good to have* ('which endows its bearer with some measure of value, or greatness, or metaphysical stature, regardless of external circumstances')[7] *and* b) *has a logical maximum*. For example, *size* isn't a great-making property. A whale isn't more valuable than me just because it's bigger than me; and however large a something you imagine, it's always logically possible to imagine a larger one. Even the universe is expanding, and there is no *logical* limit to how big it can get! On the other hand, *power* is a great-making property, one that has a logical maximum in the quality of being omnipotent. Knowledge is a great-making property, one that has a logical maximum in omniscience. And the goodness of *being* (which is a pre-condition of every other good) is a great-making property that has a logical maximum in necessary being.

Anselm's insight that 'God' *means* 'the greatest possible being' underlies not only the OA, but also the area of philosophical theology known as *perfect-being theology*: 'the core thesis of perfect being theology . . . ascribes to God the greatest possible array of *compossible* great-making properties. An array or collection of properties is compossible just in case it is possible that they all be had by the same individual at the same time, or all together.'[8] Perfect being theology is an important partner in a dialogue with natural theology and systematic theology concerning the nature of God.

The reliance of both the OA and of perfect-being theology upon the concept of great-making properties means that neither will appeal to anyone who adopts a subjective theory of value (cf. chapter 8).

✔ The ontological argument and perfect being theology both depend upon the reality of objective value

Read:
For an application of the ontological argument to perfect-being theology, cf. Peter S. Williams, 'Understanding the Trinity' www.bethinking.org/who-are-you-god/advanced/understanding-the-trinity.htm.

9.1 Ontological Argument I

One (Anselmian) version of the OA claims that, since the concept 'God' exists in the atheist's mind, and since mind-independent existence is a greater sort of existence than mind-dependent existence, then, on pain of self-contradiction, the atheist in whose mind the concept 'God' exists *can't* deny that 'God' must have mind-independent existence. Once the atheist understands both that 'God' *means* 'that than which nothing greater can be conceived' and that mind-independent existence is greater than mind-dependent existence, they can't fail to understand that God must exist! In syllogistic form:

1. It is greater for a thing to exist in the mind *and* in reality than in the mind alone
2. 'God' means 'that than which a greater cannot be conceived'
3. Supposing that 'God' exists in the mind but not in reality, then something greater than 'God' can be conceived (namely, a God who exists in reality as well as in the mind)
4. But something greater than God cannot be conceived (since God is by definition 'that than which a greater cannot be conceived')
5. Therefore, God exists both in the mind *and* in reality

However, there's an important difference between God himself and 'the concept of "God"' that this argument ignores. On the one hand, what exists 'in the mind' is *not* 'that than which nothing greater can be conceived', but rather *the mental concept of* 'that than which nothing greater can be conceived'. On the other hand, what exists 'in reality' if God exists is *not* the mental concept of 'that than which nothing greater can be conceived' (a *concept* can't exist outside a mind), but rather 'that than which nothing greater can be conceived' himself!

Question:
Does the first ontological argument (given above) commit an informal logical fallacy? If so, what fallacy is it?

9.2 Ontological Argument II

Alvin Plantinga kick-started philosophical re-evaluation of the traditional arguments for God by laying out a logically valid version of the OA in his 1974 book *The Nature of Necessity*. Plantinga drew on Leibniz's insight that the OA implicitly assumes that the concept of God (of 'that than which nothing greater can be conceived') is logically coherent. Defining God as a 'maximally great being' (a being who possesses the greatest possible set of great-making properties), Plantinga argued that a maximally great being *must exist if its existence is possible*, because 'necessary existence is a great making property.'[9] Given the additional premise that 'the existence of a maximally great being is *possible*',[10] it follows that a maximally great being therefore 'exists, and exists necessarily.'[11]

Plantinga used the philosophical vocabulary of 'possible worlds' (logically self-consistent descriptions of reality as a whole) and symbolic logic to lay out his argument in technical detail, but his OA can be summarized in ordinary language as follows:[12]

1. It is possible that a maximally great being exists
2. If it is possible that a maximally great being exists, then a maximally great being exists in at least one 'possible world'
3. If a maximally great being exists in one 'possible world', then it exists in every 'possible world'
4. If a maximally great being exists in every 'possible world', then it exists in the actual world (since the actual world is by definition a 'possible world')
5. Therefore, a maximally great being exists

Indeed, the OA can be further condensed into a single logically valid (MP) syllogism:

1. If it is possible that God (a 'maximally great being') exists, then God exists
2. It is possible that God exists
3. Therefore, God exists

This argument shows that 'the person who wishes to deny that God exists must claim that God's existence is impossible.'[13] 'God' is by definition a being whose existence is *either actual* or *impossible*. Therefore, *if* 'God' is not impossible, *then* he must be actual.

Watch:
William Lane Craig, 'What Is the Ontological Argument?' http://youtu.be/W_sCDNFJiHs.

9.2.1 Why God isn't like Nessie

Why would anyone think it is implausible to deny the crucial second premise of this OA? Denying the existence of God is not on a par with denying the existence of the Loch Ness monster. To deny the existence of the Loch Ness monster one needn't claim that its existence is logically impossible, because one can coherently claim that Nessie simply fails to exist *despite its existence being logically possible*. However, to deny the existence of God one does have to make the claim that God's existence is logically impossible (one must reject premise 2 of the above argument), because the OA shows that one cannot coherently claim that God fails to exist *despite being logically possible*.

God isn't the sort of thing that could just happen not to exist. By definition, God's existence is either necessary (and actual) or impossible (and non-actual). Hence *if* God's existence isn't impossible, *then* God's existence is necessary (and hence actual). But claiming that a thing's existence is impossible seems to be a stronger claim than the claim that its existence is possible but non-actual, at least when the thing in question isn't obviously an incoherent concept like a round square. And nobody thinks that the statement 'God exists' is like the statement 'Round squares exist'!

✔ To claim that God exists is obviously not on a par with the claim that round squares exist

Nevertheless, many non-theists are willing to pay the 'price' of making the stronger claim in order to avoid the conclusion of the OA; and this despite the fact that no independent argument has shown the concept of God to be incoherent.[14]

9.2.2 For anyone who already believes . . .

Since the OA is valid, and since the first premise is true by definition, the question is whether or not its second premise is true. If the second premise is true, then this argument is sound. Naturally, anyone who already believes that God exists will believe that it is possible for God to exist, and hence that this ontological argument is sound.

The person in this position might believe in God in a properly basic manner. They might think that a combination of theistic arguments (e.g. the moral, cosmological and design arguments) indicate the existence of a being who is plausibly to be identified as a 'maximally great being' (perhaps on grounds of simplicity). As Charles Hartshorne observes: 'the [Ontological] Argument as it stands does not suffice, except for one who grants that . . . the . . . idea of God is self-consistent. But here the other theistic arguments may help.'[15] Either way (and these 'ways' are not mutually exclusive), anyone with independent grounds for the belief that God exists also has independent grounds for thinking that it is possible for God to exist. And if one has independent grounds for thinking that it is possible for God to exist, then one has independent grounds for thinking that the ontological argument is sound.

Of course, if one's acceptance of the OA is wholly dependent upon such independent grounds, then the OA adds nothing to one's grounds for belief in God, although it might add much to one's *understanding of* God. As Charles Taliaferro writes: 'the ontological argument may be seen as a natural, formal attempt to refine a full-scale concept of excellence or greatness. The intuitions that drive the argument may not solely be intellectual . . . but located in religious life and practice.'[16]

9.2.3 Independent grounds for the possibility of God

Are there, then, any grounds for accepting the crucial second premise of the OA that don't depend wholly upon a prior belief in God, or upon other theistic arguments? Plantinga answers this question by noting that if we carefully consider the second premise, and the alleged objections to it, in the context of our overall noetic structure, and we find insufficient reason to think that the denial of this premise is more plausible than its acceptance, then 'we are within our rational rights in accepting it.'[17]

For example, it seems plausible to say that knowledge and power are both great-making properties (given that one is prepared to grant the objectivity of values, that is, since there can't be any great-making properties if values are merely subjective). And we know that these are compatible properties because humans have both of them to a limited degree. It seems plausible to think that a being could have both great-making properties to a maximal degree. And the same sort of thing goes for other great-making properties such as goodness or beauty. Hence, as Plantinga argues, the OA shows that theism is *at least rational*:

it must be conceded that not everyone who understands and reflects on its central premise – that the existence of a maximally great being is *possible* – will accept it. Still, it is evident, I think, that there is nothing contrary *to reason* or *irrational* in accepting this premise. What I claim for this argument, therefore, is that it establishes, not the *truth* of theism, but its rational acceptability.[18]

Even having the mere *rationality* of theistic belief plausibly demonstrated might be a massive step forward for some non-theists.

Let's think a little more about the position of the non-theist faced with the OA. The argument proves that *if* 'God exists' is a coherent proposition *then* it must also be a true proposition. But as Charles Taliaferro writes: 'it is at least not obvious that the belief that God exists is incoherent. Indeed, a number of atheists think God might exist, but conclude God does not.'[19] For example, atheist Klemens Kappel acknowledges that he can't provide 'reasons to think that such a being [God] could not even possibly exist', affirming, 'I don't think I can give such a reason; I think it's a possibility.'[20] However, anyone who believes with Klemens that God's existence is 'a possibility' but that God doesn't exist on the one hand, and who understands the OA on the other hand, will see that these beliefs form a self-contradictory set. One way to resolve this contradiction is by accepting the existence of God. Consider the conclusion to Trent Dougherty's discussion of the OA:

> Since all efforts to show that the concept of God is contradictory have failed heretofore I conclude, somewhat reluctantly, that God exists . . . I realize that to the average person, this seems like a trick, but the average person is not particularly accustomed to following logical arguments at all, much less highly specialized forms of logical calculi developed by professional philosophers. Most professors at the University level don't even know modal logic and many have never studied it and some have never heard of it. What do those who know it, but don't believe in God say? They say that the concept of God is incoherent. I have not yet seen an even slightly plausible argument to that effect. Until I do, the OA will be cogent to me.[21]

Thus the OA can move someone from atheism or agnosticism to theism.

9.2.4 Reverse-engineering the ontological argument

Of course, as Dougherty notes, an alternative way out of the self-contradictory position of the non-theist who believes that God could but does not exist is to deny that God could possibly exist. Indeed, anyone sufficiently committed to denying the existence of God will turn the OA on its head, as follows:

1. If it is possible that God exists, then God exists
2. God does not exist
3. Therefore, it is not possible that God exists

The OA thus tends to polarize non-believers into atheists prepared to claim that 'God exists' is an incoherent proposition, and theists! This 'negative' OA (which assumes rather than proves that God doesn't exist) is logically valid. Moreover, it shares its first premise with the positive OA. The question is whether or not the second premise is true. The person who rejects the OA on the grounds that they believe that God doesn't exist and/or that God's existence is impossible is in a position that parallels the person who accepts the OA because they believe that God exists and/or that God's existence is possible. After all, proving the *rationality* of theistic belief, which task Plantinga claims the OA accomplishes, is not automatically the same thing as proving the *irrationality* of atheism.

✔ One might think that the OA shows the rationality of theism without showing the irrationality of atheism

9.3 Three Issues to Debate and Five Objections

At this point, then, the debate between theist and atheist must involve the following issues:

1. Objections to the OA that the supporter of the argument must rebut
2. Any independent grounds for believing that God exists or does not exist (e.g. other theistic arguments versus arguments for atheism)
3. Any independent grounds for believing that God's properties are incoherent (e.g. the atheist trying to show that the concept of omnipotence is in some way incoherent, like the concept of a round square)

With respect to issue 3), we can observe that the burden of proof is clearly on the atheist. Moreover, there's no obligation to attribute *impossible* properties to the greatest *possible* being! Rather, theists can shape their understanding of the divine properties so that they don't fall foul of any proven incoherence. For example, can God create a stone he can't move? If he can, then there's something he can't do (i.e. move the stone); but if he can't, then there's still something he can't do (i.e. create something he can't move).

Either way, there's something God can't do. But this doesn't mean that God can't be 'omnipotent.' Rather, it means that omnipotence should be defined as 'the ability to do anything *that's logically possible.*' Anything that's logically impossible isn't a *thing* that could be done. Like 'creating a round square', 'creating a stone that God can't move' simply isn't a logically possible thing that anyone, including God, could do. God's inability to create a stone he couldn't subsequently move is thus no more a refutation of his omnipotence than his inability to create a round square.[22] As a general rule, then, arguments about the coherence of divine properties are arguments *within* the discipline of perfect-being theology that help us understand what it means to claim that there is a greatest possible being; they are not arguments *against* the existence of a greatest possible being. As atheist Richard Carrier acknowledges, arguments for thinking that 'God' is an incoherent concept are 'not valid, since any definition of god (or his properties) that is illogical can just be revised to be logical. So in effect, Arguments from Incoherence aren't really arguments for atheism, but for the reform of theology.'[23]

Since we cover issue ii) in other chapters of this book, we will focus our attention upon rebutting five objections to the OA.

9.3.1 Objection 1: The 'most perfect island' objection

Starting with Gaunilo of Marmoutiers in the eleventh century, philosophers have critiqued the OA by suggesting that if it were logically valid then one could use it to prove the existence of all sorts of patently ridiculous things, from 'the most perfect island conceivable' (Gaunilo's example), to fairies. The thought is that since these results are patently absurd, the OA must be invalid. That is, such 'parodies' of the OA are an attempt at a *reductio ad absurdum* of the argument.

However, such arguments fail to attend to the crucial role played by great-making properties (especially necessary existence), and/or the uniqueness of the concept of 'the greatest possible being', in the OA. As William Lane Craig observes:

> the properties that go to make up maximal excellence as Plantinga defines it have intrinsic maximum values, whereas the excellent-making properties of things like islands do not. For example, omniscience is the property of knowing only and all truths. It is impossible to know any more truths than that. By contrast, in the case of islands, there could always be more palm trees or native dancing girls! Thus there cannot be a most perfect or greatest conceivable island.[24]

Atheist philosopher Yujin Nagasawa agrees: 'For any island i it is always possible to make i greater by adding, for example, one more beautiful palm tree or one more pleasant beach. The island objection is, therefore, unsucessful.'[25]

Once, when I presented the OA in a debate at the Cambridge Union, a member of the audience objected that the same logic could surely prove the existence of 'the stupidest possible being.' My reply was brief but to the point: 'Stupidity is not a great-making property!'[26]

9.3.2 Objection 2: The 'quasi-maximal being' objection

Consider the concept of a 'quasi-maximally great' being. This might be a being that is like God in every respect except that its knowledge isn't perfect. Why treat the premise 'It is possible that God exists' as more plausibly true than the premise 'It is possible that a quasi-maximally great being exists'? If it is rational to think that 'God's existence is possible' is true, isn't it *equally* rational to think that 'The existence of a quasi-maximally great being is possible' is true? And wouldn't this undermine the claim that the crucial premise of the OA is true? Craig doesn't think so:

> Since a maximally great being is by definition omnipotent, no concrete object can exist independently of its creative power. As an omnipotent being, a maximally great being must have the power to freely refrain from creating anything at all, so that there must be possible worlds in which nothing other than the maximally great being exists. But that entails that if maximal greatness is possibly exemplified, then quasi-maximally greatness . . . would lack necessary existence . . .[27]

The same conclusion would seem to follow from the observation that 'aseity' – the property of being the cause of any and all things other than oneself – is a great-making property.[28] If Craig is right, no argument can make us believe in a quasi-maximally great being without begging the question against the OA: 'our intuition that a maximally great being is possible is not undermined by the claim that a quasi-maximally great being is also intuitively possible, for we see that the latter intuition depends upon the assumption that a maximally great being cannot possibly exist, which begs the question.'[29]

One might describe a human being as a quasi-maximally great being on the grounds that a human exhibits non-maximal degrees of several great-making properties (e.g. power, knowledge, goodness), but the existence of humans is obviously not a *reductio* of the OA. The existence of quasi-maximally great beings that might be thought to constitute a *reductio* of the OA seems to be less plausible than their non-existence inasmuch as no one actually worries about their existence until they bring them up as an *ad hoc* objection to the OA: 'quasi-deities are "cooked up" philosophical examples . . . But this is not so in the case of God. God's existence is a real question of philosophical inquiry; it is not adventitious.'[30]

Richard Swinburne observes that it's simpler 'to posit either zero or infinity as the measure of [a great-making property] than to posit some inexplicably finite measure [and this means that it] would be more plausible to think that maximal greatness is possibly instantiated than quasi-maximal greatness.'[31]

9.3.3 Objection 3: The 'you can't define God into existence' objection

Richard Dawkins summarizes Anselm's ontological argument as follows:

> It is possible to conceive, Anselm said, of a being than which nothing greater can be conceived. Even an atheist can conceive of such a superlative being, though he would deny its existence in the real world. But, goes the argument, a being that doesn't exist in the real world is, by that very fact, less than perfect. Therefore we have a contradiction and, hey presto.[32]

Dawkins clearly has in mind the invalid version of the OA that equivocates between God existing in the mind and in reality. He calls the OA 'infantile',[33] asking: 'isn't it too good to be true that a grand truth about the cosmos should follow from a mere word game?'[34] Dawkins asserts that the idea of any OA working 'offends me aesthetically.'[35] This response is clearly more of a question-begging psychological report than an argument (he simply *asserts* that the OA is 'trickery' and a 'mere word game'). Indeed, Dawkins admits he has 'an automatic, deep suspicion of any line of reasoning that reached such a significant conclusion without feeding in a single piece of data from the real world. Perhaps that indicates no more than that I am a scientist rather than a philosopher. Philosophers down through centuries have indeed taken the ontological argument seriously, both for and against.'[36] As Douglas Groothuis complains: 'As a naïve empiricist, [Dawkins] simply finds absurd the idea that an argument could prove God's existence without appeal to empirical evidence. But Dawkins' glib rejection never engages the richness or subtlety of the argument, a piece of reasoning that has intrigued some of the best minds in philosophy.'[37]

Perhaps Dawkins' suspicion of the OA would be lessened by Yujin Nagasawa's observation that 'it is known that we *can* derive *a priori* the non-existence of some beings (e.g. a square circle, a married bachelor, etc.)'.[39] If we can derive the *non*-existence of something *a priori*, why not the *existence* of something?

Maybe Dawkins' suspicion is grounded in the mistaken belief that the OA reaches its conclusion 'without feeding in a single piece of data from the real world', where 'data' and 'the real world' are taken to mean not merely *empirical* data from the *natural* world, but any propositional content at all beyond that contained within the definition of God as the 'greatest possible being.'[38] As Stephen T. Davis points out, while many critics see the OA as trying to prove the existence of God by simply analyzing the concept of God:

> This oft-repeated claim is . . . quite mistaken. It is true that Anselm's definition of God – 'that being than which no greater can be conceived' – is crucial to his argument . . . but merely analysing that concept will get one nowhere in proving the existence in reality of anything. One must also bring into consideration what Anselm surely took to be certain necessary truths (e.g. *a thing is greater if it exists both in the mind and in reality than if it exists merely in the mind* and *the existence of the* [*greatest conceivable being*] *is possible*). These claims are essential aspects of the OA, and do not follow merely from an examination of any concept of God.[39]

One *suspects* that Dawkins believes that 'non-empirical data' is a contradiction in terms. One would of course respond to such a view by pointing out that since the proposition 'non-empirical data is a contradiction in terms' isn't something that could be known though empirical data, it is itself a self-contradictory proposition!

As Jim Holt observes, Dawkins 'dismisses [Anselm's] ontological argument as "infantile" and "dialectical prestidigitation" without quite identifying the defect in its logic. He seems unaware that this argument, though medieval in origin, comes in sophisticated modern versions that are not at all easy to refute. Shirking the intellectual hard work, Dawkins prefers to move on.'[40]

Question:
Which logical fallacies does Richard Dawkins commit when he presents and critiques
Anselm's ontological argument in *The God Delusion*?

9.3.4 Objection 4: The 'existence is not a predicate' objection

According to Immanuel Kant 'existence' is not a property that can be
listed alongside other properties, such as 'omnipotence':

> 'Being' is obviously not a real predicate, that is, it is not a concept of some-
> thing which could be added to the concept of a thing . . . The proposition 'God
> is omnipotent' contains two concepts, each of which has its object – God and
> omnipotence. The small word 'is' adds no new predicate . . . If, now, we take
> the subject (God) with all its predicates . . . and say 'God is' . . . we attach no
> new predicate to the concept of God . . .[41]

Dawkins reckons that 'the most definitive refutations of the ontological
argument are usually attributed to the philosophers David Hume (1711–
76) and Immanuel Kant (1724–1804).'[42] However, the supposed 'definitive refutations' of the OA from Kant and Hume (who make essentially
the same point) are rejected by many philosophers today.

Charles Hartshorne notes that 'logicians, including some who would
rather be seen in beggars' rags than in the company of the Ontological
Argument, have held that existence is, after all, a sort of predicate, even
of ordinary things.'[43] For example, Stephen T. Davis takes issue with
Kant's claim that 'exists' is not a real predicate: 'sometimes we . . . talk
about things that are, or possibly are, non-existent – things that are,
say, mythical, extinct, legendary, dead, or fictional. And in those cases
it might well add to our knowledge of a thing to say that it does (or
does not) exist. In such cases, "exists" appears to be a property or real
predicate.'[44]

Moreover, even if saying that something 'exists' doesn't add to the list
of its properties, to say that something 'exists necessarily' certainly *does*
add to its list of properties. Atheist Yujin Nagasawa acknowledges: 'even
if existence is not a predicate, necessary existence, which is also normally
ascribed to God by theists, seems to be a predicate. Again, necessary
existence is existence in all possible worlds. This clearly seems to be a
property . . .'[45] As Keith E. Yandell explains: 'One may hold . . . that *necessary existence and contingent existence* are properties and agree with Hume
that we have no general notion of existence – i.e. of *existence, neither necessary nor contingent*.'[46] Michael L. Peterson et al. comment:

for any two objects, if one exists necessarily and the other not (that is, exists contingently, such that it could either exist or not exist), the first is greater than the second. It follows, then, that if God's existence were continent . . . he would not be the best conceivable being. But God, as the greatest possible being, possesses necessary existence. Therefore, God's existence is either logically necessary or logically impossible. God's existence is not logically impossible. Hence, it is *logically necessary*.[47]

Christopher Hitchens' attempt to dismiss the OA by noting how 'Kant objects that existence is *not* a predicate'[48] is a red herring.

9.3.5 Objection 5: The 'correct atheist' objection

Peter van Inwagen asks us to:

consider the concept of a 'correct atheist', that is, of someone who believes, and rightly, that there is no perfect being. If the concept 'correct atheist' is a possible concept, the concept 'perfect being' is an impossible concept . . . And if 'perfect being' is an impossible concept, 'correct atheist' is obviously a possible concept. One of the two concepts is therefore possible and the other impossible. But which is which?[49]

According to Inwagen:

There seems to be no way to answer this question . . . Our conclusion must be that, although there is a version of the ontological argument that is without logical flaw, the argument proceeds from a premise such that there is no way to decide whether it is true . . . it would seem, therefore, to be impossible to know that the premise of the ontological argument is true without first knowing that its conclusion is true. The ontological argument, therefore, cannot serve as a means by which someone can pass from not knowing whether a perfect being exists to knowing that a perfect being exists.[50]

Inwagen isn't arguing that the OA is unsound. He is arguing that it may or may not be sound, but that we have no independent way of knowing, because we have no way of knowing whether or not the crucial second premise is true that's independent of our already knowing whether or not God exists. And the reason he thinks that we have no independent way of knowing whether or not the crucial second premise is true is that we can't simply give the 'benefit of the doubt' to the proposition that God's existence is possible, since not to give an equal benefit of the doubt to the proposition that a 'correct atheist' is possible would make us guilty of adopting a double standard.

✔ Inwagen's 'correct atheist' objection doesn't question the OA's soundness, but its apologetic bite

For several years, Inwagen's objection convinced me that, despite being a sound argument, the OA had no apologetic use. However, it then occurred to me to ask whether Inwagen's assumption, i.e. *the only (independent) way to justify the proposition that God's existence is possible is to give it the benefit of the doubt*, is true. I think not.

9.4 Ten (or so) Reasons to Accept Premise 2

First, doesn't Plantinga's procedure of carefully considering the concept of a perfect being in relation to our noetic structure take us beyond reliance upon any methodological rule of thumb about giving claims about possibility the benefit of the doubt?

Second, mightn't someone with a properly basic intuition that God's existence is possible thereby rationally believe that a 'correct atheist' is an incoherent concept? After all, the concept of 'a correct atheist' is clearly parasitic upon the proposition (*pace* the second premise of the OA) that 'God' is not a coherent concept.

Third, religious experience might warrant belief in the existence of a transcendent being with at least two maximally degreed great-making properties (e.g. omnibenevolence and omnipotence, or omnipotence and omniscience). Alternatively, religious experience might at least warrant belief in a transcendent being in whom two or more great-making properties – properties that may, for all we know, be maximally degreed – coexist. Either way, religious experience could provide abductive support for the general hypothesis that maximal degrees of great-making properties can coexist over against the hypothesis that they cannot.

Fourth, we know from non-religious experience that great-making properties can coexist when they are at less than their maximum quantities. Humans possess non-maximal degrees of great-making properties such as power, knowledge and goodness. This provides abductive support for the hypothesis that maximal degrees of great-making properties can coexist over against the hypothesis that they cannot.

Fifth, 'Todd Buras and Mike Cantrell . . . claim that, since natural desires are a guide to possibility and human beings naturally desire at least one state of affairs for which the existence of God is a necessary condition, it is possible that God exists.'[51]

Sixth, it might be argued that at least some of God's great-making properties are in a sense identical:

> When we speak of different perfections, such as omniscience or omnipotence, we connote different things, and so the assertions have different meanings. Nevertheless, perhaps all of these different meanings have the same denotation; that is, perhaps they refer to some single capacity in God. This does not seem implausible. After all . . . perhaps being omnipotent entails being omniscient, perhaps being perfectly loving entails being perfectly just, and so forth.[52]

Yujin Nagasawa argues that '*a statement about divine omniscience can be restated in terms of a divine epistemic power*. This principle reveals a connection between divine omniscience and omnipotence . . . omniscience can be understood as God's exercising a particular part – the epistemic part – of His omnipotence.'[53] If correct, this analysis of great-making properties decreases the atheists' opportunities for claiming that 'God' has incompatible properties (although it still leaves open questions about the internal coherence of those properties). For example, this analysis entails that *if* necessary existence is compatible with omnipotence *then* it is necessarily compatible with omniscience, etc.

Seventh, suppose the atheist grants that *some* great-making properties (e.g. omnipotence and omniscience) can coexist in the same being, but makes a crucial exception for necessary existence. We might well ask what reason the atheist has to think that the former great-making properties are compatible with one another but incompatible with necessary existence? It wouldn't do to answer our question by stating that whilst, for example, omniscience is in a sense identical to omnipotence (see above), neither quality is identical with necessary existence. After all, properties can coexist in the same being without being identical. Given that no principled answer to our question is forthcoming, Occam's razor rules against making the atheist's proposed distinction. That is, to draw a distinction between great-making properties that can and can't coexist, and to insist without sufficient justification that necessary existence just happens to fall into the latter category, so that the OA is unsound, is an *ad hoc* leap of blind faith on the part of the atheist.

Eighth, consider Josef Seifert's *a priori* argument that great-making properties 'must be all compatible with each other, for it contradicts the nature of that, which it is absolutely speaking, better to possess than not to possess to exclude any other such perfection. Otherwise a logical contradiction would arise in that it would be simultaneously better to possess perfection A (a pure perfection) and not to possess it (because it would exclude another pure perfection B).'[54] The concept of 'the greatest possible being' is of course the concept of the greatest possible set of great-making properties *that can coexist*. Seifert defines great-making properties as properties that it is 'absolutely speaking, better to possess than not to possess.' Then he argues that it is self-contradictory to make a distinction between 'the set of great-making properties that *can* coexist' and 'the set of great-making properties that *cannot* coexist', since drawing this distinction means affirming the existence of properties that are *greater* than properties that it is 'absolutely speaking, better to possess than not to possess.'

Ninth, like a scientific hypothesis with verified predictions that provide grounds (via an inference to the best explanation) for accepting the hypothesis making these predictions (absent falsifying data), so the simplest theistic hypothesis, that a maximally great being exists entails various predictions, many of which have been metaphysically 'verified' by theistic arguments, and none of which have been falsified. For example, the theistic hypothesis predicts that there exists, a being with necessary existence (something verified by the cosmological argument) who is highly intelligent (something verified by the design argument) and whose essence is goodness itself (something verified by the moral argument). Without venturing too deeply into probability theory, the 'prime principle of confirmation' tells us 'that whenever we are considering two competing hypotheses, H_1 and H_2, an observation, O, counts as evidence in favour of H_1 over H_2 if O is more probable under H_1 than it is under H_2.'[55] If we compare theism (H_1) with atheism (H_2) as rival hypotheses against the metaphysical observations that there exists i) a being whose essence is goodness, ii) a necessary being, and iii) an intelligent designer of the cosmos, then the prime principle of confirmation clearly favours (H_1) theism over (H_2) atheism. But, of course, the hypothesis of theism entails that God's existence is possible. Hence, while the other theistic arguments don't prove everything one might want to say about a perfect being, they nevertheless provide cumulative, independent grounds for an inference that supports the crucial second premise of the ontological argument. As Craig writes: 'The ontological argument might play its part in a cumulative case for theism, in which a multitude of factors simultaneously conspire to lead one to the global conclusion that God exists [and wherein the ontological argument encapsulates] the thrust of all the arguments together to show that God, the Supreme Being, exists.'[56]

Finally, one might support the claim that God's existence is possible by arguing against the coherence and/or possibility of alternative conceptions of ultimate reality (such as pantheism[57] and metaphysical naturalism).[58]

I submit that, taken together, these arguments provide a sufficient cumulative answer to van Inwagen's objection and an adequate cumulative case for endorsing the crucial second premise of the ontological argument. This is *not* to say that perfect being theology provides us with an entirely perspicuous concept of divinity devoid of mystery. However, for the OA to be a sound argument with apologetic value all that is required of its crucial second premise is that it be more plausibly true than its denial in the light of our total available evidence.

Conclusion

The OA is a logically valid argument that anyone who thinks either that theism is true *or that theism is possibly true* should also take to be a sound argument that adds to the cumulative case for theism.

*   *   *

Recommended Resources

Video

Inwagen, Peter van. 'Arguing God from Being' www.closertotruth.com/video-profile/Arguing-God-from-Being-Peter-van-Inwagen-/1097.
*Williams, Peter S. and William Lane Craig vs Andrew Copson and Arif Ahmed. 'Cambridge Union: This House Believes God Is Not a Delusion' www.bethinking.org/who-are-you-god/advanced/cambridge-union-society-debate-an-analysis.htm.
*— 'The Ontological Argument for God' YouTube Playlist www.youtube.com/playlist?list=PLQhh3qcwVEWjE7hqAz3D6jp7MWjChVYKn.

Audio

Craig, William Lane. Defenders Podcast, series 2, parts 23–25 www.reasonablefaith.org/defenders-2-podcast/s4.
*Williams, Peter S. 'The Ontological Argument' www.damaris.org/cm/podcasts/231.
— and Luke Pollard. 'Ontological Class' www.damaris.org/cm/podcasts/662.
— vs Peter Cave. 'Is Belief in God Reasonable?' www.damaris.org/cm/podcasts/364.

Online papers

Last Seminary's Ontological Argument Page. www.lastseminary.com/ontological-argument/.

Craig, William Lane. 'Dawkins' Critique of the Ontological Argument' www.reasonable-faith.org/site/News2?page=NewsArticle&id=6831.

— 'Does the Ontological Argument Beg the Question?' www.reasonablefaith.org/site/News2?page=NewsArticle&id=8139.

—'God's Necessity' www.reasonablefaith.org/site/News2?page=NewsArticle&id=7301.

— 'The Ontological Argument' www.reasonablefaith.org/site/News2?page=NewsArticle&id=6155.

— 'Two Questions on the Ontological Argument' www.reasonablefaith.org/site/News2?page=NewsArticle&id=8715.

— 'Van Inwagen on Uncreated Beings' www.reasonablefaith.org/van-inwagen-on-uncreated-beings.

Dougherty, Trent. 'Conceivability, Defeasibility, and Possibility: A Defense of the Modal Ontological Argument' www.lastseminary.com/ontological-argument/A%20Defense%20of%20the%20Modal%20Ontological%20Argument.pdf.

Maydole, Robert E. 'The Ontological Argument' http://commonsenseatheism.com/wp-content/uploads/2009/10/Maydole-The-Ontological-Argument.pdf.

MessianicDrew. 'The Ontological Argument and the S5 Objection' http://messianicdrew.blogspot.com/2011/06/ontological-argument-and-s5-objection.html.

— 'The Ontological Argument for the Triune God' http://messianicdrew.blogspot.com/2011/03/ontological-argument-for-triune-god.html.

Nagasawa, Yujin. 'The Ontological Argument and the Devil' www.yujinnagasawa.com/resources/devil.pdf.

— 'Divine Omniscience and Knowledge *De Se*' www.thedivineconspiracy.org/Z3214A.pdf.

*Plantinga, Alvin. 'The Ontological Argument' www.lastseminary.com/ontological-argument/Plantinga%20-%20The%20Ontological%20Argument.pdf.

Williams, Peter S. 'Understanding the Trinity' www.bethinking.org/who-are-you-god/advanced/understanding-the-trinity.htm.

Zagzebski, Linda. 'Omnisubjectivity' www.baylor.edu/content/services/document.php/39971.pdf.

Books

Beilby, James K., ed. *For Faith and Clarity: Philosophical Contributions to Christian Theology* (Grand Rapids, MI: Baker Academic, 2006).

*Craig, William Lane. 'The Ontological Argument.' Pages 124–38 in *To Everyone an Answer: A Case for the Christian Worldview* (ed. Francis J. Beckwith, William Lane Craig and J.P. Moreland; Downers Grove, IL: IVP, 2004).

— *Reasonable Faith: Christian Truth and Apologetics* (Wheaton, IL: Crossway, 3rd edn, 2008).

— *Time and Eternity: Exploring God's Relationship to Time* (Wheaton, IL: Crossway, 2001).

— and J.P. Moreland, eds. *The Blackwell Companion to Natural Theology* (Oxford: Wiley-Blackwell, 2009).

Davies, Brian. *An Introduction to the Philosophy of Religion* (Oxford University Press, 3rd edn, 2004).

— *Philosophy of Religion: A Guide and Anthology* (Oxford University Press, 2000).

Davis, Stephen T. 'Has the Ontological Argument Been Refuted?' Pages 185–204 in *Disputed Issues: Contending for Christian Faith in Today's Academic Setting* (Baylor University Press, 2009).

— 'The Ontological Argument.' Pages 93–111 in *The Rationality of Theism* (ed. Paul Copan and Paul K. Moser; London: Routledge, 2003).

— *Logic and the Nature of God* (Grand Rapids, MI: Eerdmans, 1983).

DeWeese, Garrett J. *God and the Nature of Time* (Aldershot: Ashgate, 2004).

Ganssle, Gregory E. *God & Time: Four Views* (Dowers Grove, IL: IVP, 2001).

Groothuis, Douglas. *Christian Apologetics: A Comprehensive Case for Biblical Faith* (Nottingham: Apollos, 2011).

Hill, Daniel J. *Divinity and Maximal Greatness* (London: Routledge, 2010).

Inwagen, Peter van. 'Ontological Arguments.' Pages 54–8 in *Philosophy of Religion: A Guide to the Subject* (ed. Brian Davies; London: Continuum, 1998).

Lowe, E.J. 'The Ontological Argument.' Pages 331–40 in *The Routledge Companion to Philosophy of Religion* (ed. Chad Meister and Paul Copan: London: Routledge, 2010).

Moreland, J.P. and William Lane Craig. *Philosophical Foundations for a Christian Worldview* (Downers Grove, IL: IVP, 2003).

Morris, Thomas V. *Our Idea of God* (University of Notre Dame Press, 1991).

— *Anselmian Explorations: Essays in Philosophical Theology* (University of Notre Dame Press, 1987).

Murray, Michael J. and Michael Rea. *An Introduction to the Philosophy of Religion* (Cambridge University Press, 2008).

Nagasawa, Yujin. *The Existence of God: A Philosophical Introduction* (Oxford: Routledge, 2011).

Nash, Ronald H. *The Concept of God: An Exploration of Contemporary Difficulties with the Attributes of God* (Grand Rapids, MI: Zondervan, 1983).

Padgett, Alan G. *God, Eternity and the Nature of Time* (Eugene, OR: Wipf & Stock, 1992).

Quinn, Philip L. and Charles Taliaferro. *A Companion to Philosophy of Religion* (Oxford: Blackwell, 1999).

Swinburne, Richard. *The Christian God* (Oxford University Press, 1994).

*Taliaferro, Charles. 'The Coherence of Theism.' Pages 239–58 in *The Rationality of Theism* (ed. Paul Copan and Paul K. Moser; London: Routledge, 2003).

— *Contemporary Philosophy of Religion* (Oxford: Blackwell, 2001).

— *Philosophy of Religion* (Oxford: OneWorld, 2009).

— and Chad Meister. *The Cambridge Companion to Christian Philosophical Theology* (Cambridge University Press, 2010).

Wainwright, William J. *Philosophy of Religion* (Belmont, CA: Wadsworth, 2nd edn, 1999).

Ward, Keith. *Religion and Creation* (Oxford: Clarendon Press, 1996).

Wood, W. Jay. *God* (Durham: Acumen, 2011).

Zagzebski, Linda. *Omnisubjectivity: A Defense Of A Divine Attribute* (Milwaukee, Wisconsin: Marguette University Press, 2013).

10. Religious Experience

The fact that large numbers of people . . . appear to have had some internal experience of God should be regarded by an open-minded person as some evidence . . . for the truth of theism.
Philip Van der Elst[1]

Introduction

Timothy Keller suggests that:

> If you have known many wise, loving, kind, and insightful Christians over the years, and if you have seen churches that are devout in belief yet civic-minded and generous, you will find the intellectual case for Christianity much more plausible. If, on the other hand, the preponderance of your experience is with nominal Christians (who bear the name but don't practice it) or with self-righteous fanatics, then the arguments for Christianity will have to be extremely strong for you to concede that they have any cogency at all[2]

Indeed, according to philosopher A.C. Ewing: 'It may be very much doubted . . . whether all these arguments [for theism] would inspire a real faith in God . . . unless the man's heart were touched by some experience not the result wholly of argument or even describable fully in intellectual terms.'[3] Yet arguments for God can illuminate, and facilitate openness to, religious experience. And religious experience can ground, or at least contribute towards, warranted belief in God's existence.

10.1 Religious Experience

Religion, in its widest sense, seeks to establish a properly functioning relationship between humanity and a reality 'behind' or 'beyond' the surface of things. While all experience has a subjective aspect (in that it's something had by a subject), not all experiences are wholly subjective (at least some experiences have objective referents). *You* experience reading this book. But you experience reading *this book*. Hence religious experience might be defined as an experience concerning a reality apparently 'behind' or 'beyond' the surface of things.

Many definitions of religious experience employ the terminology of *transcendence*. Something is transcendent 'if it goes beyond or is more than one's immediate consciousness.'[4] Something is transcendent *in a religious sense* if it is believed to be *the ultimate object worthy of a total existential commitment*: 'The Transcendent is the object of a total commitment – that for which one would make even the supreme sacrifice. The Transcendent is the object of ultimate concern because it is thought to be ultimate or final . . . It is . . . the Ultimate to which one makes an ultimate commitment.'[5]

To be properly religious, an experience must involve an awareness of the transcendent *together with a response* of 'ultimate commitment to the Transcendent'[6] on the part of the one who experiences it. Hence, 'a religious experience involves at least two fundamental factors: an awareness of the Transcendent, and a total commitment to it as ultimate.'[7] Awareness of the Transcendent without a response of total commitment (what we might call a 'transcendent experience') may be an experience of something fundamental to religion, but it isn't a properly *religious* experience: 'For the religious person, the Transcendent not only discloses itself, but also evokes a [positive] response from the individual,'[8] argue Geisler and Corduan: 'A religious experience involves something beyond a mere disclosure, something unconditional and ultimate; something to which persons are willing to commit themselves with utter loyalty and devotion. That is, it involves not only an awareness of the transcendent but an awareness of it as ultimate and as demanding an ultimate commitment.'[9]

In other words, one's response to the transcendent must be *positive* in order to be properly religious. This positive response to the transcendent is called *worship*: 'Worship . . . is a response to the worth-ship of the object. In this sense, then, worship is the attitude of admiration and acceptance of the ultimate worth of the Transcendent of which it is aware . . . worship is at the very heart of religious experience.'[10]

An awareness of the transcendent as ultimate and as demanding an ultimate commitment, combined with a *negative* personal response, is obviously not, in this sense, a *religious* experience. We could perhaps call such a negative transcendent experience an *irreligious* experience! Far from detracting from whatever evidential support can be granted to the God hypothesis by religious experience, irreligious experience actually adds weight to the case for God. The argument from religious experience accommodates positive 'religious' modes of religious experience, negative 'irreligious' modes of religious experience, and neutral 'transcendent experiences' that lack clearly religious or irreligious reactions. Consider atheist H.G. Wells' admission:

> At times, in the lonely silence of the night and in rare, lonely moments, I come upon a sort of communion of myself with something great that is not myself. It is, perhaps, poverty of mind and language which obliges me to say that this universal scheme takes on the effect of a sympathetic person – and my communion a quality of fearless worship. These moments happen, and they are the supreme fact of my religious life to me. They are the crown of my religious experiences.[11]

Wells acknowledges the fact and *prima facie* religious quality of his experience even as he attempts to introduce a non-religious explanation (his own 'poverty of mind and language') that might undermine such a face-value interpretation of things. Religious experience, it might be said, covers a multitude of sins.

10.2 Five Types of Theistic Religious Experience

Theistic religious experience includes either an apparent conscious awareness of a *personal transcendent reality* (God), or at least a conscious experience taken by the person having the experience as properly grounding belief in the existence of God. We can define a *direct* theistic religious experience as 'an experience which seems . . . to the subject to be an experience of God (either of his just being there, or doing or bringing about something).'[12] And we can define an *indirect* theistic religious experience as 'an experience which seems to the subject to be an experience that they can properly take as grounding belief in God' even though it is not a direct theistic religious experience. Charles

Taliaferro thinks that 'broad theism is sufficiently extensive to describe or accommodate much of the central reported religious experiences in Judaism, Christianity, and Islam, and theistic traditions within Hinduism, Buddhism, African religions, Sikhism, aboriginal or primary religions, theistic Confucianism, and other religions.'[13]

As with everyday sensory perception, the general reliability of religious experience is compatible with a certain degree of experiential disagreement, especially in matters of secondary detail. Hence, while there may be experiential agreement 'about certain general features of the divine',[14] this agreement may be obscured by the fact that these features 'will be articulated in very different terms depending upon one's social, cultural, religious context.'[15] Moreover, as William Lane Craig argues:

> what about a case where I have no evidence that some non-Christian claimant to religious experience is mistaken other than the incompatibility of his truth-claims with Christian truth-claims? Does that give me reason to be agnostic about the veridicality of my experience? I think not. Consider, by analogy, beliefs formed on the ground of moral experience. Should I regard as unwarranted my belief that anti-Semitism is immoral just because Nazis regard it as moral? Certainly not; their warped perceptions should not lead me to think that my perceptions are warped, even though there is no court of appeal beyond moral experience itself. Similarly with religious experience . . .[16]

Richard Swinburne defines five categories of theistic religious experience:[17]

1. *Experience mediated by common public phenomena*
There's a difference between seeing and perceiving. In seeing someone's face I may or may not perceive their sadness (perhaps I am too preoccupied with my own feelings to notice theirs). 'One often perceives one thing in perceiving something else,' notes Swinburne:

> In seeing the print of such-and-such a shape in the sand I may see the footprint of a bear . . . In these cases [the] same visual or other sensations . . . which bring about my perceiving the first thing also bring about my perceiving the second thing. In perceiving the second thing one does not see anything extra in the sense of a new item which had escaped one's notice before; rather one perceives the first thing as the second thing. In these cases one man may perceive both things, and another man perceive only the first and yet both have the same visual sensations.[18]

Thus, 'a man may look at the night sky, and suddenly "see it as" God's handiwork, something which God is bringing about (in the way in

184

which a man may see a vapour trail in the sky as the trail of an aeroplane).'[19] William P. Alston's religious experience seems to fit at least partially into this category: 'My coming back [to faith] was less like seeing that certain premises implied a conclusion than it was like coming to hear some things in music that I hadn't heard before, or having my eyes opened to the significance of things that are going on around me.'[20]

2. *Experience mediated by uncommon ('odd') public phenomena*

The experience of the Israelites in the exodus,[21] or of witnesses to the resurrection appearances of Jesus,[22] fit into this category. So do the experiences of people who encounter angels or instances of demonization.[23] Likewise, Gary R. Habermas notes that 'there are numerous documented (and actually quite extraordinary) cases of healings.'[24] For example, according to *The Independent on Sunday*:

> After a visit to her local hospital in 2003, [Sharyn] Mackay was diagnosed with cancer of the kidney. The tumour was removed, but soon grew back and spread to her lungs. After being given a year to live, Mackay decided to visit a church that performed healing services. On entering the church, Mackay recalls feeling an 'enormous heat' and the cancer leaving her body. Amazingly, subsequent test results found no traces of the cancer.[25]

Andrew Wilson reports:

> A physiotherapist friend of mine who had been wearing a wrist splint, unable to move her wrist without significant pain, was healed instantly in front of me and ten others three weeks ago, and has since been able to move it completely normally without any discomfort, much to the surprise of many of her (atheist physiotherapist) colleagues. A chef in our church, who had been unable to move his arm above shoulder level for two years, prayed for it two weeks ago during a church meeting, and was instantly able to do so (last time I looked, he had not stopped waving it for several days). A short-sighted student I know, who had never been able to walk around with no glasses without suffering migraines, was instantly healed on being prayed for, and has not worn glasses since (except when, ironically, she cautiously wore them at college, and ended up getting migraines because her eyesight had been corrected). I do not mention these examples because they are the most dramatic I know . . . I mention them because I have personally witnessed them in the last few weeks . . . they are neither internalised hallucinations nor empirically untrue, but public, physical events in the space-time world, verifiable by doctors and friends.[26]

Watch:
Peter S. Williams, 'Prayer & Healing' YouTube Playlist www.youtube.com/play-list?list=PLQhh3qcwVEWi2KT0RszsmqH8xHDQWdCKN.
— 'Angelology' YouTube Playlist www.youtube.com/playlist?list=PLQhh3qcwVE-WjxHf8HUnl7sI_cvYnoRyyZ.

3. *Private experience consisting of describable sensory data*

In a dream described in Matthew 1:20ff. Joseph saw an angel. There were no public phenomena, only private sensations that could be described by means of normal sensory vocabulary: 'What made the dream a religious experience was that in having the sensations, *and* after he has woken up, it seemed to Joseph that an angel was talking to him, i.e. he took the man-in-a-dream to be a real angel and not a mere angel-in-a-dream.'[27] One might consider the course of events after Joseph's dream to verify its genuinely religious nature, an instance of private religious experience having a publicly testable dimension.

I once had an acquaintance everyone called Andy. He'd been a Christian youth worker, but had become disenchanted with the church and had consequently drifted away from Christianity. Nevertheless, Andy remained friends with several Christians, and occasionally went to church with them. At the church we both attended at the time, we often had services offering prayer for healing. Before such services a small prayer-group met to 'listen to God' for 'words of knowledge' that were then given out in the service to encourage people to come for prayer (about 70% of the 'words' were reportedly responded to by people who thought that a proffered 'word' was for them). One Sunday, someone in the prayer group believed they had received a 'word' in the form of a symbolic picture depicting someone in a tug of war but feeling they were on the wrong team. The prayer-group leader (whom I knew well) felt that this word was too vague and so asked the group to pray that God would give them a specific name to attach to it. No one in the prayer-group knew about Andy, yet someone hesitantly offered 'Andrew', which was Andy's actual name. The picture plus name were duly given out during the service, and Andy responded. He told me that, several times before, he'd heard similar 'words' that he *could* have applied to himself, but he didn't respond, reasoning that if God was really interested in him, God could put his name on an appropriate 'word.' Thus, in a congregation of some 240 people, a non-Christian named Andrew, who felt in a 'tug of war' about accepting God, challenged God to put his name on an appropriate 'word' *and God apparently responded*. Andy rededicated his life to God, and a straightforward interpretation of the data surely supports the prima facie conclusion that he was rational in so doing.

4. *Private experience consisting of indescribable sensory data*
Here 'the subject has a religious experience in having certain sensations private to himself, yet these are not of a kind describable by normal vocabulary . . . Presumably mystics and others who find it difficult if not impossible to describe their religious experiences, and yet feel that there is something to be described if only they had the words to do the describing, are having experiences of this kind.'[28]

5. *Private experience without sensory data*
For example, 'a man may be convinced that God is telling him to do so-and-so (e.g. follow such-and-such a vocation), and yet there are no auditory or other sensations occurring.'[29] (The putting of a name to the symbolic picture in the example given in category 3 would seem to have been this kind of experience.)

> **Questions:**
> Try sorting Swinburne's five types of religious experience into direct and indirect religious experiences. Do you find this exercise easy or hard? Why?
> Are the forms of religious experience that are most convincing to a believer and to a non-believer different? If so, why?

10.3 Words of Caution

First, it should be noted that the project of using religious experience as evidence for God's existence involves placing greater weight upon such experience than it is called upon to bear in the normal course of a religious believer's life. In the normal course of things a believer may call upon a complex web of beliefs that they take to warrant the acceptance of certain religious experiences as being (at least more likely than not) genuine. For example, they may call upon the beliefs that God exists and that God has revealed himself in a specific manner and that as a matter of divinely guaranteed revelation people who undertake to interact with God in a given way are likely to have religious experiences that are generally trustworthy. With Alston, 'I take it to be tolerably obvious that not every such supposition is correct, any more than every supposed sense perception of, for example, a lake is the genuine article. (Sometimes the supposed lake is a mirage.)'[30] Nevertheless, the believer may appeal to various reasons outside their religious experience in support of the *general* trustworthiness of their religious experiences. However, when religious experience is asked to form the basis of an evidential argument for the existence of God, calling upon such a web of beliefs to validate religious experience would be question begging. Hence, the context of natural theology is of necessity a context that tends to minimize the warrant attached to religious experience. However, *minimizing* the warrant attached to religious experience isn't the same thing as *eradicating* that warrant.

Second, it must be noted that the very nature of religious experience sometimes leads people to describe their experience in ways that overemphasize its evidential force. Such overemphasis can fuel a cynicism towards religious experience that's guilty of throwing the baby out with the bathwater. Saint Teresa reported: 'One day when I was at prayer . . . I saw Christ at my side'; but she immediately qualified her assertion, writing: 'or, to put it better, I was conscious of Him, for I saw nothing with the eyes of my body or the eyes of the [imagination]. He seemed quite close to me.'[31] (Teresa's experience seems to be the fifth type of experience listed by Swinburne.) It's unreasonable to expect everyone who has a religious experience to be similarly exact. Someone may report, 'God said that I should make a certain decision', when they don't mean that they *literally* heard God tell them what choice to make. It might be more accurate to say they experienced a sense of incumbency about a certain choice that seemed to them to come from God. They may be able to give reasons for interpreting their experience this way. They may have experienced an apparently objective moral obligation to undertake a course of action that wouldn't normally be considered obligatory; they may feel that this sense of obligation isn't adequately explained in terms of their own prior desires (which it might contradict), perhaps because it came about as they engaged in a number of other religious experiences, connected to acts of prayer, worship, meditation upon Scripture, etc. Describing this experience in metaphorical language as 'hearing God speak' is understandable shorthand, but it obscures the distinctions that can be drawn between different modes of religious experience. Hence C. Stephen Layman counsels:

> We have to distinguish *careful* reports of religious experience (by which I mean reports that plausibly describe just what the subject was presented with) from highly interpreted reports. But the same thing comes up with accounts of sense experience. Listen to two people describing a traffic accident. One person chooses her words carefully, sticking to a sensible account that plausibly indicates what she was presented with. Another person who saw the same incident may give a loose account, full of what are plainly judgements that go well beyond what he could possibly have been presented with. We don't throw out all accounts of an accident simply

because some of them are careless and chock-full of dubious inferences or interpretations.[32]

Read:
Michael Licona, 'Religious Experience' www.4truth.net/fourtruthcb.aspx?id=8589995562.

10.4 Mystical Experience

What should we make of so-called 'mystical' religious experiences that blur the distinction between the Creator and created, or between personal and impersonal? I think we are, once again, apt to be led astray by the religious use of language; for there's a significant difference between a) not experiencing the transcendent as being personal, and b) experiencing the transcendent as being impersonal. The former is simply the lack of a positive experience of the transcendent as personal, while the latter claims to be just as much a positive experience as is the experience of the transcendent as personal. The former claim doesn't contradict theistic religious experience, while the latter claim does: 'When a theistic mystic who supposes God to be an objective reality reports an experience of an undifferentiated unity, she is best construed not as denying the existence of any real distinctions, for example, between herself and God, but as simply reporting that she is aware of no such distinctions, or of any other, at the time.'[33]

Moreover, the pantheistic interpretation of such a mystical experience involves an individual making the self-contradictory claim to have personally experienced the non-reality of personal, individual experience. Since there can be no contradiction without differentiation, we should recognize that 'if Vedanta or Yoga mystics report that they are aware of an undifferentiated unity, that attribution in itself is not incompatible with characterizing the same being as a personal agent, unless a denial of the latter is read into the former.'[34] To read a denial of the latter (positive experience) into the former is to reject the simplest adequate explanation (that the former is simply a lack of positive experience given a certain metaphysical import) for an explanation that's self-contradictory.

10.5 Numinous Experience

Rudolf Otto introduced the concept of 'numinous experience' to the philosophy of religion. The term 'numinous' is 'derived from the Latin *numen* for divinity or divine will.'[35] In its broadest sense, a numinous experience is simply an experience in which '*a person seems to apprehend a divine reality independent of oneself.*'[36] However, Otto highlighted three types of feeling involved in numinous experience: 'the feeling of dependence [upon the numinous], the feeling of religious dread or awe [of the numinous], and the feeling of longing for the transcendent [numinous] being that fascinates us.'[37] Hence Keith Yandell defines numinous experience as experience involving 'an awesome, overpowering, majestic, holy, living, personal Being who elicits awe, a sense of one's creaturehood and dependence, an awareness of one's sinfulness, repentance, and worship.'[38]

Otto's analysis of numinous experience has the unfortunate effect of focusing discussion upon the subject of *feelings*. While theistic religious experience clearly can involve feelings of dependency, awe and longing (and other feelings besides, e.g. relief at forgiveness), it would be a mistake to think that the content of such experiences is restricted to feelings – especially if 'feelings' are interpreted as nothing but subjective, individualistic reactions. Alston cautions:

> The treatment of 'religious experience' as essentially consisting of 'feelings' or other affective states is very common. Thus in Schleiermacher, the fountainhead of concentration on religious experience in the study of religion, we find the basic experiential element of religion treated as a 'feeling of absolute dependence'. Rudolf Otto and William James also concentrate on feelings. It must be confessed that in all these cases the theorists also characterize religious experience as cognitive of objective realities in ways that seem incompatible with the classification as *affective* . . . Nevertheless, it remains true that their concentration on affect has frequently been taken out of context and as such has powerfully influenced succeeding generations.[39]

As H.D. Lewis writes, theists would describe their religious experience as encompassing 'not just a feeling . . . but a conviction or insight.'[40] The categories of 'feeling' and 'insight' aren't mutually exclusive. For example, scientists at the University of Iowa undertook a study in which volunteers were presented with four packs of playing cards, two blue and two red. Each card they turned over would either win or lose them money. They were tasked with trying to maximize their winnings. Participants weren't told that while the blue packs offered a steady diet of modest rewards and penalties, the red packs offered both high wins *and losses*. The scientists wanted to see how long it took people to figure out the difference between the red and blue packs. They found that after turning over about fifty cards, most people start developing a hunch about what's going on. After turning over about eighty cards, most people figure out the game and can explain why picking the red decks is a bad idea. People have a *hunch* about the red cards being a bad bet *before* they have an explicit understanding of why the red decks are the worse bet:

> But the Iowa scientists did something else, and this is where the strange part of the experiment begins. They hooked each gambler up to a machine that measured the activity of the sweat glands below the skin in the palms of their hands. Like most of our sweat glands, those in our palms respond to stress as well as temperature . . . What the Iowa scientists found is that gamblers started generating stress responses to the red decks by the tenth card, forty cards before they were able to say they had a hunch about what was wrong with those two decks. More importantly, right around the time their palms started sweating, their behaviour began to change as well. They started favouring the blue cards and taking fewer and fewer cards from the red decks. In other words, the gamblers figured the game out before they realized they had figured the game out . . .[41]

Scientists at Rice University used an electromagnetic device to temporarily shut down the primary visual cortex in sighted volunteers before presenting them with a series of images:

> they were asked to say whether a bar was horizontal or vertical. They were also asked to say how confident they felt about their decision . . . If people were blindfolded and simply guessed, chance alone would suggest they would get half right. But during the tests, volunteers typically got around three quarters correct. Some said they were simply guessing. But others said they had a 'feeling' of seeing something, despite having no conscious idea of what it was. This was backed up by their confidence scores. Those who felt more sure of themselves got more answers right.[42]

The researchers concluded that after disruption to the primary visual pathways other pathways and/or brain structures were functioning to provide this 'blind sight', something previously observed in certain blind people: 'One 52-year-old doctor who had lost his sight after two strokes was even able to detect different emotions on faces. This suggested to scientists there must be other connections in the brain that allow unconscious sight.'[43] Once again, the lesson is that we can know more than we can say or explain how we know. The surprisingly accurate blinded volunteers simply went on the basis of their 'feelings.'

191

Far from excluding epistemically significant insight, then, having a feeling can function *as the rational ground or conduit of cognition*, and should be treated as innocent until proven guilty. The person who prays for forgiveness and feels they are relieved of guilt has an experience that involves not merely a *feeling* (of relief), but also a *belief* (that they have received the forgiveness they are relieved about receiving). Moreover, that belief may (in part at least) be rationally warranted *by their feelings*. The person on a country walk who develops the 'hunch' that nature is created may be in a position with no less warrant than that of a gambler who, during the course of a game of cards, develops the hunch that the blue decks are a better bet than the red decks.

10.6 A Basic Argument from Religious Experience

Religious experience, like any other type of experience, is obviously more convincing in the first person than in the third person. Nevertheless, religious experience, even considered in the third person, and even taking into account the caveats issued above, clearly provides *some* warrant for theism:

> if I could not find any confirmation of the Christian message in my own experience [or in other people's experience], I would be less justified in accepting that message than I am in fact . . . suppose that no one had ever experienced communion with God, had ever heard God speaking to him or her, had ever felt the strengthening influence of the Holy Spirit in a difficult situation. In that case Christian belief would be a less rational stance than it is in fact.[44]

To deny any evidential value to religious experience considered in the third person involves a double standard:

> Much of what a particular individual knows (justifiably believes) about the world is acquired from testimony. If I had to rely on my own experience and reasoning alone, I would know little of history, geography, science, and the arts, to say nothing of what is going on in the world currently. We generally suppose that justification is transferred via testimony from someone who has learned something from perception, memory, reasoning, or some combination thereof, to society at large. Why should it be different in the religious sphere?[45]

Hence, everyone must deal with the fact that:

> a host of individuals have claimed to have known and had a personal relationship with God. This claim has been made across cultural and geographic

192

boundaries as well as over time. For the atheist's claim that there is no God to be true, every single one of these individuals must be wrong about the matter that they themselves would characterize as the most important human concern.[46]

Common consent is weak evidence; but it is evidence. Two heads are better than one. At the very least, common consent puts the burden of proof on the sceptic, as Joshua Hoffman and Gary S. Rosenkrantz affirm: 'if entities of a certain kind belong to folk ontology [the ontological presumptions of our common-sense worldview], then there is *prima facie* presumption in favour of their reality . . . Those who deny their existence assume the burden of proof.'[47]

Throughout history, people from different cultures all over the world have claimed to perceive God both indirectly and directly. For atheism to be true, each and every one of these individuals must be wrong about a central feature of their own experience. As Geisler and Corduan explain, denying God 'entails the assertion that not only some people have been deceived about the reality of God but that indeed all religious [theists] who have ever lived have been completely deceived into believing there is a God when there really is not. For if even one religious person is right about the reality of [God], then there really is a [God].'[48]

It's *possible* that theists have misinterpreted all of their religious experience, but it doesn't seem *plausible*: 'It seems much more likely that such self-analyzing and self-critical men as Augustine, Blaise Pascal, and Kierkegaard were not totally deceived than that total skepticism is right.'[49] Such self-analyzing and self-critical believers abound in the contemporary world. Alvin Plantinga testifies: 'It seems to me that I experience God . . . in a variety of ways, just as lots and lots of people do; in church, in reading the Bible, in nature, in human relationships, in a thousand different ways.'[50] Stephen T. Davis explains: 'the reason I am a theist . . . has a great deal to do with experiences I have had that I interpret in terms of the presence of God – experiences I find myself interpreting in terms of divine forgiveness, divine protection, divine guidance.'[51] We could argue:

1. Whenever a very large number of people, including a great many educated, intelligent, self-analyzing and self-critical people, regardless of culture and historical period, believe they perceive something, it's probably real
2. A very large number of people, including a great many self-analyzing and self-critical people, regardless of culture and historical period, believe they perceive God
3. Therefore, God is probably real

10.7 The Argument from Credulity

Swinburne defends the need of placing the burden of proof upon those sceptical of perceptual claims, including religious perceptual claims:

> It is a basic principle of knowledge . . . that we ought to believe that things are as they seem to be, until we have evidence that we are mistaken . . . If you say the contrary – never trust appearances until it is proved that they were reliable – you will never have any beliefs at all. For what would show that appearances were reliable, except more appearances?[52]

One cannot use Occam's razor to counter the 'principle of credulity', because the principle of credulity applies to the more important 'adequacy' part of the razor's demand that we accept the 'simplest adequate' explanation.

Swinburne notes that the 'principle of credulity' encourages us to take religious experience at face value, unless there is sufficient reason to doubt it: 'If it seems . . . to S that x is present, that is good reason for S to believe that it is so, in the absence of special considerations – whatever x may be.'[53] Swinburne also argues that if you lack religious experience yourself, the principle of credulity means that it is reasonable to trust the reports of those with such experience:

> Since (probably) others have the experiences which they report, and since (probably) things are as a subject's experience suggests that they are, then (with some degree of probability) things are as others report . . . One who has not himself had an experience apparently of God is not in as strong a position as those who have. He will have less evidence for the existence of God; but not very much less, for he will have testimony of many who have had such experiences . . .[54]

As H.H. Price argued, one should 'accept what you are told, unless you see reason to doubt it.'[55]

> **Watch:**
> William Lane Craig, 'Can We Trust Religious Experience?' www.youtube.com/watch?v=AYc4hmrHthg.

Other people's testimony regarding their religious experience carries, by the principle of credulity, *prima facie* (literally 'on-the-face-of-it') validity. Hence Philip Van der Elst contends: 'the fact that large numbers of people of all nations, types, and temperaments appear to have had some internal experience of God, should be regarded by an open-minded person as some evidence . . . for the truth of theism.'[56]

10.8 Direct Perception

The 'direct perception' argument seeks to demonstrate a close analogy between some forms of religious experience and everyday sensory experience (e.g. seeing or hearing something), in order to argue by analogy that 'since we know the latter to be cognitive and (usually) veridical [i.e. true to reality], there is justification for taking the former to be cognitive and (usually) veridical.'[57] As J.P. Moreland argues: 'there are several reasons for holding that there is a close analogy between sensory perception and numinous [religious] perception. And since we know that the former is (usually) veridical, there is good reason to take the latter as (usually) veridical.'[58]

Of course, there are disanalogies between sensory and religious experience; but merely pointing this out doesn't defeat the direct perception argument, because disanalogy is an essential feature of *all* analogy. The question is whether the analogy between sensory and religious experience is *strong enough* for an argument by analogy to work. To be strong enough, an analogy merely needs to have more points of relevant coincidence than divergence.

At least ten points of coincidence can be noted between religious experiences and the sensory experience of sight:

1. *Our belief-forming practices can't be justified without epistemic circularity but are innocent until proven guilty.*

Alston points out that none of our belief-forming practices can be justified without begging the question: 'it is a familiar story that our best attempts to establish the reliability of memory, introspection, deductive reasoning or inductive reasoning will make use of premises derived from the practice under consideration, and so fall into epistemic circularity.'

While a belief-forming practice must *be* reliable if the beliefs it produces are to *be* reliable, we need not justify the belief that our belief-forming practices are reliable in order to be justified in relying upon the beliefs they produce. After all, the demand that we do so is impossible to satisfy since it leads to an infinite regress. Hence the only rational thing to do is to take our stand *within* familiar belief-forming practices 'that have become established, psychologically and socially, in our lives'[59] and to 'follow the lead of Thomas Reid in taking all our established doxastic [belief-forming] practices to be acceptable as such, as innocent until proven guilty.'[60] These considerations apply no less to religious experience than to memory, deductive reasoning, etc: '*for any established doxastic practice it is rational to suppose that it is reliable, and hence rational to suppose that its doxastic outputs are prima facie justified* . . . [Christian religious experience] is a functioning, socially established, perceptual doxastic practice . . . As such it possesses a *prima facie* title to being rationally engaged in, and its outputs are therefore prima facie justified.'[61]

2. *If one seems to see something then this is* prima facie *evidence for the existence of that object (in the absence of relevant evidence that undermines this claim, the experience counts as evidence for the object).*

If one seems to experience God, this is *prima facie* evidence for the existence of God. Swinburne develops this point in his argument from the principle of credulity. Alston notes that while Swinburne applied the principle of credulity to individual belief-forming *events*, one can also apply it to belief-forming *practices*: 'Swinburne's principle applies to experience-belief pairs individually, in isolation, while in my approach a principle of justification that applies to individual beliefs is grounded in a defence of the rationality of socially established doxastic practices.'[62]

3. *Certain conditions must be met, both in and out of the perceiving subject, if the perception is to be possible.*

In the sensory case, the perceiving subject must not be blind, must have their eyes open and so on. In the spiritual case, the subject must usually be 'looking' for God, he or she must develop through practice and discipline the ability to 'recognize God's voice', and so on: 'Among the particular conditions for reliable religious experience, honesty and attentiveness are often singled out as necessities.'[63] Alston comments:

> A priori it seems just as likely that some aspects of reality are accessible only to persons who satisfy certain conditions not satisfied by all human beings, as that some aspects are equally accessible to all. I cannot see any a priori reason for denigrating a practice either for being universal or for being partial . . . quite apart from the religious case, we can see many belief-forming practices, universally regarded as rational, that are practiced by only a small minority. Higher mathematics and theoretical physics certainly satisfy this description . . . Relatively few persons can follow inner voices in complex orchestral performances. But such belief-forming practices are not denied epistemic credentials on the grounds of narrow distribution . . . the most basic point is that God has set certain requirements that must be met before He reveals Himself to our experience, at least consistently and with relative fullness. 'Blessed are the pure in heart for they will see God.'[64]

4. *Such experiences are about or of objects, and these objects usually exist independently of the experience itself.*

Visual experiences are usually experiences of objects that are taken to exist outside the subject. Religious experience is also experience of an object taken to exist outside the subject: 'the mode of consciousness involved is distinctively perceptual; it seems to the subject that something . . . is directly presenting itself to his/her awareness as so-and-so.'[65]

5. *Such experience is 'analogue' (a matter of degree) and not 'digital' (not all-or-nothing).*

'Just as one can sensorily perceive the same physical object with different degrees of attention, and just as a sensorily perceived object can be more or less within the focus of attention, so it would seem to be with the perception of God.'[66]

6. *Successive experiences of the object lead one from a vague experience to a clear experience of that object.*

Seeing a table from a distance is a vague perception; moving closer allows a clear perception. Religious experience occurs in a similar manner:

> The initial stage of awareness of God frequently involves an awakening of the self to a vague sense of God's presence accompanied by intense feelings of joy and exultation. This is often followed by a clearer apprehension of God's beauty and holiness with a concomitant awareness of one's own sin and guilt. Eventually, perception becomes clearer to the point that spiritual work is done on the self in that it becomes more unified, whole, and at peace. Further, God has several attributes. Just as a table could appear circular from one angle and elliptical from another, so numinous perception can fasten onto different aspects of God as he is experienced in different ways in different conditions.[67]

Hence 'one's apprehension of the divine can be self-correcting, just as one can continually correct one's vision as one sees objects from different angles and in different lights.'[68]

7. *The experience is both individual and communal.*

My friend's dog and my friend's God can both feature in the experience of many people at once, although none of these people is sharing the selfsame experience in either case: 'people in the Christian community do tend to make the same or similar attributions to God on the basis of similar experiences.'[69]

8. *There are public checks for perception.*

You can ask other people if there is a dog in the room. You can ask someone else to describe what colour it is, etc. Likewise (although it *is* harder to do), religious experiences can be cross-referenced with multiple witnesses, including testimony from members of other religious traditions and even from non-theists.[70] Several tests can be offered to distinguish true from false perceptions of God. For example: reliable experiences must be internally coherent and externally consistent with those of 'mystics' considered exemplars of religious experience. Such experiences are likely to be repeated, shared by others, and morally beneficial both for the self and for others. Such experience might be expected to conform to an objective body of revelation. Moreover, just as the experience of one sense (e.g. a straw *looks* bent when placed in a glass of water) can be corrected by another sense (e.g. the straw nevertheless continues to *feel* straight), religious experiences can be falsified if they contradict ordinary sense experience. As Layman writes: 'While I resist a dismissive attitude toward religious experience, I think we have to regard sense experience as a paradigm of reliable experience. In my view, any religious experience that conflicts with sensory experience should be considered unreliable.'[71]

9. *Perceptual doxastic practices allow for a degree of inconsistency in their output.*

Alston observes:

> Witnesses to crimes and automobile accidents often disagree as to what happened, and there are undoubtedly many other cases of disagreement that go unnoticed because they are of no practical importance. It is notorious that people's memories often conflict . . . Nevertheless, I doubt that any of our most basic doxastic practices yield enough mutually contradictory pairs to be disqualified as a rational way of forming beliefs. It is only on a fanatically rigoristic epistemology that one would be deemed irrational in holding perceptual beliefs just on the grounds that those beliefs were formed by a sort of mechanism that sometimes yields mutually contradictory beliefs.[72]

The fact that religious experience sometimes yields mutually contradictory beliefs cannot be used to invalidate the belief-forming practice of religious experience, unless one is prepared to jettison memory or sight on the same grounds. However, jettisoning belief in the general reliability of one's memory is self-contradictory. After all, one would have to assume that one had correctly remembered the reason for denying the general reliability of memory in the very process of withdrawing trust from one's memory. Hence, denying the general reliability of religious experience on the same grounds is also self-contradictory, unless one is prepared to endorse a double standard: 'sources of belief can be rationally tapped and can be sources of epistemic justification even if they sometimes yield mutually contradictory pairs of beliefs, provided this is a small propor-tion of their output.'[73]

Lest we become distracted by the analogy with sight, Alston reminds us that 'touch, unlike seeing, involves direct contact with the object; seeing reveals much more detail concerning the object and provides a much more convincing view of its nature and identity. And some mystical perceptions involve a more intimate contact with God, while others reveal him more fully.'[74] Religious experience doesn't necessarily exhibit 'the kind of clear, unmistakable, chock-full-of-information sort of awareness of God that we have of physical objects when we see them with our eyes.'[75] However, 'this has no tendency to show that we don't have any kind of perception of God. After all, feeling and smell don't give us such a clear, sharp, and loaded-with-information cognition of an object as vision does, but nonetheless they are modes of perception.'[76]

Indeed, *this is a tenth analogy between religious experience and sense expe-rience*: both can be divided into different types of experience bearing different types and amounts of information.

10.8.1 Dealing with disanalogy

The most obvious disanalogy between sensory and religious perception is that religious perception isn't empirical. God can be indirectly sensed 'in' or 'through' the beauty of nature, but God isn't part of nature (like a tree or a mountain) that can be seen or touched. Rather, belief in God is analogous to belief in other minds. No human has ever had empir-ical sensory perception of another person's experience (although we all know what it is to know what someone else is feeling or thinking). Someone else's experience just isn't the sort of thing that is open to *direct sensory perception*; and neither is God. If the fact that 'other minds' aren't directly perceivable by the empirical senses doesn't make belief in 'other minds' irrational (and clearly it doesn't) then neither does the fact that God is not directly perceivable by the empirical senses make belief in God irrational. As Keith Yandell argues: 'perceptual experiences provide evidence that there are physical objects; it is arbitrary not to add that perceptual experience provides evidence that God exists, unless there is some epistemically relevant difference between sensory and numinous experience.'[77]

The non-empirical nature of religious perception is not obviously an *epistemically relevant* difference. Indeed, setting up the empirical nature of sensory perception as a necessary condition of reliable experience (something that would undermine our experience of logical and moral truths) looks like begging the question: 'Unless the critic can give a convincing reason for supposing that the criteria available for sense perception constitute a necessary condition for any experiential access to objective reality,' observes Alston, 'he is guilty of *epistemic chauvinism*.'[78] Besides, 'it is a category fallacy to fault . . . God for not being an empirical entity . . . It is not part of the nature of a spirit to be visible empirically as a material object would be. It is a category fallacy to ascribe sensory qualities to God or fault him for not being visible.'[79] Hence, it would appear that an analogy can be drawn between sensory and religious perception in which there are more points of relevant coincidence than of relevant divergence, and that therefore religious experience does provide evidence for the existence of God. As R. Douglas Geivett concludes: 'The strong analogy between sense perception and perception of God ensures strong epistemological parity between the evidence of sense perception in grounding beliefs about the physical world and the perception of God in grounding beliefs about God.'[80]

10.9 The Causal Argument from Religious Experience

In this argument 'a person cites certain experiences of spiritual power and transformation, his changed life, his new ability to handle problems in a way not available to him before his conversion (or before some special numinous experience after conversion), and postulates God as the best explanation for his change.'[81] Alston suggests: 'one's experience of the changes in one's life that follow a conversion, or one's experience of the gradual improvement of one's character in the course of sincere attempts to open oneself up to the influence of the Holy Spirit, can be of cognitive significance, in addition to other forms of significance, as presenting explananda that are naturally explained theologically.'[82]

The causal argument can be framed in the third person, as Basil Mitchell argues:

if [religious believers] did in fact exemplify a quality of life of unusual power and grace of a kind and to a degree that their former personality gave no warrant for expecting, some weight attaches to their testimony that it was 'not I, but the grace of God that was in me', and the value to be given to it is necessarily related to whatever other reasons there may be for believing in the God whose character and purposes they purport to reflect. The situation is analogous to that in which one man claims to have been influenced by another. In assessing his claim we pay attention to such matters as his general truthfulness, the contrast between his performance before and after the alleged influence, the extent to which his words and actions altered in conformity with the other's known views and whether the other was in a position to influence him. To the extent that we are satisfied by such tests as these we are the more inclined to trust his testimony; but his testimony makes its own independent contribution to our final judgement.[83]

Watch these testimonies:
William Lane Craig http://youtu.be/KkAAE2_vLsY.
Lee Strobel http://youtu.be/2AT_bMuFBfs.

Moreland comments:

> Religious transformation has occurred for thousands of years, in primitive cultures and advanced ones, in young and old people, in those well educated and those without education, in cool, calm people and emotional, hysterical people, in those in a religious culture and those in an atheistic culture. Such differences in time, place, upbringing, temperament, and age are good evidence that the common causal factor in such cases is God.[84]

Question:
Record an episode from your own experience, or the experience of someone you know, which you think forms a strong basis for a causal argument from religious experience. Can you set out a logically valid syllogistic argument for Christian theism based upon this experience?

10.10 Rebuttal of Dawkins' Objection to Religious Experience

Richard Dawkins observes: 'the brain's simulation software . . . is well capable of constructing "visions" and "visitations" of the utmost veridical power. To simulate a ghost or an angel or a Virgin Mary would be child's play to software of this sophistication.'[85] This observation concludes Dawkins' rebuttal of the argument from religious experience: 'This is really all that needs to be said about personal "experiences" of gods or other religious phenomena. If you've had such an experience, you may well find yourself believing firmly that it was real. But don't expect the rest of us to take your word for it, especially if we have the slightest familiarity with the brain and its powerful workings.'[86]

Dawkins' attempted rebuttal of the argument from religious experience doesn't actually rise to the level of an argument, since it fails to contain more than one premise. All Dawkins gives us is:

1. Apparent experiences can be delusions created by our brains
2.
3. Therefore, all apparent religious experiences are delusions created by our brains

Merely observing that the brain *can* create illusions provides no reason for the conclusion that all religious experience *is* illusory!

> **Question:**
> Try to formulate a premise that plugs the gap in Dawkins' argument while restricting the illusion-giving power of the brain to religious experiences. If you manage to formulate such a premise, do you think it's more plausibly true than false?

Conclusion

Evelyn Underhill writes:

> Our spiritual life is God's affair, because whatever we may think to the contrary, it is really produced by God's steady attraction and our humble and self-forgetful response to it. It consists in being drawn, at God's pace and in God's way, to the place where God wants us to be, not the place we fancied for ourselves. Some people may seem to us to go to God by a moving staircase . . . Some appear to be whisked past us in an elevator, while we find ourselves on a steep flight of stairs . . . But none of this really matters. What matters is the conviction that all are moving towards God, and in that journey, accompanied, supported, checked, and fed by God . . . the solid norm of the spiritual life should be like that of the natural life: a matter of porridge, bread and butter, and a cut off the joint. The extremes of joy, discipline, vision, are not in our hands, but in the Hand of God . . . The supernatural can and does seek and find us, in and through our daily normal experience: the invisible through the visible. There is no need to be peculiar in order to find God . . . No Christian escapes a taste of the wilderness on the way to the Promised Land . . . This is all part of our training and helps us, in a disagreeable way, to realize our entire dependence on God.[87]

Recommended Resources

Video

*Williams, Peter S. 'Religious Experience' YouTube Playlist www.youtube.com/playlist?list=PLQhh3qcwVEWjccogWzetsujJ_3BtcyLJT.
*— 'Prayer & Healing' YouTube Playlist www.youtube.com/playlist?list=PLQhh-3qcwVEWi2KT0RszsmqH8xHDQWdCKN.
*— 'Angelology' YouTube Playlist www.youtube.com/playlist?list=PLQhh3qcwVEW-jxHf8HUnl7sI_cvYnoRyyZ.
*— 'Miracles' YouTube Playlist, www.youtube.com/playlist?list=PLQhh3qcwVEW-jIqwpnQZQfCxB-ZWLXNvh-.

Audio

Craig, William Lane. 'Testimony' www.bethinking.org/resource.php?ID=347&TopicID=15&CategoryID=12.
*Groothuis, Douglas. 'The Argument from Religious Experience' www.relyonchrist.com/Lecture/Audio/22.mp3.
*Habermas, Gary R. 'Is God Active in the World Today?' www.apologetics315.com/2009/07/is-god-active-in-world-today-gary.html.
— 'Is God Active in the World Today?' http://namb.edgeboss.net/download/namb/audio_files/habermas_god_in_world_today.mp3
*Moreland, J.P. 'On the Promises and Problems of Petitionary Prayer' www.jpmoreland.com/media/on-the-promises-and-problems-of-petitionary-prayer/.
Rietkerk, Win. 'Is God a Projection?' www.bethinking.org/resource.php?ID=330&TopicID=7&CategoryID=7.
*Williams, Peter S. 'Religious Experience' www.damaris.org/cm/podcasts/636.

Online papers

'Does God Answer Prayer? ASU Research Says "Yes"' www.physorg.com/news93105311.html.
Alston, William P. 'The Experiential Basis of Theism' http://afterall.net/papers/490772.
Copan, Paul. 'Is God Just a Psychological Crutch for the Weak?' http://enrichmentjournal.ag.org/201203/201203_112_Is_God_crutch.cfm.
Gray, John. 'Myths of Meaning: Breaking the Spell and Six Impossible Things before Breakfast' www.newstatesman.com/200603200044.
Brown, Candy Gunther, et al. *'Study of the Therapeutic Effects of Proximal Intercessory Prayer (STEPP) on Auditory and Visual Impairments in Rural Mozambique', Southern Medical Journal*: September 2010 - Volume 103 - Issue 9 - pp 864-869 http://journals.lww.com/smajournalonline/Fulltext/2010/09000/Study_of_the_Therapeutic_Effects_of_Proximal.5.aspx.

— 'Testing Prayer' www.psychologytoday.com/blog/testing-prayer.

Oliver, IN & Detney, A., 'A randomized, blinded study of the impact of intercessory prayer on spiritual well-being in patients with cancer', *Alternative Therapeutic Health Medicine* 2012 Sep-Oct; 18(5):18-27 www.ncbi.nlm.nih.gov/pubmed/22894887.

Habermas, Gary R. 'God's Activity in Today's World' www.garyhabermas.com/articles/phil_christi/habermas_phil_christi_Gods-Activity.htm.

— 'Our Personal God: God Interacts with Us' www.garyhabermas.com/books/why_believe/whybelieve.htm#ch29.

Koukl, Gregory. 'Intuition: A Special Way of Knowing' www.bethinking.org/resource.php?ID=26&TopicID=4&CategoryID=6.

*Kreeft, Peter. 'The Argument from Desire' www.peterkreeft.com/topics/desire.htm?vm=r.

Licona, Michael. 'Religious Experience' www.4truth.net/fourtruthcb.aspx?id=8589995562.

Lindsley, Art. 'C.S. Lewis on Freud and Marx' http://artlindsleyministries.org/c-s-lewis/c-s-lewis-on-freud-and-marx/.

Lovell, Steven. 'All in the Mind?' at www.csl-philosophy.co.uk/.

McMillan, Duncan. 'Origins of Belief' www.union.ic.ac.uk/media/iscience/article_template_typ.php?articleid=108.

Mohler, Albert. 'The God Gene: Bad Science Meets Bad Theology' www.beliefnet.com/story/154story_15458.htm.

*Swinburne, Richard. 'The Justification of Theism' www.leaderu.com/truth/3truth09.html.

Vitz, Paul C. 'The Psychology of Atheism' www.origins.org/truth/1truth12.html.

Books

Alston, William P. *Perceiving God: The Epistemology of Religious Experience* (Cornell University Press, 1993).

Brown, Candy Gunther. *Testing Prayer: Science and Healing* (Harvard University Press, 2012).

Copan, Paul and Paul K. Moser, eds. *The Rationality of Theism* (London: Routledge, 2003).

Craig, William Lane and J.P. Moreland, eds. *The Blackwell Companion to Natural Theology* (Oxford: Wiley-Blackwell, 2009).

Craig, William Lane and Walter Sinnott-Armstrong. *God? A Debate between a Christian and an Atheist* (Oxford University Press, 2004).

*Geisler, Norman L. and Winfried Corduan. *Philosophy of Religion* (Eugene, OR: Wipf & Stock, 2nd edn, 2003).

Gellman, Jerome I. *Experience of God and the Rationality of Theistic Belief* (Cornell University Press, 1997).

Habermas, Gary R. 'The Silence of God.' Pages 67–80 in *Come Let Us Reason: New Essays in Christian Apologetics* (ed. Paul Copan and William Lane Craig; Nashville, TN: B&H Academic, 2012).

Humphreys, Colin J. *Miracles of Exodus: A Scientist's Discovery of the Extraordinary Natural Causes of the Biblical Stories* (New York: HarperCollins, 2003).

Kay, William K. and Robin Parry. *Exorcism & Deliverance: Multi-Disciplinary Studies* (Milton Keynes: Paternoster, 2011).

Keener, Craig S. *Miracles: The Credibility of the New Testament Accounts* (Grand Rapids: Baker Academic, 2011).

Kreeft, Peter. *Heaven: The Heart's Deepest Longing* (San Francisco: Ignatius, 1993).

Layman, C. Stephen. *Letters to Doubting Thomas: A Case for the Existence of God* (Oxford University Press, 2007).

Lucus, Ernest, ed. *Christian Healing: What Can We Believe?* (London: Lynx, 1997).

Moreland, J.P. *Kingdom Triangle* (Grand Rapids, MI: Zondervan, 2007).

— *Scaling the Secular City* (Grand Rapids, MI: Baker, 1987).

Quinn, Philip L. and Charles Taliaferro, eds. *A Companion to Philosophy of Religion* (Oxford: Blackwell, 1999).

Scruton, Roger. *The Face of God* (London: Continuum, 2012).

Sennett, James F. and Douglas Groothuis. *In Defence of Natural Theology: A Post-Humean Assessment* (Downers Grove, IL: IVP, 2005).

Swinburne, Richard. *Is There a God?* (Oxford University Press, 1996).

*Williams, Peter S. *C.S. Lewis vs the New Atheists* (Milton Keynes: Paternoster Press, 2013).

*— *Understanding Jesus: Five Ways to Spiritual Enlightenment* (Milton Keynes: Paternoster Press, 2011).

— *The Case for Angels* (Carlisle: Paternoster Press, 2002).

Wood, W. Jay. *God* (Durham: Acumen, 2011).

Yandell, Keith E. *Philosophy of Religion: A Contemporary Introduction* (London: Routledge, 1998).

Part III

The Philosophy of Mind

Nobody has the slightest idea how anything material could be conscious.
Jerry Fodor[1]

In 'Sorry, but Your Soul Just Died' (*Forbes ASAP* in 1996), Tom Wolfe grappled with the growing influence and ethical consequences of a purely materialistic understanding of the self:

Since consciousness and thought are entirely physical products of your brain and nervous system . . . what makes you think you have free will? Where is it going to come from? What 'ghost', what 'mind', what 'self', what 'soul', what anything that will not be immediately grabbed by those scornful quotation marks, is going to bubble up your brain stem to give it to you?[2]

Wolfe observed:

the notion of a self – a self who exercises self-discipline, postpones gratification, curbs the sexual appetite, stops short of aggression and criminal behaviour – a self who can become more intelligent and lift itself to the very peaks of life by its own bootstraps through study, practice, perseverance, and refusal to give up in the face of great odds – this old-fashioned notion . . . is already slipping away.[3]

Is this loss of confidence in 'the immaterial self'[4] literally forced upon our brains by advances in neuroscience, where evidence of correlation and dependency between mind and body stealthily transmutes into presumed proof of metaphysical identity? Or is the 'death of the soul' really a consequence of the 'death of God'? After all, if the natural world is all there is then there *can't* be more to the mind than the body. On the other hand, if theism is true then belief in finite immaterial selves – whether embodied (i.e. ourselves) or unembodied (i.e. angels and demons) – becomes a live question. Conversely, if one accepts the 'old-fashioned notion' that *notions* (i.e. *ideas*) and the selves who entertain them are (at least partly) spiritual realities, then one must pay respectful attention to the theistic explanation of this data. Of course, one can dismiss the old-fashioned notion of the self with some scornful quotation marks in order to keep God out of one's worldview; but that seems like the ultimate case of 'cutting off the nose to spite the face.'[5] After all, 'What good is it for someone to gain the whole world, yet forfeit their soul?' (Mark 8:36 NIV).

11. The Mind–Body Problem

In studying man philosophy is dealing with an object which already by an
entire portion of itself transcends the corporeal world.

Jacques Maritain[1]

Introduction

Anthropology (from the Greek *anthropos* and *logos*) literally means
'knowledge of humankind.' Philosophical anthropology seeks to answer
essential questions about humanity, including the 'mind–body problem':
Is the human mind a merely material thing, or does it have a non-physical, supernatural aspect?

Theologian John W. Cooper argues that 'the biblical view of the human
constitution is some kind of "holistic dualism."'[2] The Bible presents
humans as *naturally embodied* beings (unlike angels, who are naturally
non-embodied) and looks forward to human re-embodiment at the
general resurrection of the new creation. However, Scripture also teaches
that what is essential about a human is a non-physical 'spirit' or 'soul'
that exists apart from the body in-between death and resurrection.[3] Hugo
Meynall observes that 'the principal hope of Christians from the earliest

times has been in the resurrection of the body, though they have generally also expected an interim state of survival as disembodied souls.'[4] As Paul Copan affirms: 'The Scriptures strongly favor the view [that] there is an immaterial aspect to human beings – the soul, mind, or spirit – which is potentially separable from the material body – even though this is not the final state.'[5] Christians clearly have an important stake in the debate concerning the mind.

The belief that the mind is *nothing but* the brain is called 'physicalism.' Owen Flanagan embraces physicalism when he states: 'There are no such things as souls or non-physical minds . . . the mind is the brain in the sense that perceiving, thinking, deliberating, choosing, and feeling are brain processes.'[6] Physicalism is a natural result of the naturalistic worldview, for naturalism rejects the existence of anything beyond the world of matter/energy: 'The naturalist will want to say that things ultimately possess the features that distinguish the personal, the purposive, and the mental in virtue of possessing other features that are not of these kinds. For example, in so far as the naturalist accepts the reality of mental states at all, she will think each is really just (constituted by) a certain kind of physical state.'[7] As Bertrand Russell wrote, it follows from naturalism that 'man is a part of nature, not something contrasted with Nature.'[8] Physicalism is a prime test-case for naturalism. If physicalism is false then naturalism is false.

Belief that the mind is more than the brain is called 'dualism' (because it recognizes the existence of *dual* realities: the mental and the physical). There are different types of dualism, but all dualists believe that physicalism is false and that 'persons are or include something non-physical.'[9]

The basic argument developed in this chapter runs as follows:

1. In the absence of sufficient counter-evidence, the *prima facie positive appearance* of reality is probably true
2. The *prima facie positive appearance* of reality is that mind–body dualism is true, and there's insufficient counter-evidence to undermine this appearance
3. Therefore, mind–body dualism is probably true

As Richard Swinburne argues: 'If we didn't believe that what it seems to us obvious that we are experiencing (perceiving or feeling) is really there, when there are no good reasons for doubting that that thing is really there, we couldn't believe anything.'[10] Since this 'principle of credulity' is a basic principle of rationality, and since the above argument is logically valid, everything depends upon the truth of the second premise. This premise contains two claims:

1. The *prima facie appearance* of reality is that dualism is true
2. There is insufficient counter-evidence to undermine the *prima facie* case for dualism.

We will examine both claims, before defending dualism against some well-known criticisms; but let's first consider the relationship between physicalism and naturalism on the one hand, and between dualism and theism on the other, in greater depth.

Dualism and supernaturalism

Supernaturalism is 'the invocation of an agent or force which somehow stands outside the familiar natural world and so whose doings cannot be understood as part of it.'[11] Theism is a type of supernaturalism. So too is the traditional dualistic conception of a human being as more than just biology. As C.E.M. Joad writes: 'Materialism may be defined as the denial of Supernaturalism. It holds, therefore, that what happens in the world is never the result of the agency of independent spiritual or mental powers, but is always explicable . . . "as a consequence of the composition of natural forces."'[12]

If the human mind refuses to fit into 'the familiar natural world' then naturalism is just as false as it is if God exists. The relationship between naturalism and physicalism can be described as 'top-down': If naturalism is true, physicalism must be true; whereas if physicalism is true, naturalism needn't be true. The relationship between theism and dualism, on the other hand, can be described as 'bottom-up': If theism is true then dualism needn't be true; whereas if dualism is true then naturalism is false and, moreover, there is positive reason to think that theism is true (cf. chapter 12). For as J.P. Moreland argues: 'it is hard to see how finite consciousness could result from the rearrangement of brute matter; it is easier to see how a conscious Being could produce finite consciousness.'[13]

From physicalism to naturalism?

Julian Baggini argues for atheism by trying to establish a physicalist account of the mind. He suggests that because the contents of consciousness 'correlate with particular patterns of brain activity,'[14] and since brains that cease functioning 'stop displaying all the signs of conscious life',[15] therefore consciousness 'is entirely dependent on our organic brain',[16] and hence 'the atheist view that we are mortal, biological organisms is well supported.'[17] Baggini suggests that *physicalism* is supported by his argument, and that since physicalism must be true if naturalism is true, his argument for physicalism supports belief in naturalism (and hence atheism).

However, the fact that the contents of consciousness *correlate with* brain activity doesn't mean that consciousness *is* (nothing but) brain activity. That brains which cease functioning stop *displaying* signs of consciousness doesn't mean that consciousness no longer *exists*, or that consciousness is *necessarily* (as opposed to contingently) dependent upon the brain, or that it is dependent upon the brain for anything besides *embodied functional expression*. Baggini's evidence is *consistent* with physicalism, but it doesn't show that the naturalistic view 'that we are mortal, biological organisms is well supported'[18] because all the evidence is also consistent with dualism. As Christopher R. Grace and J.P. Moreland argue:

> If something happens to the brain, memory loss occurs; if a person persists in anxious thoughts, brain chemistry changes. But none of this says anything at all about what mental states themselves are. Something is what it is in virtue of its intrinsic constituents (i.e. its properties, potentialities, and parts) and not in virtue of what caused it or what must be present for it to function.[19]

Even if Baggini's argument for physicalism were sound, it wouldn't be a problem for theism *as such*. Physicalism doesn't entail atheism, or the truth of naturalism. Physicalism must be true if naturalism is true, but naturalism could be false even if physicalism is true.

The only evidence against physicalism Baggini considers is 'the testimony of mediums, supposed appearances of ghosts, and near-death experiences',[20] evidence few cite – and certainly not the best evidence – in favour of dualism. Even so, he admits there are 'rare examples of genuinely puzzling evidence for life after death.'[21]

Watch:
Gary R. Habermas, 'Are Near Death Experiences Possible?' http://youtu.be/wUlcpRjfzfU.
Read:
Gary R. Habermas, 'Near Death Experiences' www.4truth.net/fourtruthpbjesus.aspx?pageid=8589952865.

Baggini admits that 'consciousness remains in many ways a mystery',[22] and that 'we do not have a rational explanation for how consciousness can be produced in physical brains.'[23] These admissions are significant. First, they show that *physicalism cannot afford to be dogmatic*. Second, they show that *belief in physicalism is a deduction from a pre-commitment to naturalism, not a conclusion supported by the evidence.* Third, they show that a *commitment to naturalism makes the existence of consciousness a mystery*: 'there are rational reasons to suppose consciousness exists because we are all conscious beings,' writes Baggini. 'In this sense it is rational to believe in the existence of what *cannot yet be rationally explained.*'[24]

Baggini rejects dualism for less than compelling reasons (without considering any of the philosophical arguments for the position); and he embraces physicalism while simultaneously admitting that it is unable to explain consciousness! Baggini's argument only 'hits the road' when he writes that naturalism 'is simple in that it requires us to posit only the existence of the natural world . . . it has everything in the universe fitting into one scheme of being.'[25] If naturalism *could* fit everything 'into one scheme of being' then, by Occam's razor, that would provide some reason to accept naturalism. But supernaturalists dispute the claim that everything *can* be fitted into (or adequately explained by) a naturalistic scheme of being, and consciousness is a prime example of a reality that resists incorporation into a naturalistic worldview.

Reductionism

C.S. Lewis argued that the mystery of consciousness on the assumption of naturalism results from the inherent reductionism of such a world-view usurping the *prima facie* reality of the supernatural:

> At the outset the universe appears packed with will, intelligence, life and positive qualities; every tree is a nymph and every planet a god. Man himself is akin to the gods. The advance of knowledge gradually empties this rich and genial universe: first of its gods, then of its colours, smells, sounds and tastes, finally of solidity itself as solidity was originally imagined. As these items are taken from the world, they are transferred to the subjective side of the account: classified as our sensations, thoughts, images or emotions. The Subject becomes gorged, inflated, at the expense of the Object.[26]

However, reductionism doesn't stop there: 'The same method which emptied the world now proceeds to empty ourselves. The masters of the method soon announce that we were just as mistaken . . . when we attributed "souls" . . . to human organisms, as when we attributed Dryads to the trees.'[27] The problem with pushing reductionism to its logical terminus is that it reduces the reducers: 'While we were reducing the world to almost nothing we deceived ourselves with the fancy that all its lost qualities were being kept safe . . . as "things in our own mind". Apparently we had no mind of the sort required. The Subject is as empty as the Object. Almost nobody has been making linguistic mistakes about almost nothing.'[28]

Reductionism thus makes a common mistake:

> We start with a view which contains a good deal of truth, though in confused or exaggerated form. Objections are then suggested and we withdraw it. But [then] we discover that we have emptied the baby out with the bathwater and that the original view must have contained certain truths for lack of which we are now entangled in absurdities. So here. In emptying out the Dryads and the gods (which, admittedly, "would not do" just as they stood) we appear to have thrown out the whole universe, ourselves included.[29]

While naturalists who admit to having an 'initial allegiance' to describing absolutely everything (including themselves) from 'the third person point of view' using the language of 'the physical sciences'[30] might resist such an analysis, their reductive programme ends up by reducing away the reducers. This makes the naturalist's first-person assertion that the third-person point of view is the truth, the whole truth and nothing but the truth, self-contradictory (who remains to assert the primacy of the third-person point of view?). Instead of explaining away the first-person point of view, we should take it as a given. As Moreland argues: 'A complete, third-person physical description of the world will fail to capture the fact expressed by "I am J.P. Moreland". No amount of information non-indexically expressed captures the content conveyed by this assertion. The first-person indexical "I" is not innocuous, but rather is explained by claiming that "I" refers to a non-physical entity.'[31]

In short: 'if everything is physical, it could be described entirely from a third-person point of view. And yet we know that we have first-person, subjective points of view – so physicalism can't be true.'[32]

11.1 That the *Prima Facie Appearance* of Reality Favours Dualism

According to Keith Ward: 'Materialism is immensely counter-intuitive. It conflicts with our common-sense view that all human knowledge begins from personal experience, that we have thoughts and feelings that no one else can experience, that we are free to plan the future, and that our intentions make a real difference to the world. In short, materialism has a major problem with consciousness.'[33]

Let's play 'odd one out.' If the objects were a toaster, a sandwich-maker, a microwave and a hedgehog, then obviously the hedgehog (as the only organic thing in the sequence) would be odd one out. What if the things listed were: a rock, a computer, a brain, an éclair, and 'your experience of seeing a rainbow'? Which is the odd one out now? As Moreland observes: 'When someone has an occasion of pain or an occurrence of thought, physicalists hold that these are merely physical events that can be exhaustively described in physical language.'[34] But, *prima facie*, this claim just doesn't seem to be true. 'It looks as though there is a clear distinction between the spiritual and the material,' writes Ward, 'that they are different in kind.'[35] Dualism has an *obvious intrinsic plausibility* that the physicalist claim clearly lacks. 'It's simply ridiculous,' writes Roy Abraham Varghese, 'to suppose that feelings and cognitions are nothing but photons and electrons.'[36] No wonder 'almost 70 per cent of those recently polled in Britain believe in a soul.'[37]

The *prima facie* plausibility of mind/body dualism means that the *burden of proof* should be shouldered by physicalism. As atheist Nigel Warburton admits: 'A strong motive for believing dualism to be true is the difficulty most of us have in seeing how a purely physical thing, such as the brain, could give rise to the complex patterns of feeling and thought which we call consciousness. How could something purely physical feel melancholy, or appreciate a painting? Such questions give dualism an initial plausibility.'[38]

John Searle explores the naturalist's problem:

We have a certain commonsense picture of ourselves as human beings which is very hard to square with our overall 'scientific' conception of the physical world. We think of ourselves as conscious, free, mindful, rational agents in a world that science tells us consists entirely of mindless, meaningless physical particles. Now, how can we square these two conceptions? How, for example, can it be the case that the world contains nothing but unconscious physical particles, and yet that it also contains consciousness? How can a mechanical universe contain intentionalistic human beings – that is, human beings that can represent the world to themselves? How, in short, can an essentially meaningless world contain meanings?[39]

The commonsense answer is that an essentially meaningless world *cannot* contain meanings; a mechanical universe *cannot* contain intentionalistic beings representing the world to themselves; the world *cannot* consist of nothing but unconscious physical particles and yet also contain consciousness. Our understanding of mind just doesn't fit with our understanding of matter: 'You will search in vain through a physics or chemistry textbook to find consciousness included in any description of matter,' note Craig and Moreland. 'A completely physical description of the world would not include any terms that make reference to or characterize consciousness.'[40] To acknowledge our experience-based self-understanding of 'mind', and to refuse an *ad hoc* redefinition of 'matter' so that it's really just 'mind' by another name, we must deny that the world contains only physical realities and admit that dualism is true.

Consciousness is fundamental to our self-understanding; but rather than *explaining* consciousness, physicalism ends up *explaining it away* by telling us that consciousness is really 'nothing but' this or that (or *some*) physical reality. Yet it's odd to ask whether my feeling of hunger is larger or smaller than my belief that angel cake will satisfy my hunger. Again, what mass should be attributed to my belief that angel cake would be nice to eat? Is this belief more or less massive than my memory of the texture and smell of angel cake? Are a child's thoughts about angel cake lighter than an adult's? How many thoughts about angel cake would fit on a pinhead? Does the answer to this question halve if I think about *pairs* of angel cakes? Are my thoughts about angel cake less dense than your thoughts about rock cake? If thoughts were physical one would expect such questions to be meaningful. Instead, they are absurd. The mind *appears* to be non-physical, and this appearance puts the burden of proof on the naturalist to show that *despite appearances* physicalism is true. As Swinburne muses: 'Much philosophical ink has been spent in trying to construct arguments to deny what seems to stare us in the face – that conscious events are distinct from brain events.'[41]

Philosopher of mind Jaegwon Kim once recommended that naturalists simply *deny the reality of the mental*, observing that belief in naturalism extracts a high price in terms of what one can believe about reality. However, as Moreland comments: 'If feigning anesthesia is the price to be paid to retain naturalism, then the price is too high.'[42] Even Kim acknowledged that 'if a whole system of phenomena that are *prima facie* not among the basic physical phenomena [i.e. mental phenomena] resists physical explanation, and especially if we do not even know where or how to begin, it would be time to re-examine one's physicalist commitments.'[43] Kim has since taken his own advice and has adopted a minimal form of dualism. A handful of naturalists may still say that 'there seems to be phenomenology, but it does not follow from this undeniable, universally attested fact that there really is phenomenology.'[44] But as Charles Taliaferro comments: 'generally, philosophers have come to abandon the project of eliminating consciousness. The denial of our mental life simply flies in the face of every waking moment. The subsequent philosophical task has been to explain, rather than to explain away, consciousness.'[45]

11.1.1 Qualia and self-knowledge

Chris Eliasmith observes that 'philosophers of mind have, for the past ten years begun to seriously question the possibility that science will be able to close the explanatory gap between the brain and our conscious experience, or qualia.'[46] 'Qualia' means the subjective experiential character (also known as the 'phenomenology') of a conscious experience:

> The subjective character of experience is hard to capture in physicalist terms. The simple fact of consciousness, constituted by the subjective feel or texture of experience itself, is a serious difficulty for physicalists . . . Subjective states of experience are real – people experience sounds, tastes, colors, thoughts, pains – and they are essentially characterized by their subjective nature. But this does not appear to be true of anything physical.[47]

There isn't merely an explanatory gap here that has yet to be bridged, but an explanatory gap that gives every appearance of being unbridgeable *in principle*. Although the objective 'wetness' of water as a physical property can be reductively explained in terms of the behaviour of water molecules, the phenomenology (subjective experience) of 'getting wet' seems like the sort of thing that couldn't be explained in an analogous manner. As Warburton admits:

> Although we can talk about 'water' and 'H_2O' as alternative descriptions of the same thing, 'a recollection of my first view of New York' cannot so easily be paraphrased as 'a certain brain state'. The difference is that . . . there is a particular feel to this conscious experience. Yet to reduce this thought simply to a brain state gives no explanation of how this could possibly be so. It ignores one of the most basic phenomena associated with consciousness and thinking: the existence of *qualia*.[48]

Many arguments for dualism rely upon 'Leibniz's law of the indiscernibility of identicals':

> *If you've got two truly identical things, then there is only one thing you are talking about – not two – and any truth that applies to 'one' applies to the 'other'.* This suggests a test for identity: If you could find one thing true of x that is not true of y, or vice versa, then x cannot be identical to y (or vice versa). Further, if you could find one thing that could possibly be true of x and not y (or vice versa), even if it isn't actually true, then x cannot be identical to y . . . if we can find just one thing true, or even possibly true of consciousness and the self that is not of the brain/body and its physical states, or vice versa, then dualism is established.[49]

Gary R. Habermas and J.P. Moreland argue for dualism using 'Leibniz's law of the indiscernibility of identicals' and the existence of qualia:

> Picture a pink elephant in your mind. Now close your eyes and look at the image. In your mind, you will see a pink property . . . There will be no pink elephant outside you, but there will be a pink image of one in your mind. However, there will be no pink entity in your brain; no neurophysiologist could open your brain and see a pink entity while you are having the sense image. The sensory event has a property – pink – that no brain event has. Therefore, they cannot be identical.[50]

In syllogistic form:

1. If we can find just one thing true of consciousness and the self that is not of the brain/body and its physical states, then dualism is true
2. Consciousness can include qualia (e.g. the pink of an imagined elephant), whereas the brain/body and its physical states can't (or at least don't) include qualia
3. Therefore, dualism is true

Moreover, I know (at least some of) the contents of my own mental life *incorrigibly* (without the possibility of being mistaken). It's impossible for me to mistakenly think that I am in pain: 'physical states/properties are not self-presenting, but mental states/properties are, as evidenced by the twin phenomena of private access and incorrigibility. Thus, physical states/properties are not identical to mental states/properties.'[51] In other words:

1. If we can find just one thing true of consciousness and the self that is not of the brain/body and its physical states, then dualism is true
2. Some mental states are incorrigible, but no physical state is incorrigible
3. Therefore, dualism is true

Minds are best known from the inside out, but brains are best known from the outside in. Thus the mind and the brain can't be identical.

11.1.2 First and third person

Fred I. Dretske affirms that 'for a materialist there are no facts that are accessible to only one person.'[52] But reality doesn't play the materialist's game: 'A neurophysiologist can know more about my brain than

I do, but he cannot know more about my mental life.'[53] Scientists can look at my brain with measuring and imaging devices, whereas I might know nothing about my brain. Of all people, I am in the *worst* position to know about my brain (e.g. I can't know anything about it while I'm sleeping, whereas a third party can). It seems to follow from physicalism that the person who knows most about my brain knows most about my mind. Yet, however much someone knows about my brain, they clearly wouldn't know my mental state in the unique way that I know it. As Charles Taliaferro writes:

> Is my thinking 'I am puzzled by your gaze' the same thing as electrochemical processes in my brain? Is observing my behaviour, brain, and nervous system the very same thing as observing my puzzlement? My puzzlement (and all my thoughts and emotions) may be brought on by brain and other bodily states, but it is not the very same thing as these states . . . it has been forcefully argued by a range of philosophers that knowledge of the physical does not (taken alone) constitute knowledge of consciousness . . . A growing number of philosophers have recognized the difficulty of seeing consciousness as an exclusively biological process . . . The issue is not merely a matter of the physical and mental merely appearing to be different; the physical description of the brain is not *ipso facto* a description of the person's thoughts.[54]

The qualia and incorrigible self-knowledge of mental states are incompatible with the public accessibility of physical phenomena, and this observation provides *prima facie* reason to doubt physicalism.

> **Question:**
> Is the above case for dualism undermined by distinguishing between a chunk of matter (e.g. a brain) *as known to other chunks of matter* (e.g. scientists) *and as known to itself*; between *knowing about* a chunk of matter and *being* that chunk of matter?

11.2 That There Is Insufficient Counter-Evidence to Undermine the *Prima Facie* Case for Dualism

The lack of sufficient counter-evidence required to rebut the *prima facie* case for dualism is shown by the twin facts that: i) many physicalists admit the explanatory shortcomings of physicalism, and ii) physicalists resort to begging the question against dualism in order to maintain their physicalism.

11.2.1 The explanatory failure of physicalism

Richard Carrier believes that 'the mind is solely the product of a functioning, physical brain, an active pattern of matter and energy in space-time.'[55] He claims that physicalism 'explains everything about us, and explains it well, with the fewest *ad hoc* hypotheses.'[56] However, he admits that 'we are still looking for a complete theory of consciousness'[57] and that 'there are still a lot of things left to discover about how the brain works to produce human experience.'[58] Indeed, Carrier tries to '*fill in the blanks* according to the predictions of Metaphysical Naturalism.'[59] In other words, physicalism does *not* explain 'everything about us', let alone well!

Anthony O'Hear recounts the current situation in consciousness studies:

> Evolutionary biology and psychology can give partial accounts of particular mental functions ... But these explanations, such as they are, assume that we do have consciousness, thought and experience ... What they do not explain, and what we have hardly any handle on at all, is how consciousness, thought and experience can be produced by material processes at all. The most we can do is to correlate these mental phenomena with brain activity. But however fine-grained these accounts get, they do nothing to solve the basic enigma, which is how mental states and experience can emerge from physical matter ...[60]

As Moreland observes: 'consciousness has stubbornly resisted treatment in physical terms.'[61] Physicalism fails to carry the proper burden of proof placed upon it by the principle of credulity as applied to consciousness:

- According to William Hasker: 'the prevalent materialisms concerning persons and consciousness are in a state of incipient crisis.'[62]
- C. Stephen Evans confirms: 'a careful look at recent work on the mind-body problem clearly shows that materialism is in what could be called a state of crisis.'[63]
- Grace and Moreland state: 'The simple fact is that there is turmoil today in philosophy of mind precisely because the discipline is dominated by physicalists who just do not know what to do with consciousness.'[64]

These assessments can't be dismissed as the 'biased' view of dualists, because *physicalists make the same admissions*. In 2005 philosopher of mind David Chalmers observed:

Jaegwon Kim's new book, 'Physicalism or Something Near Enough' . . . is especially notable for the fact that *Kim, often seen as an arch-reductionist, comes out of the closet as a dualist* . . . As the title suggests, Kim soft pedals his debut as a dualist a little . . . this makes at least three prominent materialists who have abandoned the view in the last few years. Apart from Kim, there's Terry Horgan and Stephen White . . . If I had to guess, I'd guess that the numbers within philosophy of mind are 50% materialist, 25% agnostic, 25% dualist.[65]

A recent survey of philosophers indicated that while 56.4% accepted or leaned towards physicalism, 27% accepted or leaned towards non-physicalist views.[66] That physicalism still gets more 'votes' than dualism is rather surprising in light of what leading naturalists say about physicalism:

- **Jerry Fodor:** 'Nobody has the slightest idea how anything material could be conscious.'[67]
- **Christof Koch:** 'exactly how organized brain matter gives rise to images and sounds, lust and hate, memories, dreams, and plans, remains unclear.'[68]
- **Susan Blackmore:** 'objects in the physical world and subjective experience of them seem to be two radically different things: so how can one give rise to the other? No one has an answer to this question.'[69]
- **Matthew D. Lieberman:** 'Given a materialist view of the universe, it makes no sense to talk about consciousness or experience at all. We have absolutely no idea what it is about the three pounds of mush between our ears that allows it to perform this trick of being conscious.'[70]
- **Steven Pinker:** 'The Hard Problem . . . is why it feels like something to have a conscious process going on in one's head... no one knows what a solution might look like or even whether it is a genuine scientific problem in the first place . . . No one knows what to do with the Hard Problem.'[71]
- **Richard Dawkins:** 'Steven [Pinker] elegantly sets out the problem of subjective consciousness, and asks where it comes from and what's the explanation. Then he's honest enough to say, "Beats the heck out of me." That is an honest thing to say, and I echo it. We don't know. We don't understand it.'[72]
- **John Searle:** 'The hard problem of consciousness is to account for how it can exist and function in a way that is private, subjective, and qualitative, in a world that consists of public, objective, physical phenomena. How . . . could the electrochemical activities of a kilogram and a half . . . of matter in my skull cause all of my conscious

experiences? . . . The equation one dollar = one hundred cents can work because both sides are sums of money. But you couldn't have one hundred cents = one month, because cents and months are in different dimensions. Mind and brain appear to be in different dimensions, because mind has qualitative subjectivity and brain does not. If you try to say, for example, that the experience of red is identical with neuron firings, the terms of the equation seem to be in different dimensions, because the conscious experience of red has the qualitative subjectivity that I described earlier, while neuron firings do not.'[73]

- **David Chalmers:** 'How are we going to be able to explain subjective experiences in terms of the objective processes which are familiar from science? How do 100 billion neurons interacting in the brain somehow come together to produce this experience of a conscious mind with all its wonderful images and sounds? I think right now nobody knows the answer to that question. One could argue about whether such a reduction of subjective experience to a physical process is going to be possible at all . . . Nobody tries to explain, say space or time in terms of something which is more basic . . . They end up taking *something* as fundamental. My own view is that to be consistent we have to say the same thing about consciousness. If it turns out that the facts about consciousness can't be derived from the fundamental physical properties we already have . . . the consistent thing to say is "OK, then consciousness isn't to be reduced. It's irreducible. It's fundamental. It's a basic feature of the world." So what we have to do when it comes to consciousness is admit it as a fundamental feature of the world – as irreducible as space and time.'[74]

No wonder materialist Mathew Iredale says: 'There appears to be something of a crisis of confidence in materialist accounts of consciousness.'[75] As Frank Dilley observes: 'The roster of the dissatisfied in contemporary philosophy of mind is impressive.'[76] Naturalistic philosopher of mind John Heil notes that 'in recent years, dissatisfaction with materialist assumptions has led to a revival of interest in forms of dualism.'[77]

Anthony Freeman, editor of the *Journal of Consciousness Studies*, admits: 'cognitive science is still long on questions and short on agreed answers . . . Meanwhile, the whole enterprise of treating the mind/brain like a computer that processes information still finds opposition at the highest level.'[78] Joshua Stern vented his frustration with the mutually contradictory 'parochialism' of consciousness studies in the journal *Psyche*: 'Physicists advocate [quantum mechanics], biologists neurons, and good computationalists like myself, computers, each looking with bemused condescension upon their eccentric neighbours. Can we get some bakers to participate in this forum, who will advocate that the roots of consciousness reside in the éclair?'[79]

Perhaps the problem isn't with deciding what physical system explains consciousness, but with the attempt to give consciousness a physical explanation in the first place. The suggestion that the roots of consciousness might reside in the éclair seems to me to be on a par with the suggestion that neurons (or any physical system) might be up to the task. As Joad said: 'This parochial [physicalist] concept of mind is, in turn, due to a parochial identification of reality with that which can be seen and touched or which is at least of the same nature as that which can be seen and touched.'[80] His review of various responses to the problem of consciousness leads Freeman to the concluding note that 'a final – but little heard – possibility might be . . . the placing of conscious thought in a different realm from the physical world.'[81] Indeed, given that dualism is the commonsense, default view, one can take the failure of naturalism to account for the mind as a failure to rebut dualism, a failure that fully justifies a return to default. As Susan Blackmore ruefully observes: 'mind and body – brain and consciousness – cannot be two different substances . . . Yet dualities of various kinds keep popping up all over the place, in spite of people's best efforts to avoid them.'[82]

If physicalism is an explanatory failure, why does anyone believe it? With Keith E. Yandell: 'I suspect . . . that the argument against . . . dualism, more draws psychological support from the current philosophical culture than from sound and valid arguments.'[83] That is, physicalism retains the status of orthodoxy because *naturalism* enjoys the same status. As Edward Fesser comments: 'the dominance of materialism in the philosophy of mind would seem to rest largely on the belief that materialism has been established everywhere *else*, so that it is reasonable to expect it to succeed where the mind is concerned. But it seems clear that materialism has not been established everywhere else.'[84] Indeed, 'over the last thirty years there have been serious challenges to the naturalistic framework . . . and a dynamic revival of philosophical theism.'[85] The revivals of theism and dualism are mutually supporting.

11.2.2 *Question begging*

Physicalism remains the principal position within the philosophy of mind, not on its explanatory merits, but because naturalism continues to rule the roost in our intellectual culture at large. As William Lycan writes: 'few theorists question the eventual truth of materialism in some form, but many see a deep principled difficulty for the materialist in giving a plausible account of consciousness.'[86] Thus Keith Ward writes about 'the materialist *faith* . . . that one day a complete materialistic account of all mental phenomena will be given.'[87] Neuroscientist Matthew D. Lieberman writes: 'I am a neuroscientist and so 99% of the time I behave like a materialist, acknowledging that the mind is real but fully dependent on the brain. But we don't actually know this. We really don't. We assume our sense of will is a causal result of the neurochemical processes in our brain, but this is a leap of faith.'[88] Likewise, Colin McGinn begrudgingly admits that his belief that only the physical exists is 'an article of metaphysical faith.'[89] Here we have clear examples of what philosopher Karl Popper disparagingly dubbed 'promissory naturalism.'[90] Searle concludes:

> Acceptance of the current [physicalist] views [in philosophy of mind] is motivated not so much by an independent conviction of their truth as by a terror of what are apparently the only alternatives. That is, the choice . . . between a 'scientific' [i.e. naturalistic] approach, as represented by one or another of the current versions of 'materialism', and an 'unscientific' [i.e. supernatural] approach, as represented by [the] traditional religious conception of the mind.[91]

Georges Rey's assertion that 'any ultimate explanation of mental phenomena will have to be in *non*-mental terms, or else it won't be an *explanation* of it'[92] is question begging. Why think that the ultimate explanation of mental phenomena X can't be mental phenomena Y (e.g. the mind of God) unless one is assuming naturalism?[93] Besides, as Lieberman admits: 'Saying that the complexity of the brain explains why we are conscious is just an article of faith – it doesn't explain anything.'[94]

Question begging unfortunately abounds in naturalistic discussions of the mind–body problem:

- Daniel Dennett begins his discussion of consciousness by adopting 'the apparently dogmatic rule that dualism is to be avoided *at all costs*.'[95] There's nothing *apparent* about the dogmatism of this rule.
- According to Ned Block: 'We have no conception of our physical or functional nature that allows us to understand how it could explain our subjective experience . . . in the case of consciousness we have nothing – zilch – worthy of being called a research programme, nor are there any substantive proposals about how to go about starting one . . . Researchers are stumped.'[96]

     However, responding to the question 'What Do You Believe Is True Even Though You Cannot Prove It?', Block writes: 'I believe that the

"Hard Problem of Consciousness" will be solved by conceptual advances made in connection with cognitive neuroscience.'[97] He explains:

> No one has a clue (at the moment) how to answer the question of why the neural basis of the phenomenal feel of my experience of red is the neural basis of that phenomenal feel rather than a different one or none at all. There is an 'explanatory gap' here which no one has a clue how to close ... The mind-body problem is so singular that no appeal to the closing of past explanatory gaps really justifies optimism, but I am optimistic none-theless.[98]

That's a clear admission that we lack a naturalistic account of consciousness and that optimism about the possibility of such an account is based upon the *assumption* of naturalism.

- A.G. Cairns-Smith begins his investigation of consciousness by assuming that consciousness has a wholly material explanation:

> The story which I will be telling . . . goes something like this. The root phenomena of consciousness are feelings and sensations . . . And I take it that the means to produce all such forms of consciousness evolved: that the ability to make sensations such as pain and hunger was perfected by natural selection because these sensations were useful . . . Now the ulti-mate means of production of any evolved function lies in material genes . . . and the only thing that DNA molecules can do is organise other molecules. It is part of the material world, the world of molecular machinery, quite as much as the ability to contract a muscle or convert the energy of sunlight into fuel. They are all evolved functions. They are all on a par.[99]

Smith's conclusion (that qualia are 'part of the material world') follows from his assumption (that qualia are part of the material world)! That 'the means to produce all such forms of consciousness evolved' because their existence was 'useful' is a non-explanation that fails to account for the initial appearance of qualia. Moreover, having asserted that qualia are part of the material world, Smith admits: 'Of course they don't seem to be. Molecular machines may explain how a muscle contracts, but how can it ever explain the sensation of a colour, or the nature and quality of a pang of guilt?'[100] How indeed? Smith's assumption condemns him to write a book that ends, as it begins, with the mere *assumption* that consciousness is physical. Smith's book is full of statements like: 'We are *supposing* that feelings are physical effects'[101] and '*I think* the phenomena of consciousness *will turn out to be* identifiable with brain processes.'[102] Hence consciousness 'remains a mystery' for Smith, and he acknowledges that he can't give 'a proper understanding of what consciousness is in physical terms.'[103]

- The same question-begging dynamic is clearly at work in Michael Lockwood's thinking:

> I count myself a materialist . . . I take consciousness to be a species of brain activity. Having said that, however, it seems to me evident that no description of brain activity of the relevant kind, couched in the currently available language of physics . . . is remotely capable of capturing what is distinctive about consciousness. So glaring, indeed, are the shortcomings of all the reductive programmes currently on offer, that I cannot believe that anyone with a philosophical training, looking dispassionately at these programmes, would take any of them seriously for a moment, were it not for the deep-seated conviction that . . . *something* along the lines of what the reductionists are offering *must* be true.[104]

As John C. Eccles and Daniel N. Robinson comment: 'Promissory materialism is simply a religious belief held by dogmatic materialists . . . who often confuse their religion with their science.'[105] For dogmatic naturalists who want to explain consciousness in purely naturalistic terms, atheist A.J. Ayer's comments remain pertinent:

> Take . . . the thesis of physicalism; that all statements which ostensibly refer to mental states or processes are translatable into statements about physical occurrences. The obvious way to refute it is to produce a counter-example, which in this case seems quite easy. There are any number of statements about people's thoughts and sensations and feelings which appear to be logically independent of any statement about their bodily condition or behaviour. But the adherent to physicalism may not recognize these examples: he may insist that they be interpreted in accordance with his principles. He will do so not because this is the meaning that they manifestly have, but because he has convinced himself on *a priori* grounds that no other way of interpreting them is possible. Our only hope then is to make the interpretations appear so strained that the assumptions on which they rest become discredited.[106]

Watch:
Alvin Plantinga, 'Is A Person All Material?' http://youtu.be/ajPaCfHFR6Y.

Question:
Formulate an argument for dualism in the form of a single disjunctive syllogism. Which premise of your argument would a naturalist deny and why? What do you make of this denial?

11.3 The Slippery Slope Objection

Richard Dawkins writes:

> A dualist acknowledges a fundamental distinction between matter and mind. A monist, by contrast, believes that mind is a manifestation of matter – material in the brain or perhaps a computer – and cannot exist apart from matter. A dualist believes the mind is some kind of disembodied spirit that *inhabits* the body and therefore conceivably could leave the body and exist somewhere else. Dualists readily interpret mental illness as 'possession by devils', those devils being spirits whose residence in the body is temporary, such that they might be 'cast out'. Dualists personify inanimate physical objects at the slightest opportunity, seeing spirits and demons even in waterfalls and clouds.[107]

What we have here is a 'slippery slope' argument, powered by the fear of social embarrassment, which simply begs the question against the reality of demons. On the one hand, plenty of dualists don't believe in demons. On the other hand, despite being a dualist who does believe in demons, I manage to avoid personifying inanimate objects 'at the slightest opportunity'. I fail to see spirits and demons 'in waterfalls and clouds.' Nor do I 'readily' interpret mental illness as possession by devils. Dawkins' slope clearly isn't very slippery.

11.4 The Interaction Objection

The main argument against dualism is the claim that it's hard to think of the mind and brain as metaphysically different things that interact one with another. Jaegwon Kim argues that 'if the causal closure of the physical domain is to be respected, it seems *prima facie* that mental causation must be ruled out.'[108] Likewise, Dennett asks how the mind can affect the brain when to imagine it doing so means contradicting the principle that nature is a causally closed system. Indeed it does; but so what? The causal closure of nature is *an assumption of naturalism*, not a necessary part of a coherent worldview!

Faced with arguments for dualism, one might conclude that mind and brain are different things, and that since they appear to interact, the naturalist's assumption that nature is a causally closed system must be mistaken: 'there is more justification for believing interaction takes place than for the various formulations of the principle that allegedly justifies the assertion that mind/body interaction is problematic.'[109] As John Foster says of Dennett:

All he has done . . . is to beg the question against the dualist by assuming that the latter will be embarrassed by having to envisage the non-physical mind having physical effects . . . all we are offered is the dogmatic assertion that 'anything that can move a physical thing is itself a physical thing' – as if this is just obvious and something that no sensible person would think of disputing. I have to confess that it is not at all obvious to me.[110]

Hasker comments:

it is often claimed that dualism must be rejected because interaction between a physical substance (a body) and a non-physical substance (the soul) is impossible . . . It is true that we do not understand how an immaterial soul can affect, and be affected by, a physical body. But it is equally true that we do not understand how causal processes operate even between physical things. Sometimes we can explain complicated physical processes by the simpler processes of which they are composed . . . But sooner or later we come to the end of such explanations, and we are left with merely a regular pattern in nature . . . [111]

C.J. Ducasse observes:

The objection to interactionism that causation, in either direction, as between psychical [mental] and physical events is precluded by the principle of the conservation of energy (or of energy-matter) is invalid for several reasons:

A. One reason is that the conservation which that principle asserts is not something known to be true without exception but is . . . only a defining-postulate of the notion of a *wholly closed* physical world, so that the question whether psycho-physical or physico-psychical causation ever occurs is (but in different words) the question whether the physical world *is* wholly closed. And that question is not answered by dignifying as a 'principle' the assumption that the physical world is wholly closed.

B. Anyway . . . it might be the case that whenever a given amount of energy vanishes from, or emerges in, the physical world at one place, then an equal amount of energy respectively emerges in, or vanishes from that world at another place.

C. And thirdly, if 'energy' is meant to designate something experimentally measurable, then 'energy' is defined in terms of causality, *not* causality in terms of transfer of energy. That is, it is not known that *all* causation, or, in particular, causation as between psychical and physical events, involves transfer of energy.[112]

As naturalist William Lycan admits: 'the standard objections to dualism are not very convincing.'[113]

Conclusion

Stewart Goetz and Charles Taliaferro note that 'if "two" things are in fact one, they must share all their properties in common',[114] and so the claim that the mind *is* the brain entails that the mind and the brain must share all their properties in common. However, there's a strong *prima facie* case for thinking that this simply isn't so: 'the mental and physical appear to be irreducibly distinct . . . The problem with identifying the mental and physical, where the physical is identified as the world as disclosed in physics, chemistry, and biology, is that conscious, mental experiences are not akin to any such physical objects, events, and processes.'[115] This *prima facie* appearance puts the 'burden of proof' on the claim that *despite appearances* mind and brain are one and the same thing. However, physicalists themselves admit that not only *haven't* they met this burden of proof (e.g. they lack a plausible solution to the 'hard problem of consciousness'), but that the prospects for a plausible physicalism are bleak: 'So glaring . . . are the shortcomings of all the reductive programmes currently on offer, that [one] cannot believe that anyone . . . would take any of them seriously for a moment, were it not for the deep-seated conviction that . . . *something* along the lines of what the reductionists are offering *must* be true.'[116] That is, physicalists deduce their physicalism from the questionable assumption that naturalism is true. Anyone who lacks a dogmatic dedication to a naturalistic worldview will not be tempted to beg the question against the arguments for dualism.

Films to watch and discuss:
Ghost in the Shell 2.0, directed by Mamoru Oshii (Manga Video, 2010) (15)
Ghost in the Shell 2: Innocence, directed by Mamoru Oshii (Dreamworks, 2004) (15)
- (Audio) Peter S. Williams, '*Ghost in the Shell 2: Innocence* and the Desire for Heaven' www.damaris.org/cm/podcasts/224
- (Paper) 'In Search of Innocence' www.damaris.org/content/content.php?-type=5&id=463

Recommended Resources

Video

Chalmers, David. 'Does Consciousness Defeat Materialism?' www.closertotruth.com/
video-profile/Does-Consciousness-Defeat-Materialism-David-Chalmers-/1172.
Searle, John. 'Consciousness, AI and Free Will' http://videobomb.com/posts/
show/13683.
*Williams, Peter S., 'Mind-Body Dualism, Free Will and Related Issues' YouTube Playlist,
www.youtube.com/playlist?list=PLQhh3qcwVEWh0MdW-hlHBPyLRWgFjzhPT.

Audio

Kreeft, Peter. 'Has Psychology Lost Its Soul?' www.peterkreeft.com/audio/39_soul.htm.
*Moreland, J.P. 'The Argument from Consciousness' www.veritas.org/mediafiles/
VTS-Moreland-1997-Georgia-97VFGA02.mp3.

Online papers

Dembski, William A. 'The Act of Creation: Bridging Transcendence and Immanence'
www.designinference.com/documents/1998.08.act_of_creation.htm.
DePoe, John. 'A Defence of Dualism' www.johndepoe.com/dualism.pdf.
Habermas, Gary R. 'Near Death Experiences' www.4truth.net/fourtruthpbjesus.aspx-
?pageid=8589952865.
Haldane, J.J. 'Sentiments of Reason and Aspirations of the Soul' http://muse.jhu.edu/
demo/logos/v007/7.3haldane.pdf.
Hasker, William. 'How Not to Be a Reductivist' www.iscid.org/papers/Hasker_NonRe-
ductivism_103103.pdf.
Koukl, Gregory. 'All Brain, No Mind' www.str.org/free/commentaries/philosophy/
nomind.htm.
*Lycan, William. 'Giving Dualism Its Due' www.unc.edu/~ujanel/Du.htm.
Moreland, J.P. 'If You Can't Reduce You Must Eliminate: Why Kim's Version of Physicalism Isn't Close Enough' www.epsociety.org/Moreland'sReviewOfKim%20(PC%20
7.2-463-473).pdf.
Willard, Dallas. 'Non-Reductive and Non-Eliminative Physicalism?' www.dwillard.org/
articles/artview.asp?artID=48.
Williams, Peter S. 'Nothing More Than Blood and Bones?' www.arn.org/docs/williams/
pw_bloodandbone.htm.
— 'Why Naturalists Should Mind about Physicalism, and Vice Versa' www.arn.org/
docs/williams/pw_whynaturalistsshouldmind.htm.
Zimmerman, Dean. 'Dualism in the Philosophy of Mind' http://fas-philosophy.rutgers.
edu/zimmerman/Dualism.in.Mind.pdf.

Books

Baker, Mark C. and Stewart Goetz, eds. *The Soul Hypothesis: Investigations into the existence of the Soul* (London: Continuum, 2011).

Beauregard, Mario and Denyse O'Leary. *The Spiritual Brain: A Neuroscientist's Case for the Existence of the Soul* (New York: HarperOne, 2007).

Corcoran, Kevin, ed. *Soul, Body and Survival* (Cornell University Press, 2001).

Craig, William Lane, ed. *Philosophy of Religion: A Reader and Guide* (Edinburgh University Press, 2002).

— and J.P. Moreland. *Philosophical Foundations for a Christian Worldview* (Downers Grove, IL: IVP, 2003).

— and —, eds. *Naturalism: A Critical Analysis* (London: Routledge, 2001).

Fesser, Edward. *Philosophy of Mind: A Short Introduction* (Oxford: OneWorld, 2005).

Gocke, Benedikt. *After Phyicalism* (University of Notre Dame Press, 2012).

*Goetz, Stewart and Charles Taliaffero. *Naturalism* (Grand Rapids, MI: Eerdmans, 2008).

Habermas, Gary R. and J.P Moreland. *Beyond Death* (Wheaton, IL: Good News Publishers, 1998).

Hasker, William. *The Emergent Self* (Cornell University Press, 1999).

Koons, Robert C. and George Bealer, eds. *The Waning of Materialism* (Oxford University Press, 2010).

Latham, Antony. *The Enigma of Consciousness: Reclaiming the Soul* (London: Janus, 2012).

Menuge, Angus. *Agents under Fire: Materialism and the Rationality of Science* (Oxford: Rowman & Littlefield, 2004).

Moreland, J.P. *The Recalcitrant Imago Dei: Human Persons and the Failure of Naturalism* (London: SCM Press, 2009).

— *Scaling the Secular City* (Grand Rapids, MI: Baker, 1987).

— and Scott B. Rae. *Body and Soul: Human Nature and the Crisis in Ethics* (Downers Grove, IL: IVP, 2000).

Nagel, Thomas. *Mind and Cosmos: Why the Materialist Neo-Darwinian Conception of Nature Is Almost Certainly False* (Oxford University Press, 2012).

Searle, John. *Minds, Brains and Science* (London: Penguin, 1991).

Swinburne, Richard. *The Evolution of the Soul* (Oxford: Clarendon Press, 1997).

Varghese, Roy Abraham, ed. *Great Thinkers on Great Questions* (Oxford: OneWorld, 1998).

Williams, Peter S. *The Case for Angels* (Carlisle: Paternoster Press, 2002).

12. The Mind and Its Creator

Although finite mental entities may be inexplicable on a naturalistic world-view, they may be explained by theism, thereby furnishing evidence for God's existence.
J.P. Moreland[1]

Introduction

Arguments for the immaterial nature of the mind have a very long history in philosophy. A more recent development is the construction of arguments from the immaterial nature of the mind for the existence of God. Chapter 11 considered some of the arguments for the immaterial nature of mind, and the present chapter will be best appreciated in light of those arguments.

A 1980 *Time* magazine story on 'Modernizing the Case for God' grouped several theistic arguments that take the existence and nature of a non-physical human soul or mind as their starting point, under the overarching label of 'The Mental Proof', in which 'an all intelligent Being is offered as the only explanation for the power of reason and for humanity's other nonmaterial qualities of mind.'[2] These mental proofs generally fall into three categories:

- Arguments from the non-material nature of consciousness (the 'mental proof from consciousness')
- Arguments from the correlation of non-physical mental experience with physical reality (the 'mental proof from correlation')
- Arguments from the rational capacities of the mind (the 'mental proof from reason')

The first argument is a sort of cosmological or causal argument concerned with the mere existence of immaterial, finite consciousness. The second and third arguments are types of teleological or design arguments concerned with the nature of immaterial, finite consciousness.

Moreover, as Charles Taliaferro observes: 'Consciousness has had a role in other arguments [for God] as well, such as arguments from religious experience . . . and beauty (aesthetic arguments).'[3] These 'other arguments' feature in chapters 10 and 15 respectively.

12.1 The Mental Proof from Consciousness

Atheist Thomas Nagel acknowledges that 'Conscious subjects and their mental lives are inescapable components of reality not describable by the physical sciences.'[4] However, rejecting physicalism (the belief that mind is material) creates an explanatory problem highlighted by atheist Colin McGinn: 'How can mere matter originate consciousness? How did evolution convert the water of biological tissue into the wine of consciousness? Consciousness seems like a radical novelty in the universe, not prefigured by the after-effects of the Big Bang; so how did it contrive to spring into being from what preceded it?'[5]

As B.F. Skinner observed: 'Evolutionary theorists . . . have never shown how a non-physical variation could arise to be selected by physical contingencies of survival.'[6] That the origin of non-physical minds and/or mental properties can be explained in wholly physical terms is *prima facie* implausible:

> It is not a particularly difficult notion that, when the nervous system reaches a certain level of complexity, it should develop new properties [or] that when the nervous system reaches a certain level of complexity it should affect something that was already in existence in a new way. But it is quite a different matter to hold that the nervous system should have the power to create something else, of a quite different nature from itself, and create it out of no materials.[7]

Susan Blackmore muses:

How can objective things like brain cells produce subjective experiences like the feeling that 'I' am striding through the grass? This gap is what David Chalmers calls 'the hard problem' [and] it seems to get worse, not better, the more we learn about the brain . . . The objective world out there, and the subjective experiences in here, seem to be totally different kinds of things. Asking how one produces the other seems to be nonsense . . . The intractability of this ['hard problem'] suggests to me that we are making a fundamental mistake in the way we think about consciousness – perhaps right at the very beginning.[8]

Naturalists see this difficulty as a reason to embrace physicalism. However, an alternative response is to reject naturalism rather than our experience of mind and matter as 'totally different kinds of thing'; and if we reject naturalism, we need an alternative worldview that doesn't lead to the same explanatory problem. Hence J.P. Moreland argues for theism from the intractability of what has been called 'the hard problem of consciousness':

At the end of the day . . . you either have 'In the beginning were the particles,' or 'In the beginning was the Logos,' which means 'divine mind.' If you start with particles . . . you may end up with a more complicated arrangement of particles, but you're still going to have particles. You're not going to have minds or consciousness . . . if you begin with an *infinite* mind, then you can explain how finite minds could come into existence. That makes sense. What doesn't make sense . . . is the idea of getting a mind to squirt into existence by starting with brute . . . mindless matter.[9]

In sum: 'Mind appears to be a basic feature of the cosmos and its origin at a finite level of persons is best explained by postulating a fundamental Mind who gave finite minds being and design.'[10] Angus J. Menuge agrees that 'if human personality cannot arise from the impersonal matter of the universe, its source surely has to be a supernatural being; and on pain of regress, this being must be supposed to be a necessary . . . being.'[11]

Watch:
J.P. Moreland, 'Arguing God from Consciousness' www.closertotruth.com/video-profile/Arguing-God-from-Consciousness-J-P-Moreland-/1168.

Question:
Is it more plausible to solve the 'hard problem' of consciousness by appealing to God than by denying the reality of consciousness?

12.2 The Mental Proof from Correlation

Christof Koch, chief science officer at the Allen Institute of Brain Science, acknowledges: 'a skeptic can always ask why does this particular NCC [neural correlate of consciousness] give rise to a conscious experience but not another one? The cause and effect between neuronal activity in the brain and conscious thought can seem as magical as rubbing a brass lamp and having a genie emerge.'[12] Richard Dawkins notes that 'perceived hues – what philosophers call qualia – have no intrinsic connection with lights of particular wavelengths',[13] but he doesn't pursue the question asked by Jaegwon Kim: 'Why is it that pain, not an itch or tickle, occurs when a certain neural condition (e.g. C-fibre stimulation) obtains? Why does not pain accompany conditions of a different neural type?'[14] Answering this question leads several philosophers to advance the following theistic argument:

1. Mental events are non-physical mental entities that exist
2. Specific mental event types are regularly correlated with specific physical event types
3. There is an explanation for these correlations
4. Personal explanation is different from natural scientific explanation
5. The explanation for these correlations is either a personal or natural scientific explanation
6. The explanation is not a natural scientific explanation
7. Therefore, the explanation is a personal one
8. If the explanation is personal, then it is theistic
9. Therefore, the explanation is theistic[15]

Robert M. Adams asks: 'Why do red things look the way they do (and not the way yellow things do)? . . . why do red things look today the way they looked yesterday?'[16] In other words: 'Why are phenomenal qualia corre-lated as they are with physical qualities?'[17] One might assume that the answer is well known and doesn't involve God: red things look red (and do so consistently) because they reflect a specific wavelength of light to our retinas, causing them to send a specific electrical signal to the brain. Assuming that such scientific descriptions are true, Adams explains:

> they do not answer the question I am asking. For suppose that the experience of seeing red is caused by brain state R, and the experience of seeing yellow by brain state Y . . . This correlation of the appearance of red with R, and of the appearance of yellow with Y, is an example of precisely the sort of thing I am trying to explain . . . Why does R cause me to see red? Why doesn't it cause

me to see yellow – or to smell a foul odor? We do not imagine that R is itself red, or Y yellow. It is hard to conceive of any reason why a particular pattern of electrical activity would be naturally connected with the peculiar kind of experience that I call the appearance of red, rather than with that which I call the appearance of yellow . . . I am not denying that R and Y are in fact constantly *correlated* with the experience of red and yellow . . . I am also not denying that R and Y *cause* me to experience red and yellow . . . What I want to know is why these relationships between brain states and phenomenal qualia obtain rather than others – and indeed why any such regular and constant relationships between things of these two types obtain at all.[18]

Granted that qualia aren't physical, it becomes clear that, as Richard Swinburne argues: 'brain-states are such different things qualitatively from experiences . . . that a *natural* connection between them seems almost impossible.'[19] Indeed, the non-physicality of qualia explains why a natural connection between qualia and brain-states is so elusive. What doesn't seem anything like as implausible, however, is the idea that an omnipotent God could create reliable correlations between certain physical states and certain non-physical qualia. Hence John Locke argued: 'the production of Sensation in us of Colours and Sounds, etc. by impulse and motion . . . being such wherein we can discover no natural connection with any *Ideas* we have [i.e. qualia we experience], we cannot but ascribe them to the arbitrary [i.e. free] Will and good pleasure of the Wise Architect.'[20] Adams likewise argues that 'a theological explanation of the correlation . . . is the only promising one that has been proposed. It is a theoretical advantage of theism that it makes possible such an explanation.'[21]

Naturalist David Armstrong argues for the reduction of qualia to physical qualities: 'at least partly on the grounds that if they are not reduced, we will be left with a mental/physical correlation that physical science probably cannot explain.'[22] But as Adams notes:

Armstrong makes no mention of a possible theological explanation of the correlation, but I think it fair to say that a main motive of his reductionism . . . is a desire to obtain an integrated naturalistic view of the world. He wants a view that neither appeals to a supernatural explanation nor leaves a central correlation unexplained. In order to obtain this integrated naturalistic worldview, he is prepared to deny what I take to be obvious facts about phenomenal qualia. Theism seems a less desperate expedient.[23]

Question:
Is the mental proof from correlation a fallacious 'argument from ignorance'?

236

12.3 The Mental Proof from Rationality

Agnostic philosopher Anthony O'Hear argues that 'there are aspects of our experience and existence more fundamental than science, and on which science depends for its possibility. So science cannot be used, as it often is, to undermine those features of our nature.'[24] O'Hear considers science as a paradigm case of humans engaging in the intentional pursuit of values (including truth) according to the canons of rational judgement:

> In seeing us as determined by material forces outside our control, materialism removes from us the possibility that what we believe and decide might be rationally decided by us after free inquiry. It thus undermines its own credentials as a doctrine to be accepted on rational grounds, for on its own account people believe things only because physical forces compel them to do so . . . [Yet] at the human level, questions about the best and acting for the best are central . . . to the way we act and the way we think about ourselves and each other. And they cannot be reduced to talk about . . . neurons and brain processes [because] brains act as they are caused to do by other physical or neurophysiological processes. They do not act because they think some things are more worth doing than others . . . [But] science itself is a human activity [and] science exists because we . . . find it good to engage in it. Moreover, in doing it, we . . . make judgements all the time about what is true, probable, supported by evidence [etc.] In making these judgements we presuppose that the structures of human intentionality are not wholly illusory. We presuppose that we do in fact make judgements, have ambitions, try to find out what is true or useful . . . and that some at least of what emerges actually is true, useful, fulfils our scientific and other ambitions, and so on. So, can an activity show that there is something amiss with the conditions which actually make it possible? Could science demonstrate that our conception of ourselves as enquirers should actually be eliminated in favour of some other story about . . . nerves reacting and neurons firing, and so on, which made no reference at all to our intentions in doing the activity or to the validity of our beliefs and judgements?[25]

O'Hear's final question is purely rhetorical, for the only coherent answer is in the negative.

The concern that naturalistic accounts of rationality are incoherent finds expression in a number of arguments commonly referred to under the overarching label of 'the anti-naturalism argument from reason.' The core of this argument can be stated as follows:

1. The naturalistic worldview reduces reasoning to a closed, mechanistic, deterministic system of physical cause and effect

2. This reduction is unable to accommodate acts of reasoning
3. Therefore, the naturalistic worldview cannot accommodate acts of reasoning
4. A worldview that cannot accommodate acts of reasoning is self-contradictory
5. Therefore, naturalism is a self-contradictory worldview

Premise 1 is accepted by naturalists, for as Paul M. Churchland writes: 'The important point about the standard [naturalistic] story is that the human species and all of its features are the wholly physical outcome of a purely physical process . . . We are creatures of matter.'[26] Premise 4 is hardly open to serious doubt; hence the crucial step in the above argument is premise 2.

12.3.1 'The cardinal difficulty of naturalism'

C.S. Lewis sets the scene for this argument by observing that 'if Naturalism is true, every finite thing or event must be (in principle) explicable in terms of the Total System [of material realities and relations] . . . If any one thing exists which is of such a kind that we see in advance the impossibility of ever giving *that kind* of explanation, then Naturalism would be in ruins.'[27] In particular, he points out that 'a theory which explained everything else in the whole universe but which made it impossible to believe that our thinking was valid, would be utterly out of court. For that theory would itself have been reached by thinking, and if thinking is not valid that theory would . . . have destroyed its own credentials.'[28]

If naturalism is incompatible with justifiably asserting naturalism to be true, then we cannot coherently claim to justifiably assert that naturalism is true. Moreover, if the truth of naturalism is incompatible with our justifiably asserting *anything* to be true, then, since we know that it is justifiable to assert that some beliefs are true, naturalism must be both false and self-contradictory as a truth-claim about reality.

An early glimmer of the 'anti-naturalism argument from reason' came from Professor Henry Melvill Gwatkin in his Gifford Lectures for 1904–05, where he argued that the denial of human free will (a denial entailed by physicalism) 'reduces every belief to a necessary effect of past states of mind which have nothing to do with truth and untruth. No means is left for distinguishing them, and reason and science disappear in idle speculation.'[29] In 1927 J.B.S. Haldane famously commented: 'If my mental processes are determined wholly by the motions of the atoms in my brain, I have no reason to suppose that my beliefs are true . . . and hence I have no reason for supposing my brain to be composed of atoms.'[30]

Contemporary philosopher Hugo Meynall agrees that 'we cannot subject our mental processes to merely physico-chemical explanation without making a nonsense of science [because] if it is really true that the scientist says what she says only due to physico-chemical causation, then the scientist does not say what she says because there is a good reason for her to do so.'[31]

12.3.1.1 It all depends on what you mean by 'because'!

The best way to exhibit the fact that naturalism discredits reason, according to C.S. Lewis, is to begin by noting that there are two different possible meanings of the term 'because' in the statement 'I believe X because of Y.' One sense is the relation of *physical cause and effect*, as in: 'Grandfather is ill today *because* (cause-effect) he ate lobster yesterday.'[32] The other is the relation of *logical ground and consequent*, as in: 'Grandfather must be ill *because* (ground-consequent) he hasn't got up yet (and we know he is an invariably early riser when he is well).'[33] Grandpa's failure to get out of bed doesn't *cause* Grandfather to be ill, nor does it *cause* us to conclude he is ill; rather, it is our *grounds* for inferring that he is ill. The cause-effect sense of *because* indicates 'a dynamic connection between events';[34] the ground-consequent sense of *because* indicates 'a logical relation between beliefs or assertions.'[35] Lewis explains:

> a train of reasoning has no value as a means of finding truth unless each step in it is connected with what went before in the Ground-Consequent relation . . . If what we think at the end of our reasoning is to be [a valid conclusion], the correct answer to the question, 'Why do you think this?' must begin with the Ground-Consequent *because*. On the other hand, every event in Nature must be connected with previous events in the Cause and Effect relation. But [if naturalism is true] our acts of thinking are events [in nature]. Therefore the true answer to 'Why do you think this?' must begin with the Cause-Effect *because*.[36]

If we reduce thinking to naturalistically acceptable categories the ground-consequent sense of *because* gets pushed out of the picture by the cause-effect sense of *because*:

> To be caused is not to be proved. Wishful thinkings, prejudices, and the delusions of madness, are all caused, but they are ungrounded . . . The implication is that if causes fully account for a belief [as they must do if naturalism is true], then, since causes work inevitably [naturalism requires determinism], the belief would have had to arise whether it had grounds or not . . . even if

grounds do exist, what exactly have they got to do with the actual occurrence of the belief as a psychological event? If it is an event, it must be caused. It must in fact be simply one link in a causal chain which stretches back to the beginning and forward to the end of time. How could such a trifle as lack of logical grounds prevent the belief's occurrence or how could the existence of grounds promote it?[37]

If naturalism is true, our thinking is *nothing but* the effect of non-rational causes connected one to another by the cause-effect sense of *because*. But 'a train of thought loses all rational credentials as soon as it can be shown to be wholly the result of non-rational causes.'[38] As William Hasker complains: '*In a physicalist world, principles of sound reasoning have no relevance to determining what actually happens.*'[39] If naturalism is true, 'our thoughts . . . are governed by biochemical laws; these, in turn, by physical laws which are themselves actuarial statements about the . . . movements of matter.'[40] Nowhere in this closed system of physical cause and effect is there room for the ground-consequent relationship to explain our arriving at this or that conclusion because we see that it is entailed by certain premises and the laws of logic:

> each mental event is [on the hypothesis of naturalism] either identical with or supervenient on a physical event. By hypothesis, the physical event in question has a complete causal explanation in terms of previous events *with which it is connected according to the laws of physics* . . . each such event has whatever causal powers it has solely in virtue of its physical characteristics . . . No causal role for the mental characteristics as such can be found . . . [Hence] *On the assumption of the causal closure of the physical, no one ever accepts a belief because it is supported by good reasons.* To say that this constitutes a serious problem for physicalism seems an understatement.[41]

This observation doubles as a devastating reply to the suggestion that dualists should be embarrassed by having to deny the causal closure of physical reality:

> rationality is called into question by a consistent materialism . . . naturalists tend to limit the reliable use of reason to the natural sciences and, in general, to what can be based fairly directly on sensory experience. But science would be impossible without logical and mathematical reasoning, and on materialistic assumptions, it turns out to be difficult or impossible to give an acceptable account of what reasoning entails. To reason properly (for instance, in a deductive argument) is . . . to accept a conclusion because it is seen to follow from the premises; the logical relationship between premises and conclusion

must play an essential role in determining the conclusion that is reached. But there is no place for this in the materialistic account of thinking. According to that account, the conclusion reached is purely the result of the actions and reactions of the elementary particles that make up our brains; principles of rational inference have no role to play.[42]

As Victor Reppert writes: 'if all thoughts are the result of non-rational causes such that, given those causes, it is impossible that the particular thought should not occur, it is incompatible with the claim that some particular thought is produced by the good reasons there are for believing it.'[43]

> **Read:**
> C.S. Lewis, 'The Cardinal Difficulty of Naturalism' from *Miracles* www.philosophy. uncc.edu/mleldrid/Intro/csl3.html.

12.3.1.2 'It does not compute'

Computers are sometimes said to be counter-examples to the claim that reason cannot be explained naturalistically. However, while we can construct physical mechanisms that act *in accordance with reason* (e.g. a chess computer), naturalism can't accommodate anything that acts *from reason* (e.g. humans programming a computer so that it will act in accordance with the chains of reasoning we perceive). Chess computer Deep Blue's ability to defeat world chess champion Gary Kasparov in their notorious 1997 match 'was not the exclusive result of physical causation, unless the people on the programming team (such as Grandmaster Joel Benjamin) are entirely the result of physical causation. And that, precisely, is the point at issue.'[44] In other words, one cannot point to computers as counter-examples to the anti-naturalism argument from reason without begging the question.

While a computer can be constructed by rational agents to manipulate symbols (symbols that can only be understood by rational agents to mean certain propositions) according to the principles of logic, it doesn't do this 'in thought.' It doesn't understand what it is doing.

✔ Computers possess some of the abilities *of* mind, but they don't *have* mind

Atheist John Searle explores this point with his famous 'Chinese room' thought experiment:

241

> Imagine that you are locked in a room, and in that room are several baskets
> full of Chinese symbols. Imagine that you (like me) do not understand a word
> of Chinese, but that you are given a rule book in English for manipulating
> Chinese symbols . . . Now suppose that some other Chinese symbols are
> passed into the room, and that you are given further rules for passing back
> Chinese symbols out of the room. Suppose that unknown to you the symbols
> passed into the room are called 'questions' by the people outside the room,
> and the symbols you pass back out of the room are called 'answers to ques-
> tions'. Suppose, furthermore, that the programmers are so good at designing
> the programs and that you are so good at manipulating the symbols, that
> very soon your answers are indistinguishable from those of a native Chinese
> speaker . . . Now the point of the story is simply this: by virtue of imple-
> menting a formal computer program from the point of view of an outside
> observer, you behave exactly as if you understand Chinese, but all the same
> you don't understand a word of Chinese.[45]

The only understanding of Chinese in the story is located in the consciousness of the programmers and questioners. Hence, according to Searle:
'You can expand the power all you want, hook up as many computers as
you think you need, and they still won't be conscious, because all they'll
ever do is shuffle symbols.'[46]
   The 'systems reply' to Searle's thought experiment – that although
none of the individual elements which allow the room to function as a
Chinese speaker actually understand Chinese, nevertheless *the room as a
whole understands Chinese* – is actually a *reductio ad absurdum* ('reduction to
absurdity') of the computational account! The 'systems reply' places the
claim that conscious understanding is explicable in terms of nothing but
neurons running computational routines on a par with the claim that (in
principle at least) one can reproduce a Chinese speaker's understanding
of Chinese by giving a rulebook and some pictograms to someone who
doesn't speak a word of Chinese! Are we *really* to believe that there is no
substantive difference between the understanding of Chinese possessed
by a native Chinese speaker on the one hand and Searle's Chinese room
on the other? Searle's thought experiment highlights the intuition that
while a Chinese speaker *possesses a conscious understanding of Chinese,*
the 'Chinese room' merely imitates this understanding (achieving the
same functional result by different means) without *exemplifying* it. The
'as a whole' rejoinder doesn't undermine this intuition. Suggesting that
it does commits a 'fallacy of composition' on a par with responding to
the epigram about the impossibility of getting blood from a stone that
you could get blood if you had a pile of stones! 'Baskets of paper don't
understand anything (including Chinese) and neither do rulebooks,'

says Searle. 'So if *you* can't figure out what any of the symbols mean, then combining you with another non-understanding entity, or even a whole slew of non-understanding entities, is not going to bring about understanding.'[47] Menuge comments: 'it looks like understanding isn't a matter of complexity but of an entirely different ontological category.'[48]

Searle explains that the increase in complexity that results from connecting together non-understanding entities fails to provide any way to move from syntax to semantics:

> why don't I understand Chinese? The answer is obvious: because I have no way to get from the syntax to the semantics; I have no way to get from the symbols to their meaning. But if I don't have any way of getting from the symbols to the meaning, neither does the room. Just imagine that I put the room inside me; imagine that I memorize the rule book and all the symbols . . . now get rid of the room, and I work outdoors in an open field and do all the calculations in my head; then there isn't anything in the system that isn't in me – and I still don't understand Chinese.[49]

A computer cannot have *beliefs*. Nor, consequently, can it have knowledge. Like a book or a map, a computer *contains* knowledge, but *has* none itself. John Polkinghorne writes: 'The human mind is indeed a computer . . . but it is much more than that – we can also "see", or understand.'[50] I agree with Polkinghorne that 'the exercise of reason is the activity of persons and it cannot be delegated to computers, however cleverly programmed.'[51] It is incoherent to view the human mind as 'nothing but a biological computer'. As Aristotle wrote: 'understanding is not an act of our brain. It is an act of our mind – an immaterial element in our makeup that may be related to, but is distinct from, the brain as a material organ.'[52]

12.3.2 Truth and aboutness

C.S. Lewis argued that 'acts of thinking are no doubt events; but they are a very special sort of events. They are 'about' something other than themselves and can be true or false.'[53] However, '[physical events] are not about anything and cannot be true or false.'[54] Being 'about' something, and being 'true' or 'false', are not properties you will find listed in any physics textbook. Hence, thinking 'events' in our minds cannot be reduced to physical 'events' in our brains.

Victor Reppert distinguishes:

> between original intentionality, which is intrinsic to the person possessing the internal state, and derived or borrowed intentionality, which is found in

maps, words, or computers. Maps, for example, have the meaning they have, not in themselves, but in relation to other things that possess original intentionality. But if they possess derived intentionality in virtue of other things that may or may not be physical systems, this does not really solve the materialist's problems.[55]

Thinking otherwise would be question begging. Original intentionality requires consciousness, and while systems lacking consciousness can 'behave in ways such that, in order to predict their behaviour, it behoves us to act as if they were intentional',[56] such ascriptions of intentionality are only analogies. If I'm playing chess against a computer, and I'm trying to figure out its next move, then it's pragmatically useful to treat it *as if* it had first-order intentionality (even though I know that its 'intentionality' is derived from the intentions of its designers): 'I act as if the computer were conscious, even though I know that it has no more consciousness than a tin can.'[57] Hence, Reppert argues: 'my paradigm for understanding [concepts of intentional content] is my life as a conscious agent. If we make these words refer to something that occurs without consciousness, it seems that we are using them by way of analogy with their use in connection with our conscious life.'[58]

Atheist Colin McGinn concedes: 'I doubt that the self-same kind of content possessed by a conscious perceptual experience . . . could be possessed independently of consciousness; such content seems essentially conscious, shot through with subjectivity.'[59] Hence Searle argues that 'any attempt to reduce intentionality to something nonmental will always fail because it leaves out intentionality.'[60] As A.E. Taylor complained, the naturalist:

> thinks of his own perceptions and inferences from them simply as a small selection from the mass of the events of nature, as events taking place in his own mind (or, as he prefers to say, in his own brain), in distinction from those which take place somewhere else. He overlooks the all-important point that *these* 'events' are not merely occurrences in the brain . . . they are pieces of *knowledge about* the 'objective' order of nature . . . How can one 'event in nature' not merely be connected by law with other events, but *be actually* the *knowledge* of those events and of that connection?[61]

Or as C.E.M. Joad asked: 'Could one piece of matter find another piece either credible or incredible? Can a piece of matter, indeed, do anything at all except move, that is, alter position in space? But if it cannot . . . the mind cannot either be, or be the same nature as, a piece of matter.'[62]

A thinking event – such as 'This anti-naturalism argument from reason is giving me a headache' – cannot be a merely physical event, because the former clearly possesses two qualities that the latter apparently cannot (note the appeal here to Leibniz's law of the indiscernibility of identicals): the quality of being *about* something, and the quality of being *true*:

> We are compelled to admit between the thoughts of a terrestrial astronomer and the behaviour of matter several light-years away that particular relation which we call truth. But this relation has no meaning at all if we try to make it exist between the matter of the star and the astronomer's brain, considered as a lump of matter. The brain may be in all sorts of relations to the star no doubt: it is in a spatial relation, and a time relation . . . But to talk of one bit of matter as being true about another bit of matter seems to me to be nonsense.[63]

'We experience,' says Lewis, 'thoughts, which are "about" or "refer to" something other than themselves . . . but physical events, as such, cannot in any intelligible sense be said to be "about" or to "refer to" anything.'[64] Electrical activity in a computer or a brain has all sorts of physical qualities, and stands in all sorts of physical relations, but no list of such physical qualities and relations would include the quality of 'being about' anything: 'no such property or combination of properties *constitutes* a representation of anything,' writes Dallas Willard, 'or qualifies their bearer as being *of* or *about* anything.'[65] Naturalism is thus 'nonsensical' as a worldview, argues Moreland, because it 'denies intentionality by reducing it to a physical relation . . . thereby denying that the mind is genuinely capable of having thoughts *about* the world.'[66] And if thoughts can't be *about* anything, then they cannot be true or false. And if thoughts cannot be true or false, then knowledge is impossible (and the claim to know that naturalism is true is self-contradictory). But since many things are known, observes Willard, 'naturalism must be false. It cannot accommodate the ontological structure of knowing and knowledge.'[67]

12.3.3 Naturalism and the end of reason

Richard Dawkins tries to reduce thinking to nothing but physics: 'The body is a complex thing with many constituent parts, and to understand its behaviour you must apply the laws of physics to its parts, not to the whole. The behaviour of the whole will then emerge as a consequence of interactions of the parts.'[68] The failure of such reductionistic explanations when applied to rationality entails the failure of naturalism, for: 'In order to avoid this kind of reductionism, one must abandon a cornerstone of contemporary naturalism, namely the causal closure of the physical domain.'[69] One must instead accept that 'human beings possess rational powers that are impossible for beings whose actions are governed entirely by the laws of physics.'[70] Indeed:

> an act [of reasoning], to be what it claims to be – and if it is not, all our thinking is discredited – cannot be merely the exhibition at a particular place and time of that total . . . system of events called 'nature' . . . acts of reasoning are not interlocked with the total interlocking system of Nature as all other items are interlocked with one another. They are connected with it in a different way; as the understanding of a machine is certainly connected with the machine but not in the way the parts of the machine are connected with each other. The knowledge of a thing is not one of the thing's parts. In this sense something beyond Nature operates whenever we reason.[71]

Lewis pointed out that naturalism is a system of thought based upon something (i.e. matter) that is *only known through thinking*: 'Reason is given before Nature and upon reason our concept of Nature depends.'[72] Naturalism insists on putting the material cart before the thinking horse, and the result is self-defeating: 'Naturalists have been engaged in thinking about Nature. They have not attended to the fact that they were *thinking*. The moment one attends to this it is obvious that one's own thinking cannot be a merely natural event, and that therefore something other than Nature exists.'[73] What naturalism gains by the simplicity of its explanation is outweighed by its inadequate neglect of this recalcitrant data:

> The validity of rational thought, accepted in an utterly non-naturalistic, transcendental (if you will), supernatural sense, is the necessary presupposition of all other theorizing. There is simply no sense in beginning with a view of the universe and trying to fit the claims of thought in at a later stage. By thinking at all we have claimed that our thoughts are more than mere natural events. All other propositions must be fitted in as best they can round that primary claim.[74]

12.3.4 From anti-naturalism to pro-theism

The argument so far is an argument against naturalism: 'The argument from reason first argues that if we are capable of rational inference, then the basic explanation for some events in the universe must be given in terms of reasons, not in terms of the blind operation of nature obeying the laws of nature. Only subsequently does the argument attempt to show that theism . . . best accounts for this explanatory dualism.'[75]

C.S. Lewis turned the conclusion of the anti-naturalism argument from reason into the first premise of an argument for theism, an argument we may call 'the mental proof from rationality':

> It is . . . an open question whether each man's reason exists absolutely on its own or whether it is the result of some (rational) cause – in fact, of some other Reason. That other Reason might conceivably be found to depend on a third, and so on; it would not matter how far this process was carried provided you found reason coming from reason at each stage. It is only when you are asked to believe in Reason coming from non-reason that you must cry Halt, for if you don't, all thought is discredited. It is therefore obvious that sooner or later you must admit a Reason which exists absolutely on its own. The problem is whether you or I can be such a self-existent Reason.[76]

Lewis thought not:

> This question almost answers itself the moment we remember what existence 'on one's own' means. It means that kind of existence which Naturalists attribute to 'the whole show' and Supernaturalists attribute to God . . . Now it is clear that my reason has grown up gradually since my birth and is interrupted for several hours each night. I therefore cannot be that eternal self-existent Reason . . . yet if any thought is valid, such a Reason must exist and must be the source of my own imperfect and intermittent rationality.[77]

He concluded: 'Human minds . . . are not the only supernatural entities that exist. They do not come from nowhere . . . each has its tap-root in an eternal, self-existent, rational Being, whom we call God.'[78] As Arthur J. Balfour argued: 'all creeds which refuse to see an intelligent purpose behind the unthinking powers of material nature are intrinsically incoherent. In the order of causation they base reason upon unreason. In the order of logic they involve conclusions which discredit their own premises.'[79]

Thomas V. Morris observes:

> Once the universe is considered as . . . not closed, the question must be asked: to what is it open? In simple terms, it could be said that what seems to be needed is some kind of Ultimate Epistemological Guarantee or Guarantor . . . Unless there is some kind of foundational epistemological . . . Guarantor, all men are in a very problematic situation which seems to pull the individual toward conclusions of radical scepticism and personal alienation from all that surrounds him. In a naturalistic or closed universe, there is no such guarantee. However, all men act as if there were a guarantee. Even the radical philosophical skeptic

has sufficiently accurate knowledge of things to be able to use a pen and paper to express his views . . . The conclusion that this is not explainable in a closed system leads directly to the consideration of the other presuppositional possibility – that the universe is an open system.[80]

12.3.5 'Welcome to Wales'

An ingenious version of the anti-naturalism argument from reason was advanced by Richard Taylor, who began with a thought experiment: Suppose you are travelling by train and, glancing out of the window, you see stones on a hillside spelling out the words 'Welcome to Wales.' If, on the basis of this observation alone, you formed the belief that you are entering Wales, 'you would, in fact, be presupposing that they were arranged that way by an intelligent and purposeful being or beings for the purpose of conveying a certain message having nothing to do with the stones themselves.'[81] It would be unreasonable to continue holding the belief that you are entering Wales if you came to believe that the stones had not been arranged on purpose to give a real insight into a reality external to themselves, but had ended up in this formation merely as a result of nothing but natural laws and/or chance: 'it would be *irrational* for you to regard the arrangement of the stones as evidence that you were entering Wales, *and at the same time to suppose that they might have come to that arrangement accidentally,* that is, as the result of the ordinary interactions of natural or physical forces.'[82]

Having made this point, Taylor argues that if you believe that *your own cognitive faculties* are the result of nothing but natural forces, it would be *just as unreasonable* to base this belief on those very faculties:

> It would be irrational for one to say *both* that his sensory and cognitive faculties had a . . . nonpurposeful origin and *also* that they reveal some truth with respect to something other than themselves . . . If, on the other hand, we do assume that they are guides to some truths having nothing to do with themselves, then it is difficult to see how we can, consistently with that supposition, believe them to have arisen . . . by the ordinary workings of purposeless forces, even over ages of time.[83]

If our trust in the stone sign for information beyond itself is to be reasonable, we must not attribute it to chance and/or necessity, but to design. Likewise, if our trust in our own cognitive faculties for information beyond them is to be rational, then we must not attribute those faculties to chance and/or necessity either. Rather, we must attribute those faculties to design.

12.3.6 Epistemology and evolution

G.K. Chesterton warned:

> Reason is itself a matter of faith. It is an act of faith to assert that our thoughts have any relation to reality at all. If you are merely a sceptic, you must sooner or later ask yourself the question, 'Why should anything go right; even observation and deduction? Why should not good logic be as misleading as bad logic? They are both movements in the brain of a bewildered ape?' The young sceptic says 'I have a right to think for myself.' But the old sceptic, the complete sceptic, says 'I have no right to think for myself. I have no right to think at all.'[84]

He argued that 'evolution is either an innocent scientific description of how certain earthly things came about; or, if it is anything more than this, it is an attack upon thought itself.'[85] For: 'The man who represents all thought as an accident of environment is simply smashing and discrediting all his own thoughts – including that one.'[86] Chesterton's concern about the perils of thinking about thought from the perspective of materialistic evolution and the dangers of 'teaching the next generation that there is no validity in any human thought'[87] prophetically foreshadowed the emergence of postmodernism. Many naturalists agree with Chesterton's reasoning while ignoring his warning:

- **Patricia Churchland** affirms: 'Boiled down to essentials, a nervous system enables the organism to succeed in the four F's: feeding, fleeing, fighting, and reproducing. The principle chore of nervous systems is to get the body parts where they should be in order that the organism may survive . . . Truth . . . definitely takes the hindmost.'[88]
- **John Gray** argues that naturalists should *not* treat science as a quest for truth: 'Now and then, perhaps, science can cut loose from our practical needs, and serve the pursuit of truth. But to think that it can ever embody that quest is pre-scientific – it is to detach science from human needs, and make of it something that is not natural but transcendental. To think of science as the search for truth is to renew a mystical faith, the faith of Plato and Augustine, that truth rules the world, that truth is divine . . . Modern humanism is the faith that through science humankind can know the truth – and so be set free. But if Darwin's theory of natural selection is true this is impossible. The human mind serves evolutionary success, not truth. To think otherwise is to resurrect the pre-Darwinian error that humans are different from all other animals . . . Darwinian theory tells us that an

interest in truth is not needed for survival or reproduction . . . Truth has no systematic evolutionary advantage over error.'[89]

- **Steven Pinker** asserts: 'Our brains were shaped for fitness, not for truth. Sometimes the truth is adaptive, but sometimes it is not.'[90]
- **Richard Rorty** argues: 'The idea that one species of organism is, unlike all the others, oriented not just towards its own increased propensity but toward Truth, is as un-Darwinian as the idea that every human being has a built-in moral compass . . .'[91] Rorty asserts the necessity of 'keeping faith with Darwin.'[92]
- **Richard Dawkins** writes: 'We are jumped-up apes and our brains were only designed to understand the mundane details of how to survive in the Stone Age African savannah.'[93]

Of course, Dawkins doesn't mean that our brains were *literally* 'designed'! He means that an *unintended* combination of *unintended* natural laws and *unguided* contingency *just happened* to throw up an ape with a brain that kept its gene-machine of a body alive long enough to reproduce and care for its progeny *in the conditions of Stone Age Africa*. That jumped-up, bewildered ape is us. Hence Colin McGinn concludes: 'given that we are recently evolved creatures with a finite brain capacity . . . it is entirely a contingent matter which facets [of reality] are knowable to us.'[94]

Insofar as this description of humans as jumped-up apes is *amazing*, so too is it *unlikely* ('surprising'[95] as McGinn says) *and therefore self-defeating*. For isn't it unlikely that brains evolved *without design* to survive in the Stone Age African savannah should understand the details of evolution? *If* human brains are shaped for 'fitness, not for truth', such that 'truth takes the hindmost', how can we have any confidence in the claim *made by these brains* that they are merely 'jumped-up apes'? Haven't naturalists laid claim to a position analogous to the person who trusts the 'Welcome to Wales' sign while believing that it is the result of nothing but natural forces? The more seriously we take the naturalists' assessment of human origins, the less seriously we can take it! Thus Eric S. Waterhouse mused:

> Bertrand Russell, in a candid moment, admitted it was a strange mystery that we could judge the works of our unthinking Mother Nature. In our philosophy and science we are so accustomed to assuming that we can, that we do not always realize how ungrounded this assumption appears when we permit ourselves to dally with the idea of a blind purposeless force behind the phenomena of the universe.[96]

Faced with the anti-naturalism argument from reason, Antony Flew once appealed to evolution, objecting that 'it looks as if evolutionary biology and human history could provide some reasons for saying that it need not be a mere co-incidence if a significant proportion of men's beliefs about their environment are in fact true.'[97] However, it's doubtful whether evolutionary biology and human history provide *sufficient* reason for believing that our beliefs about the environment are likely to be reliable, even in the minimal sense of being true *more often than not*. Stephen Stitch contends that 'there are major problems to be overcome by those who think that evolutionary considerations impose interesting limits on irrationality.'[98] Reppert observes:

> the fact that humans tend to respond positively to placebos suggests that false beliefs can, and often do, have survival value . . . If false beliefs about matters that are of immediate concern [such as health] can be false yet helpful, is it also possible natural selection could, in various ways, incline us towards a whole range of false beliefs? Could our beliefs be systematically false [more often than not] and still adaptive? I see no reason to think they could not.[99]

O'Hear acknowledges:

> the evolutionary account does not take us very far when it comes to explaining what we actually know and are interested in . . . we have the ability to find out about all sorts of things beyond what would have helped our ancestors to survive on the savannahs of Africa . . . However our intelligence originally arose, its scope and nature take us quite beyond standard evolutionary accounts of knowledge. Evolution accounts for it only insofar as it is useful for survival, and this turns out to be a very small aspect of what we are about in our search for knowledge and understanding. Against this background it becomes plausible to ask where our pure desire to know comes from, and also why our drive to know might be successful even in areas which have nothing to do with survival value.[100]

Arthur J. Balfour presses the point home:

> At first sight we might suppose that, at the worst, the cognitive series and the causal series might be harmonized on the basis of natural selection if knowledge never aspired to rise above the level which promoted race survival . . . This scheme of thought, though narrowly constricted, is apparently coherent. Yet even this modest claim must be deemed excessive: for the speculation on which it rests does violence to its own principles. Manifestly we cannot indulge ourselves in reflections upon the limits of the 'knowable' without using our intellect for a purpose never contemplated by selection. I do not allege that our intellect is therefore unequal to the task. I only say that, if it

indeed be equal to it, we are in the presence of a very surprising coincidence. Why should faculties, 'designed' only to help primitive man . . . successfully to breed and feed, be fitted to solve philosophic problems so useless and so remote? Why, indeed, do such problems occur to us? Why do we long for their solution? To such questions Naturalism can neither find an answer nor be content without one . . . No rational cure is, on naturalistic principles, within our reach.[101]

12.3.7 Plantinga's 'evolutionary anti-naturalism argument'

Evolutionary naturalism provides an account of our capacities that
undermine their reliability, and in doing so undermines itself.
Thomas Nagel.[102]

Alvin Plantinga develops an 'evolutionary anti-naturalism argument from evolution' on the grounds that 'the fact that my behaviour (or that of my ancestors) has been adaptive . . . is at best a third-rate reason for thinking my beliefs mostly true and my cognitive faculties reliable.'[103] If one assumes the conjunction of naturalism and evolution:

> What our minds are *for* is not the production of true beliefs, but the production of adaptive behavior. That our species has survived and evolved at most guarantees that our behavior is adaptive; it does not guarantee or even suggest that our belief-producing processes are for the most part reliable, or that our beliefs are for the most part true. That is because, obviously, our behavior could be adaptive, but our beliefs mainly false.[104]

After all, 'beliefs don't causally produce behavior *by themselves*; it is beliefs, desires, and other factors that do so together. Then the problem is that clearly there will be any number of *different* patterns of belief and desire that would issue in the same action; and among those there will be many in which the beliefs are wildly false.'[105]

Since naturalistic evolution is 'interested' only in what *works* and not what's *true*, a belief in naturalistic evolution eliminates any rational grounds for confidence in the truth of our beliefs, including belief in naturalism (note that Plantinga doesn't advance this as an argument against evolution, but as an argument against belief in the conjunction of evolution with metaphysical naturalism).

Watch:
Alvin Plantinga, 'The Problem With Naturalistic Evolution.' http://youtu.be/cW7CgOZXVH8.

Having distinguished between the neurophysiological properties (NP) of a *syntactic* structure in the brain and the *semantic* content of a 'belief that p', Plantinga points out that *on the naturalistic account* of mind our beliefs are either 'nothing but' syntactic neurophysiology (reductive materialism), or else the conjunction of syntactic neurophysiology with causally impotent semantic content wholly dependent upon and determined by our syntactic neurophysiology (semantic epiphenomenalism). The explanation of a belief's being adaptive *on the naturalistic view of things* is that the NP properties of the belief cause adaptive behaviour, not that the belief is true. That is, NP properties can cause adaptive behaviour *whether or not the content they constitute (or determine) is true*. Plantinga illustrates his point:

> Think about a frog sitting on a lily pad: A fly buzzes past, the frog's tongue flicks out and nails the fly. Does it matter what the frog then believes, if indeed frogs have beliefs? Clearly not: What matters is the frog's behavior and the neurophysiology that causes that behavior. Of course *something* in the frog registers or indicates the approach of the fly, the distance from fly to frog, the velocity of the fly, and so on; and those somethings are part of the cause of the frog's capturing the fly. Call those structures *indicators*. For the frog's behavior to be adaptive, for it to capture the fly, it is necessary that there be indicators, and necessary that they indicate accurately. But none of that need involve *belief* . . . We don't need to posit true beliefs in the frog to account for its adaptive behavior: what is required is only accurate indication; and accurate indication need not be accompanied by true belief. As long as the indication is accurate, the belief content can be anything whatsoever.[106]

Whether or not frogs have beliefs, humans do. Thus Plantinga points out the obvious problem with the pessimistic claims about human cognition made from the naturalistic perspective of Churchland, Dawkins, Rorty, etc., namely that *in undermining reason the conjunction of naturalism and evolution undermines itself*. On the one hand, if an orientation towards truth is un-Darwinian (as Rorty says) and we accept Darwinism, we provide ourselves with a reason to doubt our beliefs are orientated towards truth, and hence to doubt Darwinism. Naturalism, argues Plantinga, 'is self-defeating, in that if it is accepted . . . it provides a defeater for itself, a defeater that can't be defeated.'[107] On the other hand, if we accept that an orientation towards true beliefs is un-Darwinian, and we accept (as we must, on pain of self-contradiction) that we are in fact orientated towards truth, we thereby provide ourselves with a reason to doubt Darwinism (although not evolution *per se*).

The sort of self-defeating proposition affirmed by Dawkins et al. has been called 'Darwin's Doubt', since Darwin himself admitted that 'the horrid doubt always arises whether the convictions of man's mind, which has been developed from the mind of the lower animals, are of any value or at all trustworthy.'[108] Plantinga argues that Darwin's Doubt does follow from naturalistic evolution, and that it is self-defeating:

> one can't rationally accept the conjunction of naturalism with evolution . . . [But] if naturalism is true, then so, in all probability, is evolution; evolution is the only game in town, for the naturalist, with respect to the question how all this variety of flora and fauna has arisen. If *that* is so . . . then naturalism *simpliciter* is self-defeating and cannot be rationally accepted . . .[109]

Plantinga argues that the self-contradictory nature of Darwin's Doubt provides us with reason for accepting a theistic worldview over against a naturalistic one.

Question:
In what ways might a belief in physicalism be thought to undermine science?

Conclusion

Reflection upon human rationality furnishes a number of arguments against physicalism (and hence against naturalism), arguments that can be extended into arguments for the plausibility of a theistic worldview. C.S. Lewis was right: 'Naturalism . . . offers what professes to be a full account of our mental behaviour; but this account . . . leaves no room for the acts of knowing . . . on which the whole value of our thinking, as a means to truth, depends.'[110] The more naturalists affirm naturalism (and naturalistic evolution), the more they sink into a mire of self-contradiction that points to the necessity not only of a naturalism-busting 'dualism of fundamental explanations; the idea that we cannot expunge purpose from the basic level of explanation',[111] but also of theism. As Robert C. Koons argues:

> materialism, without a designer who intended man to be equipped with an aptitude for truth, leads inexorably to an epistemological catastrophe, the 'epistemic defeat' of all the materialist's aspirations for knowledge . . . There is a price to be paid for . . . the conviction that our scientific theories provide . . . models that we have some reason to believe may be approximately correct. This price is our admission that the physical realm does not exhaust reality, but that it is instead the artifact of a reasonable God who has fitted us to the task of investigating it.[112]

Victor Reppert concludes that several features of human consciousness 'make more sense on a theistic world view than on a naturalistic one, and therefore they provide substantial reasons for preferring theism to naturalism.'[113] Even non-theistic philosophers feel the force of this argument, with O'Hear admitting that 'in a contest between materialistic atheism and some kind of religious-cum-theistic view, the materialistic conclusion leaves even more mysteries than a view which sees reason and consciousness as part of the essence of the universe.'[114]

* * *

Recommended Resources

Video

*Williams, Peter S., 'Mind-Body Dualism, Free Will and Related Issues' YouTube Playlist, www.youtube.com/playlist?list=PLQhh3qcwVEWh0MdW-hlHBPyLRWg-FjzhPT.

Audio

Menuge, Angus J. 'Agents under Fire: Part One' http://intelligentdesign.podomatic.com/entry/eg/2008-08-18T17_44_24-07_00.
— 'Apologist Interview' http://j.mp/Apologetics315-InterviewAngusMenuge.
Moreland, J.P. 'The Argument from Consciousness' www.veritas.org/mediafiles/VTS-Moreland-1997-Georgia-97VFGA02.mp3.
*Plantinga, Alvin vs Daniel C. Dennett. 'Science and Religion: Are They Compatible?' www.brianauten.com/Apologetics/Plantinga-Dennett-Debate.mp3.
Williams, Peter S. and Christopher Norris. 'The Cardiff God Debate' www.damaris.org/cm/podcasts/786.
Williams, Peter S. 'How Can We Be Sure?' www.highfield.org.uk/church/index.php?id=240&sermonid=1727.

Online papers

Groothuis, Douglas. 'The Great Cloud of Unknowing' www.arn.org/docs/groothuis/dg_greatcloud.htm.
Haldane, J.J. 'Sentiments of Reason and Aspirations of the Soul' http://muse.jhu.edu/demo/logos/v007/7.3haldane.pdf.
Hasker, William.'How Not to Be a Reductivist', www.iscid.org/papers/Hasker_NonReductivism_103103.pdf.
Koons, Robert C. 'The Incompatibility of Naturalism and Scientific Realism' www.leaderu.com/offices/koons/docs/natreal.html.
Lewis, C.S. 'The Cardinal Difficulty of Naturalism' www.philosophy.uncc.edu/mleldrid/Intro/csl3.html.

A Faithful Guide to Philosophy

Lovell, Steven. 'C.S. Lewis' Case against Naturalism' at www.csl-philosophy.co.uk/.

Lucas, J.R. 'The Godelian Argument' www.leaderu.com/truth/2truth08.html.

Menuge, Angus. 'The Role of Agency in Science' www.4truth.net/site/apps/nl/content3.asp?c=hiKXLbPNLrF&b=1171681&ct=1579247.

— 'Libertarian Free Will and the Argument from Reason' www.reasonsforgod.org/wp-content/uploads/2012/09/Libertarian-Free-Will-and-The-Argument-From-Reason1.pdf.

Moreland, J.P. 'Does the Argument from Mind Provide Evidence for God?' www.boundless.org/features/a0000901.html.

*Plantinga, Alvin. 'Against Naturalism' (from *Knowledge of God*) www.thedivineconspiracy.org/Z5223A.pdf.

— 'Evolution vs Naturalism' www.christianitytoday.com/bc/2008/004/11.37.html.

— 'An Evolutionary Argument against Naturalism' http://hisdefense.org/articles/ap001.html.

Rasmussen, Josh. 'The Argument from Persons' www.untamedlion.com/ApologeticsWeek5.doc.

Reppert, Victor. 'The Argument from Reason' www.infidels.org/library/modern/victor_reppert/reason.html.

— 'Dr Reppert on the "Argument from Reason"' http://go.qci.tripod.com/Reppert-interview.htm.

— 'Taking Lewis Seriously: Apologetics and the Personal Heresy' www.narniaontour.com/articles/takinglewisseriously.htm.

Swinburne, Richard. 'The Justification of Theism' www.leaderu.com/truth/3truth09.html.

Willard, Dallas. 'Knowledge and Naturalism' www.dwillard.org/Philosophy/Pubs/knowledge_and_naturalism.htm.

Wilson, A.N. 'Why I Believe Again' www.newstatesman.com/religion/2009/04/conversion-experience-atheism.

Books

Adams, Robert M. 'Flavors, Colors, and God.' Pages 225–40 in *Contemporary Perspectives on Religious Epistemology* (ed. R. Douglas Geivett and Brendan Sweetman; Oxford University Press, 1992).

Baker, Mark C. and Stewart Goetz. *The Soul Hypothesis: Investigations into the Existence of the Soul* (New York: Continuum, 2011).

Craig, William Lane, ed. *Philosophy of Religion: A Reader and Guide* (Edinburgh University Press, 2002).

Craig, William Lane and J.P. Moreland. *Philosophical Foundations for a Christian Worldview* (Downers Grove, IL: IVP, 2003).

— and —, eds. *The Blackwell Companion to Natural Theology* (Oxford: Wiley-Blackwell, 2009).

— and —, eds. *Naturalism: A Critical Analysis* (London: Routledge, 2001).

Dennett, Daniel C. vs Alvin Plantinga. *Science and Religion: Are They Compatible?* (Oxford University Press, 2011).

Hasker, William. *The Emergent Self* (Cornell University Press, 1999).

Lewis, C.S. *Miracles* (London: Fount, 2nd edn, 1998).

Menuge, Angus J. *Agents under Fire: Materialism and the Rationality of Science* (Oxford: Rowman & Littlefield, 2004).

Moreland, J.P. 'The Argument from Consciousness.' Pages 383–4 in *The Routledge Companion to Philosophy of Religion* (ed. Chad Meister and Paul Copan; London: Routledge, 2010).

— *Consciousness and the Existence of God: A Theistic Argument* (London: Routledge, 2009).

— 'Hume and the Argument from Consciousness.' Pages 271–96 in *In Defence of Natural Theology: A Post-Humean Assessment* (ed. James F. Sennett and Douglas Groothuis; Downers Grove, IL: IVP, 2005).

— *The Recalcitrant Imago Dei: Human Persons and the Failure of Naturalism* (London: SCM Press, 2009).

— *Scaling the Secular City* (Grand Rapids, MI: Baker, 1987).

Nagel, Thomas. *Mind & Cosmos: Why The Materialist Neo-Darwinian Conception Of Nature Is Almost Certainly False* (Oxford University Press, 2012).

— *The Last Word* (Oxford University Press, 1997).

Nash, Ronald H. 'Miracles and Conceptual Systems.' Pages 115–31 in *In Defence of Miracles* (ed. R. Douglas Geivett and Gary R. Habermas; Leicester: Apollos, 1997).

O'Hear, Anthony. *Beyond Evolution: Human Nature and the Limits of Evolutionary Explanation* (Oxford: Clarendon Press, 1997).

Plantinga, Alvin. *Where the Conflict Really Lies: Science, Religion, and Naturalism* (Oxford University Press, 2011).

— and Michael Tooley. *Knowledge of God* (Oxford: Blackwell, 2008).

*Reppert, Victor. *C.S. Lewis's Dangerous Idea* (Downers Grove, IL: IVP, 2003).

Smith, R. Scott. *Naturalism and Our Knowledge of Reality* (Farnham: Ashgate, 2012).

Swinburne, Richard. *Mind, Brain and Free Will* (Oxford University Press, 2013).

West, John G., ed. *The Magician's Twin: C.S. Lewis on Science, Scientism, and Society* (Seattle: Discovery Institute Press, 2012).

Williams, Peter S. *C.S. Lewis vs the New Atheists* (Milton Keynes: Paternoster Press, 2013).

13. Freedom and Responsibility

> Only in recognizing a trans-physical centre of all our willing can we make
> sense of our experience, and also of the basis of our responsibility.
> Roy Abraham Varghese[1]

Introduction
13.1 Compatibilism, Evil and the Free Will Defence
13.2 Theological Determinism
13.3 Dawkins' Deterministic Delusion
13.4 Naturalism and the Denial of Libertarian Free Will
13.5 Freedom and Responsibility
13.6 Freedom and Rationality
Conclusion

Introduction

Do you have the sort of freedom of will which means that it is ultimately
your choice and moral responsibility that you began to read this paragraph,
even though you didn't have to do so and could have done something else
instead? Some people don't believe in this type of *libertarian free will*. Most
of these free-will denying people believe in *determinism* (sometimes called
'hard determinism'): 'Determinism is the view that for every event that
happens, there are conditions such that, given them, nothing else could
have happened. Every event [including every event in the human mind
and of the human body] is caused or necessitated by prior factors such
that, given these prior factors, the event in question had to occur.'[2] Thus
determinists disagree with libertarians, who 'embrace free will and hold
that determinism is incompatible with it.'[3]

Alternatively, 'compatibilists hold that freedom and determinism are
compatible with each other and, thus, the truth of determinism [which
compatibilists embrace] does not eliminate freedom.'[4] Compatibilists
only get away with having their cake and eating it like this by *redefining*
what they mean by 'freedom.' Compatibilists are just determinists with a
non-standard definition of 'freedom.' Hence compatibilism is also known
as 'soft determinism.'

One needn't think of libertarian free will as analogous to a light bulb attached to a switch that's either on (and you have unlimited free will that you find really easy to exercise) or off (and you have no free will). One can think of free will like a light bulb attached to a dimmer switch. A dimmer switch might be off (and you have no free will) and it might be fully on (and you have unlimited free will that you find really easy to exercise). However, it might also be at any point in-between these extremes. That's analogous to having free will that's constrained and affected by influences like genetic inheritance or environmental conditions. Even if the light bulb is barely on, there's nevertheless a big difference between darkness and even the weakest light. There's a big difference between having no free will and having some free will, however constrained. Like a light bulb attached to a dimmer switch, free will might vary in intensity from person to person and even within the life of an individual.

According to the Bible, God freely chose to create humans with the capacity to exercise at least a degree of genuine free choice. While God wants humans to freely choose the good, he nevertheless allows us to ignore this desire by rejecting good and choosing evil:

> So God created man
> > in his own image,
> in the image of God
> > he created him;
> male and female
> > he created them . . .

> And the LORD God commanded the man, '*You are free* to eat from any tree in the garden; *but you must not* eat from the tree of the knowledge of good and evil, for when you eat of it you will surely die.' (Genesis 1:27; 2:16–17, my italics)

The biblical story is predicated upon the assertion that *humans are morally blameworthy for freely choosing to do that which we know to be wrong* (sin). As H.P. Owen writes:

> Christianity presupposes free will in both the religious and the moral spheres. If our wills were not free in the religious sphere there would be no point in preaching the Gospel. Such preaching would do no more than intensify a pre-existing tendency to accept or reject God's Word. There would be no genuine offer of salvation, no genuine invitation to eternal life . . . Equally Christianity presupposes free will in the moral sphere. If our wills were not morally free we should not be responsible for our actions and so accountable to God.[5]

God desires freely chosen loving relationship with all humans (cf. 1 Timothy 2:3–4); and while, as a necessary precondition of such relationships, God has given humans the freedom to reject him (cf. Romans 11:32), he has also provided them the means to be saved from the natural consequence of sin; namely, by freely receiving his gift of forgiveness displayed in Christ (cf. Acts 4:12). Some welcome relationship with God. Others spurn his advances. Jesus laments: 'O Jerusalem, Jerusalem, you who kill the prophets and stone those sent to you, how often I have longed to gather your children together, as a hen gathers her chicks under her wings, *but you were not willing'* (Matthew 23:37; Luke 13:34, my italics).

Paul Marston and Roger Forster note that although 'free will' isn't a biblical term, it was a term coined by the early church:

> to represent the Bible's teaching that God allows man a choice of whether or not to obey him . . . Not a single church figure in the first 300 years rejected it and most of them stated it clearly in works still extant . . . Thus we find striking agreement among early church leaders over the issue of freewill. The same teaching was held by mainstream and fringe groups, by scholars and ordinary ministers, by the Greek, Latin and even Syrian traditions, by everyone, in short, except total heretics . . . it expressed their universally held belief that God made man free to accept or reject his offer of free pardon and grace.[6]

For example, Irenaeus (c. AD 130–200) wrote:

> This expression, 'How often would I have gathered thy children together, and thou wouldst not,' set forth the ancient law of human liberty, because God made man a free (agent) from the beginning, possessing his own soul to obey the behests of God voluntarily, and not by compulsion of God. For there is no coercion with God . . . in man as well as angels, He has placed the power of choice . . . man is possessed of freewill from the beginning, and God is possessed of freewill in whose likeness man was created.[7]

Christians clearly have an interest in the free will debate. So do naturalists. Note how Irenaeus *explains* free will: *we are not merely physical creatures, but have non-physical souls that reflect the nature of our Creator.* As J.P. Moreland and Scott B. Rae write: 'Persons are agents and, as such, are first-movers, unmoved movers who simply have the power to act as the ultimate originators of their actions.'[8] This makes coherent sense if persons are created in the image of an omnipotent Person with free will (God), but otherwise it appears to be an unexpected and inexplicable brute fact. Indeed, naturalists generally affirm that *given* that humans are merely physical beings, *then* they *cannot* have free will; which is as much as to admit that *if* people have free will, *then* they *cannot* be *merely* physical beings. Hence free will is a crucial testing ground for the naturalistic worldview and a potential source of evidence for a theistic worldview.

13.1 Compatibilism, Evil and the Free Will Defence

In *There Is a God* (HarperOne, 2007) former atheist Antony Flew comments: 'The other matter on which I changed my mind was free will, human freedom . . . whether expressed as a debate between free will and predestination or . . . free will and determinism, the question of whether we have free will is of fundamental importance.'[9] He illustrates the importance of the free will debate by linking it to the debate over the logical problem of evil (cf. chapter 17):

> This issue is important because the question of whether we are free lies at the heart of most major religions. In my earliest antitheological writings, I had drawn attention to the incongruity of evil in a universe created by an omnipotent, all-good Being. The theist response . . . was the claim that God gives humans free will, and that all or most of the obvious and scandalous evils are immediately or ultimately due to misuse of this dangerous gift, but that the end results will be the realization of a sum of greater goods than would otherwise be possible. I was, in fact, the first to label this the free will defence.[10]

Flew notes that he initially responded to the free will defence 'by trying to have it both ways, by introducing a position now known as compatibilism.'[11] Compatibilism starts with the distinction between being *free to act* on what one wants to do and being *free to choose* what one wants to do. Compatibilists agree with determinists that no one is *free to choose* what they want to do (what we want to do is determined by forces outside of our control); but compatibilists define 'free will' *wholly* in terms of being *free to act* upon what we have been caused to want to do. For the compatibilist, then, a human being is 'free' just so long as they are neither constrained nor compelled against their *predetermined* will. Hence the compatibilist 'maintains . . . that free choices could be both free and choices even if they were physically . . . determined by some law or laws of nature.'[12] And *this* means that God *could* have given humans 'free will' while ensuring that they never sinned (because he could have determined that they never want to sin). And *this* means (so compatibilists argue) that the free will defence, which assumes an either/ or choice between libertarian free will and determinism, collapses. For as Bishop Methodius of Olympus (c. AD 260–311) said: 'those who decide that man is not possessed of freewill, and affirm that he is governed by the unavoidable necessities of fate . . . are guilty of impiety toward God Himself, making Him out to be the cause and author of human evils.'[13] Only, of course, as Flew admits, *compatibilism means no such thing.* Indeed, compatibilism accepts that there *is* an either/or choice between the freedom to choose how one wants to act and the absence of such free will (determinism). It simply *redefines* being free *wholly* in terms of the (otherwise perfectly respectable) distinction between being free to act on what one wants or not. The claim that, *contra* the 'free will defence', God could have created humans who have significant freedom of choice but are unable to sin, invalidly exploits this ambiguity.

Flew eventually conceded that the compatibalist response to the free will defence was a failed attempt to 'have it both ways.'[14] He acknowledged that 'you cannot . . . consistently believe that these free choices are physically caused. In other words, compatibilism does not work.'[15] Flew concluded:

> Agents are creatures who . . . can and cannot but make choices: choices between the alternative courses of action or inaction that are from time to time open to them as individuals – real choices between genuine alternative possibilities . . . The nerve of the distinction between the *movings* involved in an *action* and the *motions* that constitute necessitated behaviour is that the latter behaviour is physically necessitated, whereas the sense, the direction, and the character of *actions* as such are that, as a matter of logic, they necessarily cannot be physically necessitated . . . It therefore becomes impossible to maintain the doctrine of universal physically necessitating determinism . . . my change of my mind on this matter is fully as radical as my change on the question of God.[16]

Thus theists can argue with H.D. Lewis that:

> If God were to create us free [to choose between good and evil] and enable us thereby to have the maturity and dignity of responsible being, He had to allow us to sin . . . The suggestion that God could have made us free [to choose between good and evil] and also guaranteed that we never misuse this freedom seems to me blatantly false, and it is very starkly so if freedom is taken here, as I maintain it should be, in a libertarian sense.[17]

13.2 Theological Determinism

We cannot handle the debate about free will and predestination mentioned by Antony Flew here (cf. recommended resources). As Norman L. Geisler and Paul D. Feinberg note: 'This issue, hotly debated in Christian circles . . . is based on varying interpretations of Scripture and is, therefore, a theological question more than a purely philosophical one. Nevertheless, one's views on such theological matters as the nature of God's omniscience and predestination will certainly affect what philosophical options one finds acceptable.'[18] And, I would add, vice versa. Flew records being impressed by William Lane Craig's 'rejection of . . . predestinarian ideas and his defence of libertarian free will'[19] – but whatever the result of this debate, it only pertains to free will *in relation to people's eternal destiny.* Thus a so-called 'Calvinistic' view on predestination restricts but doesn't contradict the reality of libertarian free will.

There is another debate about free will and God. This concerns the question: 'If God foreknows what I am going to do tomorrow, does that mean that I have no free will?' Answering in the positive, the 'sceptical argument' against free will goes like this:

1. Necessarily, if God knows in advance that I will do *x*, *x* will come about
2. God knows in advance that I will do *x*
3. Therefore, *x* will come about necessarily
4. Anything that will come about necessarily isn't something concerning which I have freedom of choice
5. Therefore, I have no freedom of choice

Paul Copan argues that 'God's knowledge of future actions does not by itself hinder human freedom since knowledge does not actually cause anything . . . Knowing and bringing about are distinct.'[20] Our knowledge that Jesus' 'second coming' will happen doesn't *cause* the second coming: 'In the same manner, God can have foreknowledge of free human choices without that foreknowledge causing anything. Something else – namely, human choice – must be added to the equation to cause human actions that God foreknows. In this sense, my foreknowledge is no different from God's foreknowledge since by itself foreknowledge does nothing.'[21]

> **Watch:**
> William Lane Craig, 'God's Omniscience and Man's Freedom' www.youtube.com/watch?v=HLiWDFb3cw4.

If there is a conflict between foreknowledge and freedom, it isn't a problem that can be restricted to theism. Moreover, whatever else might be wrong with the sceptical argument given above, it makes a mistake in modal logic (the logic of possibility and necessity). Atheist philosopher Peter Cave argues:

> If God knows that Peter will sin, then, yes, it does necessarily follow that Peter will sin, but it does not necessarily follow that Peter will necessarily sin. To note that something necessarily follows is *not* to note that what follows is itself necessary . . . just because someone – anyone – knows something to be true, it does not mean that what is known is a necessary truth and so could not have been otherwise. Foreknowledge alone is no threat to our acting freely.[22]

Copan explains:

> The skeptical argument – that God's foreknowledge nullifies human freedom – results from the confusion between certainty and necessity. Look at the following two statements:
>
> A. If God knows in advance that I will do x, x will necessarily come about.
> B. Necessarily, if God knows in advance that I will do x, x will come about.
>
> What is the difference between A and B? Statement A implies that the action God foreknows *had to* come about (that it *must* happen); because God foreknows it, it is necessarily so and could not have been otherwise. Statement B implies that my action that God foreknows *may* have been different (e.g. if I had chosen differently), but it *will* happen. Therefore, *if* God knows that [we will x], then we will [x], but, logically speaking, this does not mean that we *have to*. While [x] is certain, it is not *necessary*. We must be careful not to confuse these two ideas . . . While something that is necessary is also certain, what is certain may not be necessary.[23]

The upshot is that *the sceptical argument is invalid because premise 3 doesn't follow from premises 1 and 2*. When we correct the mistaken logic, the first syllogism of the sceptical argument reads:

1. Necessarily, if God knows in advance that I will do x, x will come about
2. God knows in advance that I will do x
3. Therefore, necessarily, x will come about

But nothing follows from *this* conclusion concerning human freedom. When it comes to a belief in free will, theists are apparently 'sitting pretty.' However, there is reason to think that naturalists are in a very different position . . .

13.3 Dawkins' Deterministic Delusion

While on tour in America atheist Richard Dawkins spoke at the famous Politics & Prose bookstore. One philosophically astute questioner, Joe Manzari, had an illuminating exchange with Dawkins:[24]

> **Manzari:** The thing I have appreciated most about your comments is your consistency . . . One of the areas . . . where I think there is an inconsistency . . . is that . . . you seem to take a position of a strong determinist who says that what we see around us is the product of physical laws playing themselves out; but on the other hand it would seem that you would do things like taking credit for writing this book . . . But it would seem . . . that the consistent position would be that . . . from the initial conditions of the big bang, it was set that this would be the product . . . I would take it that that would be the consistent position but I wanted to know what you thought about that.

Manzari's question suggests Dawkins is inconsistent when he both affirms that metaphysical naturalism is true and takes *credit* for writing his book, because the former assumption implies that his book is the product of a complex series of physical events stretching all the way back to the Big Bang. Dawkins cannot consistently claim *responsibility* for his book while claiming that he is 'nothing but' a subset of a vast material system of physical laws blindly playing themselves out.

In reply, Dawkins notes the existence of powerful intuitions concerning freedom and responsibility, but affirms that we may simply have to reject our intuitions to fit a naturalistic anthropology:

> The philosophical question of determinism is a very difficult question . . . I don't actually know what I actually think about that . . . What I do know is that what it feels like to me, and I think to all of us, we don't feel determined. We feel like blaming people for what they do or giving people the credit for what they do . . . None of us ever actually as a matter of fact says, 'Oh well he couldn't help doing it, he was determined by his molecules.' Maybe we should . . . when we punish people for doing the most horrible murders, maybe the attitude we should take is 'Oh they were just determined by their

265

molecules.' It's stupid to punish them. What we should do is say 'This unit has a faulty motherboard which needs to be replaced.'

As Dawkins says elsewhere: 'As scientists, we believe that human brains, though they may not work in the same way as man-made computers, are as surely governed by the laws of physics. When a computer malfunctions, we do not punish it. We track down the problem and fix it, usually by replacing a damaged component, either in hardware or software.'[25]

On the one hand, then, Dawkins places how we feel about the free will question, our intuitive belief that we are free and hence responsible for our actions. One could formalize the implicit argument here as follows:

1. In the absence of sufficient counter-evidence, the *prima facie appearance* of reality is probably true (principle of credulity)
2. The *prima facie appearance* of reality is that humans have libertarian free will, and there is a lack of sufficient counter evidence to undermine this appearance
3. Therefore, people probably have free will

Since it is generally accepted that it does *appear* to be the case that people have free will, the crucial clause in the crucial second premise is the lack of sufficient counter-evidence to the apparent reality of free will.

On the other hand, Dawkins affirms a materialistic worldview entailing that people are merely physical components of a merely physical reality. Since physical things cannot sensibly be held morally responsible for malfunctioning, Dawkins suggests that people shouldn't be held morally responsible for their actions, but should instead be treated as malfunctioning machines: 'Why do we vent such visceral hatred on child murderers, or on thuggish vandals, when we should simply regard them as faulty units that need fixing or replacing?'[26] One could formalize Dawkins' argument as follows:

1. If people are merely physical things, then they cannot have libertarian free will
2. People are merely physical things
3. Therefore, people cannot have libertarian free will
4. Things that lack libertarian free will cannot be held morally responsible or blameworthy for their actions, but they can be physically altered or replaced
5. People do not have libertarian free will (from 1 and 2)
6. Therefore, people cannot be held morally responsible or blameworthy for their actions, but they can be physically altered or replaced

> **Watch:**
> 'Free Will – Laurence Krauss & Richard Dawkins' http://youtu.be/anBxaOcZnGk
>
> **Question:**
> What would life be like under a legal system consistent with Dawkins' views about human free will?

Despite the *prima facie* case for libertarian free will, and the consequent requirement for anyone who denies the reality of freedom to produce sufficient counter-evidence to undermine this case, Dawkins begs the question against libertarian freedom by simply *asserting* the truth of naturalism. Nevertheless, Dawkins shrinks back from embracing the 'mechanical stance' towards people, saying that to adopt such a stance would be 'intolerable', while openly *admitting that such a refusal to follow through on the implications of his naturalistic anthropology is 'an inconsistency' in his worldview*:

> **Dawkins:** I can't bring myself to do that. I actually do respond in an emotional way and I blame people, I give people credit . . .
> **Manzari:** But do you personally see that as an inconsistency in your views?
> **Dawkins:** I sort of do, yes. But it is an inconsistency that we sort of have to live with otherwise life would be intolerable. But it has nothing to do with my views on religion, it is an entirely separate issue.

Dawkins seeks to limit the significance of his admission of inconsistency by asserting that the question of freedom and responsibility is a 'red herring' *when the issue is his views on religion*. However, as Dawkins himself implicitly accepts, the question of free will is *far* from being 'an entirely separate issue' from the issue of belief in God, because it goes to the heart of the worldview commitments that distinguish naturalists from non-naturalists.

Dawkins' inconsistency on this point was highlighted in a debate between Dawkins and Irish Catholic journalist David Quinn:[27]

> **Quinn:** If you're an atheist . . . you cannot believe . . . in free will . . . if a person carries out a bad action, we can call that person bad because we believe that they are freely choosing those actions . . . an atheist believes we are controlled completely by our genes and make no free actions at all.
> **Dawkins:** I certainly don't believe a word of that. I do not believe we are controlled wholly by our genes . . .
> **Quinn:** How are we independent of our genes by your reckoning? What allows us to be independent of our genes? Where is this coming from?

Dawkins: Environment for a start.
Quinn: Well hang on but that also is a product of, if you like, of matter. Okay?
Dawkins: Yes but it's not genes.
Quinn: What part of us allows us to have free will?

Quinn connects the issue of free will to the question of religion by suggesting that a naturalist shouldn't believe in free will. Dawkins corrects Quinn's oversimplification concerning genes and environment. However, Quinn rightly points out that since both genes and environment are material according to the naturalist, this correction doesn't help Dawkins evade the point in question. Quinn's question still stands, but Dawkins tries to evade it (once again) by proclaiming it a red herring:

Dawkins: Free will is a very difficult philosophical question and it's not one that has anything to do with religion . . .
Quinn: It has an awful lot to do with religion because if there is no God there's no free will because we are completely phenomena of matter.
Dawkins: Who says there's not free will if there is no God? That's a ridiculous thing to say.
Quinn: William Provine for one who you quote in your book . . . I have a quote here from him: '. . . everything that goes on in our heads is a product of genes and [as you say] environment and chemical reactions. That there is no room for free will.' And Richard if you haven't got to grips with that you seriously need to because many of your colleagues have and they deny outright the existence of free will and they are hardened materialists like yourself.
Dawkins: I'm not interested in free will . . .

Despite Quinn's rebuttal of his assertion that free will is a red herring in a discussion about God's existence, Dawkins evades Quinn's line of argumentation for a second time by changing the topic. However, many naturalists would agree with Quinn that the question of free will is a very pertinent one that should not be brushed under the carpet. For example, Marvin Minsky affirms: 'The physical world provides no room for freedom of will.'[28] If thinkers from Manzari to Minsky are right to see naturalism and libertarian free will as mutually exclusive beliefs, logical consistency demands that either we accept naturalism and reject libertarian free will or we accept libertarian free will and reject naturalism.

Question:
Does logical consistency demand that we either accept naturalism and reject libertarian free will or accept libertarian free will and reject naturalism? If so, which

should we choose to accept and which should we choose to reject? What logical fallacy is committed by anyone who says we should choose to accept naturalism and reject libertarian free will?

13.4 Naturalism and the Denial of Libertarian Free Will

Naturalism sees the mind as being identical with (or as 'supervening upon') the brain, which is a physical system running according to the laws of nature; hence Patricia Churchland declares: 'the brain is a causal machine. It goes from state to state as a result of antecedent conditions.'[29] Thomas Metzinger likewise asserts: 'The next state of the physical universe is always determined by the previous state. And given a certain brain-state plus an environment, you could never have acted otherwise.'[30] As C.S. Lewis explained, if Naturalism is true 'only Nature – the whole interlocking system – exists. And if that were true, every thing and event would, if we knew enough, be explicable without remainder . . . as a necessary product of the system.'[31] William Provine (mentioned by Quinn in his debate with Dawkins) writes: 'Humans are comprised only of heredity and environment, both of which are deterministic. There is simply no room for the traditional concepts of human free-will. That is, humans do make decisions and they go through decision-making processes, but all of these are deterministic. So from my perspective as a naturalist, there's not even a possibility that human beings have free will.'[32]

Provine's argument is logically valid:

1. Humans are systems comprised only of heredity and environment
2. Systems comprised only of heredity and environment are deterministic
3. Therefore humans are deterministic systems
4. Deterministic systems cannot have libertarian freewill
5. Therefore, there's not even a possibility that human beings have libertarian free will

The crucial premise is the first premise, and the crucial term in the first premise is the reductive 'only.'

One can't avoid Provine's conclusion by mentioning quantum indeterminacy (even if one accepts the indeterminate Copenhagen interpretation of quantum mechanics),[33] for libertarian freedom is undermined just as surely by the suggestion that human actions are to be explained in terms of *random* impersonal causes as by the suggestion that they are to be explained in terms of *regular* impersonal causes, or the combination of the two: 'Attempts have been made to link the existence of free will with the indeterminacy of quantum mechanics, but it is difficult to see how this feature of the theory makes free will more plausible. On the contrary, free will presumably implies rational thought and decision, whereas the essence of the indeterminism in quantum mechanics is that it is due to intrinsic randomness.'[34] As atheist Ned Block admits: 'free will is . . . incompatible with indeterminism because chance alone doesn't make us free: if all our actions happened by chance we wouldn't be free.'[35]

C. Stephen Layman distinguishes between libertarian free will and 'mechanism', and argues that each is incompatible with the other:

> A causal factor is *mechanistic* if it does not involve purpose, choice, volition, or the like . . . Laws of nature may be viewed as descriptions of how physical entities behave when only mechanistic factors are at work . . . Mechanists claim that the causal history of any event can be traced back ultimately to purely mechanistic factors. In particular, each part of the causal history of any human act can be traced back to purely mechanistic factors . . . True, given that the laws of nature are statistical, the universe is an indeterministic system and the past does not determine a unique future. But this does not guarantee human freedom. If each part of my act . . . has a causal history that traces back to purely mechanistic factors, then it seems I'm not in control of my act. After all, I do not control the laws of nature – whether they are deterministic or statistical. Nor do I control the past events that form the causal chains leading to the various aspects of my act . . . indeterminism opens up the possibility that I, on a given occasion, might perform *either* act A *or* some alternative act, B. *But the crucial question is whether I control which of the acts occurs.* Suppose I perform act B simply because of the operation of certain statistical laws of nature. Then I fail to see how I can be credited with controlling which act I perform. Notice that indeterminism itself doesn't give me a new kind of control over my acts; it simply replaces deterministic laws of nature with statistical ones. So I think incompatibilists *should* claim that free will is incompatible with mechanism.[36]

Moreover, the *combination* of physical regularity with physical randomness is no less incompatible with libertarian freedom. Hence Roy Abraham Varghese concludes: 'If materialism is true . . . then there's no free will.'[37] Reasons to doubt the truth of determinism are therefore also reasons to doubt the truth of physicalism and hence of naturalism.

John Searle writes that 'human freedom is just a fact of experience',[38] while according to Thomas Nagel: 'Our ordinary conception of autonomy . . . presents itself initially as the belief that antecedent circumstances, including the condition of the agent, leave some of the things we will do undetermined: they are determined only by our choices, which are motivationally explicable but not themselves causally determined.'[39] These naturalists are, I think, right about free will. As Moreland and Rae argue:

> we all seem to be aware of the fact that we are the absolute originators of our actions . . . We experience ourselves engaging in pure voluntary acts, acts that are not caused or determined by any of our own reasons or motives we have . . . When we deliberate about what we shall do, we are aware that an action is 'up to us'.[40]

These experiences can ground a properly basic belief in free will, offering (at the very least) 'prima facie justification for believing in libertarian agency,[41] and [shifting] the burden of proof onto those who deny such agency.' In other words:

1. In the absence of sufficient counter-evidence, the *prima facie positive appearance* of reality is probably true (principle of credulity)
2. The *prima facie positive appearance* of reality is that humans have free will, and there is insufficient counter-evidence to undermine this *prima facie* appearance
3. Therefore, people probably have free will

However, if, as this argument suggests, the above naturalists are right about free will, then (like Dawkins) they are inconsistent as philosophers, because (as many naturalists insist) free will doesn't cohere with naturalism. That is:

1. If naturalism is true, no one has any free will
2. Someone has some free will
3. Therefore, naturalism is false

Both thinkers recognize this problem, with Nagel simply admitting ignorance, saying that his 'present opinion is that nothing that might be a solution [to this problem of free will] has yet been described.'[42] That is, no solution has yet been described *within a naturalistic framework*. Conceptually, it seems that no such solution is possible.

Searle's commitment to naturalism means that he ends up denying the *reality* of free will, despite acknowledging the *experience* of freedom (an experience that grants the reality of freedom the presumption of truth): 'for reasons I don't really understand, evolution has given us a form of experience of voluntary action where the experience of freedom . . . is built into the very structure of conscious, voluntary, intentional human behaviour. For that reason, I believe, neither this discussion nor any other will ever convince us that our behaviour is unfree.'[43]

If determinism is true, there can be no such thing as 'voluntary, intentional human behaviour', yet the language of freedom ('For that reason, I believe . . .') slips through Searle's denial. Maybe Searle (like Dawkins) is in two minds here, but he claims too much because he bases the claim that the illusion of freedom is so strong that nothing 'will ever convince us that our behaviour is unfree' *upon the claim that our behaviour is unfree.* If Searle's claim were right, he shouldn't be able to claim that his claim is right. And yet he does make this claim. Hence his claim is wrong.

What Searle is really saying is that although free will is 'a fact of experience'[44] that is 'built into the very structure of conscious, voluntary, intentional human behaviour'[45] – and although the reality of freedom contradicts the truth of naturalism – he is so committed to naturalism that he's prepared to sacrifice belief in free will. But as Searle's language intimates, his denial of free will remains a purely theoretical commitment in the face of the everyday pragmatic realities of 'voluntary, intentional human behaviour.'[46]

Inconsistency on the issue of free will is endemic among naturalists. As Nancy Pearcey observes:

> Steven Pinker . . . acknowledges that morality depends upon the idea that humans are *more* than machines – that we are capable of making undetermined, free choices. Here is his dilemma, then: When working in the lab, Pinker adopts what he calls 'the mechanistic stance,' treating humans as complex mechanisms. But 'when those discussions wind down for the day,' he writes, 'we go back to talking to each other as free and dignified human beings.' In other words, when he goes home to his family and friends, his scientific naturalism does not work as a viable philosophy . . . Pinker admits that he has to switch to a completely contradictory paradigm. Here's how he puts it: 'A human being is simultaneously a machine and a sentient free agent, depending on the purpose of the discussion.' This is a fatal contradiction . . . . Thinkers like Pinker embrace . . . naturalism in their professional ideology . . . But it does not fit their real-life experience. So what do they do? They take a leap of faith . . . they affirm a completely contradictory set of ideas like moral freedom and human dignity – *even though these things have no basis within their own intellectual system.*[47]

Indeed, it's not simply that naturalists like Pinker make a leap of blind faith that's unsupported by their worldview; rather, they make a leap of faith *that they openly acknowledge is contradicted by their worldview:* 'Consciousness and free will seem to suffuse the neurobiological phenomena at every level,' writes Pinker. 'Thinkers seem condemned either to denying their existence or to wallowing in mysticism.'[48] Denying one's own existence is a philosophically problematical position, whereas 'wallowing in mysticism' is simply a pejorative description for the alternative, supernatural horn of this dilemma. Nevertheless, some naturalists fear pejorative labels more than they fear self-contradiction:

> Rodney Brooks of MIT provides another example. In his book *Flesh and Machines*, he argues that a person is nothing but an automaton – 'a big bag of skin full of biomolecules' interacting by the laws of physics and chemistry. It is not easy to think this way, he admits. But 'when I look at my children, I can, when I force myself . . . see that they are machines.' And yet, 'This is not how I treat them . . .' If this sounds incoherent, Brooks admits as much: 'I maintain two sets of inconsistent beliefs.'[49]

However, anyone without a dogmatic attachment to naturalism might reasonably take the experience of freedom as a strong reason for doubting naturalism. William Hasker writes:

> I find the sorts of descriptions [of free will] given by Nagel and Searle extremely compelling. These descriptions give us a perspective which seems to be *internal* to the experience of acting and making decisions; it may therefore be simply impossible for us to avoid relying on them in practice, whatever our theoretical qualms about it may be. Rejecting this understanding of experience ought to be recognized as a major form of scepticism, along with scepticism about the external world, scepticism about other minds, and other varieties. When confronted with such scepticisms we always ought to ask ourselves whether the arguments in their favour, even if apparently cogent, are really of sufficient force to outweigh what seem palpable facts of experience . . . the experience of freedom described by Nagel and Searle . . . does establish a powerful presumption in its favour . . .[50]

Jacques Maritain wrote that the freedom of the will belongs to the 'domain of common sense', beliefs that are 'immediately deducible . . . from primary data apprehended by observation and first principles apprehended by intellect. All men, unless spoiled by a faulty education or by some intellectual vice, possess a natural certainty of these truths.'[51] Moreover, this is one of the 'great truths without which man's moral life is impossible'.[52] Likewise, according to Geisler and Feinberg:

> If it is a fact that effects are totally determined and could not have been otherwise, what can we make of the traditional moral concepts of 'merit,' 'praise,'

and 'blame'? It would seem, if determinism is true, that we would never be justified in punishing any criminal, no matter how terrible the crime. Nor would it ever be appropriate to praise a person for an action, no matter how heroic.[53]

13.5 Freedom and Responsibility

To be morally responsible for one's actions means being *answerable* for those actions such that one is *the proper subject of praise or blame*. According to Immanuel Kant: 'freedom . . . must be the foundation of all moral laws and the consequent responsibility.'[54] The link between responsibility and free will can be easily illustrated and intuitively grasped.

Suppose you are walking along a beach beside a cliff, and a stone precariously perched on the cliff edge is dislodged by a gust of wind, falls through the air, and hits you on the head. Would you say that the stone *ought* not to have done that? Would you hold the stone (or the wind, or gravity) *morally responsible* for your suffering? Of course not. It wasn't up to the stone whether or not to hit you on the head. Given certain physical conditions a stone will fall to earth, and that's all there is to it. The stone had no freedom to do anything other than what it was caused to do, its activity was determined by causes over which it had no control, and so it is not a proper subject of moral blame. If humans lack free will, being nothing more than a physical object (like the rock, but more complex), then *our actions fall into exactly the same category as the action of a falling stone*. We would have no freedom to do anything other than what we are caused to do by causes outside our control (indeed, we would have no 'control'), and so we would not be the proper subjects of moral blame.

But suppose that the stone that hit you was thrown from the cliff top by someone. You might well say that they *ought* not to have done such a thing. All things being equal, people ought not to throw stones at other people; and people generally know this and are therefore blameworthy if they fail to live up to their moral obligation not to do things that they know are wrong. However, supposing our stone thrower is nothing but a complex physical system whose actions 'if we knew enough, would be explicable without remainder . . . as a necessary product of the system';[55] would such concepts as being morally blameworthy for failing to live up to one's moral obligations make any more sense when applied to such a being than they do as applied to the stone? Clearly not. A moral obligation is something you *ought* to do, something you *should* do; but what use is there for concepts like 'he ought not to do that' in a world where every human action is a 'has to do' on a par with the gravity-obeying movement of a stone falling off a cliff? Clearly, none. As Hasker asks: 'How in reason can a person be held responsible – whether for good or ill – for doing what she was ineluctably determined to do by forces that were in place long before she was born?'[56] Surely they cannot be held responsible. In which case there must be something wrong either with moral concepts (such as 'obligation', 'responsibility' and 'wrong'), or with the naturalistic account of persons that nullifies such concepts.

Most people intuitively think that the stone is *not responsible* for hitting you on the head (whether impelled by wind and gravity, or thrown by me). And most people intuitively think that *I am responsible* for throwing the stone at you. However, this distinction makes no sense if both 'the stone impelled by wind and gravity' and 'the stone impelled by Peter S. Williams' are nothing but physical systems behaving according to mechanistic laws of nature. The obvious way to justify blaming me but not the stone is to accept that, unlike the stone, *I am not a merely physical thing*. As Gary R. Habermas and J.P. Moreland write: 'It is safe to say that physicalism requires a radical revision of our common-sense notions of freedom, moral obligation, responsibility, and punishment. On the other hand, if these common-sense notions are true, physicalism is false.'[57] In syllogistic form, we may argue as follows:

1. If anyone is morally responsible for their behaviour, then libertarian free will is true
2. People are sometimes morally responsible for their behaviour
3. Therefore, libertarian free will is true

We can then extend the above argument from responsibility into an argument against naturalism:

1. If naturalism is true, no one exercises libertarian free will
2. Humans sometimes exercise libertarian free will
3. Therefore, naturalism is false

Question:
How might one extend the above argument for libertarian free will from moral responsibility into an argument for theism?

13.6 Freedom and Rationality

Tom Wolfe reports:

> at a recent conference on the implications of genetic theory for the legal system – five distinguished genetic theorists are up on stage – I stood up in the audience and asked, 'If there is no free will, why should we believe anything you've said so far? You only say it because you're programmed to say it.' You've never heard such stuttering and blathering in response to anything in your life . . .[58]

Wolfe's point is well made; the naturalist/physicalist/determinist cannot sensibly say that anyone *ought* to believe in naturalism/physicalism/determinism, or *ought not* to believe in free will. Determinists cannot consistently advance any arguments for determinism, for as Joseph H. Casey argues: 'Every viable argument proposed by determinists must appeal to the exercise of free choice . . . In one form or another such arguments insist that one ought to be reasonable enough to accept the argument.'[59] Hence Anthony O'Hear lodges the objection against physicalism that 'in seeing us as determined by material forces outside our control, materialism removes from us the possibility that what we believe and decide might be rationally decided by us after free inquiry. It thus undermines its own credentials as a doctrine to be accepted on rational grounds, for on its own account people believe things only because physical forces compel them to do so.'[60]

As C.E.M. Joad wrote: 'If freedom of willing goes by the board, so does freedom of thinking.'[61] Working at the same problem from a moral perspective Keith Ward writes: 'we cannot divorce morality from truth and reason [for] the disinterested pursuit of truth is itself a normative, a moral obligation. It is one of our chief moral obligations to seek truth and to be reasonable. But if morality no longer has any binding force, then there is no particular reason to seek truth.'[62]

Naturalism illegitimately divorces truth and rationality from morality both by a) requiring a deterministic understanding of thought that can't accommodate the fact that pursuing truth is a normative moral obligation and by b) ruling out the reality of objective moral norms in the first place.

The concept of a moral obligation only makes sense if we are *free* to live up to, or fail to live up to, our obligations. But if determinism is true (as it must be if naturalism and/or physicalism is true), then (as is admitted by many naturalists) we have no such freedom, and so cannot have any obligations. Thus, anyone who accepts an obligation 'to seek truth and be reasonable' should reject naturalism, physicalism and determinism; while anyone who accepts naturalism, physicalism or determinism should reject the claim that anyone (including those who disagree with them) has an obligation 'to seek truth and be reasonable'!

Oxford philosopher T.J. Mawson presents a neat two-stage argument 'for the rational inescapability of Objectivism about at least some values'[63] that we can usefully extend here. In Mawson's argument 'that Subjectivism about all value is indefensible . . . the first stage [is] based on a thought experiment and some intuitions which the majority will have in response to it, the second stage [is] based on how those who don't share those intuitions must think about the fact that they don't if they are to think of themselves as rational.'[64] Mawson's thought experiment concerns two friends, one of whom is Jewish, who stumble into a Fascist society wherein the law commands that the non-Jewish friend must shoot his Jewish companion dead, and where all the citizens think that this is absolutely the right thing to do. Suppose you were in this situation and were asked to shoot your friend, asks Mawson:

What ought you to do? Everyone sane knows what the wrong answer to this question is. The wrong answer is, 'Shoot your friend'. But by what standard is this the wrong answer? Not the standard that is actually enshrined in the legal codes of the society in which you've found yourselves and which enjoys the support of that society. That standard dictates that you shoot your friend. By your own, internal, standard then? But we all know that being good isn't simply a matter of doing what is in accord with one's own internal standard. We all acknowledge that individuals can go wrong in their moral assessment of actions. It seems from our reaction to this example, that we think that a whole society can go wrong in its moral assessment of actions too. If this is indeed what we think, we must be assuming that morality is independent, not only of anyone's beliefs or attitudes, but also of any society's beliefs and attitudes . . . And we think that even if we lived in a world where *everyone* believed that shooting someone merely for being Jewish was right, we'd all be wrong . . . It seems then that we do not believe in Subjectivism about all values, we endorse Objectivism about moral values.[65]

Stage one of his argument completed, Mawson focuses on the moral subjectivist who remains unconvinced:

Let me now suppose that you're unconvinced by the argument as I've presented it so far. If you take the fact that you're unconvinced as reflecting some sort of philosophical achievement on your part, you'll have to think not simply that as a psychological matter of fact you've remained unconvinced by it but that you're right to remain unconvinced. You'll have to think that this argument *shouldn't* convince one of the objectivity of value.[66]

Now the trap is sprung: 'But the sort of judgment you'll then be making itself supposes some normative principle or principles that dictate what one should or should not believe on the basis of a certain argument. So you'll be tacitly . . . thinking that there are at least objective standards determining what people should believe as a result of arguments.'[67] Hence Mawson concludes that 'objectivism about at least some value is inescapable for those reflective people who wish to believe rationally.'[68] We can build on Mawson's argument by combining it with Kant's observation that libertarian freedom is a prerequisite of moral responsibility. If one cannot count the repudiation of moral objectivity as a rational achievement without contradicting oneself (by tacitly acknowledging the existence of some objective moral norms), and if one cannot coherently acknowledge the reality of objective moral obligations binding upon humans without acknowledging the reality of libertarian freedom, then *one cannot rationally repudiate the reality of libertarian free will*!

'In the area of rationality,' writes Moreland, 'there are rational oughts . . . Reasons and evidence imply or support certain conclusions, and if one is to be objectively rational, one "ought" to accept these conclusions . . . Failure to do so makes one irrational.'[69] However, on the naturalistic account of the mind it is impossible for mental states (e.g. premises) to stand in relationships to other mental states (e.g. conclusions) which *prescribe* that one *ought* to have the latter mental state, 'because one physical state does not . . . prescribe that the other "ought" to occur . . . It either causes or fails to cause the second state.'[70] As Stephen Clark argues: 'If my opinions are just chemical events, they . . . can't be something I *ought* or *ought not* to have. And in that case my beliefs aren't rational at all.'[71] Clark concludes that 'materialists ought not to claim that their arguments are ones which anyone ought to accept.'[72]

Conclusion

I agree with H.P. Owen: 'On the one hand the objections to determinism are so strong that we are rationally compelled to withhold assent to it. On the other hand, in view of these objections, a person who finds that the consciousness of freedom is an irreducible datum of his own experience has every reason to regard this datum as a reality.'[73]

The reality of morally and rationally responsible free will directly contradicts physicalism and naturalism, and is best explained by positing the existence of immaterial human souls that are in turn best explained by the claim that humans are created in the image of God.

Watch:
J.P. Moreland, 'Do Humans Have Free Will?' www.closertotruth.com/video-profile/Do-Humans-Have-Free-Will-J-P-Moreland-/1165.

---

* * *

Recommended Resources

Video

*Williams, Peter S., 'Mind-Body Dualism, Free Will and Related Issues' YouTube Playlist, www.youtube.com/playlist?list=PLQhh3qcwVEWh0MdW-hlHBPyLRWgFjzhPT.

Online papers

Ananthaswamy, Anil. 'Brain might not stand in the way of free will', *New Scientist* (6th August, 2012), www.newscientist.com/article/dn22144-brain-might-not-stand-in-the-way-of-free-will.html.

Brice, Makini. 'Contrary to Previous Findings, Science Indicates that Free Will Does Exist', *Medical Daily* (August 7th, 2012), www.medicaldaily.com/articles/11358/20120807/science-indicates-free-will-does-exist.htm.

Craig, William Lane. 'Divine Foreknowledge and Newcombe's Paradox' www.reasonablefaith.org/site/News2?page=NewsArticle&id=5202.

— 'Middle Knowledge, Truth-Makers, and the "Grounding Objection"' www.reasonablefaith.org/middle-knowledge-truth-makers-and-the-grounding-objection.

— 'Tachyons, Time Travel and Divine Omniscience' www.reasonablefaith.org/site/News2?page=NewsArticle&id=5201.

Geisler, Norman L. 'Free Will' www.ankerberg.org/Articles/_PDFArchives/theological-dictionary/TD3W1100.pdf.

Goetz, Stewart. 'Naturalism and Libertarian Agency' www.independent.org/newsroom/article.asp?id=1756.

— and Charles Taliaferro. 'An Argument from Consciousness and Free Will' www.infidels.org/library/modern/stewart_goetz/dualism.html.

Hunt, David P. 'Contra Hasker: Why Simple Foreknowledge Is Still Useful' www.etsjets.org/files/JETS-PDFs/52/52-3/JETS%2052-3%20545-550%20Hunt.pdf.

*Johnson, Philip E. 'The Robot Rebellion of Richard Dawkins' www.arn.org/docs/johnson/pj_robotrebellion.htm.

Moreland, J.P. 'Naturalism, Postmodernism and Free Will' www.trueu.org/Academics/LectureHall/A000000918.cfm.

Pruss, Alexander R. 'Prophecy Without Middle Knowledge' www9.georgetown.edu/faculty/ap85/papers/Prophecy.pdf.

Quinn, David vs Richard Dawkins. http://catholiceducation.org/articles/science/sc0086.htm.
Swinburne, Richard. 'Free Will and Modern Science' www.britac.ac.uk/templates/asset-relay.cfm?frmAssetFileID=11006.
Williams, Peter S. 'Why Naturalists Should Mind about Physicalism, and Vice Versa' www.arn.org/docs/williams/pw_whynaturalistsshouldmind.htm.

Books

Basinger, David and Randall Basinger, eds. *Predestination and Free Will: Four Views of Divine Sovereignty and Human Freedom* (Downers Grove, IL: IVP, 1986).
Beilby, James K. and Paul R. Eddy, eds. *Divine Foreknowledge: Four Views* (Downers Grove, IL: IVP, 2001).
*Copan, Paul. *That's Just Your Interpretation* (Grand Rapids, MI: Baker, 2001).
Craig, William Lane. *The Only Wise God: The Compatability of Divine Foreknowledge and Human Freedom* (Eugene, OR: Wipf and Stock, 2000).
DeWeese, Garrett J. and J.P. Moreland. *Philosophy Made Slightly Less Difficult: A Beginner's Guide To Life's Big Questions* (Downers Grove, IL: IVP, 2005).
Inwagen, Peter van. *An Essay on Free Will* (Oxford: Clarendon Press, 1983).
*Marston, Paul and Roger Forster. *God's Strategy in Human History* (Eugene, OR: Wipf & Stock, 2000).
Murray, Michael J. and Michael Rea. *An Introduction to the Philosophy of Religion* (Cambridge University Press, 2008).
Owen, H.P. *Christian Theism: A Study in Its Basic Principles* (Edinburgh: T&T Clark, 1984).
Pearcey, Nancy. 'Intelligent Design and the Defence of Reason.' Pages 227–43 in *Darwin's Nemesis: Phillip Johnson and the Intelligent Design Movement* (ed. William A. Dembski; Downers Grove, IL: IVP, 2006).
Pinnock, Clark H., ed. *The Grace of God and the Will of Man* (Minneapolis, MN: Bethany House, 1989).
Sanders, John. *No Other Name: Can Only Christians Be Saved?* (London: SPCK, 1994).
Swinburne, Richard. *Mind, Brain and Free Will* (Oxford University Press, 2013).
Walls, Jerry L. and Joseph R. Dongell. *Why I Am Not a Calvinist* (Downers Grove, IL: IVP, 2004).

Part IV

Broadening Our Horizons

In a lawsuit the first to speak seems right,
until someone comes forward and cross-examines (Proverbs 18:17 NIV).

We begin our final section with two chapters about aesthetics, one defending the objectivity of beauty and the other tying objective beauty to God, the maximally beautiful Being. Thereafter we respond to some common objections raised against the rationality of theism in general and Christianity in particular. These concern the relationship between science and theology, and the perennial 'problem of evil.'

14. Aesthetics I: Objective Beauty

Whatever is true, whatever is honourable, whatever is right, whatever is pure, whatever is lovely, whatever is of good repute, if there is any excellence and if anything worthy of praise, dwell on these things (Philippians 4:8 NASB).

Introduction

Atheist Richard Dawkins talks a lot about beauty. He affirms: 'The real world, properly understood in the scientific way, is deeply beautiful and unfailingly interesting.'[1] In *Unweaving the Rainbow* he says:

> the urge to know more about the universe seems to me irresistible, and I cannot imagine that anybody of truly poetic sensibility could disagree. I am ironically amused by how much of what we have discovered so far is a direct extrapolation of unweaving the rainbow. And the poetic beauty of what that unweaving has now revealed, from the nature of the stars to the expansion of the universe, could not fail to catch the imagination of Keats; would be bound to send Coleridge into a frenzied reverie . . .[2]

However, Dawkins pays no attention to 'unweaving' beauty itself (i.e. to understanding beauty and considering its metaphysical implications).

Unweaving beauty is one of the tasks of aesthetics, a philosophical subject that takes its name from the Greek for 'perception': *aesthesis*.

Our consideration of aesthetics will focus on the debate about whether beauty is subjective or objective. This debate parallels the debate about the nature of moral value (cf. chapter 8). Thus atheist J.L. Mackie argues that the claim that values are subjective must include not only moral goodness, but also 'non-moral values, notably aesthetic ones, beauty and various kinds of aesthetic merit [for] clearly much the same considerations apply to aesthetic and to moral values, and there would be at least some initial implausibility in a view that gave the one a different status from the other.'[3]

14.1. An Objective Definition of Beauty

In Philippians 4:8 (NASB) Paul advises: 'whatever is true, whatever is honourable, whatever is right, whatever is pure, whatever is lovely, whatever is of good repute, if there is any excellence and if anything worthy of praise, dwell on these things.' Paul assumes an objective conception of aesthetic value, for he doesn't command Christians to dwell upon 'whatever things happen to take your own subjective fancy', but upon things that *are* true, honourable, right, pure, lovely, excellent, of good repute and, most crucially, 'worthy of praise.' As Matthew Kieran states: 'An object is of intrinsic aesthetic value if it appropriately gives rise to pleasure in our contemplation of it.'[4] I suggest that 'appropriately' should here be construed *in an objective moral sense*. Here is one reason to agree with Cambridge philosopher G.E. Moore, who wrote: 'the beautiful should be *defined* as that of which the admiring contemplation is good in itself . . . the question whether it is truly beautiful or not, depends upon the *objective* question whether the whole in question is or is not truly good.'[5] With Alvin Plantinga we can thus affirm that 'To grasp the beauty of a Mozart D Minor piano concerto is to grasp something that is objectively there; it is to appreciate what is objectively worthy of appreciation.'[6]

Question:
Survey a local church group. Do they agree or disagree with the following statements? (Ask each in turn!)

1) 'Beauty is in the eye of the beholder.'

2) 'Since beauty is in the eye of the beholder, Philippians 4:8 means that our minds should dwell on anything we happen to like.'

Are the answers given to these two questions consistent?

14.2 The Decline and Fall of Objective Beauty

Robin Collins argues that 'because . . . beauty and elegance has been so successful in guiding physicists in developing highly successful theories, it is difficult to claim that this beauty and elegance is merely in the eye of the beholder.'[7] Alexander R. Pruss likewise observes that 'If one says beauty is subjective, then the justification of scientific theories runs the danger of being too subjective, since the beauty of theories is a part of the criteria scientists employ, particularly in physics.'[8] Hence Thomas Dubay concludes: 'science and theology agree on the objectivity of beauty. While there is a subjective readiness in us, greater or lesser, for perceiving the splendid, both disciplines assume and insist that beauty is not merely in the eye of the beholder; it is primarily something "out there".'[9] Not everyone would agree. The ancient Greek philosopher Protagoras wrote: 'Man is the measure of all things; of those things that are, that they are; of those things that are not, that they are not.'[10] With the West's drift away from God in recent times, relativism has become an influential viewpoint. In the 1970s Wladyslaw Tatarkiewicz wrote an article with the title 'The Great Theory of Beauty and Its Decline', in which he declared: 'in our own century we have been witness to a crisis not merely in the theory of beauty but in the very concept itself.'[11] As C.E.M. Joad wrote in the 1950s:

> The current view of values is that they are subjective. To say 'this is good' or 'this is beautiful' means, on this view, that I, or most people who have ever lived, or most of those who have the knowledge and experience which entitles them to pass judgement, or most of the governing classes of the community to which I belong, approve of it or appreciate it or derive enjoyment from it. Thus good, bad, beautiful, ugly (and, presumably, true, false) are relational qualities, that is to say, they are related to human beings. They are also psychological in that they are defined with reference to mental states. It follows that if there were no human minds and no feelings, therefore, of appreciation, approval and the reverse, nothing would be good, bad, beautiful, ugly, true or false.[12]

C.S. Lewis, in *The Abolition of Man*, relates how the authors of an English textbook, whom he names 'Gaius' and 'Titus', comment upon a story about the poet Coleridge and a waterfall. Imagine the scene, as the water majestically cascades over the precipice, plunging into the still waters below, sparkling in the sunlight. Two tourists were present besides Coleridge. One called the waterfall 'sublime';[13] the other said it was 'pretty.' Coleridge 'mentally endorsed the first judgement and rejected the second with disgust.'[14] Gaius and Titus comment: 'When the man said

This is sublime, he appeared to be making a remark about the waterfall . . . Actually . . . he was not making a remark about the waterfall, but a remark about his own feelings. What he was saying was really *I have feelings associated in my mind with the word "Sublime"*, or shortly, *I have sublime feelings.'*[15]

According to Gaius and Titus, this confusion is common: 'We appear to be saying something very important about something: and actually we are only saying something about our own feelings.'[16] Hence beauty is reduced to *nothing but* subjective feelings. Charles Darwin likewise held that 'the sense of beauty obviously depends on the nature of the mind, irrespective of any real quality in the admired object . . . the idea of what is beautiful is not innate or unalterable.'[17] For all his talk about the beauty of nature, I suspect Richard Dawkins would agree. He certainly thinks this way when it comes to *moral* values, as revealed in an interview with *Skeptic* magazine:

Skeptic: Can we turn to evolution to answer not what is, but what ought to be?

Dawkins: I'd rather not do that . . . In my opinion, a society run along 'evolutionary' lines would not be a very nice society in which to live . . .

Skeptic: But then isn't what we ought to do (as David Hume argued a long time ago) just a matter of preference and choice, custom and habit?

Dawkins: I think that's very likely true . . .

Skeptic: So once again the discussion goes back to how do you determine whether something is good or not, other than by just your personal choice?

Dawkins: I don't even try.

Dawkins admits elsewhere: 'My view, if you think about its aesthetic . . . connotations, is a bleak and cold one.'[19] Colin E. Gunton muses: 'if only science tells us the truth, what remains to art? A doctrine of the meaninglessness of material particulars combines with scientism to deprive the artistic object of its inherent meaning and substantiality.'[20] Hence Dawkins announces: 'Beauty is not an absolute virtue in itself.'[21] Keith Ward comments:

I do not think he really means it, since he places so much emphasis on simplicity and beauty in scientific theories that he must regard it as a virtue. However . . . One of the most destructive ploys of atheism is to suggest that facts are there, in the outside world, while values are just subjective reactions, which vary from one person to another, matters of personal taste.[22]

It seems that Dawkins has adopted a philosophy of value represented by David Hume, who argued:

All sentiment is right; because sentiment has a reference to nothing beyond itself, and is always real, wherever a man is conscious of it. But all determinations of the understanding are not right; because they have a reference to something beyond themselves, to wit, real matter of fact; and are not always conformable to that standard . . . On the contrary . . . no sentiment represents what is really in the object . . . Beauty is no quality in things themselves: It exists merely in the mind which contemplates them; and each mind perceives a different beauty.[23]

For Hume, 'beauty is nothing but a form which produces pleasure.'[24] So, if masochistic acts produce in me a feeling of aesthetic pleasure, then by definition masochism *is* 'beautiful', *for me*! Beauty depends upon *my* pleasure, and is thus relative to me as a subject. No aesthetic judgements can be false, because no one can be mistaken about their own subjective aesthetic reactions. Beauty 'does not reside in any of the things of nature, but only in our own mind.'[25] This is the contemporary, common, subjective view of beauty. I think it's very ugly. The end result of this view, as Lewis saw, is that 'the emotion, thus considered by itself, cannot be either in agreement or disagreement with reason . . . the world of facts, without one trace of value, and the world of feelings, without one trace of truth or falsehood, justice or injustice, confront each other, and no rapprochement is possible.'[26]

14.3 The Resurrection of Beauty

What is beautiful by the lights of Hume is simply what is pleasing to the beholder. Yet there is surely misperception in those lights.
Peter Cave[27]

The subjective theory of value adopted by Dawkins and Hume looks very much like putting the cart before the horse. After all, aesthetic value, like moral value, is experienced as a reality beyond ourselves that impinges upon us. 'Beauty belongs, *prima facie*, to things,' observed Joad: 'It is not emotions which are beautiful but that which arouses them.'[28] As Antony Latham writes: 'I believe that flowers are *really* beautiful and therefore their beauty has an objective reality. If not, then the rose has no more *actual* beauty than a piece of coal or a rusty nail. Nevertheless, I have every reason to believe that a rose is more beautiful.'[29] Latham's objective view of beauty represents the common-sense presumption of human tradition: 'in *pre-modern* aesthetics . . . aesthetic objects and values are generally taken to be prior, with aesthetic responses and attitudes being held to be posterior to and explicable in terms of these.'[30] That is, in aesthetic experience we perceive something that draws us towards itself as an end rather than as a means. This pleasurable sense of 'being drawn' is derived from the perception of the object as one that can be appreciated *for its own sake*. Plotinus put the matter well when he observed: 'These experiences must occur whenever there is contact with any sort of beautiful thing, wonder and a shock of delight and longing and passion and a happy excitement.'[31]

Subjectivists confuse their pleasurable experience of beauty with the beauty that they take pleasure in. Augustine wrote: 'If I were to ask whether things are beautiful because they give pleasure, or give pleasure because they are beautiful, I have no doubt that I will be given the answer that they give pleasure because they are beautiful.'[32] How times have changed! Norman L. Geisler reckons that belief in 'the relativity of beauty may be more widespread than the relativity of truth or the relativity of morality.'[33] Jerry Solomon concurs that 'one of the most prevalent ways of approaching art is to simply say that "beauty is in the eye (or ear) of the beholder".'[34] However, while *the experience of beauty* is obviously in the eye (etc.) of the beholder, it hardly follows that *the beauty thus experienced* is subjective. Indeed, like our experience of moral value, our aesthetic experience appears to have an objective referent: 'Just as my experience of roundness when I see an orange is not itself round, my experience of aesthetic excellence has an objective reference beyond the experience itself,' argues Douglas Groothuis: 'To think otherwise is to fundamentally confuse the perceiving subject with the perceived object.'[35] Mortimer J. Adler thus made a crucial distinction when he wrote that 'admirable beauty is objectively present, but enjoyable beauty is in the eye of the beholder, who gets pleasure from beholding it.'[36] As Groothuis concludes: 'Beauty is not *only* in the eye of the beholder.'[37]

14.3.1 Admirable beauty

We call the object beautiful because it has certain properties that make it admirable.
Mortimer J. Adler[38]

Philosopher E.R. Emmet (a subjectivist) acknowledged:

There is not much doubt that the view [of beauty] that has been most strongly held by philosophers in the past, from Plato onwards, has been the objective one – that is that beauty in a sense is something that is there, that whether an object is beautiful or not is a matter of fact and not a matter of opinion or taste, and that value judgements about beauty are true or false, right or wrong.[39]

Despite the recent fashion for abandoning this orthodoxy, many recent and contemporary philosophers defend the objectivity of beauty (e.g. Mortimer J. Adler, Robert Audi, Peter Cave, Robin Collins, Garrett J. DeWeese,[40] Norman L. Geisler, Daniel J. Hill, David A. Horner, C.E.M. Joad, Peter Kreeft, C.S. Lewis,[41] Colin McGinn, Michael Matheson Miller, G.E. Moore, Thomas V. Morris, J.P. Moreland, Mary Mothersill,[42] David K. Naugle, Alvin Plantinga, Alexander R. Pruss,[43] John Mark Reynolds, Jerry Root, Guy Sircello,[44] Richard Swinburne, Joseph D. Wooddell,[45] Keith Yandell and Eddy M. Zemach[46]). As this list shows, the objective view of beauty is far from being the preserve of religious believers. For example, atheist Peter Cave defends the objectivity of beauty with a rhetorical question:

> if we truly think that beauty is but a matter of eyed taste, then why is there ready acceptance that a sunset is more beautiful than a car park and music by Mahler more ravishing than the beats of the all-night bar's techno? To judge that the music is rapturous is not to say that majority ears are open to such beauty; but they may be opened.[47]

A recent survey suggested that 41% of contemporary philosophers 'accept or lean toward' the objectivity of beauty, while only 34.4% 'accept or lean toward' thinking beauty is subjective.[48]

C.S. Lewis began his counter-attack on the subjective position propagated by Gaius and Titus by pointing out that 'the man who says *This is sublime* cannot mean *I have sublime feelings* . . . The feelings which make a man call an object sublime are not sublime feelings, but feelings of veneration.'[49] The correct 'translation' of the tourist's assertion, if a translation must take place, would be 'I have humble feelings.'[50] Otherwise we would end up translating assertions such as 'You are contemptible', as 'I have contemptible feelings', which is ludicrous.

If a humble feeling of veneration prompts Coleridge to agree that the waterfall is sublime, we may ask *whether that feeling was an appropriate response to its object*. In other words, aesthetic delight may be appropriate or inappropriate relative *not to the person doing the appreciating*, but *to the nature of the object being appreciated*. As Lewis explained:

> Until quite modern times all . . . men believed the universe to be such that certain emotional reactions on our part could be congruous or incongruous to it – believed, in fact, that objects did not merely receive, but could merit, our

approval or disapproval . . . The reason why Coleridge agreed with the tourist who called the cataract sublime and disagreed with the one who called it pretty was of course that he believed inanimate nature to be such that certain responses could be more 'just' or 'appropriate' to it than others . . . the man who called the cataract sublime was not intending simply to describe his own emotions about it: he was also claiming that the object was one which merited those emotions.[51]

Lewis draws upon Augustine's definition of virtue as *ordo amoris* or 'appropriate love': 'the ordinate condition of the affections in which every object is accorded that kind and degree of love which is appropriate to it.'[52] Hence he says that 'because our approvals and disapprovals are thus recognitions of objective value or responses to an objective order, therefore emotional states can be in harmony with reason . . . or out of harmony with reason.'[53]

It might be objected that since experiences of colour are subjective facts constituted by the mental states of finite minds, an experienced colour can't be objectively beautiful. However, that's like arguing that since visual experiences are constituted by mental states it isn't true to say that there are lots of stars in the Milky Way; or that since intentions are subjective facts about people's mental states, no one can have good intentions! Even if the existence of the colour *as I perceive it* is constituted by a subjective fact (my mental state), this colour can nevertheless be objectively beautiful because the fact that I can *appropriately derive aesthetic pleasure from perceiving it is an objective moral fact.* Whether the admired fact is objective or subjective, its intrinsic admirability or lack of admirability (and the moral merit attached to appreciating it) are matters of objective fact. Therefore, beauty is objective: 'To say that the cataract is sublime means saying that our emotion of humility is appropriate or ordinate to the reality, and thus to speak of something else besides the emotion.'[54] To borrow a rhetorical question posed by Wittgenstein: Would a syringe of chemicals that produces the same effects on you do just as well as the cataract?[55]

To be good, the subjective aesthetic appreciation of an intrinsically admirable fact has to be of an ordinate, appropriate character; ordinate that is, to the degree of admirability the object of contemplation possesses intrinsically. A diamond may be beautiful, but someone who finds more pleasure in appreciating a diamond than in appreciating the beauty of their 'fellow human being' has a serious problem with a moral dimension. This doesn't stop the gem being beautiful. The objective beauty of the diamond remains, but the subjective, 'enjoyed beauty' is, in this case, objectively bad. Objective moral values attach both to the *degree* of 'love' which would constitute an ordinate 'love' of x, and to the actual degree of 'love' lavished upon x by y. When the latter conforms to the former, that 'love' is ordinate.

14.3.2 Discovering 'beauties unthought of now'

There's no contradiction in saying that twelve-tone music has intrinsic admirability (and is therefore objectively beautiful) but that one personally doesn't 'get it'. Other people clearly find pleasure in this music when they perceive it, and one's own lack of appreciation needn't lead one to doubt that other people's appreciation is ordinate (morally proper). The fact that other people like twelve-tone music gives one a reason to believe that at least some such music is beautiful, and this recognition neither contradicts nor is contradicted by the fact that this type of music may give one little or no aesthetic pleasure *within one's own subjective experience.*

Watch:
'ArnoldSchoenberg's Twelve Tone Method' http://youtu.be/u5dOI2MtvbA.
Robert Conrad, 'Twelve Tone Commercial' http://youtu.be/LACCAF04wSs.

A fascinating illustration of the distinction between acknowledged objective beauty and subjective 'enjoyed beauty' comes from Sir Francis Younghusband, who, moved by the scenery of Kashmir, wrote:

There came to me this thought . . . why the scene should so influence me and yet make no impression on the men about me . . . Clearly it is not the eye but the soul that sees. But then comes the still further reflection: what may there not be staring me straight in the face which I am blind to as the Kashmire stags are to the beauties amidst which they spend their entire lives? The whole panorama may be vibrating with beauties man has not yet the soul to see. Some already living, no doubt, see beauties we ordinary men cannot appreciate. It is only a century ago that mountains were looked upon as hideous. And in the long centuries to come may we not develop a soul for beauties unthought of now?[56]

The critic may ask: 'What grounds are there for thinking that the correct view [of mountains] wasn't the one of a hundred years ago?'[57] If we asked Younghusband this question, he might well reply that his grounds for thinking that his view of the aesthetic value of mountains is the correct one is simply that he finds them beautiful (this is a 'properly basic' belief for him). Since the objective account of beauty can easily accommodate other people simply 'not getting it', Younghusband could simply find himself with the conviction that mountains are beautiful, and presume that the people of a hundred years ago simply hadn't noticed. As Jacques Maritain writes: 'however beautiful a created thing may be, it can appear beautiful to some and not to others, because it is beautiful only under certain aspects, which some discern and others do not.'[58] Indeed, Younghusband is prepared to accept that there may be unappreciated beauties that neither he, nor anyone of his generation, has 'the soul to see' as yet.

A critic might also ask: 'We find desolate landscapes beautiful; the eighteenth century found them repulsive. What facts would show one or other of us to be wrong?'[59] For example, Dr Johnson was singularly unimpressed with the Scottish scenery:

[The hills] exhibit very little variety; being almost wholly covered with dark heath, and even that seems to be checked in its growth. What is not heath is nakedness . . . An eye accustomed to flowery pastures and waving harvests is astonished and repelled by this wide extent of hopeless sterility. The appearance is that of matter incapable of form or usefulness, dismissed by nature from her care and disinherited of her favours, left in its original elemental state, or quickened only with one sullen power of useless vegetation. It will readily occur, that this uniformity of barrenness can afford little amusement to the traveller; that it is easy to sit at home and conceive rocks and heath, and waterfalls; and that these journeys are useless labours, which neither impregnate the imagination, nor enlarge the understanding.[60]

What facts would show one or other of us to be wrong? The fact that we are not stepping outside our moral rights in finding aesthetic enjoyment in contemplating desolate landscapes! It may be difficult to *prove* that there is nothing immoral about appreciating desolate landscapes, but then we're happy enough to live with the fact that moral judgements are sometimes hard to make, let alone prove. Absence of proof is no disproof of a belief. Dr Johnson seems to have been preoccupied with the demand that a beautiful landscape should match up with the familiar beauties of the English countryside. In short, Dr Johnson found the Scottish landscape too different and boring for his tastes. He just didn't 'get it.'

'But what is it about desolate landscapes which we now "see" which people in the eighteenth century couldn't see?' asks our critic. 'Isn't it more reasonable to suppose that our attitudes have simply changed, but that neither of us is objectively correct in our respective aesthetic estimations?' What is it that we now 'see' that people in the past did not 'see'? What else but *the beauty* (the intrinsic aesthetic admirability) of certain qualities that can be found in such landscapes?

Just as the aesthetic sensibility of individuals matures throughout their lives as they gain a wider aesthetic experience, so the aesthetic sensibilities of a civilization can mature over time, because the shared culture which civilization builds up incorporates a greater and greater range of aesthetic experiences. We should expect then, on the objective theory of beauty, that over time people will notice more and more about the world that is beautiful. It is a prediction of the objective theory of beauty that as time goes on, more and more beautiful facts can be discovered. It is therefore a confirmation of this theory that this should be so in, for example, the contrast between eighteenth and twenty-first-century attitudes to desolate landscapes.

If many people find something beautiful which I find ugly, I am likely to form the opinion that I simply lack good taste in this case, and that the object of dispute probably is beautiful, especially if the people disagreeing with me have a wider aesthetic experience than I do. In this way an objective concept of beauty can easily accommodate the fact that 'different persons get [aesthetic pleasure] from different objects', that 'they differ in their tastes', and that 'what one person finds enjoyable, another might behold with no pleasure at all.'[61] Still, as Aldous Huxley wrote:

> An Indian, for example, finds European orchestral music intolerably noisy, complicated, over-intellectual, inhuman. It seems incredible to him that anyone should be able to perceive beauty and meaning, to recognize an expression of the deepest and subtlest emotions, in this elaborate cacophony. And yet, if he has patience and listens to enough of it, he will come at last to realize, not only theoretically, but also by direct, immediate intuition, that this music possesses all the qualities which Europeans claim for it.[62]

And the reverse is surely true of someone brought up in the Western musical tradition listening to Indian music.

14.3.3 Subjectivism about beauty is counterintuitive

For those used to the assumption that beauty is subjective, it may appear counterintuitive to be told that the subjective theory of beauty is counterintuitive. However, I hope that a few thought experiments might help to uncover some intuitions about beauty that are at odds with the subjective theory. Consider the following snatch of dialogue by Peter Kreeft:

Sal: . . . Look at that beautiful sunset!
Chris: Oh! Thanks, Sal.

Sal: Thanks for the sunset? Who do you think I am, God? I didn't make the sunset.

Chris: No, I mean to thank you for calling my attention to it. And thanks to God for making it.

Sal: . . . I don't need your God; I have science to explain everything . . .

Chris: Since when is 'beautiful' a scientific term?

Sal: It isn't.

Chris: But you just called the sunset beautiful. You're not being scientific.

Sal: . . . I didn't really mean it.

Chris: You mean the sunset isn't really beautiful?

Sal: Right. It's just a dance of molecules. The beauty isn't really in it. It's in us, in our feelings.

Chris: The beauty is in you, not the sunset?

Sal: Yes.

Chris: But that's silly. You're not that beautiful. The sunset is!

Sal: I mean the beauty is in my feelings, not in my face.

Chris: You *felt* beautiful when you looked at the sunset?

Sal: No. I'm *not* that beautiful. But I feel the sunset is.

Chris: Then according to your feelings, the sunset really is beautiful, there really is beauty out there?

Sal: According to my feelings, yes. But my feelings are wrong. There's no real beauty out there. How can feelings tell you what the real world out there is like?

Chris: Why not? Why can't feelings be just as true as reasoning?

Sal: . . . That's just plain silly.

Chris: Why can't feelings be true?

Sal: I guess I don't know, I feel it.

Chris: And that feeling – is it true?[63]

This dialogue highlights the way in which the subjective theory of beauty says that beauty is just a matter of our feelings, even as our feelings tell us that beauty is a matter of the nature of those things outside ourselves that we appreciate as beautiful. 'When I describe something as beautiful,' writes Roger Scruton, 'I am describing *it*, not my feelings towards it – I am making a claim, and that seems to imply that others, if they see things aright, would agree with me.'[64] David Bentley Hart concurs:

> Beauty is there, abroad in the order of things, given again and again in a way that defies description and denial with equal impertinence . . . Beauty possesses a phenomenal priority . . . over whatever response it evokes . . . The beautiful is not a fiction of desire, nor is its nature exhausted by a phenomenology of pleasure; it can be recognized in despite of desire, or as that toward which desire must be cultivated.[65]

The objective theory of beauty takes our experience of beauty at face value (in line with the principle of credulity), whereas the subjectivist theory has to explain it away as a delusion, contrary to the principle of credulity; hence 'an objectivist account of our aesthetic judgements explains our experience of beauty, ugliness, and other aesthetic properties in a way the subjectivist [account] cannot.'[66] Which should we trust, our feelings about beauty or the subjective theory of beauty? We can't do both: 'when we call a sunset beautiful,' admits Anthony O'Hear, 'we unreflectively take ourselves to be speaking of the sunset and its properties. We do not, as Hume [and his followers] maintain, take ourselves to be speaking about nothing in the object, or to be merely gilding and staining it with projected sentiment.'[67] As Richard Swinburne argues:

> When people admire a beautiful work of art, they are not admiring the effect of the work on their consciousness; they do not say 'This is a wonderful painting because it produces these feelings in me and other people who look at it'. Rather, it is because they believe that it has some beautiful feature, which they have been fortunate to notice, that it does produce the *appropriate* feeling.[68]

14.3.4 Ethics and aesthetics

Moral objectivist Michael Huemer writes: 'Assume that my arguments against moral anti-realism succeed. Would arguments of the same kind demonstrate realism about beauty? Perhaps. Some philosophers accept aesthetic realism in any case; moreover, "beauty" may itself be an evaluative term – "beautiful" may imply "good" – so this result would not be terribly surprising.'[69] Indeed, one might say that this result is only to be expected; ethics and aesthetics go hand in hand because goodness is a beautiful thing and beauty is a good thing. Albertus Magnus said that 'beauty calls things to it because it is an end and a good.'[70] Thomas Aquinas thought of the beautiful 'as a way in which the good makes itself manifest'[71] and reckoned that 'anyone who desires the good, by that very fact desires the beautiful.'[72] Thus atheist J.L. Mackie observed that 'much the same considerations apply to aesthetic and to moral values, and there would be at least some initial implausibility in a view that gave the one a different status from the other.'[73] Anyone wishing to defend an objective account of moral value (cf. chapter 8) must defend an objective account of aesthetic value, and vice versa. Therefore, if moral values are objective, it's reasonable to think that aesthetic values are objective. Thus we can argue for the objectivity of beauty by parity with the objectivity of morality.

Suppose that the commander of Belsen concentration camp, observing the Holocaust, found himself aesthetically pleased by what he saw (somewhat, we may suppose, after the manner of a pyromaniac). I think most people would agree that the commander's feelings notwithstanding, the Holocaust was not a beautiful event because (to put it mildly) it wasn't a good thing. Indeed, most people would agree that the sight of helpless, innocent victims being systematically slaughtered must be an *ugly* affair, because it is an evil affair. Just as Hitler may reasonably be supposed to have approved of the Holocaust as a good thing, while yet leaving us with the intuition that the Holocaust was a bad thing, so the fact that someone (or some community) finds something 'pleasing when perceived' leaves us with the intuition that this fact alone doesn't settle the matter of whether the thing in question is beautiful or not.

Mortimer J. Adler encourages us to recognize that, 'in addition to the enjoyable, there is the admirable',[74] that the enjoyable is not necessarily admirable, the pleasant not always beautiful. So we see that the concept of aesthetic value is inextricably linked to the concept of moral value, and the objectivity of the one guarantees the objectivity of the other. While aesthetic utterances certainly have a subjective aspect, assertions of the type 'Rainbows are beautiful' are matters of objective truth or falsehood. This seems to me to be the common-sense analysis of such utterances, an analysis I don't believe we should attempt to 'explain away.' Instead, we should agree with Norman L. Geisler that 'beauty is that which is admirable for its own sake . . . it has intrinsic admirability.'[75]

> **Question:**
> Can you think of any argument against the objectivity of beauty that doesn't parallel an argument against *moral* objectivity?

14.3.5 Aesthetic disagreements count for *objectivity*

Anthony O'Hear observes: 'it is often said that taste is not to be argued about, and that matters of taste simply reflect personal preference . . . But that is surely false. The arguments we all engage in about the virtues of competing tastes are among the fiercest and most bitterly contested. We know, deep down, that these things do matter. They are important in themselves.'[76]

The prime reason given for doubting the objectivity of beauty is that people differ in what they find to be aesthetically pleasing in their subjective experience. How, it is asked, can beauty be an objective quality when people obviously disagree about what is and isn't beautiful? This objection parallels the common objection advanced against objective moral values that such values must be subjective because different people hold different moral beliefs. However, the moral objectivist may accept that different people have different moral *beliefs*, without needing to give up on the existence of objective moral *values*. Since the objection from differing opinions can be met with regards to moral value, a parallel response will prevail in the case of aesthetic value.

In the moral case: Some people may simply be wrong about what the standard of morality actually is; so the fact that not everyone agrees about what is right and wrong doesn't prove that there is no standard. Indeed, the idea that cultures differ about values doesn't carry much factual weight, for 'no culture ever existed which taught a totally different set of values.'[77] As Scruton writes: 'cultural variation does not imply the absence of cross-cultural universals.'[78] Furthermore, that people disagree about ethics indicates, not that moral values are subjective, but that they are objective. People disagree about matters of objective truth, such as whether moral values are objective or not. When it comes to subjective truths, people don't disagree. The fact that people disagree somewhat about moral values is therefore actually evidence that moral values are objective!

In the aesthetic case:

- The existence of differing subjective opinions about aesthetic matters doesn't prove that aesthetic assertions have no objective content. W.R. Sorley notes: 'We must distinguish two things: value and the consciousness of value. They do not necessarily go together.'[79]
- Aesthetic disagreements are not as widespread or divergent as the critic assumes. No one disagrees with the assertion that rainbows are beautiful and says instead that they are ugly! As Colin Lyas argues:

  it is not clear that there is massive disagreement in aesthetic judgements. When haste, ignorance, prejudice, inexperience and the like are discounted what is striking is the amount of agreement there is about what is good and great in art. Where there is disagreement it is sometimes patchy. Two people may agree on the greatness of Mozart, Beethoven and Shakespeare but disagree over Mahler. Even here the way this is put is significant: one is likely to say 'I cannot see what you see in Mahler'. This language . . . suggests that there may be something to be seen, but that one is *blind* towards it. And this blindness may be overcome by further experience and discussion . . . It is . . . possible to overestimate the amount of disagreement when seeking to show that aesthetic judgement is less objective than our ordinary perceptual judgements. Even if it were not . . . the mere fact of disagreement shows nothing . . . no more than the fact that a colour-blind man makes a different claim about the traffic lights from a fully-sighted man shows anything about the subjectivity of colour perception.[80]

- That people disagree about aesthetics indicates, not that beauty is subjective, but that it is objective. Scruton observes:

> The description of something as beautiful has the character of a judgement, a verdict, and one for which I can reasonably be asked for a justification. I may not be able to give any cogent reasons for my judgement; but if I cannot, that is a fact about me, not about the judgement. Maybe someone else, better practised in the art of criticism, could justify the verdict . . . people are constantly disputing over matters of aesthetic judgement, and constantly trying to achieve some kind of agreement. Aesthetic disagreements are not comfortable disagreements, like disagreements over tastes in food (which are not so much disagreements as differences).[81]

14.3.6 A qualification

If something is aesthetically admirable, then it *can* be enjoyed; but that something is admirable doesn't guarantee that it *will* be admired, nor does it impose any moral obligation upon those who perceive it to admire it. The 'can' in the proposition 'If something is admirable then it can be enjoyed' should be understood in the sense that *it is morally good – but not morally obligatory –* for an admirable fact to be admired. To call something 'beautiful' is to demand that others allow that the aesthetic appreciation of the object in question is *morally permissible*.

It seems more plausible to hold that aesthetic obligation is intrinsic to the process of artistic creation than that there is a general obligation upon everyone to appreciate beauty regardless of the context. If beauty is a good thing, and given that there is a general moral obligation to choose and promote good over evil, then it follows that, *all other things being equal*, we ought to choose and promote the beautiful over the ugly when the opportunity arises to do so. It is a fact of artistic experience that, for example, in composing a piece of music, a certain note will sound somehow more 'right' than any other option; it 'calls out' to be actualized. As both a writer and a composer I can endorse from experience Iris Murdoch's conclusion that 'the true artist is obedient to a conception of perfection to which his work is constantly related and re-related in what seems an external manner.'[82]

It does seems to me that we have a moral obligation to take reasonable steps to develop our aesthetic sensibilities insofar as we are able; for 'if we develop our ability to respond to art [aesthetic value] we shall develop our potential as human beings',[83] which I take to be a good thing. I am with Nicholas Wolterstorff in seeing aesthetic delight as 'a . . . species of that joy which belongs to the shalom God has ordained as the goal of human existence, and which here already . . . is to be sought and experienced.'[84]

That something is aesthetically admirable means, then, that anyone who finds an ordinate amount of aesthetic pleasure in perceiving it is, all things being equal, within their moral rights; and they are within their moral rights because the object of their appreciation objectively merits such appreciation.

I emphasize the 'all things being equal' because we can easily complicate matters by supposing, for example, that someone enjoys listening to Mozart's *Requiem* in preference to saving someone from drowning! Such an act is clearly bad, but this doesn't mean that Mozart's *Requiem* is altered by the situation into something ugly! The *Requiem* is still beautiful, because of its admirable 'determinate qualities.' The person admiring it aesthetically would be acting properly if all things were 'equal', which in the above example they are not.

Since beauty is good, it is a proper object of the general moral obligation to prefer good to evil; but obligations form a hierarchy that are context-sensitive (e.g. the goodness of deliberately deceiving someone in order to save a life) within which such aesthetic obligations may be thought to rank rather low. Furthermore, given that we have a general obligation to develop our aesthetic awareness and capacities, people with greater artistic capacities will be under greater aesthetic obligations than people who lack such capacities (cf. Luke 12:48).

14.4 Beauty and Ugliness

If 'the beautiful' is *that which it is morally good to appreciate*, then 'the ugly' must be *that which is morally bad to appreciate* (the 'obligatory-not-to-appreciate'). I think it's clear that, given the above definition of beauty, the vast majority of facts are beautiful in the sense of their being good to appreciate overall.[85] As Maritain writes:

> Like . . . the true and the good, the beautiful is being itself considered from a certain aspect; it is a property of being . . . Thus everything is beautiful, just as everything is good, at least in a certain relation. And as being is everywhere present and everywhere varied the beautiful likewise is diffused everywhere and is everywhere varied . . . each kind of being is in its own way, is good in its own way, is beautiful in its own way.[86]

This is *not* to say that everything is beautiful 'through and through', or in every aspect of its being. Rather, it's to say that everything is beautiful *in at least one aspect of its being.* Since goodness is beautiful, everything is beautiful, at least in that it exists, because existence *per se* is good. This being so, it follows that only certain facts are ugly *overall*. Beauty, as well as goodness, can be found in some measure, however small, in any fact, including those that are (overall) ugly.

14.5 Beauty and Goodness

The relationship between beauty and ugliness (like the relationship between good and evil) is asymmetrical. Facts can be beautiful without being ugly in any way, whereas nothing can be ugly without being beautiful in at least one way (although some things are ugly *overall*).

Goodness and beauty relate to each other in this: real, objective goodness is objectively beautiful, and objective beauty is objectively, intrinsically good. Thus, 'moral and aesthetic values are closely connected.'[87] Plato rhetorically asks: 'Is not the good also the beautiful?'[88] I agree. Moreover, I think it plain that all that is beautiful is good. To do a good action is therefore to do a beautiful action.

In ancient Hebrew there was a linguistically enshrined recognition that goodness and beauty have close truck one with another. In Genesis 'God saw all that he had made, and it was very good' (Genesis 1:31). The word translated here as 'good' can also mean beautiful: 'the word "good" . . . may mean "fitting" or "beautiful" amongst a wide range of meanings.'[89] ('Fitting', we may take it, in the sense of being instrumentally good, or 'fit for purpose'.) God's affirmation of creation in Genesis might therefore be translated: 'God saw all that he had made, and it was very beautiful.' Clearly there's a priority of goodness over beauty that makes the 'fit for purpose / very good' translation preferable; however, the full meaning of the text will be missed if we don't bear in mind that creation is affirmed as being both very good and very beautiful.

This affirmation resonates with my suggestion that beauty is connected to goodness and the realization that the cosmos is overwhelmingly beautiful. In the Greek translation of the Old Testament, the word *kalos* is used for the word we can translate as 'good' or 'beautiful':[90] 'The basic idea in the word *kalos* is the idea of winsome beauty . . . There is no English word which fully translates *kalos*; there is no word which gathers up within itself the beauty, the winsomeness, the attractiveness, the generosity, the usefulness, which are all included in this word. Perhaps the word which comes nearest to it is the Scots word *bonnie*.'[91]

In the New Testament Jesus says: 'Salt is good [*kalos*]' (Mark 9:50).[92] Jesus calls himself 'The Good [*Kalos*] Shepherd' (John 10:11).[93] *Kalos* is also

employed in the New Testament of character, such that 'in all his striv-
ings towards moral holiness, the Christian must never forget the *beauty
of holiness* . . . Every Christian should be *kalos*; and every activity of the
Christian life should be *kalos*.'[94]

Pushing further back into Greek history we find *kalos* used primarily
in an aesthetic sense: 'In classical Greek *Kalos* . . . referred to beauty of
form. It could be applied to any person who was lovely or to anything
that was beautiful.'[95] *Kalos* is applicable to both sensual and intellectual
facts. Laws, like people, can be *kalos*. As Paul writes in Romans 7:16: 'But
if I do what I do not will, I agree with the law, that (it is) good [*kalos*].'[96]

Kalos also has a moral connotation: '*Kalos* in Greek also means *beautiful*
and *honourable* in the *moral* sense. Homer . . . says: "It is not honourable
(*kalos*) or just to rob the guests of Telemachus" (*Odyssey* 20.294).'[97] *Kalos*
describes the objective beauty of an objectively morally virtuous character and of the objectively morally good actions that spring from such a
character:

> We may best of all see the meaning of *kalos*, if we contrast it with *agathos* which
> is the common Greek word for good . . . When a thing or person is *agathos*, it
> or he is good in the moral and practical sense of the term, and in the result of
> its or his activity; but *kalos* adds to the idea of goodness the idea of beauty . . .[98]

Agathos refers to moral and instrumental goodness. For example, the moral
sense of *agathos* is employed in John's gospel when a crowd is debating
who Jesus is: 'there was murmuring among the people concerning him: for
some said, He is a good [*agathos*] man: others said, Nay; but he deceiveth
the people.'[99] *Kalos* regards the good not only as ethically or pragmatically
good (*agathos*), but also as aesthetically good. For example, in talking meta-
phorically about how a tree is known by its fruit, Jesus says: 'Either make
the tree good [*kalos*] and its fruit good [*kalos*], or make the tree corrupt and
its fruit corrupt; for the tree is known by the fruit . . . the good [*agathos*]
man, out of the good treasures of his heart, puts forth good things.'[100] It
stands to reason that no one can be *agathos* in the moral sense without
simultaneously being *kalos*; no one can be good without being, in respect
of their goodness, beautiful. Hence Milton wrote how:

> Abash'd the devil stood,
> And felt how awful goodness is, and saw
> Virtue in her shape how lovely.

Atheist Colin McGinn notes that judgements of moral character are often
expressed using aesthetic predicates, and interprets this 'as reflecting

our implicit commitment to the view that goodness and badness of character are allied to aesthetic qualities of the person.'[102] If one pursues physical beauty above morality one will become an ugly character (cf. Proverbs 11:22); but if one seeks goodness, one will also develop a beautiful soul: 'seek first his kingdom and his righteousness, and all these things [including inner beauty] will be given to you as well' (Matthew 6:33). Hence McGinn concludes: 'The intuitive picture is that the virtues and vices *give rise* to aesthetic properties of the soul that bears them . . . Virtue equals beauty plus the soul, to put it crudely. The particular kind of beauty proper to the soul is what virtue consists in.'[103]

Many stories, particularly fairy stories, depend upon the appropriateness of modelling physical appearance upon spiritual beauty or ugliness: consider *Snow White*. Some stories, including fairy stories, depend upon this tradition whilst highlighting the distinction between outer, physical, and inner, spiritual aesthetic properties: consider *Beauty and the Beast* or *The Picture of Dorian Gray*.

Being good does indeed, on the account I am offering, make the virtuous person beautiful (in respect to their character); to contemplate goodness is indeed to contemplate something which is objectively beautiful; and to contemplate beauty is to be put into contact with objective goodness, including objective moral goodness (and vice versa). This 'aesthetic theory of virtue' has a long Christian tradition: 'Hildegard [of Bingen] described a life of virtue as taking on the brilliant beauty of the stars . . . throughout Hildegard's letters, books, and songs, the virtuous life always leads to beauty.'[104] Hildegard taught that 'knowledge of eternal life is diffused by both [awe] and love of God, which reaches from a person's inner heart to his face.'[105] Thus a beautiful spirit will tend to produce a more beautiful face than a person would otherwise possess (note, not necessarily more beautiful relative to the faces of people with ugly characters, but more beautiful relative to how an individual would be without a beautiful spirit). This view seems to comply with the common-sense view that, for example, excessively worried people develop furrowed brows while happy people develop laughter lines (here is the truth behind the reprimand: 'If the wind changes, you'll stay like that!').

If objective moral goodness depends upon (and is primarily instantiated by) the character of God, then the connection between beauty and goodness means that since contemplating beauty means being put into contact with objective moral goodness, it also means being put into contact with divinity: 'The Beautiful, says Hegel, is the spiritual making itself known sensuously. It represents, then, a direct message from the heart of Reality; ministers to us of more abundant life.'[106] As Hildegard thought: 'Art and all beauty touch the senses and, thence, the spirit . . .

art can influence spirituality because a work that is formed by the spirit actually communicates the spirit.'[107] For the Christian, the cosmos itself is a work of art that must therefore communicate something of the Holy Spirit of God. Hence Iris Murdoch is right when she writes that 'the appreciation of beauty in art or nature is . . . the easiest available spiritual exercise; [because] it is also . . . the checking of selfishness in the interest of seeing the real . . . Beauty is that which attracts this particular unselfish attention.'[108]

> **Watch:**
> Everett Berry, 'Interview with Joseph D. Wooddell' http://youtu.be/9JqERC1Q6Ds.

Conclusion

> There is right feeling, right experience and right enjoyment just as
> much as right action.
> Roger Scruton[109]

As J.P. Moreland writes: 'beauty is objective and knowable and real; it's not in the eye of the beholder, it's objective, it can be known.'[110] The subjective view of beauty is wrong because God, the maximally beautiful being of whom all lesser beauties speak, exists: 'finite beauty, as wonderful and intrinsically valuable as it is, functions not only as a good but also as a pointer to a good that lies beyond it that is our ultimate *telos* [goal]. And that is the ultimate beauty – God Himself.'[111] Plato ascended in thought from the beauty of the world to the absolute beauty of the divine:

> This is the right way of being initiated into the mysteries of love, to begin with examples of beauty in this world and use them as steps to ascend continually to absolute beauty as one's final aim . . . This above all others is the region where a truly human life should be spent, in the contemplation of absolute beauty . . . One who contemplates absolute beauty and is in constant union with it . . . will be able to bring forth not mere reflected images of goodness but true goodness, because one will be in contact not with a reflection but with the truth . . . What may we suppose to be the felicity of the man who sees absolute beauty in its essence, pure and unalloyed, who . . . is able to apprehend the divine beauty . . . ?[112]

The connection between divinity and objective value means that the concept of objective beauty loses all coherence if God is excluded from our worldview. The devaluation of objective beauty, and the consequent loss of wonder and meaning felt in society at large, is a logical consequence of the 'death of God'. To reject the maximal objective beauty of divinity (whether one begins by rejecting beauty and ends by rejecting God, or begins by rejecting God and ends with the rejection of beauty) is to reject the one sure foundation of a meaningful existence. As Keith Ward comments:

> In Plato, a connection is made between the contemplation of beauty, human goodness and love. One who contemplates beauty can rightly be said to love that which is most worth loving. And, since Plato holds that one becomes like what one contemplates, the contemplator of beauty is one whose life becomes beautiful . . . In this sense, God is supreme goodness. To love God is the highest goal of human life. To attain God is to have one's life enfolded in perfect beauty, and to become an image of goodness to others . . . Thus we can move from awe and admiration of God to love of God.[113]

Films to Watch and Discuss::
Beauty and the Beast, directed by Gary Trousdale and Gary Wise (Disney, 1991) (U)
Dorian Gray, directed by Oliver Park (Momentum, 2010) (15)
Snow White and the Huntsman, directed by Rupert Sanders (extended collector's edition) (Universal, 2012) (12)

---

* * *

Recommended Resources

Video

'Arnold Schoenberg's Twelve Tone Method' http://youtu.be/u5dOI2MtvbA.
Conrad, Robert. 'Twelve Tone Commercial' http://youtu.be/LACCAF04wSs.
Marillion. 'Beautiful' www.youtube.com/watch?v=Y-6dUzwt_0Q&feature=related.
Reynolds, John Mark. 'Finding Christ in Culture' http://vimeo.com/30333189.
*Williams, Peter S. 'Beauty' YouTube Playlist www.youtube.com/playlist?list=PLQhh-3qcwVEWiL488-SGbfODhf6kLPSZbJ.

Audio

Kreeft, Peter. 'Language of Beauty in *Lord of the Rings*' www.peterkreeft.com/audio/31_lotr_language-beauty.htm.
*— 'Truth, Goodness and Beauty' www.peterkreeft.com/audio/27_good-true-beautiful/peter-kreeft_good-true-beautiful.mp3.
*Lewis, C.S. 'Men without Chests' http://youtu.be/VTum5vajIXg.

Little, Bruce. 'Christianity and the Arts' www.bethinking.org/your-course/advanced/christianity-and-the-arts.htm.

*Reynolds, John Mark. 'Beauty' http://cdn-edu.biola.edu/torrey_honors/reynolds_beauty.mp3.

Root, Jerry. 'C.S. Lewis' Approach to Art and Literature' www.bethinking.org/your-course/advanced/c-s-lewiss-approach-to-art-and-literature.htm.

Websites

Christians in the Visual Arts http://civa.org/.

Damaris Trust www.damaris.org

Interface Arts http://uccf-arts.blogspot.co.uk/.

Online papers

Dembski, William A. 'The Act of Creation: Bridging Transcendence and Immanence' www.arn.org/docs/dembski/wd_actofcreation.htm.

Parsons, George. 'Studying Music?' www.bethinking.org/your-course/introductory/studying---music.htm.

Plantinga, Alvin. 'Two Dozen (or so) Theistic Arguments' www.homestead.com/philof-religion/files/Theisticarguments.html.

Sartwell, Crispin. 'Beauty' http://plato.stanford.edu/entries/beauty/.

Solomon, Jerry and Jimmy Williams. 'Art and the Christian' www.leaderu.com/orgs/probe/docs/artandxn.html.

Spicher, Michael. 'Medieval Theories of Aesthetics' www.iep.utm.edu/m-aesthe/.

Williams, Peter S. 'The Abolition of Man: Reflections on Reductionism with Special Reference to Eugenics' www.arn.org/docs/williams/pw_abolitionofman.htm.

—'Intelligent Design, Aesthetics and the Design Argument' www.arn.org/docs/williams/pw_idaestheticsanddesignarguments.htm.

— 'A Theistic Account of Aesthetic Value' www.leaderu.com/theology/williams_beauty.html.

Wyn, Mark. 'Beauty, Providence and the Biophilia Hypothesis' www.calvin.edu/faith/resources/faculty/beauty/providence_natural.pdf.

Books

Adler, Mortimer J. *Six Great Ideas* (London: Collier Macmillan, 1981).

— *How to Think about the Great Ideas from the Great Books of Western Civilization* (ed. Max Weismann; Chicago: Open Court, 2001).

Brown, Stephen F., ed. *Bonaventure: The Journey of the Mind to God* (trans. Philotheus Boehner; Indianapolis: Hackett, 1993).

Caldecott, Stratford. *Beauty for Truth's Sake: On the Re-enchantment of Education* (Grand Rapids, Michigan: Brazos, 2009).

— *Beauty in the World: Rethinking the Foundations of Education* (Tacoma, WA: Angelico, 2012).

Cooper, David E. *Aesthetics: The Classic Readings* (Oxford: Blackwell, 1997).

*Dubay, Thomas. *The Evidential Power of Beauty* (San Francisco: Ignatius Press, 1999).

Gilson, Étienne. *The Christian Philosophy of St. Thomas Aquinas* (University of Notre Dame Press, 2002).

Groothuis, Douglas. *Truth Decay* (Downers Grove, IL: IVP, 2000).

Hanflung, Oswald, ed. *Philosophical Aesthetics: An Introduction* (Oxford: Blackwell, 1992).

Harries, Richard. *Art and the Beauty of God* (New York: Mowbray, 1993).

Joad, C.E.M. *The Recovery of Belief* (London: Faber & Faber, 1952).

*Lewis, C.S. *The Abolition of Man* (London: Fount, 1999); cf. www.columbia.edu/cu/augustine/arch/lewis/abolition1.htm#1.

McGinn, Colin. *Ethics, Evil and Fiction* (Oxford: Clarendon Press, 1999).

Miller, Michael Matheson. 'C.S. Lewis, Scientism, And The Moral Imagination' pages 309-338 in *The Magician's Twin: C.S Lewis on Science, Scientism and Society* (ed. John G. West; Seattle: Discovery Institute Press, 2012).

Schaeffer, Francis A. *The Complete Works of Francis A. Schaeffer*, vol. 1 (Wheaton, IL: Crossway Books, 1994).

Scruton, Roger. *Beauty* (Oxford University Press, 2009).

— *Beauty: A Very Short Introduction* (Oxford University Press, 2011).

— *Culture Counts: Faith and Feeling in a World Besieged* (New York: Encounter, 2007).

*Sherry, Patrick. *Spirit and Beauty* (London: SCM Press, 2nd edn, 2002).

Swinburne, Richard. *The Existence of God* (Oxford: Clarendon Press, 2004).

Watkins, Tony. *Focus: The Art and Soul of Cinema* (Southampton: Damaris, 2007).

Wiker, Benjamin and Jonathan Witt. *A Meaningful World: How the Arts and Sciences Reveal the Genius of Nature* (Downers Grove, IL: IVP Academic, 2006).

Williams, Peter S. *I Wish I Could Believe in Meaning: A Response to Nihilism* (Southampton: Damaris, 2005).

Wolterstorff, Nicholas. *Art in Action: Toward a Christian Aesthetic* (Carlisle: Solway, 1997).

Wooddell, Joseph D. *The Beauty of Faith: Using Aesthetics for Christian Apologetics* (Eugene, OR: Wipf & Stock, 2010).

15. Aesthetics II: Beauty and Divinity

Now if a man believes in the existence of beautiful things, but not of Beauty
itself, and cannot follow a guide who would lead him to a knowledge of it,
is he not living in a dream?
Plato's *Republic*, 476c.

Introduction

Arguments for God from beauty (aesthetic arguments) constitute a broad
swathe of natural theology that overlaps with several other types of
theistic argument, especially design arguments (cf. chapters 6 and 7) and
arguments from experience (cf. chapter 10).[1]

Aesthetic reality can be divided between our subjective appreciation of beauty and the objective beauty we appreciate. Aesthetic arguments may therefore focus either upon our appreciation of beauty, or
upon the beauties we appreciate. Aesthetic arguments that focus upon
our knowledge of beauty are 'epistemological aesthetic arguments';
those that focus upon the beauty we know are 'ontological aesthetic
arguments.'

One type of epistemological aesthetic argument begins with the mere
fact that we have aesthetic awareness and seeks to show that theism
provides the best explanation of this capacity. These are epistemological
aesthetic arguments *from the fact of aesthetic experience*. Other epistemological aesthetic arguments begin with the particular nature of our aesthetic

experience, seeking to interpret this experience as revealing God's existence. These are epistemological arguments *from the content of aesthetic
experience.*

Ontological aesthetic arguments likewise fall into two subcategories. One
type of ontological aesthetic argument questions how well unintended
natural processes are at explaining the objective beauties that we discover
around us. These are ontological aesthetic arguments *from beautiful things.*
There's an overlap between this type of ontological aesthetic argument
and the design argument, although they are by no means identical. Other
ontological aesthetic arguments (arguments *from the fact of beauty itself*)
propose that only the existence of God can ground or account for objective aesthetic value, just as the moral argument proposes God's existence
as the ground of objective moral value (cf. chapter 8).

Having defended the objective nature of beauty in chapter 14, this
chapter will provide a historical tour through *the ontological aesthetic argument from the fact of beauty itself.*

15.1 Augustine's Idealistic Aesthetic Argument

Augustine argued that:

> Physical beauty . . . can be appreciated only by the mind. This would be impos-
> sible, if this 'idea' of beauty were not found in the mind in a more perfect
> form . . . But even here, if this 'idea' of beauty were not subject to change, one
> person would not be a better judge of sensible beauty than another . . . This
> consideration has readily persuaded men of ability and learning . . . that the
> original 'idea' is not to be found in this sphere, where it is shown to be subject
> to change . . . And so they saw that there must be some being in which the
> original form [of beauty] resides, unchangeable, and therefore incomparable.
> And they rightly believed that it is there that the origin of things is to be
> found, in the uncreated, which is the source of all creation.[2]

Augustine says that our judgements about beauty must be measured
against some objective standard that the human mind apprehends. This

standard cannot depend upon any individual finite mental state (or collection thereof), or else it would of necessity be a subjective standard; and objective aesthetic judgements cannot depend upon a subjective aesthetic standard. Therefore, there must exist an objective standard of beauty that is independent of finite minds. However, such an aesthetic standard isn't the sort of thing that could exist in the physical world. Therefore, the standard of beauty must exist neither in finite minds, nor in the physical world, but in an infinite non-physical reality.

Peter Kreeft observes: 'God is objective spirit, and when "God is dead", the objective world is reduced to matter and the spiritual world is reduced to subjectivity.'[3] Hence, if a rainbow, a sunset, a lily of the field or a human being possesses any objective beauty, then 'somewhere over the rainbow' there must exist an ideal and unsurpassable beauty. As Victor Cousin argued:

> ideal Beauty . . . resides neither in the individual nor in a collection of individuals. Nature or experience provides the occasion of our conceiving it, yet beauty is essentially a distinct thing. The man who has once conceived it finds all natural figures, beautiful as they may be, only images of a beauty which is not realised in them . . . the true and absolute Ideal is no other than God Himself . . . The physically beautiful serves as an envelope for the intellectually and morally Beautiful . . . God is the principle of all the three orders of the Beautiful . . . God is perfect Beauty . . . He presents to our reason the most elevated idea beyond which there is nothing, to our Imagination the most attractive Contemplation, to our Sentiment an object supremely lovely. He is therefore perfectly the Beautiful . . .[4]

15.2 Peter Lombard's Cosmological Aesthetic Argument

According to medieval theologian Peter Lombard:

> The most exalted philosophers . . . understood the beauty of a body to be sensible and the beauty of the soul to be intelligible, and they preferred intellectual to sensible beauty. We call 'sensible' such things as can be seen or touched and 'intelligible' such as can be perceived by mental vision. Once they perceived various degrees of beauty in mind and body, they realized there was something which produced these beautiful things, something in which beauty was ultimate [unsurpassed] and immutable, and therefore beyond compare. And they believed, with every right, that this was the source of all things, that source which itself was never made but is that by which all else was made.[5]

Lombard's argument appears to be that things which exhibit various degrees of beauty, but not ultimate and immutable beauty, must be caused by something that does exhibit ultimate and immutable beauty. As a causal argument, this line of thought links the aesthetic argument with the cosmological argument (cf. chapter 4).

If a thing exists then it has the ontological beauty of *being*. However, we may distinguish the ontological beauty of contingent and/or dependent being from the greater ontological beauty of necessary and/or independent being. Once this distinction is made, we may employ the cosmological argument to argue that something exists which has necessary and independent existence. Indeed, we may conclude the existence of something with the objective beauty of *maximal ontological security*. To such cosmological reasoning, Lombard adds the causal principle that 'the greater cannot come from the lesser', in order to reach the conclusion that *the beauty of creation cannot surpass the beauty of the First Cause*. The First Cause is therefore something in which beauty of every variety (ontological, moral and epistemological) is actually unsurpassed.

Lombard's argument leads us to the existence of a 'most beautiful' or 'greatest *actual*' being, rather than to a 'maximally beautiful' or 'greatest *possible*' being. It does not, therefore, lead us to the same conclusion as the ontological argument (cf. chapter 9). However, when we recall that a being with maximal ontological security must possess all of its properties without external limitation, it would seem that God's maximal beauty is guaranteed *in the absence of internal, logical limitations*.

This extension of Lombard's argument might be said to suffer from the problem that, while it may be rational to accept that there are no logical limitations preventing God's unsurpassed beauty also being unsurpassable, it may be equally rational to doubt this premise. However, since Lombard's argument leads us to a God with the beauty of maximal ontological security, and since we have good reason to attribute maximal moral goodness to God as well (cf. the moral argument), it might well be argued that it is *simpler* (and no less adequate) to conceive of God as being maximally beautiful *tout de suite* than to conceive of God as being maximally beautiful in respect of some qualities (e.g. existential security) but merely ultimately beautiful in respect of others. As Richard Swinburne argues:

> Scientists have always seen postulating infinite degrees of some quality as simpler than postulating some very large finite degree of that quality ... If the action of a person is to explain the existence and operation of the universe, he will need to be a very powerful person. It is a simpler hypothesis to postulate that his power is infinite rather than just very large. If we said that he was powerful enough to make a universe of such and such mass but not powerful

enough to make a more massive one, the question would arise as to why there was just that rather than any other limit to his power. It naturally fits the suggestion that God's power is infinite that there be no causal influences influencing how he exercises that power, and so it is simplest to hold that his freedom too is infinite. In order to exercise power effectively, you need to know what are the consequences of your actions. Hence it naturally fits the claim that God is infinitely powerful and free to claim that he is infinitely knowledgeable . . . Hence the principles which we use in science . . . and all other human enquiries into causes indicate that, if we are to explain the world in terms of personal explanation, we should postulate a personal being of infinite power, knowledge, and freedom.[6]

To broaden Swinburne's point, since we are explaining the world in terms of a being of actually unsurpassed beauty (and unsurpassable ontological security and moral goodness) we should (at least provisionally) postulate a being of infinite, unsurpassable, maximal beauty. Hence Lombard's aesthetic cosmological argument can secure a real-world foothold for Occam's razor which acts as a metaphysical ratchet that succeeds in placing the burden on proof upon anyone sceptical about God's maximal beauty.

15.3 Aquinas's Fourth 'Way'

In the fourth 'way' of his *Summa Theologica*, Thomas Aquinas argued:

Among beings there are some more and some less good, true, noble and the like. But 'more' and 'less' are predicated of different things, according as they resemble in their different ways something which is the maximum, as a thing is said to be hotter according as it more nearly resembles that which is hottest; so that there is something which is truest, something best, something noblest [i.e. something maximally beautiful] and, consequently, something which is uttermost being [i.e. maximally ontologically secure]; for those things that are greatest in truth are greatest in being, as it is written in [Aristotle's] *Metaph*. ii. Now the maximum in any genus is the cause of all in that genus; as fire, which is the maximum heat, is the cause of all hot things. Therefore there must also be something which is to all beings the cause of their being, goodness, and every other perfection; and this we call God.[7]

This argument from degrees of perfection is usually treated as a variation of the moral argument, but it is at least implicitly aesthetic. As E.L. Mascall observes:

although St. Thomas does not include beauty among the perfections enumerated, the argument will obviously apply to it too. It is therefore not true to suggest . . . that St. Thomas has no place for aesthetic considerations in his conception of God. The reason for his omission is far more probably that he did not consider beauty as a distinct perfection from those which he instances.[8]

If we conceive of Aquinas's argument in terms of beauty, and if we focus upon the way we attribute greater and lesser degrees of beauty to a multiplicity of things, then it appears to be simply an aesthetic 'feed-in' to the moral argument: If a thing's beauty is a matter of its being morally good to appreciate aesthetically, then predicating degrees of beauty to things in the world implies the existence of an objective standard of goodness that, as the moral argument shows, must be grounded in the necessary existence of a personal ground of absolute goodness. Since existence, goodness and personhood *per se* are beautiful, this necessarily existent personal ground of goodness must be beautiful at least in these respects.

I think this is right insofar as it goes. However, it doesn't capture the complexity of Aquinas's argument. For one thing, it doesn't lead to Aquinas's conclusion, that there must exist 'something which is to all beings the cause of their being, goodness, and every other perfection' and which possesses all of these perfections to maximal degree. For another, what are we to make of Aquinas's appeals to a multiplicity of qualities (goodness, truth, nobility, being), to the notion that there must exist maximal instantiations of these qualities, and to the principle that 'the maximum in any genus is the cause of all in that genus'? As F.C. Copleston comments: 'if the line of thought represented by the fourth way is to mean anything to the average modern reader, it has to be presented in a rather different manner from that in which it is expressed by Aquinas who was able to assume in his readers ideas and points of view [especially scientific ones] which can no longer be presupposed.'[9]

It seems to me that the fact singled out by Aquinas for theistic explanation in the fourth way is not the epistemological fact that we can make true aesthetic judgements about things, but *the ontological fact that things of objective but finite beauty exist.* As Mascall explains, the fourth way:

asserts the existence of a supreme degree of each perfection not merely as the pattern or exemplar of the lesser degrees [by which they are judged], but as their creative cause . . . It is not merely that the *idea* of infinite perfection implies the existence (or even the idea) of infinite perfection as its *model*, but that the *existence* of finite perfection implies the existence of infinite perfection as its *cause*.[10]

Moreover, Aquinas doesn't root his argument in the general concept of beauty, but by noting that things in the world around us exhibit, in varying degrees, certain general qualities of objective value (being, goodness, etc.). These qualities naturally fall within the broadest value category: beauty. In other words, Aquinas begins his argument with the existence of things in the world that exhibit finite degrees of transcendental, great-making properties. This is where Aquinas's appeal to the principle that there must exist maximal instantiations of the qualities he mentions comes into play. For although 'the existence of a more and a less does indeed require the existence of a . . . most',[11] we are concerned here with the existence of more and less in terms of great-making properties, properties that by definition admit of an intrinsic, logical maximum, rather than a merely contingent, factual maximum:

> the qualities Aquinas uses in this Way are what the medievals called 'transcendentals': good, true, noble, and the like. The label means that these notions apply indifferently to anything in any of the categories of the existent. This concept is not altogether unfamiliar to us: we are accustomed to regard certain notions, e.g. the central concepts of philosophical logic, such as identity, existence, reference, truth, etc., as having some application in all fields of discourse without exception. The crucial difference, though, is that St. Thomas's transcendental notions are not logical but metaphysical . . .[12]

Only by keeping the notion of transcendental values in mind can we avoid being sidetracked by Aquinas's outdated scientific example of heat and fire. Kreeft comments: 'The point of the argument is that "better" implies "best" . . . St. Thomas' example of this principle (fire) is, of course, bad science. But the invalid illustration does not invalidate the principle.'[13] As Mascall points out: 'Goodness, so the argument claims, demands as its cause a God who is good; while heat, though it necessarily demands a God whose knowledge of possible being includes an idea of heat, does not demand a God who is hot as its cause, but only a God who can create.'[14]

Étienne Gilson is on the right track when he observes that Aquinas:

> maintains that the lower degrees of perfection and being suppose a being in which perfections and being meet in their highest degree. He also maintains that to possess a perfection incompletely and to possess it from a cause are synonymous. A cause can only give what it has. Anything that does not possess a perfection of itself and only possesses it incompletely must hold it from something possessing it of itself and in the highest degree.[15]

313

Richard Dawkins' critique of the fourth way is completely derailed by his failure to notice that the argument works with great-making properties. He tries to rebut the argument via the following *reductio ad absurdum*: 'That's an argument? You might as well say, people vary in smelliness but we can make the comparison only by reference to a perfect maximum of conceivable smelliness. Therefore there must exist a pre-eminently peerless stinker, and we call him God.'[16] However, 'smelliness' isn't a great-making property. Dawkins' failure to notice the central importance of great-making properties to the fourth way means he ends up attacking a straw man.

Although Aquinas's use of great-making properties in the fourth way may put us in mind of Anselm's ontological argument, his argument is no mere gloss or variation upon that proof (with which he disagreed). Rather, it depends upon combining metaphysical principles about great-making properties and causality with the observation that certain things in the world actually fall under the purview of these concepts. Indeed, if the fourth way is related to the work of Anselm, it is related to the arguments from degrees of perfection given in the first few chapters of his *Monologium*. As Copleston recounts:

> In the *Monologium* Anselm develops a series of proofs of God's existence from degrees of perfection. It is obviously assumed as a fact that there are degrees of perfection in the universe, degrees of goodness [and beauty] for example. It is further assumed as a premise that when a number of beings possess a perfection which does not of itself involve finiteness and limitation, they derive this perfection from a being which is that perfection itself in an absolute and unlimited form. Thus degrees of goodness reveal the existence of absolute goodness [and of beauty, absolute beauty].[17]

With these observations in hand, it will prove helpful to arrange the fourth way into a sequence of propositions before expanding upon the argument, reviewing its logic and premises in more contemporary language. For as Gilson warns: 'Of all the Thomistic proofs none has been subjected to quite so many different interpretations.'[18] And as Adrian Nichols notes: 'The Five Ways have generated an enormous literature, partly because of the extreme concision with which they are expressed.'[19]

The fourth way appears to be made up of two overlapping syllogisms:

1. Among beings there are some more and some less good, true, noble and the like.
2. But 'more' and 'less' are predicated of different things, according as they resemble in their different ways something which is the maximum

3. so that there is something which is truest, something best, something noblest and, consequently, something which is uttermost being.
4. Now the maximum in any genus is the cause of all in that genus.
5. Therefore there must also be something which is to all beings the cause of their being, goodness, and every other perfection; and this we call 'God.'

Here's how I'd express the fourth way:

1. Things exist in the world around us which exhibit finite degrees of great-making properties (e.g. being, power, truth, goodness, beauty).
2. The existence of something exhibiting a great-making property to a finite degree implies the existence of something that possesses the property in question to a maximal degree.
3. Therefore, all great-making properties possessed in finite degree by beings in the world around us, including being, are possessed to a maximal degree by something.
4. An effect cannot exceed the greatness of its cause.
5. Therefore, there exists a maximally ontologically secure being that possesses every great-making property possessed by its effects to a maximal degree; and this we call 'God.'

The first premise, that 'things exist in the world around us which exhibit finite degrees of various transcendental great-making properties', draws upon an objective theory of value. As Kreeft observes: 'The fourth way presupposes something which everyone except a few Sophists in ancient Greece and Skeptics in ancient Rome accepted until modern times . . . that "values" are objective, that value judgements are judgements of fact.'[20] As Jacques Maritain affirms: 'It is a fact that there are degrees of value or perfection in things',[21] and 'goodness, beauty, being are not in their fullness in any one of the things we touch and see.'[22]

The second premise affirms a general principle which is said to apply to all transcendental great-making properties. The principle in question is that if anything possesses any such property to a finite degree, then something must possess the property in question to a maximal degree. As Mascall writes, the crucial question for the fourth way is 'whether the argument can in fact prove what it claims . . . [i.e. that] the concrete existence of finite good necessarily implies the concrete existence of an absolute maximum good. (And similarly, of course, with the other types of perfection.)'[23]

Aquinas's analogy of things being said to be hotter as they more closely resemble that which is hottest isn't helpful, because heat does not have a logical maximum, as is necessarily the case with great-making proper-ties. Aquinas's analogy isn't strong enough to support the principle in question. However, perhaps we can find better analogies or illustrations of this crucial principle. For example, if we are comparing two proposed routes from A to B, and if we can truthfully say that one of the proposed routes is more direct than the other (as we often do), then it follows that there must be a most direct route. It's not merely that the *concept* of longer and shorter distances between two points entails the *concept* of a shortest distance, but that the actual existence of longer and shorter distances between two points entails the actual existence of a shortest possible distance between them (i.e. a straight line). In other words, the existence of a route exhibiting the elegant efficiency of directness to a finite degree entails the existence of a route that exhibits this quality to a maximal degree.

Moreover, we can draw upon other theistic arguments from great-making properties to provide inferential support for Aquinas's second premise: The moral argument demonstrates that the existence of finite actions and agents that are morally better or worse than each other implies the existence of a morally perfect agent. Hence we already know that 'the concrete existence of finite good necessarily implies the concrete existence of an absolute maximum good.'[24] The cosmological argument demonstrates that the existence of anything with less than maximal onto-logical security implies the existence of something with maximal onto-logical security. Hence we already know that Aquinas's general principle holds for 'goodness' as well as for 'being' (indeed, at this stage of the fourth way Aquinas may be implicitly drawing upon the preceding cosmological argument from contingency given by his 'third way' for support). Given the interrelated nature of the transcendental values, there would seem to be good reason to assume that Aquinas's principle also holds for beauty.

Drawing upon other theistic arguments for support in this way does of course make the fourth way dependent upon those other arguments. However, since I believe those other arguments to be sound, I have little hesitation in drawing upon them for support. Since the fourth way leads to a grander conclusion than the arguments it draws upon, this move doesn't render it moot as a piece of natural theology.

But perhaps there's something to be said for treating the fourth way as an independent argument capable of standing on its own feet. It may be that such observations as that '"better" implies "best"'[25] and that the existence of more and less direct routes implies the existence of a most direct route are sufficient in and of themselves to allow the fourth way to proceed without the additional support that can be gathered from its compatriots. After all, while Aquinas seems to present his second premise as something axiomatic (thereby tempting us either to accept it as certainly true or to reject it as certainly false), the argument will work perfectly well if it is accepted simply as being *more plausible than its denial.*

The third premise is a midpoint conclusion that follows from the previous two premises. Note that the conclusion here is *not* that there exists a single being that possesses maximal degrees of every finitely instantiated great-making property. Rather, the conclusion is that every finitely instantiated great-making property has a maximal instantiation somewhere. These instantiations may or may not coincide.

The fourth premise, that 'the maximum in any genus is the cause of all in that genus', is similar, if not identical, to the principle that an effect cannot exceed the greatness of its cause. To use the sort of example Aquinas looks for, water doesn't rise higher than its source.

In the words of Jacques Maritain, Aquinas concludes from these four premises that 'the supreme degree of goodness of beauty, of being, exists [and does so] in a Prime Being which causes all that there is of goodness, beauty and being in things.'[26] Clearly, Aquinas thinks that the causal principle of premise 4 justifies tying together the maximal instantiations of great-making properties proven in premise 3 into a single, maximally beautiful being. Aquinas obviously thinks that the existence of a being with maximal ontological security, a quality that he singles out in premise 3, is crucial to this 'bundling' process. His line of thought would appear to be something like this: If anything possesses a maximal degree of some great-making property, but doesn't have maximal ontological security, it must ultimately be the effect of a maximally ontologically secure being. Since an effect cannot exceed the greatness of its cause, the maximally ontologically secure being in question must therefore be accorded the maximal degree of the great-making property in question. Hence the maximally ontologically secure being must be greater than any being that possesses a great-making property but that lacks maximal ontological security. Therefore, *on the assumption that there is only one maximally onto-logically secure being*, it follows that there must exist a single maximally ontologically secure being that possesses every great-making property possessed by its effects to a maximal degree. And *this* (as Anselm's onto-logical argument shows) is what we mean by 'God.' Hence Aquinas moves from the existence of a maximally ontologically secure being (established in premise 3) to the existence of a greatest or most beautiful possible being.

Consider the crucial assumption, implicit in Aquinas's argument, that *there is only one maximally ontologically secure being*. Aquinas was right about the existence of a being with maximal ontological security (a quality he singles out in premise 3) being crucial to the 'bundling' process that produces his monotheistic conclusion. However, his argument also makes the implicit assumption that there is only one maximally ontologically secure being. It may be understandable why Aquinas failed to make this assumption explicit in what is, after all, only a paragraph summary of an argument. Nevertheless, premise 3 does require that such an assumption be made if the fourth way is to reach its conclusion. This is because that conclusion can be avoided if the existence of multiple maximally ontologically secure beings (each possessing maximal degrees of different great-making properties) is postulated. For example, one could postulate the existence of a maximally ontologically secure being that is maximally good and the cause of finite goodness, and a different maximally ontologically secure being that is maximally true (i.e. which had a maximal capacity for knowledge), etc.

However, Aquinas could readily answer this objection. On the one hand, this alternative conclusion is of little comfort to atheists (since it appears to establish a sort of polytheism). On the other hand, Occam's razor discourages such an extravagant polytheistic conclusion in favour of belief in a single, maximally beautiful, maximally ontologically secure being. Therefore, although Aquinas's fourth way requires the inclusion of an appeal to Occam's razor, once this addition is made, his monotheistic conclusion does seem to follow validly from his premises. As Peter Kreeft and Ronald Tacelli argue:

> we arrange some things in terms of more and less. And when we do, we naturally think of them on a scale approaching most and least . . . But if these degrees of perfection pertain to being and being is caused in finite creatures [by a single ultimate source of existence], then there must exist a 'best,' a source and real standard of all the perfections that we recognize belong to us as beings. This absolutely perfect being – the 'Being of all beings,' 'the Perfection of all perfections' – is God.[27]

This conclusion greatly outstrips the conclusion of our initial reading of the fourth way, which simply produced an aesthetic feed-in to the moral argument. In point of fact, Copleston suggests that the fourth way combines both lines of argument:

> [Aquinas] argues not only that if there are different degrees of a perfection like goodness there is a supreme good to which other good things approximate but also that all limited degrees of goodness are caused by the supreme good . . . since goodness is a convertible term with being, a thing being good in so far as it has being, the supreme good is the supreme being

[i.e. it has maximal ontological security] and the cause of being in all other things.[28]

As Jacques Maritain comments, Aquinas's fourth way demonstrates that 'all our perishable treasures of being and beauty are besieged on all sides by the immensity and eternity of the One Who Is.'[29]

> **Question:**
> How can Aquinas's fourth way help us to resist temptation in the light of Jesus' comment that 'where your treasure is, there your heart will be also' (Matthew 6:21)?

15.4 Francis Schaeffer's Value Argument for Monotheism

Francis A. Schaeffer argued that only by beginning with a *personal* ultimate reality can we reasonably aspire to the use of the universal categories of value necessary to a meaningful existence; and although Schaeffer focused upon epistemological and moral beauty (truth and goodness), his argument incorporates beauty in its broadest sense: 'if you begin with the impersonal . . . there is no place for morals as morals [or beauty as beauty]. There is no standard in the universe which gives final meaning to such words as *right* and *wrong* [or *beautiful* and *ugly*]. If you begin with the impersonal, the universe is totally silent concerning any such words.'[30] As Thomas V. Morris explains: 'in a universe in which everything is reducible to a source or content of matter, or energy, or any other impersonal, there is ultimately only unity and homogeneity. This ground of being allows for no special significance to any particular configuration or formation of the basic components, over against any other actual or possible configuration of those components.'[31]

If non-human reality is 'indifferent' to us, as naturalists claim, then the only home for value is the finite, subjective individual: 'The Greeks understood that if we were really to know what was right and what was wrong [beautiful or ugly], we must have a universal to cover all the particulars.'[32] However, observes Schaeffer, while the Greek gods 'were personal gods – in contrast to the Eastern gods, who include everything and are impersonal – they were not big enough. Consequently, because their gods were not big enough, the problem [of universal categories] remained unsolved for the Greeks.'[33] Schaeffer argues that the God of monotheism provides what the Greeks lacked: an objective and personal instantiation of maximal, perfect goodness and beauty by which worldly particulars can be judged.

According to this analysis, the 'postmodern' rejection of objective value is a logical consequence of the modernistic rejection of God. Modernism initially attempted to retain belief in the 'permanent things' (truth, goodness, beauty) while rejecting God, but such a position is inherently unstable, according to Schaeffer, because God is the ontological ground of all value. As Jean Baudrillard urges: 'In the aesthetic realm of today there is no longer any God to recognize his own . . . there is no gold standard of aesthetic judgement or pleasure. This situation resembles that of a currency which may not be exchanged: it can only float, its only reference itself, impossible to convert into real value or wealth.'[34]

Indeed, once God is out of the picture there is no room in reality for objective goodness or beauty, for the objective value of truth and knowledge, or for the expectation that the human mind is capable of reliably grasping anything beyond what it is pragmatically useful to our survival that we grasp:

> While on the surface postmodernism seems to reject the artificially truncated rationalism embodied by scientific materialism, it actually adopts the materialist account of man as its starting point. Richard Rorty, dean of American postmodernists, even argues for the importance of 'keeping faith with Darwin.' It is precisely because the materialist account of man is so bleak that it creates fertile ground for postmodernism to grow . . . If human beings (and their beliefs) really are the mindless products of their material existence, then everything that gives meaning to human life – religion, morality, beauty – is revealed to be without objective basis. [In a doomed attempt to] avoid sliding into nihilism as a result of this revelation, postmodernists take a page from Nietzsche and reject reason altogether, urging people to fashion their own reality through an act of the will. In this way, the narrow 'rationalism' of scientific materialism begets utter irrationalism.[35]

There's no way for a modernist to avoid the postmodern nihilistic terminus, for as R.C. Sproul writes: 'the existence of God is the supreme *proto*-supposition for all theoretical thought . . . To deny this chief premise is to set one's sails for the island of nihilism.'[36]

15.4.1 Art and the line of despair

Schaeffer analyzed modern culture in terms of a dichotomy it has set up between the rational realm of (objective, empirical) facts and the non-rational realm of (subjective, opinion-relative) values. Schaeffer called the historical crossing-point after which this dichotomy arose 'the line of despair.'[37] The theist accepts art 'as the mediation that embodies love for the beauty of this world and desire for those far-off gleams of a higher world.'[38] The naturalist doesn't believe in any such universal-containing 'higher world', and so cannot accept such a high view of art. Instead, they must relegate those 'gleams of transcendence'[39] offered by art to the realm of pure subjectivity.

Schaeffer observed that a worldview that cuts a transcendent God out of its account of reality leads to the depersonalization of humanity in the realm of fact and the restriction of values (including moral goodness, beauty, and ultimately even truth) to the realm of subjective, relative opinion. As a secular worldview grows, value is increasingly placed in what Schaeffer dubbed 'the upper storey', where a leap of blind faith is required to avoid the obvious naturalistic conclusion that the 'death of God' leads to the 'death of value':

> Modern man, says Schaeffer, resides in a two-story universe. In the lower story is the finite world without God; here life is absurd . . . In the upper story are meaning, value, and purpose. Now modern man lives in the lower story because he believes there is no God. But he cannot live happily in such an absurd world; therefore, he continually makes leaps of faith into the upper story to affirm meaning, value, and purpose, even though he has no right to, since he does not believe in God.[40]

When Schaeffer wrote in the 1970s, postmodernism was in its infancy, and culture as a whole still clung, through a non-rational leap of faith, to the existence of objective value. Today, the implications of the 'death of God' have caught up with us:

> Where is God?' [cried the madman] 'I shall tell you. We have killed him . . . All of us are his murderers. But how have we done this? . . . Who gave us the sponge to wipe away the horizon? What did we do to unchain this earth from its sun? . . . Where are we moving now? Away from all suns? Are we not plunging continually backward, sideward, forward, in all directions? Is there any up or down left? Are we not straying through an infinite nothing?[41]

Postmodernists can tread water for a while, but eventually they will drown in a sea of relativism; for as Nietzsche recognized, one has no right to Christian morality without accepting the Christian worldview: 'When one gives up the Christian faith, one pulls the right to Christian morality out from under one's feet. This morality is by no means self-evident. Christianity is a system, a whole view of things thought out together. By breaking one main concept out of it, the faith in God, one breaks the whole. It stands or falls with faith in God.'[42] Schaeffer's insight was that *the same hard truth holds for aesthetic value.*

Peter Kreeft likewise diagnoses Western culture as suffering from an 'eclipse of "the permanent things".'[43] This eclipse has followed that of the supreme permanent thing: God. Apart from God, says Kreeft, culture has lost 'the objective and unchangeable laws of logic, metaphysics, and mathematics', together with 'objective moral laws.'[44] We can add to Kreeft's list of cultural casualties the eclipse of objective beauty. It is as if society has become exhausted with the attempt to constantly leap into Schaeffer's 'upper storey' of objective values in the face of a worldview that provides no ontological basis for their existence. Those who 'see through' the universe inevitably 'see through' their own pretensions to personal meaning: 'You cannot go on "seeing through" things for ever', wrote C.S. Lewis: 'The whole point of seeing through something is to see something through it . . . If you see through everything, then everything is transparent. But a wholly transparent world is an invisible world. To "see through" all things is the same as not to see.'[45] Postmodernism is the result of the realization that without the transcendent reference point provided by God, the 'upper storey' of value has become nothing but an incoherent miscellany of subjective, relative opinions, governed more by fashion than common sense.

Consider the similarities between the prophetic words of Nietzsche and British philosopher Roger Scruton's view of postmodern culture, which recommends that we live 'as if' life mattered:

> To understand the depth of the . . . 'as if' is to understand the condition of the modern soul. We know that we are animals, parts of the natural order, bound by laws which tie us to the material forces which govern everything . . . and that death is exactly what it seems. Our world has been disenchanted and our illusions destroyed. At the same time we cannot live as though that were the whole truth of our condition. Even modern people are compelled to praise and blame, love and hate, reward and punish. Even modern people . . . are aware of self, as the centre of their being; and even modern people try to connect to other selves around them. We therefore see others as *if* they were free beings, animated by a self or soul, and with more than a worldly destiny. If we abandon that perception, then human relations dwindle into a machine-like parody . . . the world is voided of love, [moral] duty and [aesthetic] desire, and only the body remains.[46]

Scruton writes that *postmodernism necessitates an inconsistent life.* In the realm of fact we 'know' that people are the unintended material products of material necessity, plus time, plus chance. We 'know' that there is therefore no objective value in truth, goodness, or beauty. However, we cannot live as if all this were true. Therefore, we must be inconsistent and live the lie of 'as if'! Schaeffer noted how some naturalists (such as Julian Huxley) admit that a human being 'functions better if he acts as though God is there', and he pointed out that 'this is not an optimistic, happy, reasonable or brilliant answer. It is darkness and death.'[47] A God-less philosophy has nowhere left to run but the land of illusions.

15.4.1.1 Art to the rescue?

According to Dawkins, 'if there is a logical argument linking the existence of great art to the existence of God, it is not spelled out by its proponents. It is simply assumed to be self-evident, which it most certainly is not.'[48] But as Eric S. Waterhouse wrote: 'That religion has constantly been the inspirer of art, and that art has often helped the expression of religious feeling, suggests the inner connection between the two . . . art joins with religion in opening the vision to the unseen.'[49]

With the rise of naturalism and secularism in the Enlightenment (which Kreeft wryly calls 'the Darkening'),[50] art came to the fore as a substitute religious experience. As Scruton explains: 'art became a redeeming enterprise, and the artist stepped into the place vacated by the prophet and the priest.'[51] Modernist culture rejected the recognition of the 'face of God' in nature and art, but continued to seek the transcendent experience of awe and wonder that it craved in an art devoid of any transcendent reference point: 'The high culture of the Enlightenment . . . involved a noble and energetic attempt to rescue the ethical view of human life . . . which flourished spontaneously in the old religious culture . . . The rescue was a work of the imagination, in which the aesthetic attitude took over from religious worship as the source of intrinsic values.'[52]

From the theistic point of view, one could say that the spiritual feelings of modernism were better than its philosophy. Cut off from its source, objective aesthetic value (no less than ethical value) is bound to die. Indeed, after the 'death of God' it would not be long before people realized this: 'Artistic expression over the past 400 years, the age of science, persistently returns to the man alone, lost and searching for something, though he is seldom sure precisely what,'[53] notes Bryan Appleyard. But instead of preserving the meaning of spiritual experience by re-acknowledging its transcendent source, postmodernism held on to naturalism and resigned itself to the objective meaninglessness of all value. Tobias Jones passes an insightful comment:

> I used to think that morality or high culture could defend the qualitative against the quantitative; but high culture shorn of its religious gold standard has accommodated itself to the 'revolt of inferiority'. It's no surprise that high

culture has lost any distinction from popular culture at precisely the time in which religion has lost its central role in the lives of cultural consumers . . . The real defenders of high culture eventually concede that it has to rub shoulders with the religious. It's a notion which is echoed by all of the eloquent writers on the subject, even those who don't necessarily have a religious belief.[54]

For example, Scruton acknowledges: 'When religion dies . . . the vision of man's higher nature is conserved by art. But art cannot be a substitute for religion, nor does it fill the void that is left by faith.'[55]

15.4.1.2 *Pictures at an exhibition*

Walking through a museum some years ago I was struck by the changing themes apparent in the historically ordered art collection. Many of the earlier paintings had a religious theme; paintings of nature became more prominent as time went on, but the general impression produced by these artworks was one of artistic beauty and meaning. I could sense that the artists were saying, 'Look, this person/event is important (often theologically so)', or simply, 'Look, this is beautiful.' As I reached the art of the Enlightenment, detailed still-life studies and portraits of wealthy people who had paid to be immortalized on canvas dominated the collection. Art had begun to serve humankind. Finally, I reached galleries of twentieth-century art. The change of mood was even more pronounced and all the more disturbing, for this art clearly expressed a disturbed mindset. Images of pain and depression filled me with a sense of tragic compassion, in stark contrast with the beauty and hope I had just seen filling the art of so many preceding centuries. Artist Thomas Williams contemplates the affect of naturalism upon art:

The direction that much art has taken in the past few generations tells us something about the despair of naturalism. There was a time when the goal of the artist was to display beauty. But as naturalistic philosophy became dominant, much of the art produced became increasingly pointless, despairing, and consciously devoid of beauty. The oppressive weight of the philosophy of meaninglessness has squeezed the bright colours from the brushes of many unbelieving artists. In their despair they have dismissed beauty as an illusion that cannot hide the dark void they believe will ultimately engulf all things. And their art reflects that despair.[56]

As theologian Hans Küng put it: 'Art has now become the expression of man's estrangement, his isolation in the world, of the ultimate futility of human life and the history of humanity.'[57]

If God exists, then to worship the beauty of art in the Enlightenment manner is to make art into an idol. As Kreeft warns: 'Since an idol is not God, no matter how sincere or passionately it is treated as God, it is bound to break the heart of its worshipper, sooner or later. Good motives for idolatry cannot remove the objective fact that the idol is an unreality . . . You can't get blood out of a stone or divine joy from non-divine things.'[58]

If (as commentators like Scruton claim) healthy art is inseparable from healthy religion, then either God exists and explains this connection, or God does not exist, and the world is absurd. A world in which aesthetic value depends upon the retention of belief in a non-existent God is a world that asks us to hypocritically predicate true value on a falsehood. If life isn't absurd in this way, then God both exists and grounds aesthetic value.

Schaeffer argues that the hypothesis that God is the only sufficient condition of the objectivity of aesthetic value explains (what otherwise seems inexplicable) why the flower of artistic high culture that flourished under the worldview of Christendom turned to rancour in a secular society. As Scruton admits: 'If you consider the high culture of modern times, you will be struck by the theme of alienation which runs through so many of its products . . . the high culture of our society, having ceased to be a meditation on the common religion, has become instead a meditation on the lack of it.'[59]

What is it that people miss so much that they devote a large proportion of our culture's artistic output to mourning its loss? God.

Watch:
Francis A. Schaeffer, 'The Flow of Materialism' http://youtu.be/9L_YuDSSL8A.
Peter S. Williams, 'A Pre-Modern Perspective on Postmodernism: A Tale of Three Mirrors' http://youtu.be/Mhf6_H612K4,.

Listen:
Peter S. Williams, 'A Pre-Modern Perspective on Postmodernism: A Tale of Three Mirrors' http://www.damaris.org/cm/podcasts/707.

Question:
Visit a historically ordered art gallery with Schaeffer's analysis of the line of despair in mind. Does what you see bear out his argument?

15.5 Patrick Sherry's Theological Prediction Argument

Spirit and Beauty (SCM, 2002), by Patrick Sherry, professor of philosophical theology at Lancaster University, is perhaps the best available modern introduction to theological aesthetics. Towards the end of his discussion of aesthetic concepts and the objectivity of beauty, Sherry observes that 'the theological consideration of these issues introduces certain new factors.'[60] He argues that:

> If indeed God created the world with all its beauty, and such beauties are reflections of His beauty, then it follows that there are theological grounds as well as philosophical for a broadly 'realist' or 'objectivist' position [regarding beauty]. Thus theology, it seems, rules out certain views a priori and favours others; and this is not surprising, for we find a similar situation in ethics, where, for instance, wholesale ethical relativism is precluded for a Christian, whilst certain values and principles are normative, even if there may be some flexibility in their application. In the case of aesthetics, Christian theologians, and indeed all theists, start from the assumption that the beautiful aspects of nature are properties put there by God as creator of all things . . .[61]

That is, according to Sherry, *the theology of creation predicts the objectivity of beauty*. In the sciences, when a hypothesis grounds a novel prediction and that prediction is verified, this match between prediction and reality is treated as evidence for the truth of the prediction-grounding hypothesis. In this instance, as Sherry notes, while 'the objectivity of beauty and other aesthetic properties is defensible on purely philosophical grounds . . . theologians are arguing for the case on other, theological, grounds . . . based on the doctrine of Creation.'[62] The naturalistic worldview clearly does not provide any *a priori* grounds for a realist account of beauty. If it did, why would an atheist like Dawkins, who makes great play of the beauty revealed by science, admit that his view, 'if you think about its aesthetic . . . connotations, is a bleak and cold one',[63] and announce that 'beauty is not an absolute virtue in itself'?[64] Indeed, a worldview that excludes God thereby excludes the possibility of objective beauty. Hence the objectivity of beauty is a novel prediction made by the theistic worldview. The independent philosophical justification of realist aesthetics therefore counts as evidence for the truth of the relevant prediction-grounding theological hypothesis.

Conclusion: God as Maximally Beautiful Being

> On the glorious splendour of your majesty,
> and on your wondrous works, I will meditate (Psalm 145:5 NRSV).

The fundamental problem with the objective theory of beauty for atheists is that it depends, as G.E. Moore's definition of beauty makes clear (cf. chapter 14), upon an objective theory of goodness; and an objective theory of goodness depends in turn upon the recognition of an objective standard of goodness that can ultimately only find its home in the character of God (cf. chapter 8). Without divinity – which necessarily exemplifies objective goodness (and hence objective beauty, because goodness is beautiful) – there would be no objective good. And without objective good, there would be no objective beauty; because nothing can be objectively beautiful that it is not objectively good to appreciate. As Edward Farley says: 'If God is dead, so is beauty.'[65] And if beauty is alive, then so too is God.

A mathematician contemplating Newton's equations may quite legitimately describe the object of their contemplation as beautiful. Similarly, someone contemplating God may quite legitimately describe the object of their contemplation as beautiful, and sublimely so. Patrick Sherry notes that 'beauty is probably today the most neglected of the divine attributes.'[66] This is despite the fact that 'many of the early Christian Fathers and the medievals regarded it as central in their discussions of the divine nature.'[67] Although God's beauty is infrequently mentioned in modern discussions of divinity, theists do continue to attribute beauty to God. Hence Keith Ward speaks of 'the supreme beauty, the supreme value, of the Divine self',[68] and Peter Kreeft says that 'God is infinite Beauty and the inventor of all beauty in creatures.'[69]

Scripture often attributes beauty to God. The book of Isaiah promises:

In that day the LORD Almighty
> will be a glorious crown,
a beautiful wreath
> for the remnant of his people (Isaiah 28:5).

The book of Psalms frequently ascribes beauty to God:

One thing I ask of the LORD,
> this is what I seek:
that I may dwell in the house of the LORD
> all the days of my life,
to gaze upon the beauty of the Lord (Psalm 27:4, my italics).

The Hebrew term *nō'am*, translated here as 'beauty', also means 'favour' or 'sweetness' – as in Psalm 90:17 (NRSV): 'Let the favour of the Lord our God be upon us.' Other similar terms applied to God in the Psalms are *hah-dahr* ('splendour' or 'majesty') – as in Psalm 145:5 (NRSV): 'On the glorious splendour of your majesty, and on your wondrous works, I will meditate' – and *tiphahrah* (translated as 'splendour', 'pride', 'glory', 'honour' and 'beauty'), as in Psalm 71:8. The term *yŏphee*, which in later Hebrew is probably closest to the English term 'beauty', is ascribed to God in Zechariah 9:17, and to places associated with God in Psalms 46 and 50.[70] Psalms extol us to 'ascribe to the LORD the glory due to his name [i.e. his nature]' (Psalm 29:2; 96:8). Keith Ward informs us that 'the idea of the glory and majesty of God is the idea of beauty, power and wisdom which is complete.'[71] Richard Harries adds: 'When goodness, truth and beauty are combined we have glory. When boundless goodness, total truth and sublime beauty are combined in supreme degree, we have divine glory . . . God is in himself all glory in a sublime conjunction of beauty, truth and love.'[72] God's moral holiness is one component of his beauty: 'Then Moses said, "Now show me your *glory*." And the LORD said, "I will cause all my goodness to pass in front of you"' (Exodus 33:19, my italics).

Indeed, *to say that God is objectively, maximally beautiful is to imply everything that can be said about the essential nature of God.* To say that God is maximally beautiful is to say that he is maximally good (since only good qualities are beautiful); that is, that God consists of the greatest set of great-making qualities that can exist together in one and the same being. Thus we can deduce that:

- God exhibits maximal ontological goodness (and thus independent and necessary existence).
- God possesses omniscience, that is, a maximal capacity for knowledge (since truth is good and truth is a quality of beliefs).
- God is almighty (omnipotent), that is, has maximal power with which to enact his good will.

Most appropriately, as the best of all possible personal beings (which God must be since the personal is greater than the impersonal, knowledge a facet of mind, and moral goodness a quality of persons) 'God is love' (1 John 4:8). This has the stunning implication that the Christian doctrine that God is a Trinity of divine persons in one divine personal being is not only a conclusion inferred as the best explanation for the data of revealed theology, but something that can be independently established through philosophical deduction.

Read:
Peter S. Williams, 'Understanding the Trinity' www.bethinking.org/who-are-you-god/advanced/understanding-the-trinity.htm.

> **Films to watch and discuss:**
> *American Beauty*, directed by Sam Mendes (Dreamworks, 1999) (18)
> cf. James S. Spiegel, 'The Theological Aesthetic of American Beauty' www.usask.ca/relst/jrpc/art4-americanbeauty.html.

* * *

Recommended Resources

Video

*Williams, Peter S. 'Beauty' YouTube Playlist www.youtube.com/playlist?list=PLQhh-3qcwVEWiL488-SGbfODhf6kLPSZbJ.

Audio

Barrs, Jerram. 'Francis A. Schaeffer: Christianity and Modern Art', part 1 http://covenantseminary.inmotionhosting.com/CC578_Lecture_16.mp3 (Transcript www.covenantseminary.edu/worldwide/en/CC578/CC578_T_16.pdf) and part 2 http://covenantseminary.inmotionhosting.com/CC578_Lecture_17.mp3 (Transcript www.covenantseminary.edu/worldwide/en/CC578/CC578_T_17.pdf).

— 'Francis A. Schaeffer: The Line of Despair', part 1 http://covenantseminary.inmotionhosting.com/CC579_Lecture_12.mp3 (Transcript www.covenantseminary.edu/worldwide/en/CC579/CC579_T_12.pdf) and part 2 http://covenantseminary.inmotionhosting.com/CC579_Lecture_13.mp3 (Transcript www.covenantseminary.edu/worldwide/en/CC579/CC579_T_13.pdf).

— 'Francis A. Schaeffer: Upper and Lower Story', part 1 http://covenantseminary.inmotionhosting.com/CC579_Lecture_14.mp3 (Transcript www.covenantseminary.edu/worldwide/en/CC579/CC579_T_14.pdf) and part 2 http://covenantseminary.inmotionhosting.com/CC579_Lecture_15.mp3 (Transcript www.covenantseminary.edu/worldwide/en/CC579/CC579_T_15.pdf).

*Kreeft, Peter. 'Desire' www.peterkreeft.com/audio/23_desire.htm.

— 'Truth, Goodness and Beauty' www.peterkreeft.com/audio/27_good-true-beautiful/peter-kreeft_good-true-beautiful.mp3.

Pearcey, Nancy. 'What's in a Worldview?' www.veritas.org/Talks.aspx#!/v/646.

*Williams, Peter S. 'A Pre-Modern Perspective on Postmodernism: A Tale of Three Mirrors' www.damaris.org/cm/podcasts/707.

Online papers

Dembski, William A. 'The Act of Creation: Bridging Transcendence and Immanence' www.arn.org/docs/dembski/wd_actofcreation.htm.

Howell, Russell W. 'Does Mathematical Beauty Pose Problems for Naturalism?' www.cslewis.org/ffblog/archives/2005/09/does_mathematic.html#more.

Kreeft, Peter. 'The Argument from Desire' www.peterkreeft.com/topics/desire.htm.

Martin, Christopher F.J. 'The Fourth Way' http://ftp.colloquium.co.uk/viae4.htm.

Pearcey, Nancy. 'How Darwinism Dumbs Us Down: Evolution and Postmodernism' www.4truth.net/fourtruthpbscience.aspx?pageid=8589952923&terms=nancy%20pearcey.

Plantinga, Alvin. 'Two Dozen (or so) Theistic Arguments' www.homestead.com/philof-religion/files/Theisticarguments.html.

Roccasalvo, Joan L. 'Beauty and the Sacred' www.ignatius.com/magazines/hprweb/roccasalvo_aug_sep_2008.html.

Solomon, Jerry. 'Art and the Christian' www.leaderu.com/orgs/probe/docs/artandxn.html.

Williams, Peter S. 'Aesthetic Arguments for the Existence of God' www.quodlibet.net/pdf/williams-aesthetic.pdf.

— 'Beauty and the Existence of God' www.peter-s-williams.co.uk/Existence_of_God/Argument%20from%20Beauty.doc.

— 'Intelligent Design, Aesthetics and Design Arguments' www.iscid.org/papers/Williams_Aesthetics_012302.pdf.

— 'Review: Edward Farley, *Faith and Beauty: A Theological Aesthetic* (Aldershot: Ashgate, 2001)' www.amazon.com/gp/cdp/member-reviews/A1VQXYIQBW3EIZ/ref=cm_pdp_rev_more?ie=UTF8&sort%5Fby=MostRecentReview#R27QECTJ4MRY55.

— 'A Theistic Account of Aesthetic Value' www.leaderu.com/theology/williams_beauty.html.

— 'Understanding the Trinity' www.bethinking.org/who-are-you-god/advanced/understanding-the-trinity.htm.

Wyn, Mark. 'Beauty, Providence and the Biophilia Hypothesis' http://apollos.square-space.com/aesthetic-argument/Beauty%20Providence%20and%20the%20Biophilia%20Hypothesis.pdf.

Books

Brown, Stephen F., ed. *Bonaventure: The Journey of the Mind to God* (trans. Philotheus Boehner; Indianapolis, IN: Hackett, 1993).

Cooper, David E. *Aesthetics: The Classic Readings* (Oxford: Blackwell, 1997).

*Dubay, Thomas. *The Evidential Power of Beauty* (San Francisco: Ignatius Press, 1999).

Farley, Edward. *Faith and Beauty: A Theological Aesthetic* (Aldershot: Ashgate, 2001).

Gilson, Étienne. *The Christian Philosophy of St Thomas Aquinas* (University of Notre Dame Press, 2002).

Hanfling, Oswald, ed. *Philosophical Aesthetics: An Introduction* (Oxford: Blackwell, 1992).

Harries, Richard. *Art and the Beauty of God* (New York: Mowbray, 1993).

Joad, C.E.M. *The Recovery of Belief* (London: Faber & Faber, 1952).

McGinn, Colin. *Ethics, Evil and Fiction* (Oxford: Clarendon Press, 1999).

McGrath, Alister. *The Re-Enchantment of Nature* (London: Hodder & Stoughton, 2002).

Morris, Thomas V. *Francis Schaeffer's Apologetics: A Critique* (Chicago: Moody Press, 1976).

Pearcey, Nancy. *Saving Leonardo: A Call to Resist the Secular Assault on Mind, Morals and Meaning* (Nashville, TN: B&H, 2010).

Polkinghorne, John. *Belief in God in an Age of Science* (Yale University Press, 1998).

Pratney, W.A. *The Nature and Character of God* (Minneapolis, MN: Bethany House, 1988).

Schaeffer, Francis A. *The Complete Works of Francis A. Schaeffer*, vol. 1 (Wheaton, IL: Crossway Books, 1994).

Scruton, Roger. *An Intelligent Person's Guide to Modern Culture* (London: Duckworth Press, 1998).

*Sherry, Patrick. *Spirit and Beauty* (London: SCM Press, 2nd edn, 2002).

Williams, Peter S. *I Wish I Could Believe in Meaning: A Response to Nihilism* (Southampton: Damaris, 2005).

16. Science and Theology

Since the Holy Writ is true, and all truth agrees with truth, the truth of Holy
Writ cannot be contrary to the truth obtained by reason and experiment.
Galileo[1]

Introduction

'If Christians are going to speak to the modern world and interact
with it responsibly,' observe J.P. Moreland and William Lane Craig,
'they must interact with science.'[2] Moreover, 'if believers are going
to explore God's world by means of science and integrate their theological beliefs with the results of that exploration, they need a deeper
understanding of science itself.'[3] Christians should be interested in
these tasks:

> Because Christians are interested in the truth and because they are called to
> proclaim and defend their views to an unbelieving world, it is important for
> the believing community to think carefully about how to integrate their care-
> fully formed theological beliefs with a careful evaluation of the 'deliverances'
> of science . . . Augustine noted long ago, 'We must show our Scriptures not
> to be in conflict with whatever [critics] can demonstrate about the nature of
> things from reliable sources.'[4]

The *philosophy of science* is an indispensable aid to this project, for as Garrett J. DeWeese and J.P. Moreland explain: 'Philosophy is, in part, a second-order discipline that studies the assumptions, concepts and argument forms of other disciplines, including science. By contrast science is a set of first-order disciplines. In philosophy of science, we investigate questions *of* philosophy *about* science.'[5] Likewise, in the philosophy of theology we investigate questions *of* philosophy *about* theology, including the important question of how theology relates to science. Hence philosophy plays an indispensable role in the project of integrating a scientific understanding of reality into theology.

16.1 What Is Science?

Philosophers have found it very hard to define science: 'There is no consensus among philosophers of science as to what constitutes a proper scientific explanation or what criteria a theory must possess in order to be truly scientific. Despite extensive attempts, criteria that indisputably demarcate science from non-science or pseudo-science have never been offered.'[6] Moreland and Craig explain that:

> Various criteria have been offered . . . for something to count as science: it must focus on the natural or physical world, be guided by natural law, explain by reference to natural law, be empirically testable, be held tentatively . . . be falsifiable, be measurable or quantifiable, involve predictions and be repeatable. The problem is that no one or no set of these is necessary or sufficient for counting as science. There are examples of science that do not have the criterion in question (thus it is not necessary) and there are examples of non-science that do have the criterion (thus it is not sufficient).[7]

Consequently, 'philosophers of science are much less optimistic than they were a few decades ago about the possibility of finding any really coherent demarcation criteria.'[8]

✔ There's no agreed definition of science

However, 'one does not need to know the definition of a thing before he can recognize clear cases of the thing being defined.'[9] As Del Ratzsch comments, while it might *seem* impossible to investigate the nature of science if we don't, strictly speaking, know what we're talking about:

> such problems are not insurmountable in comparable situations. For instance, it is almost a cliché that no one can define love. But that does

not stop us from proclaiming (often correctly) our undying version of love to select persons on Valentine's day . . . We can often recognize instances of and characterics of a concept even if we are unable to formulate an ironclad definition of it, and we often have a good general idea even if we cannot specify all of the details. Such is the case with the general concept of science.[10]

It's far easier to say how we *shouldn't* define science . . .

16.1.1 Scientism

Atheist Richard Dawkins defines science as 'the honest and systematic endeavour to find out the truth about the real world.'[11] In practice he uses 'science' as a term of endearment extending to any investigation of the 'real world' *to which empirical data has relevance.* Moreover, Dawkins assumes that the 'real world' can be described in *exclusively* naturalistic terms. In sum, Dawkins views science as:

- *The honest and systematic, empirically guided endeavour to find out the truth about all reality,* where (crucially) 'all reality' is *assumed to be metaphysically naturalistic.*

Science thus defined claims competence to give an account of *all reality*, and must therefore either attempt to *reduce* (to naturalistically acceptable categories) or *reject* the existence of anything supernatural. For example, since it's impossible to do science without thinking, Dawkins can't reject the reality of mind; so he deduces that mind *must* have a *reductive* naturalistic explanation (even though no such explanation is available). Since God is by definition a supernatural being, Dawkins simply *rejects* God *a priori.*

Viewing science in such omni-competent terms is a form of *scientism.* One of the problems with scientism is that *moral values* are objective realities that scientism must either reduce or reject; and to reduce the *prescriptive* reality of moral value to the purely *descriptive* realities of a metaphysically naturalistic worldview is necessarily to reject the *prescriptive* reality of moral value! What then becomes of Dawkins' dedication to science as an *honest* endeavour to find out the truth about the real world?

Watch:
John G. West, 'The Magician's Twin: C.S. Lewis and the Case against Scientism' http://youtu.be/FPeyJvXU68k.

Scientism refers to any philosophical view that elevates science above all other sources of knowledge. Scientism is self-contradictory, as Moreland explains: 'A dogmatic claim of scientism . . . is self-refuting. The statement itself is not a statement of science, but a second-order philosophical statement about science . . . Justifying science by science is question begging. The validation of science is a philosophical issue . . . and any claim to the contrary will itself be philosophical.'[12]

Watch:
William Lane Craig, 'Craig Humiliates Dr Peter Atkins' http://youtu.be/cJrM-Fv6QoX0.

Question:
Make a list of things you think you know with more certainty than you think you can have in any scientifically grounded belief. What implication does your list have for the believability of scientism?

16.1.2 Methodological naturalism

One can distinguish between 'metaphysical naturalism', which denies the existence of God, and 'methodological naturalism' as a disciplinary method that's *neutral* about God's existence. Methodological naturalism (MN) has been defined as the idea that 'scientific method requires that one explain data by appealing to natural laws and natural processes.'[13] Paul De Vries asserts that 'the natural sciences are committed to the systematic analysis of matter and energy within the context of methodological naturalism.'[14] Likewise, Nancy Murphy claims: 'science seeks naturalistic explanations for all natural processes . . . Anyone who attributes the characteristic of living things to creative intelligence has by definition stepped into the arena of either metaphysics or theology.'[15] However, 'appeal to definition cannot be the whole story.'[16]

Despite its popularity among scientists, MN is a highly problematic and widely disputed demarcation criterion: 'The inadequacy of methodological naturalism [is] widely acknowledged by philosophers of science, even among those who are atheists.'[17] For example, according to Larry Laudan: 'There is no demarcation line between science and non-science, or between science and pseudoscience, which would win assent from a majority of philosophers.'[18] Elsewhere he writes: 'If we would stand up and be counted on the side of reason, we ought to drop terms like "pseudo-science" and "unscientific" from our vocabulary; they are just hollow phrases which do only emotive work for us.'[19] Michael Ruse acknowledges: 'It would indeed be very odd were I and others to simply characterize "science" as something which, by definition, is based on (methodological) naturalistic philosophy and hence excludes God.'[20] Hence atheist Thomas Nagel argues that Intelligent Design Theory (cf. chapter 7) *is* a scientific theory:

> The denier that ID is science faces the following dilemma. Either he admits that the intervention of such a designer is possible, or he does not. If he does not, he must explain why that belief is more scientific than the belief that a designer is possible. If on the other hand he believes that a designer is possible, then he can argue that the evidence is overwhelmingly against the actions of such a designer, but he cannot say that someone who offers evidence on the other side is doing something of a fundamentally different kind . . . Critics take issue with the claims made by defenders of ID about what standard evolutionary mechanisms can accomplish . . . Whatever the merits, however, that is clearly a scientific disagreement, not a disagreement between science and something else . . .[21]

As Del Ratzsch notes, one informal definition of science is that it constitutes:

> an attempt to get at the truth *no holds barred* . . . The scientific attitude has usually been characterized as a commitment to following the evidence wherever it leads. That does not look like promising ammunition for someone pushing an official policy of refusing to allow science to follow evidence to supernatural design no matter what the evidence turns out to be . . . [Such an approach] commits science to either having to deliberately ignore major (possibly even *observable*) features of the material realm or having to refrain from even considering the obvious and only workable explanation, should it turn out that those features clearly resulted from supernatural activity . . . any imposed policy of naturalism in science has the potential not only of eroding any self-correcting capacity of science but of preventing science from reaching certain truths. Any imposed policy of methodological naturalism will have precisely the same potential consequences.[22]

Isaac Newton wrote that 'the business of science is to deduce causes from effects, till we come to the very first cause, which certainly is not mechanical.'[23] Newton's first Rule of Reasoning in [Natural] Philosophy (i.e. science), from volume 2 of the *Principia*, states: 'We are to admit no more causes of natural things than such as are both true and sufficient to explain their appearances. To this purpose the philosophers say that Nature does nothing in vain, and more is in vain when less will serve.'[24]

In other words, Newton thought of science as a search for *the best expla-nation* of material reality, and the best explanation may not be 'mechan-ical', but intelligent. As Stephen C. Meyer notes: 'there are at least two possible types of causes: mechanistic and intelligent'[25] – and ruling out either type of cause *a priori* when arguing that the other type of cause explains a given effect is simply question begging. Newton didn't beg the question against intelligent causes, and so felt free to argue that 'this most beautiful system of sun, planets, and comets could only proceed from the counsel and dominion of an intelligent and powerful Being.'[26] Paul Nelson observes:

> The founders of western science . . . knew how to recognise design. Knowl-edge of intelligent causation (design) was not placed in a separate rank from knowledge of natural causation (physical regularities and chance events), such that knowing that a stone will fall to the ground when thrown counted as genuine *scientia*, whereas knowing that a letter had an author did not. The very suggestion would have been seen by such early giants of science as Robert Boyle or Isaac Newton as laughable.[27]

Biologist Denis Alexander asserts that 'there is nothing that scientists can describe which is not part of the nexus of the secondary causes that comprise God's actions.'[28] This assertion begs the question against the true explanation of anything studied by scientists being God acting directly as a *primary* cause. Alexander writes: 'The theistic claim is that the created order, complete with its biological diversity, has been brought into being and continues to exist by God's will. The claim says nothing about the mechanisms by which this has occurred in the past or continues to occur in the present. It is the task of biologists (and others) to elucidate such mechanisms.'[29] If 'such mechanisms' are simply *defined* in a method-ologically naturalistic manner, excluding any primary actions performed by God *a priori*, then Alexander's statement begs the question against Newton's first rule of natural philosophy. Alexander thereby divorces the search for *scientific* explanations from the search for *true* explanations. As Jay Wesley Richards complains: 'Methodological naturalism . . . contra-dicts the true spirit of science, which is to seek the truth about the natural world, no holds barred.'[30] As Alexander himself argues in another context:

> The traditional Christian theist has a 'voluntaristic' doctrine of God, meaning that . . . God is free to act in any way he chooses, unrestricted and unfettered . . . this doctrine provided a powerful support for science in stimulating the early natural philosophers to investigate what God had actually done in the created order in contradistinction to the rationalistic scholastic philosophers who thought they

could derive what God ought to have done from first principles. Therefore when it comes to scientific explanations and models of how things work, the theist need have no hidden theological investment in supporting one model over another . . . Scientists are meant to be empiricists not dogmatists.[31]

But allowing scientists to be 'empiricists not dogmatists' entails rejecting methodological naturalism. Indeed, Alexander argues against methodological naturalism *in the study of history*:

The atheist who believes that the universe is essentially a closed system in which all matter 'obeys' deterministic laws is unlikely to be very open to the possibility that the material world occasionally behaves in an unexpected way . . . In contrast, the theist who believes that there is a creator-God who is actively sustaining every aspect of the created order will not be surprised if God occasionally chooses to act in an unusual way in a particular historical context . . . Ironically it is therefore the stance of the atheist that is likely to lead to a closed mind when it comes to the question of evidence for claimed miraculous events . . . it is the stance of the theist that best exemplifies the general attitude which one hopes characterizes the scientific community as a whole, namely, an openness to the way the world actually is, rather than the attitude more typical of some forms of Greek rationalism, which already knew the answer before the investigation had even begun.[32]

How can a scientific attitude of 'openness to the way the world actually is' rather than knowing the answer before investigation even begins (an attitude Alexander says should characterize 'the scientific community as a whole') be consistently endorsed regarding history but not natural history? To argue for Jesus' resurrection from the evidence of history while simultaneously endorsing a methodological rule against arguing for miracles from the evidence of natural history is inconsistent and arbitrary. As William Lane Craig argues:

It is frequently asserted that the professional scientist or historian is methodologically committed to seeking only natural causes as explanations of their respective data, which procedure rules out inference to God as the best explanation. It is puzzling that some methodological naturalists in science . . . nevertheless want to dismiss methodological naturalism when it comes to history and to affirm the historicity of the gospel miracles. One cannot, it seems to me, have it both ways.[33]

With Craig: 'I see no good reason for methodological naturalism in either science or history.'[34]

16.1.3 HMN vs SMN

One can distinguish between *hard* and *soft* versions of methodological naturalism.[35] Hard methodological naturalism (HMN) excludes all *intelligent* causation from scientific explanations – thereby a) exiling from science many fields of study currently considered scientific and b) ceding epistemological competency from science to philosophy. On the other hand, soft methodological naturalism (SMN) excludes *explicitly supernatural causation* from science, but permits explanations framed in terms of *intelligence*.

SMN permits ID Theory to count as science just as effectively as the outright rejection of 'methodological naturalism' endorsed by many contemporary philosophers of science. As Michael J. Behe explains:

> my argument is limited to design itself; I strongly emphasize that it is not an argument for the existence of a benevolent God, as Paley's was. I hasten to add that I myself do believe in a benevolent God, and I recognize that philosophy and theology may be able to extend the argument. But a scientific argument for design in biology does not reach that far. Thus while I argue for design, the question of the identity of the designer is left open . . . as regards the identity of the designer, modern ID theory happily echoes Isaac Newton's phrase, *hypothesis non fingo*.[36]

David DeWolf et al. confirm: 'Empirical science cannot determine whether the intelligent cause detected resides inside or outside of nature. That further determination requires more than empirical science. Far from merely being "rhetorical," this claim is central to the definition of intelligent design as a scientific theory . . . intelligent design does *not* require a supernatural entity.'[37]

SMN isn't a necessary condition of 'science', but there are practical reasons for practising science within the bounds of SMN. SMN allows science to continue as a 'big tent' for people of widely differing world-views. Rather than theists doing 'theistic science' and atheists doing 'naturalistic science' (HMN definition), we can all cooperate in doing science (SMN definition). SMN allows agnostics, atheists, Buddhists, Christians, deists, Jews, Mormons, Muslims, New Agers, panentheists, pantheists, Platonists and Raelians to all do science together – which is a good thing. Furthermore, SMN doesn't risk subverting the truth-seeking intent of science. SMN permits but doesn't entail ID. SMN does limit the epistemological competency of science so defined, but whether an intelligent cause is supernatural or not, it's still an *intelligent* cause, and hence still true to note it as such within scientific theory making. Hence DeWolf et al. conclude: 'Intelligent design, properly conceived, does not need to violate methodological naturalism.'[38]

16.1.4 Science is . . .

At the very least, science is *a first-order discipline that seeks to understand the truth about observable reality*. The scientific quest starts, *but doesn't end*, with the familiar world around us as accessed through the physical senses. Science quickly finds itself exploring realities that can't be observed directly, but only indirectly. At its limits (which become very philosophical), science can involve hypothetical realities that cannot be observed at all (e.g. parallel universes).

Although there is 'no set of necessary and sufficient conditions by which to define science', there are 'good "rules of thumb" that help clarify what science is.'[39] As John Lennox explains: 'certain elements crop up regularly in attempts to describe what "scientific" activity involves: hypotheses, experiments, data, evidence, modified hypothesis, theory, prediction, explanation, and so on.'[40] Robert C. Koons elaborates:

> There is no such thing as 'the scientific method.' There is, on the one hand, a cache of rules of thumb, platitudes, and homely advice drawn from common-sense and tradition, and, on the other hand, sets of specific methods and approaches that define specific research programs in science. Examples of the former include: subject your conjectures to rigorous testing; do not accept authority blindly; rely where possible on firsthand observation; be precise and careful. Examples of the latter are: batteries of statistical tests for significance; double-blind tests for medical treatments; and reliance on well-established scientific instruments . . .[41]

Samir Okasha recalls how 'Ludwig Wittgenstein argued that there is no fixed set of features that define what it is to be a "game". Rather, there is a loose cluster of features most of which are possessed by most games. But any particular game may lack any of the features in the cluster and still be a game. The same may be true of science.'[42] If some scientific disciplines and theories have more in common than others, then, given that science shares some of its objects and methods with other disciplines (e.g. philosophy and theology), there will inevitably be more and less clear examples of what counts as a scientific discipline or theory. The question of whether or not a truth-claim is *scientific* may be a bit like the question of whether or not a pile of sand is or isn't a sand dune! It's impossible to say exactly how many grains of sand it takes to make a sand dune, but that doesn't stop us distinguishing between a few grains of sand on the one hand and a sand dune on the other. As Moreland says: 'One can recognize clear examples of science without a definition . . . and clear cases of non-science . . . But these are at opposite ends of a continuum with fuzzy boundaries and several borderline cases.'[43] This state of affairs shouldn't be all that surprising when we remember that what we now call 'science' used to be recognized as a sub-discipline of philosophy called 'natural philosophy.' Perhaps scientists are philosophers who have restricted themselves to answering *first-order questions raised by the quest to understand observational reality,* the better to specialize in those methodologies appropriate to such study. While there's no single 'scientific method', it seems true to say that, in addition to the rules of logic (essential to all philosophical inquiry), scientists pay special attention to the role that empirical experience plays in confirming and/or undermining truth-claims. Hence Michael J. Murray and Michael Rea define science as *'the collective judgement of professional scholars who aim to explain the workings of the natural world through empirically testable theories.'*[44]

Empirical testing is usually a matter of *inference to the best explanation.* Influential philosophers of science have placed significant emphasis on the role ideally played by empirical *verification* and/or *falsification* in science. Ideally, a scientific theory can be used to make predictions that can be checked against reality by observation in such a way as to support (verify) or disconfirm (falsify) the theory. However, invalid predictions can be made, indirect observations rely upon assumptions that might themselves be false, direct observations can be mistaken, and verification is never conclusive (because falsification in the light of new evidence always remains a possibility). As for falsification, Koons explains:

> First, it is clear from history that scientists, practicing good science, do not immediately throw away a well-established theory at the first sign of trouble, including even falsified predictions by the theory. It is clear . . . that a rigid adherence to falsificationist dogma would have stymied scientific progress through the premature rejection of theories that appeared to be in conflict with experimental results. Second . . . no theory is ever simply falsified by a result. Instead, each theory is tested in conjunction with a host of auxiliary hypotheses, the falsity of any of which could be responsible for a negative result . . . Finally, since no empirical result is ever absolutely conclusive, it is also impossible to falsify anything absolutely . . .[45]

Moreover, Moreland notes:

> it often happens that two scientific theories are empirically equivalent . . . they have all and only the same observational consequences, and one cannot

choose between them without appealing to something besides observational considerations . . . In this case, the two scientific theories cannot be tested against one another by observation, but must be judged by an appeal to philosophical, epistemic virtues good theories presumably should have.[46]

Such epistemic virtues include: logical coherence, meeting the principle of credulity, scope of reference, fruitfulness in guiding research, theoretical simplicity and beauty.

All this should make it clear that scientists aren't infallible, and hence that science isn't infallible. After all, scientists have different philosophical beliefs, disagreements about reality that can't be settled on scientific grounds alone, but which affect how they think about science. For example, some scientists accept metaphysical or methodological naturalism. Others do not. This philosophical disagreement cannot be settled on scientific grounds, but it affects how different scientists think about a lot of things. Furthermore, however careful scientists are, they can get things wrong. Science makes progress, often by modifying or discarding previously well-regarded theories as inadequate or plain wrong. As Kirsten Birkett notes: 'Scientific ideas fall along a continuum of "certainty", and may move up or down depending on further discoveries.'[47] Scientists should always remember that it's reality that calls the shots, not science.

16.2 Theology

Christian theology is *a discipline that seeks to understand everything in terms of a specifically Christian worldview that corresponds to reality*. That is, theology is that intellectual discipline characterized a) by its universal scope and by its joint commitment to understanding reality in a way that is b) legitimately Christian and c) true. People who think that Christianity is false will inevitably think that theology is a doomed project. For example, Dawkins opines:

> university departments of theology house many excellent scholars of history, linguistics, literature, ecclesiastical art and music, archaeology, psychology, anthropology, sociology, iconology, and other worthwhile and important subjects. These academics would be welcomed into appropriate departments elsewhere in the university. But as for theology itself, defined as 'the organised body of knowledge dealing with the nature, attributes, and governance of God', a positive case now needs to be made that it has any real content at all, and that it has any place in today's universities.[48]

The word 'theology' comes from two Greek terms: *theos* ('god' or 'divinity') and *logos* ('word' or 'reason'). Theology is literally 'reasoning about god' or 'discourse about divinity' (something that also goes on in philosophy). As universities developed in the twelfth and thirteenth centuries a name had to be found for the systematic study of the Christian faith. Under the influence of writers such as Peter Abelard, the Latin word *theologia* came to mean 'the discipline of sacred learning', embracing all Christian doctrine, rather than just doctrine about God. Hence Alister McGrath defines Christian theology as 'an attempt to make sense of the foundational resources of Christianity [e.g. revelation, reason – including scientific reasoning, tradition and experience] in the light of what each age regards as first-rate methods.'[49]

Aquinas referred to theology as the 'queen of the sciences' (for Aquinas 'science' – *scientia* in Latin – simply meant 'knowledge'). Theology is the highest level of theoretical engagement with reality of which human beings are capable. This is because theology relies upon and subsumes all of the other theoretical disciplines into an overarching worldview: 'The working assumption [of the medieval university] was that all diverse particulars of knowledge discovered and analyzed in the specialized academic disciplines, found their coherence in God. It was the unifying power of theology that elevated her to the queen of sciences, being assisted by her handmaiden philosophy.'[50]

16.3 And Her Handmaiden Philosophy

Philosophy can be defined as *the wise pursuit of true answers to significant questions through the practice of good intellectual habits.* Philosophers seek to know and defend truth (most particularly truth concerning fundamental questions) by thinking carefully and arguing well. As Aquinas wrote: 'the twofold office of the wise man [is] to mediate and speak forth . . . truth . . . and to refute the opposing error.'[51] As such, philosophy requires the combined and skilled use of *logic* (the rules of rational argument) and *rhetoric* (the art of effective communication). 'Philosophy' comes from two ancient Greek terms: *philo* meaning 'brotherly love', and *sophia* meaning 'wisdom'. Hence Thomas V. Morris writes that 'philosophy is the love of wisdom, along with an unending desire to find it, understand it, put it into action and pass it on to others.'[52] As such, philosophy plays an indispensable role in the project of integrating the understanding of reality provided by science into our theology.

16.4 Integration

Theologian David Ford argues that 'the best centres of theology . . . recognize that, if God is really related to the whole of reality, then they need to engage with not only what usually comes under religious studies, but also with many other disciplines [including] the natural sciences.'[53] Theology requires dialogue with the other academic disciplines, including science, in order to fulfil its mission as the queen of sciences. Hence Christian theology is committed to a high view of science: 'Modern science arose within the bosom of Christian theism; it is a shining example of the powers of reason with which God has created us; it is a spectacular display of the image of God in us human beings. So Christians are committed to taking science and the deliverances of contemporary science with the utmost seriousness.'[54] But it is philosophy that operates as chaperone for the relationship between science and theology: 'questions about integrating science and theology are largely philosophical and not directly scientific or theological, although the latter are obviously involved.'[55]

When theologians seek to integrate an understanding of material reality into their theology, they talk of the 'two books of God': the Bible and nature. If both 'books' come from God, it makes sense to think that they don't contradict each other and that they even throw light on each other. As Galileo wrote: 'Since the Holy Writ is true, and all truth agrees with truth, the truth of Holy Writ cannot be contrary to the truth obtained by reason and experiment.'[56]

However, theologians are just as fallible as scientists. Theologians have different philosophical commitments, disagreements that cannot be settled on scriptural or scientific grounds alone, which affect how they think about theology. Moreover, however careful theologians are, they can get things wrong. Theology makes progress, often by modifying or discarding previously well-regarded theories as inadequate or plain wrong (few contemporary theologians would defend a theory of the atonement in quite the same terms as Anselm). Theologians must remember that it's reality that calls the shots, not them.

Terence L. Nichols observes: 'Science and theology . . . are similar in some respects. Both claim that there is a development in their knowledge, that is, that their theories about the world become increasingly more accurate descriptions of reality. Both would recognize that there is an element of human interpretation in their theories. That is, the theories do not perfectly describe nature.'[57] Thus it shouldn't be surprising that such fallible human quests as science and theology sometimes conflict with each other. Such conflict doesn't necessarily mean that science disproves theology, any more than it means that theology disproves science. Conflict can result from the fallibility of science, of theology, or of both, rather than from any contradiction between the 'two books of God.'

16.4.1 Models for relating science and theology

Several different models of the relationship between science and theology have been proposed. Stephen Jay Gould advocated the 'non-overlapping magisteria' (NOMA) independence model, which holds that there is no relationship between science and religion because science and religion treat distinct domains of reality with distinct methodologies: 'The net, or magisterium of science covers the empirical realm . . . The magisterium of religion extends over questions of ultimate meaning and moral value. These two magisteria do not overlap . . . To cite the old clichés, science gets the age of rocks, and religion the rock of ages; science studies how the heavens go, religion how to go to heaven.'[58]

However, if there *is* a relationship between science and theology (in that at least *some* truth-claims made by either discipline in its own terms come into contact with the other), then this relationship leads to a situation of potential conflict and the independence model is false. Some scholars who reject the independence model think there is an *inevitable conflict* between science and religion, while others think such conflict is *potential but not inevitable.*

16.4.1.1 No more NOMA

Richard Dawkins considers NOMA an act of 'bending over backwards to positively supine lengths'[59] to avoid any possibility of conflict between science and theology. In order to stand a chance of attacking Christianity using the sword of science, Dawkins must first cut through the shield of NOMA. The suggestion that science is about 'how' while religion is about 'why' contains a grain of truth (religion does deal with questions of meaning that science does not), but is too simplistic. As Dawkins says, NOMA 'sounds terrific – right up until you give it a moment's thought.'[60] He dramatizes the point by imagining that:

> forensic archaeologists unearthed DNA evidence to show that Jesus really did lack a biological father. Can you imagine religious apologists shrugging their shoulders and saying anything remotely like the following? 'Who cares? Scientific evidence is completely irrelevant to theological questions. Wrong magisterium! We're concerned only with ultimate questions and with moral values. Neither DNA nor any other scientific evidence could ever have any bearing on the matter, one way or the other.' The very idea is a joke.[61]

Christianity makes real-world claims that intersect with fields of inquiry handled by science. As Meyer argues:

> it's inherent in the Christian faith to make claims about the real world. According to the Bible, God has revealed himself in time and space, and so Christianity – for good or ill – is going to intersect some of the factual claims of history and science. There's either going to be conflict or agreement. To make NOMA work, its advocates have to water down science or faith, or both. Certainly Gould did – he said religion was just a matter of ethical teaching, comfort, or metaphysical beliefs about meaning. But Christianity certainly claims to be more than that.[62]

The problem with NOMA is that 'the rock of ages' (Jesus Christ) lived within and had effects upon the empirical world. Indeed, Christians believe that Jesus continues to have empirical effects upon the world today. Dawkins observes that 'the alleged power of intercessory prayer is at least in principle within the reach of science. A double-blind experiment can be done and was done. It could have yielded a positive result. And if it had, can you imagine a single religious apologist who would have dismissed it on the grounds that scientific research has no bearing on religious matters? Of course not.'[63] Dawkins fails to mention several scientific studies on prayer that *have* reported positive results.[64] A systematic review of the efficacy of distant healing published in 2000 concluded that 'approximately 57% (13 of 23) of the randomised, placebo-controlled trials of distant healing . . . showed a positive treatment effect.'[65] Such results aren't conclusive verification of the efficacy of prayer for healing, but they show that Dawkins fails to grapple with the full range of available evidence. It also shows that it's harder to attack Christianity using science than Dawkins thinks, because there's no simple move from 'null' results to 'negative' results, from absence of evidence (for answered prayer) to evidence for the absence (of a prayer answerer). Nevertheless, Christians should welcome Dawkins' rejection of NOMA, a rejection he applies to the questions at the heart of both ID and Christianity:

> The presence or absence of a creative super-intelligence is unequivocally a scientific question, even if it is not in practice – or not yet – a decided one. So also is the truth or falsehood of every one of the miracle stories that religions rely upon to impress multitudes of the faithful. Did Jesus have a human father, or was his mother a virgin at the time of his birth? Whether or not there is enough surviving evidence to decide it, this is still a strictly scientific question with a definite answer in principle: yes or no. Did Jesus raise Lazarus from the dead? Did he himself come alive again, three days after being crucified?

There is an answer to every such question, whether or not we can discover it in practice, and it is a strictly scientific answer. The methods we should use to settle the matter, in the unlikely event that relevant evidence ever became available, would be purely and entirely scientific methods.[66]

> **Question:**
> Is it wholly or only partly true to say that 'science is about how and religion is about why'?

16.4.1.2 Inevitable conflict or fallible integration?

Rejecting NOMA opens the door to interaction between science and theology, and hence to the possibility of conflict. However, it doesn't automatically imply the existence of any conflict between science and theology (nor which discipline's arguments will prove most persuasive if there is a conflict); not unless one assumes the (self-contradictory) *scientistic* philosophy of science adopted by Dawkins:

> While the inevitable conflict model still persists in popular discussions of the relationship between science and religion, it is easy to see that it has fatal flaws. The first flaw is that it characterizes science and religion in ways we should not accept . . . nothing from the domain of science justifies the scientist in the claim that *science alone* provides us with justified beliefs about the natural world . . . there is no reason to think that this epistemological claim is or even could be justified by sense experience and the application of the scientific method. As a result, this characterization of science is self-defeating.[67]

We should therefore view the relationship between science and theology as one of potential but not inevitable conflict, noting that where there is the possibility of conflict, so too is there the possibility of friendship. As with all human relationships, the relationship between science and theology is inevitably one of *fallible integration*. As historian Thomas Dixon reports:

> Although the idea of warfare between science and religion remains widespread and popular, recent academic writing on the subject has been devoted primarily to undermining the notion of an inevitable conflict . . . The story is not always one of a heroic and open-minded scientist clashing with a reactionary and bigoted church. The bigotry, like the open-mindedness, is shared around on all sides – as are the quest for understanding, the love of truth, the use of rhetoric, and the compromising entanglements with the power of the state.[68]

Michael Ruse acknowledges that 'this "warfare" metaphor, so beloved of nineteenth-century rationalists, has only a tenuous application to reality.'[69] It's worth noting with McGrath that 'the idea that science and religion are in perpetual conflict is no longer taken seriously by any major historian of science.'[70]

16.5 Integration and Origins

The question of our biological origins is both scientific and theological, and is perhaps the most obvious 'hot topic' in the relationship between science and religion today. Phillip E. Johnson sagely advises that 'the best way to approach a problem of any kind is usually not to talk or even think very much about the ultimate answer until I have made sure that I am asking all the right questions in the right order.'[71] So I'm not going to proffer an *answer* to the question of origins. Instead, I'm going to offer *a methodology for arriving at an answer*, a methodology that depends upon asking the right questions in the right order.

My first piece of advice is to start at the very beginning, with the first five words of Genesis: 'In the beginning God created . . .' (cf. John 1:1–3). It's important to keep in mind the distinction between the *doctrine* of creation, which is something all Christians hold in common, and different *models* of creation that Christians hold because they have different interpretations of Genesis and of the relevant scientific evidence. As Johnson remarks: 'The essential point of creation has nothing to do with the timing or the mechanism the Creator chose to employ, but with the element of design or purpose. In the broadest sense, a "creationist" is simply a person who believes that the world (and especially mankind) was *designed*, and exists for a *purpose*.'[72] The place to start thinking about origins is with the *doctrine* of creation, because once you've worked that out, you are in a good position to evaluate different Christian *models* of creation. In other words, our first question should be:

1) *'Is the doctrine of creation true?'*
According to Richard Dawkins, before Darwin there was no adequate naturalistic candidate for an explanation to fill in the problematical blank labelled '*blind* watchmaker'; but Darwin's theory of evolution fills that blank, thereby making it 'possible to be an intellectually fulfilled atheist.'[73] However, even if Darwinism does adequately fill in the '*blind* watchmaker' blank, this doesn't contradict belief in the doctrine of creation or justify atheism. Father Christmas fills in the blank left by the assumption that 'parents don't deliver Christmas presents', but that hardly proves

that parents don't exist, or that they have nothing to do with presents. Likewise, Darwinism may fill in a blank created by the assumption of naturalistic atheism, but that doesn't prove naturalism or atheism.

Why is the water getting hot? Because the flow of electrons through the kettle's heating element is causing the water molecules to vibrate. But *why* is this happening? Because I chose to make tea. You don't have to pick one explanation over the other. The fact that we can give a description of an impersonal physical mechanism that results in boiling water doesn't disprove the existence of a kettle designer! Similarly, a scientific description of a physical mechanism that results in diverse organisms wouldn't disprove the existence of a designer of that system. The theist, no less than the atheist, can acknowledge the existence of a 'blind watchmaker', simply by attributing that 'blind watchmaker' itself to God's design. The theory of evolution is irrelevant to the *doctrine* of creation.

Plato noted that 'all things do become, have become and will become, some by nature, some by art, and some by chance',[74] and he argued that either mind comes before matter (and the world is basically a work of art), or matter comes before mind (and the world is purely the result of chance and natural regularities). The doctrine of creation says that mind came before matter – the cosmos is a creation, a work of art. To be an atheist, on the other hand, means being committed to a 'matter first' view of things – the cosmos isn't a work of art, and everything *must*, therefore, be the result of nothing but natural regularities and/or chance.

The theory of evolution is an explanation of biological reality in terms of a finely balanced combination of natural regularities and chance working over long periods of time. For atheism, belief in evolution isn't so much the result of an objective assessment of the empirical evidence as it is a necessary assumption brought to its interpretation. One can contrast the intellectual freedom to follow the evidence enjoyed by someone who accepts the doctrine of creation with the *a priori* constraints imposed upon the interpretation of the evidence by a naturalistic worldview, as candidly revealed by geneticist Richard Lewontin: 'It is not that the methods . . . of science somehow compel us to accept a material explanation of the . . . world, but, on the contrary, that we are forced by our . . . adherence to material causes to create . . . a set of concepts that produce material explanations, no matter how counterintuitive, no matter how mystifying.'[75] 'Moreover,' says Lewontin, 'that materialism is absolute, *for we cannot allow a Divine foot in the door.*'[76] Lewontin's rejection of the doctrine of creation has nothing to do with science and everything to do with faith in materialism.

The *a priori* constraint of naturalism often results in its adherents engaging in question-begging arguments (often under the guise of 'science'). For example, Dawkins defines biology as 'the study of compli-cated things that give the appearance of having been designed for a purpose.'[77] So why is he so confident that the apparent design of living things is *only apparent*? Because he has a philosophical commitment to the naturalistic presupposition that 'the kind of explanation we come up with must not contradict the laws of physics. Indeed *it will make use of the laws of physics, and nothing more than the laws of physics.*'[78] But as Johnson observes, this shows that 'Darwinism is the answer to a specific question that grows out of philosophical naturalism . . . How must creation have occurred if we assume that God had nothing to do with it?'[79] Answering *this* artificially restricted question is not at all the same as answering this question: 'How did creation occur?' As Michael Ruse admitted in a speech delivered before the American Association for the Advancement of Science:

> Johnson [is] arguing [that] the kind of position of a person like myself, an evolutionist, is metaphysically based at some level, just as much as the kind of position of [the] creationist . . . And . . . I must confess . . . I've been coming to this kind of position myself . . . I was inclined to say . . . creationism is not science and evolution is . . . Now . . . I'm inclined to think that . . . we should recognize . . . that the science side has certain metaphysical assumptions built into doing science . . . Certainly, I think that philosophers like myself have been much more sensitized to these things, over the last ten years, by trends . . . in the philosophy of science . . . So . . . however we're going to deal with creationism, or new creationism [i.e. Intelligent Design Theory] . . . we should also look at evolution and science, in particular, biology, generally philosoph-ically I think a lot more critically . . . And *it seems to me very clear that at some very basic level, evolution as a scientific theory makes a commitment to a kind of naturalism, namely, that at some level one is going to exclude miracles and these sorts of things, come what may* . . . I think . . . that evolutionary theory in various forms certainly seems to be the most reasonable position, *once one has taken a naturalistic position.* So I'm not coming here and saying, give up evolution, or anything like that. But I am coming here and saying, I think that philosoph-ically . . . one should be sensitive to what I think history shows, namely, that . . . evolution, akin to religion, involves making certain *a priori* or metaphys-ical assumptions, which at some level cannot be proven empirically . . . And I think that the way to deal with creationism, but the way to deal with evolu-tion also, is not to deny these facts, but to recognize them, and to see where we can go, as we move on from there.[80]

Approaching the question of origins without 'a commitment to a kind of naturalism' doesn't mean excluding evolution as the best available scientific account of biology; but it does mean *letting the evidence speak for itself*. As Thomas Woodward notes:

> ID scientists never *prejudge* in detecting design. *They never assume design; design must be positively detected*, by analysing evidence and passing rigorous tests. Darwinism is different. It is profoundly theological in its basic operating rules, in that it lays down an *assured truth* – an axiom that amounts to a religious catechism. It is this catechism then that serves as a starting point. The Darwinian catechism states that when scrutinizing complex living systems, one can rest assured that scientific evidence and logic can never lead one to conclude that there was an intelligent cause behind life . . . Evolutionary biology, by limiting itself exclusively to material mechanisms, has settled in advance the question of which biological explanations are true, apart from any consideration of the empirical evidence. This is armchair philosophy.[81]

I therefore suggest that the next question on our agenda should be:

2) *'If we don't presuppose naturalism, is evolution the best explanation of the relevant available evidence, or is there a better explanation?'*
Question 2 is an interesting and important question – but it isn't a crucial question for everyone to answer. You could quite happily be a Christian without having an answer to it. Nevertheless, when a Christian approaches any question about the natural world, including this one, they have the luxury of rejecting armchair philosophy for open-minded inquiry. Evolution may be a wholly adequate theory, a partially adequate theory, or a wholly inadequate theory, but the right way to find out is to let the evidence speak for itself without support from the assumption that the natural world *must* be able to account for everything about itself. As Alvin Plantinga writes:

> a Christian (naturally) believes that there is such a person as God, and believes that God has created and sustains the world. Starting from this position [the doctrine of creation] . . . we recognize that there are many ways in which God could have created the living things he has in fact created: how, in fact, did he do it? . . . Did it all happen just by way of the working of the laws of physics, or was there further divine activity . . .? That's the question . . . Starting from the belief in God, we must look at the evidence and consider the probabilities as best we can.[82]

It's very important to note that 'evolution' is a broad term that subsumes several different scientific hypotheses that can and should be judged on their individual merits:

- *The Ancient Earth Hypothesis*: the earth is very old, perhaps some 4.5 billion years old.
- *The Progress Hypothesis*: life has changed, from relatively simple to relatively complex forms of life, over time.
- *The Common Ancestry Hypothesis*: each extant form of life is related by common ancestry to previous, different forms of life.
- *The Universal Common Ancestry Hypothesis*: life originated at only one place and all subsequent forms of life are related by common ancestry to one original form of life.
- *The Darwinian Hypothesis*: there is a naturalistic explanation for the macro-evolutionary development of life from simple to complex forms, and that explanation is (primarily) an extrapolation of the observed micro-evolutionary process of natural selection operating on random genetic mutations.
- *The Naturalistic Origins Hypothesis*: the claim that life itself developed from non-living matter without any special creative activity by an intelligence, but just by virtue of the ordinary laws of physics and chemistry.

The combination of these theses forms 'The Grand Evolutionary Story.' While some of these hypotheses entail others (e.g. the Darwinian hypothesis entails the Progress and Common Ancestry hypotheses), it's possible to accept some of these hypotheses while rejecting others (e.g. the Ancient Earth hypothesis doesn't entail the Naturalistic Origins hypothesis, nor vice versa). I have arranged these hypotheses in what many informed scholars consider a descending order of plausibility. Plantinga writes:

> There is excellent evidence for an ancient earth . . . Given the strength of this evidence, one would need powerful evidence on the other side – from Scriptural considerations . . . in order to hold sensibly that the earth is young. There is less evidence, but still good evidence in the fossil record for the Progress Thesis, the claim that there were bacteria before fish, fish before reptiles, reptiles before mammals, and mice before men . . . the Naturalistic Origins Thesis . . . seems to me to be for the most part mere arrogant bluster; given our present state of knowledge, I believe it is vastly less probable, on our present evidence, than is its denial.[83]

For example, atheist Peter Atkins acknowledges that 'one problem with evolution is how it began . . . how did matter step across the notional bridge from the inorganic to the organic in the first place? How did signal emerge from noise? . . . I have to admit that science is a bit stuck.'[84] Atheist Thomas Nagel is sceptical of both the 'Naturalistic Origins Hypothesis' and the 'Darwinian Hypotheses':

for a long time I have found the materialist account of how we and our fellow organisms came to exist hard to believe . . . the dominant scientific consensus . . . faces problems of probability that I believe are not taken seriously enough, both with respect to the evolution of life forms through accidental mutation and natural selection and with respect to the formation from dead matter of physical systems capable of such evolution. The more we learn about the intricacy of the genetic code and its control of the chemical processes of life, the harder those problems seem. Again: with regard to evolution, the process of natural selection cannot account for the actual history without an adequate supply of viable mutations, and I believe it remains an open question whether this could have been provided in geological time merely as a result of chemical accident . . . Whatever one may think about the possibility of a designer, the prevailing doctrine – that the appearance of life from dead matter and its evolution through accidental mutation and natural selection to its present forms has involved nothing but the operation of physical law – cannot be regarded as unassailable. It is an assumption governing the scientific project rather than a well-confirmed scientific hypothesis.[85]

If one has answers to our first two questions, one is in a good position to ask a third question:

3) *'Which* model *of creation is the most plausible?'*
This is an interesting and important question – but it isn't a crucial question for everyone to answer. You could quite happily be a Christian without having an answer to this question. Christians certainly shouldn't elevate belief in any particular model of creation into anything more than the secondary issue that it is.

If we *do* pursue this question, there's no shortage of interpretations we could adopt. In-between the 'bookends' of a so-called *literal* 'young-earth', six-day creationism and an *essentially non-literal* creationism (often associated with some kind of 'theistic evolution'), you might adopt some sort of *more or less literal* 'old-earth' or 'progressive' creationist interpretation. I doubt anyone holds to either a *completely* literal or a *completely* non-literal creationism.

Moreland warns: 'there are sufficient problems in interpreting Genesis 1 and 2 to warrant caution in dogmatically holding that only one understanding is allowable by the text.'[86] Giving a responsible answer to our third question involves asking a whole bunch of subsidiary questions: 'The phrase "The Bible says . . ." begs a lot of questions . . . What *does* the Bible say? To whom is it saying it? What is the context, background and literary form of the passage in question? Is it to be taken literally, or figuratively, or allegorically?'[87] With Plantinga I admit that 'the proper understanding of the early chapters of *Genesis* . . . is a difficult area, an area where I am not sure where the truth lies.'[88] My suspicion is that the creation accounts are much more subtle bearers of meaning than any of the standard interpretive frameworks developed thus far allow. What I am sure of is that there can't be any conflict between God's Word and God's World when both are properly understood, although there can be conflicts between incorrect human understandings of God's Word and God's World. As Charles Hodge warned: 'Theologians are not infallible in the interpretation of Scripture.'[89] Nor are scientists infallible when they think about nature.

For anyone who believes in the doctrine of creation, the fundamental question isn't 'What is the best *scientific* account of reality?' (let alone 'What is the best *naturalistic* account of reality?') but 'What is *the best* account of reality given everything we know?' This only seems odd if, with Richard Lewontin, we accept 'science as the only begetter of truth.'[90] But of course, the claim that science is the only begetter of truth *isn't something that science can establish as being true*! It's a self-contradictory philosophical claim; in which case, there must be more truth than can be known through science, and Christians are right to seek to understand reality by employing everything we think we know from thinking about God's Word as well as what we think we know from thinking about God's World. Our *model* of creation (as distinct from the *doctrine* of creation) isn't the best place to start this project of integration, but it shouldn't be *excluded* from the process. Doing that would be like deciding a murder case purely on the basis of the forensic evidence, without taking into account the testimony of witnesses. As John Stek warns: 'we cannot . . . pursue theology without bringing to that study all that we know about the world, nor can we . . . pursue science without bringing to that study all that we know about God.'[91] That's why it's important to understand that when Plantinga urges us to 'look at the evidence' he doesn't *just* mean us to look at the *scientific* evidence; he means us to look *at every source of warranted belief open to us, including theology*. Hence Murray and Rea suggest that:

> In the same way that the scientists can be mistaken in the conclusions that they draw from the empirical data, religious believers must remain open to the possibility that they have mistakenly interpreted the revelatory data. Thus, for the religious believer, the conflicts between science and religion will involve balancing evidence against evidence: the empirical evidence favouring scientific claims against the revelatory evidence favouring theological claims. The Christian critic of evolution might . . . conclude that the . . . evidence for an ancient earth seems quite strong, while the evidence for the

naturalistic origin of life is, in fact, virtually non-existent. This then needs to be balanced against the evidence of revelation. How clear is it that the Bible teaches that the earth is young, or that God directly intervened in the cosmos to bring about life?[92]

Listen:
Peter S. Williams, 'An Introduction to Intelligent Design Theory' www.damaris.org/cm/podcasts/434
— 'A Rough Guide to Creation' www.damaris.org/cm/podcasts/536.

Conclusion

It's easier to know what science isn't than what it is, but we can say that:

- Science is *a first-order discipline that seeks to understand the truth about observable reality.*
- *Scientism* is the philosophical view that elevates science above all other sources of knowledge, and it is self-contradictory.
- Science and theology do *not* constitute 'non-overlapping magisteria'.
- Methodological naturalism (whether 'hard' or 'soft') is not a necessary condition of scientific theorizing.
- Hard methodological naturalism subverts the truth-seeking nature of science, and should therefore be rejected.
- There are some practical advantages to adopting soft methodological naturalism.
- The relationship between science and theology is one of *fallible integration* in which there is potential but not inevitabile conflict.
- Philosophy 'chaperones' the relationship between science and theology (who can and should be friends).

When it comes to origins, it's important to distinguish between the *doctrine of* creation (which is primary) and different *models* of creation (which are secondary). It is also important to distinguish between the various hypotheses that make up the 'Grand Evolutionary Story' – and to judge each on its individual merits without the epistemic constraints imposed by naturalism or HMN. One can then draw upon all relevant sources of warranted belief, including scientific and theological sources, in order to form a specific *model* of creation.

> **Film to watch and discuss:**
> *Expelled,* directed by Nathan Frankowski (Premise Media Corporation / Rampant Films, 2008) (PG) – Ben Stein fronts this interesting documentary about the treatment of God and the idea of Intelligent Design within the academy (though note that Stein oversimplifies by conflating the concept of an intelligent designer with God).

*   *   *

Recommended Resources

Video

Dembski, William A. 'The Challenge of Intelligent Design to Unintelligent Evolution' http://video.google.com/videoplay?docid=-6646238627774515357&hl=en.

God: New Evidence www.focus.org.uk/?page_id=101.

Illustra Media Website www.youtube.com/user/IllustraMedia.

*Koon, Robert C. 'Science and Belief in God: Concord not Conflict' www.veritas.org/media/talks/601.

*Lennox, John. 'Has Science Buried God?' www.cis.org.uk/upload/cis20080428.mov.

*Williams, Peter S. 'Christianity & Science' YouTube Playlist www.youtube.com/play-list?list=PLQhh3qcwVEWjeYJfOKB1YYXsInZ5GIPL_.

Audio

Craig, William Lane. 'Has Science Made Faith in God Impossible?' www.reasonablefaith.org/RF_audio_video/Other_clips/A97TAMU01.mp3.

— 'Scientific Intolerance' www.reasonablefaith.org/site/News2?page=NewsArticle&id=5887.

— vs Victor Stenger. 'Does God Exist?' www.bringyou.to/CraigStengerDebate.mp3.

Lennox, John. 'God and Richard Dawkins' www.bethinking.org/science-christianity/advanced/god-and-richard-dawkins.htm.

Moreland, J.P. 'Reconciling Science and Scripture' www.apologetics315.com/2009/12/reconciling-science-scripture-mp3-audio.html.

Plantinga, Alvin. 'Faith and Science' www.calvin.edu/january/2000/ram/20000118.ram.

— 'Science and Religion: Why Does the Debate Continue?' www.calvin.edu/nagel/audio/AlPlantinga08.mp3.

— vs Daniel C. Dennett. 'Science and Religion: Are They Compatible?' www.brianauten.com/Apologetics/Plantinga-Dennett-Debate.mp3.

*Williams, Peter S. 'Hawking and the Grand Designer' www.damaris.org/cm/podcasts/566.

*— 'An Introduction to Intelligent Design Theory' www.damaris.org/cm/podcasts/434.

*— 'Is Christianity Unscientific? (Hesketh Bank Christian Centre)' www.damaris.org/cm/podcasts/534.

*— 'Is Science the Only Way to Know Anything?' www.damaris.org/cm/podcasts/619.

*— 'A Rough Guide to Creation' www.damaris.org/cm/podcasts/536.
— 'Is it Reasonable to Believe in Genesis?' www.damaris.org/cm/podcasts/795.

Websites

Access Research Network www.arn.org.
Bethinking: Science and Christianity www.bethinking.org/science-christianity/.
Christians in Science www.cis.org.uk/.
William A. Dembski's Design Inference Website www.designinference.com/.
Discovery Institute Centre for Science and Culture www.discovery.org/csc/.
The Faraday Institute for Science and Religion www.st-edmunds.cam.ac.uk/faraday/.

Online papers

Craig, William Lane. 'What Is the Relation between Science and Religion?' www.reason-ablefaith.org/site/News2?page=NewsArticle&id=5355.
Fodor, Jerry. 'Why Pigs Don't Have Wings' www.lrb.co.uk/v29/n20/fodo01_.html.
Fuller, Steve. 'Against the Faith' http://newhumanist.org.uk/1880.
Koons, Robert C. 'The Incompatibility of Naturalism and Scientific Realism' www.leaderu.com/offices/koons/docs/natreal.html.
— 'Science and Theism: Concord not Conflict' www.utexas.edu/cola/depts/philosophy/faculty/koons/science.pdf.
Luskin, Casey. 'Human Origins and Intelligent Design' www.iscid.org/papers/Luskin_HumanOrigins_071505.pdf.
Marston, Paul. 'Understanding the Biblical Creation Passages' www.asa3.org/ASA/topics/Bible-Science/understanding_the_biblical_creation_passages.pdf.
Menuge, Angus. 'The Role of Agency in Science' www.4truth.net/site/apps/nl/content3.asp?c=hiKXLbPNLrF&b=1171681&ct=1579247.
Meyer, Stephen C. 'The Origin of Biological Information and the Higher Taxonomic Categories' www.discovery.org/scripts/viewDB/index.php?command=view&id=2177&program=CSC%20-%20Scientific%20Research%20and%20Scholarship%20-%20Science.
— 'A Scientific History and Philosophical Defense of the Theory of Intelligent Design' www.discovery.org/a/7471.
— 'The Scientific Status of Intelligent Design' www.discovery.org/scripts/viewDB/index.php?command=view&id=2834&program=CSC%20-%20Scientific%20Research%20and%20Scholarship%20-%20History%20and%20Philosophy%20of%20Science.
Monton, Bradley. 'Is Intelligent Design Science? Dissecting the Dover Decision' http://philsci-archive.pitt.edu/archive/00002583/01/Methodological_Naturalism_2.pdf.
Moreland, J.P. 'Complementarity, Agency Theory, and the God-of-the-Gaps' www.afterall.net/index.php/papers/490579.
— 'Is Science a Threat or a Help to Faith? A Look at the Concept of Theistic Science' www.afterall.net/index.php/papers/18.
— 'Scientific Creationism, Science, and Conceptual Problems' www.afterall.net/index.php/papers/490578.
— 'Scientific Naturalism and the Unfalsifiable Myth of Evolution' www.afterall.net/citizens/moreland/papers/jp-naturalism1.html.
Opposing Views.com (various papers both pro and anti ID). 'Does Intelligent Design Have Merit?' www.opposingviews.com/questions/does-intelligent-design-have-merit.

Nagel, Thomas. 'Public Education and Intelligent Design' http://as.nyu.edu/docs/IO/1172/papa_132.pdf.

Nelson, Paul. 'Intelligent Design', *Nucleus* (January 2005) www.cmf.org.uk/printable/?-context=article&id=1303.

Plantinga, Alvin. 'Methodological Naturalism?' http://id-www.ucsb.edu/fscf/library/plantinga/mn/home.html.

— 'Religion and Science' http://plato.stanford.edu/entries/religion-science/.

*— 'Why Darwinist Materialism Is Wrong', *The New Republic*, 16 November 2012 www.tnr.com/print/article/books-and-arts/magazine/110189/why-darwinist-material-ism-wrong.

— et al. 'Dialogue: When Faith and Reason Clash: Evolution and the Bible' www.asa3.org/ASA/dialogues/Faith-reason/index.html.

Ruse, Michael. 'Nonliteralist Antievolution,' AAAS Symposium: 'The New Antievolutionism' 13 February 1993, Boston, MA (1993) www.leaderu.com/orgs/arn/orpages/or151/mr93tran.htm.

Thaxton, Charles. 'Christianity and the Scientific Enterprise' www.leaderu.com/truth/1truth17.html.

Trevors, J.T. and D.L. Abel. 'Three Subsets of Sequence Complexity and Their Relevance to Biopolymeric Information'. *Theoretical Biology and Medical Modelling* (2005) 2:29 www.pubmedcentral.nih.gov/articlerender.fcgi?artid=1208958.

*Williams, Peter S. 'Is Christianity Unscientific?' www.bethinking.org/science-christianity/advanced/is-christianity-unscientific.htm.

*The Alexander–Williams debate on Intelligent Design Theory

1) Alexander, Denis. 'Creation and Evolution?' www.bethinking.org/resource.php?ID=193.
2) Williams, Peter S. 'Theistic Evolution and Intelligent Design in Dialogue' www.bethinking.org/resource.php?ID=216&TopicID=2&CategoryID=1.
3) Alexander, Denis. 'Designs on Science' www.bethinking.org/resource.php?ID=260&TopicID=2&CategoryID=1.
4) Williams, Peter S. 'Intelligent Designs on Science: A Surreply to Denis Alexander's Critique of Intelligent Design Theory' www.iscid.org/papers/Williams_Intelligent-Designs_073106.pdf & www.arn.org/docs/williams/pw_designsonscience.htm.

Books

Behe, Michael J. *Darwin's Black Box: The Biochemical Challenge to Evolution* (New York: Free Press, 2nd edn, 2006).

— *The Edge of Evolution: The Search for the Limits of Darwinism* (New York: Free Press, 2007).

Campbell, John Angus and Stephen C. Meyer, eds. *Darwinism, Design, and Public Education* (Michigan State University Press, 2003).

Dembski, William A. *The Design Revolution: Answering the Toughest Questions about Intelligent Design* (Downers Grove, IL: IVP, 2004).

— ed. *Uncommon Dissent: Intellectuals Who Find Darwinism Unconvincing* (Wilmington, DE: ISI Books, 2004).

*— and Sean McDowell. *Understanding Intelligent Design: Everything You Need to Know in Plain Language* (Eugene, OR: Harvest House, 2008).

— and Jonathan Wells. *The Design of Life: Discovering Signs of Intelligence in Biological Systems* (Dallas, TX: Foundation for Thought and Ethics, 2008).

Gonzalez, Guillermo and Jay Richards. *The Privileged Planet: How Our Place in the Cosmos is Designed for Discovery* (Washington, DC: Regnery Publishing, 2005).

Hannam, James. *God's Philosophers: How the Medieval World Laid the Foundations of Modern Science* (London: Icon, 2009).

Johnson, Phillip E. *Darwin on Trial* (Downers Grove, IL: IVP, 20th anniv. edn, 2010) http://talebooks.com/images/bs/291.pdf.

*Lennox, John C. *God and Stephen Hawking: Whose Design Is It Anyway?* (Oxford: Lion, 2010).

*— *God's Undertaker: Has Science Buried God?* (Oxford: Lion, 2nd edn, 2007).

Meyer, Stephen C. *Signature in the Cell: DNA and the Evidence for Intelligent Design* (New York: HarperOne, 2009).

*Monton, Bradley. *Seeking God in Science: An Atheist Defends Intelligent Design* (Peterborough, ON: Broadview Press, 2009).

Moreland, J.P. and William Lane Craig. *Philosophical Foundations for a Christian Worldview* (Downers Grove, IL: IVP, 2003).

*Nagel, Thomas. *Mind and Cosmos: Why the Materialist Neo-Darwinian Conception of Nature Is Almost Certainly False* (Oxford University Press, 2012).

Nichols, Terence L. *The Sacred Cosmos: Christian Faith and the Challenge of Naturalism* (Grand Rapids, MI: Brazos Press, 2003).

Plantinga, Alvin. *Where the Conflict Really Lies: Science, Religion, and Naturalism* (Oxford University Press, 2011).

Ratzsch, Del. *Science and Its Limits: The Natural Sciences in Christian Perspective* (Downers Grove, IL: IVP, 2000).

Ward, Keith. *The Big Questions in Science and Religion* (West Conshohocken, PA: Templeton Foundation Press, 2008).

— *God, Chance and Necessity* (Oxford: OneWorld, 1996).

West, John G., ed. *The Magician's Twin: C.S. Lewis on Science, Scientism, and Society* (Seattle: Discovery Institute Press, 2012).

17. The Problem of Evil

The existence of God is neither precluded nor rendered improbable
by the existence of evil.
Alvin Plantinga[1]

Introduction

The premier argument against theism is surely the 'problem of evil.' To
many people it just seems obvious that the reality of evil and suffering is
a knock-down argument against theism, such that *merely to ask the question* 'If God exists, why does evil / so much evil exist?' is, in their minds,
to settle the issue. To show why this is far from being the case, we will
look at the nature of evil, at the theistic argument *from* evil (yes, there

really is one), and two different versions of 'the problem of evil.'[2] We will also learn about the difference between a 'defence' and a 'theodicy', before closing with some thoughts on the practical problem of suffering in the context of beliefs about the meaning and purpose of life.

17.1 Evil Is Parasitic upon Good

Christians cannot deny the reality either of evil or of God. As Alvin Plantinga notes: 'the central Christian message is that Christ, the second person of the Trinity, came into the world to make salvation from sin available to us human beings; Christian belief, therefore, entails that there is evil in the world.'[3]

Some people think that good and evil are 'equal opposites' that exist only in contrast with each other. But as C.S. Lewis asked: 'If a taste for cruelty and a taste for kindness were equally ultimate and basic, by what common standard could the one reprove [i.e. criticize] the other?'[4]

Christianity says that God is a wholly good necessary being, and that everything else is dependent upon God. It follows that 'evil cannot exist at all without the good [whereas] the good can exist without evil.'[5] Aquinas argued that evil is *a privation of good* which is *parasitic upon good*. It follows that 'every evil is based on some good . . . sheer evil is impossible.'[6] This means that while something can be 'pure good' (e.g. God), nothing can be 'pure evil'. As Lewis argued:

> To be bad, [Satan] must exist and have intelligence and will. But existence, intelligence and will are in themselves good. Therefore he must be getting them from the Good Power: even to be bad he must borrow or steal from his opponent. And do you now begin to see why Christianity has always said that the devil is a fallen angel? That is not a mere story for the children. It is a real recognition of the fact that evil is a parasite, not an original thing. The powers which enable evil to carry on are powers given it by goodness. All the things which enable a bad man to be effectively bad are in themselves good things – resolution, cleverness, good looks, existence itself.[7]

One cannot ask why evil exists without asking why good exists. The latter question leads into the moral argument for God.

17.2 The Theistic Argument from Evil

Atheist Friedrich Nietzsche warned: 'When one gives up the Christian faith, one pulls the right to Christian morality out from under one's feet

. . . Christianity is a system, a whole view of things thought out together. By breaking one main concept out of it, the faith in God, one breaks the whole. It stands or falls with faith in God.'[8] If objective values stand or fall with a wholly good personal deity, then it's inconsistent to use any argument against theism that assumes the objectivity of values. In other words, *if* (as Nietzsche held) naturalism excludes objective values, *then* naturalists can't argue against theism by pointing to the existence of objective evil! However, if there is *objective* evil, then there must be objective good. Given that there can't be any objective goodness without a deity who is 'the good' (cf. chapter 8), *the existence of objective evil actually proves the existence of such a deity*!

✔ The existence of objective evil actually argues *for* theism!

> **Watch:**
> 'Atheists Trying to Have Their Cake and Eat It Too on Morality' http://youtu.be/wQ-aqnDHqqA.
> Greg Koukl, 'Evil and Suffering Equals No God?' http://youtu.be/9AnjG94ZDOE.
> Brian Godawa, 'Cruel Logic' http://youtu.be/ZY9Z5LRkjkk.

17.3 The Logical Problem of Evil

> The theist believes that God is omnipotent, omniscient and benevolent. If the theist's beliefs are correct, how then can there be evil?
> J.J.C. Smart[9]

Given the existence of objective evil, is it possible for there to exist a deity who is not only all-good, but also all-powerful and all-knowing? Atheist Robin Le Poidevin thinks not: 'The fact of suffering faces theists with a truth that is both undeniable and apparently incompatible with their belief.'[10] Humans clearly have difficulty accepting that God and evil coexist. However, as we will see, there is no contradiction between belief in evil and belief in God, even if we can't comprehend the place of evil in the creation.

17.3.1 Limits of the argument

> If God exists, either He can do nothing to stop the most egregious calamities, or He does not care to. God, therefore, is either impotent or evil.
> Sam Harris[11]

The logical problem of evil claims to deduce the non-existence of a deity who is maximally good, powerful *and* knowledgeable, from the premise that evil exists. As Poidevin argues:

> If [God] is all-knowing, he will be aware of suffering; if he is all-powerful, he will be able to prevent suffering; and if he is perfectly good, he will desire to prevent suffering. But, clearly, he does not prevent suffering, so either there is no such deity, or, if there is, he is not all-knowing, all-powerful and perfectly good, though he may be one or two of these.[12]

This argument doesn't rule out belief in a supernatural being lacking one or more of these 'great-making' properties of 'maximal goodness' etc. The logical problem of evil is neither an argument for naturalism, nor an argument against theism. Rather, it's an attempt to rule out belief in a deity with all three qualities of maximal power, knowledge *and* goodness. Of course, this *is* just the sort of deity Christians believe in.

✔ The 'problem of evil' isn't an argument for atheism!

17.3.2 *The question of validity*

Philosophers of religion have cast serious doubt on whether there even is any inconsistency involving the appropriate propositions regarding evil and God's alleged properties.
Scott A. Shalkowski[13]

The logical problem of evil claims there is a *contradiction* between the propositions that God exists (when God is understood as the omnipotent, omniscient, all-good Creator of the universe) and that evil exists. However, consider these propositions:

1. God exists
2. God is omnipotent
3. God is omniscient
4. God is all-good
5. God created the world
6. The world contains evil

As Ronald H. Nash observes: 'this list lacks two contradictory propositions . . . The proponent of the deductive problem of evil must find a way to demonstrate that propositions 1 through 6 entail the claim that the world does not contain evil.'[14] In other words: 'The alleged inconsistency . . . is not obvious; it is neither explicit nor formal in nature. In order to make the [purported] implicit inconsistency explicit, some additional propositions must be specified.'[15] But as Plantinga notes: 'many . . . who confidently assert that this set is contradictory make no attempt whatever to *show* that it is. For the most part they are content just to *assert* that there is a contradiction here.'[16]

Poidevin tries to make the supposed contradiction explicit by specifying additional propositions – namely that God must be aware of evil (due to his omniscience), able to prevent evil (due to his omnipotence), and must desire to prevent evil (due to his goodness):

> It is true that there is no explicit contradiction between the statements that there is an omnipotent and wholly good god and that there is evil. But if we add the at least initially plausible premises that good is opposed to evil in such a way that a being who is wholly good eliminates evil as far as he can, and that there are no limits to what an omnipotent being can do, then we do have a contradiction. A wholly good omnipotent being would eliminate [and/or prevent] evil completely; if there really are evils, then there cannot be any such being.[17]

However, it isn't *necessarily* true that an all-good being *always* eliminates evil *as far as it can at any given time*. For example, a good dentist is justified in bringing about some pain to his patient in the present (e.g. drilling his tooth) in order to avoid a greater evil in the future (i.e. tooth decay). Indeed, a good person who is omniscient might allow the existence of *more* evil than a good person who isn't omniscient and who is thus ignorant of certain greater goods! It doesn't matter whether or not we can imagine what these 'greater goods' might be. The mere fact that good people don't *necessarily* abolish all the evil they can at any given time means that it is *possible* for God to be all-good even if *he* doesn't abolish all the evil he can at a given time. Even Poidevin admits that suffering might be part of God's design, insofar as it is an unavoidable consequence of a greater good. Moreover:

> The claim that God can do absolutely anything ['there are no limits to what an omnipotent being can do'] is not true. Christians have always recognized that an omnipotent being cannot do lots of things . . . even the Bible declares that God cannot . . . swear by a being greater than himself . . . no proponent of the deductive problem of evil ever succeeded in supplying the missing proposition needed to reveal the presumed contradiction.[18]

Atheist J.L. Mackie acknowledged the failure of the additional propositions approach to prove a contradiction between the existence of God and evil:

the opposition between good and evil may be construed in such a way that a wholly good god would not, after all, eliminate evil as far as he could, and . . . it may be argued that there are limits . . . to what even an omnipotent being can do. For example, it would usually be said that God cannot do what is logically impossible; and this, we can agree, would be no real departure from omnipotence.[19]

Mackie admitted: 'the problem of evil does not, after all, show that the central doctrines of theism are logically inconsistent with one another.'[20] Indeed, 'philosophers of religion, theists and atheists alike have agreed in recent years that this version of the problem of evil has been decisively rebutted and is therefore unsuccessful.'[21]

✔ The problem of evil has never been successfully formulated as an airtight argument against God

17.3.3 Theistic defences

William Lane Craig affirms that 'it is widely recognized among contemporary philosophers that the logical problem of evil has been dissolved. The coexistence of God and evil is logically possible.'[22] This is partly due to the failure to show any contradiction within the claim that God and evil coexist; but it's also due to the triumph of theistic *defences* in the face of the logical problem of evil.

A theistic 'defence' is an argument to the effect that the coexistence of God and evil is logically possible. A 'theodicy' is a purportedly plausible explanation of how it is (or at least may well be) that God and evil coexist. A defence only tries to show how God and evil *could* coexist, whereas a theodicy tries to show how God and evil *may in fact* coexist.

Faced with the problem of evil, theists have traditionally attempted to provide a theodicy. There's much to be said for theodicy, and we will return to the issue later. Nevertheless, advancing a defence is a perfectly adequate intellectual strategy, and it is easier than advancing a theodicy, because while a theodicy must be *plausibly true*, a defence only needs to be *possibly true*.

17.3.3.1 Proving a defence

Dean L. Overman explains that 'for [the logical argument from evil] to prevail [one] must demonstrate that God has no good reason for allowing the evil that exists in the world. No one has ever been able to demonstrate that this is true.'[23] Even atheists must grant that *if* God exists, *then*, since evil exists, there must be some reason (or reasons) why the existence of evil is compatible with the existence of God. It follows that the atheist can't simply point to evil as proof that God doesn't exist, because that move *begs the question* by simply *assuming* that no such reason (or set of reasons) exists. The following syllogism highlights the question-begging nature of the logical argument from evil:

1. Evil exists in the world
2. *If* God exists, *then*: he knows about any evil that exists (because he is all-knowing); he is opposed to evil in such a way that he would prevent or eliminate it *unless to do so, at least at this time, would contradict his nature and/or is morally undesirable or unnecessary* (because he is all-good); he can do anything *that is logically possible and which doesn't contradict his own nature* (because he is all-powerful); and he created the world
3. Therefore, *if* God exists, he is an all-good being who created the world and who knows about the evil that exists in the world, but preventing or eliminating this evil is logically impossible, and/or would contradict his nature, and/or is morally undesirable or unnecessary (at least at the present time)

This argument acknowledges the existence of evil, adds a conditional premise about God's nature that is true by definition, and then *validly deduces a conclusion that's neutral about God's existence.* Hence, *this argument proves that there's no contradiction between God and evil.*

As Ronald H. Nash muses concerning the logical problem of evil: 'it is one thing to demonstrate that no one has discovered the required missing premise up to this point. But what about the future?'[24] The atheist may still *feel* that God and evil are incompatible, even if they're unable to produce a non-question-begging argument to *show* that their intuition is correct. However:

> All that is required to prove our list of propositions [1–6] is logically consistent (and thus forever immune to the possibility of being shown to be inconsistent) is to add a new proposition that is logically possible, which means simply that it does not describe a contradictory state of affairs. The new proposition must be consistent with the other propositions in the list, and, in conjunction with the other propositions, it must entail that evil exists in the world. [Alvin Plantinga suggests] the claim that *God creates a world that contains evil and has a good reason for doing so.*[25]

Thus, it's not merely that atheists have failed to demonstrate that God and evil are logically incompatible. Rather, theists can demonstrate that God and evil are logically compatible. Craig explains:

there is no reason to think that God and evil are logically incompatible . . . there is no *explicit* contradiction between them. And if the atheist means that there is some *implicit* contradiction between God and evil, then he must be presupposing some hidden premise to bring out this implicit contradiction . . . no philosopher has been able to identify such premises . . . But more than that, we can actually prove that God and evil *are* logically compatible. You see, the atheist presupposes that God cannot have morally sufficient reasons for permitting the evil in the world. But this assumption is not necessarily true. So long as it is even *possible* that God has morally sufficient reasons for permitting evil, it follows that God and evil are logically consistent.[26]

Agnostic Paul Draper concedes: 'it is possible that there is some good reason (perhaps a reason too complicated for humans to understand) for God to permit tragedies. So tragedies don't conclusively disprove God's existence.'[27] Atheist William L. Rowe observes: 'Some philosophers have contended that the existence of evil is *logically inconsistent* with the existence of the theistic God. No one, I think, has succeeded in establishing such an extravagant claim. Indeed, granted incompatibilism, there is a fairly compelling argument for the view that the existence of evil is logically consistent with the existence of the theistic God.'[28] Rowe is referring to Plantinga's articulation of the 'free will defence':

A world containing creatures who are significantly free . . . is more valuable, all else being equal, than a world containing no [significantly] free creatures at all . . . To create creatures capable of [significant] moral good . . . [God] must create creatures capable of [significant] moral evil; and he can't give these creatures this freedom to perform evil and at the same time prevent them from doing so.[29]

Adding the implausible but *logically possible* suggestion that all 'natural evil' (cf. 17.5.1) is caused by demons misusing their free will is sufficient to *prove* the *logical compatibility* of God and evil. As Mitch Stokes concludes: 'there's no contradiction between God's existence and the existence of suffering . . . Philosophers now concede that the traditional vision of the problem of evil is entirely unsuccessful. There is no *logical* inconsistency between God's existence and the existence of evil.'[30]

Watch:
Alvin Plantinga, 'Is God Good?' http://youtu.be/Rfd_1UAjeIA.
— 'Why Does a Loving God Permit Evil in Our World?' http://youtu.be/cdW8X-F6UiUE.

17.4 The 'Evidential Argument from Evil'

The typical atheistic claim today isn't that evil *disproves* the existence of God, but than evil *counts against the rationality of belief* in God: 'In 1935 John Wisdom argued that the existence of God is logically consistent with the existence of evil; but he said that it is unlikely, given the amount of evil, that there is such a person as God.'[31] According to Wisdom (and other atheists who followed in his wake), while the existence of evil doesn't *disprove* theism, it does *count against* God. Perhaps the strongest type of evidential argument from evil concerns the existence of 'gratuitous evil' (evil that isn't necessary to secure some compensating good or prevent some worse evil), a representative form of which runs as follows:

1. The existence of God is inconsistent with the existence of gratuitous evil
2. If some evil X appears gratuitous to me, then it probably is gratuitous
3. Evil X appears gratuitous to me
4. Therefore, evil X is probably gratuitous
5. Therefore, evil X is probably inconsistent with the existence of God and thus counts as evidence against God

Several responses can be made.

17.4.1 Rejecting premise 1

Peter van Inwagen attacks the first premise with the following counter-example:

> a sentence of 10 years is no more effective at deterring future crime than is a sentence of 9 years and 364 days. So [one might think that] a just punisher would not sentence the criminal to 10 years. But then this line of reasoning can be reiterated (just as in a sorites argument) until we reach the conclusion that no jail term is just. But surely some jail term or other is just. The solution is to recognize that 'effective deterrence' is vague. A perfect moral judge must simply draw the line somewhere, and for any place he draws it, it will be true that his drawing it at a slightly different place would have been just as effective.[32]

In other words, there's no precise number or quality of evils that must exist in order to secure certain compensating goods or to prevent greater evils. God:

cannot remove all the horrors from the world, for that would frustrate his plan for reuniting [free] human beings with himself. And if he prevents only some horrors, how shall he decide which ones to prevent? Where shall he draw the line . . . between threatened horrors that are prevented and threatened horrors that are allowed to occur? I suggest that wherever he draws the line, it will be an arbitrary line.[33]

If there's no precise line of demarcation between a) evils that are necessary to secure compensating goods or prevent worse evils and b) evils that aren't necessary in this way, *any* moral agent (including God) attempting to secure those compensating goods or prevent those greater evils must permit the existence of *some* gratuitous evil. If premise 1 of the evidential argument from gratuitous evil is true, argue Daniel and Frances Howard-Snyder:

then there is a minimum amount of intense suffering God must permit in order to secure those goods involved in His purposes. But . . . there is no such minimum amount. To suppose that there is such a minimum amount is like supposing that . . . if the state's purposes required a fine to deter illegal parking, there is a minimum dollar-and-cents figure that would suffice, and if the fine were one cent less, it would not be a significant deterrent.[34]

17.4.2 An adjusted evidential argument

At this point the atheologian might suggest that while God's existence isn't incompatible with gratuitous evil as such, it is incompatible with what we might call 'excessively gratuitous evil':

1. The existence of God is inconsistent with the existence of excessively gratuitous evil
2. If evil X appears to be an excessively gratuitous evil to me, then it probably is
3. Evil X appears to be an excessively gratuitous evil to me
4. Therefore, evil X is probably an excessively gratuitous evil
5. Therefore, evil X counts as evidence against God

Even granting the first premise, this argument invites some hard questions. For example, '*How much* gratuitous evil must there be to count as excessive?' and 'Why believe the world contains excessively gratuitous evil'?

Concerning our first question, the notion of an excessively gratuitous evil is inherently vague and subjective. What unit of measurement are we to use? A ten-year prison sentence can be a morally justifiable punishment despite containing *some* gratuitous evil (evil that's contingent upon but isn't a necessary precondition of something good), so how much gratuitous time could the sentence accommodate before being 'excessively' gratuitous as a punishment? Thirteen months? Fourteen? Fifteen? It's hard to say. Likewise, how much gratuitous evil can a world accommodate before being 'excessively' gratuitous for a creation? A fifty-year sentence may clearly be excessively gratuitous *relative to the punishment a judge can justifiably permit for a given crime*; but how much gratuitous evil would clearly be 'excessive' *relative to the amount of evil God could justifiably permit within his creation*? It's hard to say – far harder than distinguishing between fair and unfair jail terms, or between piles of sand that are and aren't dunes – and that makes it hard for the evidential argument from evil to get off the ground.

Concerning our second question, the atheologian must not only justify the claim that gratuitous evil exists (which is all the first version of the argument required); they must justify the claim that there's some gratuitous evil that is, at least pretty clearly, 'excessively' gratuitous.

On both counts, the revised evidential argument saddles itself with a heavier burden of proof than the unsound argument it replaced.

17.4.3 A general weakness with the evidential argument

A weakness common to both versions of the evidential argument is that to warrant the move from premise 3 to premise 4 the argument depends upon the assumption (implicit within premise 2) that an absence of evidence translates into evidence of absence. However, the absence of evidence only translates into evidence of absence if we would probably detect the absent evidence in question if it existed. An analogy: Not seeing an elephant in the fridge is a good reason for thinking there's no elephant in there, because you'd notice if there was. On the other hand, missing a small pot of yoghurt in a crowded fridge is a weak reason for thinking there's no yoghurt in there, because it's not unlikely that you'd fail to see it even if it's there somewhere. So, the question that arises is whether looking for God's morally sufficient reason/s for evil in any given instance is more like looking for the elephant or more like looking for the yoghurt.

While as moral beings made in God's image we'd expect a high degree of moral insight, nevertheless, as finite beings made in the image of God (the maximally great being) we would nevertheless expect his comprehension of moral reality to outstrip our own on occasion. Affirming that 'our cognitive and moral powers are endowments of the creation and that neither the taint of sin nor their essential finitude renders them systematically unreliable in making judgements about God's ways with evil' is wholly compatible with thinking that 'sometimes our judgements that evils are gratuitous are mistaken.'[35] What percentage of unreliability are we talking about here? It's hard to say, but at the very least reflection upon this issue weakens the move from premise 3 to premise 4.

For example, we may lack an adequate appreciation for the value of goods we can see attaching (or plausibly see as attaching) to evil. Consider C. Stephen Layman's free-will theodicy:

> A loving God would have good reason to place persons in a situation in which they can achieve lives that are rich in meaning and significance. And, other things being equal, a life that involves significant choices is more significant than one that does not. Furthermore, the significance of a choice is linked to its consequences or expected outcomes . . . the benefit or harm the acts are apt to bring about (or prevent). Therefore, if a loving God exists, we ought to expect there to be opportunities to make choices between good acts that will provide great benefits (or prevent great harms) and evil acts that will inflict great harm (or prevent great benefits). So, if a loving God exists, it is not surprising that we have opportunities to freely perform very wicked acts.[36]

It's not that each moral evil is allowed as the necessary means to a greater good: 'Wrong acts, taken collectively, are simply the unsurprising result of creating agents with very significant moral choices; and wrong acts, taken individually, need not be the necessary means to any greater good.'[37] Wrong acts are, in that sense, gratuitous. However, on the Christian view, the existence of significant human freedom makes possible not only very wicked acts, but *eternal* relationships of freely chosen love and forgiveness between humans and, most significantly, between humans and God. There are obvious reasons why we find it difficult to *feel* the full weight of these eternal goods here and now. Nevertheless, there's nothing unreasonable about *thinking* that the goods permitted by significant human freedom will outweigh the evils permited thereby. At the very least, 'it isn't clear that our grasp of the goods we do know of is sufficiently clear to warrant assurance that those goods don't justify God's permission of horrendous evils.'[38]

Watch:
Robin Collins, 'Does Evil Refute God's Existence?' http://closertotruth.com/video-profile/Does-Evil-Refute-God-s-Existence-Robin-Collins-/717.

Read:
Robin Collins, 'The Connection Building Theodicy' www.lastseminary.com/problem-of-evil/The%20Connection%20Building%20Theodicy.pdf.

The inference from the claim that it seems as though there's no sufficient moral reason to be found for evil X to the conclusion that it's probably the case that there is no sufficient moral reason doesn't seem to be particularly robust. Such an inference would be 'like supposing that when you're confronted with the activity or productions of a master in a field in which you have [less] expertise, it is reasonable for you to draw inferences about the quality of her work just because you "don't get it".'[39] Lessons can and should be drawn here from the failure of 'sub-optimality' arguments against intelligent design theory from so-called 'junk DNA', the supposedly poor design of the Panda's 'thumb' or the vertebrate eye.

Watch:
'The Myth of Junk DNA Trailer', http://youtu.be/u7UrUuakwPI.
'ENCODE: The Encyclopedia of DNA Elements' http://youtu.be/PsV_sEDSE2o.
Ian Sample, 'What the ENCODE project tells us about the human genome and "junk DNA"' http://youtu.be/UBQ5a7mCpMs.

Read:
Reasons to Believe, 'Bad Designs' www.reasons.org/rtb-101/baddesigns.
George Ayoub, 'The Design of the Vertebrate Retina' www.arn.org/docs/odesign/od171/retina171.htm.
Michael J. Denton, 'The Inverted Retina: Maladaption or Preadaption?' www.arn.org/docs/odesign/od192/invertedretina192.htm.
Casey Luskin, 'Is the Panda's Thumb a "Clumsy" Adaptation that Refutes Intelligent Design?' www.ideacenter.org/contentmgr/showdetails.php/id/1477.
Paul Nelson, 'Jettison the Arguments, or the Rule? The Place of Darwinian Theological Themata in Evolutionary Reasoning' www.discovery.org/a/104.

Then again, it's plausible to imagine that a child whose parents are always morally praiseworthy would occasionally be perplexed by their behaviour despite (or even because of) its moral praiseworthiness. Even if the child is theoretically capable of understanding the parents' behaviour this doesn't guarantee that he or she will understand their behaviour in practice.

Read:
Kelly James Clark, 'I Believe in God the Father, Almighty' www.calvin.edu/academic/philosophy/writings/ibig.htm.

Nick Trakakis and Yujin Nagasawa build on this analogy:

Parents . . . have certain rights over their children which strangers do not . . . and these rights arise from the parents being (to some extent) the source of their children's existence as well as their role as benefactor and provider for their children. Similarly, God – in virtue of his role as our creator and benefactor – may have the right to allow us to endure abuse and murder, whereas we do not have those sorts of rights over each other . . . If, as Swinburne has suggested, God may have rights over us that we do not have over each other, then . . . we have good reason to think that (a) God may be morally justified – in virtue of occupying role R – in permitting evil E, but (b) we cannot be morally justified – in virtue of not occupying role R – in permitting E.[40]

As David Baggett argues:

God has prerogatives [rights] that we do not have, has a perspective we lack, can redeem situations we cannot, and is not afflicted with our limitations . . . God might command or allow something that, to our finite understanding, seems quite bad or radically wrong, yet he still may be good . . . In fact, it seems rather obvious that a good God may have reasons for doing or allowing certain things without being under any obligation to tell us why, and he may have excellent reasons not to. Moreover, if God's ways are above ours, we may not yet be in a position to hear, understand or appreciate those reasons.[41]

Gregory Ganssle concludes:

Given that if God exists, he has a good reason to allow the evil he allows, how likely is it that we should *know* what his reasons are? I think we should expect to be able to discern some likely candidates in some cases but not in others . . . those who press the argument against God's existence *overestimate* the percentage of cases in which we ought to be able to figure all of this out and they *underestimate* the percentage of cases in which we *actually can*.[42]

18.5 Theodicy

Providing likely candidates for God's reasons for allowing evil in as high a percentage of cases as we can is the task of 'theodicy.' Providing a comprehensive theodicy may be beyond humans, who can't hope to *comprehend* either God or even God's creation. However, we do have *some insight* into what might plausibly be thought to be God's reasons for permitting evil in various forms.

> **Watch:**
> Gregory Koukl, 'Why Does God Allow Evil and Suffering?' http://youtu.be/ KJQVaCnL-oM.

17.5.1 'Moral' and 'natural' evils

Moral evil is all the evil caused by people deliberately doing what they ought not to do, or negligently failing to do what they ought to do. Murder and failing to provide the police with information about a murderer are both examples of moral evil.

While God has the freedom to choose whether or not to create beings with whom to relate, created beings have no choice about whether or not to be created. Therefore, if created beings are to have a choice about whether or not to have a genuine relationship with God (or each other), they must be free not only to choose *between* goods, but also to choose *against* the good:

> God has chosen to make a universe in which there are many kinds of creature, including . . . self-conscious beings who have freedom as an essential part of their nature . . . Since it is part of their nature to be free, it must be possible for these creatures to choose something other than the good, for the whole point of their life is that the love whereby they can choose God has to be freely given and therefore has a value of a kind not found elsewhere in the created order. Because of the unique value of this love, a universe in which there are men, with both love and evil, is better than a universe with no men and neither human love nor human evil.[43]

Natural evil is all the evil that isn't moral evil. Events like earthquakes and tsunamis are examples of natural evils. Of course, such events are not considered evil *in themselves*, but only when they cause suffering.

These two classes of evil overlap. For example, human mistreatment or neglect of the environment can cause so-called 'natural disasters' (e.g. through war, deforestation, climate change, etc.).[44] Then again, it's not so much earthquakes that kill, but substandard building regulations perpetuated by human greed and corruption: 'The 2010 Haiti earthquake, which was 7.0 in magnitude and resulted in 230,000 deaths was starkly contrasted with the almost identical Californian earthquake – which caused only 57 deaths.'[45]

17.5.2 The interconnectedness of nature

Modern science shows us that even tiny changes in the laws of nature would result in a universe incapable of containing embodied, intelligent life-forms like ourselves (cf. chapter 7). Natural evils are the result of a universe operating according to physical laws without which embodied intelligences such as our own would be impossible. Hence we cannot separate our existence from the existence of natural evil. It would seem that natural evils at least very much like those we observe are a necessary precondition of there existing creatures like ourselves (or, indeed, our animal cousins). As Guillermo Gonzalez and Jay W. Richards point out: 'Most of us associate earthquakes with death and destruction, but ironically, earthquakes are an inevitable outgrowth of geological forces that are highly advantageous to life . . . Plate tectonics make possible the carbon cycle, which is essential to our planet's habitability.'[46]

Even if some natural evil is inevitable *given the existence of beings like us*, couldn't God have ordered physical reality so that our present suffering would have been averted or alleviated? The components of nature are so closely interlocked that a slight change in one particular would probably cause large-scale effects in others. To ask for even a slight change could mean asking for a very different, and quite possibly worse, kind of world. Our world may not be the 'best of all possible worlds' (many philosophers think 'the best of all possible worlds' is actually an incoherent concept), but it may be a physical reality well suited to achieving God's good purposes in creation.

Question:
Collect some newspaper reports about natural disasters. Sort them according to the following categories: 1) Caused by human sin, 2) Caused by natural laws we couldn't live without, 3) Caused by demonic activity, 4) A mystery. What proportion of reports fit into each category?

17.5.3 Snakes and ladders

Suppose someone decided to play 'snakes and ladders.' When the die is thrown, they have a before-the-fact desire for the result to be free of intelligent interference. It wouldn't be a fair game otherwise. However, every time the die is thrown, the player nevertheless has an after-the-fact desire that a particular, advantageous number results. If the result of throwing the die means they have to slide down a snake, then there's a sense in which that's the result the player wanted, because, before the fact, they wanted the generated numbers to be outside their control. Nevertheless, they also have an after-the-fact desire for numbers that mean they avoid snakes and land on ladders.

By analogy, we might suppose that, before the fact of creation, God wanted there to be a world where what happens depends in part upon the choices of significantly free, embodied, rational creatures. If so, many things may happen after the fact of creation that God does not, before the fact, desire. God might desire humans to make different free choices,

375

just as I might want the die to generate a five and not a six. Hence we can see how it could be the case that even God (despite omnipotence) would have to accept after-the-fact outcomes he doesn't desire before the fact, if these outcomes are the intrinsic result of an overall context he desires before the fact for good reasons.

God desires the existence of the universe for the sake of various goods that it permits. Those clearly include the existence of rational, embodied creatures with free will capable of entering into meaningful relationships (with the world they inhabit, with one another, and with God). However, as a result of these creatures' free will, and of the generally stable[47] natural order necessary to the existence of these creatures, any such universe is bound to contain moral and natural evils that God no more desires than I desire to land on a snake when playing snakes and ladders. 'Landing on snakes' is something that God doesn't desire before the fact, but something he judges to be justifiable in the light of the greater before-the-fact context.

17.5.4 Creation old and new

But in keeping with his promise we are looking forward to a new heaven and a new earth, where righteousness dwells (2 Peter 3:13 NIV).

Christians believe that God's purposes in creation will eventually blossom in the 'new heavens and earth' (cf. Isaiah 65:17–22; 2 Peter 3:13; Revelation 21:1) – a Hebrew phrase that means 'universe.' Jesus' resurrected 'spiritual body' is the first sample of this renewed universe (cf. 1 Corinthians 15:43). Just as the resurrected Jesus was a transformed or transposed pre-resurrection Jesus, so the new creation is the 'old' (i.e. current) creation transformed or transposed by God.

We could say that Jesus' resurrected body was physical without being *merely* physical: 'Paul conceived of the resurrection body as a powerful, glorious, imperishable, Spirit-directed *body*, created through a transformation of the earthly body or the remains thereof, and made to inhabit the new universe in the eschaton [i.e. in the end or goal of the present world].'[48] Analogously, the 'new heavens and earth' will be physical but not *merely* physical. There will not simply be a different 'tuning' or even a different set of merely physical laws. Rather, there will be a closer marriage between the physical and the spiritual, like that displayed in Jesus' resurrection. This data allows us to embrace a coherent and evidentially motivated hope in a future resurrected life of relationships purged of moral and natural evil (a hope the Bible links to a belief in hell, often explicated in terms of God's respect for the freedom of creatures who wish to reject him).[49]

Concerning the present, *merely* physical reality of the 'old' creation, 'the very conditions in the universe that make human life possible, if only slightly different, would not support life at all and thus no free human beings. For all we know, there may not be a more suitable world [for our existence] that is governed by [merely physical] laws that have no natural evil as a by-product.'[50] Hence Paul writes:

> I consider that our present sufferings are not worth comparing with the glory that will be revealed in us. The creation waits in eager expectation for the sons of God to be revealed. For the creation was subjected to frustration, not by its own choice, but by the will of the one who subjected it, in hope that the creation itself will be liberated from its bondage to decay and brought into the glorious freedom of the children of God.
>
> We know that the whole creation has been groaning as in the pains of childbirth right up to the present time. Not only so, but we ourselves, who have the firstfruits of the Spirit, groan inwardly as we wait eagerly for our adoption as sons, the redemption of our bodies (Romans 8:18–23).

Scripture indicates that human choice exercised in the 'old creation' plays an important role in shaping the spiritual reality of the transformed 'new creation' (cf. 1 Corinthians 3:11–15).

We may lack a *complete* grasp of how the merely physical 'old creation' phase of creation relates to the 'new creation' or why the 'old creation' is worthwhile, but since we can't reasonably expect to have a complete grasp of such matters it's nevertheless rational to believe that the 'old creation' *is* worthwhile, at least in light of the new. The new heavens and earth aren't an arbitrary compensation for the present world. Rather they are the organic final goal (or *telos*) of creation, a goal that tips the value scales of reality into (or further into) the 'worthwhile' category. Kelly James Clark writes:

> When a woman gives birth to a child she suffers terribly, but in retrospect the suffering is forgotten . . . While she is suffering, however, the good is not yet fully present to her. Perhaps the victim of horrific suffering's [eventual] perspective on suffering is like a woman's later perspective on childbirth where the good is now present and transforms her attitudes toward her suffering . . . The sufferings of this life can be defeated by sharing in God's joy in the next life.[51]

As Marylin McCord Adams writes:

> Relative to human nature, participation in horrendous evils and loving intimacy with God are alike disproportionate: for the former threatens to engulf

the good in an individual human life with evil, while the latter guarantees the reverse engulphment of evil by good. Relative to one another, there is also disproportion, because the good that God is, and intimate relationship with Him, is incommensurate with created goods and evils alike. Because intimacy with God so out-scales relations (good or bad) with any creatures, integration into the human person's relationship with God confers significant meaning and positive value even on horrendous suffering.[52]

Watch:
Robin Collins, 'A New Heaven' http://closertotruth.com/video-profile/A-New-Heaven-A-New-Earth-Robin-Collins-/720.
Gary R. Habermas, 'The Death and Resurrection of Debbie' www.youtube.com/watch?v=489i38n1gjU.
Robert Russell, 'All Things New' http://closertotruth.com/video-profile/All-Things-New-Robert-Russell-/905.
N.T. Wright, 'Clouds and Harps – Is That the Real Heaven?' http://youtu.be/yRMMelo5o5c.
— 'What Does Heaven Look Like?' http://youtu.be/v7vJ6P_r3W0.
— 'Will God Bring Heaven and Earth Together?' http://youtu.be/V1RsgKQYnTQ.

17.5.5 The scientific limits of theodicy

Austin Farrer probes the insight that within merely physical reality the existence of embodied creatures is inseparable from natural evil:

If God was pleased to create a physical universe, he was sure to set going [forces] acting upon one another in accordance with [natural laws]. Such a universe must inflict much accidental damage on the systems it contains . . . Does it follow that physical evil was unavoidable? Only if it pleased God to create a physical universe. Did he need to create such a universe? No . . . even if God wanted to have creatures, he would not have needed to make physical creatures . . . Instead of asking why God did not make his physical world free from its characteristic ills, we ask why, since such ills inevitably characterize it, he made a physical world. What are we to make of the question in its new shape? It is open to us to reject it, as totally unreal . . . We could only wish the world had been made otherwise, if we could wish to be creatures of another sort. But we cannot; we want to be ourselves; better men, no doubt, and happier, but still men. We love our physical being: we do not want to be angels . . . we are outraged by the presence of certain distressing features [in nature]; but once they are proved inseparable from its general nature, there is no further question we can rationally ask.[53]

As Herbert McCabe argues:

you cannot make material things that develop in time without allowing for the fact that in perfecting themselves they will damage other material things . . . You may be tempted to argue that it would be better not to have lions at all – but *if you think along those lines you have to end up thinking that it would be better not to have any material world at all* . . . No reasonable person objects to . . . a miracle from time to time; but a world without any natural causes . . . would not be a natural material world at all. So the people who would like [God] to have made a material world without suffering . . . would have preferred him not to have made a [natural material] world . . . But . . . *most people are pleased he made such a world* . . . *The accusation that God made it does not seem very damning.*[54]

If we consider what would be involved in offering a theodicy purporting to fully explain, in terms that we can comprehend, why God is justified in thinking that the natural world is worth all the evils it entails, we may agree with Farrer that 'we involve ourselves in great unrealities. We should be undertaking to vindicate God for making the world as he has made it, rather than otherwise. But this would involve the serious pretence to conceive the predicament of Almighty Wisdom, in choosing what sort of world to make. And is not such a pretence fantastic?'[55] Since we lack a comprehensive grasp of the nature of physical reality, it seems unreasonable to expect to construct a *comprehensive* explanation of why the world is not only compatible with the existence of God, but also chosen by him. The to-be-expected nature of our inability to provide a comprehensive theodicy means that atheists can't jump upon this inability as if it provided grounds for criticizing theism. As Plantinga writes: 'Perhaps no theodicy we can think of is wholly satisfying. If so, that should not occasion much surprise: our knowledge of God's options in creating the world is a bit limited.'[56]

Watch:
Keith Ward, 'Did God Create Evil?' www.closertotruth.com/video-profile/Did-God-Create-Evil-Keith-Ward-/812.

17.6 Belt and Braces

Suppose (for the sake of argument) that one thinks the evidential argument from evil is sound, such that the probability of God's existence (Q) relative to the existence of apparently gratuitous (or apparently excessively gratuitous) evil (P) is less than a half. As Plantinga points out: 'that wouldn't show for a moment that belief in God is unjustified' because 'there are many pairs of propositions P and Q, such that we

379

(justifiably) believe P, the probability of Q on P is very low . . . but [we] are still perfectly justified in believing Q.'[57] For example:

> We play a hand of bridge: the probability that the four of us should be dealt just the hands we are dealt is . . . about 1 out of 10 billion billion billion [P]. Yet when we lay out the cards and take a look at them, we are entirely justified in thinking that this deal [Q] did in fact occur. And of course the reason is that we perceive that it occurred. Probabilities get swamped by the deliverances of a faculty like perception. And the same goes for belief in God.[58]

In other words, the positive, properly basic religious experience of God's existence (Q) might have enough intrinsic warrant to outweigh the evidence to the contrary (P), just as a memory belief that provides an alibi for a murder suspect would swamp a great deal of forensic evidence that suggested their guilt:

> Plantinga . . . gives the example of someone accused of a crime and against whom all the evidence stands, even though that person knows he is innocent. In such a case, that person is not rationally obliged to abandon belief in his own innocence . . . The [properly basic] belief that he did not commit the crime intrinsically defeats the defeaters brought against it by the evidence. Plantinga makes the theological application by suggesting that belief in God may similarly intrinsically defeat all the defeaters that might be brought against it.[59]

Even if the evidence of evil isn't entirely 'swamped' by religious experience, it must at least be partially 'soaked up' thereby. Any residual evidence against God must then be weighed in the balance against the cumulative weight of the many arguments *for* theism (e.g. the cosmological, design, moral, experiential and mental arguments, arguments from beauty, and so on) as well as the many arguments *against* alternative worldviews.

In this context, it's worth recalling that in all its forms the problem of evil grants a crucial premise of the moral argument for theism (cf. section 17.2).[60] Moreover, while the logical problem of evil denies the possibility of God's existence, the evidential argument doesn't deny the possibility of God's existence, and is thus fully compatible with the ontological argument (cf. chapter 9).[61]

✔ The problem of evil must be weighed in the scales against all the warrant *for* theism

As Daniel Howard-Snyder observes: 'Even if evil is some evidence that there is no God, you might have better evidence to think that God exists; in that case, it wouldn't be reasonable for you to believe there is no God.'[62] Agnostic Graham Oppy agrees: 'If theists can reasonably suppose that they have lots of evidence which supports the claim that God exists, then they may reasonably believe that there is a solution to "the problem of evil", even if they do not know what that solution is.'[63] Atheist Michael Tooley concedes:

> even if it can be shown that the evils that are found in the world render the existence of God unlikely, it might still be the case that the existence of God is not unlikely *all things considered*. For perhaps the argument from evil can be overcome by appealing either to positive arguments in support of the existence of God, or to the idea that belief in the existence of God is properly basic . . .[64]

17.7 An Existential Concern

If we ask ourselves whether the pain of existence is worth the gain, answering that it isn't is equivalent to saying that it would be better if humanity were to become extinct. Indeed, we'd be saying it would have been better if humanity *had never come to pass*:

> Happy people who do not regret their own individual existence cannot meaningfully raise a problem of evil since their existence and identity are causally dependent upon certain past evil events in world history. Thus, in so far as the problem of evil is raised as a personal and moral complaint against God and the world he has created, answers to it will satisfy those who are happy that they exist and fail to satisfy those who are willing to say that they regret their existence.[65]

To say that the pain of life *isn't worth the gain* is to say to oneself and to one's fellow humans that *life isn't worth living*. But asserting the worthlessness of human existence seems a harshly nihilistic attitude to adopt. Hence we may think twice before blaming God for creation. In other words, the possession of a (properly basic) belief *that* life is worthwhile reinforces the point that it's irrational to discount God on the grounds that we don't have a complete understanding of *why* life is worthwhile. To recognize the value of human existence means making the *unselfish* decision that we'd rather the universe contain the value we embody, despite the consequent aggregate of evil, than that the universe be deprived of this value. Indeed, perhaps such selflessness is *itself* one of the many goods permitted by the existence of the cosmos that justifies its existence.

Conclusion

One can sympathize with the 44% of people who, when asked what questions they'd ask God if given the opportunity, said they would ask him to explain 'why there is evil or suffering in the world.'[66] Nevertheless, as Alvin Plantinga concludes:

> The existence of God is neither precluded nor rendered improbable by the existence of evil. Of course, suffering and misfortune may nonetheless constitute a *problem* for the theist; but the problem is not that his beliefs are logically or probabilistically incompatible. The theist may find a *religious* problem in evil; in the presence of his own suffering or that of someone near to him he may find it difficult to maintain what he takes to be the proper attitude towards God. Faced with great personal suffering or misfortune, he may be tempted to rebel against God . . . or even to give up belief in God altogether. But this is a problem of a different dimension. Such a problem calls, not for philosophical enlightenment, but for pastoral care.[67]

In light of the death and resurrection of Jesus (a subject that raises interesting philosophical and evidential questions we unfortunately don't have room to examine here)[68] we should never forget that God suffers with and for us, and that he gives eternal life to everyone who responds to his sacrificial love for them. Nor should we forget that those questioning God via the problem of evil might need practical loving care more than they need philosophical answers.

Make a practical response:
Amnesty International www.amnesty.org.uk/index.asp.
ARocha www.arocha.org/gb-en/index.html.
CAFOD www.cafod.org.uk/.
Care www.care.org.uk/.
Christian Aid www.christianaid.org.uk/.
Jubilee Centre www.jubilee-centre.org/.
The Salvation Army www.salvationarmy.org.uk/.
Samaritan's Purse www.samaritans-purse.org.uk/.
Save the Children www.savethechildren.org.uk/.
Speak www.speak.org.uk/.
Tearfund www.tearfund.org/.
Traidcraft www.traidcraft.co.uk/.
World Vision www.worldvision.org.uk/.

Films to Watch and Discuss:
The Fifth Element, directed by Luc Besson (Twentieth Century Fox, 1997) (PG) – At the climax Bruce Willis tells the Fifth Element something important; why can the film-makers bank upon the audience reaction to this revelation, and what does this tell us about the problem of evil?
Memories of Matsuko, directed by Tetsuya Nakashima (Third Window Films, 2006) (15) – Is Matsuko's existence meaningful?

* * *

Recommended Resources

Video

'ENCODE: The Encyclopedia of DNA Elements' http://youtu.be/PsV_sEDSE2o.
'The Myth of Junk DNA Trailer' http://youtu.be/u7UrUuakwPI.
Sample, Ian. 'What the ENCODE project tells us about the human genome and "junk DNA"' http://youtu.be/UBQ5a7mCpMs.
*Geivett, Douglas. 'Problems of Evil' http://hisdefense.org/video/Geivett%20-%20Problems%20of%20Evil.WMV.
Moreland, J.P. 'Eternal Life Is Like What?' http://closertotruth.com/video-profile/Eternal-Life-is-Like-What-J-P-Moreland-/1169.
*Russell, Robert. 'All Things New' http://closertotruth.com/video-profile/All-Things-New-Robert-Russell-/905.
Ward, Keith. 'Did God Create Evil?' www.closertotruth.com/video-profile/Did-God-Create-Evil-Keith-Ward-/812.
*Williams, Peter S. 'The Problem of Evil' YouTube Playlist www.youtube.com/playlist?list=PLQhh3qcwVEWjSOz8xsGXuS_VahByzSzhe.
*— 'Heaven & Hell' YouTube Playlist www.youtube.com/playlist?list=PLQhh3qcwVE-WiImwi0EwFZIiNXYAVEQpvN.
*— 'The Resurrection of Jesus' YouTube Playlist www.youtube.com/playlist?list=PLQhh3qcwVEWjF0VbpQ9sPUUivlyF5n0wB.
*— 'Debating the Resurrection' YouTube Playlist www.youtube.com/playlist?list=PLQhh3qcwVEWhAPCkcpFsSwEXrYKuBhoaq.

Audio

Copan, Paul. 'Is God a Moral Monster?' www.reclaimingthemind.org/content/files/TUP/TUPProgram139copanotmorality.mp3.
*Craig, William Lane. 'The Problem of Evil and Suffering' www.reasonablefaith.org/media/the-problem-of-evil-and-suffering-gracepoint-church.
*— 'The Historicity of the Resurrection of Jesus' www.reasonablefaith.org/media/historicity-of-the-resurrection-of-jesus-elc-hungary.
— 'Contemporary scholarship and the resurrection of Jesus' www.bethinking.org/bible-jesus/contemporary-scholarship-and-the-resurrection-of.htm.

— 'The Evidence for Christianity' www.bethinking.org/bible-jesus/the-evidence-for-christianity-reasonable-faith.htm

— vs. Gerd Lüdemann. 'Jesus' Resurrection: Fact or Figment?' w w w . b r i n g y o u . t o / CraigLüdemannResurrectionDebate.mp3.

— vs. John Dominic Crossan, 'Will the real Jesus please stand up?' www.bringyou.to/ CraigCrossanDebate.mp3.

— vs. Robert G. Cavin 'Dead or Alive?' www.bringyou.to/CraigCavinDebate.mp3.

Dougherty, Trent. 'Faith and Reason in a Broken World' http://thinkingmatters.org. nz/2011/08/audio-trent-dougherty-on-faith-and-reason-in-a-broken-world/.

Geivett, Douglas. 'Problems of Evil' www.brianauten.com/Apologetics/problems-of-evil.mp3.

Habermas, Gary R. 'The Minimal Facts Approach' www.garyhabermas.com/audio/ habermas_minimal_facts_approach.mp3.

*May, Peter. 'What About Animal Suffering?' www.highfield.org.uk/church/index. php?id=240&sermonid=1732.

Strobel, Lee. *The Case for Faith*, 'Chapter One' http://youtu.be/2zDdd-PzWZc.

Stump, Eleonore. 'Job and the Problem of Evil' www.bethinking.org/suffering/ advanced/job-and-the-problem-of-evil.htm.

— 'The Problem of Evil and Theodicy' www.youtube.com/watch?v=vLkIajOGGOY&-feature=related.

Swinburne, Richard. 'Historical Evidence for the Resurrection' www.blackhawkmedia. org/MP3/Swinburne3.mp3.

White, Bob. 'Natural Disasters: Are They Acts of God?' www.cis.org.uk/upload/south-ampton/Soton_White_Mar11.mp3.

*Williams, Peter S. 'The Problem of Evil' www.damaris.org/cm/podcasts/792.

— 'Living with Evil: Three Problems of Evil' www.damaris.org/cm/podcasts/446.

— 'Problems with Evil' www.damaris.org/cm/podcasts/793.

— 'Stephen Law's "Evil God Challenge"' www.damaris.org/cm/podcasts/750.

— 'Salvation of the Daleks' www.damaris.org/cm/podcasts/483.

— 'Understanding Jesus Seminar' www.damaris.org/cm/podcasts/714.

— 'Understanding Jesus Interview' www.damaris.org/cm/podcasts/715.

— 'Understanding Jesus: An Overview' www.damaris.org/cm/podcasts/591.

— 'The Resurrection Puzzle: Putting the Pieces Together' www.damaris.org/cm/ podcasts/317.

— 'Jesus' Resurrection: Worldview, Data and Explanation' www.damaris.org/cm/ podcasts/453.

— 'Is God Nasty?' www.highfield.org.uk/church/index.php?id=240&sermonid=1731.

Online papers

Adams, Marylin McCord. 'Horrendous Evil and the Goodness of God' www.lastsem-inary.com/problem-of-evil/Horrendous%20Evil%20and%20the%20Goodness%20 of%20God.pdf.

Ayoub, George. 'The Design of the Vertebrate Retina' www.arn.org/docs/odesign/ od171/retina171.htm.

Bergmann, Michael and Michael Rea. 'In Defense of Skeptical Theism: A Reply to Almedia and Oppy' http://nd.edu/~mrea/papers/In%20Defense%20of%20Skeptical%20Theism.pdf.

Bortolotti, Lisa and Yujin Nagasawa. 'Immortality Without Boredom' http://yujinnaga-sawa.com/resources/boredom.pdf.

Boyce, Kenny and Justin McBrayer, 'Van Inwagen on the Problem of Evil: The Good, the Bad and the Ugly' www.baylor.edu/content/services/document.php/41162.pdf.

Bruckner, Donald W. 'Against the Tedium of Immortality' www.personal.psu.edu/dwb12/blogs/donald_bruckners_webpage/Against%20the%20Tedium%20of%20Immortality.pdf.

Chappell, Timothy. 'Infinity goes on trial: must immortality be meaningless?' www.open.ac.uk/Arts/philosophy/docs/infinity_goes_up_on_trial.pdf.

— '"A logos that increases itself": response to Burley' http://oro.open.ac.uk/24587/1/logosburley.pdf.

*Clark, Kelly James. 'I Believe in God the Father, Almighty' www.calvin.edu/academic/philosophy/writings/ibig.htm.

*Collins, Robin. 'The Connection Building Theodicy' www.lastseminary.com/problem-of-evil/The%20Connection%20Building%20Theodicy.pdf.

Copan, Paul. 'God Can't Possibly Exist Given the Evil and Pain I See in the World' www.bethinking.org/resource.php?ID=30.

— 'Is the Old Testament God Evil?' http://enrichmentjournal.ag.org/201203/201203_034_Good_God.cfm.

— 'Is Yahweh a Moral Monster? The New Atheists and Old Testament Ethics' www.epsociety.org/library/articles.asp?pid=45.

— 'Yahweh Wars and the Canaanites' www.epsociety.org/library/articles.asp?pid=63.

Cowan, Steven B. 'Peering through a Glass Darkly: Responding to the Philosophical Problem of Evil' www.arcapologetics.org/articles/article09.htm.

*Craig, William Lane. 'The Problem of Evil' www.bethinking.org/resource.php?ID=60&TopicID=3&CategoryID=3.

*— 'Contemporary scholarship and the historical evidence for the resurrection of Jesus Christ' www.reasonablefaith.org/site/News2?page=NewsArticle&id=5214.

— 'Visions of Jesus: A Critical Assessment of Gerd Lüdemann's Hallucination Hypothesis' www.reasonablefaith.org/site/News2?page=NewsArticle&id=5208.

— vs Bart Ehrman, 'Is there historical evidence for the resurrection of Jesus?' www.holycross.edu/departments/crec/website/resurrection-debate-transcript.pdf.

Denton, Michael J. 'The Inverted Retina: Maladaption or Preadaption?' www.arn.org/docs/odesign/od192/invertedretina192.htm.

*Fisher, John Martin. 'Why Immortality Is Not so Bad' www.andrewmbailey.com/jmf/Immortality.pdf.

Habermas, Gary R. 'Atheism and Evil: A Fatal Dilemma' www.garyhabermas.com/books/why_believe/whybelieve.htm.

— 'The Case for Christ's Resurrection' http://digitalcommons.liberty.edu/cgi/viewcontent.cgi?article=1109&context=lts_fac_pubs.

— 'Resurrection claims in non-Christian religions' www.garyhabermas.com/articles/religious_studies/rel_stud_res_claims_in_non-christian_religions.htm.

— 'The Empty Tomb of Jesus' www.4truth.net/fourtruthpbjesus.aspx?pageid=8589952861.

— 'The Resurrection Appearances of Jesus' www.4truth.net/fourtruthpbjesus.aspx?pageid=8589952867.

— 'Experiences of the Risen Jesus' www.garyhabermas.com/articles/dialog_rexperience/dialog_rexperiences.htm.

Haig, Albert. 'A Deontological Solution to the Problem of Evil' www.arsdisputandi.org/publish/articles/000255/article.pdf.

Howard-Snyder, Daniel and Francis Howard-Snyder. 'Is Theism Compatible With Gratuitous Suffering?' www.lastseminary.com/problem-of-evil/Is%20Theism%20Compatible%20with%20Gratuitous%20Evil.pdf.

Kreeft, Peter. 'God's Answer to Suffering' www.peterkreeft.com/topics/suffering.htm.

— '35 FAQs about Eternity' www.peterkreeft.com/topics-more/35-faqs_eternity.htm.

— and Ronald Tacelli. 'Evidence for the Resurrection of Christ' http://hometown.aol.com/philvaz/articles/num9.htm.

Lewis, C.S. 'The Weight of Glory' www.verber.com/mark/xian/weight-of-glory.pdf.

Luskin, Casey. 'Is the Panda's Thumb a "Clumsy" Adaptation that Refutes Intelligent Design?' www.ideacenter.org/contentmgr/showdetails.php/id/1477.

McGrew, Timothy and Lydia McGrew, 'The Argument from Miracles: A Cumulative Case for the Resurrection of Jesus of Nazareth' www.lydiamcgrew.com/Resurrectionarticlesinglefile.pdf.

*Nelson, Paul. 'Jettison the Arguments, or the Rule? The Place of Darwinian Theological Themata in Evolutionary Reasoning' www.discovery.org/a/104.

Reasons to Believe. 'Bad Designs' www.reasons.org/rtb-101/baddesigns.

Swinburne, Richard. 'The Problem of Evil' www.lastseminary.com/problem-of-evil/The%20Problem%20of%20Evil%20-%20Swinburne.pdf.

— 'The Probability of the Resurrection of Jesus' www.epsociety.org/userfiles/pc%2015-2%20swinburne%20final(1).pdf.

Trakakis, Nick and Yujin Nagasawa. 'Skeptical Theism and Moral Skepticism: A Reply to Almeida and Oppy' www.arsdisputandi.org/publish/articles/000178/index.html.

Wiker, Benjamin D. 'The Problem of Evil' www.discovery.org/a/1673.

Williams, Peter S. 'Death and Philosophy' www.damaris.org/content/content.php?type=5&id=68.

Wisnewski, J. Jeremy. 'Is the immortal life worth living?' www.hartwick.edu/documents/philoswisnewskiimmortallife.pdf.

Wright, N.T. 'Jesus' Resurrection and Christian Origins' www.ntwrightpage.com/Wright_Jesus_Resurrection.htm.

Books

Adams, Marilyn McCord and Robert Merrihew Adams, eds. *The Problem of Evil* (Oxford University Press, 1996).

Baggett, David, Gary R. Habermas and Jerry L. Walls, eds. *C.S. Lewis as Philosopher: Truth, Goodness and Beauty* (Downers Grove, IL: IVP, Academic, 2008).

Copan, Paul. *Is God a Moral Monster? Making Sense of the Old Testament God* (Grand Rapids, MI: Baker, 2011).

— (ed.). *Will The Real Jesus Please Stand Up? A Debate between William Lane Craig and John Dominic Crossan* (Grand Rapids: Baker, 1998).

— and Paul K. Moser (ed.'s). *The Rationality of Theism* (London: Routledge, 2003).

— and Ronald K. Tacelli (ed's.). *Jesus' Resurrection: Fact or Figment? A debate between William Lane Craig & Gerd Lüdemann* (Downers Grove, Illinois: IVP, 2000).

*Craig, William Lane. *On Guard: Defending Your Faith with Reason and Precision* (Colorado Springs, CO; David C. Cook, 2010).

— ed. *Philosophy of Religion: A Reader and Guide* (Edinburgh University Press, 2002).

— and Chad Meister, eds. *God Is Good, God Is Great* (Downers Grove, IL: IVP, 2009).

— and J.P. Moreland, eds. *The Blackwell Companion to Natural Theology* (Oxford: Wiley-Blackwell, 2009).

Davis, Stephen T. *Risen Indeed: Making Sense of the Resurrection* (London: SPCK, 1993).

Farrer, Austin. *Love Almighty and Ills Unlimited* (London: Fontana, 1966).

*Ganssle, Gregory E. 'God and Evil.' Pages 259–77 in *The Rationality of Theism* (ed. Paul Copan and Paul K. Moser; London: Routledge, 2003).

Geivett, R. Douglas. 'God and the Evidence of Evil.' Pages 249–68 in *Reasons for Faith: Making a Case for the Christian Faith* (ed. Norman L. Geisler and Chad V. Meister; Wheaton, IL: Crossway, 2007).

Habermas, Gary R. and J.P. Moreland. *Beyond Death: Exploring the Evidence for Immortality* (Eugene, OR: Wipf & Stock, 2004).

Habermas, Gary R. vs Anthony Flew. *Did Jesus Rise from the Dead? The Resurrection Debate* (ed. Terry L. Miethe; Harper & Rowe, 1987).

Howard-Snyder, Daniel, ed. *The Evidential Problem of Evil* (Indiana University Press, 1996).

*Lewis, C.S. *The Problem of Pain* (London: Fount, 1977).

Licona, Michael R. *The Resurrection of Jesus: A New Historiographical Approach* (Nottingham: Apollos, 2010).

Meister, Chad. *Evil: A Guide for the Perplexed* (London: Continuum, 2012).

— and James K. Drew, eds. *God and Evil: The Case for God in a World Filled with Pain* (Downers Grove, IL: IVP, 2013).

Murray, Michael J. *Nature Red in Tooth and Claw: Theism and the Problem of Animal Suffering* (Oxford University Press, 2011).

*Nash, Ronald H. 'The Problem of Evil.' Pages 203–23 in *To Everyone an Answer: A Case for the Christian Worldview* (ed. Francis J. Beckwith, William Lane Craig and J.P. Moreland; Downers Grove, IL: IVP, 2004).

Perry, John. *Dialogue on Good, Evil, and the Existence of God* (Cambridge, MA: Hackett, 1999).

Peterson, Michael L. 'The Problem of Evil.' Pages 393–401 in *A Companion to Philosophy of Religion* (ed. Philip L. Quinn and Charles Taliaferro; Oxford: Blackwell, 1999).

Powell, Doug. *Resurrection iWitness* (Holman Reference, 2012).

Strobel, Lee. *The Case For The Real Jesus: A Journalist Investigates Current Attacks on the Identity of Christ* (Zondervan, 2007).

Stump, Eleonore. *Wandering in Darkness: Narrative and the Problem of Suffering* (Oxford University Press, 2012).

Swinburne, Richard. *The Resurrection of God Incarnate* (Oxford: Clarendon Press, 2003).

— Was Jesus God? (Oxford University Press, 2008).

*Walls, Jerry L. *Heaven: The Logic of Eternal Joy* (Oxford University Press, 2003).

*Williams, Peter S. *Understanding Jesus: Five Ways to Spiritual Enlightenment* (Milton Keynes: Paternoster Press, 2011).

— *I Wish I Could Believe in Meaning: A Response to Nihilism* (Southampton: Damaris, 2004).

Wright, Tom. *Surprised by Hope* (London: SPCK, 2007).

Wright, N.T. *The Resurrection of the Son of God* (London: SPCK, 2003).

Yandell, Keith E. 'Theology, Philosophy, and Evil.' Pages 219–42 in *For Faith and Clarity: Philosophical Contributions to Christian Theology* (ed. James K. Beilby; Grand Rapids, MI: Baker, 2006).

Recommended Resources

Peter S. Williams

My Website: www.peterwilliams.com.
YouTube Playlist www.youtube.com/playlist?list=PLQhh3qcwVEWgmFh_mVgG9r-rQl-jXyJk-z.
Audio YouTube Playlist www.youtube.com/playlist?list=PLQhh3qcwVEWgpeBUF-690fL3qnBiznNbUz.
Podcast Channel www.damaris.org/cm/podcasts/category/peterswilliams.
ID.Plus Blog http://idpluspeterswilliams.blogspot.com/.
C.S. Lewis vs the New Atheists (Milton Keynes: Paternoster Press, 2013).
Understanding Jesus: Five Ways to Spiritual Enlightenment (Milton Keynes: Paternoster Press, 2011).
A Sceptic's Guide to Atheism (Carlisle: Paternoster Press, 2009).
I Wish I Could Believe in Meaning: A Response to Nihilism (Southampton: Damaris, 2004).
The Case for Angels (Carlisle: Paternoster Press, 2002).
The Case for God (Crowborough: Monarch, 1999).

Introductions to Philosophy

Steven B. Cowan and James S. Spiegel, *The Love of Wisdom: A Christian Introduction to Philosophy* (Nashville, TN: B&H Academic, 2009).
Garrett J. DeWeese and J.P. Moreland, *Philosophy Made Slightly Less Difficult: A Beginner's Guide to Life's Big Questions* (Downers Grove, IL: IVP Academic, 2005).

Introductions to the Philosophy of Religion

Brian Davies, *An Introduction to the Philosophy of Religion* (Oxford University Press, 3rd edn, 2004).
C. Stephen Evans, *Philosophy of Religion: Thinking about Faith* (Downers Grove, IL: IVP, 1st edn, 1982).
Norman L. Geisler and Winfried Corduan, *Philosophy of Religion* (Eugene, OR: Wipf & Stock, 2nd edn, 1988).
J.P. Moreland and William Lane Craig, *Philosophical Foundations for a Christian Worldview* (Downers Grove, IL: IVP, 2003).
Michael J. Murray and Michael Rea, *An Introduction to the Philosophy of Religion* (Cambridge University Press, 2008).
Michael Peterson et al., *Reason and Religious Belief: An Introduction to the Philosophy of Religion* (Oxford University Press, 4th edn, 2009).
Charles Taliaferro, *Philosophy of Religion* (Oxford University Press, 2009).

Readings in the Philosophy of Religion

Kelly James Clark, ed., *Readings in the Philosophy of Religion* (Peterborough, ON: Broadview Press, 2000).

Paul Copan and Paul K. Moser, eds, *The Rationality of Theism* (London: Routledge, 2003).

William Lane Craig, ed. *Philosophy of Religion: A Reader and Guide* (Edinburgh University Press, 2002).

William Lane Craig and J.P. Moreland, eds, *The Blackwell Companion to Natural Theology* (Oxford: Wiley-Blackwell, 2009).

William Lane Craig and J.P. Moreland, eds, *Naturalism: A Critical Analysis* (London: Routledge, 2001).

Brian Davies, ed., *Philosophy of Religion: A Guide and Anthology* (Oxford University Press, 2000).

R. Douglas Geivett and Brendan Sweetman, eds, *Contemporary Perspectives on Religious Epistemology* (Oxford University Press, 1992).

John Hick, ed., *The Existence of God* (London: Macmillan, 1964).

Michael Peterson et al., *Philosophy of Religion: Selected Readings* (Oxford University Press, 4th edn, 2010).

James F. Sennett and Douglas Groothuis, eds, *In Defense of Natural Theology: A Post-Humean Assessment* (Downers Grove, IL: IVP, 2005).

Christian Apologetics

Francis J. Beckwith et al., eds, *To Everyone an Answer: A Case for the Christian Worldview* (Downers Grove, IL: IVP, 2004).

Boa, Kenneth D. and Robert M. Mowman Jr., *Faith Has Its Reasons: An Integrative Approach to Defending Christianity* (second edition; Milton Keynes: Paternoster, 2005).

William Lane Craig, *On Guard* (Colorado Springs, CO: David C. Cook, 2010).

The Complete C.S. Lewis Signature Classics (Grand Rapids, MI: Zondervan, 2007).

C.S. Lewis Essay Collection: Faith, Christianity and the Church (ed. Lesley Walmsley; London: HarperCollins, 2002).

J.P. Moreland, *Scaling the Secular City: A Defense of Christianity* (Grand Rapids, MI: Baker, 1987).

James E. Taylor, *Introducing Christian Apologetics: Cultivating Christian Commitment* (Grand Rapids, MI: Baker Academic, 2006).

Websites

Apologetics 315 http://apologetics315.blogspot.com/.
Bethinking www.bethinking.org/.
Discovery Institute Centre for Science and Culture www.discovery.org/csc/.
Evangelical Philosophical Society http://epsociety.org/about/.
God: New Evidence www.youtube.com/user/godnewevidence.
Last Seminary www.lastseminary.com/.

Christian Philosophers

Paul Copan www.paulcopan.com/.
William Lane Craig www.reasonablefaith.org.
William A. Dembski http://designinference.com/dembski-on-intelligent-design/dembski-writings/.
Peter van Inwagen http://andrewmbailey.com/pvi/.
Peter Kreeft www.peterkreeft.com/home.htm.
John C. Lennox http://johnlennox.org/index.php/en/.
J.P. Moreland www.jpmoreland.com/.
Stephen C. Meyer www.stephencmeyer.org/.
Alvin Plantinga http://alvinplantinga.net/.
Richard Swinburne http://users.ox.ac.uk/~orie0087/index.html.

Video

Closer to Truth www.closertotruth.com/.
William Lane Craig Audio-Visual Page www.reasonablefaith.org/site/PageServer?pagename=audio_visuals.
John C. Lennox http://johnlennox.org/index.php/en/talks/.
Lee Strobel www.leestrobel.com/index.html.
Veritas Forum Media www.veritas.org/media/.
Peter S. Williams YouTube Channel www.youtube.com/user/peterswilliamsvid.

Audio

William Lane Craig Podcasts www.reasonablefaith.org/site/PageServer?pagename=podcasting_main.
Intelligent Design: The Future http://intelligentdesign.podomatic.com/.
Unbelievable www.premierradio.org.uk/shows/saturday/unbelievable.aspx?mod_page=0.
Highfield Church: Reasonable Faith? www.highfield.org.uk/church/index.php?id=469.
Peter S. Williams Podcast Channel www.damaris.org/cm/podcasts/category/peterswilliams.

Endnotes

Introduction: A Faithful Guide to Philosophy

[1] Thomas Aquinas, *Summa Contra Gentiles, Book One: God* (trans. Anton C. Pegis; University of Notre Dame Press, 2005), p. 61.
[2] Unlike many secular textbooks, which unfortunately misrepresent theistic beliefs and arguments.
[3] A fun way to get such an overview would be to read Jostein Gaarder's novel, *Sophie's World* (London: Phoenix, 1994). A more substantial review is provided by F.C. Copleston's eleven-volume *A History of Philosophy* (London: Continuum, 2003).
[4] Peter Kreeft, *Because God Is Real* (San Francisco: Ignatius, 2008), pp. 15–16.
[5] Peter Kreeft, *Philosophy 101 by Socrates* (San Francisco: Ignatius, 2002), p. 113.

Part I: The Love of Wisdom

[1] Quoted by J.P. Moreland and William Lane Craig, *Philosophical Foundations for a Christian Worldview* (Downers Grove, IL: IVP, 2003), p. 28.
[2] ibid.
[3] Joe Carter and John Coleman, *How to Argue Like Jesus* (Wheaton, IL: Crossway, 2009), p. 44.
[4] cf. Isaac Watts, *Logic: Or the Right Use of Reason in the Inquiry after Truth with a Variety of Rules to Guard against Error in the Affairs of Religion and Human Life, as Well as in the Sciences* www.google.co.uk/books?id=5EwWAAAAYAA-J&printsec=frontcover&dq=Isaac+Watts+Logic&lr=#v=onepage&q&f=false.
[5] David A. Horner, *Mind Your Faith* (Downers Grove, IL: IVP Academic, 2011), p. 51.
[6] ibid.
[7] ibid.

1. Philosophy and Faith

1 Timothy Keller, *The Reason for God: Belief in an Age of Skepticism* (New York: Dutton, 2008), pp. xvi–xvii.

2 Carson Weitnauer, 'How Churches Can Respond to Doubt' www.apologetics315.com/2012/08/how-to-get-apologetics-in-your-church-2_30.html#more.

3 Chad Meister, ed., *The Philosophy of Religion Reader* (London: Routledge, 2008), General Introduction.

4 Thomas V. Morris, 'Foreword', in *C.S. Lewis as Philosopher: Truth, Goodness and Beauty* (ed. David Baggett, Gary R. Habermas and Jerry L. Walls; Downers Grove, IL: IVP, 2008), p. 10.

5 ibid., p. 149.

6 Paul K. Moser, *Jesus and Philosophy: New Essays* (CUP, 2009), Introduction, p. 20.

7 J.P. Moreland, 'Why I Have Made Jesus Christ Lord of My Life', in *Why I Am a Christian: Leading Thinkers Explain Why They Believe* (ed. Norman L. Geisler and Paul K. Hoffman; Grand Rapids, MI: Baker, 2nd edn, 2006), p. 300.

8 cf. Douglas Groothuis, *Christian Apologetics* (Nottingham: Apollos, 2011), p. 31 and Douglas Groothuis, *On Jesus* (London; Thomson/Wadsworth, 2003).

9 David A. Horner, *Mind Your Faith* (Downers Grove, IL: IVP Academic, 2011), p. 39.

10 Dallas Willard, *The Divine Conspiracy: Rediscovering Our Hidden Life in God* (London: Fount, 1998), p. 2.

11 Thomas Aquinas, *Summa Contra Gentiles, Book One: God* (trans. Anton C. Pegis; University of Notre Dame Press, 2005), pp. 60–61.

12 On postmodernism cf. Peter S. Williams, 'A Pre-Modern Perspective on Postmodernism: A Tale of Three Mirrors' (Eastern European Bible College) http://youtu.be/Mhf6-H6l2K4.

13 Ian Crofton, *Big Ideas in Brief: 200 World-Changing Concepts Explained in an Instant* (London: Quercus, 2011), p. 8.

14 J.P. Moreland and Mark Matlock, *Smart Faith: Loving Your God with All Your Mind* (Colorado Springs, CO: Think, 2005), p. 28.

15 Charles Taliaferro, *Philosophy of Religion* (Oxford: OneWorld, 2009), p. xi.

16 Aristotle, *The Art of Rhetoric* (trans. H.C. Lawson-Tancred; London: Penguin, 2004), p. 70.

17 Stratford Caldecott, *Beauty in the World: Rethinking the Foundations of Education* (Tacoma: Angelico, 2012), p. 92.

18 Aristotle, *The Art of Rhetoric*, p. 74.

19 Cicero, Orator 75, quoted by H.C. Lawson-Tancred, *The Art of Rhetoric* (London: Penguin Classics, 1991), p. 55.

20 Crofton, *Big Ideas*, p. 8.

21 Horner, *Mind Your Faith*, p. 47.

22 Paul W. Gooch, 'Paul, the Mind of Christ, and Philosophy', in *Jesus and Philosophy: New Essays* (ed. Paul K. Moser; CUP, 2009), p. 103.

23 Glen Schultz, *Kingdom Education* (Nashville, TN: LifeWay, 1998), p. 39.

24 Paul Copan, *Loving Wisdom: Christian Philosophy of Religion* (St Louis, MO: Chalice, 2007), pp. 3–4.

[25] Bill Smith, 'Blazing the North–South Trail', *Just Thinking*, Winter 2001, p. 11.

[26] cf. André Comte-Sponville, *The Book of Atheist Spirituality: An Elegant Argument for Spirituality without God* (London: Bantam, 2008).

[27] Alister McGrath, *The Passionate Intellect: Christian Faith and the Discipleship of the Mind* (Downers Grove, IL: IVP, 2010), p. 21.

[28] C.S. Lewis, 'Myth Become Fact', in *God in the Dock* (Grand Rapids, MI: Eerdmans, 1970), p. 66.

[29] Thomas Aquinas, *Summa Theologica*, part 1, question 16, objection 3.

[30] Cat photo by Loliloli (own work) [Public domain], via Wikimedia Commons, http://commons.wikimedia.org/wiki/File:Spielendes_Kätzchen.JPG.

[31] Quoted by Peter Kreeft, *Between Heaven and Hell* (Downers Grove, IL: IVP, 1982).

[32] Aquinas, *Quaestiones Disputatae de Veritate*, in *Aquinas: Selected Philosophical Writings* (ed. Timothy McDermott; OUP, 1998), p. 58.

[33] Aquinas, quoted by Norman L. Geisler and Paul D. Feinberg, *Introduction to Philosophy* (Grand Rapids, MI: Baker, 1987), p. 247.

[34] Douglas Groothuis, *Christian Apologetics* (Nottingham: Apollos, 2011), p. 124.

[35] Jacques Maritain, *An Introduction to Philosophy* (London: Continuum, 2005), p. xiii.

[36] Aquinas, *Summa Contra Gentiles*, *Book One*, p. 60.

[37] Parker J. Palmer and Arthur Zajonc, *The Heart of Higher Education: A Call to Renewal* (San Francisco: Jossey-Bass, 2010), p. 29.

[38] Groothuis, *Christian Apologetics*, p. 16.

[39] cf. Frank Hofmann, 'Epistemic Means and Ends: In Defense of Some Sartwellian Insights' www.springerlink.com/content/v36576173745833j/; Pierre Le Morvan, 'Epistemic Means and Ends: A Reply to Hofmann' www.tcnj.edu/~lemorvan/documents/Web_Reply_to_Hofmann.pdf; Ken Morris, 'Concerning Sartwell's Minimalist Thesis' www.stanford.edu/group/dualist/vol8/pdfs/morris.pdf.

[40] cf. Edmund L. Gettier, 'Is Justified True Belief Knowledge?' www.ditext.com/gettier/gettier.html; Stephen Hetherington, 'Gettier Problems' www.iep.utm.edu/g/gettier.htm; William G. Lycan, 'On the Gettier Problem Problem' www.unc.edu/~ujanel/Gettier.htm.

[41] J.P. Moreland in *Does God Exist?* (Buffalo, NY: Prometheus, 1993), p. 58; cf. J.P. Moreland, 'Skepticism and Epistemology' www.hisdefense.org/LinkClick.aspx?link=http%3a%2f%2fhisdefense.org%2fvideo%2fMoreland+-+Skepticism+and+Epistemology.wmv&tabid=136&mid=938.

[42] J.P. Moreland, *The Kingdom Triangle* (Grand Rapids, MI: Zondervan, 2007), p. 124.

[43] Dallas Willard, *Knowing Christ Today: Why We Can Trust Spiritual Knowledge* (New York: HarperOne, 2009), p. 15.

[44] Horner, *Mind Your Faith*, p. 49.

[45] Richard Dawkins, *The Selfish Gene* (OUP, 1976), p. 198.

[46] Alister McGrath, *Dawkins' God* (Oxford: Blackwell, 2005), pp. 91, 99.

[47] Julian Baggini, *Atheism: A Very Short Introduction* (OUP, 2003), p. 32.

[48] A.C. Grayling, *Against All Gods* (London: Oberon, 2007), pp. 15–16.

[49] Baggini, *Atheism*, p. 33.

[50] Moreland, *Kingdom Triangle*, pp. 130–31.

51 J.P. Moreland, 'Living Smart', in *Passionate Conviction* (ed. Paul Copan and William Lane Craig; Nashville, TN: B&H Academic, 2007), p. 22.

52 C.S. Lewis, *Mere Christianity* (London: Fount, 1997), p. 117.

53 ibid.

54 C.S. Lewis, 'Religion: Reality or Substitute?', in *C.S. Lewis Essay Collection: Faith, Christianity and the Church* (London: HarperCollins, 2002), pp. 136–7.

55 Tom Price, 'Faith Is Just about "Trusting God" Isn't It?' www.bethinking.org/resource.php?ID=132&TopicID=9&CategoryID=8.

56 Michael J. Wilkins and J.P. Moreland, *Jesus under Fire: Modern Scholarship Reinvents the Historical Jesus* (Grand Rapids, MI: Zondervan, 1995), p. 8.

57 cf. Peter S. Williams, 'Apologetics in 3D: Persuading across Spiritualities with the Apostle Paul', *Theofilos* (2012:1) and 'Apologetics in 3D' http://vimeo.com/33805834.

58 Peter Kreeft and Ronald Tacelli, *Handbook of Christian Apologetics* (Downers Grove, IL: IVP, 1994), p. 22.

59 ibid., pp. 21–2.

60 ibid., p. 22.

61 Norman L. Geisler and Paul D. Feinberg, *Introduction to Philosophy: A Christian Perspective* (Grand Rapids, MI: Baker, 1997), p. 73.

62 Douglas Groothuis, *On Jesus* (London: Thomson/Wadsworth, 2003), p. 35.

63 Mark Mittelberg, 'Fact and Faith' www.christianitytoday.com/ct/2008/july/15.26.html?start=2 cf. J.P. Moreland, 'How Evangelicals Became Over-Committed to the Bible and What Can Be Done about It' www.kingdomtriangle.com/discussion/moreland_EvangOverCommBible.pdf.

64 Mortimer J. Adler, *The Great Ideas: A Syntopicon of the Great Books of the Western World* (2 vols; University of Chicago Press, 1952), 1:543.

65 cf. http://en.wikipedia.org/wiki/John_Wesley.

66 John Wesley, 'An Address to the Clergy' http://wesley.nnu.edu/john_wesley/10clergy.htm.

67 Const. De Fide, II, De Rev., quoted by the *Catholic Encyclopedia* www.newadvent.org/cathen/01215c.htm.

68 John Polkinghorne, 'Where Is Natural Theology Today?', *Science and Christian Belief* 18 (2006): p. 169.

69 Norman L. Geisler, *Philosophy of Religion* (Grand Rapids, MI: Zondervan, 1974), p. 208.

70 H. Wayne House and Dennis W. Jones, *Reasons for Our Hope: An Introduction to Christian Apologetics* (Nashville, TN: B&H, 2011), p. 58.

71 C.S. Lewis, quoted by Norman L. Geisler in J.P. Moreland, *Scaling the Secular City* (Grand Rapids, MI: Baker, 1987), Foreword.

2. Making a Good Argument

1 G.K. Chesterton, 'The Blue Cross', in *The Innocence of Father Brown* (CreateSpace Independent Publishing Platform, centennial edn, 2009), p. 15.

[2] cf. Peter S. Williams, 'Apologetics in 3D: Persuading across Spiritualities with the Apostle Paul' *Theofilos* (2012:1), pp. 3–24, www.bethinking.org/what-is-apologetics/advanced/apologetics-in-3d.htm. and 'Paul in Athens and Engaging with Popular Culture' www.damaris.org/cm/podcasts/241.

[3] Douglas Groothuis, *Christian Apologetics* (Nottingham: IVP/Apollos, 2011), p. 27.

[4] Thomas Aquinas, *Summa Contra Gentiles, Book One: God* (trans. Anton C. Pegis; University of Notre Dame Press, 2005), p. 62.

[5] Thomas Nagel, *The Last Word* (OUP, 1997), pp. 61–2.

[6] A.C. Grayling, *The Meaning of Things: Applying Philosophy to Life* (London: Weidenfeld & Nicolson, 2001), p. 25.

[7] G.K. Chesterton, *St Thomas Aquinas* (London: Hodder & Stoughton, 1933), pp. 198–200, 221.

[8] Puzzles do arise concerning vagueness. cf. Roy Sorensen, 'Vagueness' http://plato.stanford.edu/entries/vagueness/.

[9] Bertrand Russell, *The Problems of Philosophy* (OUP, 1980), pp. 40–41.

[10] ibid., p. 41.

[11] Gregory E. Ganssle, *Thinking about God: First Steps in Philosophy* (Downers Grove, IL: IVP, 2004), p. 164.

[12] James Kelly Clark, *Return to Reason* (Grand Rapids, MI: Eerdmans, 1990), p. 126.

[13] ibid.

[14] ibid., p. 131.

[15] ibid., p. 127.

[16] ibid., p. 130.

[17] ibid., p. 129.

[18] Roy Clouser, *Knowing with the Heart* (Downers Grove, IL: IVP, 1999), pp. 68–71.

[19] ibid., p. 65.

[20] Aquinas, *Summa Contra Gentiles, Book One*, pp. 74–5.

[21] Roy Abraham Varghese, *Great Thinkers on Great Questions* (Oxford: OneWorld, 1998), pp. 3, 5, 11.

[22] William Lane Craig, *God, Are You There?* (Atlanta, GA: RZIM, 1999), p. 8.

[23] Craig, *God, Are You There?*, pp. 8–9.

[24] Aquinas, *Summa Contra Gentiles, Book One*, p. 78.

[25] Alvin Plantinga, 'Two Dozen (or so) Theistic Arguments' http://philofreligion.homestead.com/files/Theisticarguments.html.

[26] C. Stephen Evans, *Philosophy of Religion* (Downers Grove, IL: IVP, 2001), p. 50.

[27] Peter Kreeft and Ronald Tacelli, *Handbook of Christian Apologetics* (Downers Grove, IL: IVP, 1994), pp. 17–18.

[28] ibid.

3. Making a Bad Argument

[1] C. Stephen Layman, *The Power of Logic* (New York: McGraw-Hill, 3rd edn, 2005), Preface.

2 'Cosmological Argument' www.allaboutphilosophy.org/cosmological-argument.htm.

3 Stephen Hawking and Leonard Mlodinow, *The Grand Design* (London: Bantam, 2010), p. 5.

4 John C. Lennox, *God and Stephen Hawking: Whose Design Is It Anyway?* (Oxford: Lion, 2010), p. 18.

5 David Hume, *An Enquiry Concerning Human Understanding* 12.3.

6 Norman L. Geisler, *Christian Apologetics* (Grand Rapids, MI: Baker, 1996), p. 22.

7 Hume's fork is a forerunner to the 'verification principle' of the logical positivists – cf. Peter S. Williams, 'The Definitional Critique of Intelligent Design Theory – Lessons from the Demise of Logical Positivism' www.arn.org/docs/williams/pw_definitionalcritique.htm; William P. Alston, 'Religious Language and Verificationism', in *The Rationality of Theism* (ed. Paul Copan and Paul K. Moser; London: Routledge, 2003).

8 Norman L. Geisler and Paul D. Feinberg, *Introduction to Philosophy: A Christian Perspective* (Grand Rapids, MI: Baker, 1997), p. 59.

9 cf. Craig A. Evans, *Fabricating Jesus: How Modern Scholars Distort the Gospels* (Downers Grove, IL: IVP, 2006), pp. 43–6, 146–8.

10 John Duncan, quoted by William Knight, *Colloquia Peripatetica*, 1870.

11 *Britannica Concise Encyclopedia* www.answers.com/topic/fallacy-formal-and-informal.

12 Nigel Warburton, *Thinking from A to Z* (London: Routledge, 2nd edn, 2003), p. 63.

13 Roy Hattersley, *Essentials of Faith: Humanism* (Cambridge Educational) http://cambridge.films.com/id/13170/Essentials_of_Faith_Humanism.htm.

14 Mike King, *The God Delusion Revisited* (Lulu, 2007), p. 63.

15 cf. www.fallacyfiles.org/genefall.html.

16 Warburton, *Thinking*, p. 4.

17 Arthur Schopenhauer, *The Art of Always Being Right* (London: Gibson Square, 2005), p. 161.

18 Mortimer J. Adler, *How to Speak/How to Listen* (New York: Macmillan, 1981), p. 153.

19 Craig J. Hazen, Preface to 'My Pilgrimage from Atheism to Theism: An Exclusive Interview with Former British Atheist Professor Antony Flew' www.biola.edu/antonyflew/flew-interview.pdf.

20 Comment quoted by Gary R. Habermas, 'My Pilgrimage from Atheism to Theism: An Exclusive Interview with Former British Atheist Professor Antony Flew' www.biola.edu/antonyflew/flew-interview.pdf.

21 Antony Flew, 'My Pilgrimage from Atheism to Theism: An Exclusive Interview with Former British Atheist Professor Antony Flew' www.biola.edu/antonyflew/flew-interview.pdf.

22 cf. Richard Dawkins on Flew at http://youtu.be/bEPUn__hYso. The same accusation was hurled at French existentialist philosopher Jean-Paul Sartre when he indicated that he embraced Messianic Judaism in his last days (cf. Jean-Paul Sartre http://nobelists.net/; Ravi Zacharias, *Can Man Live without God?* [Dallas, TX: Word, 1994], p. 212).

23 Antony Flew, *There Is a God* (New York: HarperOne, 2007), p. 2.
24 John Nolt et al., *Logic* (New York: McGraw-Hill, 2006), p. 114.
25 Tertullian, 'The Apology', in *Christian Apologetics Past and Present: A Primary Source Reader*, vol. 1 (ed. William Edgar and K. Scott Oliphant; Wheaton, IL: Crossway, 2009), p. 129.
26 Adler, *How to Speak/Listen*, p. 153.
27 Nolt et al., *Logic*, p. 115.
28 ibid., p. 116.
29 cf. Peter S. Williams, 'Stephen Hawking and the Grand Designer (Winchester)' www.damaris.org/cm/podcasts/682.
30 Warburton, *Thinking*, p. 111.
31 Sean B. Carroll, 'The Big Picture', *Nature* 409 (2001): p. 669.
32 J.P. Moreland, *Love Your God with All Your Mind* (Colorado Springs, CO: NavPress, 1997), p. 123.
33 cf. Peter S. Williams, 'The Inspiration, Authority and Activity of the Bible' www.damaris.org/cm/podcasts/541.
34 Richard Dawkins, 'Darwin Triumphant', *A Devil's Chaplain* (London: Weidenfeld & Nicolson, 2003), p. 86.
35 Richard Dawkins, *Climbing Mount Improbable* (London: Viking, 1996).
36 Dawkins, *Devil's Chaplain*, pp. 211–12.
37 ibid., p. 212.
38 ibid.
39 cf. 'An Atheist with Faith – Richard Dawkins' http://youtu.be/t7OgcWNJm8w.
40 cf. www.nizkor.org/features/fallacies/special-pleading.html.
41 Richard Dawkins, *The Blind Watchmaker* (London: Penguin, 2006), p. 141.
42 Daniel Came, 'Richard Dawkins's Refusal to Debate Is Cynical and Anti-Intellectual' www.guardian.co.uk/commentisfree/belief/2011/oct/22/richard-dawkins-refusal-debate-william-lane-craig.
43 Steven Lovell, 'Evidence and Atheism' at www.csl-philosophy.co.uk/.
44 Robert A. Harris, *The Integration of Faith and Learning: A Worldview Approach* (Eugene, OR: Cascade, 2004), p. 83.
45 Richard Norman, *On Humanism* (London: Routledge, 2004), p. 16.
46 Antony Flew, *The Presumption of Atheism* (London: Pemberton, 1976), p. 14.
47 Steven Lovell, 'Evidence and Atheism' at www.csl-philosophy.co.uk/.
48 cf. http://youtu.be/2mTqopwPTvU.
49 Dawkins, *Mount Improbable*, p. 4.
50 ibid., p. 3.
51 ibid.
52 ibid., pp. 4–5.
53 ibid., p. 4.
54 Warburton, *Thinking*, p. 106.
55 ibid.
56 cf. Jack Collins, 'Miracles, Intelligent Design, and God-of-the-Gaps', *Perspectives on Science and Christian Faith* 55:1 (March 2003) www.asa3.org/ASA/

PSCF/2003/PSCF3-03Collins.pdf; Robert Larmer, 'Is There Anything Wrong with "God of the Gaps" Reasoning?' www.newdualism.org/papers/R. Larmer/Gaps.htm; J.P. Moreland, 'Complementarity, Agency Theory, and the God-of-the-Gaps' http://afterall.net/papers/490579; David Snoke, 'In Favour of God-of-the-Gaps Reasoning' www.cityreformed.org/snoke/gaps.pdf.

[57] cf. Jack Collins, 'Miracles, Intelligent Design, and God-of-the-Gaps', *Perspectives on Science and Christian Faith* 55:1 (March 2003) www.asa3.org/ASA/ PSCF/2003/PSCF3-03Collins.pdf.

[58] J.P. Moreland, 'Complementarity, Agency Theory, and the God-of-the-Gaps' http://afterall.net/papers/490579.

[59] Phil Dowe, *Galileo, Darwin and Hawking: The Interplay of Science, Reason, and Religion* (Grand Rapids, MI: Eerdmans, 2005), pp. 193–4.

[60] This principle states that we should always believe things to be the way they (positively) seem to us to be, until and unless we are given sufficient reason for doubt. If one adopted the opposite principle – that we should doubt positive appearances until given reason to believe – we would never believe anything, because we would be bound to doubt anything provided with the aim (impossible in the circumstances) of getting us to believe. The only alternative to following the principle of credulity is complete scepticism.

[61] Robert Larmer, 'Is There Anything Wrong with "God of the Gaps" Reasoning?' www.newdualism.org/papers/R.Larmer/Gaps.htm.

[62] Moreland, *Love Your God with All Your Mind*, p. 122.

[63] Warburton, *Thinking*, p. 126.

[64] Peter Kreeft, *Philosophy 101 by Socrates* (San Francisco: Ignatius, 2002), p. 21.

[65] Adler, *How to Speak/Listen*, pp. 27–28.

Part II: Some Arguments for God

[1] Robert C. Koons, 'Science and Theism: Concord, not Conflict', in *The Rationality of Theism* (ed. Paul Copan and Paul K. Moser; London: Routledge, 2003), p. 73.

[2] H. Wayne House and Dennis W. Jowers, *Reasons for Our Hope: An Introduction to Christian Apologetics* (Nashville, TN: B&H Academic, 2011), p. 250.

[3] James F. Sennett and Douglas Groothuis, *In Defence of Natural Theology: A Post-Humean Assessment* (Downers Grove, IL: IVP, 2005), p. 10.

[4] William Lane Craig and J.P. Moreland, eds, *The Blackwell Companion to Natural Theology* (Oxford: Wiley-Blackwell, 2009), p. x.

[5] David Berlinski, 'God, Man and Physics', in *The Deniable Darwin and Other Essays* (Seattle: Discovery Institute, 2009), p. 263.

[6] ibid.

[7] Craig J. Hazen, 'My Pilgrimage from Atheism to Theism: An Exclusive Interview with Former British Atheist Professor Antony Flew' www.biola.edu/ antonyflew/flew-interview.pdf.

[8] Flew, ibid.

9 William C. Davis, 'Theistic Arguments', in *Reason for the Hope Within* (ed. Michael J. Murray; Cambridge: Eerdmans, 1999), p. 21.
10 ibid., pp. 21–2.

4. Cosmological Arguments I

1 C. Stephen Evans, *Pocket Dictionary of Apologetics and Philosophy of Religion* (Downers Grove, IL: IVP, 2002), p. 29.
2 cf. Paul Copan, 'Is Creatio Ex Nihilo a Post-Biblical Invention? An Examination of Gerhard May's Proposal' www.earlychurch.org.uk/article_exnihilo_copan.html.
3 Evans, *Pocket Dictionary of Apologetics*.
4 C. Stephen Evans and R. Zachary Manis, *Philosophy of Religion: Thinking about Faith* (Downers Grove, IL: IVP Academic, 2nd edn, 2009), p. 62.
5 J.P. Moreland, ed., *The Creation Hypothesis: Scientific Evidence for an Intelligent Designer* (Downers Grove, IL: IVP, 1994), p. 22.
6 Nigel Warburton, *Philosophy: The Basics* (London: Routledge, 4th edn, 2004), p. 17.
7 ibid.
8 Philip Van der Elst, *C.S. Lewis: A Short Introduction* (London: Continuum, 2005), p. 29.
9 Sam Harris, *Letter to a Christian Nation* (London: Bantam, 2006), pp. 72–3. Attacking how an argument 'more or less' goes doesn't cut the philosophical mustard.
10 Daniel Dennett, *Breaking the Spell* (New York: Penguin, 2006), p. 242.
11 For example, cf. Norman L. Geisler, *Christian Apologetics* (Grand Rapids, MI: Baker, 1995), in which Geisler argues both that 'the theist need not claim that everything has a cause' (p. 238) and that 'a self-caused being is impossible' (p. 241).
12 Edward Feser, 'The New Philistinism' www.american.com/archive/2010/march/the-new-philistinism.
13 Richard Dawkins, *The God Delusion* (London: Bantam, 2006), p. 77.
14 ibid.
15 J.L. Mackie, *The Miracle of Theism* (OUP, 1982), p. 7.
16 Richard Taylor, *Metaphysics* (Englewood Cliffs, NJ: Prentice-Hall, 3rd edn, 1974), pp. 105–10.
17 '*Reductio ad absurdum* is a mode of argumentation that seeks to establish a contention by deriving an absurdity from its denial, thus arguing that a thesis must be accepted because its rejection would be untenable.' – Internet Encyclopedia of Philosophy www.iep.utm.edu/r/reductio.htm.
18 Peter Kreeft and Ronald K. Tacelli, *Handbook of Christian Apologetics* (Downers Grove, IL: IVP, 1994), p. 51.
19 W. David Beck in *In Defence of Miracles* (ed. R. Douglas Geivett and Gary R. Habermas; Leicester: Apollos, 1997), p. 151.
20 Patterson Brown, quoted by Beck, ibid.
21 Beck, ibid.

22 David S. Oderberg, 'The Cosmological Argument', in *The Routledge Companion to Philosophy of Religion* (ed. Chad Meister and Paul Copan; London: Routledge, 2010), p. 347.

23 William Lane Craig, 'Argument from Contingency' www.reasonablefaith. org/site/News2?page=NewsArticle&id=5847.

24 ibid.

25 ibid.

26 ibid.

27 ibid.

28 ibid.

29 ibid.

30 ibid.

31 ibid.

32 Richard Purtill quoted by Charles Taliaferro, *Contemporary Philosophy of Religion* (Oxford: Blackwell, 2001), pp. 358–9.

33 ibid.

34 Alexander R. Pruss http://alexanderpruss.blogspot.co.uk/2012/08/god-and-principle-of-sufficient-reason.html.

35 cf. Alexander R. Pruss, 'A Restricted Principle of Sufficient Reason and the Cosmological Argument' www.georgetown.edu/faculty/ap85/papers/RPSR. html.

36 ibid.

5. Cosmological Arguments II

1 Plato, *Timaeus*, quoted by David Sedley, *Creationism and Its Critics in Antiquity* (London: University of California Press, 2007), p. 101.

2 William Lane Craig, 'Design and the Cosmological Argument', in *Mere Creation: Science, Faith and Intelligent Design* (ed. William A. Dembski; Downers Grove, IL: IVP, 1998), p. 333.

3 cf. Stephen T. Davis, *God, Reason and Theistic Proofs* (Edinburgh University Press, 1997); R. Douglas Geivett, 'The Kalam Cosmological Argument', in *To Everyone an Answer* (ed. Francis J. Beckwith, William Lane Craig and J.P. Moreland; Downers Grove, IL: IVP, 2004); Shandon L. Guthrie, 'Theism and Contemporary Cosmology' http://sguthrie.net/theism_and_contemporary_cosmology.htm; Robert C. Koons, 'Theism and Big Bang Cosmology' www.leaderu.com/offices/koons/docs/lec5.html; J.P. Moreland, *Scaling the Secular City* (Grand Rapids, MI: Baker, 1987).

4 William Lane Craig, *Reasonable Faith* (Wheaton, IL: Crossway, 2nd edn, 1994), p. 92.

5 Mortimer J. Adler, *How to Think about God* (New York: Bantam, 1988), p. 38.

6 J.P. Moreland and William Lane Craig, *Foundations for a Christian Worldview* (Downers Grove, IL: IVP, 2003), pp. 468–9.

7 David Hume in *The Letters of David Hume* (2 vols; ed. J.Y.T. Grieg; New York: Garland, 1983), 1:187.

8 Craig, *Reasonable Faith*, p. 119.

9 Norman L. Geisler and Frank Turek, *I Don't Have Enough Faith to Be an Atheist* (Wheaton, IL: Crossway, 2004), p. 91.

10 William Lane Craig, *God? A Debate between a Christian and an Atheist* (OUP, 2004), p. 58.

11 David Hilbert, 'On the Infinite', quoted by Craig, *God?*, p. 4.

12 Moreland and Craig, *Foundations*, pp. 472–3.

13 Dean L. Overman, *A Case for the Existence of God* (New York: Rowman & Little-field, 2009), p. 51.

14 Moreland and Craig, *Foundations*, p. 473.

15 David S. Oderberg, 'The Cosmological Argument', in *The Routledge Companion to Philosophy of Religion* (ed. Chad Meister and Paul Copan; London: Rout-ledge, 2010), p. 348.

16 Craig, *Reasonable Faith*, pp. 113–14.

17 Arthur Eddington, quoted by Geisler and Turek, *I Don't Have Enough Faith*, p. 78.

18 Craig, *Reasonable Faith*, p. 114.

19 Geisler and Turek, *I Don't Have Enough Faith*, p. 76.

20 ibid., p. 79.

21 John Lennox, *God's Undertaker: Has Science Buried God?* (Oxford: Lion, 2007), p. 6.

22 Cliff Walker, 'An Interview with Particle Physicist Victor J. Stenger' (November 1999) www.positiveatheism.org/crt/stenger1.htm.

23 cf. www.ctc.cam.ac.uk/hawking70/multimedia.html.

24 Alexander Vilenkin quoted by Lisa Grossman, 'Death of the Eternal Cosmos', *New Scientist*, 14 January 2012, p. 7; cf. Alexander Vilenkin, 'Did the Universe Have a Beginning?' http://youtu.be/NXCQelhKJ7A.

25 'In the Beginning', *New Scientist*, 14 January 2012, p. 3.

26 Alexander Vilenkin, *Many Worlds in One: The Search for Other Universes* (New York: Hill and Wang, 2006), p. 176; cf. William Lane Craig, 'Vilenkin's Cosmic Vision: A Review Essay of Many Worlds in One' www.reasonablefaith.org/vilenkins-cosmic-vision-a-review-essay-of-many-worlds-in-one.

27 Anthony Kenny, *The Five Ways: St Thomas Aquinas' Proofs of God's Existence* (New York: Schocken, 1969), p. 66.

28 Peter Atkins, *On Being* (OUP, 2011), pp. 11–12.

29 Sam Harris, 'Everything and Nothing: An Interview with Lawrence M. Krauss' http://richarddawkins.net/articles/644472-everything-and-noth-ing-an-interview-with-lawrence-krauss.

30 Lawrence M. Krauss, *A Universe from Nothing: Why There Is Something Rather than Nothing* (London: Free Press, 2012), p. 174.

31 Craig, *Reasonable Faith*, p. 92.

32 For a survey of philosophical arguments for the finitude of the past, cf. William Lane Craig, 'Philosophical and Scientific Pointers to Creation Ex

Nihilo' www.asa3.org/ASA/PSCF/1980/JASA3-80Craig.html; Shandon L. Guthrie, 'Russell, Infinity, and the Tristram Shandy Paradox' http://sguthrie. net/infinity.htm; Tim Holt, 'Maths and the Finitude of the Past' www.philos-ophyofreligion.info/mathsfinitepast.html; William Lane Craig, *Reasonable Faith: Christian Truth and Apologetics* (Wheaton, IL: Crossway, 3rd edn, 2008); J.P. Moreland, *Scaling the Secular City* (Grand Rapids, MI: Baker, 1987).

33 It is thus more accurate to formulate the *kalam* argument with Norman L. Geisler as stating that 'Everything that had a beginning had a cause, The universe had a beginning, Therefore the universe had a cause.' – Geisler and Turek, *I Don't Have Enough Faith*, p. 75. It is from the conclusion that the universe had a cause, because it had a beginning, that one may deduce the present truth of the proposition that the cause of the universe exists.

34 cf. William Lane Craig, 'Must the Beginning of the Universe Have a Personal Cause? A Rejoinder' www.leaderu.com/offices/billcraig/docs/morriston.html.

35 cf. William Lane Crag vs Stephen Law, 'Does God Exist?' www.bethinking.org/who-are-you-god/does-god-exist-william-lane-craig-debate-with-ste-phen-law-audio.htm.

36 Paul Davies, *The Goldilocks Enigma: Why Is The Universe Just Right for Life?* (London: Penguin, 2007), p. 80.

37 Richard Swinburne, *The Existence of God* (Oxford: Clarendon, revd edn, 1991), p. 121.

38 J.P. Moreland, *Scaling the Secular City* (Grand Rapids, MI: Baker, 1987), p. 38.

39 ibid., p. 41.

40 Dallas Willard, *Knowing Christ Today: Why We Can Trust Spiritual Knowledge* (New York: HarperOne, 2009), p. 101.

41 ibid., pp. 101–2.

42 ibid., p. 103.

43 Moreland, *Secular City*, p. 39.

44 Dallas Willard, 'The Three-Stage Argument for the Existence of God', in *Contemporary Perspectives on Religious Epistemology* (ed. Douglas Geivett and Brendan Sweetman; OUP, 1992).

45 Oderberg, 'The Cosmological Argument', pp. 341–50.

46 Moreland, *Secular City*, pp. 38–9.

47 R. Douglas Geivett, 'The *Kalam* Cosmological Argument', in *To Everyone an Answer* (ed. Francis J. Beckwith, William Lane Craig and J.P. Moreland; Downers Grove, IL: IVP, 2004), p. 72.

48 cf. William Lane Craig, 'God and the Initial Cosmological Singularity: A Reply to Quentin Smith' www.reasonablefaith.org/site/News2?page=News-Article&id=5160.

49 Craig, *God?*, pp. 56–7.

50 Quentin Smith, 'The Uncaused Beginning of the Universe', *Philosophy of Science* 55 (1988): p. 50.

51 Geivett, 'The *Kalam* Cosmological Argument', p. 73.

52 Overman, *Case for the Existence of God*, p. 51.

53 Paul Davies, 'The Birth of the Cosmos', in *God, Cosmos, Nature and Creativity* (ed. Jill Gready; Scottish Academic Press, 1995), pp. 8–9.

54 Moreland and Craig, *Foundations*, pp. 479–80.

6. Teleological Arguments I: Paley, Hume and Design

1 David Hume, *Natural History of Religion*, quoted in Dave Armstrong, 'Was Skeptical Philosopher David Hume an Atheist?' http://ic.net/~erasmus/RAZ515.HTM.

2 Plato, *Laws* 12.966e.

3 cf. Michael Shermer, 'Why People Believe in God: An Empirical Study on a Deep Question', *The Humanist* 59:6 (November/December 1999): pp. 20–26.

4 Henry Melvill Gwatkin, *The Knowledge of God and Its Historical Development* (Edinburgh: T&T Clark, 3rd edn, 1918), p. 60.

5 Bertrand Russell, *History of Western Philosophy* (New York: Simon & Schuster, 1945), p. 589.

6 Immanuel Kant, quoted by H.D. Lewis, *Philosophy of Religion* (London: English Universities Press, 1965), p. 183.

7 cf. Robin Collins, 'The Teleological Argument', in *The Routledge Companion to Philosophy of Religion* (ed. Chad Meister and Paul Copan; London: Routledge, 2010), pp. 352–61.

8 William Paley, *Natural Theology* (OUP, 2006), p. 7.

9 ibid.

10 ibid.

11 Michael J. Behe, *Darwin's Black Box* (New York: Free Press, 2nd edn, 2006), p. 39.

12 cf. Michael J. Behe, *Darwin's Black Box* (New York: Free Press, 2nd edn, 2006); Michael J. Behe, 'Darwinism Gone Wild: Neither Sequence Similarity nor Common Descent Address a Claim of Intelligent Design' www.evolutionnews.org/2007/04/darwinism_gone_wild_neither_se.html; William A. Dembski, *No Free Lunch: Why Specified Complexity Cannot Be Purchased without Intelligence* (New York: Rowman & Littlefield, 2001); Stephen Griffith, 'Irreducible Complexity' www.iscid.org/papers/Griffith_IrreducibleComplexity_052504.pdf; Scott Minnich and Stephen C. Meyer, 'Genetic Analysis of Coordinate Flagellar and Type III Regulatory Circuits', *Proceedings of the Second International Conference on Design and Nature*, Rhodes, Greece (ed. M.W. Collins and C.A. Brebbia; WIT Press, 2004) www.discovery.org/scripts/viewDB/filesDB-download.php?id=389; William A. Dembski, 'Still Spinning Just Fine: A Response to Ken Miller' www.designinference.com/documents/2003.02.Miller_Response.htm; William A. Dembski, 'Irreducible Complexity Revisited' www.designinference.com/documents/2004.01.Irred_Compl_Revisited.pdf; Unlocking the Mystery of Life (Illustra Media, 2002).

13 J.P. Moreland, *Love Your God with All Your Mind* (Colorado Springs, CO: NavPress, 2012), p. 175.

14 cf. www.bristol.ac.uk/mecheng/people/person.html?id=14218.

15 Paley, *Natural Theology*, p. 7.

16 Stuart Burgess, *Hallmarks of Design* (Epsom: Day One, revd edn, 2002), pp. 73–4.

17 You can read his fascinating paper on 'The Beauty of the Peacock Tail and the Problems with the Theory of Sexual Selection' www.creationontheweb.com/content/view/1832.

18 Paley, *Natural Theology*, p. 8.

19 ibid., p. 16.

20 Empiricism is the belief that human knowledge comes only or primarily through the physical senses.

21 Nicholas Capaldi, *David Hume* (Boston: Hall & Co., 1975), ch. 9; Dave Armstrong, 'Was Skeptical Philosopher David Hume an Atheist?' http://ic.net/~erasmus/RAZ515.HTM.

22 cf. Peter S. Williams, 'Design and the Humean Touchstone' www.arn.org/docs/williams/pw_humeantouchstone.htm.

23 cf. Richard Swinburne, 'The Argument from Design', in *Contemporary Perspectives on Religious Epistemology* (ed. R. Douglas Geivett and Brendan Sweetman; OUP, 1992); Brian Davies, *An Introduction to the Philosophy of Religion* (OUP, new edn, 1993).

24 David Hume, *Dialogues Concerning Natural Religion* (Mineola, NY: Dover, 2006), p. 39.

25 Stephen T. Davis, *God, Reason and Theistic Proofs* (Edinburgh University Press, 1997), p. 103.

26 Richard Swinburne, 'The Argument from Design', in *Contemporary Perspectives on Religious Epistemology* (ed. R. Douglas Geivett and Brendan Sweetman; OUP, 1992), pp. 209–10.

27 David Hume, *Natural History of Religion*, quoted in Dave Armstrong, 'Was Skeptical Philosopher David Hume an Atheist?' http://ic.net/~erasmus/RAZ515.HTM.

28 David Hume, *An Enquiry Concerning Human Understanding* (Stilwell, KS: Digireads.com, 2005), p. 78.

29 John Earman, *Hume's Abject Failure: The Argument against Miracles* (OUP, 2000), p. 4.

30 Paley, *Natural Theology*, p. 8.

31 ibid.

32 ibid.

33 ibid., pp. 8–9.

34 cf. 'ENCODE: Encyclopedia of DNA Elements' http://youtu.be/Y3V2thsJ1Wc; W. Wayt Gibbs, 'The Gems of "Junk" DNA' www.arn.org/docs2/news/JunkDNA111903.htm; Jonathan Wells, *The Myth of Junk DNA* (Seattle: Discovery Institute, 2011).

35 Gordan C. Mills et al., 'Origin of Life and Evolution in Biology Textbooks – A Critique' www.arn.org/docs/mills/gm_originoflifeandevolution.htm.

36 Paley, *Natural Theology*, p. 9.

[37] ibid.

[38] ibid.

[39] ibid.

[40] ibid.

[41] ibid., p. 10.

[42] As Richard Swinburne argues: 'It is a basic principle of knowledge . . . that we ought to believe that things are as they seem to be, until we have evidence that we are mistaken . . . If you say the contrary – never trust appearances until it is proved that they were reliable – you will never have any beliefs at all. For what would show that appearances were reliable, except more appearances?' – 'Evidence for God', in *Beyond Reasonable Doubt: Evidence for God in the 1990's* (ed. Gillian Ryeland; Norwich: Canterbury Press, 1991), pp. 13–14.

[43] William Lane Craig, *Reasonable Faith: Christian Truth and Apologetics* (Wheaton, IL: Crossway, 3rd edn, 2008), p. 102.

[44] cf. Peter S. Williams, 'The War on Science: How Horizon Got Intelligent Design Wrong' http://arn.org/docs/williams/pw_horizonreview.htm; 'Focus on Intelligent Design: Some Advice on Avoiding Journalistic Embarrassment' http://arn.org/docs/williams/pw_focusonid.htm.

[45] Stephen C. Meyer, 'Not by Chance: From Bacterial Propulsion Systems to Human DNA, Evidence of Intelligent Design Is Everywhere', *National Post of Canada* (10 December 2005) www.discovery.org/a/3059.

7. Teleological Arguments II: Intelligent Design Theory

[1] Bradley Monton, *Seeking God in Science: An Atheist Defends Intelligent Design* (Peterborough, ON: Broadview, 2009), p. 39.

[2] J.P. Moreland and William Lane Craig, *Philosophical Foundations for a Christian Worldview* (Downers Grove, IL: IVP, 2003), p. 356.

[3] Intelligent Design Network www.intelligentdesignnetwork.org/.

[4] William A. Dembski, 'On the Scientific Status of Intelligent Design' www.designinference.com/documents/2002.03.kennedy_on_ID.htm.

[5] cf. Francis J. Beckwith, *Law, Darwinism, and Public Education* (New York: Rowman & Littlefield, 2003); William A. Dembski, 'In Defence of Intelligent Design' in *Oxford Handbook of Religion and Science* (ed. Philip Clayton; OUP, 2006) www.designinference.com/documents/2005.06.Defense_of_ID.pdf

[6] cf. Beckwith, *Law, Darwinism, and Public Education*; Casey Luskin, 'Is Intelligent Design Theory Really an Argument for God?' www.ideacenter.org/contentmgr/showdetails.php/id/1341.

[7] Beckwith, *Law, Darwinism, and Public Education*, p. xiii.

[8] Michael J. Behe, *The Edge of Evolution* (New York: Free Press, 2007), p. 229.

[9] William Lane Craig, *Reasonable Faith: Christian Truth and Apologetics* (Wheaton, IL: Crossway, 3rd edn, 2008), p. 157.

[10] cf. William A. Dembski, 'The Logical Underpinnings of Intelligent Design', in *Debating Design: From Darwin to DNA* (ed. William A. Dembski and

Michael Ruse; CUP, 2004) www.designinference.com/documents/2002.10.
logicalunderpinningsofID.pdf; William A. Dembski, *The Design Inference*
(CUP, 1999).

[11] cf. Michael J. Behe, *Darwin's Black Box* (New York: Free Press, 10th anniversary
edn, 2006); William A. Dembski, 'Irreducible Complexity Revisited' www.
designinference.com/documents/2004.01.Irred_Compl_Revisited.pdf.

[12] cf. Robin Collins, 'The Fine-Tuning Design Argument' http://home.messiah.
edu/~rcollins/finetech.htm; Robert C. Koons, 'Are Probabilities Indispensable to the Design Inference?' www.utexas.edu/cola/depts/philosophy/
faculty/koons/ontocomplex.pdf

[13] Henry Melvill Gwatkin, *The Knowledge of God and Its Historical Development*
(Edinburgh: T&T Clark, 3rd edn, 1918), p. 72.

[14] William A. Dembski, 'Another Way to Detect Design?' www.arn.org/docs/
dembski/wd_responsetowiscu.htm.

[15] cf. William A. Dembski, 'The Logical Underpinnings of Intelligent Design',
in *Debating Design: From Darwin to DNA* (ed. William A. Dembski and
Michael Ruse; CUP, 2004); William A. Dembski, 'Reinstating Design
within Science', in *Darwinism, Design, and Public Education* (ed. John Angus
Campbell and Stephen C. Meyer; Michigan State University Press, 2003);
William A. Dembski, 'Naturalism and Design', in *Naturalism: A Critical
Analysis* (ed. William Lane Craig and J.P. Moreland; London: Routledge,
2000).

[16] Stephen C. Meyer, 'Teleological Evolution: The Difference It Doesn't Make'
www.arn.org/docs/meyer/sm_teleologicalevolution.htm.

[17] Richard Dawkins, OP-ED, *Free Inquiry* 24:6 (October/November 2004): pp.
11–12.

[18] Richard Dawkins, *The Blind Watchmaker* (London: Penguin, 1990), p. 9.

[19] Behe, *Darwin's Black Box*, p. 39.

[20] Charles Darwin, *Origin of Species* (1872) (New York University Press, 6th edn,
1988), p. 154. Darwin sets the bar rather too high when he stipulates that
one needs to find something that 'could not possibly' be formed in this way.
Finding something that is highly unlikely to form in this way is sufficient.

[21] Richard Dawkins, *The God Delusion* (London: Bantam, 2006), p. 125.

[22] Richard Dawkins, 'Darwin Triumphant', *A Devil's Chaplain* (London: Phoenix,
2004), p. 86.

[23] Behe, *Darwin's Black Box*, p. 40.

[24] 'Self-Assembly of Bacterial Flagella' www.aip.org/mgr/png/2002/174.htm.

[25] William A. Dembski, 'Reinstating Design within Science', in *Unapologetic
Apologetics* (ed. Jay Wesley Richards; Downers Grove, IL: IVP, 2001), p. 253.

[26] Behe, p. 194.

[27] Monton, *Seeking God*, p. 115.

[28] Behe, *Darwin's Black Box*, pp. 265–6. This point is also made by Robert C.
Koons, 'The Check Is in the Mail: Why Darwinism Fails to Inspire Confidence', in *Uncommon Dissent: Intellectuals Who Find Darwinism Unconvincing*
(ed. William A. Dembski; Wilmington, DE: ISI, 2004).

[29] Franklin Harold, *The Way of the Cell: Molecules, Organisms and the Order of Life* (OUP, 2001), p. 205.

[30] William A. Dembski, *The Design Revolution* (Downers Grove, IL: IVP, 2004), p. 113.

[31] ibid., pp. 112–13.

[32] Stephen Hawking and Leonard Mlodinow, *The Grand Design* (London: Bantam, 2010), pp. 130, 144.

[33] William Lane Craig, *On Guard* (Colorado Springs, CO: David C. Cook, 2009), p. 119.

[34] Robin Collins, 'Design and the Many Worlds Hypothesis' http://home.messiah.edu/~rcollins/finetune/Craig7.htm.

[35] Gwatkin, *Knowledge of God*, p. 18.

[36] Stephen C. Meyer, 'The Scientific Status of Intelligent Design', in *Science and Evidence for Design in the Universe* (ed. Michael J. Behe, William A. Dembski and Stephen C. Meyer; San Francisco: Ignatius, 1999), p. 193.

[37] Del Ratzsch, *Science and Its Limits* (Leicester: Apollos, 2000), pp. 123–4.

[38] Bradley Monton, 'Is Intelligent Design Science? Dissecting the Dover Decision' http://philsci-archive.pitt.edu/archive/00002592/01/Methodological_Naturalism_Dover_3.doc, pp. 1, 2, 9–10.

[39] cf. Peter S. Williams, 'Reviewing the Reviewers: Pigliucci et al. on Darwin's Rotweiller and the Public Understanding of Science' www.arn.org/docs/williams/pw_designsonscience.htm; Stephen C. Meyer, 'Sauce for the Goose' in *The Nature of Nature: Examining the Role of Naturalism in Science* (ed. Bruce L. Gordon and William A. Dembski; Wilmington, DE: ISI, 2011), p. 123, n. 99.

[40] David DeWolf et al., *Traipsing into Evolution* (Seattle: Discovery Institute), pp. 32, 35.

[41] ibid., p. 35.

[42] J.P. Moreland, 'Theistic Science and Methodological Naturalism', in *The Creation Hypothesis* (ed. J.P. Moreland; Downers Grove, IL: IVP), p. 55.

[43] Larry Laudan, *Beyond Positivism and Relativism* (Boulder, CO: Westview, 1996), p. 210.

[44] Michael Ruse, *Can a Darwinian Be a Christian?* (CUP, 2004), p. 101.

[45] Dawkins, *God Delusion*, p. 59; cf. Bradley Monton, 'Is Intelligent Design Science? Dissecting the Dover Decision', http://philsci-archive.pitt.edu/archive/00002583/01/Methodological_Naturalism_2.pdf; Alvin Plantinga, 'Whether ID Is Science Isn't Semantics' www.discovery.org/scripts/viewDB/index.php?command=view&id=3331; Alvin Plantinga, 'Methodological Naturalism?', *Perspectives on Science and Christian Faith* 49 (1997): 'Part 1' www.arn.org/docs/odesign/od181/methnat181.htm and 'Part 2' www.arn.org/docs/odesign/od182/methnat182.htm; Peter S. Williams, 'If SETI Is Science and UFOlogy Is Not, Which Is Intelligent Design Theory?' www.arn.org/docs/williams/pw_setivsufology.htm; Peter S. Williams, 'The Definitional Critique of Intelligent Design Theory – Lessons from the Demise of Logical Positivism' www.arn.org/docs/williams/pw_definitionalcritique.htm.

[46] Victor J. Stenger, *The New Atheism: Taking a Stand for Science and Reason* (Amherst, NY: Prometheus, 2009), p. 102.

[47] Richard Dawkins, *Playboy* interview, 20 August 2012 http://richarddawkins. net/articles/646818-playboy-interview-with-richard-dawkins.

[48] Sam Harris, *Letter to a Christian Nation* (London: Bantam, 2007), p. 73.

[49] Michael J. Behe, 'The Modern Intelligent Design Hypothesis', *Philosophia Christi*, series 2, 3:1 (2001): p. 165.

[50] Michael J. Behe, 'Whether Intelligent Design Is Science: A Response to the Court in Kitzmiller vs Dover Area School District' www.discovery.org/ scripts/viewDB/filesDB-download.php?command=download&id=697, p. 8.

[51] 'Getting the Facts Straight: A Viewer's Guide to PBS's Evolution' (Discovery Institute, 2001) www.arn.org/docs/pbsevolution/vguide.pdf.

[52] William A. Dembski, 'Preface', *Darwin's Nemesis: Phillip Johnson and the Intelligent Design Movement* (Downers Grove, IL: IVP, 2006), pp. 17, 20.

[53] cf. Peter S. Williams, 'Raelians Successfully Clone Naturalism' www.arn.org/ docs/williams/pw_raeliansclonenaturalism.htm.

[54] cf. Wikipedia, 'Ad hoc' http://en.wikipedia.org/wiki/Ad_hoc.

[55] Monton, *Seeking God*, pp. 7–8.

8. The Moral Argument

[1] Luke Pollard, 'Does Morality Point to God?' www.bethinking.org/resource. php?ID=305&TopicID=10&CategoryID=9.

[2] William Lane Craig, *God? A Debate between a Christian and an Atheist* (OUP, 2004), p. 17.

[3] Thomas L. Carson and Paul K. Moser, *Moral Relativism: A Reader* (OUP, 2001), Introduction, p. 2.

[4] This is termed the 'cultural differences argument' by James Rachels; however, this is misleading, as its first premise could be about individual instead of cultural attitudes.

[5] Anne Jordan, Neil Lockyer and Edwin Tate, *Philosophy of Religion for A Level* (Cheltenham: Nelson Thornes, 2004), p. 88. Note that this quote appears to endorse the second premise of the moral argument.

[6] Russ Shafer-Landau, *Whatever Happened to Good and Evil?* (OUP, 2004), pp. 68, 70.

[7] Rebecca Massey-Chase, 'An Argument on the Moral Argument', in *Philosophy Now* 57 (September/October 2006): p. 29 www.philosophynow.org/issue57/ 57pollard-masseychase.htm.

[8] Paul Copan, *True for You, but Not for Me* (Minneapolis, MN: Bethany House, 1998), p. 35.

[9] Peter Kreeft and Ronald Tacelli, *Handbook of Christian Apologetics* (Crowborough: Monarch, 1995).

[10] Francis J. Beckwith and Gregory Koukl, *Relativism: Feet Firmly Planted in Mid-Air* (Grand Rapids, MI: Baker, 1998), p. 63.

[11] Stephen Law, *The War for Children's Minds* (London: Routledge, 2006), pp. 88–9.

12 Kai Nielson www.leaderu.com/offices/billcraig/docs/craig-nielsen2.html.

13 C.S. Lewis, *Mere Christianity* (London: HarperCollins, 2001), p. 21.

14 Michael Ruse, 'Evolution and Ethics', in *The Nature of Nature: Examining the Role of Naturalism in Science* (ed. Bruce L. Gordon and William A. Dembski; Wilmington, DE: ISI, 2011), p. 862.

15 Beckwith and Koukl, *Relativism*, p. 166.

16 H.P. Owen, 'Why Morality Implies the Existence of God', edited extract from *The Moral Argument for Christian Theism* (George Allen & Unwin, 1965) in *Philosophy of Religion: A Guide and Anthology* (ed. Brian Davies; OUP, 2000), p. 648.

17 William Lane Craig, *Is Goodness without God Good Enough? A Debate On Faith, Secularism, And Ethics* (ed. Robert K. Garcia & Nathan L. King; New York: Rowman & Littlefield, 2009), p. 169.

18 Jordan, Lockyer and Tate, *Philosophy of Religion*, p. 89.

19 Copan, *True for You*, p. 45.

20 Richard Dawkins, 'God's Utility Function', *Scientific American*, November 1995, p. 85, my italics.

21 Richard Dawkins, *The God Delusion* (London: Bantam, 2006), p. 232.

22 Stephen Unwin, 'Dawkins Needs to Show Some Doubt', *Guardian Online* www.guardian.co.uk/commentisfree/story/0,,1883586,00.html.

23 Plato, *Euthyphro* 10a, *Plato: The Collected Dialogues of Plato* (ed. Edith Hamilton and Huntingdon Cairns; trans. Lane Cooper; Princeton University Press, 1961), p. 178.

24 William Lane Craig, *God, Are You There?* (Atlanta, GA: RZIM, 1999), pp. 38–9.

9. The Ontological Argument

1 Stephen T. Davis, *God, Reason and Theistic Proofs* (Edinburgh University Press, 1997), p. 42.

2 Colin McGinn, *The Making of a Philosopher* (London: Scribner, 2002), p. 11.

3 ibid.

4 ibid.

5 ibid., p. 237.

6 Trent Dougherty, 'Concise Introduction to the Modal Ontological Argument for The Existence of God' quoted at www.doxa.ws/Ontological/modal.html.

7 Thomas V. Morris, *Our Idea of God* (University of Notre Dame Press, 1991), p. 35.

8 ibid., p. 37.

9 Alvin Plantinga, *God, Freedom and Evil* (Grand Rapids, MI: Eerdmans, 1977), from Michael Peterson et al., *Philosophy of Religion: Selected Readings* (OUP, 1996), p. 158.

10 Plantinga, *God, Freedom and Evil*, p. 163.

11 ibid., p. 159.

12 cf. William Lane Craig, 'The Ontological Argument', in *To Everyone an Answer: A Case for the Christian Worldview* (ed. Francis J. Beckwith, William Lane Craig and J.P. Moreland; Downers Grove, IL: IVP, 2004), p. 128.

13 C. Stephen Evans, *Philosophy of Religion* (Downers Grove, IL: IVP, 2001), p. 50.

14 On the coherence of the concept of God, cf. Thomas V. Morris, *Our Idea of God* (University of Notre Dame Press, 1991) and Charles Taliaferro, 'The coherence of theism', in *The Rationality of Theism* (ed. Paul Copan and Paul K. Moser; London: Routledge, 2003).

15 Charles Hartshorne, 'A Recent Ontological Argument', in *The Philosophy of Religion Reader* (ed. Chad Meister; London: Routledge, 2008), p. 311.

16 Charles Taliaferro, *Contemporary Philosophy of Religion* (Oxford: Blackwell, 2001), p. 381.

17 Alvin Plantinga, *The Nature of Necessity* (OUP, 1974), p. 221.

18 Plantinga, *Nature of Necessity*, p. 163.

19 Taliaferro, *Contemporary Philosophy of Religion*, p. 379.

20 Klemens Kappel in the Q&A time of his debate with William Lane Craig (18 April 2012); cf. www.youtube.com/watch?v=uauZy6FDRXA.

21 Trent Dougherty, 'Concise Introduction to the Modal Ontological Argument for the Existence of God' www.abarnett.demon.co.uk/atheism/ontol.html.

22 cf. www.existence-of-god.com/paradox-of-the-stone.html.

23 Richard Carrier, *Sense and Goodness without God* (Bloomington, IN: Author House, 2005), p. 276.

24 Craig, 'The Ontological Argument', pp. 129–30.

25 Yujin Nagasawa, *The Existence of God: A Philosophical Introduction* (Oxford: Routledge, 2011), p. 31.

26 Peter S. Williams, 'Peter S. Williams PWNS Cocky Student on the Ontological Argument' www.youtube.com/watch?v=c6o7UEPODVU.

27 Craig, 'The Ontological Argument', pp. 130–31.

28 cf. William Lane Craig, 'Biblical Basis of God's Unique Aseity' www.reasonable-faith.org/site/News2?page=NewsArticle&id=8793; 'Van Inwagen on Uncreated Beings' www.reasonablefaith.org/site/News2?page=NewsArticle&id=9203.

29 Craig, 'The Ontological Argument', p. 131. cf. William Lane Craig, 'Question 51: The Ontological Argument' www.reasonablefaith.org/site/News2?page=NewsArticle&id=6155 and Thomas P. Flint and Alfred J. Freddoso, 'Maximal Power' www.nd.edu/~afreddos/papers/mp.htm.

30 Douglas Groothuis, *Christian Apologetics* (Nottingham: Apollos, 2011), p. 202.

31 Craig, 'The Ontological Argument', p. 136.

32 Richard Dawkins, *The God Delusion* (London: Bantam, 2006), p. 80.

33 ibid.

34 ibid., p. 81.

35 ibid.

36 ibid., p. 82.

37 Groothuis, *Christian Apologetics*, p. 186.

38 Nagasawa, *The Existence of God*, p. 33.

Endnotes

[39] Stephen T. Davis, 'The Ontological Argument', in *Rationality of Theism* (ed. Copan and Moser), p. 94.

[40] Jim Holt, 'Beyond Belief', *New York Times*; cf. Trent Dougherty, 'Concise Introduction to the Modal Ontological Argument for the Existence of God' www.abarnett.demon.co.uk/atheism/ontol.html.

[41] Immanuel Kant, *Critique of Pure Reason* (ed. Norman Kemp Smith; London: Macmillan, 1929), p. 61.

[42] Dawkins, *God Delusion*, p. 83.

[43] Hartshorne, 'A Recent Ontological Argument', p. 311.

[44] Davis, 'The Ontological Argument', pp. 98–9.

[45] Nagasawa, *The Existence of God*, p. 25.

[46] Keith Yandell, 'David Hume on Meaning, Verification and Natural Theology', in *In Defence of Natural Theology: A Post-Humean Assessment* (ed. James F. Sennett and Douglas Groothuis; Downers Grove, IL: IVP, 2005), p. 72.

[47] Michael Peterson et al., *Reason and Religious Belief* (OUP, 1991), p. 73.

[48] Christopher Hitchens, *God Is Not Great* (London: Atlantic, 2007), p. 265.

[49] Peter van Inwagen, 'Ontological Arguments', in *Philosophy of Religion: A Guide to the Subject* (ed. Brian Davies; London: Continuum, 1998), pp. 57–8.

[50] ibid., p. 58.

[51] Nagasawa, *Existence of God*, p. 40.

[52] Jay Wesley Richards, 'Divine Simplicity: The Good, the Bad, and the Ugly', in *For Faith and Clarity: Philosophical Contributions to Christian Theology* (ed. James K. Beilby; Grand Rapids, MI: Baker Academic, 2006), p. 169.

[53] Yujin Nagasawa, 'Divine Omniscience and Knowledge De Se' www.thedivineconspiracy.org/Z3214A.pdf.

[54] Josef Seifert in *Great Thinkers on Great Questions* (ed. Roy Abraham Varghese; Oxford: OneWorld, 1998), p. 131.

[55] Robin Collins, 'God, Design and Fine-Tuning' http://home.messiah.edu/~rcollins/Fine-tuning/Revised%20Version%20of%20Fine-tuning%20for%20anthology.doc. (Collins notes: 'To avoid certain potential counterexamples, one might need to restrict the principle to apply only to those cases in which H_1 has some independent plausibility apart from evidence E, or was at least not merely constructed to account for E. This is certainly the case with theism'.)

[56] Craig, 'The Ontological Argument', p. 136.

[57] cf. Norman L. Geisler, *Baker Encyclopedia of Christian Apologetics* (Grand Rapids, MI: Baker, 1999), pp. 580–83; Douglas Groothuis, *Christian Apologetics: A Comprehensive Case for Biblical Faith* (Nottingham: Apollos, 2011), pp. 326–9.

[58] cf. William Lane Craig and J.P. Moreland, eds, *Naturalism: A Critical Analysis* (London: Routledge, 2000); Stewart Goetz and Charles Taliaferro, *Naturalism* (Cambridge: Eerdmans, 2008); Angus Menuge, *Agents under Fire* (Oxford: Rowman & Littlefield, 2004); Victor Reppert, *C.S. Lewis' Dangerous Idea: In Defence of the Argument from Reason* (Downers Grove, IL: IVP, 2003).

411

10. Religious Experience

[1] Philip Van der Elst, *C.S. Lewis: A Short Introduction* (London: Continuum, 2005), p. 33.

[2] Timothy Keller, *The Reason for God* (New York: Riverhead, 2008), p. 53.

[3] A.C. Ewing, *The Fundamental Questions of Philosophy* (London: Routledge & Kegan Paul, 1968), p. 238.

[4] Norman L. Geisler and Winfried Corduan, *Philosophy of Religion* (Eugene, OR: Wipf & Stock, 2nd edn, 2003), p. 16.

[5] ibid., p. 17.

[6] ibid., p. 28.

[7] ibid., p. 37.

[8] ibid., p. 35.

[9] ibid.

[10] ibid., p. 37.

[11] H.G. Wells, quoted by Leslie D. Weatherhead, *Psychology, Religion and Healing* (London: Hodder & Stoughton, 1955), p. 413.

[12] Richard Swinburne, *The Existence of God* (Oxford: Clarendon, revd edn, 1991), p. 246.

[13] Charles Taliaferro, *Contemporary Philosophy of Religion* (Oxford: Blackwell, 2001), p. 277.

[14] ibid., p. 279.

[15] ibid.

[16] William Lane Craig, 'A Reply to Objections', in *Does God Exist?* (ed. Stan W. Wallace; Aldershot: Ashgate, 2003), p. 181.

[17] cf. Richard Swinburne, *The Existence of God* (Oxford: Clarendon, revd edn, 1991), p. 252.

[18] Swinburne, *Existence of God*, p. 249.

[19] ibid., p. 250.

[20] William P. Alston, 'Why I Am a Christian', *Truth Journal* http://leaderu.com/truth/1truth23.html.

[21] cf. Colin J. Humphreys, *Miracles of Exodus: A Scientist's Discovery of the Extraordinary Natural Causes of the Biblical Stories* (New York: HarperCollins, 2003).

[22] cf. Peter S. Williams, *Understanding Jesus: Five Ways to Spiritual Enlightenment* (Carlisle: Paternoster, 2011).

[23] cf. Peter S. Williams, *The Case for Angels* (Carlisle: Paternoster, 2002).

[24] Gary R. Habermas, 'Our Personal God: God Interacts with Us' www.garyhabermas.com/books/why_believe/whybelieve.htm#ch29.

[25] *The Independent on Sunday*, 7 January 2007, p. 15.

[26] Andrew Wilson, *Deluded by Dawkins? A Christian Response to the God Delusion* (Eastbourne: Kingsway, 2007), pp. 47–8.

[27] Swinburne, *Existence of God*, p. 251.

[28] ibid.

[29] ibid.

[30] William P. Alston, *Perceiving God: The Epistemology of Religious Experience* (Cornell University Press, 1993), p. 11.

[31] Saint Teresa, quoted by Alston, *Experience of God*, p. 13.

[32] C. Stephen Layman, *Letters to Doubting Thomas* (OUP, 2007), pp. 55–6.

[33] Alston, *Perceiving God*, p. 24.

[34] ibid., p. 257.

[35] Taliaferro, *Contemporary Philosophy of Religion*, p. 265.

[36] ibid.

[37] Michael Peterson et al., *Philosophy of Religion: Selected Readings* (OUP, 1996), p. 5.

[38] Keith E. Yandell, 'Religious Experience', in *A Companion to the Philosophy of Religion* (ed. Philip L. Quinn and Charles Taliaferro: Oxford: Blackwell, 1999), p. 371.

[39] Alston, *Perceiving God*, p. 16, n. 5.

[40] H.D. Lewis, *Philosophy of Religion* (London: English Universities Press, 1973), p. 144.

[41] Malcolm Gladwell, *Blink* (London: Penguin, 2005), pp. 9–10.

[42] Julie Wheldon, 'The Blind's "Sixth Sense"', *Daily Mail*, 1 November 2005, p. 3.

[43] ibid.

[44] William P. Alston, 'Christian Experience and Christian Belief' in *Faith and Rationality: Reason and Belief in God* (ed. Alvin Plantinga and Nicholas Wolterstorff, London: University of Notre Dame Press, 1983), p. 103.

[45] Alston, *Perceiving God*, p. 280.

[46] Paul D. Feinberg, *Five Views on Apologetics* (ed. Steven B. Cowan; Grand Rapids, MI: Zondervan), p. 161.

[47] Joshua Hoffman and Gary S. Rosenkrantz, *Substance: Its Nature and Existence* (London: Routledge, 1997), p. 7.

[48] Norman L. Geisler and Winfried Corduan, *Philosophy of Religion* (Eugene, OR: Wipf & Stock, 2nd edn, 2003), p. 76.

[49] ibid.

[50] Alvin Plantinga in *Great Thinkers on Great Questions* (ed. Roy Abraham Varghese; Oxford: OneWorld, 2009), p. 120.

[51] Stephen T. Davis, *God, Reason and Theistic Proofs* (Edinburgh University Press, 1997), p. 193.

[52] Richard Swinburne, 'Evidence for God', in *Beyond Reasonable Doubt: Evidence for God in the 1990's* (ed. Gillian Ryeland; Norwich: Canterbury Press, 1991), pp. 13–14.

[53] Swinburne, *Existence of God*, p. 260.

[54] ibid., pp. 273–4.

[55] H.H. Price, quoted by Charles Taliaferro, *Contemporary Philosophy of Religion* (Oxford: Blackwell, 2001), p. 272.

[56] Van der Elst, *C.S. Lewis*, p. 33.

[57] J.P. Moreland, *Scaling the Secular City* (Grand Rapids, MI: Baker, 1987), p. 235.

[58] ibid., p. 240.

[59] Alston, *Perceiving God*, p. 146.

[60] ibid., p. 153.

[61] ibid., pp. 183.

[62] ibid., p. 195.

[63] Taliaferro, *Contemporary Philosophy of Religion*, p. 274.

[64] Alston, *Perceiving God*, pp. 198–9.

[65] ibid., p. 67.

[66] ibid., p. 33.

[67] Moreland, *Secular City*, p. 238.

[68] Taliaferro, Contemporary *Philosophy of Religion*, p. 274.

[69] Alston, *Perceiving God*, p. 201.

[70] For example, Paul didn't believe in Jesus before meeting him on the road to Damascus; some atheists report experiencing angels or God (which experience can play a role in their conversion to Christianity); some Muslims report meeting Jesus in dreams that lead them to convert to Christianity, etc.

[71] Layman, *Letters to Doubting Thomas*, p. 61.

[72] Alston, *Perceiving God*, pp. 170–71.

[73] ibid., p. 171.

[74] ibid., p. 52.

[75] ibid., p. 61.

[76] ibid.

[77] Keith E. Yandell quoted by Taliaferro, *Contemporary Philosophy of Religion*, p. 267.

[78] William P. Alston, 'Why Should There Not Be Experience of God?', in *Philosophy of Religion: A Guide and Anthology* (ed. Brian Davies; OUP, 2000), p. 386.

[79] Moreland, *Secular City*, p. 227.

[80] R. Douglas Geivett, 'The Evidential Value of Religious Experience', in *The Rationality of Theism* (ed. Paul Copan and Paul K. Moser; London: Routledge, 2003), p. 183.

[81] Moreland, *Secular City*, p. 232.

[82] Alston, *Perceiving God*, p. 35.

[83] Basil Mitchell, *The Justification of Religious Belief* (London: Macmillan, 1973), p. 42.

[84] Moreland, *Secular City*, pp. 233–4.

[85] Richard Dawkins, *The God Delusion* (London: Bantam, 2006), p. 90.

[86] ibid., p. 92.

[87] Evelyn Underhill, *The Soul's Delight: Selected Writings of Evelyn Underhill* (ed. Keith Beasley-Topliffe; Nashville, TN: Upper Room, 1998), pp. 13, 45, 68.

Part III: The Philosophy of Mind

[1] Jerry Fodor, 'The Big Idea: Can There Be a Science of Mind?', *Times Literary Supplement*, 3 July 1992, p. 5.

[2] Tom Wolfe, 'Sorry, but Your Soul Just Died' www.independent.co.uk/arts-entertainment/sorry-but-your-soul-just-died-1276509.html.

[3] ibid.

⁴ cf. John Foster, *The Immaterial Self: A Defence of the Cartesian Dualist Conception of the Mind* (London: Routledge, 2005).
⁵ cf. http://en.wikipedia.org/wiki/Cutting_off_the_nose_to_spite_the_face.

11. The Mind–Body Problem

¹ Jacques Maritain, *An Introduction to Philosophy* (New York: Continuum, 2005), p. 111.
² John W. Cooper, *Body, Soul and Life Everlasting: Biblical Anthropology and the Monism–Dualism Debate* (Leicester: Apollos, 1989), p. xvi.
³ cf. Matthew 10:28; Luke 12:4–5; 20:38; 23:43; 2 Corinthians 5; Philippians 1:23–24; Revelation 6:9–10.
⁴ Hugo Meynall, 'People and Life after Death', in *Philosophy of Religion: A Guide to the Subject* (ed. Brian Davies; New York: Continuum, 2003), p. 286.
⁵ Paul Copan, *How Do You Know You're Not Wrong?* (Grand Rapids, MI: Baker, 2005), p. 96.
⁶ Owen Flanagan, *The Problem of the Soul: Two Visions of the Mind and How to Reconcile Them* (New York: Basic Books, 2002), pp. 3, 77.
⁷ Steven Lovell, 'C.S. Lewis's Case against Naturalism' at http://myweb.tiscali.co.uk/cslphilos/CSLnat.htm.
⁸ Bertrand Russell, 'What I Believe', *Why I Am Not A Christian* (London: Routledge, 1996), pp. 42, 47.
⁹ Stewart Goetz and Charles Taliaffero, *Naturalism* (Grand Rapids, MI: Eerdmans, 2008), p. 7.
¹⁰ Richard Swinburne, *Was Jesus God?* (OUP, 2008), p. 15.
¹¹ Barry Stroud, 'The Charm of Naturalism', *Proceedings and Addresses of the American Philosophical Society* 70 (1996): p. 44.
¹² C.E.M. Joad, *Guide to Philosophy* (London: Victor Gollancz, 1946), p. 496.
¹³ J.P. Moreland, 'Physicalism, Naturalism and the Nature of Human Persons', in *To Everyone an Answer: A Case for the Christian Worldview* (ed. Francis J. Beckwith, William Lane Craig and J.P. Moreland; Downers Grove, IL: IVP, 2004), p. 225.
¹⁴ Julian Baggini, *Atheism: A Very Short Introduction* (OUP, 2003), p. 18.
¹⁵ ibid.
¹⁶ ibid., p. 19.
¹⁷ ibid.
¹⁸ ibid.
¹⁹ Christopher R. Grace and J.P. Moreland, 'Intelligent Design Psychology and Evolutionary Psychology on Consciousness: Turning Water into Wine', *Journal of Psychology and Theology* (22 March 2002).
²⁰ Baggini, *Atheism*, p. 19.
²¹ ibid., p. 21. cf. Gary R. Habermas and J.P Moreland, *Beyond Death* (Wheaton, IL: Good News, 1998).
²² ibid., p. 18.

23 ibid., p. 77.

24 ibid., my italics.

25 ibid., p. 28.

26 C.S. Lewis, 'The Empty Universe', *Present Concerns* (London: Fount, 1991), p. 81.

27 ibid.

28 ibid., p. 83.

29 ibid., p. 85.

30 Daniel Dennett, *A Companion to the Philosophy of Mind* (Oxford: Blackwell, 1995), quoted by William Hasker, *The Emergent Self* (Cornell University Press, 1999), Preface, p. x.

31 J.P. Moreland, 'The Soul and Life Everlasting', in *Philosophy of Religion* (ed. William Lane Craig; Edinburgh University Press, 2002), p. 435.

32 J.P. Moreland in Lee Strobel, *The Case for a Creator* (Grand Rapids, MI: Zondervan, 2007), p. 255.

33 Keith Ward, *The Big Questions in Science and Religion* (West Conshohocken, PA: Templeton, 2008), p. 28.

34 Moreland, 'Physicalism, Naturalism and the Nature of Human Persons', p. 226.

35 Ward, *Big Questions*, p. 134.

36 Roy Abraham Varghese, *The Wonder of the World* (Fountain Hills, AZ: TYR, 2003), p. 298.

37 John Haldane, *An Intelligent Person's Guide to Religion* (London: Duckworth, 2003), p. 23.

38 Nigel Warburton, *Philosophy: The Basics* (London: Routledge, 2004), pp. 129–30.

39 John Searle in Varghese, *Wonder of the World*, p. 13.

40 William Lane Craig and J.P. Moreland, *Philosophical Foundations for a Christian Worldview* (Downers Grove, IL: IVP, 2003), p. 231.

41 Richard Swinburne, 'The Origins of Consciousness', in *Cosmic Beginnings and Human Ends* (ed. Clifford N. Matthews and Roy Abraham Varghese; Chicago: Open Court, 1994), p. 358.

42 J.P. Moreland, 'The Argument from Consciousness', in *The Rationality of Theism* (ed. Paul Copan and Paul K. Moser; London: Routledge, 2003), p. 217.

43 Jaegwon Kim, *Mind in a Physical World*, p. 96, quoted by Moreland, 'The Argument from Consciousness', p. 217.

44 Daniel Dennett, *Consciousness Explained* (London: Penguin, 1993), p. 365.

45 Charles Taliaferro, 'Where Do Thoughts Come From?', in *The Big Argument: Does God Exist?* (ed. John Ashton and Michael Westcott; Green Forest, AR: Master Books, 2006), pp. 156–7.

46 Chris Eliasmith, 'Dualism' http://en.wikipedia.org/wiki/Dualism_(philosophy_of_mind).

47 Craig and Moreland, *Foundations*, p. 236.

48 Warburton, *Philosophy*, p. 136.

49 Moreland, 'Physicalism, Naturalism and the Nature of Human Persons', pp. 229–30.

50 Habermas and Moreland, *Beyond Death* (Wheaton, IL: Good News, 1998), p. 49.

51 ibid., p. 51.

52 Fred I. Dretske, *Naturalizing the Mind* (MIT Press, 1995), p. 65.

53 Habermas and Moreland, *Beyond Death*, p. 50.

54 Taliaferro, 'Where Do Thoughts Come From?', p. 158.

55 Richard Carrier, *Sense and Goodness without God* (Bloomington, IN: Author House, 2005), p. 150.

56 ibid.

57 ibid.

58 ibid., p. 146.

59 ibid., p. 135, my italics.

60 Anthony O'Hear, *Philosophy* (London: Continuum, 2001), p. 87.

61 Moreland, 'Physicalism, Naturalism and the Nature of Human Persons', p. 211.

62 William Hasker, 'Persons as Emergent Substances', in *Soul, Body and Survival* (ed. Kevin Corcoran; Cornell University Press, 2001), p. 107.

63 C. Stephen Evans, 'Separable Souls: Dualism, Selfhood, and the Possibility of Life after Death', *Christian Scholar's Review* 34:3 (Spring 2005).

64 Christopher R. Grace and J.P. Moreland, 'Intelligent Design Psychology and Evolutionary Psychology on Consciousness: Turning Water into Wine', *Journal of Psychology and Theology* (22 March 2002).

65 David Chalmers http://fragments.consc.net/djc/2005/09/jaegwon_kim_com.html, my italics.

66 cf. http://philpapers.org/surveys/results.pl.

67 Jerry Fodor, 'The Big Idea: Can There Be a Science of Mind?', *Times Literary Supplement*, 3 July 1992, p. 5.

68 Christof Koch, 'Consciousness Is Everywhere' www.huffingtonpost.com/christof-koch/consciousness-is-everywhere_b_1784047.html.

69 Susan Blackmore, *Conversations on Consciounsess* (OUP, 2005), pp. 3–4.

70 Matthew D. Lieberman, 'Free Will: Weighing Truth and Experience: Do Our Beliefs Matter?' *Psychology Today*, 22 March 2012 www.psychologytoday.com/blog/social-brain-social-mind/201203/free-will-weighing-truth-and-experience.

71 Steven Pinker, 'The Mystery of Consciousness', *Time*, 19 January 2007 www.time.com/time/magazine/article/0,9171,1580394-1,00.html.

72 Richard Dawkins, quoted by Varghese, *Wonder of the World*, p. 56.

73 John Searle, 'Minding the Brain', *New York Review of Books*, 2 November 2006.

74 David Chalmers in Blackmore, *Conversations on Consciousness*, pp. 38, 42.

75 Mathew Iredale, 'Putting Descartes before the Horse', *The Philosopher's Magazine* 42:3 (2008): p. 40.

76 Frank Dilley, quoted by Iredale, 'Putting Descartes before the Horse', p. 40.

77 John Heil, *Philosophy of Mind: A Contemporary Introduction* (London: Routledge, 1998), p. 53.

78 Anthony Freeman, 'What Is a Thought?', in *Big Questions in Science* (ed. Ward), p. 48.

[79] Joshua Stern, quoted by Larry Witham, *By Design: Science and the Search for God* (San Francisco: Encounter, 2003), p. 196.

[80] C.E.M. Joad, *The Recovery of Belief* (London: Faber and Faber, 1951), pp. 189–90.

[81] Freeman, 'What Is a Thought?', p. 49.

[82] Blackmore, *Conversations on Consciousness*, p. 4.

[83] Keith E. Yandell, 'A Defence of Dualism', in *Philosophy of Religion* (ed. Craig), p. 482.

[84] Edward Fesser, *Philosophy of Mind: A Short Introduction* (Oxford: OneWorld, 2005), p. 62.

[85] Goetz and Taliaffero, *Naturalism*, p. 9.

[86] William Lycan, quoted by Mathew Iredale, 'Putting Descartes before the Horse', p. 40.

[87] Ward, ed., *Big Questions*, p. 29, my italics.

[88] Lieberman, 'Free Will: Weighing Truth and Experience: Do Our Beliefs Matter?'.

[89] Colin McGinn, quoted by Mathew Iredale, 'Putting Descartes before the Horse', p. 40.

[90] Karl Popper and John C. Eccles, *The Self and Its Brain* (London: Routledge, 1984), p. 97.

[91] John Searle, *Rediscovery of the Mind* (Cambridge, MA: MIT Press, 1992), pp. 3–4.

[92] Georges Rey, *Contemporary Philosophy of Mind* (Oxford: Blackwell, 1997), p. 21.

[93] One wonders how Rey would handle the suggestion that any ultimate explanation of material phenomena 'will have to be' in non-physical terms, or else it wouldn't be an explanation of it? Rey appears to be assuming that any ultimate explanation of one type of reality must be framed in terms of a different type of reality – but this seems to me to be a highly questionable definition of explanation.

[94] Lieberman, 'Free Will: Weighing Truth and Experience: Do Our Beliefs Matter?'

[95] Daniel Dennett, quoted by John Foster in Varghese, *Wonder of the World*, p. 61.

[96] Ned Block, 'Consciousness', in *A Companion to Philosophy of Mind* (ed. Samuel Guttenplan; Malden, MA: Blackwell, 1994), p. 211.

[97] Ned Block, www.edge.org/q2005/q05_3.html.

[98] ibid.

[99] A.G. Cairns-Smith, *Evolving the Mind* (CUP, 1996), Preface.

[100] ibid., Preface.

[101] ibid., p. 248.

[102] ibid., p. 249, my italics.

[103] ibid., Preface.

[104] Michael Lockwood, 'Consciousness and Quantum Worlds', in *Consciousness: New Philosophical Perspectives* (ed. Q. Smith and A. Jokic; Oxford: Clarendon, 2003), p. 447.

[105] John C. Eccles and Daniel N. Robinson, *The Wonder of Being Human: Our Brain and Our Mind* (New York: Free Press, 1984), p. 36.

[106] A.J. Ayer, 'The Concept of a Person and Other Essays', quoted by Basil Mitchell, *The Justification of Religious Belief* (London: Macmillan, 1973), p. 72.

[107] Richard Dawkins, *The God Delusion* (London: Bantam, 2006), pp. 179–80. It is of course incorrect to say that monists *per se* believe mind to be a manifestation of matter, as the existence of spiritual/idealist monists like Hindus or Spinoza demonstrates. It would be pedantic to point out that a spirit inhabiting a body is precisely not a disembodied spirit. What Dawkins presumably means is that many dualists conceive of the mind as something that can become disembodied.

[108] Jaegwon Kim, *Philosophy of Mind* (Boulder, CO: Westview, 1996), quoted by Goetz and Taliaferro, *Naturalism*, p. 29.

[109] Moreland, *Philosophy of Religion* (ed. Craig), p. 438.

[110] Foster, in Varghese, *Wonder of the World*, pp. 65–7.

[111] William Hasker, 'Philosophical Contributions to Theological Anthropology', in *For Faith and Clarity* (ed. James K. Beilby; Grand Rapids, MI: Baker, 2006), p. 248.

[112] Curt Ducasse, 'In Defense of Dualism', in *Dimensions of Mind* (ed. Sidney Hook; New York: Collier, 1961), pp. 88–9.

[113] William Lycan, 'Giving Dualism Its Due' www.unc.edu/~ujanel/Du.htm.

[114] Goetz and Taliaferro, *Naturalism*, p. 49.

[115] ibid., p. 32.

[116] Lockwood, 'Consciousness and Quantum Worlds', p. 447.

12. The Mind and Its Creator

[1] J.P. Moreland, 'The Argument from Consciousness', in *The Rationality of Theism* (ed. Paul Copan and Paul K. Moser; London: Routledge, 2003), p. 204.

[2] *Time*, 7 April 1980, p. 66.

[3] Charles Taliaferro, 'Where Do Thoughts Come From?' in *The Big Argument: Does God Exist?* (ed. John Ashton and Michael Westcott; Green Forest, AR: Master Books, 2006), p. 159.

[4] Thomas Nagel, *Mind and Cosmos: Why the Materialist Neo-Darwinian Conception of Nature Is Almost Certainly False* (Oxford University Press, 2012), p. 41.

[5] Colin McGinn, *The Mysterious Flame* (New York: Basic Books, 1999), pp. 13–14.

[6] B.F. Skinner, 'Can Psychology Be a Science of the Mind?', *American Psychologist* 45:1207 (1990).

[7] D.M. Armstrong, *A Materialist Theory of Mind* (London: Routledge & Kegan Paul, 1968), p. 30.

[8] Susan Blackmore, 'What Is Consciousness?', in *Big Questions in Science* (ed. Harriet Swain; Jonathan Cape, 2002), pp. 39–40.

[9] J.P. Moreland in *The Case for a Creator* (ed. Lee Strobel; Grand Rapids, MI: Zondervan, 2007), p. 264.

[10] J.P. Moreland, 'Searle's Biological Naturalism and the Argument from Consciousness', in *Philosophy of Religion: A Reader and Guide* (ed. William Lane Craig; Edinburgh University Press, 2002), p. 103.

[11] Angus J. Menuge, *Agents under Fire* (Oxford: Rowman & Littlefield, 2004), p. 84.

[12] Christof Koch, 'Consciousnesses Is Everywhere' www.huffingtonpost.com/christof-koch/consciousness-is-everywhere_b_1784047.html.

[13] Richard Dawkins, *The God Delusion* (London: Bantam, 2006), p. 373.

[14] Jaegwon Kim, *Minds in a Physical World* (MIT Press, 1998).

[15] Moreland, 'Searle's Biological Naturalism and the Argument from Consciousness', p. 157.

[16] Robert M. Adams, 'Flavors, Colors, and God', in *Contemporary Perspectives on Religious Epistemology* (ed. R. Douglas Geivett and Brendan Sweetman; OUP, 1992), p. 225.

[17] ibid., p. 226.

[18] ibid., pp. 226–7.

[19] Richard Swinburne, *The Existence of God* (Oxford: Clarendon, 2004), p. 171.

[20] John Locke, *An Essay Concerning Human Understanding* (ed. Peter H. Nidditch; Oxford: Clarendon, 1975), IV, iii, p. 29.

[21] Adams, 'Flavors, Colors, and God', p. 231.

[22] ibid., p. 238.

[23] ibid.

[24] Anthony O'Hear, *Philosophy* (London: Continuum, 2001), p. 13.

[25] ibid., pp. 12, 19, 85, 86.

[26] Paul M. Churchland, *Matter and Consciousness* (MIT Press, 1988), p. 21.

[27] C.S. Lewis, *Miracles* (London: Fount, 1998), p. 11.

[28] ibid., p. 14.

[29] Henry Melvill Gwatkin, *The Knowledge of God* (Edinburgh: T&T Clark, 3rd edn, 1918), p. 65.

[30] J.B.S. Haldane, 'When I Am Dead', *Possible Worlds and Other Essays* (London: Chatto & Windus, 1927), p. 209.

[31] Hugo Meynall, in *Great Thinkers on Great Questions* (ed. Roy Abraham Varghese; Oxford: OneWorld, 1998), p. 46.

[32] Lewis, *Miracles*, p. 14.

[33] ibid.

[34] ibid., p. 15.

[35] ibid.

[36] ibid.

[37] ibid, pp. 15–20.

[38] ibid., p. 26.

[39] William Hasker, *The Emergent Self* (Ithaca: Cornell University Press, 1999), p. 71.

[40] C.S. Lewis, 'Religion without Dogma?', *Timeless at Heart* (London: Fount, 1991), p. 92.

[41] Hasker, *Emergent Self*, pp. 67–8.

[42] William Hasker, 'Philosophical Contributions to Theological Anthropology' in *For Faith and Clarity* (ed. James K. Beilby; Grand Rapids, MI: Baker, 2006), p. 246.

⁴³ 'Dr Reppert on the "Argument from Reason"' http://go.qci.tripod.com/ Reppert-interview.htm.

⁴⁴ Victor Reppert, 'Several Formulations of the Argument from Reason', *Philosophia Christi* 5:1 (2003), p. 24.

⁴⁵ John Searle, *Minds, Brains, and Science* (Harvard University Press, 1984), pp. 32–3.

⁴⁶ John Searle, 'Do Brains Make Minds?', on *Closer to Truth*, quoted in Lee Strobel, *The Case for a Creator* (Grand Rapids, MI: Zondervan, 2007), p. 248.

⁴⁷ Matt Lawrence, *Like a Splinter in Your Mind: The Philosophy behind the Matrix Trilogy* (Oxford: Blackwell, 2004), p. 51.

⁴⁸ Angus Menuge, personal correspondence, January 2007.

⁴⁹ John Searle in Blackmore, *Conversations on Consciousness* (OUP, 2005), p. 210.

⁵⁰ John Polkinghorne, *Reason and Reality* (London: SPCK, 1992), p. 10.

⁵¹ ibid.

⁵² Aristotle, quoted by Mortimer J. Adler, *Aristotle for Everybody* (New York: Simon & Schuster, 1997), pp. 183–4.

⁵³ Lewis, *Miracles*, p. 16.

⁵⁴ ibid.

⁵⁵ Victor Reppert, 'Defending the Dangerous Idea: An Update on Lewis's Argument from Reason', in *C.S. Lewis as Philosopher: Truth, Goodness and Beauty* (ed. David Baggett, Gary R. Habermas and Jerry L. Walls; Downers Grover, IL: IVP Academic, 2008), p. 58.

⁵⁶ ibid.

⁵⁷ ibid.

⁵⁸ Reppert, 'Defending the Dangerous Idea', p. 59.

⁵⁹ Colin McGinn, *The Problem of Consciousness* (Oxford: Blackwell, 1991), p. 34.

⁶⁰ John Searle, *The Rediscovery of the Mind* (MIT Press, 1992), p. 51.

⁶¹ A.E. Taylor, *Does God Exist?* (London: Fontana, 1961), pp. 37–8.

⁶² C.E.M. Joad, *The Recovery of Belief* (London: Faber and Faber, 1951), p. 42.

⁶³ C.S. Lewis, 'De Futilitate', *Christian Reflections* (London: Fount, 1991), pp. 87–8.

⁶⁴ C.S. Lewis, *The Discarded Image* (CUP, 1964), pp. 165–6.

⁶⁵ Dallas Willard, 'Knowledge and Naturalism', in *Naturalism: A Critical Analysis* (ed. William Lane Craig and J.P. Moreland; London: Routledge, 2001), p. 39.

⁶⁶ J.P. Moreland, *Scaling the Secular City: A Defense of Christianity* (Grand Rapids, MI: Baker, 1987), p. 96.

⁶⁷ Willard, 'Knowledge and Naturalism', p. 44.

⁶⁸ Dawkins, *The Blind Watchmaker* (London: Penguin, 1990), p. 10.

⁶⁹ William Hasker, 'How Not to Be a Reductivist' www.iscid.org/papers/ Hasker_NonReductivism_103103.pdf.

⁷⁰ Victor Reppert, *C.S. Lewis's Dangerous Idea* (Downers Grove, IL: IVP, 2003), pp. 87, 101.

⁷¹ Lewis, *Miracles*, pp. 23, 25.

⁷² ibid., p. 23.

⁷³ ibid., p. 43.

[74] Lewis, 'Religion without Dogma?', p. 95.

[75] ibid., p. 53.

[76] Lewis, *Miracles*, p. 28.

[77] ibid.

[78] ibid., p. 29.

[79] Arthur J. Balfour, *Theism and Humanism* (Seattle: Inkling, 2000), p. 147.

[80] Thomas V. Morris, *Francis Schaeffer's Apologetics: A Critique* (Chicago: Moody, 1976), p. 57.

[81] Richard Taylor, *Metaphysics* (Englewood Cliffs, NJ: Prentice-Hall, 1974).

[82] ibid.

[83] ibid.

[84] G.K. Chesterton, *Orthodoxy* (London: House of Stratus, 2001), pp. 20–21.

[85] ibid., p. 21.

[86] G.K. Chesterton, 'The Wind and the Trees' [1909], *Stories, Essays and Poems* (London: J.M. Dent and Sons, 1939), p. 183.

[87] Chesterton, *Orthodoxy*, p. 20.

[88] Patricia Churchland, quoted by Alvin Plantinga, 'An Evolutionary Argument Against Naturalism' www.calvin.edu/academic/philosophy/virtual_library/articles/plantinga_alvin/an_evolutionary_argument_against_naturalism.pdf.

[89] John Gray, *Straw Gods: Thoughts on Humans and Other Animals* (London: Granta, 2002), pp. 20, 26, 27.

[90] Steven Pinker, *How the Mind Works* (New York: Norton, 1997), p. 305.

[91] Richard Rorty, 'Untruth and Consequences', *The New Republic,* 31 July 1995, p. 36.

[92] ibid.

[93] Richard Dawkins, *Sunday Telegraph*, 18 October 1998.

[94] McGinn, *Problem of Consciousness*, p. 181.

[95] ibid.

[96] Eric S. Waterhouse, *The Philosophical Approach to Religion* (London: Epworth, 1933), p. 91.

[97] Anthony Flew, 'Determinism and Validity Again', *The Rationalist Annual*, 1958, p. 47.

[98] Stephen Stitch, 'Evolution and Rationality', *The Fragmentation of Reason* (MIT Press, 1990), p. 56.

[99] Reppert, 'Defending the Dangerous Idea'.

[100] Anthony O'Hear, *Philosophy* (London: Continuum, 2001), pp. 139–41.

[101] Balfour, *Theism and Humanism*, pp. 147–8.

[102] Nagel, *Mind & Cosmos*, p.27.

[103] Alvin Plantinga, *Warranted Christian Belief* (OUP, 2000), p. 235.

[104] Alvin Plantinga, 'Evolution versus Naturalism', *The Nature of Nature: Examining the Role of Naturalism in Science* (ed. Bruce L. Gordon and William A. Dembski; Wilmington, DE: ISI, 2011), p. 139.

[105] Alvin Plantinga, http://hisdefense.org/articles/ap001.html.

[106] Alvin Plantinga, *Science and Religion: Are They Compatible?* (ed. James P. Sterba; OUP: 2011), pp. 69–70.

107 Plantinga, *Warranted Christian Belief*, p. 238.
108 Charles Darwin, letter to William Graham, 3 July 1881, *The Life and Letters of Charles Darwin* (ed. Francis Darwin; University Press of the Pacific, 2001).
109 Plantinga, 'Evolution versus Naturalism', p. 148.
110 Lewis, *Miracles*, p. 18.
111 Reppert, 'Several Formulations of the Argument from Reason', p. 32.
112 Robert C. Koons, 'Science and Theism', in *The Rationality of Theism* (ed. Paul Copan and Paul K. Moser (London: Routledge, 2003) p. 83.
113 Reppert, 'Defending the Dangerous Idea'.
114 Anthony O'Hear, *Philosophy in the New Century* (London: Continuum, 2001), p. 125.

13. Freedom and Responsibility

1 Roy Abraham Varghese, *The Wonder of the World* (Fountain Hills, AZ: TYR, 2003), p. 309.
2 Garrett J. DeWeese and J.P. Moreland, *Philosophy Made Slightly Less Difficult: A Beginner's Guide to Life's Big Questions* (Downers Grove, IL: IVP, 2005), p. 123.
3 ibid.
4 ibid.
5 H.P. Owen, *Christian Theism: A Study in Its Basic Principles* (Edinburgh: T&T Clark, 1984), p. 117.
6 Paul Marston and Roger Forster, *God's Strategy in Human History* (Eugene, OR: Wipf & Stock, 2000), pp. 131, 296, 305.
7 Irenaeus, *Against Heresies*, quoted by Marston and Forster, *God's Strategy*, p. 298.
8 J.P. Moreland and Scott B. Rae, *Body and Soul: Human Nature and the Crisis in Ethics* (Downers Grove, IL: IVP, 2000), pp. 129–30.
9 Antony Flew, *There Is a God* (New York: HarperOne, 2007), pp. 58–9.
10 ibid.
11 ibid, p. 59.
12 ibid.
13 Methodius of Olympus quoted by Marston and Forster, *God's Strategy*, p. 302.
14 Flew, *There Is a God*, p. 59.
15 ibid., p. 60.
16 ibid., pp. 63–4.
17 H.D. Lewis, *Philosophy of Religion: A Concise Introduction* (London: English Universities Press, 1965), p. 309.
18 Norman L. Geisler and Paul D. Feinberg, *Introduction to Philosophy: A Christian Perspective* (Grand Rapids, MI: Baker, 1997), p. 205.
19 Flew, *There Is a God*, p. 73.
20 Paul Copan, *That's Just Your Interpretation* (Grand Rapids, MI: Baker, 2001), p. 78.
21 ibid.

22 Peter Cave, *This Sentence Is False: An Introduction to Philosophical Paradoxes* (London: Continuum, 2010), p. 133.

23 ibid., p. 80.

24 For a transcript of this exchange, cf. 'Who Wrote Dawkins' New Book?' www.evolutionnews.org/2006/10/who_wrote_richard_dawkinss_new.html#more.

25 Richard Dawkins, quoted by Mario Beauregard and Denyse O'Leary, *The Spiritual Brain* (New York: HarperOne, 2007), p. 118.

26 Richard Dawkins, www.edge.org/q2006/q06_9.html#dawkins.

27 cf. 'David Quinn and Richard Dawkins Debate' www.freerepublic.com/focus/f-news/1727564/posts.

28 Marvin Minsky, *The Society of Mind* (New York: Simon & Schuster, 1985), p. 307.

29 Patricia Churchland in *Conversations on Consciousness* (ed. Susan Blackmore; OUP, 2006), p. 61.

30 Thomas Metzinger, 'The Forbidden Fruit Intuition', in *What Is Your Dangerous Idea?* (ed. John Brockman; London: Pocket Books, 2006), p. 145.

31 C.S. Lewis, *Miracles* (London: Fount, 1998), p. 11.

32 William Provine in *Science and Wonders* (ed. Russell Stannard; London: Faber, 1996).

33 cf. James Daniel Sinclair, 'The Metaphysics of Quantum Mechanics' www.reasons.org/resources/apologetics/other_papers/the_metaphysics_of_quantum_mechanics.shtml.

34 cf. www.britannica.com/eb/article-77521/quantum-mechanics.

35 Ned Block in *Conversations on Consciousness* (ed. Blackmore), p. 30.

36 C. Stephen Layman, *Letters to Doubting Thomas: A Case for the Existence of God* (OUP, 2007), p. 143–5.

37 Varghese, *Wonder of the World*, p. 309.

38 John Searle, *Minds, Brains and Science* (Harvard University Press, 1984), p. 88.

39 Thomas Nagel, *The View from Nowhere* (OUP, 1986), p. 114.

40 Moreland and Rae, *Body and Soul*, p. 133.

41 ibid., pp. 132–3.

42 Nagel, *View from Nowhere*, p. 112.

43 Searle, *Minds, Brains and Science*, p. 98.

44 ibid., p. 88.

45 ibid., p. 98.

46 ibid.

47 Nancy Pearcey, 'Intelligent Design and the Defence of Reason', in *Darwin's Nemesis: Phillip Johnson and the Intelligent Design Movement* (ed. William A. Dembski; Downers Grove, IL: IVP, 2006), pp. 236–7.

48 Steven Pinker, *The Blank Slate: The Modern Denial of Human Nature* (New York: Viking, 2002), p. 240.

49 Pearcey, 'Intelligent Design and the Defence of Reason', p. 237.

50 William Hasker, *The Emergent Self* (Cornell University Press, 2009), pp. 84–5.

51 Jacques Maritain, *An Introduction to Philosophy* (London: Continuum, 2005), p. 79.

52 ibid.

53 Norman L. Geisler and Paul D. Feinberg, *Introduction to Philosophy: A Christian Perspective* (Grand Rapids, MI: Baker, 1997), p. 196.

54 Immanuel Kant, *Critique of Practical Reason* (1788) http://praxeology.net/kant4.htm.

55 Lewis, *Miracles*, p. 16.

56 Hasker, *Emergent Self*, p. 85.

57 Gary R. Habermas and J.P. Moreland, *Beyond Death* (Wheaton, IL: Good News, 1998), p. 60.

58 Carol Iannone, 'A Critic in Full: A Conversation with Tom Wolfe' www.nas.org/polArticles.cfm?doc_id=296.

59 Joseph H. Casey, *God Is: From Question to Proof to Embracing the Truth* (University Press of America, 1998), quoted in a review by Ronald K. Tacelli, *Philosophia Christi*, series 2, 3:2 (2001): pp. 565–6.

60 Anthony O'Hear, *Philosophy* (London: Continuum, 2001), p. 12.

61 C.E.M. Joad, *The Recovery of Belief* (London: Faber & Faber, 1955), p. 140.

62 Keith Ward, *The Battle for the Soul* (London: Hodder & Stoughton, 1985), p. 70.

63 T.J. Mawson, 'The Rational Inescapability of Value Objectivism', *Think* (Spring/Summer 2008): p. 17.

64 ibid.

65 ibid., pp. 18–19.

66 ibid., p. 19.

67 ibid.

68 ibid., p. 21.

69 J.P. Moreland, *Scaling the Secular City: A Defense of Christianity* (Grand Rapids, MI: Baker, 1987), p. 93.

70 ibid.

71 Stephen R.L. Clark, *God, Religion and Reality* (London: SPCK, 1998), p. 98.

72 Stephen R.L. Clark, *From Athens to Jerusalem* (OUP, 1984), pp. 96–7.

73 Owen, Christian, *Theism*, p. 119.

14. Aesthetics I: Objective Beauty

1 Richard Dawkins, *A Devil's Chaplain* (London: Weidenfeld & Nicholson, 2003), p. 42.

2 Richard Dawkins, *Unweaving the Rainbow* (London: Penguin, 1999), p. 63.

3 J.L. Mackie, *Ethics: Inventing Right and Wrong* (London: Penguin, 1990), p. 15.

4 Matthew Kieran, 'Aesthetic Value, Beauty, Ugliness and Incoherence', *Philosophy* 72 (281) (1997): pp. 387–99.

5 G.E. Moore, *Principia Ethica* (CUP, 1993), p. 249.

6 Alvin Plantinga, 'Two Dozen (or so) Theistic Arguments' www.homestead.com/philofreligion/files/Theisticarguments.html.

7 Robin Collins, 'The Teleological Argument', in *The Routledge Companion to Philosophy of Religion* (ed. Chad Meister and Paul Copan; London: Routledge, 2010), p. 359.

[8] Alexander R. Pruss, 'Beauty' (comments section) http://alexanderpruss. blogspot.co.uk/2010/09/beauty.html.

[9] Thomas Dubay, *The Evidential Power of Beauty* (San Francisco: Ignatius, 1999), pp. 16–17.

[10] Protagoras, quoted by Holmes, *Fact, Value and God* (Grand Rapids, MI: Eerdmans, 1997), p. 8.

[11] Wladyslaw Tatarkiewicz, 'The Great Theory of Beauty and Its Decline', *Journal of Aesthetics and Art Criticism* 31 (1972–3): p. 169.

[12] C.E.M. Joad, *The Recovery of Belief* (London: Faber & Faber, 1952), p. 212.

[13] In the Romantic era, 'sublime' replaced 'beauty' as the pre-eminent aesthetic term of praise.

[14] C.S. Lewis, *The Abolition of Man* (London: Fount, 1999), p. 7.

[15] Quoted, ibid.

[16] Quoted, ibid., p. 8.

[17] Charles Darwin, *Origin of Species* (6th edn, 1872), ch. 6, p. 160, quoted by George Hayward Joyce SJ, *Principles of Natural Theology*, 'Proofs of God's Existence (ii. Physical Arguments)' www.nd.edu/Departments/Maritain/ etext/pnt04.htm.

[18] Frank Miele, 'Darwin's Dangerous Disciple – An Interview with Richard Dawkins', *The Skeptic* 3:4 (1995).

[19] Richard Dawkins, quoted in Keith Ward, *The Turn of the Tide* (London: BBC, 1986), p. 32.

[20] Colin E. Gunton, *The One, the Three and the Many* (CUP, 1996), p. 67.

[21] Richard Dawkins, *River out of Eden* (London: Weidenfeld & Nicholson, 1995), p. 120.

[22] Ward, *Turn of the Tide*, p. 142.

[23] David Hume, *On the Standard of Taste*, www.econlib.org/library/LFBooks/ Hume/hmMPL23.html.

[24] David Hume, *A Treatise of Human Nature*, section viii http://ebooks.adelaide. edu.au/h/hume/david/h92t/B2.1.8.html.

[25] ibid.

[26] Lewis, *Abolition of Man*, p. 13.

[27] Peter Cave, *How to Outwit Aristotle* (London: Quercus, 2012), p. 330.

[28] Joad, *Recovery of Belief*, p. 145.

[29] Antony Latham, *The Naked Emperor: Darwinism Exposed* (London: Janus, 2005), p. 157.

[30] John Haldane, 'Admiring the High Mountains', in *The Philosophy of the Environment* (ed. T.D.J. Chappell; Edinburgh University Press, 1997), p. 81.

[31] Plotinus, 'Enneads', *Aesthetics: The Classic Readings* (ed. David E. Cooper; Oxford: Blackwell, 1997), p. 60.

[32] Augustine, quoted by Umberto Eco, *The Aesthetics of Thomas Aquinas* (trans. Hugh Bredin; Cambridge, MA: Harvard University Press, 1988), p. 49.

[33] Norman L. Geisler, *The Issue of Beauty* (audio cassette tape), side 1.

[34] Jerry Solomon, 'Art and the Christian' www.leaderu.com/orgs/probe/docs/ artandxn.html.

[35] Douglas Groothuis, *Truth Decay* (Downers Grove, IL: IVP, 2000), p. 257.

[36] Mortimer J. Adler, *Adler's Philosophical Dictionary* (Pocket Books, 1996), p. 39.

[37] Groothuis, *Truth Decay*, p. 258.

[38] Mortimer J. Adler, *Six Great Ideas* (London: Collier Macmillan, 1981), p. 112.

[39] E.R. Emmet, *Learning to Philosophise* (London: Longmans, 1964), p. 119.

[40] cf. Garrett J. DeWeese, *Doing Philosophy as a Christian* (Downers Grove, IL; IVP Academic, 2011), ch. 7.

[41] 'If our minds are totally alien to reality then all our thoughts, including this thought, are worthless. We must, then, grant logic to the reality; we must, if we are to have any moral standards, grant it moral standards too. And there is really no reason why we should not do the same about standards of beauty. There is no reason why our reaction to a beautiful landscape should not be the response, however humanly blurred and partial, to a something that is really there. The idea of a wholly mindless and valueless universe has to be abandoned at one point – i.e. as regards logic: after that, there is no telling at how many other points it will be defeated nor how great the reversal of our nineteenth-century philosophy must finally be.' – 'De Futilitate', *Christian Reflections* (London: Fount, 1991).

[42] cf. Mary Mothersill, *Beauty Restored* (OUP, 1984).

[43] cf. Alexander R. Pruss, 'Beauty' http://alexanderpruss.blogspot.co.uk/2010/09/beauty.html.

[44] cf. Guy Sircello, *A New Theory of Beauty* (Princeton University Press, 1975).

[45] cf. Joseph D. Wooddell, *The Beauty of Faith: Using Aesthetics for Christian Apologetics* (Eugene, OR: Wipf & Stock, 2010).

[46] cf. Eddy M. Zemach, *Real Beauty* (University Park, PA: Pennsylvania State University Press, 1997).

[47] Cave, *Outwit Aristotle*, p. 329.

[48] cf. http://philpapers.org/surveys/results.pl.

[49] Lewis, *Abolition of Man*, p. 8.

[50] ibid.

[51] ibid., p. 14.

[52] ibid.

[53] ibid., p. 16.

[54] ibid.

[55] cf. Cave, *Outwit Aristotle*, p. 333.

[56] Quoted by H.E. Huntley, *The Divine Proportion* (New York: Dover, 1970), p. 89.

[57] Dr Nicholas Everitt, personal communication.

[58] Jacques Maritain, *Art and Scholasticism* (University of Notre Dame Press, 1974), p. 3.

[59] Dr Nicholas Everitt, personal conversation.

[60] Samuel Johnson, *A Journey to the Western Islands* (ed. R.W. Chapman; OUP, 1994), pp. 34–5.

[61] Adler, *Six Great Ideas*, p. 37.

[62] Aldous Huxley, *Ends and Means* (London: Greenwood, 1969), p. 287.

[63] Peter Kreeft, *Yes or No?* (San Francisco: Ignatius, 1991), pp. 41–2.

[64] Roger Scruton, *Beauty: A Very Short Introduction* (OUP: 2011), pp. 26–7.

[65] David Bentley Hart, *The Beauty of the Infinite: The Aesthetics of Christian Truth* (Cambridge: Eerdmans, 2003), pp. 16–17.

[66] Anthony O'Hear, *Beyond Evolution* (Oxford: Clarendon, 1997), p. 187.

[67] ibid., p. 191.

[68] Richard Swinburne, *Providence and the Problem of Evil* (Oxford: Clarendon, 1998).

[69] Michael Huemer, *Ethical Intuitionism* (Basingstoke: Palgrave Macmillan, 2008), p. 211.

[70] Quoted by Eco, *Aesthetics of Thomas Aquinas*, p. 113.

[71] ibid., p. 32.

[72] ibid., p. 33.

[73] Mackie, *Ethics*, p. 15.

[74] Adler, *Philosophical Dictionary*, p. 37.

[75] Geisler, *Issue of Beauty*, side 1.

[76] Anthony O'Hear, *Philosophy in the New Century* (London: Continuum, 2001), p. 102.

[77] Peter Kreeft and Ronald Tacelli, *Handbook of Christian Apologetics* (Oxford: Monarch, 1999).

[78] Scruton, *Beauty*, p. 119.

[79] W.R. Sorley, *Moral Values and the Idea of God* (CUP, 1921), p. 124.

[80] Colin Lyas, 'The Evaluation of Art', in *Philosophical Aesthetics: An Introduction* (ed. Oswald Hanfling; Oxford: Blackwell, 1992), pp. 371–2.

[81] Scruton, *Beauty*, p. 197.

[82] Iris Murdoch, 'On "God" and "Good"', *The Sovereignty of the Good* (London: Routledge, 1970), p. 62.

[83] Anne Sheppard, *Aesthetics: An Introduction to the Philosophy of Art* (OUP, 1987), p. 154.

[84] Nicholas Wolterstorff, *Art in Action: Toward a Christian Aesthetic* (Carlisle: Solway, 1997), p. 169.

[85] cf. Alexander R. Pruss, 'Where Are the Ugly Galaxies?' http://alexander-pruss.blogspot.co.uk/2010/04/where-are-ugly-galaxies.html.

[86] Jacques Maritain, *Art and Scholasticism* (Filiquarian, 2007), p. 24.

[87] Sorley, *Moral Values*, p. 31.

[88] Plato, *Symposium*.

[89] Paul Marston and Roger Forster, *Reason, Science and Faith* (Crowborough: Monarch, 1999) p. 258.

[90] 'The relation of ethics and art is bound to be close, for in a certain sense the good must be beautiful and the beautiful good, as the Greeks recognized by their compound word the "beautiful-good".' – Eric S. Waterhouse, *The Philosophical Approach to Religion* (London: Epworth, 1933), p. 163. The Authorised Version of the Bible usually translates *kalos* as 'good', and occasionally as 'honest' (e.g. Romans 12:17; 2 Corinthians 8:21). 'Honest' in this context does not primarily mean 'telling the truth', but is used in its Latin sense of *honestus*, meaning '*handsome, gracious, fair to look upon*' – William Barclay, *New Testament Words* (Westminster John Knox Press, 1974), p. 151.

244444444

44444444444

Honestus refers to an objective attribute of things. Cicero defined that which is *honestus* as being 'such that even if its utility is taken away, and even if any rewards and fruits which come from it are removed, it can still be praised for its own sake.' That which is *honestus* – and by implication, that which is *kalos* – is an end in itself and not merely a means, intrinsically and not merely instrumentally good.

91 ibid., p161.
92 Mark 9:50, Literal Translation, *Interlinear Greek–English New Testament* (ed. Jay P. Green Sr; Grand Rapids, MI: Baker, 3rd edn, 2007), p. 141.
93 ibid., p. 322.
94 William Barclay, *New Testament Words* (Louisville, KY: Westminster John Knox, 1974), pp. 157, 159.
95 ibid., p. 151.
96 Romans 7:16, Literal Translation, *Interlinear Greek–English NT*, p. 489.
97 Barclay, *New Testament Words*, p. 153.
98 ibid., p. 145.
99 John 7:12, King James Version, *Interlinear Greek–English NT*, p. 308.
100 Matthew 12:33,35, Literal Translation, *Interlinear Greek–English NT*, p. 38.
101 Paradise Lost, book 4, l. 846, quoted in *The Macmillan Dictionary of Religious Quotations* (comp. Margret Pepper; London: Macmillan, 1989), p. 214.
102 ibid.
103 ibid., p. 97.
104 Gloria Durka, *Praying with Hildegard of Bingen* (Winona, MN: Saint Mary's, 1991), pp. 53, 55.
105 ibid., p. 54.
106 Evelyn Underhill, *The Essentials of Mysticism* (London: J.M. Dent & Sons, 1920), p. 113.
107 Durka, *Praying with Hildegard*, pp. 83, 85.
108 Murdoch, 'On "God" and "Good"', p. 65.
109 Scruton, *Beauty*, p. 197.
110 J.P. Moreland in *Communiqué*, Robert K. Garcia, '*Communiqué* Interview: J.P. Moreland' http://communiquejournal.org/q4_moreland.html
111 ibid.
112 Plato, *Symposium*.
113 Keith Ward, *God, Faith and the New Millennium* (Oxford: OneWorld, 1999), p. 97.

15. Aesthetics II: Beauty and Divinity

1 cf. Alexander R. Pruss, 'The Argument from Beauty' http://alexanderpruss.blogspot.co.uk/2009/09/argument-from-beauty.html.
2 St Augustine, *City of God* (London: Penguin Classics, 1984), p. 308.
3 Peter Kreeft, *Heaven: The Heart's Deepest Longing* (San Francisco: Ignatius, 1989), pp. 23, 25, 112, 247.

[4] Victor Cousin, 'God Seen in the Beautiful', in *Selections from the Literature of Theism* (ed. Alfred Caldecott and H.R. Mackintosh; Edinburgh: T&T Clark, 1931), pp. 309–11.

[5] Peter Lombard, *The Sentences* 1.3.1. The Sentences were a standard medieval university textbook, upon which it was common to make commentaries.

[6] Richard Swinburne, *Is There a God?* (OUP, revd edn, 2010), pp. 40–42.

[7] Thomas Aquinas, *Summa Theologica* www.newadvent.org/summa/100203.htm.

[8] E.L. Mascall, *He Who Is* (London: Longmans, Green and Co., 1954), p. 54.

[9] F.C. Copleston, *Aquinas* (Harmondsworth: Penguin, 1957), p. 121.

[10] Mascall, *He Who Is*, pp. 53–4.

[11] cf. Christopher F.J. Martin, 'The Fourth Way' http://users.colloquium.co.uk/~BARRETT/Viae4.htm.

[12] ibid.

[13] Peter Kreeft, *A Shorter Summa* (San Francisco: Ignatius, 1993), p. 63.

[14] Mascall, *He Who Is*, p. 53.

[15] Étienne Gilson, *The Christian Philosophy of St Thomas Aquinas* (University of Notre Dame Press, 2002), p. 74.

[16] Richard Dawkins, *The God Delusion* (London: Bantam, 2006), p. 79.

[17] F.C. Copleston, *A History of Medieval Philosophy* (University of Notre Dame Press, 1972), p. 73.

[18] Gilson, *Christian Philosophy of Aquinas*, p. 70.

[19] Adrian Nichols, *Discovering Aquinas* (London: Darton, Longman & Todd, 2002), p. 45.

[20] Kreeft, *Shorter Summa*, p. 62.

[21] Jacques Maritain, 'God and Science' www.ewtn.com./library/THEOLOGY/JM2404.HTM.

[22] ibid.

[23] Mascall, *He Who Is*, p. 53.

[24] ibid.

[25] Kreeft, *Shorter Summa*, p. 63.

[26] Maritain, 'God and Science'.

[27] Peter Kreeft and Ronald Tacelli, *Handbook of Christian Apologetics* (Downers Grove, IL: IVP, 1994), p. 54.

[28] Copleston, *Aquinas*, p. 121.

[29] Maritain, 'God and Science'.

[30] Francis A. Schaeffer, *He Is There and He Is Not Silent* in *The Complete Works of Francis A. Schaeffer*, vol. 1 (Wheaton, IL: Crossway, 1994).

[31] Thomas V. Morris, *Francis Schaeffer's Apologetics: A Critique* (Chicago: Moody, 1976), p. 29.

[32] Schaeffer, *He Is There*, p. 306.

[33] ibid.

[34] Jean Baudrillard, *The Transparency of Evil: Essays on Extreme Phenomena* (trans. James Benedict; London: Verso, 1990), pp. 14–15.

[35] John G. West Jr, 'The Regeneration of Science and Culture', in *Signs of Intelligence: Understanding Intelligent Design* (ed. William A. Dembski and James M. Kushiner; Grand Rapids, MI: Brazos, 2001), p. 65.

[36] R.C. Sproul, *The Consequences of Ideas* (Wheaton, IL: Crossway, 2000), p. 171.

[37] cf. 'A Christian View of Philosophy and Culture', *The Complete Works of Francis A. Schaeffer*, vol. 1 (Wheaton, IL: Crossway, 1994).

[38] Janet Leslie Blumberg, *The Literary Background of The Lord of the Rings: Celebrating Middle Earth* (Oxford: Inkling, 2002), pp. 79–80.

[39] ibid., p. 80.

[40] William Lane Craig, *Reasonable Faith* (Wheaton, IL: Crossway, 1994), p.65.

[41] Friedrich Nietzsche, 'Skirmishes of an Untimely Man', in *Twilight of the Idols* www.handprint.com/SC/NIE/GotDamer.html.

[42] Friedrich Nietzsche, quoted by Ravi Zacharias in *A Shattered Visage* (Grand Rapids, MI: Baker, 1990), p. 49.

[43] Peter Kreeft, *C.S. Lewis for the Third Millennium* (San Francisco: Ignatius, 1994), p. 42.

[44] ibid., pp. 42–3.

[45] C.S. Lewis, *The Abolition of Man* (London: Fount, 1999), p.50.

[46] Roger Scruton, *An Intelligent Person's Guide to Modern Culture* (London: Duckworth, 1998), p. 68.

[47] Francis Schaeffer, *The God Who Is There* in *The Complete Works of Francis A. Schaeffer*, vol. 1 (Wheaton, IL: Crossway, 1994), p. 95.

[48] Richard Dawkins, *The God Delusion* (London: Bantam, 2006), p. 87.

[49] Eric S. Waterhouse, *The Philosophical Approach to Religion* (London: Epworth, 1933), p. 34.

[50] Peter Kreeft, *Back to Virtue* (San Francisco: Ignatius, 1992), p.100.

[51] Schaeffer, *He Is There*, p. 36.

[52] ibid.

[53] Bryan Appleyard, *Understanding the Present* (London: Picador, 1993), p. 15.

[54] Tobias Jones, *Utopian Dreams* (London: Faber, 2007), pp. 74–5.

[55] Scruton, *Guide to Modern Culture*, p. 49.

[56] Josh McDowell and Thomas Williams, *In Search of Certainty* (Wheaton, IL: Tyndale, 2003), p. 83.

[57] Hans Küng, *Art and the Problem of Meaning* (New York: Crossroad, 1981), p. 29.

[58] Peter Kreeft, *Heaven: The Heart's Deepest Longing* (San Francisco: Ignatius, 1989), p. 21.

[59] Scruton, *Guide to Modern Culture*, p. 17.

[60] Patrick Sherry, *Spirit and Beauty* (London: SCM, 2002), p. 47.

[61] ibid.

[62] ibid.

[63] Richard Dawkins, quoted in Keith Ward, *The Turn of the Tide* (London: BBC, 1986), p. 32.

[64] Richard Dawkins, *River out of Eden* (London: Weidenfeld & Nicholson, 1995), p. 120.

[65] Edward Farley, *Faith and Beauty: A Theological Aesthetic* (Aldershot: Ashgate, 2001), p. 64.

[66] Patrick Sherry, 'Beauty', in *A Companion to Philosophy of Religion* (ed. Phillip L. Quinn and Charles Taliaferro; Oxford: Blackwell, 1999), p. 279.

[67] ibid.

[68] Keith Ward, *Religion and Creation* (Oxford: Clarendon, 1996), p. 198.

[69] Peter Kreeft, *Angels (and Demons)* (San Francisco: Ignatius, 1995), p. 72.

[70] cf. Patrick Sherry, *Spirit and Beauty* (SCM, 2002), p. 57.

[71] Ward, *Religion and Creation*, pp. 267–8.

[72] Richard Harries, *Art and the Beauty of God* (New York: Mowbray, 1993), p. 54.

16. Science and Theology

[1] Galileo Galilei, *The Authority of Scripture*, quoted by Paul Nelson and John Mark Reynolds, 'Young Earth Creationism', in *Three Views on Creation and Evolution* (ed. J.P. Moreland and John Mark Reynolds; Grand Rapids, MI: Zondervan, 1999), p. 68.

[2] J.P. Moreland and William Lane Craig, *Philosophical Foundations for a Christian Worldview* (Downers Grove, IL: IVP, 2003), p. 307.

[3] ibid.

[4] J.P. Moreland and John Mark Reynolds, eds, *Three Views on Creation and Evolution* (Grand Rapids, MI: Zondervan, 1999), Introduction, p. 8.

[5] Garrett J. DeWeese and J.P. Moreland, *Philosophy Made Slightly Less Difficult* (Downers Grove, IL: IVP, 2005), p. 133.

[6] Bruce L. Gordon, 'Is Intelligent Design Science?', in *Signs of Intelligence: Understanding Intelligent Design* (ed. William A. Dembski and James M. Kushiner; Grand Rapids, MI: Brazos, 2001), p. 201.

[7] Moreland and Craig, *Foundations*, p. 359.

[8] Thomas Dixon, *Science and Religion: A Very Short Introduction* (OUP, 2008), p. 99.

[9] J.P. Moreland, *Christianity and the Nature of Science* (Grand Rapids, MI: Baker, 1998), p. 19.

[10] Del Ratzsch, *Science and Its Limits: The Natural Sciences in Christian Perspective* (Leicester: Apollos, 2000), p. 11.

[11] Richard Dawkins, *The God Delusion* (London: Bantam, 2006), p. 361.

[12] Moreland, *Christianity and the Nature of Science*, p. 107.

[13] DeWeese and Moreland, *Philosophy Made Slightly Less Difficult*, p. 133.

[14] Paul de Vries, 'Naturalism in the Natural Sciences', *Christian Scholar's Review* 15 (1986): pp. 388–96.

[15] Nancy Murphy, 'Phillip Johnson on Trial: A Critique of His Critique of Darwin', *Perspectives on Science and Christian Faith* 45:1 (1993): p. 33.

[16] Del Ratzsch, *Nature, Design and Science: The Status of Design in Natural Science* (State University of New York Press, 2001), p. 94.

[17] DeWeese and Moreland, *Philosophy Made Slightly Less Difficult*, p. 146.

[18] Larry Laudan, *Beyond Positivism and Relativism* (Boulder, CO: Westview, 1996), p. 210.

[19] Larry Laudan, 'The Demise of the Demarcation Problem', in *But Is It Science?* (ed. Michael Ruse; Buffalo, NY: Prometheus, 1983), p. 349.

[20] Michael Ruse, *Can a Darwinian Be a Christian?* (CUP, 2004), p. 101.

[21] Thomas Nagel, 'Public Education and Intelligent Design', *Wiley InterScience Journal Philosophy and Public Affairs* 36:2, quoted by Denyse O'Leary, 'Philosopher Says Teaching Students about Intelligent Design Should Be Okay' www.arn.org/blogs/index.php/2/2008/09/21/intelligent_design_and_high_culture_phil.

[22] Ratzsch, *Science and Its Limits*, pp. 123–4.

[23] Nancy R. Pearcey and Charles B. Thaxton, *The Soul of Science: Christian Faith and Natural Philosophy* (Wheaton, IL: Crossway, 1994), p. 72.

[24] Isaac Newton, *Principia*, vol. 2, quoted by Michael Friedlander, 'Intelligent Design and the Workings of Science', *Skeptical Inquirer* 30:3.

[25] Stephen C. Meyer, 'The Methodological Equivalence of Design and Descent', in *The Creation Hypothesis* (ed. J.P. Moreland; Downers Grove, IL: IVP, 1994), p. 97.

[26] Pearcey and Thaxton, *Soul of Science*, p. 72. For a contemporary presentation of the design argument from the fine-tuning of our solar habitat, cf. Guillermo Gonzalez and Jay Richards, *The Privileged Planet: How Our Place in the Cosmos Is Designed for Discovery* (Washington, DC: Regnery, 2005).

[27] Paul Nelson, 'Intelligent Design', *Nucleus* (January 2005) www.cmf.org.uk/printable/?context=article&id=1303

[28] Denis Alexander, *Rebuilding the Matrix* (Oxford, Lion, 2001), p. 436.

[29] ibid., p. 340.

[30] Jay Wesley Richards, 'How Phil Johnson Changed My Mind', in *Darwin's Nemesis: Phillip Johnson and the Intelligent Design Movement* (ed. William A. Dembski; Leicester: IVP, 2006), p. 58.

[31] ibid., pp. 341, 444.

[32] Alexander, *Rebuilding the Matrix*, p. 444.

[33] William Lane Craig, 'A Classical Apologist's Response', in *Five Views on Apologetics* (ed. Steven B. Cowen; Grand Rapids, MI: Zondervan, 2000), p. 124.

[34] William Lane Craig, *Reasonable Faith* (Wheaton, IL: Crossway, 1994), p. 190.

[35] A proposal I first made in 'Reviewing the Reviewers: Pigliucci et al. on Darwin's Rottweiler and the Public Understanding of Science' www.arn.org/docs/williams/pw_pigliucci_reviewingreviewers.htm.

[36] Michael J. Behe, 'The Modern Intelligent Design Hypothesis', *Philosophia Christi*, series 2, 3:1 (2001): p. 165.

[37] David DeWolf, John West, Casey Luskin and Jonathan Witt, *Traipsing into Evolution: Intelligent Design and the Kitzmiller vs Dover Decision* (Seattle: Discovery Institute, 2006), pp. 31–3.

[38] ibid.

[39] J.P. Moreland, 'Intelligent Design and the Nature of Science', in *Intelligent Design 101* (ed. H. Wayne House; Grand Rapids, MI: Kregel, 2008), p. 52.

[40] John Lennox, *God's Undertaker: Has Science Buried God?* (Oxford: Lion, 2nd edn, 2009), p. 32.

[41] Robert C. Koons, 'Science and Theism: Concord not Conflict', in *The Rationality of Theism* (ed. Paul Copan and Paul K. Moser; London: Routledge, 2003), pp. 75–6.

[42] Samir Okasha, *Philosophy of Science: A Very Short Introduction* (OUP, 2002), pp. 16–17.

[43] Moreland, *Christianity and the Nature of Science*, p. 57.

[44] Michael J. Murray and Michael Rea, *An Introduction to the Philosophy of Religion* (CUP, 2008), p. 194.

[45] Koons, 'Science and Theism: Concord not Conflict', p. 76.

[46] Moreland, *Christianity and the Nature of Science*, p. 28.

[47] Kirsten Birkett, *Unnatural Enemies: An Introduction to Science and Christianity* (Sydney: Matthias Media, 1997), p. 11.

[48] Richard Dawkins, 'Theology Has No Place in a University' http://richard-dawkins.net/article,1698,Letters-Theology-has-no-place-in-a-university, Richard-Dawkins; cf. Richard Dawkins, 'The Emptiness of Theology' www.simonyi.ox.ac.uk/dawkins/WorldOfDawkins-archive/Dawkins/Work/Articles/emptiness_of_theology.shtml.

[49] Alister McGrath, *Christian Theology: An Introduction* (Oxford: Blackwell, 2001), p. 120.

[50] R.C. Sproul, John Gerstner and Arthur Lindsay, *Classical Apologetics* (Grand Rapids, MI: Zondervan/Academic Books, 1984), pp. 9–10.

[51] Thomas Aquinas, *Summa Contra Gentiles, Book One: God* (trans. Anton C. Pegis: University of Notre Dame Press, 2005), pp. 60–61.

[52] Tom Morris, 'Foreword', in *C.S. Lewis as Philosopher: Truth, Goodness and Beauty* (ed. David Baggett, Gary R. Habermas and Jerry L. Walls; Downers Grove, IL: IVP, 2008), p. 10.

[53] David Ford, *Theology: A Very Short Introduction* (OUP, 1999), p. 19.

[54] Alvin Plantinga, 'Evolution and Design', in *For Faith and Clarity* (ed. James K. Beilby; Grand Rapids, MI: Baker, 2006), p. 212.

[55] Moreland, *Christianity and the Nature of Science*, p. 44.

[56] Galileo, *Authority of Scripture*, quoted by Nelson and Reynolds, 'Young Earth Creationism', in *Three Views on Creation and Evolution* (ed. Moreland and Reynolds), p. 68.

[57] Terence L. Nichols, *The Sacred Cosmos* (Grand Rapids, MI: Brazos, 2003), p. 207.

[58] Stephen Jay Gould, *Rock of Ages*, quoted by Dawkins, *God Delusion*, p. 55.

[59] Dawkins, *God Delusion*, p. 55.

[60] ibid.

[61] ibid., p. 59.

[62] Stephen C. Meyer in Lee Strobel, *The Case for a Creator* (Grand Rapids, MI: Zondervan, 2004), p. 76.

[63] Dawkins, *God Delusion*, p. 65.

[64] For example, cf. BBC News, 'Heart Patients "Benefit from Prayer"' http://news.bbc.co.uk/1/hi/health/1627662.stm; Phyllis McIntosh, 'Faith Is Powerful Medicine', *Reader's Digest* (May 2000); R.C. Byrd, 'Positive Therapeutic Effects of Intercessory Prayer in a Coronary Care Unit Population', *Southern Medical Journal* 81 (1988): pp. 826–9.

[65] J.A. Astin, E. Harkness, E. Ernst MD, 'The Efficacy of "Distant Healing": A Systematic Review of Randomized Trials', *Annals of Internal Medicine* 132 (2000): pp. 903–10.

[66] Dawkins, *God Delusion*, p. 59.

[67] Murray and Rea, *Introduction to Philosophy of Religion*, pp. 195–6.

[68] Dixon, *Science and Religion*, pp. 2–3.

[69] Michael Ruse in *The Philosophy of Biology* (ed. David L. Hull and Michael Ruse; OUP, 1998), p. 671.

[70] Alister McGrath, *The Twilight of Atheism* (London: Rider & Co., 2005), p. 87.

[71] Phillip E. Johnson, *The Right Questions* (Downers Grove, IL: IVP, 2002), Introduction.

[72] Phillip E. Johnson, *Darwin on Trial* (Downers Grove, IL: IVP, 1993), p. 115.

[73] ibid., p. 6.

[74] Plato, *Laws*, book 10.

[75] Richard Lewontin, 'Billions and Billions of Demons', *New York Review of Books*, 9 January 1997.

[76] ibid., my italics.

[77] Richard Dawkins, *The Blind Watchmaker* (London: Penguin, 1991), Preface, p. x.

[78] Dawkins, *Blind Watchmaker*, p. 151, my emphasis.

[79] Phillip E. Johnson, 'What Is Darwinism?', *Objection Sustained* (Downers Grove, IL: IVP, 1998), p. 33.

[80] Michael Ruse, 'Nonliteralist Antievolution,' AAAS Symposium: 'The New Antievolutionism,' 13 February 1993, Boston, MA (1993) www.leaderu.com/orgs/arn/orpages/or151/mr93tran.htm, my emphasis.

[81] Thomas Woodward, *Darwin Strikes Back: Defending the Science of Intelligent Design* (Grand Rapids, MI: Baker, 2006), pp. 52–3.

[82] Alvin Plantinga, 'Evolution, Neutrality, and Antecedent Probability: A Reply to Van Till and McMullen', *Christian Scholar's Review* 21:1 (September 1991), pp. 80–109; www.calvin.edu/academic/philosophy/virtual_library/articles/plantinga_alvin/evolution_neutrality_and_antecedent_probability.pdf.

[83] Alvin Plantinga, 'When Faith and Reason Clash' www.asa3.org/ASA/dialogues/Faith-reason/CRS9-91Plantinga1.html.

[84] Peter Atkins, *On Being* (OUP, 2011), p. 38; cf. Stephen C. Meyer, 'DNA and the Origin of Life' www.discovery.org/a/2184.

[85] Thomas Nagel, *Mind and Cosmos: Why the Materialist Neo-Darwinian Conception of Nature Is Almost Certainly False* (OUP, 2012), pp. 5, 9, 11.

[86] J.P. Moreland, *Scaling the Secular City* (Grand Rapids, MI: Baker, 1987), p. 214.

[87] David Winter, *But This I Can Believe* (London: Hodder & Stoughton, 1980), p. 112.

[88] Plantinga, 'Evolution, Neutrality, and Antecedent Probability', p. 2.

[89] Charles Hodge, *Systematic Theology* (3 vols: Grand Rapids, MI: Baker, 1992), 1:59.

[90] Richard Lewontin, 'Billions and Billions of Demons', *New York Review of Books*, 9 January 1997.

[91] John Stek, quoted by Alvin Plantinga, 'Methodological Naturalism? Part 2', *Origins and Design* 18:2 (1997) www.calvin.edu/academic/philosophy/

virtual_library / articles / plantinga_alvin / methodological_naturalism_
part_2.pdf.
[92] Murray and Rea, *Introduction to Philosophy of Religion*, p. 211.

17. The Problem of Evil

[1] Alvin Plantinga, *God, Freedom, and Evil* (Grand Rapids, MI: Eerdmans, 1974), pp. 63–4.
[2] We won't examine the argument, popular in much neo-atheist literature, that the God of Christian Scripture is obviously a straightforward moral monster. At best, this is only an argument against one interpretation of a specific theistic revelation claim, not an argument against Christianity per se, let alone an argument against theism per se. For a range of responses to typical neo-atheist assertions along these lines cf. Paul Copan, 'Is Yahweh a Moral Monster? The New Atheists and Old Testament Ethics' www.epsociety.org / library / articles.asp?pid=45; 'Yahweh Wars and the Canaanites' www.epsociety.org / library / articles.asp?pid=63; 'Is the Old Testament God Evil?' http://enrichmentjournal.ag.org/201203/201203_034_Good_God.cfm and *Is God a Moral Monster? Making Sense of the Old Testament God* (Grand Rapids, MI: Baker, 2011); William Lane Craig and Chad Meister, *God Is Good, God Is Great* (Downers Grove, IL: IVP, 2009); Richard S. Hess, 'Apologetic Issues in the Old Testament', in Douglas Groothuis, *Christian Apologetics: A Comprehensive Case for the Biblical Faith* (Nottingham: Apollos, 2011).
[3] Alvin Plantinga, *Knowledge of God* (Oxford: Blackwell, 2008), p. 152.
[4] C.S. Lewis, 'Evil and God', *Christian Reunion* (London: Fount, 1990), p. 49. See also *Mere Christianity* (London: Fount, 1986), pp. 42–7.
[5] Augustine, from *Confessions and Enchiridion* (ed. and trans. Albert C. Outer: Philadelphia: Westminster, 1955), in *Philosophy of Religion: Selected Readings* (ed. Michael Peterson et al.; OUP, 1996), p. 234.
[6] Thomas Aquinas, *Summa Contra Gentiles* 3.7 and 11.
[7] C.S. Lewis, *Mere Christianity* (London: Fount, 1997), p. 37.
[8] Quoted by Ravi Zacharias, *A Shattered Visage: The Real Face of Atheism* (Grand Rapids, MI: Baker, 1990), p. 49.
[9] J.J.C. Smart, *Atheism and Theism* (Oxford: Blackwell, 2nd edn, 2003), p. 60.
[10] Robin Le Poidevin, *Arguing for Atheism* (London: Routledge, 1996), p. 88.
[11] Sam Harris, *Letter to a Christian Nation* (London: Bantam, 2007), p. 55.
[12] Poidevin, *Arguing for Atheism*, p. 88.
[13] Scott A. Shalkowski, 'Atheological Apologetics', in *Contemporary Perspectives on Religious Epistemology* (ed. R. Douglas Geivett and Brendan Sweetman; OUP, 1992), p. 66.
[14] Ronald H. Nash, 'The Problem of Evil', in *To Everyone an Answer: A Case for the Christian Worldview* (ed. Francis J. Beckwith, William Lane Craig and J.P. Moreland; Downers Grove, IL: IVP, 2004), p. 214.

15 Michael L. Peterson, 'The Problem of Evil', in *A Companion to the Philosophy of Religion* (ed. Philip L. Quinn and Charles Taliaferro; Oxford: Blackwell, 1999), p. 393.

16 Alvin Plantinga, *God, Freedom, and Evil* (OUP, 2001), p. 23.

17 J.L. Mackie, *The Miracle of Theism* (Oxford: Clarendon, 1982), p. 150.

18 Nash, 'The Problem of Evil', p. 215.

19 Mackie, *Miracle of Theism*, p. 151.

20 ibid., p. 154.

21 Chad Meister, 'God, Evil and Morality' in *God Is Great, God Is Good* (ed. William Lane Craig and Chad Meister; Downers Grove, IL: IVP, 2009), p. 108.

22 William Lane Craig www.leaderu.com/offices/billcraig/docs/craig-nielsen1.html.

23 Dean L. Overman, *A Case for the Existence of God* (New York: Rowman & Littlefield, 2009), p. 94.

24 Nash, 'The Problem of Evil', p. 215.

25 ibid., pp. 215–216.

26 ibid.

27 Paul Draper, 'Seeking but Not Believing', in *Divine Hiddenness: New Essays* (ed. Daniel Howard-Snyder and Paul K. Moser; CUP, 2002), p. 204.

28 William L. Rowe, 'The Problem of Evil and Some Varieties of Atheism', *American Philosophical Quarterly* 16 (1979).

29 Alvin Plantinga, 'The Free Will Defence', in *The Philosophy of Religion* (ed. Basil Mitchell; OUP, 1971).

30 Mitch Stokes, *A Shot of Faith to the Head* (Nashville, TN: Thomas Nelson, 2012), pp. 192–3.

31 Plantinga, *Knowledge of God*, p. 153.

32 Kenny Boyce and Justin McBrayer, 'Van Inwagen on the Problem of Evil: The Good, the Bad and the Ugly' www.baylor.edu/content/services/document.php/41162.pdf.

33 Peter van Inwagen, quoted ibid.

34 Daniel and Francis Howard-Snyder, 'Is Theism Compatible with Gratuitous Suffering?' www.lastseminary.com/problem-of-evil/Is%20Theism%20Compatible%20with%20Gratuitous%20Evil.pdf.

35 Michael L. Peterson, 'C.S. Lewis on the Necessity of Gratuitous Evil', in *C.S. Lewis as Philosopher: Truth, Goodness and Beauty* (ed. David Baggett, Gary R. Habermas and Jerry L. Walls; Downers Grove, IL: IVP Academic, 2008), p. 179.

36 C. Stephen Layman, *Letters to Doubting Thomas: A Case for the Existence Of God* (OUP, 2007), pp. 184, 187.

37 Layman, *Letters to Doubting Thomas*, p. 186.

38 William J. Wainwright, *Philosophy of Religion* (Belmont, CA: Wadsworth, 1999), p. 98.

39 Daniel Howard-Snyder and Michael Bergman, 'Evil Does Not Make Atheism More Reasonable than Theism', in *Contemporary Debates in Religion* (ed. Michael L. Peterson and Raymond J. VanArragon; Oxford: Blackwell, 2003), p. 19.

[40] Nick Trakakis and Yujin Nagasawa, 'Skeptical Theism and Moral Skepticism: A Reply to Almeida and Oppy' www.arsdisputandi.org/publish/articles/000178/article.pdf.

[41] David Baggett, 'Is Divine Iconoclast as Bad as Cosmic Sadist?', in *C.S. Lewis as Philosopher: Truth, Goodness and Beauty* (ed. David Baggett, Gary R. Habermas and Jerry L. Walls; Downers Grove, IL: IVP, 2008), pp. 116, 127.

[42] Gregory Ganssle, 'God and Evil', in *The Rationality of Theism* (ed. Paul Copan and Paul K. Moser; London: Routledge, 2003), p. 264.

[43] Michael J. Langford, *Unblind Faith* (London: SCM, 1982), p. 87.

[44] While the suggestion that all natural evil could be caused by demons is implausible as a theodicy, it may be suggested that the activity of demons may somewhat extend the area of moral evil into the territory of natural evil. That is, although the 'free will defence' is simply an unpacking of what God's morally sufficient reason for permitting evil might possibly be, it can also be advanced as a partial explanation of God's actual reason for permitting evil, thereby constituting a theodicy. And such a theodicy can cover at least some examples of natural evil by explaining them in terms of the free will of both embodied and disembodied persons (i.e. humans and demons); cf. Peter S. Williams, *The Case for Angels* (Carlisle: Paternoster, 2003).

[45] 'The Bible and Modern Science: Conference Report', PreCiS (Winter 2011/12); cf. Bob White, 'Natural Disasters: Are They Acts of God?' www.cis.org.uk/upload/southampton/Soton_White_Mar11.mp3.

[46] Guillermo Gonzalez and Jay W. Richards, *The Privileged Planet* (Washington, DC: Regnery, 2004), pp. 55–8.

[47] Frequent miraculous intervention by God to prevent evil would negate the creation of a natural world in the first place, and might be thought to unduly impact the exercise of human free will. Miracles must be the exception rather than the rule in this context.

[48] William Lane Craig, 'The Bodily Resurrection of Jesus' www.reasonablefaith.org/site/News2?page=NewsArticle&id=5215

[49] cf. Stephen T. Davis, 'Universalism, Hell, and the Fate of the Ignorant', *Modem Theology* 6:2 (January 1990) http://ekklesiahellweek.wordpress.com/2011/03/16/universalism-hell-and-the-fate-of-the-ignorant-stephen-t-davis/; Bruce R. Reichenbach, 'Inclusivism and the Atonement' www.faithandphilosophy.com/article_atonement.php.

[50] Paul Copan, *That's Just Your Interpretation* (Grand Rapids, MI: Baker, 2001), p. 99.

[51] Kelly James Clark, 'I Believe in God the Father, Almighty' www.calvin.edu/academic/philosophy/writings/ibig.htm.

[52] Marylin McCord Adams, 'Horrendous Evil and the Goodness of God' www.lastseminary.com/problem-of-evil/Horrendous%20Evil%20and%20the%20Goodness%20of%20God.pdf.

[53] Austin Farrer, *Love Almighty and Ills Unlimited* (London: Fontana, 1966), pp. 60–61.

[54] Herbert McCabe, *God Matters* (New York: Mowbray, 1987), pp. 31–3, my italics.

[55] Farrer, *Love Almighty*, pp. 61–2.

[56] Alvin Plantinga, *Where the Conflict Really Lies: Science, Religion, and Naturalism* (OUP, 2011), p. 59.

[57] ibid, p. 174.

[58] ibid.

[59] William Lane Craig, *Reasonable Faith* (Wheaton, IL: Crossway, 3rd edn, 2008), p. 41.

[60] Some philosophers think that one can frame a problem of suffering that doesn't mention evil, but it seems to me that any such argument implicitly assumes that suffering is an evil that it is wrong of God to permit, etc.

[61] cf. 'Answering Objections to the Ontological Argument' http://youtu.be/ixqsZP7QP_o.

[62] Daniel Howard-Snyder, 'God, Evil and Suffering', in *Reason for the Hope Within* (ed. Michael J. Murray; Grand Rapids, MI: Eerdmans, 1999), pp. 76–115.

[63] Graham Oppy, 'Review: Suffering Belief' www.infidels.org/library/modern/graham_oppy/weisberger.html.

[64] Michael Tooley in Alvin Plantinga and Michael Tooley, *Knowledge of God* (Oxford: Blackwell, 2008), p. 70.

[65] Peterson, 'Problem of Evil', p. 400.

[66] Poll results reported by Luis Palau, *Is God Relevant?* (London: Hodder & Stoughton, 1997), p. 174.

[67] Alvin Plantinga, *God, Freedom, and Evil* (Grand Rapids, MI: Eerdmans, 1974), pp. 63–4.

[68] To pursue these issues, cf. Peter S. Williams, *Understanding Jesus: Five Ways to Spiritual Enlightenment* (Milton Keynes: Paternoster, 2011). See also: Peter S. Williams, 'Understanding Jesus' http//youtu.be/Fz1qkBMFFqa.

Paternoster:
thinking faith

We trust you enjoyed reading this book
from Paternoster. If you want to be informed
of any new titles from this author and other
releases you can sign up to the Paternoster
newsletter by contacting us:

By Post:
Paternoster
52 Presley Way
Crownhill
Milton Keynes
MK8 0ES

E-mail
paternoster@authenticmedia.co.uk

Follow us: